# Teaching and Learning in Art Education

In this student-centered book, Debrah C. Sickler-Voigt provides proven tips and innovative methods for teaching, managing, and assessing all aspects of art instruction and student learning in today's diversified educational settings, from pre-K through high school. Up-to-date with the current National Visual Arts Standards, this text offers best practices in art education, and explains current theories and assessment models for art instruction.

Using examples of students' visually stunning artworks to illustrate what children can achieve through quality art instruction and practical lesson planning, *Teaching and Learning in Art Education* explores essential and emerging topics such as:

- managing the classroom in art education;
- artistic development from early childhood through adolescence;
- catering towards learners with a diversity of abilities;
- integrating technology into the art field; and
- understanding drawing, painting, paper arts, sculpture, and textiles in context.

Alongside a companion website offering Microsoft PowerPoint presentations, assessments, and tutorials to provide ready-to-use-resources for professors and students, this engaging text will assist teachers in challenging and inspiring students to think creatively, problem-solve, and develop relevant skills as lifelong learners in the art education sector.

**Debrah C. Sickler-Voigt** is a professor of art education at Middle Tennessee State University with 20+ years of pre-K–18 art teaching experience. She is an active member of international and national art education organizations. She served as the Senior Editor for the National Art Education Association's popular white papers on assessment. Her professional website is www. arted.us.

# Teaching and Learning in Art Education

Cultivating Students' Potential
from Pre-K through High School

Debrah C. Sickler-Voigt

Routledge
Taylor & Francis Group

NEW YORK AND LONDON

First published 2020
by Routledge
52 Vanderbilt Avenue, New York, NY 10017

and by Routledge
2 Park Square, Milton Park, Abingdon, Oxon, OX14 4RN

*Routledge is an imprint of the Taylor & Francis Group, an informa business*

*Library of Congress Cataloging-in-Publication Data*
A catalog record for this book has been requested

ISBN: 978-1-138-54931-9 (hbk)
ISBN: 978-1-138-54932-6 (pbk)
ISBN: 978-1-351-00096-3 (ebk)

Typeset in Berling
by Apex CoVantage, LLC

Visit the companion website: www.routledge.com/cw/sickler-voigt

Dedicated to the Lidice Memorial's International Children's Exhibition of Fine Art Lidice (ICEFA Lidice) and its diligent work in educating society about the Lidice massacre and all children who are victims of war. Its exhibitions present children's diversified artistic interpretations through global themes that raise cultural awareness and promote children's perspectives of peace. While I was working on this textbook, its leadership, including Ivona Kasalická and Martina Lehmannová, invited me to be a part of its jury to experience firsthand the stellar work they do. My involvement with ICEFA Lidice has augmented my teaching and research practices, as well as given me special friendships. I am most honored to include artworks, teachings, and stories inspired by ICEFA Lidice within *Teaching and Learning in Art Education*.

Collaborative K–8 project (detail). © Carlos Alves and JC Carroll. United Arts Council of Collier County.

# Contents

# Artists' Lessons to Thrive!

# Spotlight on Student Art

# Models

# Preface

*Teaching and Learning in Art Education* invites readers to share in the best practices that motivate and inspire teachers and students to thrive and succeed in classroom settings and beyond. It is written for all people interested in art education and is designed for use in undergraduate and graduate courses as well as a reference for practicing educators. This textbook's comprehensive, student-centered approach explains current theories and practices for visual art instruction. It presents cutting-edge and established information that practitioners need to know in a user-friendly, approachable style to augment their existing knowledge and cultivate students' full potential. Its exemplary and thoughtful collection of internationally acclaimed pre-K–12 student artworks embody what children can achieve through quality art instruction and community support.

With the belief that we all share in the education of children and society, I have integrated a journey theme throughout this textbook. When we take journeys, we carry aspects of our past with us. As we move forward, we meet new people and acquire new information. On my journey to becoming an educator, I felt fortunate to have the support of mentors who assisted me as I learned how to teach and students who motivated me to better my teaching practices. Given that foundational support, I strive to provide guidance to teachers and students and listen to their interests and concerns. It is comforting to know other educators have experienced similar rewards and challenges and have shared their insights to help others. I also emphasize a "Yes, We Can!" approach, so that readers feel empowered as they learn this textbook's innovative methods for teaching, managing, and assessing art instruction.

Early in my art education studies, I learned how outstanding teaching correlates with quality student artwork and idea development. Ever since, I have spent significant time examining children's artworks, watching children's art making processes, and observing great teachers in action. With these inspirations, I learned how to access specialized art materials for my students and try new art methods so that we could create meaningful works and share special experiences. I am a firm believer in teaching students life skills using artists' exemplars. This textbook's **Spotlight on Student Art** features correlate with the chapters' guiding themes to take up-close looks at international student artworks and their meanings. Its **Artists' Lessons to Thrive!** features contain narrative texts on contemporary international artists (ones collected by famous museums and ones located in everyday communities) and the big ideas that drive their works. Together these resources serve as original inspirations for readers to develop into detailed lesson plans. Their open-ended format offers flexibility in planning for students' ages, lesson durations, class procedures, materials, and types of assessments.

*Teaching and Learning in Art Education's* five parts represent a comprehensive approach to art education:

- **Part I** begins with an overview of teaching and learning in today's diversified classroom and community spaces. It explains how educators implement a choice-based art curriculum to provide students with ongoing opportunities to make personally-driven curricular decisions, feel connected to learning tasks, and achieve positive results. It explains how to become assessment literate teachers who can assess and manage all aspects of teaching and learning.

- **Part II** teaches about diversified student learners. It describes children's development from early childhood through adolescence so that readers develop an understanding of where students have come from and where they are going in their physical, cognitive, social/emotional, and artistic development. Recognizing that students are unique individuals, it focuses on students' abilities and explains how to make modifications and accommodations so that all students can build new skills and succeed.

- **Part III** presents art inquiry methods through the study of aesthetics, art criticism, art history, and visual culture. It teaches how students of all ages can explore art's meanings, make informed judgments about art, study art's history, and identify how all types of people make art. It offers strategies to build students' visual literacy skills that broaden their ways of seeing and knowing to invoke greater understandings of the human experience.

- **Part IV** offers an array of fine art and crafts methods to guide students' creation of art using diverse art media. Its chapters are filled with spectacular exemplars created by adult and student artists to use as curricular inspirations. It emphasizes teaching artistic behaviors so that students learn the reasons why artists create and how their works communicate meanings. Readers can apply its

teachings to promote students' cognitive and creative skills.

- **Part V** concludes *Teaching and Learning in Art Education*, offering practical guidance for teachers to maintain career success by explaining the skills needed to be effective leaders and creators who build community partnerships and gain support for teaching and learning through a high quality art program. Its arts advocacy strategies discuss ways to bring positive recognition to the art program and explain why we need to teach art to students. It identifies pathways for teachers to explore their creativity and participate in professional development.

Ultimately, readers will discover ways to utilize and adapt *Teaching and Learning in Art Education's* informative resources to suit their instructional needs. Its **Chapter Questions and Activities** encourage readers to reflect upon what they have learned, make connections, and identify ways to thrive in their unique teaching circumstances. Its **companion website** offers rich resources that simplify textbook adoption for higher-education professionals and provide readers with supplemental resources and downloadable materials. Given its practical exemplars, readers will identify ways to employ their personal creativity to foster student achievement and career satisfaction.

I cordially invite you to utilize *Teaching and Learning in Art Education* and share in its educational journey to thrive and succeed in the classroom and beyond!

# Acknowledgements

*Teaching and Learning in Art Education* resulted from the contributions of many individuals, including the teachers, students, artists, and organizations identified within its pages and those who inspired me throughout my personal and professional development.

I thank the entire Routledge team, especially my editors, Simon Jacobs and Karen Adler. Both recognized the need for this comprehensive art education methods textbook. Simon Jacobs provided effective leadership and ongoing support. He guided *Teaching and Learning in Art Education* from its manuscript submission to its production and publication. He was always available to answer my questions and provide encouragement. We shared many laughs as we worked with editorial assistant Marie Andrews to reach our collective goals. Senior project manager Kate Fornadel kindly facilitated production. Karen Adler welcomed me to the Routledge family. She understood and fostered my creative vision for this textbook. I am most grateful to Simon and Karen who made my experience so positive and rewarding!

I dedicate this textbook to the International Children's Exhibition of Fine Arts Lidice (ICEFA Lidice; www.mdvv-lidice.cz/en/) for its outstanding work in promoting the value of children's art throughout the world. Its vast collection of children's artworks results from the organization's visionary leadership and the dedication of thousands of teachers and students. I am most grateful to ICEFA Lidice's entire staff and jury team (including Čeněk Hlavatý, Alena Zupková, Renata Mečkovskiené, Ilze Rimicane, Zuzana Hrubošová, Ivana Junková, Kateřina Krutská Vrbová, Pavel Rajdl, Jaroslava Spěváčková, Ivan Stoyanov, Lenka Zmeková), with special support from Ivona Kasalická, Martin Homola, Josef Zedník, Romana Štajerová, Vsevolod Romankov, Simply Art's Lau Family, Emi de Graeve, Dana Vondrušková, and Martina Lehmannová.

Artists and museum collections from around the world kindly offered the use of their artworks. It is an honor to include their works as teaching tools. International teachers and students shaped the development of this textbook. Quality teacher–student relationships motivate teachers and students to achieve great things. I offer heartfelt thanks to my teachers and students. Pablo Cano, Carlos Alves, JC Carroll, Tom Anderson, Mike Muller, Lynn Ezell, Heidi Powell, Julee Latimer, Rebecca Hunter, James McLean, Nancy Kelker, Lisa Wee, Gilbert Anglin, Shane McGinnis, Colin Looney, Jonathan Griffith, Lydia Horvath, David Chang, Nick Cave, Bob Faust, Signe Aarhus, Kimsooja, Bit, Nan Liu, Yichien Cooper, James McLean, Lorinne Lee, Suzanne St. John, and Monica Leister offered special support.

My family imparts the gifts of love, art, creativity, and culture. My grandmothers, Aileen and Mildred, set strong and nurturing foundations. Barbara, Betty, Ailee, and Tracey shared memorable artistic experiences. My stepfather, Howard, patiently taught me writing skills. My father, Richard, encouraged me to travel and work with tools to create. My husband, Norbert, supports me each day. My mother, Pamela, is my daily muse and inspiration. My family's love and support means the world to me.

I thank the readers of this textbook who will apply its teachings and their own unique styles to make a positive difference in people's lives.

I have deep gratitude for each of you!

# PART I

# Art Education

## Thriving in Teaching and Learning

# Chapter 1

# Teaching and Learning in Art Education

## An Overview

**FIGURE 1.1** Tamara Samveli Kocharian, 11-years-old, Dilizhanskaya Detskaya Khudozhestvenaia Shkola i. O. Sharambeiana, Dilizhan, Armenia.
*Source: ICEFA Lidice, 39th Exhibition.*

Welcome to *Teaching and Learning in Art Education: Cultivating Students' Potential From Pre-K Through High School*. This textbook provides pre-service and practicing teachers—and all others interested in art education—with the skills and insights needed to teach successfully in today's diversified learning environments. It addresses the ways that art contributes to humanity's overall well-being as a necessary and meaningful part of life (Dissanayake, 1995). *Teaching*

*and Learning in Art Education* presents teaching and advocacy methods to educate students and the greater society about the visual arts' purposes and functions. It contains an outstanding collection of international artworks and instructional resources that connect contemporary and established theories with best practices in art education. The student artworks shown in Figures 1.1–1.4 illustrate some of the ways that the visual arts are an essential part of life. Through this

**FIGURE 1.2** Elementary through high school students produce a stop-motion film. United States.

*Source: Author, Monica Leister, and Emily James.*

**FIGURE 1.3** Azimowa Dilaferuz Azimowowna, 14-years-old, Shkola N. 1, S. A. Nyyazow, Turkmenistan.

*Source: ICEFA Lidice, 39th Exhibition.*

**FIGURE 1.4** Lau You Gi, 8-years-old, Simply Art, Hong Kong, China.

*Source: ICEFA Lidice, 44th Exhibition.*

textbook's teachings, we will embark on a journey to discover effective teaching methods to cultivate students' full potential through art. We will participate in its comprehensive activities to meet chapter objectives like the following for this chapter:

- Describe the importance of art education in classroom and community settings.
- Explain how quality instruction fosters students' lifelong learning skills.
- Identify the value of comprehensive art education in students' lives with its connections to the National Visual Arts Standards (NVAS) and big ideas.

## CULTIVATING STUDENTS' FULL POTENTIAL THROUGH ART EDUCATION

Art education belongs to each of us. The positive attributes we remember from our educational experiences represent some of the characteristics that define quality art instruction. Great teachers care about students' personal growth and development. Their art curriculum challenges students to pose and answer serious questions, make connections among disciplines, and apply classroom knowledge to situations that extend beyond school (Trafi-Prats & Woywod, 2013). Great teachers enjoy teaching and inspire students to grow as individuals. They design meaningful lessons and establish open communications with students. All students have a voice. Students learn that it is okay for people to have different opinions as they participate in substantial conversations and learning tasks to answer questions about art, global topics, and life.

Teaching art in today's diversified learning environments, educators need to be prepared for the practicalities, rewards, and challenges that teachers and students face across our planet. Due to educational institutions' different missions, philosophies, resources, and levels of support, no one-size-fits-all approach or master key exists that can solve all teaching and learning obstacles. For example, classrooms and community settings for teaching art range from having fewer than ten to more than fifty students per teacher. Some learning spaces have the latest-and-greatest technologies, with ample room, supplies, and furnishings to nurture students' development. Others have inadequate resources and facilities. Many range between the two extremes. Teachers and students may come from different social, economic, ethnic, and religious backgrounds, and therefore must learn the subtleties of how people from differing backgrounds interact. Some students speak different languages; some are preparing for college; some are at risk for dropping out of school; some have disabilities; and some are highly accomplished (gifted and talented). When confronted with oversized classes, working with inadequate budgets and resources, and struggling with classroom management skills, teachers' enthusiasm can become frustration. This textbook provides practical solutions and helpful exemplars to support educators in being better prepared to teach art in all types of settings and advocate for students' access to a quality education through art, even when challenges arise.

To cultivate students' full potential, we need to carry a full set of keys and use each one to guide students on the path to success. Our teaching moves students away from solely memorizing rote information and parroting the teacher. We collaborate with students as parallel partners in learning. Students explore artistic behaviors, processes, and media to communicate ideas, such as modeling clay to replicate the human form or producing a still life (Figures 1.5 and 1.6).

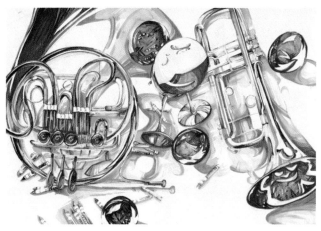

FIGURE 1.6 Chee Ying Ng, 16-years-old, Yeow Chye Art Centre, Penang, Malaysia.
Source: ICEFA Lidice, 43rd Exhibition.

They apply their varied life experiences to relate to class teachings (Freire, 2009). We make adaptations to our curriculum and instructional methods so that all students can achieve quality learning outcomes. This by no means entails dummying down the curriculum. When students have difficulty understanding topics or making personal connections to instruction, we help them overcome difficulties.

## COMPREHENSIVE ART EDUCATION

**Comprehensive art education** is a holistic student-centered approach to visual arts instruction (Anderson & Milbrandt, 2005; Parsons, 2004; Stewart & Walker, 2005). It developed in response to fast-paced technologies. Our world has progressed into an integrated, multicultural society with instant access to data in written, audible, and visual formats. Using technologies and other resources, comprehensive art education encourages students to learn how themes in art and diverse disciplines come together to invoke greater understandings. Students study the contextual reasons behind art production to make connections among disparate content to foster deeper understandings of local and global issues. Many educators teach comprehensive art education in conjunction with a **choice-based curriculum** so that students have ongoing opportunities to make personally-driven curricular decisions, feel connected to learning activities (Figure 1.7) and achieve positive results (Figure 1.8; Douglas & Jaquith, 2018).

FIGURE 1.5 Barbora Římalová, 10-years-old, Dům dětí a mládeže Praha 3–Ulita, Praha 3–Žižkov, Czech Republic.
Source: ICEFA Lidice, 39th Exhibition.

**FIGURE 1.7** Stephan Libwoni Shionda, 10-years-old, Kenya.
*Source: Lisa Wee, teacher.*

**FIGURE 1.8** Lee Min Hye, 13-years-old, Busan Middle School of Arts, Busan, South Korea.
*Source: ICEFA Lidice, 43rd Exhibition.*

Students learn effective ways to make curricular choices that include selecting concepts, processes, materials, and learning strategies. Rather than teachers giving students all the solutions, these practices

inspire students to answer questions and solve problems related to the theories, issues, and beliefs that shape humanity. Classrooms and community spaces become exploratory laboratories in which to cultivate students' acquisitions of knowledge. As a result, students have the ability to explore topics in depth and transfer class scholarship to the different contexts they encounter in life.

## Comprehensive Art Education and the National Visual Arts Standards

Comprehensive art education aligns with the NVAS. **Standards** signify the learning outcomes teachers expect students to achieve. Comprehensive art education provides an in-depth curricular plan that guides students in achieving learning outcomes as lifelong learners (McTighe & Wiggins, 2012). The **NVAS** (National Coalition for Core Arts Standards [NCCAS], 2014a) are voluntary standards developed by leading arts organizations with input from art educators and visual artists including Jaune Quick-to-See-Smith and Lawrence Gartel, who served on its National Artists Advisory Committee (these artists are featured in this textbook's Artists' Lessons to Thrive! 12.1 and 3.1). The NVAS writing team examined standards and arts practices from fifteen countries including the United States to identify best practices in art education. The team restructured the original 1994 standards to respond to changes in technology and address contemporary trends and theories. The NVAS model advocates that students gain quality arts experiences through the processes of creating, presenting, responding, and connecting. The NVAS prompts educators to design art curricula with end goals in mind, a practice called *backwards design* (Wiggins & McTighe, 2005), and to contemplate how students can apply learning outcomes to diversified contexts. Instead of viewing each grade and subject in isolation, the NVAS brings disparate ideas within the school curriculum together so that students learn content and meaning in depth to achieve long-term personal, educational, and professional goals.

**Big ideas** are broad topics that students study in depth to address significant human issues that remain relevant regardless of the times and cultures in which people live (Stewart & Walker, 2005; Wiggins & McTighe, 2005). The enduring understandings and essential questions presented in the NVAS and comprehensive art education assist students in grasping the meaning and reasoning behind the big ideas that drive learning tasks. **Enduring understandings** "are statements summarizing important ideas and core processes that are central to a discipline and have lasting value beyond the classroom;" they identify "what students should value about the content area over the course of their lifetimes" (NCCAS, 2014b, p. 14). An enduring understanding serves as an instructional resource for students to make sense of the curriculum and comprehend issues thoroughly. Students revisit topics to build on prior knowledge, contemplate varying perspectives, and transfer new information to other situations. **Essential questions** are broad-based questions that guide students as they attain knowledge about enduring understandings. The essential questions presented in the NVAS focus on topics relating to art, artists, creativity, events in time, global phenomena, and more. For example, Figures 1.9 and 1.10 provide visual stimuli for students to answer essential questions about the built environment, including: "How do built environment structures assist us in daily life?" or "In which ways do built environment designs shape communities?" They connect with the National Visual Arts Creating Standard #VA.CR.2.3, "Generate and conceptualize artistic ideas and work" (NCCAS, 2014a). When students participate in inquiry-driven learning tasks through essential questions, they learn to recognize how people have multiple and varied responses to essential questions and can generate additional inquiries based on what they have learned.

## Comprehensive Art Education's Framework and 21st Century Skills

Comprehensive art education's framework developed in response to previous ways of teaching art. For much of the 20th century, art educators taught creativity in isolation through studio art production practices. In the 1980s the Getty Institute collaborated with art education scholars to develop **Discipline-Based Art Education** (DBAE), a method for teaching art that extended beyond studio art production to provide students with deeper levels of artistic understandings (Clark, Day, & Greer, 1987). The DBAE model added

**FIGURE 1.9** Coley Lee, 13-years-old, United States.
*Source: Mike Muller, teacher.*

**FIGURE 1.10** Group project, 7–14-years-old, ZUŠ Václava Talicha, Beroun, Czech Republic.
*Source: ICEFA Lidice, 39th Exhibition.*

the disciplines of aesthetics, art criticism, and art history to the school curriculum.

- **Art production** represents the creation of artworks, including drawings, paintings, sculptures, textiles, installations, digital products, and performances.

- **Aesthetics** is a branch of philosophy that focuses on the nature of art and beauty. It asks: "What is art?" Artists and designers apply their understanding of local and global art concepts, traditions, and beauty to form aesthetic works.
- **Art criticism** is a method of talking and writing about art to form educated opinions about artworks. Individuals look for details and meanings within artistic products.
- **Art history** is the study of artists, including people of all genders, cultures, races, ethnic backgrounds, and religions who have made artworks and crafts throughout time.

DBAE presented art as a core subject in schools. It focused on teaching students how to make and respond to art competently by combining the four disciplines (art production, aesthetics, art criticism, and art history) to give students a broader understanding of art's meaning. In the subsequent decades, art educators expanded DBAE into **comprehensive art education** to reach beyond visual art and include multicultural and contextual studies so that the visual arts did not appear disconnected from students' fuller school and life experiences. Added disciplines included visual culture studies, contemporary technologies, and creative self-expression in a social context (Anderson & Milbrandt, 2005).

- **Visual culture studies** deconstruct the meanings of all types of images within global society, including the visual arts and graphic works, such as magazine ads, websites, and media images. Individuals seek to understand the reasons behind their production and how their messages might invoke actions and inactions among viewers.
- **Contemporary technologies** bring awareness to our global interconnectedness and society's use of technological information to receive visual, auditory, written, and multimedia data.
- **Creative self-expression in a social context** is based on the belief that students have the ability to research and explore issues, identify problems, and figure out solutions through art processes, media, and integrated subject matter.

With the implementation of the National Core Arts Standards (NCCAS, 2014a), arts practitioners developed a framework that consists of creating, presenting, responding, and connecting to guide the comprehensive choice-based art curriculum. The framework builds on the visual arts' disciplines from the DBAE and the earlier model of comprehensive art education.

- **Creating** is the act of conceptualizing, making, and manipulating art and other works. Like artists, students explore art media and art production processes to communicate ideas (Figures 1.11–1.13). Their creative products include fine art, designs, crafts, digital technologies, diagrams, installations, performances, writings, compilations, and more.

**FIGURE 1.11** Jovana Tomanovič, 4-years-old, Kindergarden Zagorka Ivanović, Cetinje, Montenegro.
*Source: ICEFA Lidice, 40th Exhibition.*

**FIGURE 1.12** G.U.D. Abgywardana Maggona, 10-years-old, Sri Lanka National Foundation for Child Art, Rajagiriya, Sri Lanka.
*Source: ICEFA Lidice, 39th Exhibition.*

**FIGURE 1.13** J. Joyce Khu, 13-years-old, St. Stephen's High School, Manila, St. Cruz, Philippines.
*Source: ICEFA Lidice, 39th Exhibition.*

- **Presenting** is the process of introducing, explaining, and/or showing artworks, performances, products, collections, and ideas to impart knowledge and prompt interpretations. Students present artworks, portfolios, and other creative products during class discussions and critiques. They display works in physical locations and virtual spaces, and they examine how curators present and exhibit art and artifacts.
- **Responding** occurs when students reply to big ideas, essential questions, and content in art history, aesthetics, visual culture, the environment, and/or other subjects. Student responses include participating in class discussions as well as creating artworks, journals, portfolios, writings, and multimedia presentations. These products and processes provide structures for students to ask questions, give feedback, cite evidence, and make informed evaluations.
- **Connecting** represents students' abilities to make associations and synthesize information about art

and topics in daily life to generate new ideas, link disparate concepts, elaborate upon what already exists, explain context, and develop creative works. Students make personally-driven connections as they create, present their works and perceptions, and make informed responses to curricular content.

Comprehensive art education's framework builds **21st century skills** that include students becoming competent in one or more disciplines, synthesizing information, applying creativity to diverse situations to construct a foundation of knowledge that is applicable to their present lives, and continuing to investigate and expand on what they know as lifelong learners (Dean et al., 2010). The *Teaching and Learning in Art Education* model of implementing comprehensive art education is a choice-based, hybrid approach that recognizes that teachers and students have varying wants and needs. It references artists' ways of knowing. Just as artists choose among different pathways to research ideas, explore, and create, the comprehensive, choice-based art curriculum offers flexibility in mixing and matching methods of instruction, learning, and assessment to demonstrate best practices in art education. Students cultivate ideas through creative practices, experimentation, dialogue, play, and research. Educators facilitate student learning by offering more or less structure depending on the nature of learning tasks so that students can gain skills and insights while having independent and collaborative exploration opportunities. This textbook's Spotlight on Student Art features provide in-depth looks at student artworks that result from the comprehensive study of art and student choices. Spotlight on Student Art #1 describes how students examined international childhood creativity through the NVAS framework. Teachers can apply and adapt its model to suit their classroom needs.

## Spotlight on Student Art #1

### Big Idea: Creativity

Children across our planet create artworks to communicate ideas and express creativity. While children sometimes present similar content in their art, their artistic styles and applications of art media can vary from region to region according to customary beliefs and aesthetic preferences. To examine these phenomena in depth, students in the United States studied global artworks from the International

Children's Exhibition of Fine Arts Lidice (ICEFA Lidice), including 11-year-old Tamara's painting, which depicts the vital role of creativity and imagination in children's lives (Figure 1.1). Since 1967, ICEFA Lidice has exhibited students' artworks to honor child victims of war. The organization is a worldwide participant in the United Nations Educational, Scientific, and Cultural Organization's (UNESCO) Intangible Cultural Heritage program to preserve cultural traditions.

Given this information, the students participated in multidisciplinary learning activities to broaden their perceptions about childhood creativity in the following ways.

1.  **Responding**: The students participated in a presentation featuring artworks in the ICEFA Lidice collection. They learned how the organization categorized its exhibitions according to the United Nations' annual themes. They discussed the qualities that made the artworks pleasing and relevant. They developed informed opinions about possible meanings of the international children's artworks.
2.  **Creating**: Inspired by the ICEFA Lidice's international children's artworks and themes, the students produced original sketches and designs using the media of their choice. They incorporated the information they learned from the class presentation and their research on global topics and aesthetic values to form artistic designs that communicated their understandings of childhood creativity.
3.  **Connecting**: The school's art and international clubs formed a new community by partnering for this project. The students compared and contrasted the cultural iconography presented in the international artworks and made informed judgments about their designs, functions, and qualities. They made connections between what they observed in American and other cultures. As researchers and producers of art, they expressed personal connections to the students who created the artworks.
4.  **Presenting**: The students presented their works as part of a class critique. They interpreted and evaluated the quality and content of their work and its connections to ICEFA Lidice collection of children's artworks.

## ARTISTS' LESSONS TO THRIVE! CHOICE-BASED RESOURCES FOR TEACHING AND LEARNING

This textbook's Artists' Lessons to Thrive! features are instructional resources that contain narrative texts on contemporary artists and the big ideas that drive their work. Studying artworks by contemporary artists informs students about issues that matter to society. Students learn firsthand how artists communicate important ideas through art media. Artists' Lessons to Thrive! features include essential/guiding questions to lead class discussions, oral/written reflections, and art production activities. They provide substantial content and context with sample daily learning targets and standards as inspirations for educators to develop into detailed lesson

plans (see Chapter 2). Their open-ended format offers teachers flexibility in planning for students' ages, lesson durations, class procedures, materials, and types of assessment. Artists' Lessons to Thrive! features bring awareness to issues of social ethics through art; assist students in gaining knowledge of artistic concepts, behaviors, and techniques; and augment student learning through multidisciplinary art studies (Weisman & Hanes, 2002).

## Social Ethics Through Art

Curricular topics in **social ethics through art** teach students about the civic and moral issues that impact people locally and globally. They are relevant because students of all ages have an ability to discuss the social and ethical issues they see in the media and in civic life. Artists have a long history of developing artworks in response to social and ethical concerns. Studying social ethics is rooted in **postmodernism,** a social philosophy developed in the later half of the 20th century. Postmodernism centers on equality, community, environmental protection, multiculturalism, and gender. Postmodernism brings awareness to life's inequities and calls for action to correct injustices to create more egalitarian societies. The postmodernists presented a more accurate representation of global art and its creators, who include people of all gender, racial, religious, socioeconomic, and ethnic backgrounds. They encouraged educators to teach students about local artists and employ **contextualism,** a method for learning the stories and circumstances behind artistic creations (Congdon, 2004; Efland, Freedman, & Stuhr, 1996).

**Art Education for Social Justice** is a mindful approach to teaching art that grew out of postmodernism and promotes social well-being and equity for all people. It embraces the **Art for Life** philosophy, which teaches students how to value the skills and dispositions acquired through comprehensive art studies and apply what they have learned to their present lives and future roles as well-rounded adults (Anderson, 2010; Anderson & Milbrandt, 2005). Lessons about social justice can be important outlets for students experiencing society's contemporary challenges. For instance, cultural shifts resulting from instant virtual technologies and greater exposure to violent terror attacks against civilians have moved us into a **post-postmodern** era (McHale, 2015). Post-postmodernism retains its predecessor's social values, while recognizing the impacts that technology and extreme violence have on the world. Working in a safe and supportive learning environment, students can apply social topics to cope with and make ethical decisions about the meanings and messages that artworks and other visual examples transmit and form constructive responses. Teachers can guide students as they learn to overcome obstacles and find solutions to the problems humans share. For example, Artists' Lessons to Thrive! 1.1, "Nick Cave: We All Need Protection," focuses on social ethics through art and the big idea of protection. It teaches students how Cave created art in response to his personal need for protection as an African American

male living in the United States during a time of racial tension (Finkel, 2009). His art is a vehicle for students to contemplate protection's different meanings and encourages them to make personal connections to all living beings' need for protection.

While children regularly see issues relating to social ethics depicted in the media, some educators may feel hesitant teaching about social ethics, especially controversial topics. A safe introduction is for teachers to select subjects that have established historical contexts. They can advance to more challenging ones when they feel ready. When educators feel unsure about the appropriateness of social ethics subject matter for their students and community, they can check with their administration to find the most effective means to address sensitive age-appropriate topics within the curriculum.

When students gain experience analyzing social ethics through art, educators might align further investigations through **participatory action research,** a multidisciplinary research method that calls upon teachers and students to collaborate as equal partners while posing pertinent questions and working with community members to solve problems and make fair and ethical decisions (Maguire, 2000; Sickler-Voigt, 2002). Its philosophy is rooted in providing underserved populations with a voice, which can include children whose voices may be ignored by adults. This model is appropriate for teaching students because young people are at risk for greater emotional, health, and societal problems than adults, and they need to have their needs met (see Chapter 6). Through participatory action research, students identify the challenges they are experiencing as a class and/or as individuals. Educators listen to students' opinions and concerns, and collaborate with them to devise possible solutions to problems. Students begin their research by identifying the issues at hand, then conducting a review of literature. They may conduct interviews to learn what others have to say about similar problems and their solutions. Artists' works function as exemplars to address important topics and find solutions. Students can use journals to collect relevant notes, sketches, photographs, and other related data. After their data collection, analysis, and interpretation, they can share their ideas, discoveries, and answers with others through discussions, art productions, writing activities, and multimedia presentations.

## Artists' Lessons to Thrive! 1.1 Nick Cave: We All Need Protection

### Big Idea: Protection

We all need protection. Throughout history, humans have developed protective shelters, seasonal clothing, and body armor to ensure survival and comfort. Nick Cave is a fine artist, designer, and dancer who creates wearable sculptural art forms called *Soundsuits* that serve as a metaphor for protective skin. In 1992, Cave reflected on his identity as an African American male after watching media reports of riots in the Los Angeles community by African Americans who were outraged when a jury acquitted police officers who brutally beat Rodney King, an African American suspect in a car chase. Sitting in a park, Cave noticed twigs lying on the ground and compared their sense of abandonment with his own, and the similar feelings other members of his ethnicity might have also experienced, and picked them up. At that moment, Cave discovered the inspiration for his artwork *Soundsuit Made From Twigs* (Figure 1.1.1). He cut twigs into 3-inch long pieces, drilled holes into their bases, and sewed them onto an undergarment that he designed. While working on this project, he realized that he could actually wear the piece as body armor. "When I was inside a suit, you couldn't tell if I was a woman or man; if I was black, red, green or orange; from Haiti or South Africa," he said. "I was no longer Nick. I was a shaman of sorts" (Finkel, 2009, p. AR22). Cave felt inspired by the sounds of the twigs in motion as he wore his suit. They resonated with his passion and training in

**FIGURE 1.1.1** Nick Cave, *Soundsuit Made From Twigs.*
*Source: Photo by James Prince, courtesy of the artist and Jack Shainman Gallery. http://nickcaveart.com/Main/Intro.html*

dance and he decided to use his *Soundsuit* as a performance piece in addition to designing it as a sculptural artwork.

Since his initial *Soundsuit* creation, Cave has designed numerous suits using brightly colored objects from material culture including buttons, hair, figurines, crocheted pieces, sweaters, socks, hats, purses, and other hand-me-downs, which were common in Cave's upbringing. His family, like many families, had limited financial resources and Cave learned how to work with the materials he had available to him (Finkel, 2009). Watching Cave perform in his *Soundsuits*, viewers witness Cave's inspiration from African ceremonial dances, similar to ones in which a performer calls upon sacred ancestral powers through ritual practice to obtain protection from the environment and promote a sense of well-being. Cave continued to evolve his *Soundsuit* designs and performances; he has incorporated teams of dancers wearing his visually stunning suits into magnificent productions. Since creating his initial *Soundsuit*, Cave has developed numerous *Soundsuits* that exemplify his cheerful style. While these *Soundsuits* have moved away from sharp and potentially harmful edges, they continue to serve as cultural protectors.

## Essential/Guiding Questions

1. Why do certain individuals or groups of people receive less access to protection than others? What role did a lack of protection play in Cave's development of his *Soundsuit Made From Twigs*? How do your feelings on forming and maintaining socially just societies and treating others ethically guide your answers?
2. Conduct an Internet search to view Cave's *Soundsuit* performances. Of what do they remind you? Reflect on a time when you sought protection. Would you have liked to have worn one of Cave's *Soundsuits* to feel more protected?

## Preparation

Students will discuss bullying and the need for protection from bullying. Students will make correlations between anti-bullying strategies and Nick Cave's *Soundsuits*. Students will work individually or in small groups to create their art project and performance.

## Daily Learning Targets

I can create a protective device, shelter, or symbol that focuses on anti-bullying.

- I can incorporate found objects that represent anti-bullying into my design.
- I can create a unified design that includes repetition and rhythm.
- I can create a short performance (2–5 minutes) that explains the meaning of my protective device, shelter, or symbol.

**National Core Arts Anchor Standards** 1, 5, 8, and 11

www.nationalartsstandards.org

## Artistic Concepts, Behaviors, and Techniques

The comprehensive art curriculum teaches **artistic concepts, behaviors, and techniques**. Art students have long studied the history of art, artistic styles, subject matter, media, and design. Beginning in the early 20th century, Arthur Wesley Dow's principles for teaching composition and the Bauhaus' emphasis on the design theory of the elements of art and principles of design to analyze artworks strongly impacted the way people have produced, talked, and written about art (Brainard, 2006; Dow, 1914). Influenced by these practices, educators taught art-making skills using a formalist approach that focused on the media and the formal qualities of the elements of art and the principles of design, the visual components artists combine and arrange to produce effective compositions (Efland et al., 1996). The **elements of art** include the basic units that make up an artwork: line, color, shape, form, space, texture, and value. When artists arrange the elements they produce the **principles of design,** which consist of balance, contrast, emphasis, movement, pattern, proportion, repetition, rhythm, variety, and unity (see Model 1.1).

Artists', educators', and scholars' focus on the manipulation of art media and the elements and principles was grounded in a popular philosophy called ***modernism*** that emphasized the role of the creative and original artist who made art for art's sake. This paradigm, which predates postmodernism, emphasizes the artwork's design and the artist's manipulation of materials. It differs from studying the contextual meanings that extend beyond

## Model 1.1
## Elements of Art and Principles of Design

| Elements of Art | |
|---|---|
| **Line** | The basic element of art, line is made from a series of dots moving in one or more directions. |
| **Color** | The amount of reflected light on a surface determines its hue, value, and intensity. |
| **Shape** | Shape is the two-dimensional area created by an enclosed, line, space, or color. |
| **Form** | Form refers to a three-dimensional object having height, width, and depth. |
| **Space** | Space refers to the two- or three-dimensional area within or surrounding a work of art. It shows the distance between or within objects in an artwork. |
| **Texture** | The way a surface feels or looks like it would feel is its texture. |
| **Value** | Value describes the range of lights and darks within an artwork. It is used to show shading and mood. |
| **Principles of Design** | |
| **Balance** | The stable distribution of visual weight within an artwork provides a feeling of equilibrium and organizes a composition. Balance can be symmetrical (formal), asymmetrical (informal), or radial. |
| **Contrast** | The relationship of opposite elements in an artwork, called *contrast*, is used to show emphasis and organize spatial relationships. |
| **Emphasis** | This is also known as **dominance,** and it refers to an area or object within an artwork that stands out the most and grabs the viewer's attention. |
| **Movement** | The actual or implied motion in an artwork is referred to as *movement*. |
| **Pattern** | The repetition of the elements of art within a composition is called its *pattern*. |
| **Proportion** | This refers to the relationship of different elements or different sizes within an artwork. |
| **Repetition** | The arrangement of similar elements or objects within an artwork is called *repetition*. All patterns show repetition, but not all repeated elements form patterns. |
| **Rhythm** | The visual movement within an artwork that dictates the direction the viewer's eye will travel, rhythm is influenced by repeated elements in a composition. |
| **Variety** | *Variety* refers to the visually satisfying arrangement of different elements and objects within an artwork. |
| **Unity** | Also known as **harmony,** unity provides a sense of order in which all elements and principles effectively come together in a composition and give the work a sense of completion. Nothing needs to be added to or taken away from the composition. All parts belong together. |

physical artworks and the comprehensive art activities presented throughout this textbook. The comprehensive art curriculum teaches students how to connect artistic styles, art media, and design qualities with big ideas, enduring understandings, and essential and guiding questions (Gude, 2004; NCCAS, 2014a). Teachers guide students in contemplating the mindsets and artistic behaviors that are necessary to produce anticipated and unanticipated meanings (Hetland, Winner, Veenema, & Sheridan, 2013). Students study artistic ways of knowing to respond to and produce art. They become involved in higher-level thinking and move beyond basic art exercises of studying art elements, principles, and media in isolation. Artists' Lessons to Thrive! 1.2, "Geese of Good

Fortune," centers on artistic concepts, behaviors, and techniques expressed through the big ideas of good fortune and prosperity. Three artists, living in different times and cultures, applied their knowledge and professional skills to produce artworks representing the same subject. The lesson's examples teach students why the artists selected particular media and methods to produce each artwork while examining the shared meanings of good fortune and prosperity as portrayed through the geese represented in these works. Understanding the context that drove the artworks' production, students can examine them to pinpoint artists' suggested meanings as depicted through their form, surface treatments, and the unique qualities of each medium.

## Artists' Lessons to Thrive! 1.2 Geese of Good Fortune

### Big Ideas: Good Fortune and Prosperity

Artists may share similar subject matter as their inspiration when creating artworks, even when they live far apart, have access to different art materials, and value distinct aesthetic preferences. The artworks *Belt Hook With Goose Head* from China's Middle Qing Dynasty (Figure 1.2.1), *Water Dropper in the Form of a Goose* from 19th century Japan (Figure 1.2.2), and the contemporary sculpture *Geese Marionettes* (Figure 1.2.3) by Pablo Cano all represent three-dimensional goose forms, yet they vary in their materials, meanings, and functions. In Eastern and Western cultures, the geese signify messengers of good fortune, fidelity, marital bliss, and prosperity (Welch, 2008).

**FIGURE 1.2.1** *Belt Hook With Goose Head*. China, Middle Qing Dynasty, about 1700–1800. Abraded jade 3 3/4 × 5/8 × 5/8 in. (9.5 × 1.6 × 1.6 cm). Gift of Patricia G. Cohan (M.2001.179.14). LACMA Public Domain.

*Source: www.lacma.org*

**FIGURE 1.2.2** *Water Dropper in the Form of a Goose*. Japan, 19th century. Hirado ware; porcelain with white glaze 3 × 3 1/4 × 1 1/2 in. (7.62 × 8.26 × 3.81 cm). Gift of Allan and Maxine Kurtzman (M.2005.79.14). LACMA Public Domain.
*Source: www.lacma.org*

**FIGURE 1.2.3** Pablo Cano, *Geese Marionettes, The Toy Box*, 2004.
*Source: Courtesy of the artist.*

For centuries, Chinese imperial society valued jade carvings as an elite status symbol because of their beauty and the labor-intensive reduction method used in their production. Jade stones were equivalent in worth to diamonds in Western society, and Chinese authorities prohibited ordinary people from collecting the stones from riverbeds. Because jade is too hard to carve with a knife, the Chinese artisan who designed and created the belt hook used an abrasive technique that rubbed hard sand particles into the jade's surface to wear it down into its highly stylized and elongated goose form. An artisan's skill in combination with the prized jade made this Chinese art form highly valuable (Zhang, 2004).

Rather than removing particles from a hard surface, a Japanese ceramicist manipulated soft, creamy porcelain clay to form the goose water dropper. The artist then applied a fine white transparent glaze to add an elegant sheen to the plump goose form. The goose water dropper, created in the Hirado region, was valued for its excellent quality porcelain with its delicate consistency and fine craftspersonship (Huish, 2005).

Unlike the Chinese and Japanese sculptures created from costly materials, Cano assembled his geese using repurposed squirt bottles, wood scraps, and tissue boxes. The artist's abstracted forms move away from the grace of the Chinese *Belt Hook With Goose Head* and the innocent expression of the Japanese *Water Dropper in the Form of a Goose*. Cano's arrangements of everyday household objects present his unique understanding of the geese's form and function. Whereas the Asian geese sculptures had a specific purpose attached to their ornate designs, Cano abandoned the functionalities of the squirt bottles and tissues that form the geese bodies and turned them into art for pure enjoyment.

## Essential/Guiding Questions

1. Do these artworks communicate ideas about good fortune and prosperity equally? How do artists' choice of media impact our understanding and responses to art? How might our perceptions and preferences change when we see various artists present the same subject matter in different ways? For example, do we naturally prefer the artworks created with costly art materials or become excited by seeing something new and unusual?
2. How have geese been presented in your community? Do you see them in nature, hear about them in stories such as those in *Mother Goose*, imagine them in games such as *Duck, Duck, Goose*, or hear them in everyday expressions including "gone on a wild goose chase"? How have these concepts been presented in fine art and visual culture? (Consider examples including flying geese patterned quilts and *Mother Goose* illustrations.)

## Preparation

Students will discuss the meanings of good fortune and prosperity. They will describe how curators exhibit collections of artworks containing animals as subject matter. They will conduct an Internet and book scavenger hunt to research animals that have symbolic meaning in multiple cultures. Each student will collect three different pictures of his/her selected animal in his/her journal to show how the animal has appeared in art and visual culture.

## Daily Learning Targets

I can create an artwork that incorporates an animal's symbolic meaning in a given culture.

- I can use art media to emphasize the animal, apply texture, and demonstrate unity and craftspersonship in my completed design.
- I can describe how my choice of media impacted my communication of the animal's symbolic meaning.
- I can write a narrative that describes the animal's cultural meaning and identify how the symbolic meaning connects to my life.

**National Core Arts Anchor Standards** 2, 4, 8, and 11
www.nationalartsstandards.org

## Multidisciplinary Art Studies: STEAM and the Humanities

**Multidisciplinary art studies** integrate the visual arts with **STEM** (<u>s</u>cience, <u>t</u>echnology, <u>e</u>ngineering, and <u>m</u>athematics) and the **humanities** (language arts, social studies, history, and the performing arts). With arts integration, STEM becomes **STEAM** (<u>s</u>cience, <u>t</u>echnology, <u>e</u>ngineering, <u>a</u>rts, and <u>m</u>athematics). Congress (2015) identified STE(A)M as part of a well-rounded education and advocates that students participate in a STE(A)M curriculum that offers "rigorous, relevant, and integrated learning experiences," while "providing hands-on learning" opportunities. Quality STEAM learning tasks have the potential to move students forward in augmenting their creative and scientific reasoning skills. One approach to teaching STEAM is through **E<u>a</u>rth Education** (Earth Art Education), a model informed by humanity's ethical stewardship of the planet (Anderson & Guyas, 2012). Students study scientific topics such as environmental protection, biodiversity, and sustainability through art. They learn how environmental artists employ sensory awareness and individual perceptions to become mindful of their role within ecosystems and the places that surround them. In practicing E<u>a</u>rth Education, students can repurpose postconsumer products into their art to reduce waste. They might spend time in nature to create art and develop environmentally inspired writings and sketches in their journals.

Academic language is at the heart of oral and written communication about art. Students apply language arts skills as they talk and write about art and visual culture through aesthetics, art criticism, and art history learning tasks to gain greater understanding of subject matter. They read stories about artists and other subjects, many of which are infused with illustrations. The visual arts lend themselves to social studies as students learn about cultures' norms, symbols, and belief systems. Students can compare and contrast the meanings and functions that inspire global art productions given their ongoing studies in the visual arts. Artists' Lessons to Thrive! 1.3 on Sher Christopher's *The Pied Piper* (Figure 1.3.1) integrates language arts and the visual arts to teach about honesty using characters in a popular children's story. Its subject matter prompts students to compare the artwork with the original story. In doing so, students apply language arts skills that include learning new vocabulary, storytelling, and analyzing art and book illustrations. The lesson can be extended to include medieval studies and STEAM content, such as Christopher's ability to produce a balanced and proportioned paper sculpture based on mathematical principles.

### Artists' Lessons to Thrive! 1.3 Sher Christopher's *The Pied Piper*: Honesty Is the Best Policy

#### Big Idea: Honesty

Children are excited by narrative texts, including fairytales and biographies, that feature characters and storylines with which children can relate. Many children have read *The Pied Piper,* which describes a medieval town infested with rats that had eaten all of the people's food and damaged their homes. In desperation, they implore the mayor to find a solution to rid the town of its rats. When all hope seems to fail, a stranger called the Pied Piper approaches the mayor and promises to remove the rats from the town for a fair payment. The mayor agrees to pay the Pied Piper for his services, and the Pied Piper plays his melodic pipe to lure the rats away. When the Pied Piper comes to collect his payment, the mayor pays him much less than originally promised because he feels that the Pied Piper's job was too easy. Enraged and disillusioned, the Pied Piper believes that the town's children should not grow up in a place where they would become dishonest adults. He plays his pipe and lures the children away to a distant land where they can sing, play, and live meaningful lives (Jackson & Disney, 1933). The Pied Piper accomplished his mission by freeing the children from an immoral life, but he left the town's people disheartened because they missed their children.

2009 Dicipline Based Art Education: thats what you did in H.S
formula on pg. 9
Teaching and Learning in Art Education    **19**
Now Comprehensive art teaches life skills: honesty, cultures, protection
education
Builton

**FIGURE 1.3.1** Sher Christopher, *The Pied Piper* ©.
*Source: Courtesy of the artist; www.sherchristopher.com.*

Like children, adults respond to the *Pied Piper* tale. Building on childhood memories, British paper sculptor Sher Christopher constructed her *Pied Piper* figure in a squatting position, playing his magical tune to an audience of rats, by manipulating colored paper into lifelike forms (Figure 1.3.1). She twisted black paper into tight curls to create his hair and strategically placed folds into his cape so that they would drape over his body. To express the *Pied Piper's* unyielding confidence in his rat-ridding abilities, Christopher depicted him concentrating steadily with the rats gleefully listening to his musical notes.

## Essential/Guiding Questions

1. How do Christopher's *Pied Piper* sculpture and book illustrations help people understand the story better? What, if any, new words did you hear in the *Pied Piper* story?
2. What does the *Pied Piper* communicate about honesty? What would you have done if you were the mayor or the Pied Piper? How might have your actions changed the story?

## Preparation

Students learn how to tell their own stories by hearing other people's stories. The class will read the story of the Pied Piper, discuss Sher Christopher's artwork, and define honesty. They will develop and share original short stories about honesty with their classmates.

## Daily Learning Targets

I can develop a two- or three-dimensional illustrated story that teaches honesty is the best policy.

- I can integrate at least one reference from the *Pied Piper* and Sher Christopher's art in my design.
- I can show emphasis, unity, and craftspersonship in my completed illustrated story.
- I can exhibit my illustrated story in a public setting and read my story during the opening reception.

**National Core Arts Anchor Standards** 1, 6, 8, and 11
www.nationalartsstandards.org

## MAKING CONNECTIONS THROUGH COMPREHENSIVE ART EDUCATION

In varying degrees, comprehensive art lessons address social ethics through art; artistic concepts, behaviors, and techniques; and multidisciplinary studies. They provide students with rich learning experiences and choices as they synergize information to understand subject matter in context. Model 1.2, "Weaving Big Ideas Into the Comprehensive Choice-Based Art Curriculum," deconstructs and builds upon Artists' Lessons to Thrive! 1.1 on Nick Cave to present possibilities for developing comprehensive learning tasks that combine social ethics through art; artistic concepts, behaviors, and techniques; and multidisciplinary art studies. The model includes sample essential/guiding questions that encourage class discussions, reflective writing, and art production activities. It also incorporates the NVAS framework of creating, presenting, responding and connecting (NCCAS, 2014a), as well as social justice, Earth Education, and participatory action research. It assists educators in visualizing how this chapter's teachings come together to structure choice-based comprehensive learning tasks.

### Model 1.2
### Weaving Big Ideas Into the Comprehensive Choice-Based Art Curriculum

| **Artist: Nick Cave** | **Big Idea: Protection** | |
|---|---|---|
| **Essential/Guiding Questions** | | |
| 1. What is protection? Why is protection a basic human need?<br>2. Why do humans protect people and the things they care about? How have you protected and been protected by others?<br>3. How is protection presented in the media and visual culture? Are the things that we see in the media always meant to make us feel safe and protected? How might they harm, rather than protect us? | | |
| • **Art Education for Social Justice**: Why is the issue of protection an important social issue in my community and the broader world? How can I present these concepts in my art?<br>• **Earth Education**: How can I extend my study of protection to include strategies to protect our planet?<br>• **Participatory action research**: Which steps can my class take to protect each other and others within our community (or beyond)? | | |
| **Creating, Presenting, Responding, and Connecting** (NCCAS, 2014a) | | |
| **Social Ethics Through Art** | **Artistic Concepts, Behaviors, and Techniques** | **Multidisciplinary Studies: STEAM and the Humanities** |
| • Given examples of Cave's *Soundsuits*, I can create an artwork that identifies why protection is a basic human need. I can make connections that identify how I need protection in my own life.<br>• I can describe (in paragraph form) a time that I protected someone else.<br>• I can research three different examples of how protection is presented in the media and orally summarize my findings to the class. | • I can explain why Nick Cave's *Soundsuits* are protective even though they are artworks made from harmless found objects.<br>• I can identify some of the artistic processes Cave used to construct his *Soundsuits*.<br>• I can select the appropriate materials to create a wearable protective artwork.<br><br>Elements and Principles:<br>• color<br>• texture<br>• form<br>• contrast<br>• emphasis<br>• repetition<br>• unity | • **Language arts:** Given a group discussion on protection, I can create a one-page written and illustrated journal page that defines protection in my own words and includes my reflection on the role of protection in my own life.<br>• **Mathematics:** I can identify and count the key words repeated within a commercial promoting protection. (Advertisers jam marketing information into short segments, such as thirty seconds, and repeat key words and phrases.) I can explain how repetition impacts a commercial's message.<br>• **Theatre:** I can write and perform a skit about protection that contains characters that communicate the need for protection. |

## OUR JOURNEY TO THRIVE CONTINUES . . .

This chapter provided an overview for cultivating student learning in the classroom and beyond. We discussed methods to offer students personally-driven curricular choices, encourage them to raise questions, and find creative solutions as they connect artistic concepts, behaviors, and techniques with issues of social ethics and multidisciplinary studies. Given this information, we are learning how do the following:

- Provide students with a choice-based art curriculum using established guidelines and teach students how to articulate their ideas to make curricular choices.
- Collaborate with students to develop individual and group learning tasks.
- Encourage students to explore art processes and media through big ideas.
- Promote students' deeper understandings through integrated subjects. Art is not an isolated subject. Students make connections and cluster ideas to form new knowledge.
- Explain the contextual motivations behind global art productions and how they contribute to our understandings of the world. All types of people from all societies produce art.
- Incorporate research- and inquiry-based learning tasks to develop students' 21st century skills. Students are active learners who pose questions and solve problems.

In forthcoming chapters, we will delve further into choice-based comprehensive art education and learn effective strategies for developing an art curriculum and assessments. We will identify effective classroom management skills and contemplate how to set high expectations and create a nurturing classroom environment. In Part II of this textbook, we will develop curricular activities that are appropriate for students' age and skill levels and make accommodations for diversified learners. In Part III, we will develop instructional resources and techniques that encourage students to respond to art through aesthetics, art criticism, art history, and visual culture. In Part IV, we will examine which art media and processes are best suited for students' different ages and apply artist exemplars to cultivate students' artistic behaviors and mindsets as they explore studio art methods. *Teaching and Learning in Art Education* concludes in Part V with strategies to assist us in making the most of our teaching careers as arts advocates, creative professionals, and lifelong learners.

## CHAPTER QUESTIONS AND ACTIVITIES

1. Describe art education in classrooms and beyond. Which theories and practices influence quality teaching and learning? How would you apply them to shape your teaching practice?
2. What is comprehensive art education? How do the NVAS and its framework work in collaboration with comprehensive art education?
3. Answer Artists' Lessons to Thrive! 1.1–1.3 essential/guiding questions in written form or as part of a group discussion. Complete their daily learning targets.

---

## References

Anderson, T. (2010). An introduction to art education for social justice. In T. Anderson, D. Gussak, K. Hallmark, & A. Paul (Eds.), *Art education for social justice* (pp. 2–13). Reston, VA: National Art Education Association.

Anderson, T., & Guyas, A. S. (2012). Earth education, interbeing, and deep ecology. *Studies in Art Education, 53*(3), 223–245.

Anderson, T., & Milbrandt, M. (2005). *Art for life*. Boston, MA: McGraw Hill.

Brainard, S. (2006). *A design manual* (4th ed.). Upper Saddle River, NJ: Prentice Hall.

Clark, G. A., Day, M. D., & Greer, W. D. (1987). Disciplined-based art education: Becoming students of art. *Journal of Aesthetic Education, 21*(2), 129–193.

Congdon, K. G. (2004). *Community art in action*. Worcester, MA: Davis Publications.

Dean, C., Ebert, C. M. L., McGreevy-Nichols, S., Quinn, B., Sabol, F. R., . . . Shuler, S. C. (2010). *21st century skills map: Arts*. Tucson, AZ: Partnership for 21st Century Skills.

Dissanayake, E. (1995). *Homo aestheticus: Where art comes from and why*. Seattle: University of Washington Press.

Douglas, K. M., & Jaquith, D. B. (2018). *Engaging learners through artmaking: Choice-based art education in the classroom (TAB)* (2nd ed.). New York, NY: Teacher's College Press.

Dow, A. W. (1914). *Composition: A series of exercises in art structure for the use of students and teachers* (9th ed.). Garden City, NY: Double Day, Page, and Company.

Efland, A., Freedman, K., & Stuhr, P. (1996). *Postmodern art education: An approach to curriculum.* Reston, VA: The National Art Education Association.

Finkel, J. (2009, May 31). I dream of clothing electric. *The New York Times*, p. AR22. Retrieved from www.nytimes.com/2009/04/05/arts/design/05fink.html?pagewanted=1

Freire, P. (2009). *Pedagogy of the oppressed: 30th anniversary edition.* New York, NY: Continuum.

Gude, O. (2004). Postmodern principles: In search of a 21st Century art education. *Art Education, 57*(1), 6–14.

Hetland, L., Winner, E., Veenema, S., & Sheridan, K. (2013). *Studio thinking 2: The real benefits of visual arts education.* New York, NY: Teacher's College Press.

Huish, M. B. (2005). *Japan and its art* (2nd ed.). New York, NY: Routledge.

Jackson, W. (Director), & Disney, W. (Producer). (1933). *The pied piper.* [Traditional animation]. United States: Walt Disney Studios.

Maguire, P. (2000). *Doing participatory research: A feminist approach.* (Originally printed in 1987). Amherst: The Center for International Education School of Education University of Massachusetts.

McHale, B. (2015). *The Cambridge introduction to postmodernism.* New York, NY: Cambridge University Press.

McTighe, J., & Wiggins, G. (2012). *From common core standards to curriculum: Five big ideas.* Retrieved from http://nccas.wikispaces.com/file/view/From%20Common%20Core%20Standards%20to%20Curriculum%20%20Five%20Big%20Ideas.pdf/375975758/From%20Common%20Core%20Standards%20to%20Curriculum%20-%20Five%20Big%20Ideas.pdf

National Coalition for Core Arts Standards. (2014a). *National Core Arts Standards.* Retrieved from www.nationalartsstandards.org

National Coalition for Core Arts Standards. (2014b). *National Core Arts Standards: A conceptual framework for arts learning.* Retrieved from www.nationalartsstandards.org/sites/default/files/NCCAS%20%20Conceptual%20Framework_4.pdf

Parsons, M. (2004). Art and integrated curriculum. In E. Eisner & M. Day (Eds.), *Handbook of research and policy in art education* (pp. 775–794). Mahwah, NJ: Lawrence Erlbaum Associates.

Sickler-Voigt, D. C. (2002). *Faces in the community: An examination of the Florida Arts and Cultural Enrichment program* (Doctoral dissertation). Retrieved from ProQuest. (3336078). Tallahassee, FL: The Florida State University.

Stewart, M. G., & Walker, S. R. (2005). *Rethinking curriculum in art.* Worcester, MA: Davis Publications.

Trafi-Prats, L., & Woywod, C. (2013). We love our public schools: Art teachers' life histories in a time of loss, accountability, and new commonalities. *Studies in Art Education, 55*(1), 7–17.

U.S. Congress. (2015). *S. 1177: Every Student Succeeds Act (ESSA).* Retrieved from www.congress.gov/bill/114th-congress/senate-bill/1177/text?overview=closed

Weisman, E., & Hanes, J. M. (2002). Thematic curriculum and social reconstruction. In Y. Gaudelius & P. Speirs (Eds.), *Contemporary issues in art education* (pp. 170–179). Upper Saddle River, NJ: Prentice Hall.

Welch, P. B. (2008). *Chinese art: A guide to motifs and visual imagery.* North Clarendon, VT: Tuttle.

Wiggins, G., & McTighe, J. (2005). *Understanding by design* (2nd ed.). Upper Saddle River, NJ: Pearson.

Zhang, M. (2004). *Chinese jade: Power and delicacy in a majestic art.* San Francisco: Long River Press.

# Chapter 2

# The Choice-Based Art Curriculum

**FIGURE 2.1** Jana Swastik, 12-years-old, The Park Institution, Kolkata, India.
*Source: ICEFA Lidice, 38th Exhibition.*

Throughout life, students will make important choices and navigate the rewards and consequences of their decisions. The **choice-based art curriculum** is an instructional plan driven by contemporary teaching and learning practices that anticipates the performances, skills, and dispositions that students are expected to achieve over a given period. It provides ample room and flexibility for students to make personal decisions as lifelong learners. This textbook's choice-based model combines the visceral sensations and freedom that students experience when creating art for personal satisfaction with the structure of a safe learning environment facilitated by teachers who ask guiding questions, teach skills, and encourage inquiry, wonderment, and exploration to foster student growth in ways unattainable without teacher guidance. Instead of telling students what to feel and believe, the choice-based art curriculum presents rich context and artists' exemplars to foster students' enduring understandings of life's topics. Our curriculum will identify some of the people, places, materials, and methods students will encounter during their studies. We will collaborate with students to explore curricular possibilities and plan the best pathways to achieve learning goals. We will also prepare for unanticipated challenges that may arise along the way.

We will meet the following objectives by participating in this chapter:

- Summarize the purposes and values of a choice-based art curriculum.
- Plan a choice-based art curriculum using learning goals.

- Develop original comprehensive lesson and unit plans.

Spotlight on Student Art #2 (Figure 2.1) presents an exemplary artwork inspired by the United Nations' theme of biodiversity that aligns with teaching students comprehensive art methods with curricular choices. Its exploratory subject matter reinforces the creative and cognitive adventures that can transpire when we implement a meaningful, choice-based art curriculum.

---

## Spotlight on Student Art #2

### Big Idea: Biodiversity

I can create my biodiverse world! Twelve-year-old Jana, from India, developed a lush artwork (Figure 2.1) in response to the United Nations Decade on Biodiversity's call to raise awareness about the value of preserving our planet's biodiversity. With its theme "living in harmony with nature" Jana's artwork provides visual evidence as to why humanity should preserve the world's flora and fauna. Examining the content of his design, viewers can instantly recognize the boy's harmonious connection with the jungle environment. His shirt mimics the patterns of India's Bengal tiger. It provides a visual metaphor that symbolizes that he is one with nature and belongs in the natural habitat. Colorful bugs and butterflies abound. With his wide smile and binoculars, he is ready to explore his biodiverse world.

This outstanding example of Earth Education represents a culmination of Jana's studies. He was able to produce this exemplary artwork due to his comprehensive understanding of biodiversity. Jana referenced the characteristics of bugs, butterflies, and plant life. He drew the boy's figure using realistic proportions, which demonstrated his practice in rendering the human form. Similarly, he showcased his skill in building up layers of color to produce the verdant jungle environment filled with rich tints and shades. Jana's combination of artistic skills, carefully planned composition, and illustration of scientific inquiry identifies the value of living in harmony with nature.

---

## DESIGNING A CHOICE-BASED ART CURRICULUM

*Teaching and Learning in Art Education* offers approaches for designing a choice-based art curriculum driven by standards, goals, learning targets, and an effective scope and sequence so that students become competent in creating worthy projects, presenting ideas in context, responding to global artworks and themes, and making personal connections. Many schools and districts require curricular plans that outline clear and logical pathways for teaching and learning. For some educators, designing a choice-based curriculum seems paradoxical because offering student choices may lead to unpredictable outcomes. When put into action, however, even the most structured plans can

result in changes due to unforeseen circumstances and the uniqueness of each student. A well-designed choice-based art curriculum, with its predictable and unpredictable outcomes, feels professionally rewarding to teach and invigorating for students to learn. Suggestions for integrating comprehensive choices into the art curriculum follow (Hetland, Winner, Veenema, & Sheridan, 2013; Strauss, 2015; Teaching for Artistic Behaviors [TAB], 2018).

- Integrate opportunities for artistic play, experimentation, curiosity, and practice. This gives students the freedom to try new things, learn from mistakes, and refine their work.
- Focus on students as individuals. Identify where students are and help them grow. Consider students'

ages, maturity levels, and abilities. Ask them about their hobbies and interests and discuss possible ways to incorporate some of them into the curriculum.

- Develop learning centers organized with art media, visual data, and topics for students to use as inspirations to produce original and collaborative works.

- Encourage students to take leadership roles and teach each other skills to add personal touches to the curriculum. Students can locate existing resources on subjects to augment their knowledge.

- Make resources available for students to participate in self-guided learning. These include teacher exemplars, handouts, diagrams, websites, sample projects, and instructional videos.

- Look to students' communities and the qualities that make them unique, including local artists and cultural events, for inspirations. Students can apply their knowledge about their communities to learning tasks.

- Teach artistic behaviors such as developing craft, making observations, and expressing meanings to develop students' autonomous behaviors and help them understand why they are learning curricular content.

- Present exemplars that motivate students to solve problems. Students can identify capstone and participatory-action research projects to study topics they deem important. Educators may also form teams of specialists to work with students. For example, interdisciplinary project-based learning courses in Finland join small groups of students and teams of teachers with diverse specialties to collaborate and solve problems students have identified.

Teachers will consider their goals, available resources, and specialized skills to construct a choice-based art curriculum. This textbook's structured model of a choice-based art curriculum is a balanced approach that builds students' skills and helps them expand beyond their comfort zones. It allows for circumstances when all students will learn how to work in a certain art medium and study particular artists and big ideas as a class to build foundational knowledge and skills that they can later apply to participate in purely student-driven learning tasks of choice. Its balanced approach is beneficial because sometimes, under the guise of choice, students choose only safe options for fear of failure. As a result, they avoid new tasks and artistic behaviors including experimentation and creative risk taking. In

the choice-based art curriculum, it is okay to have students try tasks that they might not normally choose on their own to build competencies while still offering them some choices. For example, students might be required to learn a particular art process, but can select the project's subject matter. Teachers recognize that sometimes students require more structure and guidance before they blossom on their own and at other times they feel ready to soar. The choice-based art curriculum gives teachers and students these opportunities.

## Standards

Standards are organized by grade level and present the skills students can achieve at various stages in their education. They assist educators in developing a choice-based art curriculum. Many school districts, regions, and states use the voluntary NVAS as a model for developing mandated, rigorous visual arts standards (McTighe & Wiggins, 2012). Viewing pre-K–12 standards as a whole, teachers have a reference for understanding where students have come from and are going in their development. The open-ended format of the NVAS offers educators opportunities to bring in personal ideas, expertise, and interpretations in designing a curriculum using artists, activities, concepts, and processes that best serve students' needs. The NVAS includes process components to guide classroom practices. Its sample essential questions and enduring understandings spark ideas for designing learning tasks (which could result in works like those shown in Figures 2.2 and 2.3). The NVAS **anchor standards** communicate the level of general knowledge that students need to become proficient and literate in art (NCCAS, 2014b). See Model 2.1 for a listing of the arts anchor standards.

The anchor standards offer flexibility and multiple interpretations for choice-based curriculum design because teachers and students can examine a variety of artists, processes, and big ideas to meet the standards. This textbook's Artists' Lessons to Thrive! features provide pathways for integrating choice into the curriculum. They include anchor standards for creating, presenting, responding, and connecting. Teachers reference the Artists' Lessons to Thrive! anchor standards to develop grade-level lesson plans that include visual arts **performance standards** that "translate the anchor standards into specific, measurable learning

FIGURE 2.2 Lee Da Young, 14-years-old, Busan Middle School of Arts, Busan, South Korea.
*Source: ICEFA Lidice, 39th Exhibition.*

FIGURE 2.3 Dagnija Butlere, 8-years-old, Livänu bërnu un jauniešu centrs, Livani, Latvia. Agnis Salminš, 9-years-old, Livänu bërnu un jauniešu centrs, Livani, Latvia.
*Source: ICEFA Lidice, 38th Exhibition.*

## Model 2.1
### National Coalition for Core Arts Standards Artistic Processes and Anchor Standards

| | | | | |
|---|---|---|---|---|
| | *Artistic Processes* **are the cognitive and physical actions by which arts learning and making are realized.** *Anchor Standards* **describe the general knowledge and skill that teachers expect students to demonstrate throughout their education in the arts. The Anchor Standards are parallel across arts disciplines and grade levels, and they serve as the tangible educational expression of artistic literacy.** | | | |
| **Artistic Process (and Definition)** | <u>Creating</u><br><br>Conceiving and developing new artistic ideas and work. | <u>Performing/Presenting/ Producing</u><br><br>**Performing (dance, music, theatre):** Realizing artistic ideas and work through interpretation and presentation<br>**Presenting (visual arts):** Interpreting and sharing artistic work<br>**Producing (media arts):** Realizing and presenting artistic ideas and work | <u>Responding</u><br><br>Understanding and evaluating how the arts convey meaning | <u>Connecting</u><br><br>Relating artistic ideas and work with personal meaning and external context |
| **Anchor Standards** Students Will Be Able To: | 1. Generate and conceptualize artistic ideas and work.<br>2. Organize and develop artistic ideas and work.<br>3. Refine and complete artistic work. | 4. Select, analyze and interpret artistic work for presentation.<br>5. Develop and refine artistic techniques and work for presentation.<br>6. Convey meaning through the presentation of artistic work. | 7. Perceive and analyze artistic work.<br>8. Interpret intent and meaning in artistic work.<br>9. Apply criteria to evaluate artistic work. | 10. Synthesize and relate knowledge and personal experiences to make art.<br>11. Relate artistic ideas and works with societal, cultural, and historical context to deepen understanding. |

*Source: © 2015 NCCAS*

goals" (NCCAS, 2014b, p. 13). For example, this chapter's Artists' Lessons to Thrive! 2.1 on Vannoy Streeter includes Anchor Standard #10. When teaching it to a 4th-grade class, teachers would locate its performance standard (VA:Cn10.1.4) for that particular grade: "Create works of art that reflect community cultural traditions" (NCCAS, 2014a). The performance standard is applicable to developing a Vannoy Streeter lesson because the students have the possibility to construct a wire sculpture inspired by

Vannoy Streeter and their community. The NVAS performance standards provide detailed competencies for pre-kindergarten through 8th-grade students and proficient, accomplished, and advanced competencies for high school students. Curriculum designers at local, regional, and state levels apply performance standards to set **benchmarks** that identify levels of student achievement within a given period for each grade level. Educators collect benchmarked student work samples as evidence to identify what same-aged students have achieved and assist other students in reaching learning targets.

## Goals

**Goals** are clear aims that drive the choice-based art curriculum. They focus on relevant and attainable learning outcomes. Using a backwards-design approach, teachers identify class content that is important and applicable to students. They refer to standards to set short- and long-term goals within the curriculum. Goals assist teachers in planning daily learning targets for students and identifying student learning outcomes. For example, teachers may have the goal that students practice art making skills in various media and want them to learn how to make revisions to their work to produce quality final designs, such as the examples in Figures 2.4 and 2.5. Goals build on students' prior knowledge and thread together big ideas, concepts, and art processes appropriate for students' age and skill levels. Teachers anticipate how students will meet goals within given periods. Some goals extend well beyond a given school year and the times in which administrators evaluate teaching and evidence of student learning outcomes. As lifelong learners students will pull from their combined educational experiences as artistically literate practitioners who care about our world's diverse cultures, traditions, and histories and will apply their creative thinking and problem solving skills to life's varied situations (Dean et al., 2010; NCCAS, 2014b; Pennisi, 2013; Steward, 2010).

## Learning Targets

With an awareness of the standards and short- and long-term goals in place, teachers are ready to integrate learning targets into the choice-based art curriculum.

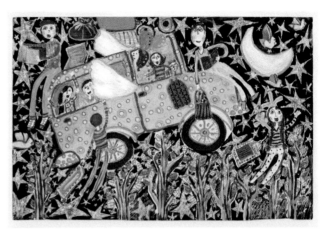

**FIGURE 2.4** Setayesh Sadeghi, 13-years-old, Kanoon–Institute for Intellectual Development of Children and Young Adults, Tehran, Iran.
*Source: ICEFA Lidice, 45th Exhibition.*

**FIGURE 2.5** Júlia Olekšáková, 11-years-old, ZUŠ, Spišská Belá, Slovak Republic.
*Source: ICEFA Lidice, 43rd Exhibition.*

**Learning targets** pinpoint the essential knowledge and achievements that educators expect students to attain through active participation in the choice-based art curriculum. Chappuis, Stiggins, Chappuis, and Arter (2012) classified five types of learning targets: knowledge, reasoning, skill, product, and disposition.

**Knowledge targets** identify factual knowledge students should know in relation to studying art. They pinpoint students' comprehension of facts about art history, art media, art processes, design concepts (including the elements and principles of art), and other pertinent information. To demonstrate knowledge, students might list artistic procedures, remember facts, and identify concepts relating to art and big ideas in written and oral formats.

**Reasoning targets** identify the cognitive processes necessary for students to solve problems and make reasoned judgments. Through reasoning targets students make predictions, such as contemplating what would happen if they were to mix different paint colors together. Students' reasoning skills include content from knowledge targets. For example, students apply factual knowledge to analyze art, make inferences (educated guesses), and evaluate artworks using set criteria as they participate in art criticism reasoning activities. Students learn to classify art through the aesthetic categories and group artworks according to art history genres. When making creative products, students synthesize concepts inspired by big ideas, artists, artistic processes, art media, and other factors. They employ reasoning skills to develop essays about art and write art history and visual culture comparison papers. Students apply reasoning skills to refine an in-progress artwork after participating in a formative critique and can summarize ideas by developing portfolios and written artist statements about completed artworks.

**Skill targets** integrate knowledge and reasoning targets. Students' skill targets range from utilizing introductory or foundational skills to proficient and advanced skills. In art, students regularly demonstrate skills to perform with art media and processes, present artworks for a display, and talk about their work. They apply skills to various targets, such as manipulating a carving instrument safely and giving a captivating presentation on a topic they selected. Students' demonstrate their ability to build skills over time. For example, they might practice with a particular tool at a learning center, such as a paintbrush, and then synthesize knowledge about different types of paintbrushes, paints, and various brushstroke techniques to generate further painting skills. Their skills burgeon with continued practice and exposure to art media and processes. Teachers should guide students as they navigate divergent pathways to advance their skills and create within safe learning environments.

**Product targets** correspond with the products that students create. Students' artistic creations build on their artistic knowledge and reasoning abilities to synthesize disparate concepts and knowledge of art media, artists, contexts, and big ideas to produce artworks and other creative products. They apply skills to communicate ideas through diverse art media and processes. For example, to create a proficient artwork, students need to become skilled in artistic processes and operating tools and equipment. The NVAS student product targets begin in early childhood with a focus on artistic play and mature to include products inspired by the professional practices that artists use. Students' product targets also include the collections they create in journals and portfolios, as well as their reports on art topics and big ideas.

**Disposition targets** identify the expressive outcomes and affective behaviors and attitudes students cultivate given their active involvement in the choice-based art curriculum. Educators identify the expressive outcomes that motivate students, including igniting students' curiosity and creative risk taking. In circumstances when teachers are just getting to know students, they might begin by asking students questions about their interests to build disposition targets. They can also research students' communities and integrate concepts from child development theories (see Chapter 5) to connect the art curriculum to students' lives. Some dispositions result from long-term goals that take time to foster, such as forming deep understandings of and appreciation for world cultures based on the comprehensive study of art. Ultimately, teachers want students to have a sense of belonging and identify the classroom environment as a safe place to explore, create, ask questions, and share opinions. While these benefits are not assessed on a report card, they have tremendous value to students.

## Scope and Sequence

An effective choice-based art curriculum has a logical order and builds on prior learning so that all components are unified. Teachers pace the curriculum and instruction so that students do not feel overwhelmed and have opportunities to receive descriptive feedback, as well as make necessary changes and revisions to their work. **Scope** refers to the parameters of the content that teachers and students cover in the curriculum and the time it will take for most students to develop identified competencies and complete tasks, lessons, and units. For example, students might explore paper processes and study contemporary paper artists for several weeks, including those featured in Artists' Lessons to Thrive! 1.3, 8.1, and 13.1 to develop paper arts skills and study the big ideas that drive artists' works through multidisciplinary learning activities. Teachers also plan the **sequence** (progression) of the curriculum, break down curricular content into manageable components, and build on students' prior learning. Even when working with a choice-based art curriculum, it is necessary to plan the curriculum's sequence so that students have a general pathway forward. The sequence might progress students towards long-term goals such as creating an individual portfolio and personally-driven capstone projects. Using the Artists' Lessons to Thrive! 1.3, 8.1, and 13.1, for example, students would begin learning two-dimensional paper techniques before moving into more complex three-dimensional paper processes.

The Weekly Art Curriculum Planning Template on this textbook's companion website is a useful guide for developing a curriculum that aligns with grade-level standards. Before writing each weekly plan completely, teachers may begin by writing preliminary ideas and organizing them to find the best sequence to plan a full grading period, semester, or year curriculum. The NVAS offers a wealth of inspiration to span a complete curriculum. A balanced curriculum includes an equal representation of the world's artists. Teachers also bring in local artists and customs as inspirations for students to make connections as they discuss art, write reflections, and experiment with art media and processes (such as wood and batik as shown in Figures 2.6 and 2.7). Teachers will actively integrate students' interests and expertise into the curriculum's design, as well

FIGURE 2.7 Maria Smuneva, 16-years-old, GUDO Vitebskii Oblastnoi Dvorets Detei i Molodozhi, Vitebsk, Belarus.
*Source: ICEFA Lidice, 45th Exhibition.*

as their own. For example, when teachers are highly skilled in textile arts they could share their knowledge with students and create related choice-based learning tasks. A curricular plan will also contain assessments, such as journaling activities and exams (see Chapter 3). Once teachers develop a curricular plan with key content, they can begin writing the curriculum's lesson and unit plans.

## LESSON AND UNIT PLANS

A **lesson plan** documents and explains how teachers propose to teach students a task, concept, process, or big idea. It guides teachers throughout the course of a lesson. Lesson plan formats vary according to school and organization requirements. Visit the textbook's companion website to access this chapter's model lesson plan and unit plan, along with templates for designing original lesson and unit plans. The model lesson plan includes a big idea, essential questions, rationale, objectives, learning targets, vocabulary, materials, instructional resources, procedures, assessments, standards, and references. It was inspired by Artists' Lessons to Thrive! 2.1 on Vannoy Streeter and a marionette project created by children living in Streeter's community. Students applied their personal understandings of community to design marionettes. When one lesson is not enough to cover class concepts in depth, teachers write a **unit plan**, a series of two or more lessons that are connected by big ideas, concepts, media, artists, subject, and/or other content. The

FIGURE 2.6 Markéta Matoušková, 6-years-old, MŠ, Dolní Cerekev, Czech Republic.
*Source: ICEFA Lidice, 42nd Exhibition.*

model unit plan, provided on the companion website, includes essential questions that drive all lessons within the unit, a unit rationale, title and sequence of the lessons within the unit, and references. For example, the aforementioned students participated in a school-wide unit of study based on the big idea of community and participated in three lesson plans in which they examined local art, including Vannoy Streeter's wire sculptures. They painted a mural, created original puppets, and participated in grade-level puppet productions (see Figures 2.8 and 2.9). The three lesson plans formed this chapter's model unit plan, "Where We Come From: An Examination of Our Local Community." The lesson plan, unit plan, and Artists' Lessons to Thrive! 2.1 on Vannoy Streeter place this chapter's teachings in context and serve as models for teachers to emulate in developing lesson plans, unit plans, and artists' narratives.

## Writing a Rationale

Teachers develop a **rationale**, a written statement that explains the value of a lesson or unit. The rationale states the relevance of lesson and unit assignments to students' growth and development. It identifies the big idea and essential questions that drive the lesson or unit and provides brief contextual information with citations to explain the topics at hand. A rationale may also include an explanation of how applicable social justice, Earth Education, and participatory action research activities can augment learning tasks.

FIGURE 2.8 Marionette performance video still. Elementary students, United States.
*Source: Author and Abbey Logan, teachers.*

FIGURE 2.9 Community mural. Elementary students, United States.
*Source: Author and Abbey Logan, teachers. Pamela McColly, photo.*

### Artists' Lessons to Thrive! 2.1 Vannoy Streeter:
### The Tennessee Wire Man

#### Big Idea: Community

Born in Manchester, Tennessee, in 1919, Vannoy Streeter moved to nearby Wartrace at age 3 and spent his entire life in this rural community, which was known for its horses and crafts. He began making wire sculptures as a child, inspired by the magnificent toys in storefront windows that were too expensive for his family to afford. Streeter studied their details and collected wire and other materials so that he could make their exact replicas and give them to his siblings as gifts (Moses, 1999; Sellen, 2000). Through this practice, Streeter developed a keen eye for detail and applied his observational skills to create wire sculptures that had moving parts and made them all the more fun.

Streeter returned to his passion for creating wire sculptures upon his retirement and became known for his depictions of the famous Tennessee Walking Horses from his community. He used only his

FIGURE 2.1.1 Vannoy Streeter, *Tennessee Walking Horse*.
*Source: Jonathan Griffith, photo.*

hands, pliers, and wire to form intricate designs. Streeter began selling his wire sculptures at a local arts and crafts fair for about $10 each to earn extra cash. He never considered his hundreds of sculptures to be art because he believed that wire bending was simply a hobby:

> Some people calls it art, I don't even think about it except as somethin' I'm just doin. It's a habit or somethin'. I don't know, I ain't got nothin' else to do. It don't mean nothin' . . . It's so easy it's pitiful. Just give me a coat hanger and I'll bend 'em on up.
>
> (Moses, 1999, p. 133)

In the last decades of his life, Streeter became a Tennessee folk art sensation, as his art found its way into the collections of local business owners, senators, governors, and former presidents (Sickler-Voigt, 2006). His family recalled how influential people would visit Streeter at his home to purchase his art and bring him more wire hangers. Surrounded by his creations while sitting on Streeter's living room floor, they played with his wire sculptures and reflected on their own childhoods. Streeter's passion for creating wire sculptures continued until his passing in 1998.

## Essential/Guiding Questions

1. How did Vannoy Streeter's small rural community impact the type of art that he created? How has your community shaped your life and the things that you create?
2. Is it okay for a person to think that Vannoy Streeter's wire sculptures are art, even when the artist himself did not think they were art? Do artists always know what constitutes art? Explain your answers.

## Preparation

Students will brainstorm the meaning of the local community. Each student will identify and make sketches of at least three personal symbols representing his/her local community to transform into a wire sculpture.

## Daily Learning Targets

I can create a wire sculpture inspired by Vannoy Streeter and my community.

- I can form a wire sculpture (i.e. toy, structure, person, animal, or object) that has a sturdy construction.
- I can create a unified sculpture that has a balanced design and at least one moving part.
- I can document the revisions I made to produce this artwork. I can orally present my process for making the artwork during a class critique.

**National Core Arts Anchor Standards** 1, 4, 9, and 10

www.nationalartsstandards.org

## Objectives

**Learning objectives** are clear, measurable student behaviors that identify learning goals and expectations. Whether writing an objective for a lesson plan, unit plan, or evaluation model, teachers analyze and interpret key concepts identified within the standards to develop objectives and produce predetermined student performances. McTighe and Wiggins (2012) refer to this process as "unpacking" the standards. Objectives challenge students as active learners to produce outcomes that span the full range of learning activities within the curriculum, including synergizing disparate information and context to create art (such as the glassware shown in Figures 2.10 and 2.11). Many teachers apply **Bloom's Taxonomy**, which classify learning objectives into cognitive, affective, and psychomotor domains to stimulate students' full minds, emotions, and bodies (Anderson et al., 2001; Bloom, Engelhart, Furst, Hill, & Krathwohl, 1956; Gronlund, 2004; Franco & Unrath, 2014). The **cognitive domain** refers to students' development of mental abilities and intelligence. Students analyze big ideas in art, recall facts about art history, and evaluate art during class critiques. For example, Figure 2.12 represents students' cognitive abilities to link art and narrative texts. The **affective domain** involves personal feelings and human emotion. Examples of affective learning include students' creation of artworks that show emotion, such as the

FIGURE 2.10 Lída Hašlarová, 15-years-old, Eliška Hlavatá, 10-years-old, Štěpánka Hlavatá, 7-years-old, Anna Machová, 10-years-old, Tamara Nádassy, 14-years-old, Anna Vetešníková, 11-years-old, ZUŠ, Mšeno, Czech Republic.
*Source: ICEFA Lidice, 43rd Exhibition.*

FIGURE 2.11 Eliška Hlavatá, 9-years-old, ZUŠ, Mšeno, Czech Republic.
*Source: ICEFA Lidice, 42nd Exhibition.*

FIGURE 2.12 Barbora Verešová, 8-years-old, Súkromná ZUŠ, Trenčín, Slovak Republic.
*Source: ICEFA Lidice, 41st Exhibition.*

FIGURE 2.14 Sophie Kazecká, 10-years-old, Viktorie Kazecká, 7-years-old, ZUŠ, Plzeň, Czech Republic.
*Source: ICEFA Lidice, 42nd Exhibition.*

FIGURE 2.13 Park So Jin, 15-years-old, Busan Middle School of Arts, Busan, South Korea,.
*Source: ICEFA Lidice, 41st Exhibition.*

artwork in Figure 2.13, and their ability to identify artists' portrayal of emotion in art. It also includes developing an appreciation of people's varying perspectives and showing empathy when studying

different cultures' artistic symbols. The **psychomotor domain** centers on students' kinesthetic learning through physical motions, such as forming ceramic sculptures (Figure 2.14). Students activate their bodies to make discoveries and generate knowledge using motor skills.

Bloom's Taxonomy of Educational Objectives focuses on the cognitive domain and includes six cognitive skills in hierarchal order to categorize the learning that students can achieve as a result of instruction: (a) knowledge, (b) comprehension, (c) application, (d) analysis, (e) synthesis, and (f) evaluation. Forty-five years later, Anderson and Krathwohl (Anderson et al., 2001) revised Bloom's Taxonomy. They presented cognitive processes in the form of active verbs: (a) remember, (b) understand, (c) apply, (d) analyze, (e) evaluate, and (f) create. They renamed Bloom's "knowledge" to "remember"; his "comprehension" to "understand"; and his "synthesize" to "create." These terms appear frequently in local, state, and national standards. Additionally, Anderson and Krathwohl's Revision of Bloom's Taxonomy of Educational Objectives applied four different types of knowledge: **factual knowledge** (basic knowledge), **conceptual knowledge** (interrelationships, how things connect); **procedural knowledge** (methods and inquiry); and **metacognitive knowledge** (awareness of cognition, especially one's own cognition) to their six cognitive processes to specify learning practices (Krathwohl, 2002).

Teachers write objectives so that students can achieve predetermined learning outcomes that align with standards. Measurable objectives identify summative tasks students are to accomplish. These include art production activities, writing, research, presentations, discussions, and other targeted actions. This textbook's Model 2.2, "Designing Measurable Art Objectives," divides an objective into four components: **The student will + measurable behavior + stimulus + criteria**.

## Model 2.2
## Designing Measurable Art Objectives

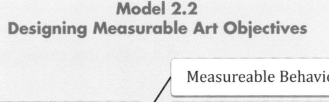
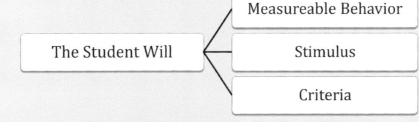

1. **The Student Will.** Students are at the heart of objectives because objectives center on measurable student actions. Some teachers write variations to "the student will" for the objective's subject. Examples include *the learner will, the students will, the learners will, the group will,* and *the class will*. Teacher actions are never stated in objectives because objectives focus solely on student performances.

2. **Measurable Behavior**. Teachers plan students' measurable behaviors in the objective by selecting the most appropriate action verb to identify student performances that they can observe and measure. Building on the student subject of the objective, teachers might write: The student will (+ action verb), such as *The student will paint*. In developing objectives, teachers should incorporate actions from the cognitive, affective, and psychomotor domains to activate students' minds, bodies, and emotions. They should also clearly identify how students will achieve broad outcomes associated with learning, understanding, and appreciating. Examples might read as follows.

   * *The student will explain a story in his/her own words.*
   * *The student will give a ten-minute multimedia presentation on a contemporary social justice issue.*
   * *The student will self-reflect on a learning activity in his/her journal by stating his/her opinion in paragraph form.*

   The lather represents a measurable action that correlates with the affective domain and appreciating because its outcome will clearly reflect a student's feelings/emotions about a work.

3. **Stimulus**. The stimulus includes the materials, instructional resources, and events that assist students in performing the measurable actions listed in objectives. Materials identify the art supplies and other school supplies and tools necessary to complete an objective, such as *watercolor paper* or *recycled materials*. Instructional resources include supplies that convey information required for the objective such as textbooks, multimedia presentations, technology devices, posters, class handouts, and more. An objective might include statements such as *given a handout on an artist, given an art reproduction,* or *given a research assignment on the computer* to identify instructional resources. Events include a performance, a reading, a field trip, and other circumstances that drive the objective, such as *a wire bending demonstration by a local artist.*

4. **Criteria**. The objective's criteria identify the distinct paths students can take to reach a learning goal based on a standard. Objective criteria involve the skills students are expected to attain, such as responding to a big idea in an artwork, demonstrating craftspersonship, applying lesson vocabulary, and presenting design qualities. They can also include quantifiable data, such as measurements, number of required components, and percentages. Examples include: *draw a composition* that represents the big idea of community, shows overlapping objects, contains objects running off at least three sides of the page, and has a unified design; *or define and illustrate 100% of the art terms correctly*.

Teachers can apply this textbook's Model for Designing Measurable Art Objectives to write both open- and closed-ended objectives. **Open-ended objectives** allow for student choices and personal interpretations. Through open-ended objectives teachers set perimeters for measuring student behaviors, yet provide students with flexibility so that the outcomes of their work will not look identical to products created by their classmates. The following open-ended objective is inspired by the artwork shown in Figure 2.15: *Given a trip to a nature reserve and a class presentation on contemporary artists that portray animals in their art, students will select at least one of the reserve's animals to create an artwork using the medium of their choice that represents an aspect of the animal's (animals') behavior(s) and habitat(s), has a sense of unity, and demonstrates effective craftspersonship*. This differs from **closed-ended objectives** such as this one, in which all students produce the same results: *Given an example of a color wheel, students will use tempera paint to mix the three secondary colors*. Closed-ended objectives can be useful in teaching special skills, but they should never drive the curriculum because the comprehensive study of art calls upon students to develop creative solutions, which are best achieved through open-ended objectives.

**FIGURE 2.15** Choi Wai Kiu, 11-years-old, Simply Art, Hong Kong, China.
*Source: ICEFA Lidice, 42nd Exhibition.*

## Transforming Objectives Into Daily Learning Targets

Teachers assist students in reaching learning objectives by transforming them into daily learning targets. Teachers apply knowledge, reasoning, skill, product, and disposition learning targets to plan the learning outcomes they intend for students to attain given their full and ongoing participation in the choice-based art curriculum. They also set **daily learning targets** to identify the short-term tasks that students are to achieve during a lesson plan, unit plan, or learning segment to meet a learning objective (Chappuis et al., 2012; Crockett, 2013; Moss & Brookhart, 2012). They are written in student-friendly language and can include picture symbols to help communicate information to students. Like objectives, daily learning targets align with the grade-level standards that drive the curriculum.

The concept of using daily learning targets began with the belief that students need to understand the performances they are expected to achieve. Instead of focusing only on summative learning outcomes, which can be complex and challenging—especially when first introduced to students—teachers offer students manageable units of information presented as daily learning targets. Guided instruction helps students understand the meanings of daily learning targets from the onset. Using daily learning targets, teachers present students with a pathway to build upon their existing knowledge. The daily learning targets they create need not be static products with a one-size-fits-all approach. Teachers adapt daily learning targets to accommodate diversified students so that they can learn and grow at paces that best suit their needs. Throughout the learning process, teachers monitor student progress formatively, as it happens. They provide supplemental instruction and resources as necessary to assist students in moving towards learning targets.

Teachers write daily learning targets in the form of "I can" statements in developmentally appropriate student language, broken down or unpacked from objectives. If students will be working collaboratively, daily learning targets may read as "we can" statements. An objective based on the artwork shown in Figure 2.1 might read: *The student will create an artwork that portrays his/her personal connection to a biodiverse environment using the medium of his/her choice. The student's artwork will have a unified composition, show craftspersonship, and apply effective design qualities to represent the environment (i.e. space, foreground, middle ground, background, and value).* The following list identifies some of the daily learning targets that align with the aforementioned objective.

- *As an artist, I can create an artwork that portrays my personal connection to a biodiverse environment.*
  - *I can select the medium of my choice.*
  - *I can create a composition that shows unity and craftspersonship.*
  - *I can portray the environment using design qualities of my choice. (These may include space, foreground, middle ground, background, and value.)*

When introducing these daily learning targets to students, teachers deconstruct each target component before asking students to begin a task. This way they can check that all students understand daily learning targets' full meanings. As demonstrated in the sample daily learning targets, many visual arts performance tasks require multiple skills and diverse forms of knowledge to accomplish. Some daily learning targets may span several days or class periods for students to attain.

The leading "I can" statement (*As an artist, I can create an artwork that portrays my personal connection to a biodiverse environment.*) identifies the main concepts behind the art performance. Students will need to know what teachers mean by a personal connection and be able to recognize different types of biodiverse environments. Teachers could begin instruction by showing students examples of biodiverse environments and have them research additional ones to discover the various qualities biodiverse environments possess and why people need to maintain the health of biodiverse environments. They could post images of biodiverse environments on the board, create handouts, and save digital images on computer devices as

student references. Building on these examples, students can brainstorm ways that they could integrate a personal connection to the biodiverse environment. Looking at the inspiration artwork in Figure 2.1, students could identify how the boy wears a tiger-striped shirt, has binoculars, and has a smile on his face to show his connection to the biodiverse environment.

Once students understand the big idea that drives the artwork, teachers can move into the remaining daily learning targets that identify the objective's criteria. For the target *I can select the medium of my choice,* the class can review the art media they have already worked with and discuss how artists select from different art materials and processes to communicate ideas about their work. Students will apply this information to select the most appropriate medium for their biodiverse design. To assist students in meeting the final three learning targets that introduce design criteria, teachers and students might give demonstrations, display posters, and make available multimedia tutorials that illustrate how to produce an effective composition, demonstrate unity and craftspersonship, and create space through value, a foreground, a middle ground, and a background. Depending on students' prior art experiences, some of these skills may be easier than others for students to attain. For example, students may need to practice making value drawings in their sketchbooks before adding value to the targeted artwork, where they will show evidence of how they combined the various skills listed in the daily learning targets to reach the objective. Teachers will also ask students to pinpoint the steps they will take to reach daily learning targets by actions such as answering questions in their journals and in small group discussions: *I will take the following actions to achieve this learning target* or *Before we can _____ we must _____.* The clear guidelines that daily learning targets outline help students become personally responsible for reaching class objectives.

## Deconstructing Objectives and Learning Targets

By deconstructing art objectives and learning targets, teachers can clearly present the different types of learning they teach students. This process also prepares teachers to communicate learning within the curriculum to students, parents, administrators, and policy makers, who may not fully understand how the arts correlate with anticipated learning expected in schools. The following example deconstructs an art objective and learning targets that integrate Bloom's Taxonomy of Learning Domains, the revised Bloom's Taxonomy of Educational Objectives, and the NVAS framework.

- **Objective**: Given a wire sculpture by Vannoy Streeter, the student will write a journal entry in paragraph form that analyzes the wire sculpture through his/her initial reaction, description, interpretation, and informed judgment; and summarize his/her findings during a class discussion.
- **Learning Target:** I can write an art criticism journal entry in paragraph form that analyzes a wire sculpture by Vannoy Streeter.
  - I can apply the art criticism steps initial reaction, description, interpretation, and judgment in my journal entry.
  - I can summarize the content in my art criticism journal entry during a class discussion.
- **Objective and Target Components**
  - The objective and targets include the acts of *creating* (a journal entry), *presenting* (orally summarizing before the class), *responding* (to the artist and the analytical art criticism format), and *connecting* (combining information about the artist, art criticism, and their local community).
  - They can be categorized as *conceptual knowledge* and the cognitive skill *analyze* because they show the students' ability to analyze artworks based on the interrelationship of parts.
  - They can also be categorized as *procedural knowledge* and the cognitive skill *create* because students will create a written art criticism journal entry by following the established procedures: reaction, description, interpretation, and evaluation (Anderson, 1997) to make an informed judgment about art.
  - They combine the *cognitive* and *affective domains* because students are using cognitive processes to answer art criticism questions and provide a personal judgment about the artwork.

## Procedures

**Procedures** identify the steps that teachers have determined to be necessary for students to complete a lesson or unit so that they can reach learning targets and class objectives. They differ from objectives because objectives identify only the end result of student actions. Procedures include both teacher and student actions throughout a lesson or unit. Well-organized, pre-planned procedures minimize downtime and student off-task behaviors. Students appreciate teachers' explanations of class ideas, artistic selections, and possible alternatives to tasks as part of class procedures and instructional methods. During instruction, effective teachers place ideas in context and present information clearly. They reinforce and connect what students have already learned to prepare them for what is to come next. If students ask questions teachers do not know the answers to, they are honest and collaborate with students to find answers to their inquiries. The following examples represent teaching and learning procedures commonly identified in lesson plans.

## Set

The **set** (anticipatory set) is a brief activity or event teachers present at the beginning of a lesson to capture students' full attention. Teachers introduce a lesson's big idea and essential questions during the set to spark students' interest in the subject matter and assist them in making personal connections to the lesson. Set activities include:

- responding to art and a big idea,
- brainstorming topics,
- making authentic connections to prior life and learning experiences,
- participating in a storytelling session,
- watching and participating in demonstrations,
- partaking in an interactive class reading,
- making predictions,
- performing reviews, and
- engaging in self-reflective activities.

Sets can take place in different classroom locations to stimulate student learning, such as a reading center one time and a demonstration table another time. Teachers should regularly integrate the learning modalities into sets and forthcoming lesson procedures to keep students focused (Glanz, 2009; Thompson, 2018). **Learning modalities**—visual, auditory, kinesthetic, and

FIGURE 2.16 Maria Popova, 4-years-old, Detskaya khudozhest-vennaya galereya, Volgograd, Russia.
*Source: ICEFA Lidice, 38th Exhibition.*

tactile learning—define the ways that students learn through their senses. For example, **visual learners** benefit from seeing teacher demonstrations, watching instructional videos, and examining works of art. **Auditory learners** profit from hearing how teachers alter voice tone to place emphasis on key information. They also enjoy integrated music activities, such as creating art to music. **Kinesthetic learners** like to move their bodies to learn information and benefit from physically demonstrating lesson procedures and acting out roles. Referencing Figure 2.16, young children could act out the movements of a polar bear in conjunction with this lesson. **Tactile learners** want to touch materials, such as assorted fabrics for textile lessons, and write down class notes to understand material better.

## Instructional Strategies

Teachers use instructional strategies to impart key information to students. Forms of instruction change according to curricular content and students' needs. Common instructional practices include:

- informing students about a lesson's daily learning targets, goals, and objectives;
- explaining a lesson's academic vocabulary;
- identifying student assessments;
- sharing pertinent information with students, while at the same time probing students to answer questions thoughtfully and independently;

- integrating multimedia instructional resources to expand students' current knowledge; and
- connecting the standards to lifelong learning skills.

Teachers monitor students' actions during instruction to verify that they are participating in the learning process, such as answering questions at appropriate times, taking notes, modeling appropriate behaviors, and reflecting on curricular content.

## Group Learning

Students collaborate during guided group practice tasks under teachers' watchful supervision. Group activities will vary according to established learning goals and objectives. Common routines for small groups or the entire class include:

- deconstructing daily learning targets and practicing task procedures together before working on a larger project;
- responding to content and context related to big ideas, essential questions, and classroom challenges;
- making connections between disparate ideas to seek new possibilities;
- taking alternative positions and posing "what if" questions; and
- assessing their current knowledge to set new goals.

Teachers check for class understanding and provide additional feedback to assist students during group learning.

## Independent Practice

Teachers call upon a range of independent student learning practices, including class activities and homework assignments, so that students can achieve learning outcomes. These experiences assist students in acquiring 21st century skills. Examples of independent student learning practices include:

- reflecting on what they want to achieve and their performances;
- using daily learning targets, books, notes, technology, information on the board, and other instructional resources to achieve tasks;

- creating art while using materials and equipment properly;
- contemplating the best means to present artworks;
- applying problem solving skills to find solutions and overcome challenges; and
- self-assessing works in a journal or portfolio.

## Accommodations

Teachers plan carefully to meet the needs of all students. Common accommodations include:

- modifying daily learning targets to suit students' abilities;
- breaking down academic vocabulary and steps needed to complete a task so that all students understand;
- supplementing oral descriptions with visual demonstrations, charts, posters, images, multimedia resources, and content posted on the board;
- meeting with students individually to review important information;
- moving students closer to the teacher so that they can follow with greater ease or be removed from possible distractions;
- assigning knowledgeable student peers to assist fellow students;
- providing students with a clear list of procedures that contain both text and images;
- offering students additional time to complete assignments;
- checking for student understanding by planning breaks at specific points during the lesson; and
- developing extended activities to aid students in taking learning to the next level.

## Closure

**Closure** summarizes the lesson, a unit, or a day's activities, during which teachers and students review the lesson's big idea, essential questions, objectives, and key content. Teachers check for understanding to ensure that students learned the necessary material and determine if students need to revisit concepts and/or spend additional time on a learning task. Students self-reflect on the learning process and share their ideas with the class. They can also identify how they might apply what they have learned to future situations, which

may extend beyond the classroom. Closure is a suitable time for students to present their in-progress and completed works and assess their creations through class critiques. Students might also reflect in journals during the closure. Because students will be creating with various art supplies, cleanup is a vital part of closure. Cleaning up teaches students responsibility and stimulates a positive learning environment.

## OUR JOURNEY TO THRIVE CONTINUES . . .

In this chapter we learned what a choice-based art curriculum is and how various components come together to form meaningful lesson and unit plans. In Chapter 3, we will learn how to apply assessment results to shape our teaching practices and curriculum design. The assessments we design will assist students in checking the quality of their performances and determining when and how to make revisions and changes to their work to produce even greater learning outcomes.

## CHAPTER QUESTIONS AND ACTIVITIES

1. What is a comprehensive art curriculum? How do teachers use the choice-based art curriculum to develop students into lifelong learners?
2. Develop a comprehensive unit plan outline that consists of three lesson plans. Then, write one of the three lesson plans that you described in your comprehensive unit plan outline that incorporates (a) the NVAS framework of creating, presenting, responding, and connecting; (b) the cognitive, affective, and/or psychomotor domain(s); and (c) at least one of the four learning modalities: visual, auditory, kinesthetic, and tactile. Use the templates provided on the textbook's companion website.
3. Work individually or in a small group to design a year's curriculum with a logical scope and sequence using the Weekly Art Curriculum Planning Template that is provided on the textbook's companion website. Use a new template for each week in the school year.
4. Answer Artists' Lessons to Thrive! 2.1's essential/guiding questions in written form or as part of a group discussion. Complete its daily learning targets.

# References

Anderson, L. W. (Ed.), Krathwohl, D. R. (Ed.), Airasian, P. W., Cruikshank, K. A., Mayer, R. E., Pintrich, P. R., . . . Wittrock, M. C. (2001). *A taxonomy for learning, teaching, and assessing: A revision of Bloom's Taxonomy of Educational Objectives* (Complete ed.). New York, NY: Longman.

Anderson, T. (1997). Talking with kids about art: A model for art criticism. *School Arts, 97*(1), 21–24.

Bloom, B. S., Engelhart, M. D., Furst, E. J., Hill, W. H., & Krathwohl, D. R. (1956). *Taxonomy of educational objectives: The classification of educational goals.* Handbook I: Cognitive Domain. New York, NY: David McKay.

Chappuis, J., Stiggins, R., Chappuis, S., & Arter, J. (2012). *Classroom assessment for student learning: Doing it right: Using it well* (2nd ed.). Upper Saddle River, NJ: Pearson.

Crockett, H. (2013). *How I CAN statements can work for you.* Retrieved from www.theartofed.com/2013/02/21/how-i-can-statements-can-work-for-you/

Dean, C., Ebert, C. M. L., McGreevy-Nichols, S., Quinn, B., Sabol, F. R., Schmid, D., . . . Shuler, S. C. (2010). *21st century skills map: Arts.* Tucson, AZ: Partnership for 21st Century Skills.

Franco, M., & Unrath, K. (2014). Carpe diem: Seizing the common core with visual thinking strategies in the visual arts classroom. *Art Education, 67*(1), 28–32.

Glanz, J. (2009). *Teaching 101: Classroom strategies for the beginning teacher.* Thousand Oaks, CA: Corwin Press.

Gronlund, N. E. (2004). *Writing instructional objectives for teaching and assessment* (7th ed.). Upper Saddle, NJ: Pearson.

Hetland, L., Winner, E., Veenema, S., & Sheridan, K. (2013). *Studio thinking 2: The real benefits of visual arts education.* New York, NY: Teacher's College Press.

Krathwohl, D. R. (2002). A revision of Bloom's Taxonomy: An overview. *Theory into Practice, 41*(4), 212–218.

McTighe, J., & Wiggins, G. (2012). *From Common Core Standards to curriculum: Five big ideas.* Retrieved from http://grantwiggins.files.wordpress.com/2012/09/mctighe_wiggins_final_common_core_standards.pdf

Moses, K. (1999). *Outsider art of the south.* Atglen, PA: Schiffer.

Moss, C. M., & Brookhart, S. M. (2012). *Learning targets: Helping students aim for understanding in today's lesson.* Alexandria, VA: Association for Supervision and Curriculum Development.

National Coalition for Core Arts Standards. (2014b). *National Core Arts Standards: A conceptual framework for arts learning.* Retrieved from www.nationalartsstandards.org/sites/default/files/NCCAS%20%20Conceptual%20Framework_4.pdf

Pennisi, A. C. (2013). Negotiating to engagement: Creating an art curriculum with eighth-graders. *Studies in Art Education, 54*(2), 127–142.

Sellen, B. (2000). *Self-taught, outsider, and folk art: A guide to American artists, locations, and resources.* Jefferson, NC: McFarland.

Sickler-Voigt, D. C. (2006). Southern African American art: Chronicles of shared history, religious zeal, and personal expression. *Journal of Cultural Research in Art Education, 24,* 71–82.

Steward, V. (2010). A classroom as wide as the world. In H. H. Jacobs (Ed.), *Curriculum 21: Essential education for a changing world* (pp. 97–114). Alexandria, VA: ASCD.

Strauss, M. (2015, March 26). No, Finland isn't ditching traditional school subjects: Here's what's really happening. *The Washington Post.* Retrieved from www.washingtonpost.com/news/answer-sheet/wp/2015/03/26/no-finlands-schools-arent-giving-up-traditional-subjects-heres-what-the-reforms-will-really-do/?utm_term=.c3ee2c41a1ffEndFragment

Teaching for Artistic Behavior. (2018). *Teaching for artistic behavior.* Retrieved from https://teachingforartisticbehavior.org

Thompson, J. G. (2018). *The first-year teacher's survival guide: Ready-to-use-strategies, tools, & activities for meeting the challenges of each school day* (4th ed.). San Francisco, CA: Josey-Bass.

# Chapter 3

# Assessment and Evaluation for the Visual Arts

FIGURE 3.1 Coley Lee, 13-years-old, United States.
*Source: Mike Muller, teacher.*

Teachers need to know where students are and where they are going in their education. Assessments and evaluations guide teachers, students, administrators, and policy makers in making informed judgments about the quality and effectiveness of teaching and student learning. **Assessment** measures anticipated and unanticipated student learning outcomes, appraises the expressive outcomes that result from participation in the choice-based art curriculum, and directs teaching and learning practices at all phases of the learning process. Whereas assessment delivers ongoing measurements and appraisals, **evaluation** is a judgment of student, teacher, and program effectiveness. Educators, administrators, and policy makers collect, analyze, and interpret the results of assessments to make informed evaluations. They use evaluation results to make comparisons and form conclusions about what different students, teachers, programs, and/or districts have achieved.

We can use the analogy of riding a bicycle as we learn how to apply the best assessments and evaluations. Hearing about required assessments and evaluations can initially feel like learning how to balance on a bicycle without the aid of training wheels. We might feel unsteady at first, but then ride with confidence and ease. We select the best gears (assessment tools), accelerate (move students forward), and ultimately cross the finish line (reach goals). On our journey to thrive, we will learn strategies to become proficient in assessing art related learning tasks and reporting outcomes in the language and formats that administrators and policy makers expect.

We will meet the following objectives by participating in this chapter:

- Characterize how assessment, assessment literacy, and evaluation correlate with learning targets.
- Explain the benefits of teachers and students assessing their own performances.
- Develop an art assessment action plan.

Spotlight on Student Art #3 describes how a student and teacher utilized assessments to produce high-quality outcomes. Figures 3.1–3.3 present a sampling of photographs within the student's portfolio.

FIGURE 3.2 Coley Lee, 13-years-old, United States.
*Source: Mike Muller, teacher.*

FIGURE 3.3 Coley Lee, 13-years-old, United States.
*Source: Mike Muller, teacher.*

## Spotlight on Student Art #3

### Big Idea: Inner Drive

"I want to do my very best" and "I can do even better" are mindsets that motivate humans to assess their performances and achieve great results based on their inner drive to produce successful outcomes. They self-assess their creations using their existing knowledge and seek ways to grow beyond their current skills. Figures 3.1–3.3 are photographs by award-winning student photographer Coley Lee, who applied his inner drive to create a body of works and improve his photographic abilities. To build his impressive collection of photographs, Coley participated in his school's photography club and took photographs in his free time. He developed his artistic intuition using the skills he learned in class and by working with mentors. He regularly met with his art teacher to discuss his photographs and sought ways to augment his works' aesthetic appeal by learning new techniques and improving his technical abilities. For example, he learned how to choose effective lighting and camera angles to capture moments in time. He applied this knowledge to select photographs to submit to the Scholastic Art Contest, for which he won a Silver Key Award. He also took the initiative to present and sell his photographs at a local art fair. Coley's portfolio documents his growing skills, efforts, and knowledge. He participated in multiple assessments (portfolio development, formative critiques, and self-assessments) to produce successful results and achieve advanced proficiencies and competence as a young photographer.

## ASSESSMENT

Visual arts assessments present discipline-specific challenges that differ from other academic subjects. They measure and appraise artistic behaviors including acquiring artistic skills, applying art production methods to communicate ideas, and generating deep understandings about the meaning of art and its functions in society (such as working effectively with themes; see examples in Figures 3.4 and 3.5). A single assessment cannot measure or appraise all that students need to achieve because assessments have different functions. **Assessment literacy** in the visual arts occurs when teachers know how to use, create, and implement different assessments. When educators become assessment-literate teachers, they apply their knowledge and professional intuitions to design and

FIGURE 3.5 This artwork is inspired by the theme of light. Lau You Gi, 7-years-old, Simply Art, Hong Kong, China.
*Source: ICEFA Lidice, 43rd Exhibition.*

implement assessments. They select assessments that produce the most accurate results to inform instruction, accommodate students' needs, and improve teaching and learning practices. Teachers communicate learning expectations and explain assessments to students so that they will understand what they need to accomplish and can monitor the quality of their performances. They analyze assessment results and reflect on ways to continue to augment students' development and attainment of learning targets. Great teachers recognize the importance of assessment literacy as a core component of their teaching practices because they help students reach competencies that have intrinsic values to students.

**Performance assessments** measure learning targets that result in students' creative products and performances derived from lesson objectives, student learning outcomes, and curricular goals. These are

FIGURE 3.4 This artwork has an agriculture theme. Hiba Khamlichi, 13-years-old, Rabat, Morocco.
*Source: ICEFA Lidice, 42nd Exhibition.*

FIGURE 3.6 Veronika Kolářová, 15-years-old, Dům dětí a mládeže Praha 3–Ulita, Praha 3–Žižkov, Czech Republic.
*Source: ICEFA Lidice, 39th Exhibition.*

the assessments most people know because they often result in grades. Performance assessments include students' art productions, communications in journals and interviews, written responses, and knowledge derived from selected answers on tests. Not all that teachers want and need to know about students and their teaching practices can be **measured quantitatively** through numeric scores (Meier, 2018). In school settings and beyond, educators collect, analyze, and measure quantitative and appraise qualitative data resulting from learning tasks over an expanded time, such as a grading period or a school year. Focusing on the whole student, they use **qualitative assessments** to appraise students' expressive outcomes (e.g. dispositions, feelings, processes, inquiries, and experiences) that result from participating in comprehensive learning tasks (Eisner, 2002). For example, constructing the sculpture in Figure 3.6 in clay required skill and persistence. Expressive outcomes, such as the pride that results from creating

quality artworks, do not necessarily produce grades, but they have tremendous value in students' lives. **Authentic assessments** appraise student learning outcomes and expressive outcomes that reach beyond the classroom with real-world applications (Anderson & Milbrandt, 2005). Teachers collaborate with students to make curricular decisions and assess performances, work samples, and dispositions. Their appraisals may include observations of students working, teacher–student conferences, anecdotal records, and personally-driven works' in students' journals and portfolios. Authentic assessment does not mean that other forms of assessment are inauthentic (Chappuis, Stiggins, Chappuis, & Arter, 2012). Rather, its model simply demonstrates the value of learning knowledge for itself, not just for the sake of earning a grade.

## DEVELOPING AN ART ASSESSMENT ACTION PLAN

Designed to accelerate teachers and students forward, this textbook's art assessment action plan (Model 3.1) offers teachers pathways to assessment literacy. Its open-ended structure stimulates innovative approaches for students to achieve the learning outcomes presented within the choice-based art curriculum. The art assessment action plan:

- integrates best practices and contemporary research on assessment to measure and appraise teaching and learning through art;
- provides a practical blueprint using quantitative and qualitative assessment methods to set goals, select assessments, manage assessments, and plan performance analyses;
- prepares teachers to identify and explain relationships;
- illustrates visual arts assessments to administrators and policy makers;
- substantiates professional teaching and assessment methodologies; and
- summarizes findings for teaching evaluations and authentic teaching practices.

Its holistic approach contrasts with assessment models that focus solely on what students' final products will look like.

# Model 3.1
## Art Assessment Action Plan

**Directions: Answer the prompts with narrative descriptions and check the appropriate boxes as applicable.**

**Timeline:**

☐ Grading Period          ☐ Semester          ☐ Academic Year          ☐ Other

## 1. Setting Achievable Goals Through Learning Targets

The following explains how I have identified achievable student learning goals that align with learning targets and standards as part of a choice-based art curriculum that challenges students. They build on students' prior knowledge and life experiences in the following ways:

## 2. Selecting Assessments

Check all that apply:

| | | |
|---|---|---|
| ☐ Informal Assessment | ☐ Holistic Scoring Rubric | ☐ Portfolio |
| ☐ Formative Assessment | ☐ Test/Quiz | ☐ Self-Assessment |
| ☐ Interim Assessment | ☐ Essay | ☐ Peer Assessment |
| ☐ Summative Assessment | ☐ Oral Exam | ☐ Group Assessment |
| ☐ Formal Assessment | ☐ Rating Scale | ☐ Discussion/ Interview/Conference |
| ☐ Numeric Scoring | ☐ Checklist | ☐ Observation |
| ☐ Analytic Rubric | ☐ Journal | ☐ Authentic Assessment |
| ☐ Other | ☐ Other | ☐ Other |

Using multiple assessments, I plan to measure and appraise student learning targets and expressive outcomes in the following ways:

## 3. Managing and Analyzing Assessment Data

Check all that apply:

| | | |
|---|---|---|
| ☐ Valid Assessment | ☐ Class Critique | ☐ Teacher Reflection Journal |
| ☐ Reliable Assessment | ☐ Student Self-Assessment | ☐ Teacher Reflection Portfolio |
| ☐ Ongoing Assessment | ☐ Peer Assessment | ☐ Summative Performance |
| ☐ Monitor Student Behavior | ☐ Group Assessment | ☐ Reteach |
| ☐ Accommodate All Students | ☐ Teacher Self-Assessment | ☐ Small Group Teaching |
| ☐ Review Formative Tasks | ☐ Observation | ☐ Individual Teaching |
| ☐ Discussion/Interview/Conference | ☐ Photographs/Videos/Documents | ☐ Curricular Change |
| ☐ Authentic Assessment | ☐ Other | ☐ Other |

I will regularly analyze quantitative and qualitative data from valid and reliable assessments to identify strengths and make necessary instructional and curricular changes/improvements in the following ways:

## Setting Goals Through Learning Targets

The first step in creating an art assessment action plan is to apply backwards design (Wiggins & McTighe, 2005) to identify the learning goals that are important for students to accomplish. Assessment-literate teachers set achievable, yet challenging, short- and long-term goals to assess and appraise what students should know and be able to do. Goals align with benchmarks, grade level performance descriptors, and objectives unpacked from curricular standards. Effective goals are age-appropriate, build on students' prior knowledge, and foster students' abilities. They include knowledge, reasoning, skill, product, and disposition learning targets (Chappuis et al., 2012). For example, Figures 3.7 and 3.8 present evidence of students' skills in conceptualizing ideas about art media, production methods, and subject matter to produce creative artworks. Teachers plan opportunities for students to revisit and refine creative learning skills to form enduring understandings (Pennisi, 2013).

## Selecting Assessments

The second step in designing an art assessment action plan is to align targets with the most appropriate

FIGURE 3.8 Yap Melissa Chia Chean, 9-years-old, Yeow Chye Art Centre, Penang, Malaysia.
*Source: ICEFA Lidice, 39th Exhibition.*

FIGURE 3.7 Asal Yar-Ahmadi, 6-years-old, Kanoon–Institute for Intellectual Development of Children and Young Adults, Tehran, Iran.
*Source: ICEFA Lidice, 38th Exhibition.*

assessments to measure and appraise what students have accomplished and still need to attain. This chapter and its companion website present model assessments for measuring learning tasks that integrate the works of Laurence Gartel, an artistic advisor for the National Core Arts Standards (see Artists' Lessons to Thrive! 3.1). Similar to Gartel applying his inner drive to work through challenges associated with producing digital artworks, assessment-literate teachers apply their inner drive to steer clear from obstacles and maintain best practices. Students utilize their inner drives to produce the very best outcomes and positive dispositions.

## Artists' Lessons to Thrive! 3.1 Laurence Gartel: When an Inner Drive Becomes a Driving Force

### Big Idea: Inner Drive

Computer technology drives daily life with its high-speed access and vast online images. It can be difficult to imagine the challenges that pioneering digital artist Laurence Gartel experienced to produce some of the very first digital artworks. Gartel says that the obstacles were enormous." In the late 1970s and early 1980s gaining access to high-performance, multimillion-dollar Cray computers for his art was nearly impossible. Gartel knew of only three such computers that were available outside of government research laboratories. He also had the daunting task of convincing the art world that digital art was a true art form.

Early on, Gartel had an ability to create what seemed to be the impossible using complex analogue computer systems. In 1980, artists could not save digital images on transferrable memory storage devices. Therefore, Gartel reproduced his digital works by photographing their images on his computer monitor, as seen in *Triumph Car* (Figure 3.1.1). Such photographs capture the linear

FIGURE 3.1.1 Laurence Gartel, *Triumph Car*, 1980.
*Source: © Laurence Gartel 2018. All rights reserved.*

moiré patterns that run throughout a design displayed on a computer screen. Normally, they would be considered an undesired byproduct. However, the moiré patterns in *Triumph Car's* add meaning to the work because the linear patterns mimic an animated racecar with speeding lines that indicate movement.

Gartel's inner drive led him to prominence as a digital artist because he overcame the challenges associated with computer technology and helped change perceptions about digital art as a valid art form. His determination to conquer obstacles led him to receive many accolades and commissions for his work. In 1989, the Joan Whitney Payson Museum replaced Vincent van Gogh's *Irises* with Gartel's *Nuvo Japonica* series. Two years later Gartel designed a popular Absolut® advertisement that ran for ten years and adorned more than 100 million magazines. Gartel explained that this significant work "changed the face of advertising art" with its groundbreaking digital art focus. Additionally, Gartel served as an artistic advisor in the writing of the National Core Arts Standards for Digital Media and was the official artist of the 57th Annual Grammy Awards. Since producing *Triumph Car*, Gartel has received commissions to create unique art cars, including *Mercedes Benz Globus SLK 320 Art Car* (Figure 3.1.2). He attached printed glossy papers, metallic papers, and tape to the vehicle's exterior to produce a playful automotive design. Reflecting on his career, Gartel acknowledged how his childhood collection of ceramic cars inspired his artistic creations and his *Roget's Thesaurus* helped him acquire new vocabulary, make sense of the world, and describe his artistic vision. Gartel continues to promote the validity of digital art and to create art cars. His inner drive has made him a leading force in shaping digital art media.

FIGURE 3.1.2 Laurence Gartel, *Mercedes Benz Globus SLK 320 Art Car*, 2014.
*Source: © Laurence Gartel 2018. All rights reserved.*

## Essential/Guiding Questions

1. How did Gartel's inner drive make him a pioneer in the digital art movement? Which obstacles did he overcome to become a successful artist?
2. Why would Gartel choose to photograph *Triumph Car* and *Mercedes Benz Globus SLK 320 Art Car*? Would you prefer to see *Triumph Car* on its original computer monitor and *Mercedes Benz Globus SLK 320 Art Car* from behind the wheel? How do artists' presentations and displays of their work shape their meanings and functions in society?

## Preparation

Using the big idea of inner drive, students will identify a time when they overcame an obstacle. They will write and sketch about this moment in their journals.

## Daily Learning Targets

I can create an artwork focusing on my inner drive.

- I can connect research on how artists such as Gartel have applied their inner drive to produce art, and select the media of my choice to communicate my ideas.
- I can create a unified design to produce a quality composition.
- I can select the best format/location to present my artwork and share my story.

**National Core Arts Anchor Standards** 1, 6, 8, and 11
www.nationalartsstandards.org

*Quoted artists' statements not listed in the reference section result from personal communications with the author (personal communications, 2014–2018).*

## Informal Assessment

**Informal assessment** is the process of assessing student behaviors formatively and checking for understanding without assigning grades. It transpires through one-on-one, small group, and whole-class interactions. Through informal assessments, teachers do the following:

- Make adaptations, monitor student behaviors, and correct potential difficulties before they occur.
- Talk to students and observe their behaviors to check for understanding and ascertain if students are on-task.
- Teach students how to use hand symbols to indicate levels of understanding, such as thumbs up to represent "I can" or "I understand."
- Prompt students to hold up cards to denote proficiency levels (i.e. beginner art apprentice, proficient artist, and highly skilled artist) and indicate readiness to move forward.

- Call volunteers and non-volunteers to answer questions. Teachers randomly pull index cards with individual students' names on them so that all students have an opportunity to answer.
- Group students as **elbow partners** who turn to the person next to them and exchange ideas during learning activities.
- Have students create name markers to place into cups at their tables to identify that they have completed tasks and are ready to move forward.

Informal assessments begin when students enter the classroom and continue throughout the duration of the learning tasks.

## Formative Assessment

**Formative assessment** is a process of collecting data during a learning activity to identify what students understand and have yet to comprehend. Formative assessments provide teachers and students with immediate feedback before assigning summative grades. Teachers use formative assessments for these purposes:

- Determine when to modify instruction and reteach pertinent information.
- Reintroduce and build upon targets associated with standards that require greater practice and knowledge over a series of sequential lesson plans before summatively measuring target attainment.
- Give students concrete suggestions to reach goals through descriptive feedback.
- Encourage students who are already on target to continue on track to attain new skills.

Through formative assessments, teachers assist students in reaching targets that were unpacked from complex standards that require multiple tasks and time to attain, such as understandings about global cultures and traditions. Teachers cluster complex learning targets with simpler ones so that students can grasp the concepts more readily.

Formative assessments contribute to students' autonomous behaviors and personal investment in learning. Students work individually, with peers, and/ or with groups to assess learning formatively:

- **Formative self-assessment** refers to individual students measuring their own performances using self-reflection and class assessment instruments as applicable to make necessary adaptations to tasks at hand.
- **Formative peer assessment** transpires when students offer fellow students constructive feedback about a learning target or behavior during a project.
- **Formative group assessment** occurs when students and other relevant participants collaborate as a team to assess learning targets.

Given formative assessment tasks, students practice skills, ask questions, self-reflect, and participate in in-progress critiques to find solutions to challenging problems. They can gain greater self-confidence using formative assessments when projects, exams, and grades are due as **formal assessments** (ones that result in numeric scores and grades) because students have predetermined that they can demonstrate required skills (Chappuis et al., 2012).

## Summative Assessment

Teachers combine formative and summative assessments for optimum results. **Summative assessment** measures learning targets at the completion of one or more

tasks. It includes results from art lessons, journals, portfolios, essays, and capstone projects. It differs from evaluations including standardized test results, report card grades, and evaluated performances. Summative assessment results are useful in identifying levels of student achievement, assigning diagnostic grades, and providing feedback with the intention of helping students grow.

Like professional artists, students' creative works undergo formative revisions before becoming finished products. Students can consider the revisions that Figures 3.9 and 3.10 may have needed to become final artworks. For example, paintings may require multiple layers of paint to achieve desired colors and textures. Ceramic sculptures may need adjustments to become

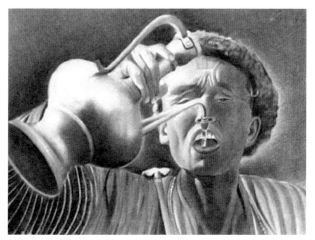

FIGURE 3.9 Auimad Zubair, 16-years-old, Institute of Construction and Local Industries, Kabul, Afghanistan.
*Source: ICEFA Lidice, 37th Exhibition.*

FIGURE 3.10 Jiří Manďák, 12-years-old, ZUŠ, Zlín–Malenovice, Czech Republic.
*Source: ICEFA Lidice, 39th Exhibition.*

freestanding works. When teachers assess student products summatively only for grades, students miss opportunities to practice skills and receive formative feedback that assists them in reaching learning targets. Assessment-literate teachers teach students how to use content on assessment instruments to assess their in-progress performances and make changes as necessary before submitting assignments for summative grades. For example, they provide assessment instruments that formatively and summatively measure performance and skill targets in the visual arts (see the "Rubrics" and "Rating Scales and Checklists" sections in this chapter). They also teach students how to apply **summative self, peer, and group assessments** to reflect on learning processes, assess completed works, and decide how to move forward given their current knowledge.

Teachers may develop **informal summative assessments** at the completion of learning tasks that do not result in grades. They include teacher–student interviews and written appraisals of students' completed works. Quality summative assessments communicate teachers' fair, transparent, and as-objective-as-possible assessment practices, which assist all students in achieving learning goals. Many schools require numeric grades for students based on **summative formal assessments**. Numeric grades clarify and quantify aspects of student achievement. They identify improvements necessary to close learning gaps. Traditionally, many formal assessments have focused on measuring students'

lower cognitive skills, including memorizing facts and recalling basic information. Developers of the NVAS (NCCAS, 2014b) articulated the need for substantial assessments in the arts that measure higher cognitive skills, such as to analyze, evaluate, and create as identified in the revised Bloom's Taxonomy (Anderson et al., 2001). A choice-based art curriculum and open-ended formal summative assessments provide pathways for students to employ higher cognitive skills when grades are necessary.

## Simplified Numeric Scoring

Busy teachers can use a **simplified numeric scoring** model to assign numeric grades using objectives or "I can" target statements unpacked from standards. For example, Model 3.2 presents a lesson's main target "I can create an artwork using the big idea of inner drive." The minimum successful completion of a task at a proficient level would earn 70 points, which is equivalent to a C grade for a project that has a maximum 100-point value (Henry, 1990). The model's final 30 points align with the project's remaining learning targets. These include design skills, application of media, and relevant context. For an even more simplified version, teachers can briefly summarize the learning targets' key words and list their point values (see Model 3.3 and the templates on this textbook's companion website).

## Model 3.2
## Simplified Numeric Scoring With Full Targets

| Inner Drive Artwork Targets | Points Value |
|---|---|
| I can create an artwork using the big idea of inner drive.<br>• I can select the media of my choice to communicate my personal concept of inner drive.<br>• I can combine two or more artistic skills to produce an innovative work. | _____ of 70 Points |
| I can research how Laurence Gartel and at least one other artist used their inner drive to create art.<br>• I can examine artistic creations, visual culture imagery, articles, and creative writings on artists' inner drive.<br>• I can incorporate at least one aspect of my research into my artwork to provide evidence of what I have learned. | _____ of 15 Points |
| I can demonstrate craftspersonship in my use of art media, tools, and techniques. | _____ of 15 Points |
| Comments: | Total Score:<br><br>_____ of 100 Points |

**70-Point Scale:** Approaching Basic Proficiency, 42–48.9; Basic Proficiency, 49–55.9; Accomplished Proficiency, 56–62.9; Exemplary Proficiency, 63–70
**15-Point Scale:** Approaching Basic Proficiency, 9–10.4; Basic Proficiency, 10.5–11.9; Accomplished Proficiency, 12–13.4; Exemplary Proficiency, 13.5–15

## Model 3.3
## Simplified Numeric Scoring With Abbreviated Targets

| Inner Drive Artwork Targets | |
| --- | --- |
| Inner Drive Artwork; Media of Choice; Combine 2+ Artistic Skills | _____ of 70 Points |
| Research Artists' Inner Drive; Evidence Presented in Artwork | _____ of 15 Points |
| Craftspersonship | _____ of 15 Points |
| Total Score: | _____ of 100 Points |

## Rubrics

A **rubric** is a scoring device in table format that contains measurable objectives or daily learning targets written in student-friendly language with "I can" statements. An **analytic rubric** (Model 3.4), also called a **scoring rubric,** presents rubric criteria on its far left column, with each criterion placed in a separate row. A **holistic scoring rubric** differs from an analytic rubric because it displays all criteria clustered together, which teachers use to assess a final product or performance as a whole (Burke, 2006; Puckett & Black, 2000). This textbook's companion website provides a model analytic, a model holistic rubric, and templates for creating original rubrics for visual art learning tasks.

A rubric's **performance scale** includes numbers, descriptor words, icons, and/or percentage points. The higher the number or level on the rubric, the better the student has satisfied the learning expectation. Many rubrics contain a 3–5 performance scale. This textbook's model analytic rubrics (Model 3.4 and the models on the companion website) have a four-level performance scale that can be aligned with the grading practices used in many schools. Given a rubric's criteria and performance scale, teachers can define levels and qualities of student performances through the **descriptive indicator of performance.** On an analytic rubric, the descriptive indicators of performance are listed in subsequent columns to the right of the itemized criteria. Well-designed rubrics include detailed performance descriptors in descriptive language that identify possible

target achievement inaccuracies, limitations, partial achievements, and full mastery so that students can understand what indicates a particular level of performance. Performance descriptors move beyond stand-alone indicators that simply name the quality of a target, such as average or excellent, and fail to describe what target attributes should look like. With this in mind, teachers can collect sample student products—including benchmarked artworks—that show students the degrees to which anonymous peers have met targets or experienced challenges in reaching the targets presented on rubrics. If teachers notice that student performances rank between two levels of attainment presented on a descriptive indicator of performance when calculating rubric scores, teachers may simply indicate which targets a student hits on each indicator and assign a value between the two points, such as 2.5 or 3.5. In circumstances in which students have not yet reached target attainment or their full potential, teachers can continue to work with students to improve their scores. If grades are due and students have not yet met proficiencies, but have completed some work, teachers can calculate scores for the partial tasks they have attained to move students beyond the level of 0.

At the onset of instruction, teachers should model how to use rubrics as formative assessment tools to guide students as they work towards targets. Students can review rubrics during self-reflection activities, formative peer assessments, and teacher conferences to make adjustments to in-progress works. For students who cannot utilize a rubric independently, such

## Model 3.4
## Analytic Rubric Components

| Criteria | Performance Scale: Approaching Basic Proficiency (1 point) | Performance Scale: Basic Proficiency (2 points) | Performance Scale: Accomplished Proficiency (3 points) | Performance Scale: Exemplary Proficiency (4 points) | Scores: Student (S) Peer (P) Teacher (T) |
|---|---|---|---|---|---|
| Criterion #1 I can . . . | Descriptive Indicator of Performance | Descriptive Indicator of Performance | Descriptive Indicator of Performance | Descriptive Indicator of Performance | (S) _____ (P) _____ (T) _____ |
| Criterion #2 I can . . . | Descriptive Indicator of Performance | Descriptive Indicator of Performance | Descriptive Indicator of Performance | Descriptive Indicator of Performance | (S) _____ (P) _____ (T) _____ |

Notes:
The criteria identify objectives or daily learning targets written as an "I Can" statements unpacked from the standards.
The descriptive indicator of performance identifies the level of quality and performance associated with the objective listed in the row.

as early childhood learners and students developing language skills, teachers can make accommodations by orally describing rubric content and checking with students throughout the learning process. As students work towards skill attainment, they might focus on individual targets within a rubric before tackling its other targets. For example, students may need to conduct preliminary research, practice, and experiment before delving fully into a criterion identified on a rubric.

Teachers can create a multipurpose rubric to reuse for different assignments or develop ones that relate to specific tasks. This textbook's model analytic rubric #1 on the companion website was designed for multiple tasks. As they deem necessary, teachers can highlight key content listed in the criteria column and create supplemental checklists to target more specified learning tasks. For example, if a class is working on the rubric's presenting target, a lesson's presenting task may focus on students developing an exhibition. For a different lesson, the class can apply the rubric's presenting target for a portfolio presentation. Once a rubric is in practice, teachers may notice that it needs revisions to become more efficient or student-friendly. They can consult with a teaching team and collaborate with students to modify rubric content (Chappuis et al., 2012).

### Rating Scales and Checklists

A **rating scale** lists learning outcomes next to symbols that represent the level of performance students can achieve. Teachers and students mark the appropriate symbol to categorize the degree of performance on a particular target. Like a rubric, a rating scale has several levels of aptitude and achievement. For example, Model 3.5 presents a rating scale for students' participation in a class discussion. One of its criteria reads: "I identified the discussion's big idea and key points." On the rating scale, students would select the appropriate symbol to self-assess their performances.

A **checklist** measures specific actions and observable behaviors students should be able to achieve on a task without rating the quality of the performance indicator like a rating scale does. Teachers may use checklists when grades are not required, but specified student actions need to be documented. Checklists also assist students in formatively self-assessing the quality of their work before they turn in assignments because they can check off required components as they complete them. For example, Model 3.6 presents a checklist to guide students' presentation of artwork for display. One of its criteria reads: "I included an artist's statement that explains the ideas behind my artwork's production, purpose, and meaning." Students would check Yes, Somewhat, or No to indicate if they met the requirement.

## Model 3.5
## Rating Scale

### Art Discussion Self-Assessment

| 1. I identified the discussion's big idea and key points. | | |
|---|---|---|
| I could have done better.<br>○ | Good<br>✿ ✿ | Great!<br>✿ ✿ ✿ |
| 2. I raised my hand to speak. I listened respectfully to the teacher, guests, and/or fellow students as they spoke. | | |
| I could have done better.<br>○ | Good<br>✿ ✿ | Great!<br>✿ ✿ ✿ |
| 3. I took efforts to answer questions appropriately. | | |
| I could have done better.<br>○ | Good<br>✿ ✿ | Great!<br>✿ ✿ ✿ |
| 4. I added my interpretations to the discussion. | | |
| I could have done better.<br>○ | Good<br>✿ ✿ | Great!<br>✿ ✿ ✿ |
| 5. I summarized class findings and ideas at the end of the discussion. | | |
| I could have done better.<br>○ | Good<br>✿ ✿ | Great!<br>✿ ✿ ✿ |

## Model 3.6
## Checklist

### Presenting Student Art for Display

| Directions: Check Yes, No, or Somewhat (as applicable) to indicate your performance on the listed criteria. | Yes ☺ | Somewhat ☺ | No ⊘ |
|---|---|---|---|
| 1. I displayed my artwork in an appropriate place to communicate its message. | | | |
| 2. My artwork's display includes my name, the work's title, its medium, and its size. | | | |
| 3. I included an artist's statement that explains the ideas behind my artwork's production, purpose, and meaning. | | | |
| 4. I gave directions on how to care for my artwork. | | | |

## *Comprehensive Art Journals*

**Art journals** are personal spaces in which to create artworks and written statements, respond to art and visual culture, make interpretations, present ideas, and build connections over time. Journals offer glimpses into students' thoughts and demonstrate knowledge that teachers may not normally have access to (Anderson & Milbrandt, 2005). Comprehensive art journals are resources to identify students' metacognitive thinking because they provide a format for students to record observations and reflect on life's circumstances. As assessment instruments, they provide formative and summative evidence of student achievement of learning targets. They document the steps that students take as they work towards reaching complex targets that require practice, inquiry, and self-reflection to attain. Many teachers develop rubrics to assess journals formally and provide students with a checklist for self-assessment.

When creating journals, some students fear that they might "mess up" blank pages. Students can get positive results by investing as few as fifteen or twenty minutes a day journaling (Ludwig, 2010). Teachers can help students overcome concerns by employing artists' journaling methods. Like artists, students can develop page backgrounds by painting, drawing, or collaging them before adding new content to a page. They can experiment with doodling, mark making, color application, printmaking, popups, cutouts, and free writing, as well as apply the following methods.

1. **Self-reflection**: Journal artist Perrella (2004) observed: "A strong connection exists between current-day art journals and the time-honored traditions of writer diaries" (p. 71). Students can self-reflect by writing and creating art about their current ideas and feelings. They can transform their preliminary ideas into fuller products. For example, students can develop preliminary sketches, brainstorming lists, webbing charts, and a data collection to create a new artwork, study social justice or Earth Education themes, or implement a participatory action research project based on self-reflections presented within their journals.
2. **Prompts:** Prompts stimulate students' journal creations and assist them in making connections, reaching targets, and developing enduring understandings about big ideas. They include discussions, demonstrations, multimedia presentations, and scavenger hunts.
3. **Souvenirs and personal collections**: Egyptian artist Mohieddin Ellabbad (2006) affixed souvenirs to journal pages to produce meaningful designs. Students can collect trinkets, labels, and sentimental memorabilia to collage in their journals. Souvenirs can give memories new life and help students recall details.
4. **Vocabulary**: Students can integrate academic art vocabulary by spelling out letters with wires, stencils, stamps, and magazine cutouts.

Comprehensive art journals can become intimate spaces where students express their thoughts and concerns. Anderson and Milbrandt (2005) recommended offering students the opportunity to conceal pages to keep certain information private. In most cases, such pages do not contain evidence of harm (or potential harm) to students. Rather, they are private spaces for students to visualize their thoughts and ideas. Because troubling information may appear in journals, teachers need to make students aware of journal rules before beginning (Armstrong, 1994). A rule might state that teachers will assess all journal pages or that students can block out private spaces so that the teacher and classmates will not examine them. Another rule might state that all content must be Pre-K-12 appropriate and not depict graphic violence and sexuality. If teachers come across concerning journal entries and/or suspect abuse or students harming themselves, they must report their concerns to their administration and/or child protective services immediately.

## Portfolios

Portfolios originated in the visual arts as professional artists and designers assembled portfolios to showcase their creative skills and styles to potential clients. Portfolios should not be confused with **working folders,** which store all of the materials that students collect and create (Chappuis et al., 2012). Working folders are useful resources for gathering data that may later become integrated into a portfolio. In the choice-based art curriculum, **portfolios** are assessment instruments that contain a collection of student selected artifacts created over an extended time (for example, see Figures 3.11 and 3.12). Teachers assess portfolios' individual artifacts formally as they are developed. Traditional portfolios provide an intimate format for audiences to view original artworks up close and experience their tactile properties. Multimedia digital portfolios have the potential advantage of reaching wider audiences. Like a storybook, when teachers flip or click through well-organized content within a portfolio, they learn students' perspectives. Portfolios are a core component of the NVAS because they provide physical evidence of pre-K–12 students' performances.

Before students begin creating portfolios, teachers should identify and explain their purposes, identify which content and learning targets will be demonstrated, and generate a working timeline. For example, a portfolio's purpose might be to document student competencies, such as artistic skill development. Or, it

FIGURE 3.11 Nirel Kadzo, 14-years-old, Kenya. Works in Nirel's portfolio represent her interest in drawing stylized human forms.
*Source: Lisa Wee, teacher.*

FIGURE 3.12 Nirel Kadzo, 14-years-old, Kenya.
*Source: Lisa Wee, teacher.*

might center on a big idea or document student work on a capstone art project, experiential learning activity, or participatory action research project. Students will select the best artifacts that align with the type of portfolio they plan to create. For example, if students wanted to showcase artistic competence, they might present a collection of artifacts that highlight their artistic skills and develop an artist statement that describes the meaning of their portfolio collection (see Chapter 8). Students will participate in teacher conferences and peer and group assessments to receive formative feedback and identify where they want to go next. Students should have multiple opportunities to discuss and present their portfolios, as knowing how to develop, organize, and present portfolios teaches valuable communication, educational, and career skills.

## Managing and Analyzing Performance Data

The third step in implementing an art assessment action plan is to document how to manage and analyze performance data and dispositions based on assessments and appraisals. Teachers maintain physical and/or virtual spaces, including folders and grade books, to collect, organize, and store the results of formative and summative assessments. To manage and analyze performance data, teachers do the following:

- Preselect intervals to analyze data that they derive from multiple assessments. This analysis provides a structure to identify patterns and draw inferences that may not have been initially recognizable.
- Find trends in student achievement and learning gaps.
- Categorize assessment data according to learning targets and by coding other applicable information into relevant themes.
- Make informed interpretations and judgments based on careful analyses.
- Identify where students were before instruction, during a learning task, and after summative assessments.
- Clarify how planning, instruction, and assessment methods impact the level of target attainment and dispositions.

## Validity and Reliability

**Analysis** confirms that the assessments that teachers implement are valid and reliable. **Validity** refers to the ability of an assessment to measure or appraise what it intends to. Teachers:

- use evidence generated from valid assessments to analyze data and make concrete judgments about student performances;
- predetermine realistic levels of student achievement to ensure validity, including selecting developmentally appropriate targets and knowing how to make modifications and accommodations for diversified learners so that all students can achieve desired outcomes; and
- write rubrics, rating scales, and checklists in student-friendly language and explain their meanings and purposes to students.

Poorly designed tasks that students have inadequate time, directions, or resources to complete do not produce valid assessment results and can cause students to feel self-doubt (Chappuis et al., 2012). Assessment instruments must be reliable to be valid. **Reliability** refers to an assessment's ability to produce similar results, given comparable circumstances and students' unchanged baseline knowledge. For example, if an assessment's instructions were vague or confusing, the assessment would not be reliable because it could cause students to work towards different targets. If a team of assessment-trained teachers scored a student's artwork using the same assessment measure and came up with substantially different scores, there would be a problem with reliability and therefore, the assessment would be invalid. Invalid measures or appraisals do not provide teachers with adequate assessments. When teachers discover invalid or unreliable assessments, they should reject their results, omit them from analyses of student performances, and prepare new valid and reliable assessments as alternatives. All inferences from assessments must be valid to benefit students (Sabol, 2018b).

## Quantitative and Qualitative Methods

Teachers' analysis of quantitative and quantitative assessment results provide stakeholders with evidence that demonstrates how the teachers applied assessment data to close learning gaps and move students towards target attainment and positive dispositions. Numerically scored performances provide quantitative data, including performances rated through point accumulation on tests, basic numeric grading practices, rubrics, and checklists. A **target map** is a quantitative guide to identify and report the targets that students attain at scheduled intervals. This textbook's model target map on the companion website identifies a sample curriculum's targets, big ideas, essential questions, and student learning outcomes that transpired over a grading period. Its format assists teachers in determining the degree to which a whole class demonstrated target proficiency. where the class experienced gaps, and where subject matter did not build upon itself from one lesson to the next (Kallick & Colosimo, 2009; Langa & Yost, 2007; Wiles, 2009).

Qualitative assessment data include reflective communications, observations, and anecdotal evidence. Teachers collect and interpret qualitative data to understand concepts and student dispositions that cannot be measured by quantitative methods alone. Qualitative assessment methods and their results correlate with informal assessment practices by helping teachers understand students' perspectives, recognizing students' achievements, and closing learning gaps. Teachers might keep a log to document when they provided students with oral and written feedback about their work and encouraged students to make revisions to assignments before submitting them for formal summative grades. For example, if students struggled, teachers could offer **focused revision** so that students do not feel overwhelmed and could see success in small increments as they worked to complete one task or target at a time (Chappuis et al., 2012). Through qualitative analyses, teachers can identify how students assessed their metacognitive thinking patterns and performances, as presented in class critiques, comprehensive art journals, and portfolios. These examples provide evidence of students' abilities to work through challenges, make revisions, and set goals to improve on forthcoming tasks. Students might look to the NVAS essential questions to augment their artistic skills and mindsets, such as: "What role does persistence play in revising, refining, and developing work?" (NCCAS, 2014a; #VA:Cr3.1). They could examine their portfolios to identify which artifacts are most successful and which ones need additional work. They could document progress by taking before and after photographs of their work, as well as write about and discuss the positive changes they made based on their research (Andrade, Hefferen, & Palma, 2014; Chin, 2013).

## EVALUATION

Evaluation includes grades on a report card; results from a standardized test; summative results from combined performances; and a school, school district, or organization's measurement of overall progress. Educational experts use evaluations to assemble data over a given time, analyze findings, identify strengths and weaknesses, and develop strategies to improve effectiveness. Since the establishment of the **Elementary and Secondary Education Act** (ESEA) in 1965, the U.S. Government has allocated funds to support children's education and, in return, has required states to evaluate student learning through standardized tests. In 2015, Congress implemented the **Every Student Succeeds Act (ESSA)** with the reauthorization of ESEA (U.S. Congress, 2016). Some of ESSA's components resemble educational practices modeled in Finland and Singapore, which are recognized for their outstanding education systems that place less emphasis on standardized testing, focus on students, and provide substantial teacher leadership opportunities (Berry, 2015; Sahlberg, 2015). ESSA identifies the visual arts as part of a **well-rounded education**. ESSA's evaluative measures move beyond one-size-fits-all "bubble" tests and include portfolios and project-based assessments, which are commonly used in the arts. The National Art Education Association (NAEA, 2016) policy advocates for quality visual arts performance assessments as clear alternatives to standardized tests. Assessing and evaluating student learning in the visual arts promotes the value of a high-quality art program because it demonstrates the visual arts' importance in the school curriculum and provides evidence of student learning to students, parents, administrators, and other stakeholders (NCCAS, 2014b).

### Evaluative Grading

**Evaluative grading** reports summative judgments of student learning in art, often using qualitative descriptors such as A for "excellent" (Quinn, 2013). Grade books contain recorded formative and summative

assessments and calculations of summative evaluations. Teachers organize grade book scores under assignment names, formal assessment names (i.e. test, essay), and/or learning targets. When evaluating students with special needs for a report card grade, teachers refer to the students' IEP (individualized education program), as the goals identified in modified assessment plans may differ from standard grade-level targets (see Chapter 6). Best teaching practices call upon teachers to limit evaluation grades to students' achievements only. Grades lose their effectiveness as accurate communication tools when teachers manipulate grades with the intention of motivating and/or sending punitive warnings to students (Chappuis et al., 2012). Teachers' effective assessment methods, teaching styles, knowledge of subject matter, professionalism, and ability to create a nurturing and stimulating learning environment motivate students as autonomous learners and help them to earn the highest and most accurate grades possible. A student's conduct and level of effort should not positively or negatively his/her impact actual grades. Students need to understand that they cannot reach many learning targets and achieve their fullest potential without behaving appropriately and exerting their best effort. To guide students towards target attainment in the visual arts, teachers can develop extra tasks and assess them to replace older assessments taken prior to a student's proficiency. They may also choose between mean scores (the average sum of all weighted scores) and median scores (showing the numeric score in the middle of selected formal assessments) to produce evaluative grades. Median scores may be the most accurate representation of performance for students who have received extreme scores, such as a zero, that significantly lowered their grades.

### Model Cornerstone Assessments

**Model Cornerstone Assessments** (MCAs) are embedded in the choice-based art curriculum at 2nd, 5th, 8th, and high school grades (NCCAS, 2014a). They include grade-level targets, rubrics, checklists, and student self-assessments. Teachers can summarize the results of student outcomes measured and appraised using MCAs' diverse assessments to form evaluations. The MCAs in the NVAS advocate for the importance of the visual arts in the broader school curriculum and exemplify how learning in the arts reaches beyond what can be measured by standardized tests alone. They span different grades so that students will develop key knowledge, higher-order thinking skills, and creative learning skills. MCAs' instruments "anchor the curriculum around the most important performances that students should be able to do (on their own) with acquired content knowledge and skills" (NCCAS, 2014b, p. 15). Students' accumulation of knowledge becomes evident through meaningful bodies of works collected in visual arts portfolios, which document students' growth and performances over time (McTighe & Wiggins, 2011). Educators can conduct these evaluations individually and/or work in teams at school and district levels to evaluate student performances. They can also adapt the MCAs to suit their particular evaluation needs (Sabol, 2018a).

## Teacher Evaluations

School districts, universities, and other educational organizations evaluate pre-service teachers and professional teachers to identify their planning abilities, instructional skills, professional knowledge, use of assessments, and ability to challenge and engage students fully. The best pre-K-12 teacher evaluations have merit beyond the evaluation period and encourage teachers to apply their results to advance their teaching practices and student learning (Sickler-Voigt, 2018). Several pre-service teacher education programs utilize the edTPA performance assessment, developed by education professionals, to evaluate pre-service educators, called *teacher candidates*, for competency in planning, instructing, and assessing (Pearson Education, 2018). Teacher candidates must provide evidence of pre-K–12 student achievement during their clinical teaching residency. They develop a portfolio that contains written personal reflections, teaching videos, and other applicable planning, instructional, and assessment artifacts. Their participation lays a foundation to self-reflect as a normative professional practice and grow from future teacher evaluations.

In pre-K–12 schools, administrators perform formal observations of instruction to evaluate teachers. Evaluations may be developed internally by a school district or state, or externally, such as The Marzano Focused Teacher Evaluation Model (Marzano, 2018), for the purpose of improving instruction and student attainment of learning outcomes. Many teacher evaluations evaluate teacher competencies in planning, instruction, and assessment while also referencing student performances and the effectiveness of the learning environment. Administrators review lesson plans, assessments, gradebooks, and other applicable resources to check for quality and identify if lessons are well organized and managed. After their evaluations, teachers meet with administrators and describe how their instruction was most successful and how they could improve their own and student performances to guide further instruction. Districts and states may also evaluate teacher effectiveness using **student growth portfolios**. They are particularly useful for non-tested subjects, including visual art. Based on their instruction, teachers collect student artifacts produced over a given period from diversified learners to show evidence of all learners' progress, including students with emerging, proficient, and advanced skills (Tennessee Department of Education, 2017). The student artifacts that teachers submit must align with the evaluation's standards-based criteria and are numerically scored.

## OUR JOURNEY TO THRIVE CONTINUES . . .

This chapter provided practical approaches to applying assessment and evaluation in the visual arts for educators to become assessment-literate teachers who know how to implement a choice-based art curriculum, design an art assessment action plan, and employ effective teaching methods. Chapter 4 addresses how we can prepare a well-managed classroom learning environment that assists teachers and students in achieving quality outcomes and dispositions.

## CHAPTER QUESTIONS AND ACTIVITIES

1. Define "assessment" and "evaluation" in your own words. Describe what it means to be an assessment-literate teacher. What are the benefits of teachers and students assessing their own performances? What are the benefits of using a teaching and learning target map?
2. Develop an art assessment action plan (Model 3.1) using the template from this textbook's companion website.

*use online book power-point*

*Due Next week*

3. Select four student artworks within this textbook. Identify the artworks by their figure numbers. Each one will serve as inspiration for developing a different assessment instrument: (a) simplified scoring method, (b) a rubric, (c) a rating scale, and (d) a checklist. Use the templates from this textbook's companion website.

4. Answer Artists' Lessons to Thrive! 3.1's essential/guiding questions in written form or as part of a group discussion. Complete its daily learning targets.

*any artwork in text    holistic or analytic choose    checklist    use templates others don't here*

## References

Anderson, L. W. (Ed.), Krathwohl, D. R. (Ed.), Airasian, P. W., Cruikshank, K. A., Mayer, R. E., Pintrich, P. R., . . . Wittrock, M. C. (2001). *A taxonomy for learning, teaching, and assessing: A revision of Bloom's Taxonomy of Educational Objectives* (Complete ed.). New York, NY: Longman.

Anderson, T., & Milbrandt, M. (2005). *Art for life.* Boston, MA: McGraw Hill.

Andrade, H., Hefferen, J., & Palma, M. (2014). Formative assessment in the visual arts. *Art Education, 67*(1), 34–40.

Armstrong, C. L. (1994). *Designing assessment in art.* Reston, VA: National Art Education Association.

Berry, B. (2015). Teacherpreneurs: Cultivating and scaling up a bold brand of teacher leadership. *The New Educator, 11*(2), 146–160. doi:10.1080/1547688X.2015.1026786

Burke, K. (2006). *From standards to rubrics in 6 steps: Tools for assessing student learning, K-8.* Thousand Oaks, CA: Corwin Press.

Chappuis, J., Stiggins, R., Chappuis, S., & Arter, J. (2012). *Classroom assessment for student learning: Doing it right: Using it well* (2nd ed.). Upper Saddle River, NJ: Pearson.

Chin, C. (2013). Cultivating divergent thinking: Conceptualization as a critical component of artmaking. *Art Education, 66*(6), 28–32.

Eisner, E. (2002). *The arts and the creation of mind.* New Haven, CT: Yale University Press.

Ellabbad, M. (2006). *The illustrator's notebook.* Toronto, ON: Groundwood Books and House of Anansi Press.

Henry, C. (1990). Grading student artwork: A plan for effective assessment. In B. E. Little (Ed.), *Secondary art education: An anthology of issues* (pp. 61–68). Reston, VA: National Art Education Association.

Kallick, B., & Colosimo, H. (2009). *Using curriculum mapping and assessment data to improve learning.* Thousand Oaks, CA: Corwin Press.

Langa, M. A., & Yost, J. L. (2007). *Curriculum mapping for differentiated instruction, K-8.* Thousand Oaks, CA: Corwin Press.

Ludwig, J. K. (2010). *Creative wildfire: An introduction to art journaling: Basics and beyond.* Gloucester, MA: Quarry Books.

Marzano, R. J. (2018). *iObservation.* Retrieved from www.iobservation.com

McTighe, J., & Wiggins, G. (2011). *Cornerstone tasks.* Retrieved from www.nccaswikispaces.com/_media/mctighe_on_cornerstones.pdf

Meier, M. E. (2018). *Assess what matters most: Recommendations for gathering information about student learning.* Retrieved from www.arteducators.org/learn-tools/assessment-white-papers-for-art-education

National Art Education Association. (2016). *Impact of high stakes and standardized testing on visual arts education: NAEA platform and position statement.* Retrieved from www.arteducators.org/advocacy/articles/191-impact-of-high-stakes-and-standardized-testing-on-visual-arts-education

National Coalition for Core Arts Standards. (2014a). *National Core Arts Standards.* Retrieved from www.nationalartsstandards.org

National Coalition for Core Arts Standards. (2014b). *National Core Arts Standards: A conceptual framework for arts learning.* Retrieved from www.nationalartsstandards.org/sites/default/files/NCCAS%20%20Conceptual%20Framework_4.pdf

Pearson Education. (2018). *edTPA.* Retrieved from www.edtpa.com/Home.aspx

Pennisi, A. C. (2013). Negotiating to engagement: Creating an art curriculum with eighth-graders. *Studies in Art Education, 54*(2), 127–142.

Perrella, L. (2004). *Artists' journals and sketchbooks: Exploring and creating personal pages.* Gloucester, MA: Quarry Books.

Puckett, M. B., & Black, J. K. (2000). *Authentic assessment of the young child: Celebrating development and learning* (2nd ed.). Upper Saddle River, NJ: Merrill.

Quinn, T. (2013). *On grades and grading: Supporting student learning through a more transparent and purposeful use of grades.* Lanham, MD: Rowman & Littlefield Education.

Sabol, F. R. (2018a). *Model Cornerstone Assessments (MCAs): A powerful tool for measuring student achievement in visual arts education.* Retrieved from www.arteducators.org/learn-tools/assessment-white-papers-for-art-education

Sabol, F. R. (2018b). *Some guiding principles for conducting assessments in visual arts education.* Retrieved from www.arteducators.org/learn-tools/assessment-white-papers-for-art-education

Sahlberg, P. (2015). *Finnish lessons 2.0: What can the world learn from educational change in Finland.* New York, NY: Teacher's College Press.

Sickler-Voigt, D. C. 2018). *Changing mindsets about edTPA: From test anxiety to demonstrating teacher competencies through authentic teaching and assessment practices.* Retrieved from www.arteducators.org/learn-tools/assessment-white-papers-for-art-education

Tennessee Department of Education. (2017). *Tennessee educator acceleration model: Fine arts.* Retrieved from http://team-tn.org/non-tested-grades-subjects/fine-arts/

U.S. Congress. (2016). *S.1177: Every Student Succeeds Act (ESSA).* Retrieved from www.congress.gov/bill/114th-congress/senate-bill/1177/text?overview=closed

Wiggins, G., & McTighe, J. (2005). *Understanding by design* (2nd ed.). Upper Saddle River, NJ: Pearson.

Wiles, J. (2009). *Leading curriculum development.* Thousand Oaks, CA: Corwin Press.

# Classroom Management in the Visual Arts

FIGURE 4.1 Svetlana Andreevna Verbickaya, 9-years-old, Gorodskoy Dvorec Detskogo Tvorchestva Goricvit, Krivoj Rog, Ukraine.
*Source: ICEFA Lidice, 41st Exhibition.*

FIGURE 4.2 Anastasia Vitalievna Banshikova, 13-years-old, Gorodskoy Dvorec Detskogo Tvorchestva Goricvit, Krivoj Rog, Ukraine.
*Source: ICEFA Lidice, 41st Exhibition.*

**Classroom management** in the visual arts encompasses the organizational procedures that teachers apply to all stages of the learning process so that students attain learning outcomes and reach their fullest potential in a safe, structured, and predictable learning environment. Managing visual arts instruction is unique in that it involves teachers facilitating students' responsible usage of specialized (and sometimes messy) art supplies and equipment. When teachers understand best practices in classroom management, they can plan effective instructional methods, identify the challenges students face, and teach students how to be responsible for demonstrating on-task behaviors.

Cultivating classroom management skills plays a major role in our journey to thrive. This chapter presents clear pathways to build, refine, and/or restructure classroom management techniques. Great classroom management feels like wearing a prized medallion or badge of honor. It showcases our ability to provide students with quality learning experiences and demonstrates our professional abilities, care for, and commitment to students.

We will meet the following objectives by participating in this chapter:

- Summarize the purposes and benefits of effective classroom management in teaching art.
- Contemplate strategies to overcome classroom management challenges.
- Design a classroom management plan for teaching art.

Spotlight on Student Art #4 (Figures 4.1 and 4.2) demonstrates how students applied on-task behaviors, practiced skills, and followed safety procedures to produce intricate beaded artworks. Similarly, students combined their concentrated skills and determined efforts to produce exceptional results in paint and carved wood (Figures 4.3 and 4.4). Such quality works would be impossible to achieve in disordered learning environments.

FIGURE 4.3 Elizaveta Kapitsa, 15-years-old, Art School, Grodno, Belarus.
*Source: ICEFA Lidice, 40th Exhibition.*

FIGURE 4.4 Josefína Vávrová, 15-years-old, ZŠ, Praha 1, Czech Republic.
*Source: ICEFA Lidice, 40th Exhibition.*

## Spotlight on Student Art #4

### Big Idea: Practice Makes Perfect

Practice makes perfect! Artists and designers apply distinct procedures to create artistic products and make adaptations to perfect their skills. Following Ukrainian beading practices to produce traditional folk costumes, 9-year-old Svetlana formed a choker called a *sylyanka*, a matching purse, and a long multi-stringed necklace (Figure 4.1), while 13-year-old Anastasia created two necklaces in a design called *gerdany*, which refers to a garland or collar around the neck (Figure 4.2). Their creations correlate directly with the big idea of practice because of the mindful acts they took to learn beading processes and create beautiful designs. The students focused their attention to maneuver thin needles and string tiny glass beads into intricate patterned designs. They applied safety procedures to protect their hands, fingers, and faces to produce each piece, while preventing the threads and beads from entangling and damaging their work. Their stunning array of accessories resulted from their dedication, time investment, and abilities to follow procedures to see their artworks through to their completion. The students' work ethic and the practiced skills that they demonstrated to create these artworks represent some of the on-task behaviors teachers expect students to achieve in their well-managed classrooms.

## MANAGING TEACHING AND LEARNING

All teachers experience classroom management challenges at one point or another. Experienced teachers can tell firsthand accounts of the mistakes they made when first entering the profession. Pre-service teachers can recall teacher classroom management challenges from their own pre-K–12 experiences. Effective classroom management begins before students enter the classroom. Teachers with proficient classroom management skills predetermine class guidelines, rules, and consequences to suit students' needs, learning environments, and their personal teaching styles (Greytak, Kosciw, & Boesen, 2013; McKeown, 2011). They plan learning targets with clear objectives, procedures, and assessments to guide teaching and learning in art.

Teachers must keep students engaged during all stages of learning for classes to operate smoothly. Similarly, students must know what teachers expect so that they are able to achieve learning targets. Effective classroom managers treat students fairly, even when students challenge them. They create an environment in which students feel comfortable trying new art learning tasks and asking for help when they do not understand. Given best teaching practices, honest discourse, and feedback from formative assessments, students learn to recognize how their own and other students' behaviors impact class dynamics and their abilities to reach learning targets (Queen & Algozzine, 2010). When visual arts learning environments are punitive and controlling, students have limited opportunities to communicate and collaborate with peers and teachers in productive ways (Cinquemani, 2014;

Espelage et al., 2013; Fredland, 2008; McKeown, 2011).

The majority of classroom behavior problems (approximately 98%) result from minor infractions, which include talking, procrastinating, wandering, and mishandling art supplies (Tileston, 2004). Children and adolescents, like adults, experience challenging life circumstances that impact their behaviors and emotions. For some students, schools may be the only places where adults consistently model positive behaviors. Some students act out because their basic needs are unmet; some want attention; and some may be having a bad day. A small percent of students (about 3%) need assistance that extends beyond the scope of typical teachers' professional training and expertise (Queen & Algozzine, 2010). Life's hardships can result in students feeling hurt and cause them to blurt out, refuse to work, and seek excessive attention from classmates and teachers. Instead of overreacting and amplifying negative situations, effective classroom managers seek constructive ways to channel student behaviors. They take steps to prevent minor transgressions from escalating into further behavior problems. They understand that one student's off-task behaviors can cause other students to mimic negative behaviors and lead to greater distractions. When off-task behaviors consume the classroom, teachers have less time to teach art and students have fewer opportunities to learn (Crews, Crews, & Turner, 2008; Fredland, 2008; Wong & Wong, 2009).

Classroom management skills align with personal job satisfaction. As effective classroom managers, teachers use self-reflection to identify what works well and what went wrong so that they can handle future situations appropriately (McKeown,

2011). They apply formative assessments to keep students on-task and motivate students to achieve more than anticipated. If one approach does not work, they try something new. Effective classroom management practices share similarities with creative professional environments in which people work individually and in teams to produce excellent results. Artists' Lessons to Thrive! 4.1 presents Oleana's (Figure 4.5) company policy of "fair made [sic] procedures" for creating beautifully designed knitted goods and accessories. Classrooms run most efficiently when the learning environment is fair and collaborative, as is the case with Oleana's work environment.

FIGURE 4.5 Photo by Solveig Hisdal, Oleana©.
*Source: https://en.oleana.no*

## Artists' Lessons to Thrive! 4.1 Oleana: A Fairytale Reality Through Fair Made Procedures

### Big Idea: Fair Procedures

Founded in 1992 by Signe Aarhus, Kolbjørn Valestrand, and Hildegunn Møster, Oleana is an award-winning Norwegian company that produces clothing, blankets, and accessories using eco-friendly raw materials including wool, silk, alpaca, and cashmere. Solveig Hisdal, one of Norway's leading designers, creates Oleana's exquisite designs. From its inception, its founders intended for Oleana to be different from other companies. Their dream was to create quality products that people loved and to produce good jobs in Norway. This was at a time when unemployment was high and most of the nation's clothing factories had moved overseas (Valestrand, Aarhus, & Hisdal, 2010).

FIGURE 4.1.1 Photo by Solveig Hisdal, Oleana©.
*Source: https://en.oleana.no*

FIGURE 4.1.2 Photo by Solveig Hisdal, Oleana©.
*Source: https://en.oleana.no*

The Oleana brand represents fair made procedures. Its leaders have invested "in creativity and pleasure of work, equality, and fairness" (Valestrand et al., 2010, p. 14). They oppose unfair labor practices that treat people as machinery, which are prevalent in sweatshops and excessively profit-driven companies. Fifty percent of the company's costs go to employee salaries and another 30% covers production. Oleana hires the best skilled individuals who also have a good sense of humor. Age is not important, as its employees range from their twenties to their eighties. Its leaders trust their employees and do not require time clocks. In the spring, all employees share a good part of the company's profits equally. Each spring, the whole company participates in a fully paid study tour to historic cities such as Salzburg, Alhambra, and Istanbul or other textile factories producing yarn, buttons, and cloth "to understand the greater picture; why we do what we do" (Valestrand et al., 2010, p. 112). The excursions and bonuses add inspiration to the ordinary workdays at the factory.

Situated on a Norwegian fjord just outside of Bergen in Ytre Arna, Oleana's state-of-the-art facility has plenty of natural light and breathtaking views. High-tech Japanese knitting machines hum in the background as skilled workers add delicate hand details to Oleana's designs. On a factory tour, Aarhus explained Oleana's design philosophy while holding a child-sized pair of hand-knit wool gloves in a traditional Norwegian style. She revealed how the back of the gloves, which her grandmother knit for her, had been mended several times. Prior to bargain-priced industrialized clothing, individuals would repair their clothing to wear them as long as possible. She explained that in today's society people purchase too much cheap clothing, which harms the environment and leads to unfair labor practices. Oleana's designers create quality products that last.

With more than twenty-five years of experience, Oleana has beaten the odds to become a successful company that produces products that people love and make their wearers feel proud. Visitors are welcome to tour the factory, where they can see Oleana's well-treated factory workers in action. All members of Oleana's team have collaborated to transform an artistic dream into a fairytale reality using fair made procedures.

### Essential/Guiding Questions

1. Why do Oleana's founders believe that it is important to use fair made procedures to create their products?
2. What can schools and communities learn from Oleana? In which ways does their business model relate to fair classroom management practices?

### Preparation

Students will learn the following information. Solveig Hisdal researches museum collections to inspire her contemporary designs. Some of her inspiration has come from historic paintings, porcelain wares, vintage buttons, and decorative lace. Upon completing each spring and fall collection, Hisdal articulates her full artistic vision for its catalogues by photographing Oleana's models, which have included her and Aarhus' daughters, in stunning locations. Every few years, Aarhus, Valestrand, and Hisdal showcase Oleana's collections with extraordinary artistic productions that feature live music, dancers, and their creative designs to share their love of the arts with the community.

### Daily Learning Targets

I can design a catalogue, tri-fold brochure, or presentation that focuses on the big idea of fair procedures for a cause that is personally meaningful to me.

- I can incorporate influences from one or more artworks, as well as my original photographs and/or drawings in my product's design.
- I can include at least three factual statements that inform viewers about the fair procedures that relate to the cause I have selected for my design.
- I can create a unified design that emphasizes my cause and demonstrates my use of craftspersonship.

**National Core Arts Anchor Standards** 2, 6, 7, and 10
www.nationalartsstandards.org

## CLASSROOM MANAGEMENT STRATEGIES FOR TEACHING ART

Students notice if teachers greet them at the door and if classroom atmospheres are conducive to learning (Wong & Wong, 2009). Based on these preliminary assessments, students make predeterminations about their role in the classroom. Effective classroom managers recognize students' expectations and prepare students for success by creating a classroom management plan that students can understand and follow, as well as reinforce its teachings through the choice-based art curriculum. Using available resources, they design safe and inviting classroom spaces that encourage student learning. For example, Figure 4.6 illustrates how a

FIGURE 4.6 School hallway, United States.
Source: Cassie Stephens, teacher.

teacher decorated her classroom hallway to create a welcoming learning environment.

## Creating a Classroom Management Plan

Creating a personalized classroom management plan involves introspection (Wong & Wong, 2009). Teachers need to anticipate how students will achieve learning outcomes and identify possible barriers that might hinder progress. Their classroom management plans should align with students' age levels and their learning environments. This textbook's Model 4.1, "Classroom Management Plan for Teaching Art," includes a mission statement that focuses on the big idea of care that can be adapted for all ages and teaching circumstances. The plan's guiding acronym, CARE, represents anticipated student and teacher actions: care, awareness, respect, and embrace. It includes a list of positive consequences that reward on-task behaviors and identifies plans to correct off-task behaviors. The consequences show students that teachers are prepared to maintain a caring classroom environment driven by high expectations. The CARE model is just one example of what a classroom management plan for teaching art might look like. In developing a plan, teachers and students can collaborate to identify the best actions to guide their teaching and learning practices. Teachers should reinforce the classroom management plan's mission and anticipated behaviors by teaching students positive actions that promote good citizenship.

Classroom management specialists recommend limiting classroom management actions to five or less so that students can concentrate on desired actions (Wong & Wong, 2009). Positive classroom actions go deeper than basic classroom rules. They promote open-ended values that teach students how to take ownership of their behaviors to achieve learning outcomes. Students learn to recognize how positive and negative consequences result from specific actions and inactions. For example, students could identify how a "job well done" produces feelings of personal satisfaction. Receiving positive teacher and peer feedback becomes an intrinsic reward through which students strive to take learning to the next level.

## Model 4.1
### Classroom Management Plan for Teaching Art

The choice-based art curriculum offers effective practices that engage students in the comprehensive study of art. Learning activities extend beyond the classroom and connect to students' lives in meaningful ways. Students apply big ideas to research significant questions and seek answers to global topics through the processes of creating, presenting, responding, and connecting to art (NCCAS, 2014a). They experiment with art media and processes to explore new ideas. Because total group participation benefits the entire class, students are expected to put forth maximum effort, share experiences, and eagerly participate in class discussions and activities. The act of caring drives the art curriculum. When we show care to each other, we reinforce how people should be treated and how we wish to have others treat us.

### Class Actions

The teacher and students will utilize positive behaviors that promote a caring class community. Class members will demonstrate the positive actions of care, awareness, respect, and embrace (CARE) to achieve quality-learning outcomes. The CARE model promotes a positive learning environment, teaches empathy, and minimizes off-task behaviors.

- **Care** represents the positive values and actions students demonstrate to each other, their teachers, and other living beings.

- **Awareness** teaches students how to become mindful about their minds, bodies, and spirits; learning objectives/targets; goals; and the class environment. When students are aware they make conscious behavior choices and apply metacognition.
- **Respect** promotes a positive learning environment and includes respect for oneself, others, materials, school, learning, and the community. It extends beyond the classroom and reaches into all aspects of students' lives. When students treat themselves and others with respect they model constructive behaviors.
- **Embrace** fuses the concepts of care, awareness, and respect because it calls upon students to embrace learning processes and the big ideas that drive the curriculum. They take ownership of their learning and recognize how comprehensive learning experiences connect to their daily lives.

## Consequences

In order to maintain a safe and nurturing classroom environment it is essential that all students understand class actions and procedures. Beginning on the first day, students will review class actions, sign a behavior contract to acknowledge their understanding of on-task behaviors, and learn class consequences. The teacher will acknowledge students' diligent work ethics, acts of kindness, and other on-task behaviors. In circumstances in which students' behaviors disrupt the class and/or students' work, the teacher and students will join forces to find a solution to correct off-task behaviors.

| Consequences to Reward On-Task Behaviors | Consequences to Correct Off-Task Behaviors |
|---|---|
| I can: <br> • feel personal accomplishment for achieving positive class actions; <br> • gain positive peer recognition; <br> • receive teacher praise (oral or written, including a handwritten note); <br> • know that my teacher will contact my parents/guardians to inform them of my positive actions; <br> • earn a certificate of appreciation; <br> • serve as a class leader; <br> • engage in special personally-driven learning activities; <br> • mentor others; <br> • create quality products; and/or <br> • participate in expanded learning experiences. | I can: <br> • review positive class actions; <br> • receive a teacher warning; <br> • offer a sincere apology for my off-task behavior; <br> • participate in an honest discussion with my teacher; <br> • find solutions to fix the problem(s); <br> • work at a different location; <br> • complete a CARE Action Plan; <br> • lose free time (time out, detention); <br> • understand that my teacher will contact my parent/guardian; <br> • participate in a conference with my parent/guardian and teacher; and/or <br> • meet with administration. |

Off-task behaviors impede student learning. When teachers require corrective actions for students' off-task behaviors, students must learn how to rectify undesirable behaviors and avoid them in the future. For example, Model 4.2, "My CARE Action Plan," encourages students to take actions to improve off-task behaviors through reflective drawing and writing tasks, and to make positive choices to move forward. Class consequences for off-task behaviors must be fair, correspond with the off-task behavior, and suitable for students' ages. These actions work better than severe punishments that push students away, because they value students as class members (Manning & Bucher, 2007; Queen & Algozzine, 2010). Teachers can prepare for possible student disruptive behaviors before they occur by listing fair consequences for off-task behaviors (including stalling and disrespecting class materials). This practice demonstrates that disruptive behaviors will not be tolerated and allowed escalate into habitual problems. When teachers create a nurturing learning community with consistent expectations, students want to use their time productively. They feel personally invested in their work and appreciate positive class interactions (Wong & Wong, 2009).

## Model 4.2
## My CARE Action Plan

Name: _____

**Draw a picture that illustrates your improvement plan through the actions of care, awareness, respect, and/or embrace.**

[blank box for drawing]

**I have a plan to improve on one or more of the following:**

I can show better care. _____
_____
_____
_____

I can become more aware. _____
_____
_____
_____

I can show greater respect. _____
_____
_____
_____

I can embrace (learning, responsibility, etc.). _____
_____
_____
_____

Additional comments: _____
_____
_____
_____

## Presenting Well-Designed Classroom Environments

Classroom spaces impact students' physical and psychological safety, ability to focus, and participation in learning activities (Broome, 2013). Teachers assess classroom spaces to make the learning environment as productive as possible for teaching art. They identify where furniture, supplies, and equipment belong. Figures 4.7 and 4.8 show how a teacher arranged

FIGURE 4.7 Art classroom, United States.
*Source: Ted Edinger, teacher.*

FIGURE 4.8 Student art supplies are located in clear plastic bins. United States.
*Source: Ted Edinger, teacher.*

student seating, organized art supplies, and created original displays to produce functional and inviting spaces for teaching and learning.

## Organizing Learning Zones

Having flexible and mobile classroom layouts permits teachers and students to move pieces of furniture and their bodies to the best locations for learning tasks (Araca, 1990; Broome, 2013; Susi, 1990). Teachers consider how fixed classroom structures, including whiteboards, cabinets, and countertops, impact desk and learning center arrangements. If a classroom has a sink, teachers plan the best flow of student traffic to navigate them towards the sink. For classrooms without a water source, teachers determine where to collect water and store it in large buckets to fill smaller water containers for class projects and to clean dirty water containers. If a classroom is carpeted, they generate a plan to protect the flooring. They design learning centers, such as a reading center in a cozy corner; a spacious drawing horse bench center (Figure 4.9); pottery wheels in spaces that can sustain splashes of wet clay and water; and technology centers that remain cool, dry, and clean. Effective designs permit students to see instruction and relevant teaching aids (including smart boards and displays) at all times so that they can focus their attention. Students might move chairs or sit in a carpeted area for whole-class readings and discussions to see, hear, and respond effectively. They might participate in small group activities at tables that seat four to six students to discuss ideas, collaborate on projects, and share art supplies. While teaching art in a designated art classroom lab is optimal, some learning environments have educators teach art from a cart designed to store art supplies, including paint and clay, that can be moved from classroom to classroom. In circumstances in which teachers with an art cart teach in other teachers' classrooms, it is necessary that those teachers provide adequate space to bring in the cart, offer demonstration and board space for instruction, and identify locations to store student artworks. Schools that require art teachers to use carts should provide a spacious closet for storing art supplies.

Many teachers create seating charts to learn students' names, facilitate attendance, and provide structure. Teachers revise seating charts when students'

FIGURE 4.9 This learning center with drawing horse benches is designed for figure drawing studies. United States.
*Source: Frist Art Museum.*

FIGURE 4.10 A student uses supplies organized in clear boxes. Kenya.
*Source: Lisa Wee, teacher.*

initial placements disrupt the learning process or when students have learning needs that require accommodations (Manning & Bucher, 2007; McKeown, 2011; Wong & Wong, 2009). Some students prefer or need to work alone or sit close to the teacher's desk due to difficulties maintaining on-task behaviors. In situations in which students prefer to sit with peers, but need time away from the group, teachers can model the correct behaviors to emulate so that they can return to the group at the proper time.

## Managing Art Supplies and Equipment

Teachers save time and teach students independence by planning the storage and distribution of art supplies. Many teachers purchase containers for each table to store miscellaneous art supplies. They label the boxes and/or color code their contents to keep supplies in order (Figure 4.10). With practice, students learn how to use the supplies properly and keep supply containers tidy. Teachers facilitate this process by demonstrating how supply containers should remain closed, unless directed otherwise. This reduces students' temptations to handle the materials inside until the appropriate moments.

Given their engagement with art production tasks, teachers and students need to be aware of art supply and equipment safety hazards. U.S. Public Law 100–695 Labeling of Hazardous Art Materials mandates that toxicologists identify chronic hazards in products from art supplies. Manufacturers are required to place warning labels on art products and provide consumers with detailed safety instructions (Art and Creative Materials, 2018; USCPSC, n.d.). The Art and Creative Materials Institute (ACMI; 2018) certifies the safety of art supplies through rigorous toxicological evaluations by medical professionals who determine if products are non-toxic. Products with its **approved product (AP)** seal are certified to be made with safe materials. The **cautionary label (CL)** seal authenticates that the products are safe when users carefully follow the package directions. For example, when working with certain paints and glazes, users may be directed to wear gloves when handling the products or cleanse areas of skin contact with soap and water. ACMI recommends that early childhood and elementary-aged children, and people with special needs who cannot read and/or understand packaging directions use AP labeled products only. Many manufacturers and distributors post product-specific **material safety data sheets (MSDS)** online for public access. Potential mechanical and chemical hazards associated with art production include inhalation, cuts, crushes, burns, and ingestion (Hagaman, 1990; U.S. Consumer Product Safety Commission [USCPSC], n.d.).

Teachers should check that all classroom products are correctly labeled and stored (Qualley, 2005). Products that are past their labeled expiration dates need to be discarded. Students need to know how to use art material and equipment safely. For example, when creating a mosaic (Figure 4.11), students need to wear a protective mask to avoid inhaling dust from thinset and grout, as well as handle tile edges carefully and use cutting tools properly. They would wear gloves when applying wet thinset and grout and protective eyewear when breaking tiles. Creating specialized ceramic artworks with a kiln (Figure 4.12) and prints with a printing press (Figure 4.13) would

require different safety procedures. Many teachers display warning signs to reinforce safety procedures, such as one that reads "caution hot" to remind students to use a heating element properly when creating a batik (Figure 4.14). Teachers might pre-assess

FIGURE 4.12 Nikola Rabiňáková, 11-years-old, ZŠ, MŠ, ZUŠ, Jesenice, Czech Republic.
*Source: ICEFA Lidice, 40th Exhibition.*

FIGURE 4.13 Innes Withersová, 8-years-old, Sdružení Roztoč, Roztoky, Czech Republic.
*Source: ICEFA Lidice, 42nd Exhibition.*

FIGURE 4.11 Elementary students design a mosaic. United States.
*Source: Author, teacher. Pamela McColly, photo.*

FIGURE 4.14 Students heed hot pink warning signage. United States.
*Source: LeAnne Deats, teacher.*

students' safety knowledge before allowing them to work with potentially harmful materials and equipment. Teachers should individually review safety requirements with students who need additional guidance and provide detailed demonstrations so they can use materials and equipment properly. After learning safety procedures, students need to know the routines for collecting and storing supplies and equipment and cleanup, including using the sink and placing works on the drying rack. Many teachers have students take turns passing out and collecting supplies to avoid classroom congestion and potential accidents from too many students walking around at once.

## Preparing Visuals and Displays

Visual resources identify the types of learning that teachers anticipate from students. The best displays have practical purposes and incorporate resources that reinforce learning objectives (Queen & Algozzine, 2010; Wong & Wong, 2009). Powerful bulletin board designs often include art, big ideas, contextual information, and academic vocabulary (Figure 4.15). Titles capture students' attention from a distance. Fine details and interactive parts encourage students' up-close examinations. Students' displayed creative works enhance the classroom and provide students with a sense of ownership. Teachers also create displays in broader school and community spaces to advocate for the art program.

FIGURE 4.15 This bulletin board features kindergarten artworks and a teacher-made character. It teaches about diversity and texture. United States.
*Source: Selina Hyzer, teacher.*

## Responding to Classroom Management Through the Choice-Based Art Curriculum

Teachers can reinforce each of the positive actions identified in a classroom management plan (such as care, respect, awareness, and embrace) through the choice-based art curriculum. For example, a lesson might focus on the concept of embracing on-task class participation. By participating in class discussions and producing creative projects, students can identify personal reasons for embracing learning tasks to achieve desired results. They can also make connections to artists that embrace particular methods and concepts to produce meaningful bodies of work. The NVAS' essential questions are exemplars that teachers can connect to their curriculum and classroom management plan. One example is Anchor Standard #VA:Cr2.2's essential questions:

> How do artists and designers care for and maintain materials, tools, and equipment? Why is it important for safety and health to understand and follow correct procedures in handling materials, tools, and equipment? What responsibilities come with the freedom to create?
>
> (NCCAS, 2014a)

With practice, students learn to become responsible for managing their behaviors and generating powerful ideas as they answer essential questions and produce creative products that can benefit themselves and others.

## Connecting in a Safe Learning Community

Efforts to create a classroom management plan, present a well-designed classroom, and respond to students' needs through the choice-based art curriculum come together so that students can connect in a safe learning community. Well-managed classrooms are places for students to form positive relationships and learn empathy and fairness for all people. Teachers can provide opportunities for students to address the meanings and purposes of healthy relationships, empathy, social ethics, and other constructive behaviors. For example, students can benefit from studying age-appropriate lessons about challenges and hardships that people their age experience in a safe and responsible manner through art. Teachers might begin by collaborating with a school's guidance counselor to develop thematic lessons to answer questions that concern students. Class discussions offer constructive opportunities for students to share feelings about the things they witnessed at school, in the broader community, and in the media. For example, depending on students' ages and maturity, they might confuse the boundaries between violence in reality and fiction given their exposure to violence in popular culture, factual news reports, movies, and video games. Without adult direction, students may be forced to decipher meanings on their own without understanding the facts (Chapin, 2008). Lack of understanding can cause students to be unaware of the negative impacts that acting out harmful behaviors might entail. Safe learning environments are productive places where teachers can offer students guidance and direction using developmentally appropriate art learning tasks.

## ADDRESSING CLASSROOM MANAGEMENT CHALLENGES

Teachers must be adept in their roles as inspirational leaders who minimize classroom management challenges. A lack of classroom management skills that remains uncorrected can result in a greater chance of job dissatisfaction, burnout, and a willingness to abandon the profession (Manning & Bucher, 2007; McMahon et al., 2014; Tileston, 2004). The following sections identify strategies to avoid common classroom management mistakes so that teachers can focus on the joys of teaching.

### Managing Students With Confidence

Standing in front of students who stare blankly, ignore instruction, goof off, or give grimacing looks can feel intimidating. Some teachers worry that students will not like them, think that they are mean, and/or not want to learn if they manage their classes. Addressing student infractions—even minor requests such as asking students not to waste art supplies—causes

some teachers to feel self-doubt. Teachers who look uncomfortable, who are fidgety, and/or speak without confidence signify that they are afraid to manage their classrooms. When such apprehensions continue, teachers create a classroom environment of chaos, permissiveness, and indecision. Their inactions translate into lack of care for students (Fredland, 2008; McKeown, 2011). Queen and Algozzine (2010) addressed the implications of not correcting off-task behaviors: "Rather than expect a change in the child's behavior, the adult alters her own behavior to avoid the child's unhappiness. The adult thus acts irresponsibly, forgetting the more important issue of providing guidance" (p. 32). Students recognize teacher confidence and authority when they see them in action. Teachers with confidence and authority command students' attention respectfully, speak confidently and smile naturally. Their body language shows that they are comfortable teaching art, as seen with the pre-service teachers shown in Figure 4.16. They calm students when they are upset, listen to their concerns, and teach them how to become responsible for their behaviors. They exude class control and check that students follow class routines (Queen & Algozzine, 2010). Self-awareness and practice can help teachers boost their confidence when managing students. For example, teachers can practice positive self-talk and student–teacher discourse. They can also develop reflective journals to document their thoughts about their classroom management practices. Journal entries can include triggers that have disrupted learning and

FIGURE 4.16 Pre-service teachers from the United States give a demonstration to elementary children in Norway.
*Source: Author, teacher.*

their solutions so that teachers can overcome them and project the confidence needed to manage students.

## Setting High Expectations for All Students

Setting high expectations begins with teachers who want to make a positive difference in all students' lives. Teachers fail students when they apply stereotypes and lower their expectations of student capabilities. Some students need extra support to achieve in school because they come to school with their basic needs unmet. Focusing on students' abilities, great teachers strive to help diversified learners achieve quality learning outcomes by teaching them how to overcome obstacles and set attainable goals. They recognize that it is normal behavior for students to challenge authority and occasionally break rules (Wong & Wong, 2009). When these acts occur, they address and correct inappropriate behaviors. Great teachers also take steps to shelter students from hearing harmful comments from peers and adults. Their authentic teaching methods and awareness of classroom management procedures provide students with the stability and skills they need to be successful.

## Instructing Students When They Are Ready to Learn

Teachers should not begin instruction until students are ready to learn because students cannot learn with diverted attention (Tileston, 2004; Wong & Wong, 2009). Some teachers feel eager to start art lessons and begin without checking to see if students are ready to learn. Others feel rushed for time because they have much information to cover. Teachers who move through instruction without gaining students' full attention will most likely spend much class time running around and repeating the lesson's directions. Effective classroom managers begin a class routine the first day of class to teach students the behaviors they anticipate. Perhaps students will have a seat and work in their journals when entering the classroom or answer essential questions written on the board as part of a small group discussion. Students learn to watch and participate in demonstrations so that they

can reach learning targets and produce successful outcomes, as alternatives to diving into learning tasks haphazardly without direction, or stalling. Effective classroom managers know how to direct students' attention at all points during instruction and motivate students to participate in the full learning process. Students learn the class routine for redirecting their attention when their teachers request their focus.

## Demonstrating Professionalism

Students have high expectations for teachers. They expect teachers to look and act like professionals. Professional teaching attire means that teachers maintain a neat and clean appearance that follows the employer's dress code. When a teacher's clothing is too casual, suggestive, or inappropriate in other ways, it distracts from the learning process. Students will focus on the teacher's attire (or body) and not what is being taught (Freeburg & Workman, 2010). A teacher's clothing should fit properly, and a teacher should wear shoes that are comfortable for walking around the classroom. Teachers' professional behaviors, like their attire, must set positive examples. Great teachers demonstrate kindness and respect for students, while differentiating the line between teacher mentoring and friendship with peers. Teaching differs from being students' intimate peers and confidants. Instead, students must know that teachers care about them, but also feel safe enough to know that they will provide them with security and guidance. If individual students are having difficulty making friends and latch on to teachers as substitutes for peer relations, teachers can help them build healthy peer interactions by pairing them with classmates during learning activities (Manning & Bucher, 2007). Collaborative art projects based on big ideas can be effective means to encourage students to find commonalities and build positive peer relationships.

Administrators recommend that teachers avoid being alone with individual students on and off school property, especially for extended periods, to reduce the potential of placing themselves and students in risky situations. Abuse allegations against teachers are real. An innocent tap on the shoulder can be misinterpreted as a threat and reported. A crush that is not discouraged can escalate into inappropriate actions. In circumstances when a student enters a classroom with no one else around but an individual teacher, the teacher can make others aware by calling the office, bringing in another student or adult into the classroom space, and/or keeping the classroom door open and standing in or next to the hallway so that others can witness their actions. Some schools and community sites have surveillance cameras installed in classroom spaces to monitor teacher–student interactions.

Although social media can be a wonderful resource for sharing artworks and community art happenings, teachers must use caution. Some school and organizational policies forbid teachers from socializing with students online. This, however, may not be enough to protect teachers. The media is quick to show teachers' inappropriate remarks and photographs made public through social media, even when teachers thought their actions were private. To protect their privacy on social media sites, some teachers conceal their identities, monitor how their names appear online, and remove potentially harmful or misinterpreted content immediately. They also keep work communications separate from personal ones.

## Appropriate Responses to Negative Comments and Behaviors

Some students might intentionally and unjustly direct hurtful behaviors toward teachers to invoke anger and extreme emotion. When this occurs, teachers should remain calm and redirect off-task behaviors using a firm and clear voice. For example, if a student's inappropriate actions cause teachers stress or strong emotions, they can use calming deep breathing exercises and wait a few seconds before responding in a professional manner. In situations that are particularly challenging, they might pair up with peer teachers who can supervise a student for a few minutes so that the class will stay on-task. This gives teachers and students time to regain focus and feel calm so they can discuss what transpired and take corrective actions (Queen & Algozzine, 2010; Tileston, 2004; Wong & Wong, 2009). Without intimidating students, raising their voices, or arguing, teachers who are confident with their classroom management abilities explain to students how a particular rule was broken and identify the consequences for the behavior. They apply fair disciplinary actions to correct the off-task behavior. At all times during the discussion, teachers focus on

maintaining student dignity and deescalating problems (Queen & Algozzine, 2010; Tileston, 2004). If discipline problems continue or escalate, teachers can inform parents and administrators so that the problems can be solved collaboratively.

## CONFRONTING VIOLENCE, BULLYING, AND VICTIMIZATION

All students can experience violence, bullying, and victimization. Teachers can take steps to confront and prevent some incidents of violence and bullying by teaching students the difference between right and wrong, demonstrating the types of behaviors expected in the classroom and beyond through positive role modeling, developing meaningful comprehensive art learning tasks that teach about these subjects, and demonstrating excellence in classroom management. Violence in schools and communities is a common concern for teachers, children, parents, administrators, policy makers, and societies across the globe. Acts of violence and victimization include harassment through obscene gestures and/or language; intimidation; property damage; stealing; and minor to major acts of physical harm, including hitting, throwing objects, and aggravated assault (Espelage et al., 2013; McMahon et al., 2014; U.S. Department of Justice, 2013). Each year, one billion children worldwide are victimized by violence, with the most serious acts of violence usually taking place outside of school (Centers for Disease Control and Prevention, 2014; Robers, Zhang, & Truman, 2012). When acts of horrific school violence occur, namely school shootings, they receive full media attention and can invoke deep fear and anxiety (Espelage et al., 2013). On a daily basis students are most commonly threatened by other students kicking, pushing, and hitting them; humiliating them; instilling fear in them; and stealing their personal belongings (Fredland, 2008). These threats appear at all school levels and in all socioeconomic brackets.

Bullying is the intentional act of harming another person (Jacobson, 2013; Olweus, 1993). It is generally ongoing. Bullying includes harmful verbal statements and social exclusions. Those who bully often conceal their behaviors from authorities. They know bullying is wrong. Some do it to gain power and social acceptance. Some do it at a distance through cyber bullying. Students who bully inflict harm based on a peer's age, race, ethnicity, culture, gender, social status, and personalities, as well as having perceived weaknesses, limited friendships, and noticeable differences in their abilities and physical forms. Middle school students aged 12–14 are more likely to be victimized at school than are elementary and high school peers (U.S. Department of Justice, 2013). Students who are lesbian, gay, bisexual, transgender, and queer (LGBTQ+) are often the recipients of the harshest bullying attacks (Check & Ballard, 2014; Greytak et al., 2013; Jacob, 2013).

Teachers can also be targets of victimization. McMahon and colleagues (2014) identified the percentages of teacher victimizations within a school year: harassment (approximately 75%), property offenses (approximately 50%), and physical offenses (44%). Other studies found that elementary teachers were more likely to be physically attacked than colleagues teaching upper grades (Robers et al., 2012) and that most attacks against teachers happen in the classroom when they discipline students (Tiesman, Konda, Hendricks, Mercer, & Amandus, 2013). Espelage and peers (2013) explained: "the effectiveness of teachers' classroom management skills is a strong indicator of the extent to which student violence is directed toward teachers" (pp. 77–78). Schools are safer when principals and policy makers recognize the challenges that teachers and students face, seek strategies and resources to support learning essentials, foster a school community of care and respect for all, and provide teachers with student-centered classroom management trainings (Fredland, 2008; Greytak et al., 2013). When teachers know how to calm rather than escalate students' off-task behaviors, they help students refocus their attention and gain control of their emotions (Tileston, 2004). Effective classroom managers understand that when students speak with anger and use hurtful language, their behavior can escalate into harassment of others and ultimately lead some students to become violent (Crews et al., 2008). By reinforcing class rules (such as through Model 4.1, "Classroom Management Plan for Teaching Art") and applying fair consequences for student off-task behaviors, teachers do their part to make school and community environments safer for everyone.

The choice-based art curriculum plays a special role in helping students cope with stress, rage, and insecurity through hands-on learning, substantial conversations, and tasks that address relevant subject matter. Age-appropriate examples from art history and visual culture are excellent resources for introducing lessons that focus on violence, bullying, victimization, and healthy living to students (see Artists' Lessons to Thrive! 1.1; Derby, 2014). Within a safe learning environment, students have opportunities to self-reflect, seek assistance, and make behavior modifications. In other circumstances, teachers might notice violent imagery in students' artworks and writings. Violence in students' art can be normal play, such as responses to things they see in the media. However, violence in children's artworks might reveal past occurrences, inner fears, and/or possible desires to harm others (Cinquemani, 2014; Diket & Mucha, 2002). Teachers must determine if violent symbols in student art is simply influenced by visual culture or a warning sign stemming from situations occurring at home or amongst a student's peers. When teachers see imagery that appears alarming and are unsure about its meaning, they should talk to students in a non-confrontational way and ask them what the artworks are about. Administration can offer further guidance when students' actions and images are concerning. When teachers have reasonable cause to suspect abuse, they are legally obligated as mandated reporters of child abuse to contact child protective services to begin an investigation. Noticing students' behaviors and working to find solutions in school and/or with additional support demonstrate teachers' care for students' well-being. When students know that they can trust and confide in teachers and other adults who will not harm them, they will more readily work through challenges and speak up if personal incidents and abuses occur.

## OUR JOURNEY TO THRIVE CONTINUES . . .

This chapter has addressed effective classroom management procedures for teaching art. Becoming a teacher is not about selecting the easiest career. It is about choosing a profession in which we can impart lifelong learning skills and touch students' lives through subject matter that we care about deeply. Our care, awareness, and dedication help students reach the best possible learning outcomes and foster a community of mutual respect and achievement. Moving into Part II of this textbook, we will examine how theories of child development (Chapter 5) shape our teaching practices and student learning.

# CHAPTER QUESTIONS AND ACTIVITIES

1. What is effective classroom management? What are the rewards and challenges associated with classroom management? How do teachers overcome classroom management challenges?

2. Refer to Model 4.1, "Classroom Management Plan for Teaching Art," to design a personal classroom management plan that includes your class mission statement, actions, and consequences. Present your plan to educational peers and/or students.

3. Answer Artists' Lessons to Thrive! 4.1's essential/guiding questions in written form or as part of a group discussion. Complete its daily learning targets.

## References

Araca, A. (1990). Environment of middle and secondary art classrooms: Becoming aware of, designing, and implementing changes in furniture, facilities, and spaces. In B. E. Little (Ed.), *Secondary art education: An anthology of issues* (pp. 69–92). Reston, VA: National Art Education Association.

Art and Creative Materials. (2018). *Safety tips: What you need to know.* Retrieved from https://acmiart.org/index.php/art-material-safety/safety-tips-what-you-need-to-know

Broome, J. L. (2013). A case study in classroom management and school involvement: Designing an art room for effective learning. *Art Education, 66*(3), 39–46.

Centers for Disease Control and Prevention. (2014). *Violence against children surveys (VACS).* Retrieved from www.cdc.gov/violenceprevention/vacs/index.html

Chapin, J. (2008). Youth perceptions of their school violence risks. *Adolescence, 43*(171), 461–471.

Check, E., & Ballard, K. (2014). Navigating emotional, intellectual, and physical violence directed toward LGBTQ students and educators. *Art Education, 67*(3), 6–11.

Cinquemani, S. (2014). "I look cool; He's dead now": Reconsidering children's violent play art. *Art Education, 67*(3), 13–18.

Crews, K., Crews, J., & Turner, F. (2008). School violence is not going away so proactive steps are needed. *College Teaching Methods & Styles Journal, 4*(1), 25–28.

Derby, J. (2014). Violent video games and the military: Recruitment, training, and treating mental disability. *Art Education, 67*(3), 19–25.

Diket, R. M., & Mucha, L. G. (2002). Talking about violent images. *Art Education, 55*(2), 11–17.

Espelage, D., Anderman, E. M., Brown, V., Jones, A., Lane, K. L., McMahon, S. D., & Reynolds, C. R. (2013). Understanding and preventing violence directed against teachers: Recommendations for a national research, practice, and policy agenda. *American Psychologist, 65*, 75–87.

Fredland, N. M. (2008). Nurturing hostile environments: The problem of school violence. *Family & Community Health, 31*(1), S32–S41.

Freeburg, B. W., & Workman, J. E. (2010). Media frames regarding teacher dress: Implications for career and technical education teacher preparation. *Career and Technical Education Research, 35*(1), 29–45. doi:10.5328/cter35.103

Greytak, E. A., Kosciw, J. G., & Boesen, M. J. (2013). Educating the educator: Creating supportive school personnel through professional development. *Journal of School Violence, 12*, 80–97.

Hagaman, S. (1990). Health hazards in secondary art education. In B. E. Little (Ed.), *Secondary art education: An anthology of issues* (pp. 143–150). Reston, VA: National Art Education Association.

Jacob, U. (2013). Creating safe and welcoming schools for LGBT students: Ethical and legal issues. *Journal of School Violence, 12*, 98–115.

Jacobson, R. B. (2013). *Rethinking school bullying: Dominance, identity, and school culture.* Routledge: New York, NY.

Manning, M. L., & Bucher, K. T. (2007). *Classroom management: Models, applications and cases* (2nd ed.). Upper Saddle River, NJ: Pearson.

McKeown, R. (2011). *Into the classroom: A practical guide for starting student teaching.* Knoxville, TN: The University of Tennessee Press.

McMahon, S., Martinez, A., Espelage, D., Rose, C., Reddy, L., Lane, K., & Brown, V. (2014). Violence directed against teachers: Results from a national survey. *Psychology in the Schools, 51*(7), 753–766. doi:10.1002/pits.21777

National Coalition for Core Arts Standards. (2014a). *National Core Arts Standards.* Retrieved from www.nationalartsstandards.org

Olweus, D. (1993). *Bullying at school: What we know and what we can do.* Malden, MA: Blackwell.

Qualley, C. A. (2005). *Safety in the artroom* (Rev. ed.). Worcester, MA: Davis Publications.

Queen, J. A., & Algozzine, B. (2010). *Responsible classroom management, grades K-5: A schoolwide plan.* Thousand Oaks, CA: Corwin Press.

Robers, S., Zhang, J., & Truman, J. (2012). *Indicators of school crime and safety, 2011* (NCES 2012–002/ NCJ 236021). Washington, DC: National Center for Education Statistics, U.S. Department of Education, and Bureau of Justice Statistics, Office of Justice Programs, U.S. Department of Justice. Retrieved from www.bjs.gov/content/pub/pdf/iscs11.pdf

Susi, E. D. (1990). The art classroom as a behavior setting. In B. E. Little (Ed.), *Secondary art education: An anthology of issues* (pp. 93–105). Reston, VA: National Art Education Association.

Tiesman, H., Konda, S., Hendricks, S., Mercer, D., & Amandus, H. (2013). Workplace violence among Pennsylvania education workers: Differences among occupations. *Journal of Safety Research, 44,* 65–71.

Tileston, D. W. (2004). *What every teacher should know about classroom management and discipline.* Thousand Oaks, CA: Corwin Press.

U.S. Consumer Product Safety Commission. (n.d.). *Art and craft safety guide.* Retrieved from www.cpsc.gov/s3fs-public/pdfs/blk_media_5015.pdf

U.S. Department of Justice, Bureau of Justice Statistics. (2013). *National crime victimization survey, 1992–2012.* Retrieved from http://nces.ed.gov/programs/coe/indicator_cld.asp#info

Valestrand, K., Aarhus, S., & Hisdal, S. (2010). *Oleana: From dream to fairytale reality* (J. Eriksen, Trans.). Oslo, Norway: Cappelen Damm.

Wong, H. K., & Wong, R. T. (2009). *How to be an effective teacher: The first days of school* (4th ed.). Mountain View, CA: Harry K. Wong.

# PART II

# Student Learners

# Chapter 5

# Artistic Development

## Early Childhood Through Adolescence

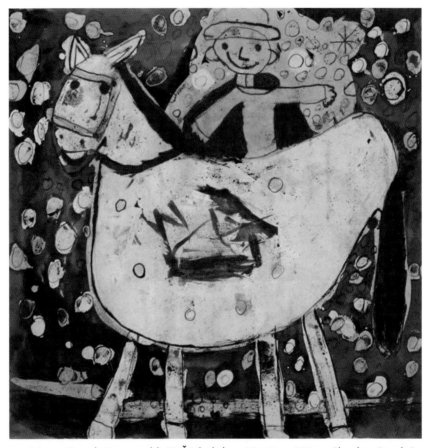

**FIGURE 5.1** Martin Bortel, 5-years-old, ZUŠ Vladislava Vančury, Háj ve Slezsku, Czech Republic.
*Source: ICEFA Lidice, 41st Exhibition.*

**Artistic development** in childhood refers to children's creative growth and acquisition of skills in the visual arts from early childhood through adolescence. It is based on measurements of children's normative behaviors and includes children's ability to manipulate art media, as well as their reasoning and decision-making skills in learning tasks related to art. This chapter explains how contemporary and established theories have shaped our understanding of artistic development and provides a foundation for identifying children's normative behaviors. Understanding development theories assists us in knowing where students have come from and where they are going in their full development (NCCAS, 2014b). As facilitators to student growth and development through art, we will reference development theories to plan lessons, select art materials and tools that students can operate safely, and guide students in experimenting and building upon existing skills.

We will meet the following objectives by participating in this chapter:

- Explain artistic development and its leading concepts.
- Summarize characteristics of whole-child development in early childhood, middle childhood, early adolescence, and adolescence.

- Apply development theories to guide choice-based art curriculum design, instruction, and assessments.

Spotlight on Student Art #5 describes the developmental characteristics presented in Figure 5.1's graphic representations of a horse, rider, and environment. We can apply its model and our knowledge of artistic development to analyze the symbols and meanings of all types of children's artworks.

---

### Spotlight on Student Art #5

### Big Idea: Inspirations

Children delight in using their imaginations and making artworks about experiences and folk legends that hold significance in their lives. A mixed media artwork by 5-year-old Martin depicts a large white horse with a golden boy riding on his back (Figure 5.1). This dynamic artwork, inspired by folk legends, results from Martin's ability to manipulate painting and drawing instruments to form the symbolic marks that illustrate his scene's narrative. Perched high on top of the horse, Martin's boy rider has outstretched arms and a wide smile that invite viewers into the picture plane. Martin made the horse the focal point of his artwork, rather than the rider. Using the graphic symbols he knew, he rendered the horse from a sideways position to make it fully recognizable to viewers. He presented his boy figure from a frontal view, yet concealed the boy's legs, to keep the horse's form intact.

On this magnificent evening, the horse's coat shines brightly against the dark blue sky. The illustrated scene contains many details, including separate spaces indicated on the horse's ears, reigns in the horse's mouth, and all four of the horse's legs planted firmly on the ground. The color red outlines both the horse and rider, while the golden yellow paper saturates the rider's body and creates a golden halo in the surrounding area. Martin separated the spaces that represent the earth and sky by drawing a yellow horizontal line just above the horse's hooves across the length of his paper. He placed white and yellow snowflakes around the horse and rider to complete his scene. This presentation of graphic symbols provides insights into student artistic development and childhood inspirations for creating art.

---

## WHOLE-CHILD DEVELOPMENT THROUGH ART

Contemporary artistic development centers on the whole-child. Teachers guide students in their development from early childhood to adolescence by espousing effective instructional methods, a choice-based art curriculum, and ongoing assessments so that they can become visually literate practitioners. Teachers must be able to recognize the characteristics that most same-aged children share to design **age-appropriate** learning tasks that are suited for children's knowledge and development. Studies on children's artistic development began in 1947, when Viktor Lowenfeld designed the Stages of Artistic Development. He

organized his model into six stages to describe the characteristics of children's artwork from early childhood through adolescence: scribbling (2 to 4 years old), preschematic (4 to 6 years old), schematic (7 to 9 years old), dawning realism (9 to 11 years old), pseudo naturalistic (11 to 13 years old), and the period of decision (14 to 18 years old). His aim was to create a universal model that guided teachers in constructing developmentally appropriate art lessons (Efland, 2002). He believed that students nurtured their creative instincts by responding to emotional and sensory stimuli in the environment.

Over time, scholars reconsidered the dominant role of Lowenfeld's model in teaching art because it did not address the full complexities associated with children's artistic development (Fineberg, 2006; Kindler, 2004, 2010; Kindler & Darras, 1997; Wilson, 2004; Wilson & Wilson, 2010). For example, Lowenfeld's (1947) model emphasized that children progress naturally in their artistic development from one stage to the next, leaving the prior stage behind. His paradigm overlooked the impact of children's stylistic choices in communicating meanings and how their representations perform specific functions in their art. Research by Kindler and Darras (1997) showed that students revisit earlier drawing processes and recycle visual symbols from previous stages to solve visual arts problems and communicate ideas to suit their needs as they progress in their artistic development (compare the similarities in Figures 5.2 and 5.3, which show artworks produced by children five years apart in age). Choice-based lessons encourage students to learn how to produce skillful artworks using diverse art media and processes, while applying their artistic intuitions, exploring ideas to their fullest, and taking creative risks.

Lowenfeld's (1947) model focused primarily on children's acquisition of realistic drawing skills by adolescence. Contemporary artistic development theories extend beyond graphic depictions and include three-dimensional creations (Figure 5.4), technological art media, abstract works, and non-objective creations (Figure 5.5; Kindler & Darras, 1997). Students study art to identify meaning through

**FIGURE 5.2** Volodymyr Maiko, 7-years-old, Center for Child and Youth Creativity, MZHK-1, Lvov, Ukraine.
*Source: ICEFA Lidice, 41st Exhibition.*

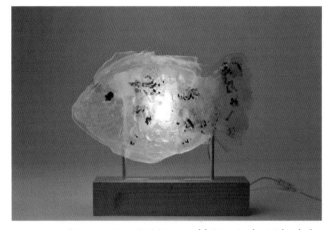

**FIGURE 5.4** Group project, 9–12-years-old, Riga Juglas Vidusskola, Riga, Latvia.
*Source: ICEFA Lidice, 43rd Exhibition.*

**FIGURE 5.3** Andrius Bertašius, 12-years-old, Skaudvile Gymnasium, Skaudvile, Lithuania.
*Source: ICEFA Lidice, 41st Exhibition.*

**FIGURE 5.5** Eliška Hlavatá, 10-years-old, ZUŠ, Mšeno, Czech Republic.
*Source: ICEFA Lidice, 43rd Exhibition.*

artistic behaviors, comprehensive discussions, writing, research, and art production activities (Hetland, Winner, Veenema, & Sheridan, 2013; Kindler, 2010; Wilson & Wilson, 2010). Students' critique their art to articulate the processes and ideas behind their productions and learn about the meaning of classmates' creations. Current artistic development theories integrate professional artists' reflections on their personal artistic development as resources to guide art instruction (Hetland et al., 2013; Kindler, 2010; NCCAS,

2014b). Professional artists are qualified experts in identifying the nature of artistic development and can broaden psychologists' and educators' perspectives on children's artistic development. They are skilled practitioners who demonstrate a heightened visual awareness and thorough knowledge of art media to produce quality creative productions. Artists' Lessons to Thrive! 5.1 on Julee Latimer provides an example of how the development of artistic behaviors began in childhood for this artist.

### Artists' Lessons to Thrive! 5.1 Julee Latimer: Artistic Inspiration

#### Big Idea: Inspirations

Artists design works based on inspirations that are sentimental, deeply significant, and/or motivated by others. Born in the United Kingdom, Australia-based artist Julee Latimer creates dynamic mosaic forms inspired by her upbringing, passion for communicating meaningful content, and desire to create with tactile materials. Having studied interior design, Latimer felt drawn to mosaics because they served as a means for her to create challenging three-dimensional artworks that blended her knowledge of creative color schemes, textures, and fine details.

*Rosaic* (Figure 5.1.1) and *Sit Your Art Down* (Figure 5.1.2) are functional armchairs that Latimer constructed from foam substrates with layers of fiberglass mesh and concrete to create hard and sturdy surfaces for sitting. She then decorated their surfaces with mosaics (Latimer, 2017). Their curvilinear forms replicate the look of upholstered armchairs with bold fabrics, plush padding, and elegant trim. Latimer applied hand-cut glass tiles and gems in patterned designs to the chairs' surfaces. The dark glass gems that form the contours in *Rosaic* and *Sit Your Art Down* mimic the look of upholstery tacks that trim the edges of quality furniture pieces and reference Latimer's keen eye for detail. Latimer's art practice is labor-intensive, with each chair requiring more than 200 hours to produce.

FIGURE 5.1.1 Julee Latimer ©. *Rosaic*. 26 × 34 × 30 in. (66.04 × 86.36 × 76.2 cm).

*Source: Courtesy of the artist; www.juleelatimer.com. Image by HONE photography.*

FIGURE 5.1.2 Julee Latimer ©. *Sit Your Art Down*. 30 × 46 × 36 in. (76.2 ×116.84 × 91.44 cm).

*Source: Courtesy of the artist; www.juleelatimer.com. Image by HONE photography.*

As art forms, *Rosaic* and *Sit Your Art Down* represent the artist's inspirations. Latimer's motivation for *Rosaic* came from reflecting on special childhood memories of collecting rose petals in the summer with her grandmother to produce fresh rosewater for facials and foot soaks (Latimer, 2017). *Rosaic* pays tribute to her grandmother and their shared love of roses. Latimer's inspiration for creating *Sit Your Art Down* came from living in Australia's arid climate. With fresh water being in short supply, the artwork's vivid flowers and cool colored background serve as visual metaphors for the large amounts of water required to produce exquisite blooms in nature. *Sit Your Art Down* communicates that water is a precious resource that we should cherish and use wisely. Through the process of creating these artistic armchairs, Latimer has invited viewers to have a seat, contemplate each work's meaning, and take actions to ensure that they value the things in life that count, including remembering special moments shared with loved ones and protecting our natural resources. By designing art based on inspirations, artists like Latimer convey significant ideas, as well as provide viewers with opportunities to feel connected to and inspired by creative artistic works.

## Essential/Guiding Questions

1. What role do inspirations play in Latimer's art and life? Why are inspirations an important part of life? What inspires you?
2. How does art inspire others? Describe an artwork that inspires you. What qualities does the work contain that make you feel inspired?

## Preparation

Students will learn the following contextual information. Latimer experienced diverse artistic inspirations in childhood. She recalled being 9-years-old when her art teacher brought in a local artist's paintings of Disney characters. She felt so excited by these works that she copied their designs during school lunch breaks to perfect her rendering skills. Around the same time, she studied with three classmates who were also named Julie and decided to change the spelling of her name to Julee to separate her from the crowd and feel original. With her desire to be unique, Latimer decorated her childhood bedroom in orange and purple hues, when most other childrens preferred neutral palettes. Examining Latimer's *Rosaic* and *Sit Your Art Down*, students will brainstorm possible ways that Latimer's early inspirations translated into her original, vibrant, and captivating designs.

## Daily Learning Targets

I can create a mosaic inspired by one of my childhood memories.

- I can form a mosaic with paper, tiles, or mixed media.
- I can present my memory as a representational and/or abstract design.
- I can create a balanced composition that shows contrast between the mosaic's pieces (the tesserae).

I can write a summative self-assessment in my journal in paragraph form that describes my completed mosaic and its visual message about my memory.

**National Core Arts Anchor Standards** 2, 6, 9, and 10

www.nationalartsstandards.org

Lowenfeld's (1947) model placed children's artistic production in isolation from society because he believed that others should not influence children's art. Contemporary scholars recognize that children's development does not occur in isolation. Students learn by copying and imitating peers and adult role models, including content they see in visual culture (Kindler, 2004; Fineberg, 2006; Wilson, 2004). Moving students beyond passive mimicry, teachers can guide students in employing conceptual, procedural, and metacognitive knowledge as they create art from inspirational sources (Anderson et al., 2001). For example, as students acquire choice-based painting and ceramic skills (Figures 5.6 and 5.7), teachers can teach them how to analyze forms, content, and context in artists' works, watch demonstrations, practice, and apply unifying concepts so that they can produce desired outcomes and move

beyond what they could achieve without instruction. Adults also influence children's artistic development by providing art supplies, demonstrating how to handle materials properly, and offering feedback on their creative works. They facilitate children's perceptions about what constitutes art. Students should have ample opportunities to study the art of the world's cultures in context. Through comprehensive learning tasks, teachers teach them how to employ research methodologies to make connections to the artistic products that people of the world in past in present times have created.

Model 5.1 places whole-child development through art in context using declarative statements: "I am growing" (physical development), "I am thinking" (cognitive development), "I am feeling" (social/emotional development), and "I am creating" (artistic development). The integration of children's growth, cognition, and feelings in this model align with The College Board's (2012) research on child development and arts education for the National Core Arts Standards. Children's development in these areas results from internal and external factors that include genetics, environment, diet, and cultural stimuli. Same-aged children's varying life experiences, cognitive abilities, physiques, dispositions, learning opportunities, and exposure to curricular context impact what they know and are able to achieve (Fineberg, 2006; Wood, 2007).

**FIGURE 5.6** Duanbuppha Kiattisak, 16-years-old, HRH Princess Sirindhorn Art Center, Wangsaphung, Thailand.
*Source: ICEFA Lidice, 43rd Exhibition.*

**FIGURE 5.7** Justina Baltrūnaite, 14-years-old, The Art School, Kretinga, Lithuania.
*Source: ICEFA Lidice, 43rd Exhibition.*

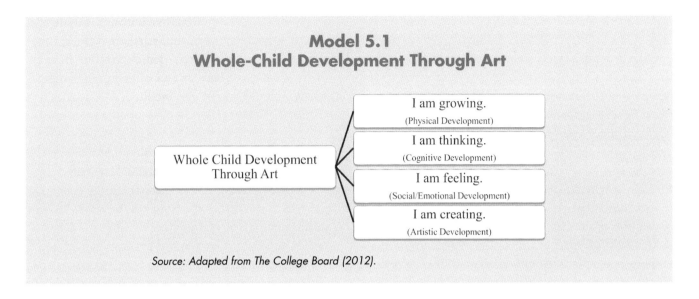

**Model 5.1**
**Whole-Child Development Through Art**

| | I am growing. |
|---|---|
| | (Physical Development) |

Whole Child Development Through Art

I am growing.
(Physical Development)

I am thinking.
(Cognitive Development)

I am feeling.
(Social/Emotional Development)

I am creating.
(Artistic Development)

*Source: Adapted from The College Board (2012).*

## I Am Growing (Physical Development)

Children's physical growth impacts their ability to participate in visual arts learning activities (Levine & Munsch, 2011). **Physical development** refers to children's bodily growth and their development of motor skills as they learn how to control muscle and nerve functions simultaneously to perform controlled actions. Gross motor skills reference children's manipulation of their large muscles to perform tasks, such as strolling through a museum. They apply fine motor skills when moving small muscles to perform detailed tasks, such as cutting minute shapes with scissors. Objectives that integrate the psychomotor domain encourage students to employ the kinesthetic methods that artists apply to produce artworks that demonstrate craftspersonship (Anderson et al., 2001; Hetland et al., 2013). Children expand their frames of reference by using their senses to receive and process new information. Elliot Eisner's (2002) research linked children's physical development with emotional and sensory perceptions experienced through art. For example, sculpting in clay (Figure 5.8), a tactile medium, stimulates children's sensory perceptions as they apply their motor skills to create dynamic forms. Children continue to refine their artistic skills by activating their bodies and senses to manipulate art media. Using their bodies, they learn to expand their graphic repertoire to include metaphorical symbols.

**FIGURE 5.8** Law Cheuk Nam, 5-years-old, Hong Kong In-form Art Education Center, Hong Kong, China.
*Source: ICEFA Lidice, 40th Exhibition.*

## I Am Thinking (Cognitive Development)

Children acquire knowledge through the advancement of organizing systems within their brains. **Cognitive development** refers to children's abilities to gain intelligence to process information, solve problems, make decisions, recall information, transfer knowledge, and utilize advanced reasoning skills. Developmental psychologist Jean Piaget (Piaget & Inhelder, 1972) developed a theory of cognitive development that describes how humans attain knowledge by progressing from lower levels of knowledge to higher levels of understanding. He explained that children procure knowledge through a process called **assimilation** (Piaget, 1983). They absorb data in their brains, respond to surrounding environmental factors, and perceive through a **schema**, which is a cognitive symbol that assists individuals in understanding and organizing new information. In art, children develop **schemata** in the form of visual symbols that represent objects, feelings, and actions. As children's frames of reference change and they accumulate further knowledge, they adapt or abandon their current schemata using a process known as **accommodation**.

**Constructivism** is a cognitive development theory that identifies children as active learners who explore their environments to acquire knowledge by assimilating and accommodating information (Bruner, 1966, 1973; Dewey, 1938; Piaget & Inhelder, 1972; Vygotsky, 1978). Students assess and validate the relevance of new data input by reinforcing what they already know, expanding their perspectives on subjects, or abandoning prior beliefs to acquire new ones (Piaget & Inhelder, 1972). They ask pertinent questions, explore possibilities, and apply metacognition to self-reflect on their acquisition of knowledge. Their initial inquiries can lead to further student-driven investigations that include essential questions presented in the visual arts standards. Even when studying the same big ideas, artists, and artistic concepts as peers, students can retain their individual perspectives by forming individualized hypotheses, analyses, and interpretations of the data they acquired (Larochelle & Bednarz, 2009).

Despite research that correlates children's cognitive development with the arts, many educational systems have overlooked this information and focused primarily on children's propensities in linguistics and mathematics. Psychologist Howard Gardner (1983, 2006) urged educators to utilize a wider array of intelligences to strengthen students' learning capabilities and address their cognitive strengths. He developed the theory of **Multiple Intelligences** to identify children's learning aptitudes through eight and a half learning intelligences: linguistic, logical-mathematical, musical, spatial, body-kinesthetic, interpersonal, intrapersonal, naturalist, and existential. His model links cognitive learning in the visual arts through spatial intelligence and addresses the cognitive benefits of self-reflection, communication, and group interactions, which are core components of comprehensive art studies.

## I Am Feeling (Social/Emotional Development)

Sociocultural learning strengthens children's development because children acquire knowledge and social skills by interacting and sharing with others. **Social/emotional development** refers to children's need to interact with and respond emotionally to other living beings and the environment. Rather than dismissing emotions from the curriculum, teachers encourage meaningful discussions, creative writing assignments, role-playing games, and art production activities to explore social development concepts including ethics, morality, and empathy. These learning experiences can lead to improved academic performance, greater self-confidence, and better emotional control (Riley, San Juan, Klinkner, & Ramminger, 2008). Lev Vygotsky's (1962) Zones of Proximal Development explains how children watch others, imitate behaviors, and discuss ideas and processes to attain new information. This model is particularly useful in studying students' development in art because it identifies the value of teaching art and differs significantly from Lowenfeld's belief that children's creativity burgeons naturally in isolation from external influences (Efland, 2002; Wilson, 2004). Students can investigate how artists, such as those identified in this textbook's Artists' Lessons to Thrive! features and others, present their cultural values through art. They can also study children's examples such as Figures 5.9–5.11. These educational experiences encourage students to be more accepting of people's varying perspectives on life's topics and gain feelings of camaraderie, care, and empathy for others, which are necessary attributes in today's global society. Students should also have access to arts professionals and other skilled individuals through class partnerships, field trips, experiential learning opportunities, volunteer work, internships (as applicable), and community art projects. These real-world exchanges demonstrate how people interact with and respond creatively, professionally, and emotionally to other

FIGURE 5.9 Suzuki Haruka, 12-years-old, Kamon Children Art School, Tokyo, Japan.
*Source: ICEFA Lidice, 41st Exhibition.*

FIGURE 5.11 Ezgi Sahin Türk, 11-years-old, Nurí Bayar Ilkogretim Okulu, Sakarya–Adapazari, Turkey.
*Source: ICEFA Lidice, 41st Exhibition.*

FIGURE 5.10 Nikita Ivanov, 11-years-old, ZŠ praktická, ZŠ speciální a MŠ speciální, Kladno 2, Czech Republic.
*Source: ICEFA Lidice, 41st Exhibition.*

living beings within the environment. Such experiences can foster feelings of positive dispositions, self-worth, and empowerment (Eisner, 2002).

## I AM CREATING: DEVELOPMENTALLY APPROPRIATE PRACTICES FOR TEACHING ART

Children develop the ability to observe, interpret, and transform what they know into visual art products (Arnheim, 1954). Progressing at their own individual pace, they become competent in producing visual symbols to express meaning while working within the confines of a given art medium (compare Figures 5.12 and 5.13). The following sections on artistic development in early childhood, middle childhood, early adolescence, and adolescence provide a foundation to identify common behaviors, artistic processes, and graphic repertoires for students' varying ages (Eisner, 2002). Teachers apply this information in conjunction with grade-level performance standards, essential questions, and big ideas to spark age-appropriate student learning opportunities.

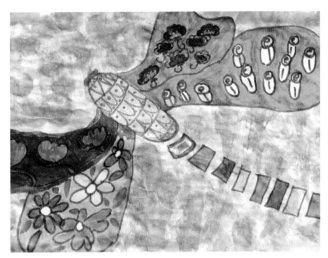

FIGURE 5.12 Siana Nyachae, 7-years-old, Kenya.
*Source: Lisa Wee, teacher.*

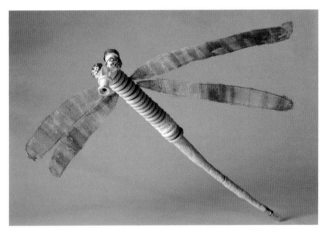

FIGURE 5.13 Ondřej Tvrdý, 12-years-old, ZUŠ Vladimíra Ambrose, Prostějov, Czech Republic.
*Source: ICEFA Lidice, 42nd Exhibition.*

## Development in Early Childhood (Pre-K–2nd Grade)

Becoming acquainted with the very youngest children's acts of creation sets teachers on a pathway to understand how children's artistic development begins. Early childhood students have a limited vocabulary and cannot read documents and understand abstract symbols (Fineberg, 2006). Art making assists young children in communicating their thoughts. At around 12 to 18 months old, children produce their first scribbles, called **disordered scribbles,** by clenching a drawing instrument in their fist and making shoulder movements (Lowenfeld, 1947). Producing these very first marks is a challenging physical process because young children are developing large muscles and do not possess the fine motor skills necessary to control a drawing instrument. They simultaneously make bodily gestures, babble, and/or play as they draw (Kindler, 2004). By 18 to 24 months old, children create **longitudinal scribbles** by holding a drawing instrument in their fist and making linear motions with their arms. They gain the ability to form **circular scribbles** with further muscle development. Young children enjoy the kinesthetic act of producing scribbles and seeing their marks on paper and other surfaces (Kindler & Darras, 1997). They begin to name their scribbles, called **naming,** and to describe their meanings. Adults frequently ask "who" and "what" questions about the content in their artworks and expect their marks to represent particular objects. Children increasingly discover that the more identifiable their artworks become, the more adults will compliment their creations.

When children learn how to draw a **mandala,** a circular shape with intersecting lines, they produce their first preschematic symbol (Figure 5.14; Lowenfeld, 1947). Children's mandalas signify common forms, including people and animals. The mandala is a more complicated graphic representation than the scribble. It indicates that children have developed better control holding and manipulating mark-making instruments. Around age 3 or 4, children can clench a pencil with four fingers. They develop the ability to hold a pencil with three fingers, called a **tripod grip,** around age 5 (Case-Smith & O'Brien, 2015; Wood, 2007). In early childhood, teachers can stimulate the development of young children by introducing them to materials such as crayons, block and stick beeswax crayons, beginner scissors, papers for collaging, water-based paints (including finger paint and tempera paint), natural and synthetic clays, manipulatives (such as pipe cleaners), textured clay rollers, and blocks.

Pre-kindergarten through 2nd grade students can share their perspectives on art. They like to tell stories and appreciate praise from teachers. They learn more deeply when teachers introduce big ideas, concepts, and processes in small, manageable units of study through daily learning targets so that they will not feel overwhelmed by learning tasks. Young children cannot sit still for long because they need to move their bodies. They appreciate physical art activities including constructing and painting. Between preschool and 1st grade, children can focus on a given activity for approximately five to ten minutes. Second-graders have greater independence and can focus a little longer. To sustain students' interests, lessons should center on open-ended concepts and kinesthetic learning activities that enable children to experiment and feel comfortable as they gain new skills and learn about various art supplies and their functions (Eisner, 2002).

Art is an expressive act for young children (Eisner, 2002). Early childhood students develop artworks using basic symbols that represent the things that influence their world. Pre-kindergarteners through 1st graders typically draw and paint with colors they like. Their color choices are not intended to depict reality; instead, they are based on students' emotional preferences. For example, instead of a dark night's sky they may choose to draw a fuchsia sky because they like the color (Figure 5.15). Adults need to be mindful of this normative behavior and should not force young children to select one color over another. By the time they reach 2nd grade, most children have gradually moved away from applying purely emotional color choices; they begin to draw and paint solid blocks of color that appear closer to nature, such as fields of monochromatic green grass or a bright yellow sun. Teachers can augment early childhood learners' understandings of color by teaching art inquiry lessons that describe how artists, illustrators, and designers choose among different color palettes to produce their designs and create meaning.

Students in preschool through 1st grade typically design compositions using non-representational space with forms that lack volume. They arrange objects arbitrarily and draw the objects that they believe to be most important as the largest figures in their compositions (Eisner, 2002). By 2nd grade, students have greater manipulative skills and a stronger handgrip.

They have developed a wider repertoire of schematized graphic symbols and seek to organize the space using a single baseline or multiple baselines within the two-dimensional picture plane (Lowenfeld, 1947). A **baseline** (Figure 5.16) arranges objects (including people, houses, flowers, and trees) on a single platform line that runs horizontally across the artwork's composition. An artwork with **multiple baselines** (Figure 5.17) has more than one baseline and

FIGURE 5.15 Mao Wenxin, 5-years-old, VKIDS Creative, Hong Kong, China.
*Source: ICEFA Lidice, 41st Exhibition.*

FIGURE 5.16 Ilija Bobrov, 7-years-old, CVR "Pramen," Grodno, Belarus.
*Source: ICEFA Lidice, 38th Exhibition.*

FIGURE 5.14 Kittithat Srisuk, 4-years-old, Bansilapa taklom club, Surat Thani, Thailand.
*Source: ICEFA Lidice, 36th Exhibition.*

FIGURE 5.17 Melika Soltan-zadeh, 8-years-old, Kanoon–Institute for Intellectual Development of Children and Young Adults, Tehran, Iran.
*Source: ICEFA Lidice, 36th Exhibition.*

FIGURE 5.19 Jakub Folda, Domov Raspenava, Raspenava, Czech Republic.
*Source: ICEFA Lidice, 42nd Exhibition.*

FIGURE 5.18 Ghazal Jelviani, 7-years-old, Kanoon–Institute for Intellectual Development of Children and Young Adults, Tehran, Iran.
*Source: ICEFA Lidice, 40th Exhibition.*

FIGURE 5.20 Adeline Steliana Krauze, 5-years-old, Family Academy of Bethesda, United States.
*Source: ICEFA Lidice, 42nd Exhibition.*

usually includes a baseline at the horizon line to show greater depth in the composition. Children also create **fold-over views** with vertical objects (including trees, people, or buildings) lying flat on parallel sides of the picture plane in a mostly symmetrical mirrored design to depict a broader view of space in their composition (Figure 5.18). Students may also present **X-ray views** to show interior and exterior views of an

object simultaneously (Figure 5.19). Choice-based art lessons can introduce students to the various ways that artists arrange their compositions to depict space. Students can learn to identify features that include placement of objects, size relationships, overlapping, and perspective in artworks.

By 2nd grade, students will have assimilated a wider range of sociocultural symbols in their art (Fineberg, 2006). For example, they repeat schemata they see peers draw, such as a particular style for drawing a house. They also draw people with similar features and make small changes to the hairstyles and clothing to show individual identities. When rendering schemata, they have the ability to place forms in various positions (such as a person standing or bending, Figure 5.20) and can incorporate more detailed patterns in their designs (Case-Smith & O'Brien, 2015; Kindler, 2004; Wilson, 2004).

# Development in Middle Childhood (3rd–5th Grades)

Students in the 3rd through 5th grades have developed a greater sense of independence given years of school experience and their advanced physical and cognitive skills. They have established a broader network of friends, and they collaborate with others (Wood, 2007). Compared to their peers in early childhood, they have greater communication skills, advanced vocabularies, and more concrete reasoning skills. Students are interested in learning content that has relevance to their lives and want to know more about real-world issues, including global concepts, the environment, and diversity. They are beginning to develop abstract thinking skills. When talking about art, students can explore art's various functions and meanings, as well as make predictions and speculate outcomes (NCCAS, 2014a).

Visual art becomes less of a communication tool in middle childhood due to students' advanced verbal and written communication skills (The College Board, 2012). They become proud of their artistic achievements and like to showcase their best efforts. Although they typically approach new art production activities with enthusiasm, teachers need to allow them ample time to practice and learn new art skills and techniques. Students can feel discouraged when they cannot grasp introductory concepts right away. Positive reinforcement helps them overcome challenges and feel successful. Formative assessments including journals, portfolios, class art critiques, and displays of students' in-progress works assist students in taking learning tasks to the next level.

By the time students are in 3rd grade they can hold a pencil like an adult and have developed the fine motor skills necessary for producing finer details in their work (Wood, 2007). In the upper elementary grades, students may continue to create graphic representations using flat areas of color. However, they have a greater ability to mix and layer colors, and they can integrate them into their art to show value and depth. Middle-childhood students still incorporate sociocultural schemata from early childhood into their graphic representations, yet also notice differences and details (Eisner, 2002). Their drawings present a more representational visual verisimilitude than their previous works. They have refined their visual repertoire to produce more proportional imagery (Eisner, 2002; Lowenfeld, 1947). Teachers can teach students how to reach beyond their habitual repertoire of schematic symbols by demonstrating observational drawing techniques and teaching them how to analyze content in artists' representational works. These learning tasks serve as foundations to teach students how to illustrate what they see rather than what they know.

While observational drawing is a useful skill, the upper elementary art curriculum should not teach observational drawing in isolation. Some middle-childhood students shy away from observational drawing because they feel concerned that their artwork does not look realistic enough. To mitigate these feelings, teachers can present lessons using multiple approaches to drawing and reinforce the message that artists use a variety of art media and processes that extend beyond representational drawing (Kindler & Darras, 1997). These include artists' stylizations and abstractions, three-dimensional works, crafts, and technology. Creating non-representational products including maps, diagrams, and abstractions (Figure 5.21) exposes students to a broader set of drawing skills. Students also benefit from kinesthetic learning experiences that engage their whole bodies, such as role-playing activities. They like to draw celebrities, trendy products, and cartoon/gaming characters, as did this chapter's feature artist, Julee Latimer, at age 9. Students appreciate lessons that incorporate their

**FIGURE 5.21** Tereza Štechrová, 9-years-old, ZUŠ Fr. Kmocha, Kolín II, Czech Republic.
*Source: ICEFA Lidice, 43rd Exhibition.*

FIGURE 5.22 Seanna Sosa Lopéz, 9-years-old, Casa de Cultura Luis Jorge León, Quemado de Guines, Cuba.
*Source: ICEFA Lidice, 41st Exhibition.*

interests in popular culture. Such lessons invite students to share their personal interests with the class (Figure 5.22; Fineberg, 2006).

Students in 3rd through 5th grades are developing greater inquiry skills and can pursue more in-depth assignments than in previous years. Students have an expanded interest in international and sociocultural concerns. They can write artist statements and defend their decisions about art (Eisner, 2002; Kindler & Darras, 1997; NCCAS, 2014a). Furthermore, they can combine content they have learned in diverse subjects to identify the broader picture and study context in greater depth. Like their younger peers, 3rd- and 4th-grade students absorb small chunks of information at a time. By 5th grade, they can comprehend multiple concepts at once and become skilled at remembering facts and classifying data (Wood, 2007).

## Development in Early Adolescence (6th–8th Grades)

Adolescence marks the transition between childhood and adulthood. During early adolescence students are undergoing vast changes in their physical, cognitive, and emotional development. Their bodies experience rapid skeletal growth, muscle development, and hormonal changes (Brown & Knowles, 2014). Early adolescents enter middle school with varying artistic abilities, based on their elementary

art experiences, interest in the discipline, and artistic skills. If they had a strong elementary foundation in art, they will be competent in mixing colors, incorporating details in their artworks, and representing three-dimensional spaces in two-dimensional works (Eisner, 2002; The College Board, 2012). They can create compositions using diverse angles and perspectives, including close-up views, overlapping busy scenes (Figure 5.23), and wide-open spaces. They can use academic vocabulary to speak knowledgeably about art.

Early adolescents strive for group belonging and want to socialize with peers. Lessons should incorporate learning tasks in which they can collaborate with students who belong to different backgrounds and cliques than their own. Without teacher intervention, young adolescents may spend little time interacting with students who are outside of their immediate group of friends, which can lead to disconnects in the classroom and beyond. When teachers assign each student individual responsibilities during group assignments and teach on-task peer dialogue and interactions, early adolescents are better prepared to stay on-task. Each member assists the team in reaching curricular goals.

At the middle school level, teachers may encounter erratic student behaviors that include mood swings, self-absorption, thrill seeking, carelessness, and feeling invincible. These behaviors ensue because the prefrontal cortex section of the early adolescent brain is not fully developed (Walsh, 2014). This region of the brain is responsible for a person's ability to concentrate, reason, organize information, and control emotions. As part of their classroom management procedures, teachers can teach young adolescents time management skills to minimize off-task behaviors, as excessive stalling can reduce students' abilities to reach learning targets. Middle school students may also be unable to focus in class due to sleep deprivation; they may not have received the nine and a half hours of sleep that their developing bodies require each night. Although early adolescents are known to multitask between social activities, multitasking is ineffective at school because it reduces students' abilities to concentrate and retain information.

By early adolescence, many students have developed an individualized artistic style (Figure 5.24) and can create didactic works that communicate their personal interests (Figure 5.25). Whereas elementary students generally demonstrate great enthusiasm for making art, early adolescents require ongoing motivation and creative instructional methods. They will avoid looking inferior to their peers at all cost. Young adolescents typically want to perfect

FIGURE 5.23 Lam Wing Hay Tori, 12-years-old, Simply Art, Hong Kong, China.
*Source: ICEFA Lidice, 42nd Exhibition.*

FIGURE 5.25 Tanaka Ryóta, 13-years-old, Japonská škola v Praze, Praha 6, Řepy, Japan.
*Source: ICEFA Lidice, 39th Exhibition.*

FIGURE 5.24 Lyricka Robinson-Smith, 8th grade, United States.
*Source: Lydia Horvath, teacher.*

art-related tasks they already know how to do well and will shy away from processes with which they are less familiar. They question teacher authority and seek independence from adults. Although early adolescents want autonomy and may initially resist authentic teaching efforts, they want to learn from teachers who model proper behaviors and care about their concerns (Wood, 2007). They require the ongoing support of their parents, teachers, and other adult mentors who can help them navigate confusing changes in their lives and reinforce positive behaviors (Walsh, 2014). The teacher's role is to embolden students to feel safe as they take creative risks, articulate their opinions, and ask questions. Teachers can help build students' self-confidence by identifying their individual strengths and demonstrating how others like them have taken creative risks to produce art (Eisner, 2002).

The middle school art curriculum should balance contemporary issues with fantasy and jovial topics to encourage students to express their individual personalities and sense of humor. Many students like to create fantasy drawings, cartoons, images from gaming, graffiti art, and zentangles. They are keen on technology and are aware of the latest trends and gadgets (Brown & Knowles, 2014). Middle schoolers are drawn to lessons that center on current events and issues they care about, including ethics, fairness, justice, and morality (Brown & Knowles, 2014; Wood, 2007). Active, open-ended learning activities stimulate students' long-term memory development (Walsh, 2014). Students can brainstorm multifaceted ideas with teachers and peers, participate in class debates, and develop multimedia campaigns to communicate personal and group messages. Many early adolescents experience peer and media pressures that impact their lives. They may feel that their bodies are inadequate due to growth spurts, pimples, teasing, and comparison with the unrealistic body types presented in visual culture. They may sense sexual urges induced by raging hormones and feel pressure to act out adult behaviors. Most girls reach puberty in middle school and boys enter puberty by the end of 8th grade (Wood, 2007). Teachers can implement visual culture studies, class discussions, and creative activities that assist young people in analyzing what they see in the media and their daily lives so that they will know how to make wise choices. Because students can see multiple sides of an issue and select pertinent context to build cases, teachers can develop choice-based learning tasks in which students present their varied ideas through role-playing, media communications, and theme-based exhibitions.

## Development in Adolescence (9th–12th Grades)

By high school, adolescents who have participated in comprehensive pre-kindergarten through 8th-grade art programs have had in-depth exposure to various art media. They can utilize big ideas and contextual studies to produce meaningful bodies of creative works, as well as analyze and judge art using established criteria and technical vocabulary (Eisner, 2002; NCCAS, 2014b). Students who have had limited art experiences in elementary and middle school typically lack the formal art knowledge and skills that same-aged peers possess. Because of these vast differences, teachers should offer a choice-based art curriculum with open-ended objectives that allows students to grow and mature at unique paces (Hetland et al., 2013). High school students

can take a single art class to fulfill fine arts credits or pursue advanced art courses. After taking an introductory course, students may register for specialized classes that teach a particular medium or advanced art techniques. When these courses are available at their schools, some students select college preparatory courses including the College Board's Advanced Placement program in art history and studio courses, and the International Baccalaureate Diploma Program's visual arts course. Students are more likely to choose art electives when they are offered by great teachers who teach course content that is meaningful and applicable to students' lives (Anderson & Milbrandt, 2005; Hume, 2014).

High school students are envisioning their place in the world and want to take on new responsibilities and gain leadership skills. They face many of the same social challenges as their middle school peers, but have become more settled into their physical forms and have a greater understanding of their personal identities. They can work effectively with traditional art media and enjoy communicating through digital media, such as claymation and video storytelling. Teachers should regularly motivate students to test theories, think abstractly, explore ideas in depth, and reflect on their personal decisions. As students create and respond to art, they become more adept in making connections to synergize original ideas. Teachers can encourage students to apply artists' cognitive and creative processes to produce unique art forms that have personal meaning (Figures 5.26 and 5.27; Hetland et al., 2013). The choice-based art curriculum challenges adolescents to make informed decisions by integrating research methodologies, artistic intuition, experimentation, and sociocultural interactions. Educators teach students how to refine their skills, work through challenges, and accept mistakes as part of the learning process as artists do. Students explore how artists are a part of a wider social system and identify how art is intertwined with the broader human experience.

The choice-based art curriculum should incorporate students' interests in creative professions, teach adult responsibilities, introduce college and career pathways, and provide opportunities for students to visit professional spaces, including artists' studios, art centers, museums, and galleries. Teachers can implement service learning art projects in which students

FIGURE **5.27** Danita Šķila, 14-years-old, J. Čakstes Liepajas pilsétas 10. vidusskola, Liepāja, Latvia.
*Source: ICEFA Lidice, 43rd Exhibition.*

FIGURE **5.26** Zorana Dukić, 16-years-old, JU Srednja Likovna Škola Petar Lubarda, Cetinje, Montenegro.
*Source: ICEFA Lidice, 43rd Exhibition.*

perform as leaders who are responsible for applying their skills to benefit others. Service learning helps students identify their role within the community and builds a sense of camaraderie. Additionally, teachers can talk to students about the value of volunteering and/or working in professional settings that relate to their future careers, and encourage them to take action. Another means to put students in touch with the broader community is to have students plan exhibitions of their work using themes, narrative texts, and signage. The choice-based art curriculum can teach students how to establish an exhibition's criteria like curators do to attract audiences and showcase particular moods (NCCAS, 2014a).

Journals and portfolios play a substantial role in the high school art curriculum. They reveal information about who students are and the things that they care about. Teachers can facilitate students'

journal and portfolio development by presenting related artists' exemplars, showing students how to further develop research topics, and brainstorming strategies to take their creative ideas to the next level. Figures 5.28 and 5.29 present works from a student's portfolio that illustrate the ability to communicate UNESCO themes through effective color and composition choices. When students submit portfolios for college credit or college admittance, evaluators want to see students' full commitment to a particular concept (Colston, 2008). Strong portfolios showcase students' flexibility in thought. Instead of repeating the same idea over and over again, each portfolio demonstrates the student's aptitude in interpreting a concept skillfully, while presenting multiple possibilities. As a collection of works, a portfolio showcases a student's predispositions for experimenting, researching subject matter, communicating context, and designing appealing compositions. Ultimately, adolescents who possess these skills can recognize their own capabilities as autonomous individuals, take creative risks, and produce powerful results (Hetland et al., 2013).

**FIGURE 5.28** Egor Zagrebelnii, 14-year-olds, KGU Komplex Kolledzh Iskusstv–Shkola Odarennyh Detei, Petropavlovsk, Kazakhstan.
*Source: ICEFA Lidice, 43rd Exhibition.*

**FIGURE 5.29** Egor Zagrebelnii, 14-years-old, KGU Komplex Kolledj Iskusstv–Shkola Odarennih Detei, Petropavlovsk, Kazakhstan.
*Source: ICEFA Lidice, 42nd Exhibition.*

## OUR JOURNEY TO THRIVE CONTINUES . . .

Chapter 6 builds upon this chapter's concepts and provides effective strategies for teaching art to diversified students. We will apply children's artistic development theories as references to make accommodations and set attainable learning targets for students whose proficiencies are above or below same-aged peers so that they remained challenged and engaged throughout comprehensive learning processes. This textbook's forthcoming parts on art inquiry and art production methods identify developmentally appropriate art learning tasks for children's different abilities, ages, and skill levels.

## CHAPTER QUESTIONS AND ACTIVITIES

1. Explain children's development in art and its leading concepts. Summarize whole-child development in early childhood, middle childhood, early adolescence, and adolescence.
2. Describe how your knowledge of children's artistic development will shape your curriculum design, instruction, and selection of classroom assessments.
3. Answer Artists' Lessons to Thrive! 5.1's essential/ guiding questions in written form or as part of a group discussion. Complete its daily learning targets.

# References

Anderson, L. W. (Ed.), Krathwohl, D. R. (Ed.), Airasian, P. W., Cruikshank, K. A., Mayer, R. E., Pintrich, P. R., . . . Wittrock, M. C. (2001). *A taxonomy for learning, teaching, and assessing: A revision of Bloom's Taxonomy of Educational Objectives* (Complete ed.). New York, NY: Longman.

Anderson, T., & Milbrandt, M. (2005). *Art for life.* Boston: McGraw Hill.

Arnheim, R. (1954/2004). *Art and visual perception: A psychology of the creative eye.* Berkeley, CA: University of California Press.

Brown, D. F., & Knowles, T. (2014). *What every middle school teacher should know* (3rd ed.). Portsmouth, NH: Heinemann.

Bruner, J. (1966). *Toward a theory of instruction.* Cambridge, MA: Harvard University Press.

Bruner, J. (1973). *Going beyond the information given.* New York, NY: Norton.

Case-Smith, J., & O'Brien, J. C. (2015). *Occupational therapy for children and adolescents* (7th ed.). St. Louis, MO: Mosby.

The College Board. (2012). *Child development and arts education: A review of recent research and best practices.* New York. Retrieved from https://nccas.wikispaces.com/file/view/NCCAS+Child+Development+Report.pdf

Colston, V. (2008). *Aspire 200 projects to strengthen your art skills.* Hauppauge, NY: Barron's Education Series.

Dewey, J. (1938). *Experience and education.* New York, NY: Macmillan.

Efland, A. D. (2002). *Art and cognition: Integrating the visual arts in the curriculum.* New York, NY: Teacher's College Press.

Eisner, E. W. (2002). *The arts and the creation of the mind.* New Haven, CT: Yale University Press.

Fineberg, J. (2006). *When we were young: New perspectives on the art of the child.* London: University of California Press.

Gardner, H. (1983). *Frames of mind: The theory of multiple intelligences.* New York, NY: Basic Books.

Gardner, H. (2006). *Multiple intelligences: New horizons in theory and practice.* New York, NY: Basic Books.

Hetland, L., Winner, E., Veenema, S., & Sheridan, K. (2013). *Studio thinking 2: The real benefits of visual arts education.* New York, NY: Teacher's College Press.

Hume, H. D. (2014). *The art teacher's survival guide for secondary schools* (2nd ed.). San Fransisco, CA: Jossey-Bass.

Kindler, A. M. (2004). Researching impossible? Models of artistic development reconsidered. In E. W. Eisner & M. D. Day (Eds.), *Handbook of research and policy in art education* (pp. 233–252). Mahwah, NJ: Lawrence Erlbaum Associates.

Kindler, A. M. (2010). Art and art in early childhood: What can young children learn from "a/art activities?" *International Art in Early Childhood Research Journal, 2*(1), 1–14.

Kindler, A. M., & Darras, B. (1997). Map of artistic development. In A. M. Kindler (Ed.), *Child development in art* (pp. 17–44). Reston, VA: The National Art Education Association.

Larochelle, M., & Bednarz, N. (2009). Constructivism and education: Beyond epistemological correctness. In M. Larochelle, N. Bednarz, & J. Garrison (Eds.), *Constructivism and education* (pp. 3–22). New York, NY: Cambridge University Press.

Latimer, J. (2017). *Sculptural secrets for mosaics: Creating 3-D bases for mosaic application.* Atglen, PA: Schiffer.

Levine, L. E., & Munsch, J. A. (2011). *Child development: An active learning approach.* Thousand Oaks, CA: Sage Publications.

Lowenfeld, V. (1947). *Creative and mental growth: A textbook on art education.* New York, NY: Macmillan.

National Coalition for Core Arts Standards. (2014a). *National Core Arts Standards.* Retrieved from www.nationalartsstandards.org

National Coalition for Core Arts Standards. (2014b). *National Core Arts Standards: A conceptual framework for arts learning.* Retrieved from www.nationalartsstandards.org/sites/default/files/NCCAS%20%20Conceptual%20Framework 4.pdf

Piaget, J. (1983). Piaget's theory. In P. Mussen (Ed.), *Handbook of child psychology* (4th ed., Vol. 1). New York, NY: Wiley.

Piaget, J., & Inhelder, B. (1972). *The psychology of the child.* New York, NY: Basic Books.

Riley, D., San Juan, R. R., Klinkner, J., & Ramminger, A. (2008). *Social and emotional development: Connecting science and practice in early childhood settings.* St. Paul, MN: Red Leaf Press.

Vygotsky, L. S. (1962). *Thought and language.* Cambridge, MA: MIT Press.

Vygotsky, L. S. (1978). *Mind in a society.* Cambridge, MA: Harvard University Press.

Walsh, D. (2014). *Why do they act that way? A survival guide to the adolescent brain for you and your teen* (2nd ed.). New York, NY: Atria.

Wilson, B. (2004). Child art after modernism: Visual culture and new narratives. In E. W. Eisner & M. D. Day (Eds.), *Handbook of research and policy in art education* (pp. 299–328). Mahwah, NJ: Lawrence Erlbaum Associates.

Wilson, M., & Wilson, B. (2010). *Teaching children to draw* (2nd ed.). Worcester, MA: Davis Publications.

Wood, C. (2007). *Yardsticks: Children in the classroom ages 4–14.* Turners Falls, MA: Northeast Foundation for Children.

# Chapter 6

# Diversified Learners

**FIGURE 6.1** Collaborative K–8 mosaic project. United States.
*Source: Carlos Alves and JC Carroll, artists-in-residence. United Arts Council of Collier County.*

**Diversified learners** represent the wide variety of students whom teachers educate across our planet. As unique individuals, students have varying abilities and come from different cultural, racial, socioeconomic, and linguistic backgrounds (Gargiulo & Metcalf, 2017). Diversified learners include students with high abilities (gifted and talented), students with disabilities, students with at-risk tendencies, English learners, and LGBTQ+. This textbook applies the term *at-risk* to bring awareness to the risk factors that impact students in their education, recognizing that all people experience risks in life, such as health and financial risks. When teaching art, we take students' differences into account so that all students can experience equal opportunities and achieve learning outcomes. We strive to make a positive difference in all students' lives through quality instruction, a choice-based art curriculum, fair assessments, and genuine care for students.

This chapter teaches about diversified students in context, identifies factors that influence their abilities to learn, and explains how to accommodate their needs through quality art instruction. It focuses on teaching students' **self-efficacy** skills, which refer to their beliefs about their capabilities to produce effective results based on their abilities to overcome obstacles, rebound from setbacks, observe people similar to themselves succeed, and hear from someone else that they have the ability to attain new skills (Bandura, 1997). When we instruct diversified learners, we will teach about **resiliency**, which refers to people's abilities to succeed despite obstacles. Students who are resilient take efforts to develop positive relationships with mentors and use their creative skills to

see alternative possibilities than their current realities might present (Wolin & Wolin, 1993). Through the comprehensive choice-based art curriculum, students will learn about artists who share similar backgrounds to themselves and overcame risk factors.

We will meet the following objectives by participating in this chapter:

- Define diversified learners and explain how diversity is a universal part of the human experience.
- Identify the characteristics of diversified learners and accommodate their needs.
- Contemplate strategies to teach diversified learners about self-efficacy and resiliency.

Spotlight on Student Art #6 showcases a collaborative art project (Figure 6.1) created by diversified learners. It is an example of how students collaborated with professional artists to develop a public artwork about life in their community.

## Spotlight on Student Art #6

### Big Idea: Equality

Elementary and middle school students applied their talents, skills, and knowledge to create *Immokalee Morning* (Figure 6.1) as part of a wall mosaic series to pay homage to the role of agriculture and the environment within their Everglades community. While attending school, many of the children's parents, who come from various cultures, pick the produce that supply grocery stores and restaurants. In this group of diversified learners, several of the students do not speak English as their first language, and several live below the poverty level. Some have disabilities, and some have been identified as learners with high ability (gifted and talented). The students' mosaics represent their perspectives on community and iconify the important roles that agriculture and the environment play in society. Their community is home to an acclaimed farming coalition that has made positive changes for migrant farm workers through its Anti-Slavery Campaign and Fair Food Program to ensure rights, social responsibility, and livable wages (Coalition of Immokalee Workers, 2018). The coalition advocates that the workers who grow the food people eat deserve fair and equal treatment for their vital work. The students' designs reinforce their community's positive achievements through their bright yellow sun, lush landscape, fruits and vegetables, and animal life.

Throughout the project, artists-in-residence Carlos Alves and JC Carroll, and schoolteachers, utilized multiple approaches and accommodations to communicate with and teach the children. The students examined the artists' past projects as visual inspirations, watched demonstrations to become acquainted with mosaic techniques, and participated in class discussions. Students with advanced English language skills translated key information to peers who were still learning English. Those with advanced artistic skills took a leadership role on the project's visual design. Upon the project's completion, the students' wall mosaics became vibrant symbols of community pride.

# GIFTED AND TALENTED: LEARNERS WITH HIGH ABILITIES

**Gifted and talented** children have high ability in one or more disciplines. Gifted and talented education provides students with the resources and learning environments necessary to excel at accelerated rates and depths of learning. Around the world, governments implement legislative acts to define gifted and talented education and determine which services children who qualify as gifted and talented will receive. In some communities giftedness focuses solely on intellectual skills. Other communities expand the definition to include **talent**, children's propensities, and above-average accomplishments in disciplines including the visual arts (as exemplified in Figures 6.2 and 6.3). The U.S. Congress (U.S. Department of Education, 2002) identifies learners who are gifted and talented as:

> students, children, or youth who give evidence of high achievement capability in areas such as intellectual, creative, artistic, or leadership capacity, or in specific academic fields, and who need services or activities not ordinarily provided by the school in order to fully develop those capabilities.

Children identified as gifted and talented learn faster than same-aged peers and can apply learning content in greater depth. **Enrichment** is the practice of providing students who are gifted and talented with experiences that reach beyond the scope of typical age-appropriate lessons. The art enrichment activities that teachers develop should stimulate student learning as a natural part of the learning process rather than feel like punitive measures that force students to produce more than classmates. Art enrichment activities include students conducting independent research on big ideas, artists, or methods; participating in extension activities related to lessons; creating at learning centers with talented peers who share similar skills; and collaborating with mentors. Teachers might also design community art projects, such as a mosaic mural (Figure 6.4), to satisfy their students' desire to participate in specialized art learning tasks.

Teachers should look for students' high artistic abilities and talents based on aptitudes such as refined artistic skills and sophisticated cognitive abilities. In the late 19th century, psychologist Alfred Binet asked

FIGURE 6.2 Lau Kin Gi, 4-years-old, Simply Art, Hong Kong, China.
*Source: 38th ICEFA Lidice.*

FIGURE 6.3 Ema Pršalová, 9-years-old, ZUŠ, Praha 5, Czech Republic.
*Source: 43rd ICEFA Lidice.*

**FIGURE 6.4** 8-and-9-year-old students, Australia.

*Source: Courtesy of the artist, Julee Latimer ©; www.juleelatimer.com*

teachers to identify children's normative skills and behaviors to develop his **intelligence testing** model, which compared a child's mental age to his/her chronological age and determined if a child's cognitive intelligence was at the same level or below same-aged peers. Lewis Terman expanded upon Binet's research to identify intellectually gifted children and adults. **Intelligence quotient (IQ)** tests have a median score of intelligence set at 100 points. Individuals with an IQ score of 130 or more are classified as gifted (Hunt, 2011). The Torrance Test of Creative Thinking measures a child's mental characteristics including fluency, flexibility, originality, elaboration, resistance to premature closure, and abstractness of titles. While it effectively measures general creativity and its tested skills link to creativity in the visual arts, contemporary scholars want to see assessments that reliably measure creativity in specialized professional domains (Zeng, Proctor, & Salvendy, 2011). Such measures would be highly relevant to visual arts and design professions in identifying possible career choices for students proficient in the arts.

In addition to using IQ and creativity tests, teachers may recognize intellectual giftedness or artistic talents through observations of students working; students' finished artworks; sketches made in students' free time; and students' leadership skills and aptitudes for future success. Children's artistic talent comes in many forms, including:

- developing deep interests in the visual arts at young ages,
- focusing on art projects longer than peers,
- designing more complicated and innovative creations,
- wanting to participate in extracurricular arts activities,
- producing a larger body of works in a shorter time span than peers,
- creating comprehensive art journals and portfolios as learning resources,
- having a keen ability to write and talk about art,
- becoming motivated when working with talented peers, and
- seeing art professionals as role models.

The choice-based art curriculum provides gifted and talented students with opportunities to work with advanced artists' media, tools, and equipment to meet their learning needs (Figures 6.5 and 6.6).

Giftedness and talent belong to all cultures, genders, and classes. A student's high abilities may go

**FIGURE 6.5** Lau You Gi, 5-years-old, Simply Art, Hong Kong, China.

*Source: 41st ICEFA Lidice.*

FIGURE 6.6 Štěpánka Hlavatá, 7-years-old, ZUŠ, Mšeno, Czech Republic.
*Source: 43rd ICEFA Lidice.*

unnoticed if school faculty and administration focus solely on children's achievements and productivity. Unidentified students often come from lower socioeconomic households, are female and/or minority students, and/or their native language is different than the dominant language spoken at school. Their creative abilities can be hidden due to environmental, physical, or cognitive factors. Some students lack talented role models to emulate, experience test bias, and fear being ridiculed by peers for being different, which may cause them to underachieve (Silverman & Miller, 2009). Statistical data collected over 100 years indicates that males and females are equally gifted and talented. Silverman and Miller (2009) explained that more boys are identified as gifted than girls because parents are more likely to have their sons tested. Female students should be identified as talented or gifted through an individual non-timed IQ test before they are 8-years-old. After this age, social relationships become more important in their lives and they might hide their abilities to blend in with peers. Teachers can help combat this tendency for students to mask their talents by developing art learning tasks that provide all students with opportunities to take leadership roles that demonstrate their creativity and unique forms of intelligence.

Some people express concerns about segregation and favored treatment for one group over another within specialized gifted and talented instruction, as occurred in former sub-Saharan African colonies. Maree and van der Westhuizen's (2009) research

provides an environmentally specific model of gifted and talented education that varies from the dominant ideals and standards of gifted education set in North America and Europe, which can be ethnocentric or biased when applied to other societies. Their model of gifted and talented education focuses on career preparation based on cultural understandings and narrative dialogues to serve their communities. In alignment with this model, choice-based art programs teach talented students professional artists' creative skills (such as the realistic drawing and glassblowing designs shown in Figures 6.7 and 6.8) and mindsets to develop 21st century skills that prepare them for their roles as future leaders in our local and global communities. To strengthen these outcomes, communities should contribute to educators' efforts by supporting students through professional partnerships, experiential learning activities, and arts-based internships for adolescents.

Educators and policy makers must remain aware that a disability can mask a student's gifted and talented capabilities and take precautions not to leave the student's high ability unidentified (Smith, Polloway, Patton, & Dowdy, 2012). Students who are gifted or talented and also identified with having a disability are referred to as **twice exceptional**. For example, Figures 6.9 and 6.10 illustrate the creative practices of a twice-exceptional artist who has speech and learning disabilities. She applies her art talents to communicate some of her perspectives on life.

FIGURE 6.7 Lee Seon Joo, 14-years-old, Busan Middle School of Arts, Busan, South Korea.
*Source: 38th ICEFA Lidice.*

FIGURE 6.8 Václav Böhm, 8-years-old, ZUŠ, Mšeno, Czech Republic.
*Source: 42nd ICEFA Lidice.*

FIGURE 6.10 Khushi Malde, 14-years-old. Kenya.
*Source: Lisa Wee, teacher.*

FIGURE 6.9 Khushi Malde, 14-years-old. Kenya.
*Source: Lisa Wee, teacher.*

## CHILDREN WITH DISABILITIES

The term **children with disabilities** applies to students who have been diagnosed with a disability, multiple disabilities, or an exceptional circumstance. The severity of a disability varies from student to student. Worldwide, 93 million children ages 14 and under have a moderate or severe disability (United Nations Children's Fund, 2013). Most teachers teach students with disabilities, as they account for approximately 13% of the school population (U.S. Department of Education Institute of Education Sciences [USDEIES], 2018). The U.S. Congress explained:

> Child with a disability means a child evaluated . . . as having an intellectual disability, a hearing impairment (including deafness), a speech or language impairment, a visual impairment (including blindness), a serious emotional disturbance (referred to in this part as "emotional disturbance"), an orthopedic impairment, autism, traumatic brain injury, an other health impairment,

a specific learning disability, deaf-blindness, or multiple disabilities, and who, by reason thereof, needs special education and related services.

(U.S. Department of Education
Individuals with Disabilities
Education Act [USDEIDEA],
2006, 300.8 (a) (1))

The World Health Organization's International Classification of Functioning, Disability, and Health (ICF; 2002) definition of disability expands beyond medical diagnoses. It emphasizes a multidimensional perspective that focuses on a person's ability to function and participate in society, rather than concentrating on a disability and its related impairments and limitations. The ICF classification recognizes disabilities as a normal and universal part of the human experience, not an exception, because all people have the potential for developing a disability at some point in their lives. A population that views disability as a regular part of the human experience is better prepared to advocate for all human's equal rights as valuable members of society (UNICEF, 2013). Best practices for teaching students with disabilities place emphasis on capable teachers who focus on children's individual learning needs and make modifications as necessary so that students acquire the skills they need to be successful and reach learning goals. Teachers provide children with disabilities access to equal opportunities that enrich their lives. For example, Figures 6.11 and 6.12 show that students with disabilities can participate in comprehensive art learning tasks.

In 1975, the U.S. Congress passed Public Law 94–142, the Education for All Handicapped Children Act, which became the **Individuals with Disabilities Education Act (IDEA)** fifteen years later (see this textbook's companion website for IDEA disability definitions). IDEA serves approximately seven million children. The law requires that children with disabilities obtain a **free, appropriate, public education (FAPE)** in the **least restrictive environment** (LRE). Of students in the United States who qualify under IDEA's definition of children with a disability, 35% have been diagnosed with a specific learning disability, 21% with a speech or language impairment, 12% with a disability labeled as other health impairment, 8% with autism, 6% with an intellectual delay, and 6% with an emotional/behavioral disability. Two percent of children have been diagnosed with multiple

FIGURE 6.11 Aneta Ampapová, 4-years-old, MŠ a spec. pedagog. centrum, Jihlava, Czech Republic.
*Source: 41st ICEFA Lidice.*

FIGURE 6.12 Ján Bartoš, 16-years-old, Špeciálna ZŠ internátna, Topol'čany, Slovak Republic.
*Source: 40th ICEFA Lidice.*

disabilities. Children with hearing impairments, orthopedic impairments, deaf-blindness, traumatic brain injury, and visual impairments each account for 1% or less of students served by IDEA. Students with an IQ below 70 points are identified as having an intellectual disability (Hunt, 2011).

IDEA requires that students with disabilities receive an instructional plan to determine how they can best reach learning objectives in all subjects of study. This is achieved through an **individualized education program (IEP)**: "a written statement for each child with a disability that is developed, reviewed, and revised in accordance with" the law (USDEIDEA, 2006, 300.22). An **IEP team** that includes educational experts, parents, and the child (as appropriate) assesses the child's educational needs and abilities at regular intervals. The IEP team listens to members' input and concerns, analyzes teacher observations and anecdotal information, and reviews recent student evaluations. The IEP that the team develops identifies any modifications, accommodations, actions, and/or special resources that the student needs to meet desired learning outcomes. For example, a student may benefit from instruction in Braille or use assistive technologies such as screen readers or dictation software to read and write about art subject matter. Without IEPs, a student's needs may not be identified and/or may remain unmet. Regular IEP meetings allow the team to reassess changes in a student's disability status, identify student progress, and make further recommendations. The IEP team keeps parents informed and requires parental consent when making decisions. If parents disagree with the IEP, they can request **procedural due process,** a legal safeguard to mediate differences. They will receive notice of any changes to the child's IEP in language they can understand (Gargiulo & Metcalf, 2017).

IDEA mandates that student learning takes place in the **least restrictive environment,** which the IEP team identifies as the most appropriate educational setting to accommodate students' learning needs. Ninety-five percent of children served by IDEA attend regular schools and the remaining students attend specialized schools or receive their education at home or in a residential learning center, hospital facility, or correctional institution (USDEIES, 2018). For the most part, students with disabilities attending regular schools spend approximately 80% of their school day in classes shared with students without disabilities.

The IEP team may identify that certain students require the assistance of a teacher aid in the general classroom or benefit from supplementary learning opportunities, such as tutoring. Students with disabilities may also learn part time or full time in a resource classroom with a qualified resource teacher who delivers instruction. In some situations, such as with conditions related to a severe disability, a child's least restrictive environment might be a specialized school or care facility with services not available in typical schools.

## STUDENTS WITH AT-RISK TENDENCIES

**Students with at-risk tendencies** are children who are more likely than other students to drop out of school. They belong to all racial groups and live in big cities, rural communities, and in the suburbs. The main risk factors that impair students' academic success include (a) poverty; (b) reading below grade level; (c) poor school attendance, truancy, delinquency, and feeling disconnected from school; and (d) speaking a different language at home. While many students have at least one risk factor, students with at-risk tendencies possess two or more risk factors. Despite the risk factors that they face, students with at-risk tendencies can be successful in school. For example, Christopher Williams (Artists' Lessons to Thrive! 14.2 and Figure 6.13) loved art as a child and also had at-risk tendencies. Given his resiliency and the support of his family and teachers, who believed in his capabilities,

**FIGURE 6.13** Christopher Williams, 5th grade, United States.
*Source: Author, teacher.*

Williams improved his grades in elementary school, graduated high school with honors, and earned a full scholarship to study art in college.

**Poverty** is a multidimensional deprivation that extends beyond material resources and contributes to children's risk factors. Living in poverty means that individuals have limited access to basic human needs including an education, nutritious foods, health care, housing/affordable housing, sanitation, clean water, school supplies, and spiritual/emotional well-being (Gorski, 2008). When children do not receive the care they need, even short-term deprivations can harm their cognitive and physical development. The poverty rate amongst children rises considerably when they live with only one parent and doubles when living with their mother, as single parents often have only one income to support their children (Ackerman, Brown, & Izard, 2004). Many single parents who work for low wages spend less time with their children because their jobs require them to work during the non-school hours. Some teachers create a school art club and other extracurricular activities to provide students with a safe place to learn after school. Community centers can also provide enriching art activities, safe peer relations, and adult supervision for children.

On average, students living in poverty score significantly lower on reading tests than children living in middle class and affluent homes. Students who have acquired limited or partial grade-level reading skills or read below grade level face greater academic risks (McFarland et al., 2018). Some children enter school with little exposure to books, few role models who read, and poor knowledge of how to read visual symbols in books, including pictures and fonts. They may not have had the same opportunities as students who read on grade level to answer literature-based questions and build their vocabularies due to their limited exposure to reading role models and/or books (Rothstein, 2008). When children cannot read at grade level by the end of 3rd grade, they will most likely continue to read below grade level throughout their schooling, as this period marks the transition from learning how to read to utilizing written text to understand class material (Mead, 2010).

Students' risk factors increase with absences, especially unexcused ones (National Center for School Engagement, 2008). Some children with disabilities may miss school and fall behind classmates because they have difficulty completing learning tasks due

to physical pain, fatigue, and medicine side effects. Other children might be prevented from attending school by their parents, because they require the children's assistance at home. In addition, children living in dangerous neighborhoods may fear commuting to school because they can become victims of crime and bullying (Rothstein, 2008).

**Truancy** is an unexcused absence from school and can be punishable by law, as officials hold students and parents accountable. Studies indicate that children who have greater feelings of rejection, poor grades, and lack of support from their parents are more likely to become truant (National Center for School Engagement, 2008). Schools may receive less funding from state and federal funding agencies when students miss school, which can impact the quality of children's educations (Fiel, 2002). Without intervention, truancy can lead to **delinquency**, which refers to a variety of negative social behaviors that includes acting out, gang involvement, committing violent offenses, and participating in illegal behaviors (United Nations, 2005).

## ENGLISH LEARNERS

**English learners (ELs)** are children living in English-speaking countries who are learning to speak English. This definition differs from children learning English as a foreign language in their native countries. Across our planet, 221 million children learn class content in a non-native language (United Nations Global Education First [UNGEFI], 2012). Teachers of students who speak other languages need to recognize how language is an important part of students' identities and social interactions. It is part of what defines who people are. Artists' Lessons to Thrive! 6.1 describes how Helle Storvik discovered that her cultural heritage and her ancestors' native language had been erased by a dominant society that viewed its own language and cultural traditions as superior. Such forced assimilation has been undertaken in many societies throughout history. Storvik used her art as a means to return some of what had been taken away and reconstruct a collective identity within her community.

In the United States, ELs may be born in the country or they may come from all over the world. They have parents who may or may not be fluent in English. ELs belong to different cultures, practice different religions, have diverse ethnicities, and come from different socioeconomic backgrounds. Congress passed the English Language Acquisition, Language Enhancement, and Academic Achievement Act so that ELs receive a quality education. Students typically spend two to three years in specialized language programming, which may be taught by EL specialists. The act also requires schools to test ELs to determine if they have made yearly progress in reading, writing, speaking, and listening to English. On average, ELs require five to seven years to become completely fluent in English (Hill & Bjork, 2008; Latta & Chan, 2011). If ELs have had interruptions in their formal education, they may struggle with reading, writing, and formal speaking in their native languages. This may cause students to be two academic years behind same-aged peers. Language barriers may also cause children to repeat grades and lead to dropping out of school (UNGEFI, 2012). Alternatively, students who learn multiple languages fluently develop flexible and abstract thinking patterns that allow them to navigate between langauages and focus on the most important information necessary for learning. Compared to monolinguistic learners, bilinqual students can also have career advantages due to their broader communication abilities (U.S. Department of Education, 2017).

### Artists' Lessons to Thrive! 6.1 Helle Storvik: Sites of Assimilation and Rejuvenation

#### Big Ideas: Assimilation and Rejuvenation

At 30 years old, while attending a family reunion in Northern Norway's Vesterålen Islands, artist Helle Storvik first discovered her Sami heritage. The Sami are an indigenous people from the Arctic Sápmi region in Norway, Sweden, Finland, and Russia's Kola Peninsula. Their population is ethnically different from other Scandinavians. Sami speak their own languages and have unique traditions. For centuries, the Sami experienced harsh discrimination and cultural assimilation. Sami children were sent to boarding schools taught by non-Sami educators to eradicate Sami language and culture. Sami youth were forced to embrace the dominant Scandinavian cultures, which were deemed superior to their own culture (Benko, 2011). In Norway, many Sami felt extreme pressure to assimilate into Norwegian culture because of the country's strict laws that prohibited individuals who did not speak Norwegian and/or have Norwegian names from purchasing land. These discriminatory practices caused many Sami to hide their true identities (Blix, Hamran, & Normann, 2013). By the end of the 20th century, Scandinavian countries ended discriminatory practices against the Sami. However, the long-term assimilation had caused great damage. Sami languages had become extinct or threatened, and countless individuals had little or no knowledge of their Sami heritage (Weinstock, 2013).

Storvik organized a collaborative art project with Mari Boine, Rune Johansen, and Åslaug Krokann Berg titled *Are We still Here? (Er vi her ennå?)* to learn more about their Sami heritage. *Are We Still Here?* resulted in their production of a narrative body of works that include film, photographs, performances, and interviews. The artists invited Vesterålen's residents to share their experiences and knowledge of their Sami origins. These events led to many questions including: "What is this culture we are a part of?" "How should we be Sami?" and "How does one reinvent one's story?" (Storvik, Boine, Johansen, & Berg, 2012, p. 45). Storvik's photographs capture the sites of Sami culture and allude to the culture's sounds, chants, and stories. Her images also portray the loneliness that the Sami must have felt due to decades of forced assimilation (Figures 6.1.1–6.1.3).

The artists used their project and its physical location in the Vesterålen Islands as a form of autoethnography. They "simply felt it imperative to produce it, for their own sakes, as persons with links to the site, both physically and discursively" (Storvik et al., 2012, p. 44). The artists' collective works have opened up dialogue about Sami culture. They function as rejuvenating forces that bring to light the values of Sami culture and ways to move forward after assimilation. Storvik and Berg explained that

FIGURE 6.1.1 Helle Storvik, "And Me, Am I Not a Part of It?" *The Fjord,* 2012, Photoshop-painted photo printed on canvas, 47.24 × 47.24 × 1.18 in. (120 × 120 × 3 cm).

FIGURE 6.1.2 Helle Storvik, "And Me, Am I Not a Part of It?" *The Sami Dress,* 2012, Photoshop-painted photo printed on canvas, 47.24 × 47.24 ×1.18 in. (120 × 120 × 3 cm).

FIGURE 6.1.3 Helle Storvik, "And Me, Am I Not a Part of It?" *The Sami Headgear,* 2012, Photoshop-painted photo printed on canvas, 47.24 × 47.24 × 1.18 in. (120 × 120 × 3 cm).

their research practices and creative works have presented an open platform to "live with their Sami heritage in everyday life, as a natural part of life" (Figenschau, 2011, para. 3). Additionally, their artistic practices have provided future Sami generations with effective methods to instill cultural pride.

## Essential/Guiding Questions

1. In your opinion, why do groups of people feel the need to assimilate others into their own cultures? How do these practices impact communities? What role do ethics play in assimilation?
2. How might the processes of creating art lead to the rejuvenation of a culture?

## Preparation

For this group project, students will discuss the artists' processes for creating *Are We Still Here?* Working in groups, students will brainstorm ways to utilize art media to communicate their group's story. They will identify the criteria they will use to evaluate the quality of their collective work's message and how it will provide deep knowledge of their chosen subject matter.

## Daily Learning Targets

We can develop a multimedia production that addresses assimilation and rejuvenation.

- We can select the media of our choice.
- We can integrate aspects of our collective research into our completed artwork.
- We can show craftspersonship and unity in our production.

**National Core Arts Anchor Standards** 1, 4, 9, and 11
www.nationalartsstandards.org

## LGBTQ+

**LGBTQ+** identifies diversified lesbian, gay, bisexual, transgendered, and queer people, as well as individuals who question their sexual and/or gender identities. Contemporary society has developed greater awareness and sensitivity to LGBTQ+ causes with supporting laws and institutional policies. These changes have resulted from the tireless efforts of LGBTQ+ advocates. Students see LGBTQ+ role models in powerful positions and learn LGBTQ+ stories in popular culture including movies, television series, and children's books. Given greater community acceptance, LGBTQ+ students have begun identifying themselves publically or to small supportive groups at earlier ages, typically in high school (Russell & Fish, 2016). While identifying as LGBTQ+ has become easier than in previous decades, students remain part of a minority school population and can experience greater harassment, bullying, and suicide risks for being different.

LGBTQ+ risk factors are significantly reduced when students have the support of school policies, teachers, parents, and peers. Educators play a vital role in creating bully-free learning environments that teach human rights and the resiliency and accomplishments of diversified populations, including LGBTQ+ (Greteman, 2017; Sanders & Gubes Vaz, 2014). Teachers can make students aware of resources, including community organizations for LGBTQ+ youth, and sponsor an LGBTQ+ club.

While many teachers understand the importance of supporting LGBTQ+ students, some may feel concerned to advocate, talk about, and teach LGBTQ+ topics due to possible parent, administrator, and community disapproval that can negatively impact their job security, particularly in conservative environments (Hseih, 2016). Rather than emphasizing sexuality, the art curriculum can address age-appropriate subject matter that leads to happier, healthier, and more productive lives, including students forming healthy (loving) relationships, treating themselves and others kindly, and respecting their bodies. Teachers can develop curricular tasks that address social justice and ethics to teach about fairness and equity for all. Studying the contributions of LGBTQ+ artists (including Nick Cave; see Artists' Lessons to Thrive! 1.1 and Figure 6.14) and the conditions that people share can inspire students who might be initially reluctant to move away from stereotypes and broaden their perspectives. Students who are aware of issues of fairness and equality can become leaders who discourage peers from harassing and bullying LGBTQ+ and others.

## TEACHING AND ACCOMMODATING DIVERSIFIED LEARNERS THROUGH ART

When teachers, including pre-service teachers, have ongoing opportunities to work directly with diversified learners as part of their professional development, they are better prepared to be flexible in their teaching methodologies and make accommodations

(Figure 6.15; Bain & Hasio, 2011; Clark & Zimmerman, 2004). Great teachers design curricular tasks that teach students about the commonalities people share (Deiner, 2013; Gargiulo & Metcalf, 2017). The United Nations (UNGEFI, 2012) articulated:

> Education must be transformative and bring shared values to life. It must cultivate an active care for the world and for those with whom we share it. Education must also be relevant in answering the big questions of the day.
>
> (p. 20)

Great teachers design safe learning environments in which students can communicate, create, and address important life topics.

## Inclusive Classroom Design

Students learn best when their physical, psychological, and emotional needs are met. **Universal design** is a practice employed by built environment

FIGURE 6.14 Nick Cave. *Heard-NY*.

*Source: Original Photo by Patrick Cashin. Image courtesy of Metropolitan Transportation Authority of the State of New York. Flickr, CC BY 2.0. https://creativecommons.org/licenses/by/2.0/*

work independently, in groups, and come together as a whole class for learning tasks. All students need accessible passageways and clutter-free art learning environments. This can be particularly helpful for students who use specialized equipment to navigate classroom spaces. Art supplies, equipment, and books need to be within students' reach. In addition, teachers can display signage identifying their classrooms as safe and inclusive spaces for students. Teachers can also plan seating arrangements to accommodate students' diverse learning needs. For example, some students may need to sit at the front of the class to understand tasks more readily. Some students benefit from having their desks facing away from lights or windows because the brightness irritates their eyes.

## Adaptive Art Supplies

Teachers utilize specialized art supplies, equipment, instructional resources, and procedures to help all students learn. They select the best materials for students to use for particular tasks. The following list provides a sampling of possible accommodations.

- Some students have difficulties holding or manipulating traditional writing and art supplies. They can have better results by writing on computer devices and creating artworks using materials (pencils, pens, markers, and scissors) that have thick grips. Teachers can purchase specialized supplies with grips and also make their own to customize materials to meet students' preferences. Some students might use the assistance of a mouthstick to control pencils, markers, paintbrushes, and other art supplies.
- Some students may require assistance locating art supplies. Teachers can arrange art supplies at students' desks to align with numerical positions on a clock and describe their positioning so that students will know where they are located and can access them without further assistance. Teachers can also stand behind a student and simultaneously hold the student's hands on top of their own to give the student feelings of control during demonstrations (Lewis & Allman, 2014).
- Students can work with clay (pulling and squeezing) and blocks (stacking and arranging) to develop hand strength, grip, and coordination.

FIGURE 6.15 A student works with a pre-service teacher to examine peers' artworks through touch during a gallery exhibition. United States.
*Source: Author and Monica Leister, teachers.*

specialists who develop environmental spaces in which all humans can interact comfortably without obstacles that leave people out. See Artists' Lessons to Thrive! 17.1 on architect Karen L. Braitmayer that describes how she designs built environment spaces for all people to share. **Universal Design for Learning** builds on universal design by built environment specialists and is a curricular approach that utilizes customized spaces and resources to promote individual student success while reducing barriers to learning (Center for Applied Special Technology, 2019). Teachers prepare **inclusive classrooms**, learning environments that are supportive and accessible to all students through their planned arrangements of furniture, equipment, materials, and learning tasks. In inclusive settings students have opportunities to move around the classroom to different learning centers and relocate furniture as necessary to

- Students can draw with black permanent markers rather than pencils to produce bolder, more visible lines. Students can create textured drawings and feel the lined surfaces by placing a sheet of paper on screen and drawing with crayons that leave a raised wax surface.
- Students may benefit by having paper secured to a work surface. Teachers can tape paper to tabletops and utilize drawing boards with clips and slant boards to secure papers.
- Some students may feel uncomfortable touching wet and sticky art materials such as clay, paper pulp, and glue. Teachers can provide gloves, paintbrushes, and spreading utensils so that students need not touch the materials directly. They might place pieces of clay and wet plaster in plastic bags for students to manipulate (Loesl, 2010). With ongoing exposure and the option to participate in small increments, students may become desensitized to processes and materials that they initially rejected.
- Students can utilize sensory boxes for learning. Sensory boxes can be themed, such as one designed to calm children and promote positive thoughts. Figure 6.16 illustrates a teacher presenting a stained glass artifact from a sensory box to a student with a visual impairment during a lesson on Gothic cathedrals.
- Students can use picture schedules that show class routines in a timetable format and checklists to know what is expected of them to reach daily learning targets and stay on-task (Eren, 2010; Jantz, Davies, & Bigler, 2014). Instructional resources in visual formats, including posters and video clips, can be highly effective in helping some students process new information and reach objectives (Huesmann, 2010).

## Safe and Empowering Communications

Safe communications are essential to creating successful learning environments for all students. Diversified students can be the recipients of other people's negative comments and actions, as described in Artists' Lessons to Thrive! 18.1 on graphic designer Madalyne Marie Hymas and her artwork *The Dyslexic Advantage*. **People-first language** focuses on people's abilities rather than limitations. Instead of using

**FIGURE 6.16** A middle-childhood student works with a preservice teacher. United States.
*Source: Author, Monica Leister, and Nichole Dawson Rich, teachers.*

medical terminology as the sole human descriptor, it identifies the person first and adds an appropriate descriptor or tool such as students with disabilities and students who use wheelchairs. It rejects **ableism**, which refers to discriminating against people who do not fit limited perceptions of what people's minds and bodies should be able to do (Derby, 2011). Teachers can expand upon their instruction of people-first language to safeguard students who may be called derogatory names for being different, including LGBTQ+, ELs, and learners with high abilities, to discuss how all people deserve care and respect. Following are some strategies that teachers can apply to foster safe communications and give every student a voice.

- Small group interactions provide students with opportunities to work closely with peers and articulate their thoughts (Eubanks, 2002). Classes can come together as whole units to share in discussions. Working together to solve problems is highly effective for children who need assistance in gaining self-control and building a sense of camaraderie (Greene, 2014).

- Classmates who possess strong verbal skills can clarify concepts and/or words that other students may not understand and assist them in articulating their ideas (Curran, 2003).
- Students who are self-conscious about their accents or English grammar usage may fear speaking in front of the whole class. Small group discussions offer students greater opportunities to share their opinions and can be less intimidating.
- Students need to be in touch with their bodies and what they are communicating to them. Teachers can discuss and model calming behaviors to help students reduce feelings of fear and anxiety that can result from a disorder as well as environmental and social factors. Teachers might integrate two-to-three minute deep abdominal breathing exercises into the class routine that teach students how to concentrate on their breath, release their worries, and receive the oxygen their brains need to function (Semple, Lee, Rosa, & Miller, 2010). This can be particularly helpful for students who may find it difficult to cope with changes and manage their behaviors. With practice, students can use breathing exercises throughout the day to rejuvenate, as well as reduce anxiety and feelings of anger. They can apply breathing exercises to reduce outbursts.
- Teachers can incorporate quiet reflective moments into lessons for students to observe art, interpret what they see, and find the appropriate words to articulate their thoughts.
- Journaling and art tasks assist students in communicating their thoughts. Creative tasks that focus on specific memories can assist students in recalling details and communicating their stories.
- Some students strive for perfection and become frustrated when their work is not perfect. Teachers and students can discuss how artists practice, experiment, manipulate materials and make revisions before their works become final products. This can be helpful for students who may think that their first efforts must always produce successful outcomes.

Given positive class communications, students build a sense of **collective efficacy** (self-efficacy among all participants within a given community) and learn how they can achieve more together (Bandura, 1997; Kraft & Keifer-Boyd, 2013). Individual members take steps to abandon personal interests as necessary to assist the group in meeting its collective goals. Collective efficacy empowers students to achieve large goals that require multiple members to complete, such as community artworks. Participatory action research correlates with collective efficacy because students work as teams to identify problems and produce positive changes. Collective efficacy can benefit classroom management practices as well because all students recognize their individual and shared responsibilities. When students face challenges, teachers reinforce that people have different skills and must sometimes work harder at a particular task than others to receive positive results.

## Building Art Vocabulary and Inquiry Skills

Each subsequent school year the academic language that students are expected to know becomes more difficult. Baker et al. (2014) suggest that teachers present class content at grade level using language that students understand, and then break down the meaning of key terms to accommodate for students' proficiencies. They recommend that students study five to eight new words in depth at one time. Teachers can prepare lists of academic terms associated with lessons for students to refer to during class demonstrations, discussions, and writing assignments. For example, kindergarteners preparing to create a collaborative collage and class reading about care identify vocabulary words beginning with the letter C, including care, circle, and collage (Figure 6.17). When working with ELs, teachers can look up important phrases and art terms in students' native languages to communicate lesson content. Figure 6.18 shows an American pre-service teacher studying abroad in Denmark using signage in Danish and English to teach an art lesson to early adolescents.

Teachers build and reinforce students' academic vocabulary by connecting artistic tasks with substantial conversations, art-based readings, creative writings, and reflective journaling. Integrating artists' specialized language can encourage students to utilize advanced vocabularies in their communications. For example, students who hide their advanced linguistic skills to avoid standing out from peers, may feel motivated to share what they know because applying advanced vocabulary becomes a normal classroom

FIGURE 6.17 Early childhood students participate in a story. United States,

*Source: Author, Brittany Gonzalez, and Sara Nixon, teachers.*

FIGURE 6.18 Early adolescents in Denmark receive instruction in English with Danish signage.

*Source: Author and Todd Tosten, teachers.*

practice. Teachers also teach students how to analyze the meanings of artworks and multimedia products in popular culture, including websites, advertisements, gaming, and clothing that combine the visual arts and text so that students understand how visual images and their corresponding texts communicate meaning (Beavis, 2012). Teachers can develop lessons that have students create storylines to accompany literacy-based art projects, including handmade books, story quilts, claymations, and puppet shows. These projects can assist children who are exposed to fewer vocabulary words at home (Spencer & Marschark, 2010).

## OUR JOURNEY TO THRIVE CONTINUES . . .

This chapter described teaching and learning practices for diversified students. Moving into Part III of this textbook, we will identify art inquiry methods that teach students language and observation skills. Aesthetic, art criticism, art history, and visual culture

inquiry tasks enrich students' learning experiences by providing them with opportunities to study art in depth and see people like themselves strive and succeed as creative individuals.

## CHAPTER QUESTIONS AND ACTIVITIES

1. Who are diversified learners? Explain how diversity is a normal and universal part of the human experience. What is people-first language? Why is it important?
2. Describe your plans for teaching art to diversified learners. How will you use the choice-based art curriculum to teach students resiliency and self-efficacy?
3. Answer Artists' Lessons to Thrive! 6.1's essential/guiding questions in written form or as part of a group discussion. Complete its daily learning targets.

# References

Ackerman, B. P., Brown, E. D., & Izard, C. E. (2004). The relations between persistent poverty and contextual risk and children's behavior in elementary school. *Developmental Psychology, 40*(3), 367–377.

Bain, C., & Hasio, C. (2011). Authentic learning experience prepares preservice students to teach art to children with special needs. *Art Education, 64*(2), 33–39.

Baker, S., Lesaux, N., Jayanthi, M., Dimino, J., Proctor, C. P., Morris, J., . . . Newman-Gonchar, R. (2014). *Teaching academic content and literacy to English learners in elementary and middle school* (NCEE 2014–4012). Washington, DC: National Center for Education Evaluation and Regional Assistance (NCEE), Institute of Education Sciences, U.S. Department of Education. Retrieved from the NCEE website: http://ies.ed.gov/ncee/wwc/publications_reviews.aspx

Bandura, A. (1997). *Self-efficacy: The exercise of control.* New York, NY: W. H. Freeman & Company.

Beavis, C. (2012). Video games in the classroom: Developing digital literacies. *Practically Primary, 17*(1), 17–20.

Benko, J. (2011). SAMI: The people who walk with reindeer. *National Geographic, 220*(5), 62–81.

Blix, B., Hamran, T., & Normann, H. (2013). Struggles of being and becoming: A dialogical narrative analysis of the life stories of Sami elderly. *Journal Of Aging Studies, 27*(3), 264–275.

Center for Applied Special Technology. (2019). *About universal design for learning.* Retrieved from http://www.cast.org/our-work/about-udl.html?utm_source=udlguidelines&utm_medium=web&utm_campaign=none&utm_content=homepage#.XTlexi2ZN0s

Clark, G., & Zimmerman, E. (2004). *Teaching talented art students.* New York, NY: Teacher's College Press.

Coalition of Immokalee Workers. (2018). *About CIW.* Retrieved from http://ciw-online.org/about/

Curran, M. E. (2003). Linguistic diversity and classroom management. *Theory into Practice, 42*(4), 334–340.

Deiner, P. L. (2013). *Inclusive early childhood education: Development, resources, and practice* (6th ed.). Belmont, CA: Wadsworth.

Derby, J. (2011). Disability studies and art education. *Studies in Art Education, 52*(2), 94–111.

Eren, R. B. (2010). Understanding and teaching children with autism spectrum disorders in the classroom: A special education perspective. In B. L. Gerber & J. Kellman (Eds.), *Understanding students with autism through art* (pp. 56–70). Reston, VA: National Art Education Association.

Eubanks, P. (2002). Students who don't speak English: How art specialists adapt curriculum for ESOL students. *Art Education, 55*(2), 41–45.

Fiel, P. (2002). Battling truancy. *American School & University, 83*(9), 29–30.

Figenschau, M. (2011). *Helle Storvikneset and Åslaug Krokann Berg.* Retrieved from https://translate.google.com/translate?sl=no&tl=en&js=y&prev=_t&hl=en&ie=UTF-8&u=http%3A%2F%2Fwww.lassagammi.no%2Fhelle-storvik-og-aslaug-krokann-berg.4956247-97565.html&edit-text=&act=url

(Original Norwegian www.lassagammi.no/helle-storvik-og-aslaug-krokann-berg.4956247-97565.html).

Gargiulo, R. M., & Metcalf, D. (2017). *Teaching in today's inclusive classrooms: A universal design for learning approach* (3rd ed.). Boston, MA: Cengage Learning.

Gorski, P. (2008). The myth of the "culture of poverty." *Educational Leadership, 65*(7), 32–36.

Greene, R. W. (2014). *Lost at school: Why our kids with behavioral challenges are falling through the cracks and how we can help them.* New York, NY: Scribner.

Greteman, A. J. (2017). Helping kids turn out queer: Queer theory in art education. *Studies in Art Education, 58*(3), 195–205.

Hill, J. D., & Bjork, C. L. (2008). *Classroom instruction that works with English language learners: Facilitator's guide.* Alexandria, VA: Association for Supervision and Curriculum Development.

Hseih, K. (2016). Preservice art teachers' attitudes toward addressing LGBTQ issues in their future classrooms. *Studies in Art Education, 57*(2), 120–138.

Huesmann, G. R. (2010). How understanding the neurobiology of autism can help you choose effective teaching strategies. In B. L. Gerber & J. Kellman (Eds.), *Understanding students with autism through art* (pp. 38–53). Reston, VA: National Art Education Association.

Hunt, E. (2011). *Human intelligence.* New York, NY: Cambridge University Press.

Jantz, P. B., Davies, S. C., & Bigler, E. D. (2014). *Working with traumatic brain injury in schools: Transition, assessment, and intervention.* New York, NY: Routledge.

Kraft, M., & Keifer-Boyd, K. (2013). *Including difference: A communitarian approach to art education in the least restrictive environment.* Reston, VA: National Art Education Association.

Latta, M. M., & Chan, E. (2011). *Teaching the arts to engage English language learners.* New York, NY: Routledge.

Lewis, S., & Allman, C. B. (2014). Instruction and assessment: General principles and strategies. In C. B. Allman & S. Lewis (Eds.), *ECC essentials: Teaching the expanded core curriculum to students with visual impairments.* New York, NY: American Foundation for the Blind Press.

Loesl, S. D. (2010). Understanding and interpreting the ASD "puzzle". In B. L. Gerber & J. Kellman (Eds.), *Understanding students with autism through art* (pp. 71–82). Reston, VA: National Art Education Association.

Maree, J. G. K., & van der Westhuizen, C. N. (2009). Giftedness and diversity: Research and education in Africa. In L. Shavinina (Ed.), *International handbook on giftedness* (pp. 1409–1425). New York, NY: Springer.

McFarland, J., Hussar, B., Wang, X., Zhang, J., Wang, K., Rathbun, A., . . . Bullock Mann, F. (2018). *The Condition of Education 2018* (NCES 2018–144). U.S. Department of Education. Washington, DC: National Center for Education Statistics. Retrieved [date] from https://nces.ed.gov/pubsearch/pubsinfo.asp?pubid=2018144

Mead, S. (2010). Reading for life. *American Prospect, 21*(6), A2–5.

National Center for School Engagement. (2008). *What is truancy?* Retrieved from http://ojjdp.ncjrs.org/truancy/pdf/FactsonTruancy.pdf

Rothstein, R. (2008). Whose problem is poverty? *Educational Leadership, 65*(7), 8–13.

Russell, S. T., & Fish, J. N. (2016). Mental health in lesbian, gay, bisexual and transgender (LGBT) youth. *Annual Review of Clinical Psychology, 12,* 465–487.

Sanders, J., & Gubes Vaz, T. (2014). Dialogue on queering arts education across the Americas. *Studies in Art Education, 55*(4), 328–341.

Semple, R. H., Lee, J., Rosa, D., & Miller, L. F. (2010). A randomized trial of mindfulness-based cognitive therapy for children: Promoting mindful attention to enhance social-emotional resiliency in children. *Journal of Child & Family Studies, 19,* 218–229.

Silverman, L. K., & Miller, N. B. (2009). A feminine perspective of giftedness. In L. Shavinina (Ed.), *International handbook on giftedness* (pp. 99–128). New York, NY: Springer.

Smith, T. E., Polloway, E. A., Patton, J. R., & Dowdy, C. A. (2012). *Teaching students with special needs in inclusive settings* (6th ed.). Boston, MA: Pearson.

Spencer, P. E., & Marschark, M. (2010). *Evidence-based practice in educating deaf and hard-of-hearing students.* New York, NY: Oxford University Press.

Storvik, H., Boine, M., Johansen, R., & Berg, Å. K. (2012). *Er vi her ennå?* Norway: Aslaug Krokann Berg and Helle Storvik.

United Nations. (2005). *World youth report 2005: Young people today and in 2015.* Retrieved from www.un.org/esa/socdev/unyin/documents/wyr05book.pdf

United Nations Children's Fund (UNICEF). (2013). *The state of the world's children 2013: Children with disabilities.* Retrieved from www.unicef.org/sowc2013/files/SWCR2013_ENG_Lo_res_24_Apr_2013.pdf

United Nations Global Education First. (2012). *Global education first initiative: An initiative of the United Nations Secretary-General.* Retrieved from www.globaleducationfirst.org/files/GEFI_Brochure_ENG.pdf

U.S. Department of Education. (2002). *Public law print of PL 107–110, the No Child Left Behind Act of 2001.* (Title IX, Part A, Section 9101(22), p. 544). Retrieved from www2.ed.gov/policy/elsec/leg/esea02/107-110.pdf

U.S. Department of Education. (2017). *The benefits of being bilingual—A review for teachers and other early education program providers.* Retrieved from https://www2.ed.gov/documents/early-learning/talk-read-sing/bilingual-en.pdf

U.S. Department of Education Individuals with Disabilities Education Act. (2006). *Subpart A: General.* Retrieved from https://sites.ed.gov/idea/regs/b/a/300.8

U.S. Department of Education Institute of Education Sciences. (2018). *Children and youth with disabilities.* Retrieved from http://nces.ed.gov/programs/coe/indicator_cgg.asp

Weinstock, J. (2013). Assimilation of the Sámi: Its unforeseen effects on the majority populations of Scandinavia. *Scandinavian Studies, 85*(4), 411–430.

Wolin, S. J., & Wolin, S. (1993). *The resilient self: How survivors of troubled families rise above adversity.* New York, NY: Villard Books.

World Health Organization. (2002). *Towards a common language for functioning, disability, and health: THE ICF.* Geneva, Switzerland: World Health Organization. Retrieved from www.who.int/classifications/icf/training/icfbeginnersguide.pdf

Zeng, L., Proctor, R. W., & Salvendy, G. (2011). Can traditional divergent thinking tests be trusted in measuring and predicting real-world creativity? *Creativity Research Journal, 23*(1), 24–37.

# PART III

# Art Inquiry Methods

# Chapter 7

# Aesthetics

## Art's Meaning

FIGURE 7.1 Elementary installation, United States.

*Source: Brittany Gardner and David Reynolds, teachers. The quotes in Spotlight on Student Art #7 on art's meanings by Brittany Gardner, Skyler Atwell, Violet Breedlove, and Van Breedlove were derived from lessons taught by Brittany Gardner, Eric Breedlove, Rebecca Hunter, Mike Muller, Suzanne St. John, and the author.*

**Aesthetics** is the sensory and intellectual philosophy that defines art and the nature of beauty. Its guiding questions include "What is art?" and "What is beauty?" In 1735, German philosopher Alexander Baumgarten adapted the Greek word *aisthetikos*, meaning sensation, to explain aesthetic taste and beauty in art. **Aestheticians** (philosophers who disseminate knowledge of established standards in art) employ theories, specialized vocabulary, and their expertise to describe art's meanings and evolutions on thoughts about what constitutes art. Aesthetic inquiry encourages students to articulate definitions of art, search for meaning, and broaden their perspectives by learning other people's views about what art might be. When viewing meaningful and/or beautiful artworks, students often want to share their perspectives with others so that they too can experience similar feelings to their own (Parker, 2010; Vandenabeele, 2008). Through aesthetic inquiry, we can guide students in becoming competent in articulating their perspectives on art using critical thinking skills and artistic vocabulary. Studying aesthetics in context, students come in contact with exciting artworks and learn to identify meanings in global artistic creations. We teach them how to develop a broader understanding of art's roles and relevance in society. Identifying art as an **open concept**, students learn that societies' definitions of art change over time and people's perceptions about art evolve. They become acquainted with societies' diversified aesthetic values and beliefs.

We will meet the following objectives by participating in this chapter:

- Define aesthetics and explain its purpose in the choice-based art curriculum.
- Identify best practices for teaching students aesthetic inquiry methods.
- Develop instructional resources for teaching aesthetics.

Spotlight on Student Art #7 (Figure 7.1) provides a sampling of pre-K–12 students' perspectives on art through class discussions, writing activities, and art production tasks. It presents examples of how students connect aesthetic inquiry to life.

### Spotlight on Student Art #7

### Big Idea: Art

"Art is all around us," enthusiastically explained a teacher preparing to lead an art inquiry lesson for students to create an art installation using only straws (Figure 7.1). She exclaimed: "Anything you see in your daily life has the potential to become art. All it takes is imagination." The teacher reinforced these concepts by showing students artworks by Tara Donovan, who uses gigantic quantities of a single found object, such as toothpicks, to create sculpted designs. The teacher prepared aesthetic questions about Donovan's work so that students could consider possible meanings about the artist's creative choices and think about their own art production methods. This included how their arrangement of approximately 20,000 colorful drinking straws around a school water fountain would impact their installation's design.

In teaching a choice-based art curriculum, educators ask students of all ages to contemplate art's meaning through aesthetic inquiry. During an aesthetics discussion in an early childhood classroom, students described art as beautiful and valued art's role in making people feel better. During an upper elementary lesson in the non-school hours, a student explained, "Art is when you express yourself." She identified art as something that people share with others. Another student added, "I believe art is, the expression of thoughts and feelings through creativity using any tools, or material, even JUNK!" In a middle school art class, students equated art with magic because of the sensations and feelings that artworks can produce. At a high school, a student connected art with humanity, stating, "It expresses emotions and thoughts of a society."

These students' varied responses resulted from their exposure to quality art instruction that included aesthetic learning tasks. Students' reflected on art's meanings, visual qualities, materials, emotions, and value. In planning the art installation lesson, the teacher's goal was to inspire students to think about art's role in life and demonstrate how art can be accessible to all students when creating with repurposed materials. Students made personal connections to the artworks they studied, listened to peer's perspectives, and solved creative problems through aesthetic inquiry. Their arrangement of colorful straws, a material not typically recognized as an art supply, beautified and added meaning to the negative space around a school water fountain. It became a site for discussions about art and its roles in society.

## AESTHETICS

Aestheticians construct new knowledge and theories to aid society in determining which artistic products to value and preserve (Leddy, 2005; Sepänmaa, 2010). Their practice of contemplating experiences relating to art and its production has caused disputes about what is art and what is not art. Teachers can explain to students that some scholars have decided that art cannot be defined because people disagree if certain products are art. Other scholars apply their expertise to define art, including Anderson (2000), who outlined the global artistic traits that make something art:

> They are the result of human production; they are created through exceptional physical, conceptual, or imaginative skill in a public medium, with the intention of provoking a sensuous effect; and they share stylistic conventions with other works from the same time and place.
>
> (p. 8)

**Institutionalism** is a theory that deems that for an artwork to be considered art, it must be recognized by the members of the art world who determine art's worth (Dickie, 1971, 1974). This perspective maintains that individual artists cannot validly identify their works as art without the art world's recognition. Artists may disagree.

**Conceptualism** is a theory that opposes institutionalism. It considers artists' perspectives in determining the nature of art. Some artists break away from established artistic dogmas to affront the art world. They intentionally challenge accepted perceptions of what is considered art by pushing boundaries and may shock audiences to redefine

what is acceptable as art. They claim the idea for making artwork is just as valuable as what makes the work itself. For example, Marcel Duchamp made **readymade** art, conceptual art "created" with everyday objects taken out of their original contexts and functions. His 1917 readymade, *Fountain*, an upside down urinal signed R. Mutt, shocked the art world at the time. It has since become part of a museum collection and inspired many artists (see Figure 7.1.1). As new generations of artists create artworks and new technologies emerge, artists' products build upon previous artists' works, form hybrid designs, and further expand society's knowledge and understanding of what art can be (Baker, Schleser, & Molga, 2009). Like Duchamp, Pablo Cano creates with found objects, which has become an accepted artistic practice. The contemporary art world recognizes Cano's marionettes as art due to his creative designs, multimedia performances, use of materials, and subject matter (Figures 7.2 and 7.3).

**Appropriation** is an aesthetic topic that addresses artists' use of other artists' works as inspiration to produce their own art. Artists appropriate for various reasons. Some honor artists' creations by designing new works that clearly reference inspiration works. For example, Cano's *The Blue Ribbon* production pays tribute to famous artworks that inspired him (see Artists' Lessons to Thrive! 7.1 and Figures 7.4 and 7.5). The inspiration artworks are recognizable, yet Cano's marionettes and puppets differ in their functions and materials. Some artists appropriate to perfect artists' advanced techniques. Some artists anticipate instant recognition by building on already famous works; however, when copying works too closely, artists risk copyright infringement for stealing others' intellectual property.

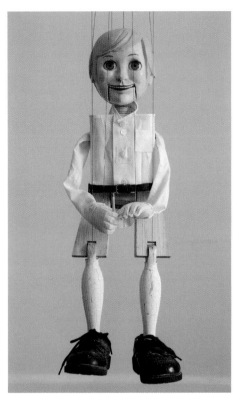

FIGURE 7.2 Pablo Cano, *Calum Marionette, The Blue Ribbon Marionette Production*, 2009.
*Source: Jose Rodriguez, photo.*

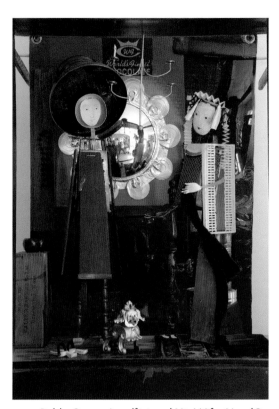

FIGURE 7.4 Pablo Cano, *Arnolfini and His Wife, Hand Puppets, The Blue Ribbon Marionette Production*, 2009.
*Source: Jose Rodriguez, photograph.*

FIGURE 7.3 Pablo Cano, *Queen Elizabeth Marionette, The Blue Ribbon Marionette Production*, 2009.
*Source: Jose Rodriguez, photo.*

FIGURE 7.5 Pablo Cano, *Campbell's Tomato Soup Can, Marionette, The Blue Ribbon Marionette Production*, 2009.
*Source: Jose Rodriguez, photo.*

FIGURE 7.1.1 Pablo Cano, *R. MUTT, Hand Puppet, The Blue Ribbon Marionette Production*, 2009. Author: Margarita Cano. Choreography: Katherine Kramer. Artist and Film Maker: Clifton Childree. Artist: Pablo Cano. Original Music: Max Farber, Mike Gold, Miriam Stern, Kenneth Metzker, and Diogo Olivera. MOCA, Executive Director Bonnie Clearwater, North Miami FL.

*Source: Jose Rodriguez, photo.*

FIGURE 7.1.2 Pablo Cano, *Mona Lisa, Hand Puppet, The Blue Ribbon Marionette Production*, 2009. Author: Margarita Cano. Choreography: Katherine Kramer. Artist and Film Maker: Clifton Childree. Artist: Pablo Cano. Original Music: Max Farber, Mike Gold, Miriam Stern, Kenneth Metzker, and Diogo Olivera. MOCA, Executive Director Bonnie Clearwater, North Miami FL.

*Source: Jose Rodriguez, photo.*

Pablo Cano creates spectacular marionette productions inspired by his Cuban heritage, family stories, and the artists he studied in college. He began making puppets in childhood and has continued this tradition since graduating with his Master of Fine Arts degree. When Cano first started making art as a professional artist he relied upon found objects to produce marionettes because he could not afford expensive art supplies. He achieved international recognition for his art shortly afterwards, yet continued to create with found objects because he appreciated the aesthetic qualities they produce and the challenge of finding the right materials.

In 1968, Cano's mother Margarita, who is also an artist, wrote him a story about a boy named Calum who visits an art gallery filled with master artworks (Figure 7.2). Her story inspired Cano's marionette production, called *The Blue Ribbon*, in which Cano has transformed ten master artworks—including Marcel Duchamp's *Fountain* (Figure 7.1.1), Leonardo da Vinci's *Mona Lisa* (Figure 7.1.2), Jan van Eyck's *The Arnolfini Portrait* (Figure 7.4), and Andy Warhol's *Campbell's Soup Cans* (Figure 7.5)—into marionettes. At the story's beginning, Calum feels so inspired by the master artworks that surround him that he places one of his drawings on the wall next to the famous artworks. Calum has broken the rules by hanging his art on the gallery walls and a security guard removes his work, causing Calum to cry. His sorrow captures the attention of the artworks and brings them to life in the form of marionettes. The *Queen Elizabeth* marionette sympathizes with Calum and announces the children's blue ribbon drawing competition (Figure 7.3). As the story unfolds, Cano, his cast of puppeteers, and musicians perform *The Blue Ribbon* before an audience that sit around large round tables filled with art supplies and paper placements. The marionettes approach the different tables so the audience can get a closer view. Meanwhile, the children in the audience learn that they have 20 minutes to draw a replica of one of the master artworks. Upon completion, the staff hangs the artworks on the gallery walls. Cano then selects a winner and awards a child with a beautiful handmade blue ribbon.

Cano's *The Blue Ribbon* centers on the concept of recognition because the artist fully acknowledged the value of his mother's creative storytelling and artworks by inspiration artists, whose designs he appropriated, to develop his production. Although Calum was initially prohibited from displaying his art in the gallery, he ultimately received the recognition he deserved when the *Queen Elizabeth* marionette announced the blue ribbon competition. For the production's happy ending, Calum received a blue ribbon for his drawing, just like children did in Cano's *The Blue Ribbon* live audiences.

## Essential/Guiding Questions

1. What role does recognition play in the creation of art? How did Cano recognize other artists in *The Blue Ribbon* production?
2. How would the meaning of Cano's *The Blue Ribbon* production change if he did not appropriate master artworks?

## Preparation

Students will review how to classify art using aesthetic categories (see this chapter's section titled Aesthetic Inquiry Methods for more information). They will be able to explain how artists use appropriation to create art.

## Daily Learning Targets

I can explain how Pablo Cano appropriated master artworks to form *The Blue Ribbon* production.

* I can identify at least five examples of how his work is similar and different than the master works. I can classify Pablo Cano's *The Blue Ribbon* using two aesthetic categories (i.e. mimesis, contextualism, etc.).
* I can write my answers in paragraph form.
* I can provide concrete examples to justify my classifications.

**National Core Arts Anchor Standards** 1, 6, 7, and 11

www.nationalartsstandards.org

Certain aesthetic theories describe how the senses relate to humanity's perspectives on life, as artworks have the power to express beauty and bring pleasure. In the 1960s artists began equating art with life, leading to the question, "What is life?" (Dezeuze, 2006). The philosophical unification of art and life caused philosophers to apply the same questioning to contemplate the human condition through an ecological approach, which values artmaking as a core component of the human experience (Dissanayake, 1995). Philosophers have also broadened aesthetics to develop the paradigms of **environmental aesthetics** and the **aesthetics of everyday life**, which identify the role of sensory pleasures in daily lives (Dowling, 2010; Erzen, 2005; Leddy, 2005; Sepänmaa, 2010; Vandenabeele, 2008). These philosophies teach people to value the simplest joys that life has to offer. A person may experience delight in noticing the beauty in textured patterns created by paint chipping off of an old building, the sensation of smooth porcelain against one's lips drinking aromatic coffee, and the pleasures of one's home environment. For example, Merete Rein's glassworks correlate with concepts of environmental aesthetics because they make utilitarian items more pleasurable and brighten built environment spaces (Figure 7.6 and Artists' Lessons to Thrive! 17.2). Aestheticians apply many of the same processes of discovery for analyzing art and connect these pleasurable experiences to

FIGURE 7.6 Merete Rein's glassware products reference nature with their organic, translucent designs.
*Source: Trond Are Berge, photo.*

FIGURE 7.7 Karolína Keiko Nakashima, 9-years-old, ZUŠ M. Stibora, Olomouc, Czech Republic.
*Source: ICEFA Lidice, 43rd Exhibition.*

environmental aesthetics. Teachers can point out that aestheticians suggest that people study contemporary art to understand the aesthetics of everyday life because it addresses current societal issues in the form of environmental artworks, installations, digital media, and performance pieces. Students can apply this information to make connections between artists' works in context and the things they experience in life.

Life provides special moments when people feel physically and emotionally moved by an artwork and have an **aesthetic experience**. Time and other concerns seem to slip away. An aesthetic experience might occur when a person feels astounded by nature's beauty during a walk or becomes breathless while staring at a painting. People develop a greater understanding of what objects and moments mean when they see and reflect mindfully (Csikszentmihalyi & Robinson, 1990). Thinking about art through aesthetics correlates with people's ideals of beauty, emotions, physical sensations, and cultivated taste. Sometimes people are moved by artworks that they previously disliked (Dewey, 1958). As individuals have more opportunities to examine and question the nature of art, they broaden their perspectives on what they consider art to be. The realm of aesthetics in art education has broad meanings and builds on Dewey's pragmatic understanding that aesthetics is connected to societies' beliefs and cultural mores. For example, Figures 7.7–7.9 present a collection of student photographs that illustrate a shift from photography's original purpose of depicting realism with their expressive background lighting, monochromatic colors, and silhouette forms.

FIGURE 7.8 Valerie Šafářová, 9-years-old, ZUŠ M. Stibora, Olomouc, Czech Republic.
*Source: ICEFA Lidice, 43rd Exhibition.*

FIGURE 7.9 Rudolf Pipal, 10-years-old, ZUŠ M. Stibora, Olomouc, Czech Republic.
*Source: ICEFA Lidice, 43rd Exhibition.*

## AESTHETIC INQUIRY METHODS

Teachers set students on the path to aesthetic literacy using diverse inquiry methods. Aesthetic inquiry invites students to investigate art subject matter, ask pertinent questions, explore ideas, and research meanings in art. Students' aesthetic knowledge builds gradually. Teachers integrate more complex learning tasks and introduce aesthetic theories and academic vocabulary each academic year. Given quality aesthetic learning experiences, when students reach adulthood they are well-versed in aesthetics and can do the following tasks (Erzen, 2005; Parker, 2010; Parsons, 1987).

- Ask pertinent questions about how art is categorized.
- Defend their positions on art and offer valid opinions. Their perspectives can differ from other people's views.
- Examine artworks in context and determine how their styles align with the times in which they were created.
- Identify how philosophical meanings are relative to the human condition and artists' creation of art.

Students develop rich proficiencies when they participate in aesthetic inquiry learning tasks starting in early childhood (Clark, Day, & Greer, 1987). In preschool, students see art from their personal perspectives (Parsons, 1987). They enjoy viewing bright colors and happy subject matter. They appreciate realistic and abstract art equally. Although young students do not understand art from other people's perspectives, teachers should encourage them to talk about their artistic perceptions as they examine art. In elementary school, children value art that is beautiful and contains realistic subject matter. They believe a subject is beautiful when they think an artwork is good. They typically disapprove of ugly subjects, even when rendered realistically. They prefer content that they can understand easily. To move students beyond their natural preferences, teachers can ask students to compare and contrast artworks they enjoy with selected abstract and non-beautiful artworks.

With a strong elementary foundation, early adolescents move beyond understanding art's subject matter in isolation and surpass their assumptions and presuppositions. They begin to recognize the importance of artistic expression. Students can see artworks from the subjective perspective of both a spectator and the artist, as well as recognize that people may understand artworks differently (Parsons, 1987). They can connect the artist's intentions with the overall expression of an artwork. However, unless they further their aesthetic development, young adolescents may never learn to ask questions about the accuracy of their interpretations. Adolescents who continue to augment their aesthetic knowledge in high school will develop an understanding of how content shapes art's meaning. They can read artworks' iconography and see how artists' intentionally manipulate art media to communicate ideas. They make connections using historical and social perspectives. Students learn to develop advanced aesthetic insights by categorizing art, answering aesthetic questions, and creating works inspired by aesthetic inquiry.

## Aesthetic Categories

Aestheticians develop aesthetic categories to investigate art's meaning and teach viewers to value art beyond personal preferences. Teachers apply aesthetic categories to cultivate students' multiple perspectives when studying art. This textbook uses a contextual approach to teaching the aesthetic categories that explains the stories and meanings behind the artworks' productions while providing a format for students to reflect on the formal and expressive qualities that shape artistic productions. It contains model essential/guiding questions and learning tasks using artists' works to assist teachers in creating original curricular activities that integrate the aesthetic categories. By categorizing art through aesthetics, students learn to broaden their perspectives and contemplate how artistic behaviors have inspired art's production (Anderson & Milbrandt, 2005; Hetland, Winner, Veenema, & Sheridan, 2013).

**Mimesis** is the most widely recognized and appreciated aesthetic category. The Greek philosopher Plato first expressed that art was the imitation of real-world objects. He equated artists with forgers because of their ability to copy accurately from life (Rosen, 2005). The purpose of mimetic art is to mimic reality so that the objects within artworks look realistic. Oftentimes, mimetic artists strive to create objects that look better than they really do, as seen in idealized Greek and Roman sculptures, portraits, and depictions of religious and historic events. Teachers can use the following questions and tasks for students to compare and contrast Le Nain, *Three Young Musicians* (Figure 7.10) with David Y. Chang's pastel painting *Pipa Solo* (Figure 7.11) to study mimesis in context. Both artworks depict realistic representations of the human form.

- Why might mimetic accuracy be the most appropriate artistic method to convey these artworks' meanings, which the artists created more than 300 years apart?
- Create a realistic artwork using the theme of your choice. Determine why realism would be

FIGURE 7.10 Antoine Le Nain, *Three Young Musicians*, c. 1630. Oil on wood panel: 10 3/4 × 13 1/2 in. (27.31 × 34.29 cm). LACMA Public Domain.
*Source: www.lacma.org*

FIGURE 7.11 David Y. Chang, *Pipa Solo*. Pastel.
*Source: Courtesy of David Y. Chang, artist.*

the best form to communicate what you have to say about this particular topic. How might the meaning of your art change if it were not mimetic?

**Formalism** is the category that values artists' unique and highly proficient application of design through the elements and principles of art. Aestheticians see worth in the artist's self-expression, quality composition, and use of media. Formalist theory began with philosophers Immanuel Kant, Roger Fry, and Clive Bell, who viewed art objectively. Kant (1952), a leading 18th century philosopher, examined art through a **disinterested** stance, meaning that the philosopher ignored the circumstances revolving around an artwork's creation and focused solely on its formal elements. Artists create formalist art for art's sake, as issues outside of the artwork and emotions are unimportant to its understanding. Formalist aestheticians look at an artwork's design qualities only to interpret its meaning. Formalist theory remains disconnected from daily life experiences and is limited to thorough examination of the artwork itself. Formalist aestheticians have the knowledge and skills to ignore external forces that might distract the viewer from understanding the artwork and concentrate solely on the application of art media and the artist's representation of significant form (Parsons & Blocker, 1993). Many early formalists rejected realistic art and preferred abstract and nonrepresentational art. Teachers can use the following questions and tasks for students to compare and contrast Robert Delaunay's *Circular Forms* (Figure 7.12) with David Patchen's *Foglio* (Figure 7.13) to study formalism in context.

- Delaunay and Patchen designed colorful abstract forms that reveal artistic skill in their chosen media. Use a formalist perspective to identify the works' similarities. Did applying a purely formalist technique provide you with a full understanding of these artworks? Is there any other information you need to know that extends beyond their formal designs?
- Create an artwork using the media of your choice that incorporates at least two of the artists' shared design features. After completing your work, explain why you selected the art media and design qualities that you did.

FIGURE 7.12 Robert Delaunay, *Circular Forms*, 1930. Oil on canvas. 26.4 × 43.2 in. (67.3 × 109.8 cm). Solomon R. Guggenheim Museum, New York Gift, Andrew Powie Fuller and Geraldine Spreckels Fuller Collection, 1999. CC0 Public Domain via Wikimedia Commons.
*Source: https://creativecommons.org/publicdomain/zero/1.0/deed.en*

FIGURE 7.13 David Patchen, *Foglio*, blown glass.
*Source: Courtesy of the artist; www.davidpatchen.com.*

**Expressionism** is the category that aestheticians use to evaluate emotion in art. Individuals may become overwhelmed with feelings as they recognize the artist's pure emotions placed within the work, or feel moved by the artwork's subject matter. Dickie (1974) argued against a disinterested examination and considered how emotions impact viewers' thoughts and psychological reactions to art. Collingwood (1983) interpreted art as a self-expressive medium that arouses human emotion. People learn how to explore their unique emotions by talking about art. Tolstoy (1932) appreciated art for its ability to express human spirituality and viewed art as a natural part of humanity. The emotions people feel about an artwork are like a spiritual force that guides them. People experience

emotional responses as they interpret the meaning of artists' expressive symbols. Langer (1971) argued that teaching aesthetics instructs students to examine artists' expressive works as resources to communicate subjective feelings (Parsons & Blocker, 1993). Teachers can use the following questions and tasks for students to compare and contrast Franz Marc's *Dreaming Horse* (Figure 7.14) with Meghan O'Connor's *Birds of a Feather Blend Together* (Artists' Lessons to Thrive! 7.2). Although both artworks have animal subject matter, the artists presented their expressive content using different media and styles.

- Marc and O'Connor presented animal forms to articulate ideas about humanity. Based on your initial observations, what emotions do you think the artworks portray? What visual qualities can you cite as evidence to support your beliefs? How might knowing the contextual stories behind their production change the way they make you feel? (Students can research Franz Marc and reference Artists' Lessons to Thrive! 7.2 to learn more.)
- Reflect on a strong emotion you experienced. Illustrate this emotion using symbols, colors, and marks. Describe its meaning privately as a written response or share it with others.

FIGURE 7.14 Franz Marc, *Dreaming Horse*, 1913. Watercolor, gouache, ink, and graphite on paper. 15.5 × 18.4 in. (39.6 cm × 46.8 cm). Solomon R. Guggenheim Museum, New York Solomon R. Guggenheim Founding Collection. CC0 Public Domain via Wikimedia Commons.
*Source: https://creativecommons.org/publicdomain/zero/1.0/ deed.en*

FIGURE 7.2.1 Meghan O'Connor, *Birds of a Feather Blend Together*, 2010. Woodcut with framing.
*Source: Courtesy of the artist; www.curlymeg88.com.*

Birds of a feather flock together, in life and in Meghan O'Connor's expressive artworks. Flocks of
birds represent safety in numbers. When referencing human nature, the proverb identifies how like-
minded individuals prefer each other's companionship. O'Connor regularly incorporates birds as iconic
symbols for humanity in her drawings, prints, and mixed media works. While her birds have beautiful,
fluffy feathers and intricate details, O'Connor incorporates visual references, including heavy marks
and juxtaposition of irregular objects, to signify that something unusual is taking place within the birds'
immediate vicinities. Her woodcut *Birds of a Feather Blend Together* (Figure 7.2.1) depicts three birds
surrounded by a bright red window frame. The birds, resting on perches, stare directly at the viewer.
They serve as physical barriers that prevent onlookers from entering the kitchen, which is normally
meant to be an open and welcoming home environment. O'Connor has designed the kitchen as a
crowded space filled with seven blenders that bear the brand name Aviary, indicating that they were
developed especially for the birds.

While O'Connor's flock symbolizes humanity, her blenders signify sources of power. The artist's large
grouping of this seemingly banal household appliance shows their strength in numbers and alludes
to a mechanical flock. The blenders have the power to influence human behavior with their electrical
charges. Their powerful force has taken over one of the birds, whose core lacks its original organic
components. O'Connor explained that the two remaining organic birds recognize the mechanized
bird's physical and emotional transformation. Yet, despite their identification of these drastic changes,
O'Connor has illustrated hope for humanity by providing the organic birds with a possible way out of
the situation. The pair can decide to remain on their perches or take their power back as fully aware,

conscious beings willing to navigate bravely through the scenario O'Connor has presented and escape through the window above the faucet or through the artwork's foreground. O'Connor explained: "They know it will be a difficult path: making a choice that is the best for self, but not necessarily the most convenient or easy choice." Will they provide the blenders with additional power through further self-destructive behaviors? Or will they show that they can control their unhealthy impulses and emotions? As individuals, each bird must determine if the flock provides healthy companionship or if they have indeed joined the wrong flock, as people sometimes fall into the wrong crowd and lose their sense of self. By making the decision to fly away to a better environment, the pair will have demonstrated to themselves that they have strength of character to begin anew.

## Essential/Guiding Questions

1. What does strength of character mean to you? Why do people sometimes say that they need to regain their power and inner strength?
2. How has O'Connor presented a power struggle in *Birds of a Feather Blend Together*? Why do you think she has chosen to represent animals and machines instead of people to depict human concerns?

## Preparation

Students will discuss the big idea of strength of character and show their understanding of the subject by providing their own examples. They will also discuss the meaning of a metaphor and identify ways to present a metaphor through art.

## Daily Learning Targets

I can write a paragraph that explains how O'Connor's *Birds of a Feather Blend Together* correlates with the aesthetic category expressionism.

- I can provide at least two examples to defend my position.
- I can present my response in my journal.

I can create an artwork that depicts the concept strength of character using the media of my choice.

- I can incorporate a metaphor into my design.
- I can show craftspersonship and unity in my creation.

**National Core Arts Anchor Standards** 2, 4, 9, and 11

www.nationalartsstandards.org

*Quoted artists' statements not listed in the reference section result from personal communications with the author (personal communications, 2014–2018).*

**Contextualism** asks viewers to examine art from social, historical, and/or political perspectives. The human stories and cultural information that surround artworks provide clues for understanding art's meaning and the things that society values. This approach differs from the formalist model because it advocates that context, regardless of an artwork's form, is always present, whether one chooses to acknowledge it or ignore it (Parsons & Blocker, 1993). Aestheticians investigate the stories and times that influenced an artwork's production. They research artists' life experiences and examine the role of artists' cultures, environments, and personal interactions in shaping art. Aestheticians begin contextual investigations by selecting an entry point to examine a single artwork or related artworks to form judgments (McFee, 2011). Teachers can use the following questions and tasks for students to compare and contrast Maya Lin's Vietnam Veterans Memorial (Artists'

Lessons to Thrive! 7.3) with Vannoy Streeter's *Feldhaus Hearse* (Figure 7.15) to study contextualism in context. Both works convey stories about the loss of human life.

- How might understanding funeral rituals, memorials, loss, and traditions help explain Lin's and Streeter's artworks? From what other perspectives might you explore their meanings?
- Research the big ideas of loss, tradition, or memory to create an artwork. Explain how Lin's and Streeter's art impacted your reflection and interpretations of the topic you selected. How were you able to make personal connections to what you studied?

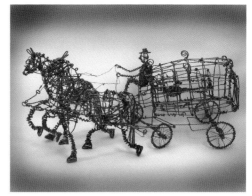

FIGURE 7.15 Vannoy Streeter's *Feldhaus Hearse* illustrates a funeral ritual in his rural community. Collection of David Feldhaus of Feldhaus Memorial Chapel.
*Source: Jonathan Griffith, photo.*

## Artists' Lessons to Thrive! 7.3 Maya Lin: Remembrance, Hope, and Inspiration Through the Vietnam Veterans Memorial

### Big Idea: Remembrance

Memorials serve as symbols of remembrance, hope, and inspiration to commemorate those who lost their lives. Maya Lin designed the Vietnam Veterans Memorial as an apolitical tribute to fallen soldiers. Loss can be especially difficult to overcome for loved ones who are left behind. Taking this into account, Lin formed an original memorial design that simultaneously provides memorial visitors the opportunity to grieve and a means to find a sense of inner peace. She invoked these emotional qualities through her monument's minimalistic V-shaped design, reminiscent of a bird flying through the sky (Figure 7.3.1). One wing, approximately 250 feet (76.2 m) in length, points to the Washington Monument and the other (of equal length) points to the Lincoln Memorial. Her alignment of the Vietnam Veterans Memorial with these landmarks identifies their historic relevance. The memorial's highly polished black granite surface rises from the ground and stands in unison with the surrounding earth. It bears the names of more than 58,000 fallen and missing soldiers. Lin arranged their names in uniform, chronological rows that date the loss of life to bestow feelings of simple elegance, dignity, and honor for the soldiers.

The Vietnam Veterans Memorial departs from typical war memorials that depict idealized human forms and weaponry. Due to its lack of figurative content, Lin provided a contextual narrative to accompany her design proposal so that people could understand its meaning. She explained: "The memorial is composed not as an unchanging monument, but as a moving composition to be understood as we move into and out of it" (Vietnam Veterans Memorial Fund [VVMF], 2018). One must participate in its space to comprehend it fully. Individuals feel smaller as they descend into the memorial. The surrounding landscape gradually slopes downward and the memorial's stone slabs peak at 10 feet (3.048 m) from the ground surface at its vertex. As visitors become one with the environment, visitors grieve the enormous loss of life. Lin explained: "For death, is in the end a personal and private matter, and the area contained with this memorial is a quiet place, meant for personal reflection and private reckoning" (VVMF, 2018). The reflective black stone panels gently mirror visitors' reflections. Visitors feel enticed to reach out and touch the panels to come in direct contact with the names of the fallen (Figure 7.3.2). The experience can feel overwhelming, causing an aesthetic experience as they glance

FIGURE 7.3.1 Maya Lin, *Vietnam Veterans Memorial*, 1982.
Carol M. Highsmith's America. Cropped photo.
*Source: Library of Congress, Prints and Photographs Division.*

FIGURE 7.3.2 Maya Lin, *Vietnam Veterans Memorial*, 1982.
*Source: Photo by E.J. Hersom. (The appearance of U.S. Department of Defense [DoD] visual information does not imply or constitute DoD endorsement.)*

upon what appears to be an infinite sea of names. The reflections of the living are superimposed on the names of the deceased, creating an additional link between the past and present. Ultimately, Lin's *Vietnam Veterans Memorial* offers a semblance of peace for those left behind.

## Essential/Guiding Questions

1. In your opinion, what qualities should a memorial possess? What qualities make Lin's *Vietnam Veterans Memorial* an effective work?
2. What role do traditions play in honoring the loss of life? How might the act of remembrance enable those left behind to cope with the loss of their loved ones?

## Preparation

Students will discuss how remembrance can help people cope with losses, as well as identify examples of memorials they have seen in their own communities and in the media. They will review McRorie's (1996) six classifications of aesthetic questioning in this chapter's Aesthetic Questioning section.

## Daily Learning Targets

I can research the big ideas remembrance, loss, hope, and tradition to create an artwork that pays homage to a person and/or event from the past.

- I can provide contextual details to explain how Lin's Vietnam Veterans Memorial and my understanding of remembrance, loss, hope, and tradition impacted my interpretation of the subject matter.
- I can refine my work to hone my ideas, as well as show craftspersonship, emphasis, and unity in my completed design.

I can write six aesthetic questions on Maya Lin's *Vietnam Veterans Memorial* using Sally McRorie's model.

- I can create one question for each of McRorie's six classifications.
- I can answer my original questions in my journal, using complete sentences.

**National Core Arts Anchor Standards** 3, 5, 8, and 10

www.nationalartsstandards.org

---

**Instrumentalism** is associated with contextualism. It identifies art made with the intention of serving a purpose beyond itself. It addresses issues relating to religion, ethnicity, gender, politics, and marketing in art and mass-produced products (Lankford, 1992). Instrumentalist works include informative and helpful artworks, posters, billboards, and signs that benefit society. It also identifies artworks that are used for propaganda to sway people's opinions (such as mandated images of a dictator in private and public spaces). **Pragmatism** is an instrumentalist theory that

philosophers apply to study images in visual culture. Dewey (1938) was a leading advocate for pragmatic aesthetic theory because he believed that the arts extended beyond high art and had the ability to promote fairness and quality living. Pragmatic thinking recognizes that art functions as a vehicle to encourage society to produce actions (Duncum, 2008, 2010). Building on Dewey's pragmatic beliefs, contemporary aestheticians use multiple approaches to interpret pragmatic theory, which can revolve around issues including social justice, democracy, self-enrichment, and equality (Shusterman, 2006). Teachers can apply institutionalism and pragmatic theories to introduce students to the ways in which visual culture influences daily living (Anderson & Milbrandt, 2005). They can also use the following questions and tasks for students to compare and contrast the two environments and the slogan presented within *Discover the Forest Public Service Advertising Campaign* by the U.S. Forest Service and Ad Council (Figure 7.16). It is an example of institutionalism and pragmatism because the Ad Council designed it as a public service announcement to educate children and better their lives.

- What visual qualities does *Discover the Forest Public Service Advertising Campaign* contain to encourage children to spend time in nature? In which ways is its design most successful in communicating this message?
- Using the media of your choice, design a public service announcement that teaches constructive recreational activities. After its completion, identify the visual qualities you incorporated into your design to make your advertisement appealing to its targeted audience.

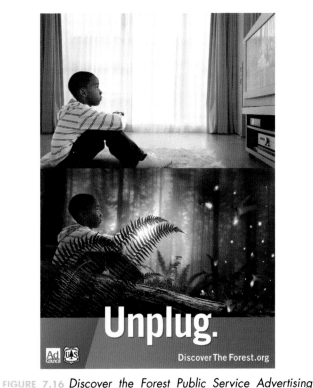

FIGURE 7.16 *Discover the Forest Public Service Advertising Campaign* by U.S. Forest Service and the Ad Council.
Source: *Forest Public Service Advertising Campaign by U.S. Forest Service and the Ad Council.*

FIGURE 7.17 Teams of early adolescents identify artworks using aesthetic categories. United States.
Source: Author, Cara Brown, and J. Quinton Creasy, teachers.

With guidance, students learn how to apply **multiple aesthetic categories** to discuss a single artwork as an alternative to examining each aesthetic category in isolation. To foster this ability, teachers might introduce lessons that present a single aesthetic category (ideal for young learners) or a few categories at a time. Students will become acquainted with each category's unique qualities and apply their building knowledge to inquiry activities. For example, students could describe Pablo Cano's *Calum* (Figure 7.2) through contextualism because they could describe how appropriation, his mother's story, and artistic inspirations shaped its production. Students could also classify *Calum* as an expressionist artwork because Cano entertains audiences through his marionette productions. They could analyze *Calum* according to the marionette's formal qualities, including its form, movement, and color. In addition to talking and writing about the aesthetic categories, teachers can develop matching games in which teams of students identify the aesthetic category that they believe matches a particular artwork best and then justify their positions to the class (Figure 7.17).

## Aesthetic Questioning

Sally McRorie (1996) developed six classifications of aesthetic questioning to contemplate art's possible meanings. They include (a) definitions of art, (b) artist centered issues, (c) audience centered issues,

(d) cultural context, (e) criticism and interpretation, and (f) values in art. The following list describes each classification using model questions inspired by Pablo Cano's *Matilda Hippo* (Figure 7.18). Matilda is looking for love, and sings *Where the Boys Are*. Students can answer the model questions on *Matilda Hippo* in oral and written forms.

1. **Definitions of Art**: McRorie's (1996) model invites students to investigate art's definitions and meanings using guiding questions such as "What is art?" and "What is beauty?". To begin, students can examine an artwork's unique features to determine the qualities that make the product art. These characteristics may reflect the features that make art pleasing to look at, or may reflect its materials. Students call upon the aesthetic categories to answer questions about the definitions of art and make judgments. For example, they can apply formalism to consider the function of art media in producing the finished design or contextualism to

FIGURE 7.18 Pablo Cano, *Matilda Hippo*, marionette/hand puppet, *For Heaven's Sake*, 2003.
*Source: Jose Rodriguez, photo.*

investigate how social influences have shaped the meaning of the artwork.

- If *Matilda Hippo* did not have any strings or moving pieces, would she still be art?
- Is *Matilda Hippo* an artwork, a performance piece, or something else? Explain your answer.

2. **Artist-Centered Issues**: Students answer questions about artists' roles when considering artist-centered issues. These questions provide students with a means to determine the artist's decisions and intents. Students explore the criteria that make a person an artist and how an artist's style impacts an artwork.

- Why did Cano choose to make *Matilda Hippo* with found objects?
- What is *Matilda Hippo's* best feature? Do you think that Cano would agree with you?

3. **Audience-Centered Issues**: Viewers take the spotlight in audience-centered issues. Students enjoy delving into audience-centered questions because they give them a chance to identify their perspectives on art. Audience-centered issues examine the materials and knowledge that students bring to an artwork. For example, an artwork may include representations of things students prefer, such as colors, objects, or materials. It might also relate to students' memories.

- If you love hippopotami, does that mean that you love *Matilda Hippo*?
- Would you want to operate *Matilda Hippo*? Or would you prefer to watch Cano perform with her? What song would you like her to sing to you?

4. **Cultural Context**: Questions within a cultural context might include a person's geographical association, spiritual beliefs, age, race, gender, social groups, and other criteria. The culture a person belongs to influences the way that person defines objects as art. Through contextual examinations, students may identify how traditions might relate to art's production. Students need not belong to a specific group described in the cultural questions to answer them. For example, students can contemplate what they thought life might have been like for people living within different times, places, or groups in response to what they see depicted in art.

- How might children view *Matilda Hippo* differently than adults? Who would have more fun with *Matilda Hippo*?
- Does *Matilda Hippo* belong on display at a museum, singing on stage, performing at a birthday party, or somewhere else?

5. **Criticism and Interpretation**: This approach has students consider the differences between preferences and judgments in art. Interpretations about art lead students to ask "what if" questions. Students learn to contemplate art from different perspectives. They consider how meanings might change if an artwork would be presented in a different way, or contained other subject matter. Based on their artistic preferences, students may judge an artwork as important, even though they may not like it. Or, they may have a special preference for an artwork that they know would never hang in a museum or appear in an art history book because it moves them or was created by someone special to them.

- Is *Matilda Hippo* happy? How can you judge?
- How would the meaning of *Matilda Hippo* change if Cano carved her in stone?

6. **Values in Art**: People make value judgments about art. They read headlines about art in newspapers and online, hear citizens' comments regarding the value of art in their communities, and observe how people pay money to purchase art. A work deemed a masterpiece costs a lot of money; whereas most children's drawings hold sentimental value. Community values determine the look of an environment and what types of artworks belong within that community. For example, many people feel that public art purchased with taxpayer money should fit the wishes and aesthetic tastes of the majority of community members. Aesthetic values can lead to censorship, which prevents artworks from being shown to the general public. They may even result in their destruction. Another value in art includes identifying a work's authenticity. Is a forged artwork worth as much or more than an original? Values also call upon society to make ethical considerations and identify how much money should be spent on art.

- Should artists like Cano be rewarded for creating art with repurposed objects and reducing waste? If so, how might you reward them?
- If you saw *Matilda Hippo* in a museum and would not be allowed to touch her, would you think it was fair? Why do many museums have no-touch policies?

As an extension to McRorie's (1996) aesthetic questions, teachers can design an art inquiry card collection by developing a box that contains index cards with aesthetic questions and related context and visuals written in student-friendly language (Model 7.1). They can use the index cards to guide whole class discussions and students could pick and choose different cards for journal assignments and group learning tasks.

## Model 7.1
## Art Inquiry Card

Does art made as a hobby have equal worth to art made by professional artists? Explain your answer.

FIGURE 7.4.1 Richard Sickler, *St. George Lighthouse*, 2017.
*Source: Richard Sickler, photo*

## Defining and Ranking Art

Students in early childhood through adolescence can define their opinions about what constitutes art. Teachers might have students describe their definition of art in oral and/or written form at the beginning of the school year and see how their definition evolves over time. During this process, students can identify how learning tasks have shaped their perceptions of what art can be (see Spotlight on Student Art #7). Teachers and students can collect objects for class learning tasks for students to categorize as art, possibly art, and not art (Stewart, 1997). Selected objects may focus on a theme or be a collection of random objects, such as advertisements, handmade quilts, and drawings. Once students decide if the objects are art, teachers can ask them to explain their decisions. As an extension, students can choose an object they listed as not art and try to convince the class the exact opposite, that they think it is art. After the debate, teachers can ask students if the work they originally thought was not art has suddenly become art. As a separate activity, teachers can introduce students to the aesthetics of everyday life and have students collect personal items that hold value to them, such as sports cards and stuffed animals. Using their collections, teachers will ask students to explain why their personal items feel sentimental, identify their artistic qualities, and describe how they might correspond with a moment. Students will then write about and illustrate their sensory feelings towards their collectable.

Aestheticians identify how artworks suit particular purposes better than others. They answer questions about their meanings and functions, as well as make appraisals using selected criteria. **Object ranking** is an aesthetic activity that teaches students this professional skill by ranking a group of art objects according to a predetermined criterion (Stewart, 1997). For example, students could develop a list ranked from 1 to 10, with 1 being the greatest, to identify concepts such as the best communication of a big idea, the best choice for their school's art collection, or the most effective design.

## BEST PRACTICES FOR TEACHING AESTHETICS

Best practices in teaching aesthetics values students' voices in examining art in context and defining its meaning. Well-managed aesthetic inquiry lessons are practical and enjoyable activities that augment students' knowledge about the philosophy of art, whether designed as the sole focus of a lesson or unit of study or as part of a studio art lesson. Teachers' perspectives about art have the potential to impact their instructional methods. Lankford (1992) explained: "Teachers should adopt an open-minded attitude, a willingness to tolerate diverse ideas—even those that may not agree with their own" (p. 29). Students should feel comfortable expressing constructive, well-thought-out viewpoints about art, which may or may not be similar to teachers' perceptions. Before initiating aesthetic conversations, teachers should articulate ground rules that explain the types of behaviors that they anticipate. This includes maintaining a learning environment in which students feel supported as they take dissimilar stances and infuse personally-driven responses to aesthetic discussions and debates.

## OUR JOURNEY TO THRIVE CONTINUES . . .

In Chapter 8, we will learn effective methods for teaching art criticism to augment students' inquiry skills. Through comprehensive art criticism learning tasks, students become versed in making informed judgments about art and learn how to apply their knowledge of aesthetic theories to express their perspectives on art.

## CHAPTER QUESTIONS AND ACTIVITIES

1. Describe your personal definition of art and explain how you plan to teach aesthetics as part of a choice-based art curriculum.
2. Develop an original comprehensive aesthetic lesson that integrates the inquiry method(s) and artist(s) of your choice. Use the lesson plan template provided on the textbook's companion website and refer to Chapter 2 for more information on lesson plan development.
3. Begin an art inquiry card collection (Model 7.1) by decorating an index card box using the media of your choice. Then, create 25 well-designed index cards filled with aesthetic questions, issues, and art reproductions for pre-K–12 students. (Note: The

finished box (based on activities from Chapters 7–10) will contain a total of 100 cards with 25 aesthetic cards, 25 art criticism cards, 25 art history cards, and 25 visual culture cards for classroom use.)

4. Answer Artists' Lessons to Thrive! 7.1–7.3's essential/guiding questions in written form or as part of a group discussion. Complete their daily learning targets.

## References

Anderson, R. L. (2000). *American muse: Anthropological excursions into art and aesthetics.* Upper Saddle River, NJ: Prentice Hall.

Anderson, T., & Milbrandt, M. (2005). *Art for life.* Boston: McGraw Hill.

Baker, C., Schleser, M., & Molga, K. (2009). Aesthetics of mobile media art. *Journal of Media Practice, 10*(2/3), 101–122.

Clark, G., Day, M., & Greer, W. D. (1987). Discipline-based art education: Becoming students of art. *Journal of Aesthetic Education, 21*(2), 129–193.

Collingwood, R. G. (1983). *The principles of art.* Oxford: The Clarendon Press.

Csikszentmihalyi, M., & Robinson, R. E. (1990). *The art of seeing: An interpretation of the aesthetic encounter.* Malibu, CA: The J. Paul Getty Trust.

Dewey, J. (1938). *Experience and education.* New York, NY: Macmillan.

Dewey, J. (1958). *Experience in nature.* New York, NY: Dover.

Dezeuze, A. (2006). Everyday life, relational aesthetics and the transfiguration of the commonplace. *Journal of Visual Art Practice, 5*(3), 143–152.

Dickie, G. (1971). *Aesthetic: An introduction.* Indianapolis, IN: Bobbs-Merrill.

Dickie, G. (1974). *Art and the aesthetic: An institutional analysis.* Ithaca, NY: Cornell University Press.

Dissanayake, E. (1995). *Homo aestheticus: Where art comes from and why.* Seattle: University of Washington Press.

Dowling, C. (2010). The aesthetics of daily life. *British Journal of Aesthetics, 50*(3), 225–242.

Duncum, P. (2008). Holding aesthetics and ideology in tension. *Studies in Art Education, 49*(2), 122–135.

Duncum, P. (2010). The promiscuity of aesthetics. *The Journal of Social Theory in Art Education, 30,* 16–22.

Erzen, J. (2005). An ecological approach to art education: Environmental aesthetics. *International Journal of Education through Art, 1*(2), 179–186.

Hetland, L., Winner, E., Veenema, S., & Sheridan, K. (2013). *Studio thinking 2: The real benefits of visual arts education.* New York, NY: Teacher's College Press.

Kant, I. (1952/1928). *The critique of judgment* (J. C. Meredith, Trans. with analytical indexes). Oxford: The Clarendon Press.

Langer, S. (1971). The cultural importance of the arts. In R. A. Smith (Ed.), *Aesthetics and problems of education* (pp. 86–94). Urbana: University of Illinois Press.

Lankford, E. L. (1992). *Aesthetics: Issues and inquiry.* Reston, VA: National Art Education Association.

Leddy, T. (2005). The nature of everyday aesthetics. In A. Light & J. M. Smith (Eds.), *The aesthetics of everyday life* (pp. 3–22). New York, NY: Columbia University Press.

McFee, G. (2011). *Artistic judgement: A framework for philosophical aesthetics.* New York, NY: Springer.

McRorie, S. (1996). *Questioning the work of Sandy Skoglund: Aesthetics.* Retrieved from www.getty.edu/artsednet/resources/Skoglund/mcrorie.html

Parker, D. H. (2010). *The principles of aesthetics.* Charleston, SC: BiblioLife.

Parsons, M. J. (1987). *How we understand art: A cognitive developmental account of aesthetic experience.* New York: Cambridge University Press.

Parsons, M. J., & Blocker, H. G. (1993). *Aesthetics and education.* Chicago: University of Illinois Press.

Rosen, S. (2005). *Plato's republic: A study.* New Haven, CT: Yale University Press.

Sepänmaa, Y. (2010). From theoretical to applied environmental aesthetics: Academic aesthetics meets real-world demands. *Environmental Values, 19*(2010), 393–405.

Shusterman, R. (2006). Aesthetics. In J. R. Shook & J. Margolis (Eds.), *A companion to pragmatism* (pp. 352–360). Malden, MA: Blackwell.

Stewart, M. G. (1997). *Thinking through aesthetics.* Worcester, MA: Davis Publications.

Tolstoy, L. (1932). *What is art? and essays on art by Tolstóy* (A. Maude, Trans.). London: Oxford University Press.

Vandenabeele, B. (2008). The subjective universality of aesthetic judgements revisited. *British Journal of Aesthetics, 48*(4), 410–425.

Vietnam Veterans Memorial Fund. (2018). *Maya Lin's original proposal.* Retrieved from www.vvmf.org/maya-lin-design-submission

# Chapter 8

# Art Criticism

## Making Informed Judgments

**FIGURE 8.1** *We BEE-lieve in Our Multicultural Community!* suitcase exterior. Third-grade students. United States.

*Source: Author and Neely James, teachers.*

**FIGURE 8.2** Suitcase interior with self-portrait dolls and art criticism passports. Third-grade students. United States.

*Source: Author and Neely James, teachers.*

**Art criticism** refers to oral and written discussions about art for the purpose of making informed judgments about art, design, and visual culture using set criteria. Professional art critics, who hold advanced degrees in the arts, summon their expert knowledge to interpret and explain local and global artworks to their audiences. They identify how external influences—including culture, religion, geography, politics, race, ethnicity, and gender—shape our perspectives and actions in response to art. Through the choice-based art curriculum, we can introduce students to these concepts and the role of critics' subjectivities in understanding art. Art criticism is a necessary discipline for students to study because without learning how to justify opinions about art, inexperienced observers will often pass judgment on artworks without trying to comprehend their full meanings. We will apply effective art criticism learning tasks to stimulate student inquiry using relevant context and content. The comprehensive art criticism learning tasks we implement will solicit students' answers to essential questions and guide them in building enduring understandings.

We will meet the following objectives by participating in this chapter:

- Define art criticism and explain its purpose in the choice-based art curriculum.
- Identify best practices for teaching students art criticism inquiry methods.
- Develop instructional resources for teaching art criticism.

Spotlight on Student Art #8 (Figures 8.1 and 8.2) describes how students studied their class' cultures through art criticism to learn more about their collective identities and hear multicultural perspectives. Its example combines art production activities with art criticism discussions and writing activities.

## Spotlight on Student Art #8

### Big Idea: Multicultural Community

Diverse cultures and traditions abound our world. One 3rd grade class packed a suitcase and created mock passports to study multiculturalism to learn more about the cultures within their class and examine their personal and collective identities (Figures 8.1 and 8.2). The students' heritages included European, African, Mexican, Korean, and Jordanian. More than a third of the students spoke English as a second language and some were born in different countries. The students began this choice-based study by selecting the bee as their class symbol. This decision referenced a motivational sign in their classroom that read: "Welcome to our beehive, the place to bee!" They decorated the suitcase's exterior with 22 bees that swarmed around the project's slogan: "We BEE-lieve in Our Multicultural Community!" Each class member drew a second bee to symbolize their individual identity within the swarm and arranged the bees within the suitcase's interior. They filled the class suitcase with handmade self-portrait dolls.

The students documented the cultures they studied in art criticism journals and their mock passports. Each passport included the student's passport photo, name, birthday, and birthplace. For each culture they studied, students glued in wallet-sized reproductions of the multicultural artworks they selected to write about and discuss in greater depth. They compared and contrasted artworks' characteristics, contemplated their possible meanings, and articulated their judgments to earn passport stamps. The passports served as analogies for landing in international airports and receiving stamps from customs agents who authenticated their work. Similar to real passports, each one looked different due to the artworks that individual students chose to investigate. Once the students completed studying the cultures in their class, they asked to continue the project to learn about additional cultures.

## ART CRITICISM

In the 1980s, when art criticism was first implemented into the art curriculum, Ron Mitra (1986) observed that if it were not for art criticism being a required discipline identified in visual arts standards, most children would be passive observers of art. For example, they might be satisfied glancing at an artwork and forming quick opinions without contemplating why they feel the ways they do. The choice-based art curriculum is a resource to challenge students as dynamic learners who can actively examine and question art's meaning. They can make critical examinations by cogently describing, interpreting, and judging the worth of the visual images they see. When teachers teach students to examine art critically, students develop the skillsets necessary to find visual evidence within artworks and explain the reasons that guide their opinions about art. They can transfer their knowledge to create art and apply related context to understand big ideas more fully.

Art criticism, like aesthetics, enhances students' verbal and reasoning skills as they articulate viewpoints that move beyond "yes" and "no" answers. Its study bridges language arts with the visual arts because students transfer their careful observations of visual information into oral and written language. During art criticism critiques, students employ listening skills and reference the academic art vocabulary they have learned (Barrett, 2003; Feldman, 1994). Art history informs art criticism learning tasks because teachers and students utilize historical data to discuss contextual information related to visual products, including knowledge about artistic styles, dates when artists produced works, artistic influences, symbols, and cultural inspirations. Art criticism connects to aesthetics because people make critical judgments about art using aesthetic categories as their criteria (e.g. mimesis and expressionism). However, aesthetics differs from art criticism because it focuses on broad topics that address the nature and meaning of art and beauty. Art criticism involves reflective interpretations and comparative judgments about art. Students gain deeper understandings of art through informed art criticism judgments, which can lead to greater aesthetic experiences (Heid, 2005).

Like aestheticians, professional art critics set standards in art. They develop methodologies to guide their investigations of all types of art and share their judgments with the public to assist others in understanding art's meaning and value. They communicate their expert opinions about art through newspaper reviews, journal articles, blogs, books, media reports, and museum and gallery catalogues. **Persuasive criticism** is a method used by art critics to present their singular interpretations and judgments about an artwork, series of works, or exhibition for the purpose of swaying audiences' feelings and perspectives. Some contemporary art critics prefer to erase the distance between the expert critic and average person by inviting members of the public to share their opinions about art, creating collective dialogues in which people learn from each other as equal partners. Some art critics have developed expert analyses with the intentions of prompting viewers' actions in response to artworks (Cross, 2017). Art critics also combat censorship in the arts and work to accept and beget greater empathy for societies' diverse perspectives on art and life. Their opinions influence the

artworks that societies collect and value. Art critics' reviews can encourage artists as well as provide them with feedback to make their works more successful. In some cases the artists and artworks that art critics praise or reject appear to be ahead of their time (Plagens, 2005).

**Portrayal criticism** is an educational art criticism method that educators apply to teach students to interpret the meaning of artworks and form opinions (Wachowiak & Clements, 2006). Class portrayal criticism discussions encourage students to listen to, build upon, and be respectful of other people's perspectives. Students learn that there is no one right answer when forming opinions about art because people can have multiple interpretations about the same artwork. Given teacher feedback and practice, students become skilled at defending their perspectives by making connections to visual, historical, and contextual evidence (Anderson & Milbrandt, 2005; Feldman, 1967, 1994). **Visual Thinking Strategies** is a model of portrayal art criticism used by teachers and museum educators to guide students who are developing contextual knowledge of art, particularly in museum settings (Housen & Yenawine, 2001). This model asks three questions to guide student inquiries: "What is going on in this picture?" "What do you see that makes you say that?" and "What else can you find?"

To study the creations of Danish artist Karen Bit Vejle, called Bit (see Artists' Lessons to Thrive! 8.1), who practices **psaligraphy** (the art of cutting paper), teachers could prepare students for a class discussion by explaining how Bit's art form using scissors differs from papercutting in which artists cut with a sharp blade on a flat surface. Figure 8.3 demonstrates how Bit positions large sheets of paper and makes cuts close to her body using great care and patience. Given this information, students could begin silent reflections to look for visual information within her artworks. When students are ready to talk about Bit's psaligraphy displayed in a museum (Figure 8.4), they might point to evidence they see to share their findings with classmates. They could identify how Bit's psaligraphy is suspended between glass panels that allow viewers to see both sides of her artworks. Throughout a criticism discussion, teachers can encourage students to make inferences and interpretations. They can probe students to identify further details and incorporate other students' perspectives by asking if everyone agrees with a statement a student has just made. As students continue to talk about Bit's displayed art, they might notice how strategically placed lights cast elegant shadows of her psaligraphy on the museum floor, which extends each artwork's physical space and adds aesthetic appeal. At the end of a discussion, students can draw conclusions that support their

statements and teachers can reinforce key information by challenging students to link disparate ideas to understand artworks' profound meanings. With ongoing practice, students learn to become more flexible in their thinking and see alternative perspectives as they explore the unknown, reinterpret ideas, and apply critical-thinking skills.

FIGURE 8.3 Karen Bit Vejle creating a psaligraphy.
Source: Marjaana Malkamakli, photo.

FIGURE 8.4 Karen Bit Vejle exhibition space.
Source: Helle S. Andersen, photo.

## Artists' Lessons to Thrive! 8.1 Karen Bit Vejle: *Ballerina Bulldog*

### Big Idea: Wisdom

Sometimes life feels like walking on a tightrope. Danish artist Karen Bit Vejle, known as Bit, understands this concept and has created a series of works called *Ballerina Bulldog* to help people navigate life's challenges (Figure 8.1.1). *Ballerina Bulldog* in its psaligraphy form consists of a collection of ballerinas, each holding a symbolic power tool, such as the bulldog, to represent the ballerina's individual attributes. Her butterfly symbolizes change; her drill empowers her to move through mountains; Nelson Mandela's prison number (46664) assists her in forgiveness, and her violin reminds her to listen to her inner voice. Bit's concept for *Ballerina Bulldog* was inspired by the work of the Danish philosopher Søren Kierkegaard, who believed in a person's ability to make responsible and wise decisions when life's obstacles present themselves. At moments when life is like a tightrope, one must learn to balance to survive. Bit's animated *Ballerina Bulldog* reinforces this perspective by illustrating how the ballerina has a few wobbles along her pathway, but retains her strength and keeps her balance to roam the heavens and earth with grace and ease (Figure 8.1.2).

With a style of her own, Bit has become an international sensation. She practices psaligraphy as a daily habit. Her works range from small intimate designs to panels that extend nearly 35 feet (12 m) in length and require more than 200,000 accurate cuts to come to life. The artist is quick to explain that psaligraphy is an unforgiving art form. If she makes a mistake, she cannot erase what she has done. Bit makes psaligraphy look easy with her intricate patterns and eye for detail. While Bit's ballerinas may

**FIGURE 8.1.1** Karen Bit Vejle, *Ballerina Bulldog*, psaligraphy, 2011.

*Source: B.S. Hove, photo.*

**FIGURE 8.1.2** Karen Bit Vejle, still frame from the *Ballerina Bulldog* animation.

*Source: Klipp & Lim, animation.*

**FIGURE 8.1.3** Karen Bit Vejle, *Me*, 2006.

*Source: Helle S. Andersen, photo.*

have delicate forms, they symbolize dedication and hard work. Her bulldog, Bit's most beloved power tool, reminds people to stay composed and reveal their inner strengths when life gets challenging.

Bit, who has been diagnosed with chronic fatigue syndrome (myalgic encephalomyelitis), is an artistic role model who demonstrates perseverance to create art. Her psaligraphy *Me* (Figure 8.1.3) illustrates some of the hardships she faced because at the time the condition rendered her unable to work and to accomplish many of her daily routines (Opstad, 2013). The work's main figure sits with her head facing downwards. Tears roam freely in the space beneath her and a bird wishes to fly away. Bit's psaligraphy and positive mindset have assisted her in finding a new path in life. *Ballerina Bulldog* and her full set of power tools serve as analogies for the stellar wisdom that Bit has accrued through her life's journeys.

Although Bit has been practicing psaligraphy since childhood, the world might not have been exposed to her self-taught artistic productions had it not been for a friend who noticed the spectacular psaligraphy that Bit kept stored underneath a carpet and encouraged her to exhibit her creations publicly. Bit had her first exhibition in 2008. Since then, she has developed a full body of work that includes elegant collections of housewares and public commissions. As a public figure, Bit has offered *Ballerina Bulldog* as a protectoress of society. *Ballerina Bulldog* provides all people with a full set of power tools to find joy, beauty, and inspiration in daily living. Bit motivates others to find their inner voices and balance life's many tightropes.

## Essential/Guiding Questions

1. How does *Ballerina Bulldog* communicate her wisdom to others? Explain a time when you felt like you were walking on a tightrope and used your balance to make it across to the other side.
2. With which of Bit's power tools do you most identify? Explain your answer.

## Preparation

Students will discuss the meaning of wisdom and examine the *Ballerina Bulldog* series. They will review Anderson's (1997) art criticism model.

## Daily Learning Targets

I can critique one or more artworks from the *Ballerina Bulldog* series using Anderson's model of art criticism.

- I can write questions utilizing all four categories of Anderson's art criticism model.
- I can answer my original questions in my journal.

I can create a papercut design using a character of my choice that carries an attribute that represents wisdom.

- I can create a character that possesses at least three different symbolic power tools.
- I can refine my design so that my final products show effective line qualities, positive and negative space, and unity.

**National Core Arts Anchor Standards** 3, 6, 8, and 10
www.nationalartsstandards.org

---

**Analytical art criticism** is a structured model that divides art criticism questions into predetermined segments for students to classify ideas and meanings in art. This analytic model is based on four questions: "What is this?" "What does it mean?" "What is it worth?" and "What is it for?" (Anderson & Milbrandt, 2005, p. 102). Analytical art criticism begins with the simplest steps and advances to more complex ones to guide students in making logical judgments about art. Feldman's (1994) and Anderson's (1997) analytical art criticism models are two of the most widely used in education.

Feldman's (1967, 1994) model consists of four parts: description, analysis, interpretation, and judgment. **Description** names and identifies objects and elements in an artwork. **Analysis** determines how the elements are combined to form a composition and unify the work through the principles of design. **Interpretation** provides an educated hypothesis about what the artwork means. **Judgment** is an evaluation of an artwork based on a description, analysis, and interpretation of an artwork. Using a formalist approach,

Feldman argued in favor of the importance of drawing on factual knowledge to critique art. He believed that personal feelings about artworks must be suppressed during the first stages of a critique and revealed only during the judgment stage.

Some scholars restructured Feldman's original art criticism model to include relevant contextual information (Anderson, 1993; Prater, 2002). Where Feldman's model looked to an artwork's significant form through the application of the elements and principles of art, contemporary scholars feel that it is especially important to understand the context surrounding art to give viewers a fuller understanding of what particular artworks mean. Another argument that scholars have made against Feldman's original model is that people are not value free and may prefer to share their knowledge immediately rather than suppress their feelings and opinions about what they see until the end of a critique. Noting this distinction, Anderson (1997) designed a model of analytical art criticism that considers viewers' initial reactions and personal responses to artworks as they progress through four stages: reaction, description, interpretation, and evaluation. To understand what an image means, viewers analyze its structure to determine how its content, context, and themes come together.

1. **Reaction** pays homage to students' first impressions and reactions to the image presented, which may be as simple as "awesome" or "how unusual!" Students' initial responses to a creative work will guide the flow of the art criticism process. Further examinations will cause them to build upon or move away from their initial reactions.

2. **Description** calls upon students to identify key features within and surrounding the image, including the artist who made the work, its title and medium, subject matter, and obvious components within its structure, such as people, objects, and emotional qualities. Anderson's (1993) model combines Feldman's description and analysis stages. Students study the work's overall composition to examine how the elements of art and principles of design form the artistic creation. At this stage, teachers and other art experts may provide students with some of the contextual information that surrounds a work, as well as elaborate on its style, the time period in which it was made, and how history shaped its production. This can be particularly helpful when looking at abstract works, visual culture, and art from distant cultures, which may be challenging for students to describe.

3. **Interpretation** provides a basis for students to present their best guess at what an image means based on the reaction and description stages. To make sense of an artwork's meaning and produce an interpretation, teachers encourage students to combine their life experiences with the contextual information they have learned about the creation. Teachers challenge students to explain the work's purpose and answer "how" and "why" questions about it.

4. **Evaluation** occurs when teachers prepare students to give their final judgment about the artwork after stating their initial reaction, description, and interpretation. The difference between the initial reaction and the final evaluation is that students have had the opportunity to slow down and look for meanings. Their opinions may remain the same or differ from their initial reaction. For instance, based on their first impressions, students may still think a work is sad,

but they will understand why the artist might have portrayed it in such a way. Or, they realize that they may not want to place a particular artwork in their home, but understand why it is important to society and belongs in a public collection. Teachers ask students to provide valid reasons and evidence to support their final evaluations. The visual evidence that students bring to a judgment will depend on their age and their experience in talking about art. For example, some students may not be able to name a particular aesthetic category during a critique, but can access knowledge that involves an aesthetic category to justify their statements by judging a work according to its realistic features, their emotional responses, or the artist's imaginative use of materials.

Teachers and students can apply Anderson's (1997) art criticism model to examine a single artwork or multiple artworks simultaneously. Model 8.1 presents art criticism questions based on Bit's *Paper Dialogues: The Dragon and Our Stories* (Figures 8.5–8.7) using Anderson's art criticism model. It also includes introductory contextual information on the artist for teachers to share with the class. Students can answer the art criticism questions in oral or written forms. The questions are organized to guide students in addressing pertinent contextual information while referencing the works' formal and technical qualities. Students will integrate their personal experiences and judgments in response to Bit's artworks.

**Socially driven art criticism** promotes equality and understanding by addressing real-world topics, including politics, ethnicity, gender issues, class, and economic struggles. Its critical study incorporates **biopolitics**, the analysis of how politics and human biology interconnect and impact all aspects of life. Biopolitics identifies humanity's patterns for forming communities, establishing rules, and creating boundaries (Lewis, 2007; Yusoff, 2010). Art critics employ socially driven art criticism methods to raise people's mindfulness of special causes, as well as to correct injustices and misunderstandings (Broome, Pereira, & Anderson, 2018; Graham, 1997; Schur, 2007). Their socially inspired critiques center on issues that bring awareness to the public, such as the loss of environmental habitat through human destruction (Figure 8.9); the ways in which groups might move forward after experiencing oppression and hardships; and means for promoting democracy, social justice, and equality. When critiquing artworks from a social perspective,

**FIGURE 8.5** Karen Bit Vejle, *Paper Dialogues: The Dragon and Our Stories. Dragon Eggs Number One*, 2012.
*Source: Adam Grønne, photo.*

**FIGURE 8.7** Karen Bit Vejle, *Paper Dialogues: The Dragon and Our Stories. Dragon Eggs Number Five*, 2012.
*Source: Adam Grønne, photo.*

**FIGURE 8.6** Karen Bit Vejle, *Paper Dialogues: The Dragon and Our Stories. Dragon Eggs Number Two*, 2012.
*Source: Adam Grønne, photo.*

**FIGURE 8.8** Kok Ching Lam, 5-years-old, Los Ninos Art Workshop, Hong Kong, China.
*Source: ICEFA Lidice, 41st Exhibition.*

## Model 8.1
## Bit's Paper Dialogues: The Dragon and Our Stories in Context

Bit is a master psaligrapher. Her smooth and free-flowing process of cutting lines in paper resembles the work of a painter gliding a paintbrush along moistened paper. Bit developed an interest in Chinese psaligraphy and arranged a collaborative project with renowned Chinese psaligrapher Xiaoguang Qiao. The two artists selected dragons, prevalent in both Scandinavian and Chinese folklore (Figure 8.8), as the theme for their partnership. Bit created a series of seven dragon eggs to represent the past, present, and future. She explained that her dragons of the future hoard knowledge rather than characteristic jeweled treasures.

### Reaction

1. What do Karen Bit Vejle's *Dragon Eggs* remind you of?

### Description

Obvious Thematic, Formal, and Technical Qualities

2. What images do you see in Bit's *Dragon Eggs*?

Formal Relationships of Shapes and Images

3. What is the focal point of Bit's *Dragon Eggs*? What causes you to look there?

Formal Characterization

4. What if Bit painted her eggs instead of cut them? How does her choice of psaligraphy add meaning to the artworks she produces?

Contextual Examination

5. What influenced Bit's creation of *Dragon Eggs*?

### Interpretation

6. If you were a character in one of Bit's *Dragon Eggs*, what would you be thinking or feeling?

### Evaluation

Personal Experience

7. If you could own one of Bit's *Dragon Eggs*, which one would you select? Explain your answer.

Aesthetic Judgment

8. How do you think that Bit achieved the technical skill necessary to produce this series of works? Explain your answer.

Contextual Judgment

9. What do Bit's *Dragon Eggs* tell us about knowledge?

Final Judgment

10. Bit's *Dragon Eggs* include many details that encourage people to invest time in looking at the artworks. How did your thorough examination of *Dragon Eggs* cause you to notice key information? What content did you focus on the most? Explain your answers.

**FIGURE 8.9** Students' creative works can spark meaningful debates that teach others about socially driven themes, such as conservation. Anna Lajšnerová, 12-years-old, ZŠ Sedmikráska o.p.s., Rožnov pod Radhoštěm, Czech Republic.
*Source: ICEFA Lidice, 43rd Exhibition.*

**FIGURE 8.10** Aileen Niemi Joyner's crocheted blanket comforts Cinnamon.
*Source: Richard Sickler, photo.*

teachers can encourage students to answer reflective questions including: "From whose perspective am I looking?" "Is the situation presented realistically?" and "Is there a solution to this problem?" These questions challenge students to identify significant issues presented in art and life, discuss situations in depth, and explore alternatives.

When critiquing socially driven themes, students can use a structured analytical model or **feminist art criticism**, which promotes open-ended conversations that follow the natural flow of a discussion without a predetermined structure and builds upon students' understanding of art and social issues. Its approach is applicable to social causes because its advocates seek to reduce oppression in all forms by shedding light on injustices and making positive changes whenever possible. Feminist scholars' research includes their examinations of how women and people of color have been left out of art history books, museums, and galleries because of the types of art they produce, namely crafts. Noting this inequality, they have provided a more realistic representation of all the peoples who make art within professional art settings and scholarly publications. Additionally, feminist art critics have analyzed the portrayal of women in Western art and visual culture. They have identified how women have been depicted differently than men—all too commonly as sexual objects. Working with themes related to equality, feminist art critics, including influential writer Arlene Raven (1988), have developed feminist models as interdisciplinary paradigms that pull from diverse subjects including art,

history, psychology, literature, and sociology to paint a fuller picture of feminist and social issues. In doing so, feminist art criticism breaks the boundaries between public and private life by inviting participants to share personal life experiences as they talk and write about art (Augsburg, 2008; Congdon, 1991; Garber, 2008). For example, Figure 8.10 shows a crocheted blanket (a family heirloom) that brings comfort and warmth to family members, including an elderly pet that suffered a stroke. A critique of this tender moment through its visual representation and sentimental story links art in private life to a public domain.

**Class critiques of student art** differ from examinations of professional artworks that focus on judgments about art because their purpose is to assist students in augmenting their artistic development and discovering meaning. Students discuss each other's artworks as a group and learn from each other's reflections and their personal insights (Figure 8.11). Using the familiar format of description, interpretation, and judgment, Barrett's (1997) model for critiquing student art focuses on interpretations and asks: "What do I see?" "What is the artwork about?" "How do I know?" (pp. 48–49). Modeling effective student-centered art criticism interpretations using constructive criticism teaches students how to support their observations of peers' artworks using relevant descriptions and judgments. When students experience obstacles in their art, teacher and classmates' interpretations can provide possible solutions to overcome challenges and help them to develop plans to move forward. Model 8.2 presents strategies for guiding effective class critiques of student art.

# Model 8.2
## Effective Class Critiques of Student Art

**Effective class critiques of student art are:**

- located where all students can see the artworks presented and hear all participants speak;

- focused (teachers identify main questions to stimulate student discussions and monitor the flow of students' answers and questioning to keep discussions on-task);

- student-centered (teachers guide students as they investigate issues presented in their art and the art of others, while the students do most of the talking);

- times to reflect on the process of making art and the decisions students use to make visual statements (discussions present new information and different perspectives; they do not focus solely on final products);

- conducted in a supportive learning environment using constructive language (teachers and students offer suggestions and ideas to problem-solve difficulties associated with the artwork's production and/or message);

- based on questions that invoke students to respond with well-thought out, meaningful statements (students' responses focus on higher order thinking that moves beyond "yes" and "no" answers); and

- centered on interpreting art (students strive to understand the meaning of an artwork through their interpretations; they describe the features they see and ultimately make informed and sensitive judgments about the work) (Barrett, 1997).

**FIGURE 8.11** First-graders critique their clay sculptures. United States.

*Source: Author and Suzanne St. John, teachers.*

## ART CRITICISM INQUIRY METHODS

The choice-based art curriculum provides students with a wealth of comprehensive learning tasks that promote inquiry. These range from class discussions, journaling activities, written artist statements, letters to artists, games, and role-playing to art production. Early childhood students bring great enthusiasm and their vivid imaginations to interpreting art. They are eager to talk about their artistic creations. Teachers can develop age-appropriate art criticism questions

using simplified language that ask young students to describe, interpret, and evaluate artists' works. Early childhood and elementary students commonly seek positive reinforcement from teachers as they learn to articulate their opinions, support statements using visual evidence, and apply applicable vocabulary words. Middle-childhood students share an enthusiasm in talking about their own and other people's art, but can apply advanced communications skills to describe their observations and interpretations about art more fully. They have developed better listening skills and can communicate ideas in writing with greater confidence. Given a strong art foundation, early adolescents can combine their developing analytical thinking skills with their growing knowledge of art history, art processes, and aesthetic categories to judge art orally and in writing. They enjoy talking about things they have experienced and integrating their personal perspectives to interpret art. By high school, adolescents educated in the visual arts in elementary and middle school can defend their independent positions on art. They desire to address real-world problems during inquiry lessons. For example, they can identify how artists take stances through their art and can apply applicable context as they participate in analytical, socially driven, and feminist art criticism learning tasks.

Regardless of their ages, pre-K–12 students have the ability to point to visual evidence in art and may sway classmates' opinions in their favor during art criticism discussions (Stolnitz, 2001). Teachers can probe students to answer essential questions about art during such discussions and address how factors including who people are, where they come from, and what they believe can shape individuals' understandings and interpretations of art. Teachers should also teach students to identify their possible biases and listen to other people's perspectives as they evaluate art's worth and meanings.

## Art Criticism Discussions

Teachers can prepare analytical, feminist, and socially driven art criticism discussions as whole-class and small-group learning tasks. Art criticism discussions bring students together to form learning communities as they make their private ideas about art public and build knowledge through classmates' opinions and interpretations about art. To guide students in moving beyond personal artistic preferences, lessons will teach students how art critics answer questions using standards of judgment. Teachers can reinforce this concept by developing **judgment standard criteria** that challenge students to examine artworks from particular perspectives. These criteria may be projected on the board or prepared as cards for students to use at their desks. A judgment criterion might include questions such as how effectively an artist can (a) tell a story, (b) advocate for a cause, (c) demonstrate craftspersonship, (d) portray history, or (e) apply media and elements and principles of art (Katter & Stewart, 2001b). Although students might prefer an artwork because of its beauty, if a judgment standard criterion calls upon them to evaluate it based on its ability to communicate a story, they will need to move beyond personal preferences to evaluate the artwork. With practice, students will be able to select among judgment standard criteria to evaluate artworks from different perspectives. They will see how the changes in a criterion can impact their final judgment of an artwork. Figures 8.12 and 8.13 illustrate how the Oleana company (Artists' Lessons to Thrive! 4.1) presents its knit products in environments that enhance the textile products it markets. Using these images as a guide, a sample judgment standard criterion question might ask: "How effective are these images in presenting a mood?" As new issues present themselves during class discussions, teachers can ask students to brainstorm additional judgment standard criteria about the same artworks. They might also expand the activity into a written assignment.

**FIGURE 8.12** This photograph presents Oleana pillows and a blanket in a comfortable cabin setting.
*Source: Photo by Solveig Hisdal, Oleana©. https://en.oleana.no*

**FIGURE 8.13** A model wearing Oleana knitwear and accessories is surrounded by garden flowers.
*Source: Photo by Solveig Hisdal, Oleana©. https://en.oleana.no*

## Journaling and Art Criticism

Journals provide a constructive space for students to process the visual images they study, record factual information, analyze context and content, and articulate their opinions about art. Figure 8.14 shows a teacher working with a student as he prepares to write in his journal about an ancient Egyptian sculpture (see Spotlight on Student Art #8). Teachers can initiate student journal tasks on art criticism by presenting guiding analytical art criticism questions that challenge students to pull from their collected life experiences

**FIGURE 8.14** A student studies a hippopotamus given the nickname "William" during an art criticism lesson. United States. Sculpture, Middle Egypt, circa 1961–1878 BCE, faience, 7 7/8 × 2 15/16 × 4 7/16 in. (20 × 7.5 × 11.2 cm). CC0 1.0.
*Source: Author and Michelle Griffith, teachers. www.metmuseum.org*

have progressed over time (Tucker, 2002). As extension activities, students can create sketches and write creative stories and poems about particular artworks inspired by their journal entries (White, 2011.)

## The Artist Statement

An **artist statement** is a written narrative that describes an artist's work or a body of works, including a series or a completed portfolio. Artists write artist statements in the first person, using the word "I" when providing facts about their works and describing the reasons for making them. Because an artist statement is a personal description, it provides a subjective account of the meaning of the artist's work. Teachers can develop learning tasks in which students write summative artist statements about their art that include (a) the factual knowledge they learned from the projects they created, (b) the processes they used to complete their art, (c) how they selected each project's big idea, and (d) the emotional impact of their body of works. Teachers can show them artist statements by professional artists and peers as inspirations for developing their own. Model 8.3 presents a student artist statement about an artwork titled *Burn* that centers on a social justice theme.

to answer. With exposure to writing about analytical art criticism, students can also become skilled in incorporating the free-flowing feminist art criticism model. They might also try writing and answering original art criticism questions that they develop. Teachers will ask students to review and reflect upon their art criticism entries to self-assess how their ideas

## Model 8.3
## Student Artist Statement

**FIGURE 8.2.1** John Paul Custodio, 13-years-old. Yichien's art studio. United States.
*Source: Dr. Yichien Cooper, teacher.*

The theme of this piece was derived from my art instructor, Dr. Yichien Cooper, who prompted me to create a work of art that portrayed "social justice." According to Toowoomba Catholic Education, part of social justice is "promoting a just society by challenging injustice." That phrase reminded me of the burning of flags, which is sometimes done as an act of protest, especially when people feel they are subjected to oppression or inequality.

To create *Burn*, I painted two separate canvases with acrylic paint and then overlapped them, so that the overall picture was a fist holding a burning cloth, while still remaining unique. My vision was a painting that was striking, in shape, subject, and color. The palette I used was inspired from Barack Obama's iconic "Hope" poster. I thought it appropriate to use colors related to a powerful political figure in a social justice painting.

Through my artwork, I hope to reach the heart and mind. If my piece can inspire even just one person, if it can influence a tiny thought in the corner of the mind, if it can motivate the heart to experience even the slightest of feelings, then I am satisfied with my work.

## Letters to the Artist

If students could ask a particular artist any question, what would they ask? Young people's imaginations inspire them to develop interesting questions about art to which they would like to know the answers. Teachers can arouse students' natural curiosity by having classes write letters to artists. For example, students can write real letters to living artists, as well as fictitious ones to artists from the past. When writing to living artists, to confirm that all communications are appropriate, teachers should supervise and facilitate communications (digital and traditional) with artists instead of having students write independently. If students will be writing make-believe letters to artists of the past, they might work in teams. One student could write the letter to the artist and the other, pretending to be that artist, could research facts and information about the artist and write back to the student. The next time, they would switch roles.

## I Spy Art Clues

I Spy Art Clues is an art criticism game that challenges students to solve great art mysteries by interpreting descriptions of an artwork that the class cannot see. Leading this task, teachers ask students to imagine what a work looks like, visualize its theme, and contemplate how its design components come together to form a completed artwork (Katter & Stewart, 2001a). This activity activates students' listening and comprehension skills because they must visualize the artworks that game leaders describe to them. Teachers and students can take turns leading the I Spy Art Clues activity. Game leaders identify the specific details that make the work unique and provide references that students can understand. The best I Spy Art Clues activities incorporate kinesthetic learning by having students strategically move their bodies to investigate an artwork. For example, game leaders describing the work will move their bodies into the position of an object in the artwork to demonstrate what its form looks like and ask the class to mimic the exact pose. After students have used their listening skills and their bodies to interpret the artwork's appearance, they will make a sketch of what they think it looks like (Figures 8.15–8.17). From the onset of the activity,

**FIGURE 8.15** A third-grade class plays I Spy Art Clues. United States.

*Source: Author and Neely James, teachers.*

FIGURE 8.16 *Shiva as the Lord of Dance.* India, Tamil Nadu, circa 950–1000. Copper alloy, 30 × 22 1/2 × 7 in. (76.20 × 57.15 × 17.78 cm). LACMA Public Domain.
*Source: www.lacma.org*

FIGURE 8.17 Lisa Goyer, 13-years-old, Shiva sketch, United States.
*Source: Mike Muller, teacher.*

teachers should inform students that their sketches function as interpretations of the original artwork and will look slightly different than the original. When they have completed their sketches, the game leader will reveal what the actual artwork looks like.

## Role-Playing

Art criticism role-playing consists of dynamic activities that call upon students to examine artworks from different perspectives, including critics, artists, and curators. For example, role-playing activities can take the form of an interview conducted as a news report, a streaming media broadcast, and/or acted out in front of the class as a dramatic presentation. Students should study the facts to defend their characters' positions and practice their individual roles within their groups to produce strong performances.

## *The Professional Art Critic*

Teachers can collaborate with students to locate noteworthy reviews of art exhibitions. Elementary students and other beginners benefit from shorter, easier-to-read examples. Once students understand a critics' review, they will discuss whether or not the review persuaded them to want to visit the exhibition. Then, teachers can divide the class into small groups. Each group might contain a host who interviews three guests: an artist, art critic, and a museum representative. The groups will take turns performing in front of the class, with the remaining groups serving as their audience. The host and guests will add unique perspectives about the exhibition as they perform before the class audience.

## *The Curator*

Curators work in museums and galleries. Those working in museums with permanent art collections may be responsible for purchasing new artworks. Art curators use their expertise to acquire artworks that will enhance a museum's collection and satisfy the museum's audience. They also select the best exhibitions to bring to their museums and galleries so that they will attract large audiences to their facility. The exhibitions may include solo shows with single artists, or be grouped by a time period, theme, or similar artists.

After teaching students about curators, their job responsibilities, and related vocabulary, students will be ready to play the role of curators who are developing a new exhibition. They might contemplate answers to the following questions to create their show:

- What will the exhibition be about? Does it focus on a particular theme, art medium, or time period?
- Where will students house their exhibition? How many artworks can the space accommodate? Is there a size limit to the artworks? Can the space display two-dimensional, three-dimensional, and technological artworks?
- Will the show be a solo exhibition or focus on a group of artists?
- Is the purpose of the exhibition to bring as many people as possible into the exhibition space? Does it have a different purpose, such as to teach an important topic or to introduce local artists in the community?

The answers to some of these questions will depend upon available space at a school or other community venue. If space is an issue, students can create a virtual gallery in which the images they select are displayed online. Or, students can arrange small reproductions on a large paper that mimics wall space. If students are working with famous artists, they should select quality art reproductions of their work. With extra effort, administrative approval, and community support, students can design an exhibition using original artworks. They might ask community artists that include professionals, art league members, fellow students, and art clubs for permission to display their art for their class exhibition. Teachers will supervise students and provide feedback during learning tasks. Students will be responsible for keeping the work protected; hanging and taking down the art; and creating labels with artists' names, titles of the artworks, dates they were created, and the art media used (Katter & Stewart, 2001a). As an extension of this activity, students can also develop **curator notes**, a written essay or blog entry that describes an exhibition with the intention of shaping public perceptions and attracting audiences to the exhibition space.

## The Classroom Studio Art Tour

The classroom studio art tour is an effective art criticism learning task in which students are asked to interpret the meaning of classmates' art and to

receive valuable feedback about their own art productions. For this activity students will place their in-progress or completed artworks at their desks along with paper and writing instruments. Then, all students in the class will walk around the room, acting as art critics to provide fellow classmates with written constructive criticisms about what is effective with their projects and also provide them with suggestions on how to work through challenges they have identified. When students return to their desks they will read and reflect upon their classmates' feedback.

Another alternative classroom studio tour activity is to have the students write a postcard-size description about their work, then place it face down. On the front of their card, they will write a single word to describe their project. Then, each class member will also write a one-word description about each student's artwork on a separate card. They will review existing classmates' cards placed face up to ensure that they have selected a different word (Figure 8.18). As needed, teachers can supply a word bank and reinforce the meanings of vocabulary words for students developing language skills. Once the students have generated a word list, they will discuss their ideas as a whole class and define how

FIGURE 8.18 Pre-service teachers learned how to conduct a classroom studio art tour by practicing it at the conclusion of their class lesson titled *Journey With the Ostrich: A Personal Exploration into the San Culture.* Leslie Brown's sculpture generated words from her classmates including "celestial," "opposites," and "mesmerizing." United States.
*Source: Author, teacher and lesson plan developer.*

the class' interpretations were similar to or different than their own thoughts.

## BEST PRACTICES FOR TEACHING ART CRITICISM

Students want to participate in art criticism discussions with meaningful content that sparks their interests and imaginations. The key is for teachers to keep students engaged and on-task to ensure that students get the most out of these learning opportunities. This begins with demonstrating how to offer thoughtful interpretations and constructive feedback when examining and critiquing art. All students must feel respected as they share their opinions. Teachers can keep students focused during class critiques by referring to individuals by name, walking around the classroom or community space to monitor their actions, maintaining eye contact, and stopping inappropriate student responses and behaviors before or as they occur. Teachers should also moderate the tone of their voice to emphasize important points. All students must be able to see the artworks being discussed and hear other students' responses, moving their seating as necessary.

When developing lessons, teachers can preplan questions they want students to answer, while recognizing that students are likely to add new ideas to an art criticism discussion that they may not have anticipated. Teachers should be ready to ask additional questions that are not on their initial lists of questions to discuss main points further. They should look for cues in students' body language to determine if they are processing answers to questions. Wait time can add depth to class discussions because it gives students an opportunity to reflect upon the questions asked and formulate what they want to add to the conversation (Barrett, 1997). This time can be beneficial to students who are shy and/or developing language skills. For example, one study found that students whose native language is Spanish spent more time looking at paintings, acquiring visual information, and interpreting their meanings than native English speakers, because they could not rely on their verbal skills alone (Vargas, Zentall, & Wilbur, 2002). If students appear fidgety and tired because a subject has been exhausted, teachers should move to a

different question or conclude the critique. In circumstances when teachers developed quality questions, but a discussion felt too long or rushed, they can spread art criticism questions over multiple class sessions to accommodate students' attention spans.

## OUR JOURNEY TO THRIVE CONTINUES . . .

Chapter 9 builds on our studies of aesthetics and art criticism and focuses on teaching art history inquiry methods to pre-K–12 students. It presents best practices to guide students as they examine global artworks through the history of art to learn art in context and gain understandings about humanity's diversity and interconnectedness.

## CHAPTER QUESTIONS AND ACTIVITIES

1. Describe how you plan to teach art criticism as part of a choice-based art curriculum. Which art criticism models and learning tasks will you introduce to students? What steps will you take to keep class discussions on-task?
2. Teach an I Spy Art Clues lesson to pre-K–12 students. Select an artwork that is developmentally appropriate through its subject matter and make a thorough list of its details. Consider the kinesthetic movements you will use to explain the artwork. Take pictures of the students' completed sketches and share your pictures and teaching experience with classmates or peers.
3. Continue to build your art inquiry card collection (Model 7.1). For this chapter's assignment, create 25 well-designed index cards filled with art criticism questions, issues, and art reproductions for pre-K–12 students. (Note: The finished box (based on activities from Chapters 7–10) will contain a total of 100 cards with 25 aesthetic cards, 25 art criticism cards, 25 art history cards, and 25 visual culture cards for classroom use.)
4. Answer Artists' Lessons to Thrive! 8.1's essential/guiding questions in written form or as part of a group discussion. Complete its daily learning targets.

# References

Anderson, T. (1993). Defining and structuring art criticism for education. *Studies in Art Education, 34*(4), 199–208.

Anderson, T. (1997). A model for art criticism: Talking with kids about art. *School Arts, 97*(1), 21–24.

Anderson, T., & Milbrandt, M. (2005). *Art for life.* Boston: McGraw Hill.

Augsburg, T. (2008). From blurred genres to the integrative process: Arlene Raven's interdisciplinary feminist art criticism. *Critical Matrix, 17,* 106–113.

Barrett, T. (1997). *Talking about student art.* Worcester, MA: Davis Publications.

Barrett, T. (2003). *Interpreting art: Reflecting, wondering, and responding.* Boston: McGraw Hill.

Broome, J., Pereira, A., & Anderson, T. (2018). Critical thinking: Art criticism as a tool for analysing and evaluating art, instructional practice and social justice issues. *The International Journal of Art & Design Education, 37*(2), 265–276. doi:10.1111/jade.12111

Congdon, K. G. (1991). Feminist approaches to art criticism. In D. Blandy & K. G. Congdon (Eds.), *Pluralistic approaches to art criticism* (pp. 15–23). Bowling Green, OH: Bowling Green State University Popular Press.

Cross, A. (2017). Art criticism as practical reasoning. *British Journal of Aesthetics, 57*(3), 299–317. doi:10.1093/aesthj/ayx016

Feldman, E. B. (1967). *Art as image and idea.* Englewood Cliffs, NJ: Prentice Hall.

Feldman, E. B. (1994). *Practical art criticism.* Upper Saddle River, NJ: Prentice Hall.

Garber, E. (2008). The voice of Arlene Raven in art and visual culture education. *Critical Matrix, 17,* 125–131.

Graham, G. (1997). The Marxist theory of art. *The British Journal of Aesthetics, 37*(2), 107–118.

Heid, K. (2005). Aesthetic development: A cognitive experience. *Art Education, 58*(5), 48–53.

Housen, A., & Yenawine, P. (2001). *Basic VTS at a glance.* Retrieved from www.vtshome.org/pages/vts-downloads

Katter, E., & Stewart, M. G. (2001a). *Art and the human experience: A community connection.* Worcester, MA: Davis Publications.

Katter, E., & Stewart, M. G. (2001b). *Art and the human experience: A global pursuit.* Worcester, MA: Davis Publications.

Lewis, T. (2007). Biopolitical utopianism in educational theory. *Educational Philosophy and Theory, 39*(7), 683–702.

Mitra, R. (1986). Why criticism? In E. J. Kern (Ed.), *Collected papers Pennsylvania's symposium on art education, aesthetics, and criticism* (pp. 81–91). Harrisburg, PA: Pennsylvania Department of Education.

Opstad, J. L. (2013). *Karen Bit Vejle: Master of paper-cut.* Stockholm: Arvinius + Orfeus.

Plagens, P. (2005). At a crossroads: Peter Plagens on the "post-artist". *Artforum International 43*(6), 61–62.

Prater, M. (2002). Art criticism: Modifying the formalist approach. *Art Education, 55*(5), 12–17.

Raven, A. (1988). *Crossing over: Feminism and art of social concern.* Ann Arbor, MI: UMI Research Press.

Schur, R. (2007). Post-soul aesthetics in contemporary African American art. *African American Review, 41*(40), 641–654.

Stolnitz, J. (2001). The educative function of criticism. In R. A. Smith (Ed.), *Aesthetics and criticism in art education* (pp. 364–372). Reston, VA: National Art Education Association.

Tucker, A. (2002). *Visual literacy: Writing about art.* Boston: McGraw Hill.

Vargas, A. U., Zentall, S. S., & Wilbur, J. D. (2002). Responses to art attention-training by English and bilingual Spanish-speaking students with and without ADHD. *Studies in Art Education, 43*(2), 158–174.

Wachowiak, F., & Clements, R. C. (2006). *Emphasis art: A qualitative art program for elementary and middle schools* (8th ed.). Boston: Pearson Education.

White, B. (2011). Embodied aesthetics, evocative art criticism: Aesthetically based research. *Studies in Art Education, 52*(2), 142–153.

Yusoff, K. (2010). Biopolitical economies and the political aesthetics of climate change. *Theory, Culture & Society, 27*(2–30), 73–99.

# Art History

## Inclusive Approaches

**FIGURE 9.1** *Kids' Guernica Peace Mural*, 4th-grade students. Denmark.
*Source: Author, Isaac Larison, Lone Bodæker, and Anna Trolles Skole (School) faculty, teachers. Tom Anderson, photo.*

**Art history** is the study of artworks spanning from prehistoric to contemporary times. It chronicles artists' and societies' perspectives by documenting how artists have communicated stories about the human condition and people's sacred beliefs, expressed through visual representations and performances. Teachers guide students on journeys of inquiry to discover world cultures; ways of seeing; and the times, places, and cultures in which people have lived and imagined. Using factual data, art historians explain the circumstances in which artists

manufacture their work, including historical events, geographic influences, cultural traditions, access to resources, and aesthetic preferences in context. This chapter presents inclusive approaches to teaching students art historical inquiry so that students may discover artistic innovations, practices, and multiple ways of knowing. Our instruction will move students beyond thinking about art history only in terms of memorizing artists' names, dates, and art movements. We will facilitate students' ability to take the lead as investigators who search for meaning by examining the clues presented in art and the contextual factors that surround its development.

We will meet the following objectives by participating in this chapter:

- Define art history and explain its purpose in the choice-based art curriculum.
- Identify best practices for teaching students art history inquiry methods.

- Develop instructional resources for teaching art history.

Spotlight on Student Art #9 (Figures 9.1–9.3) describes how students studied art history to develop an international peace mural. Their examination of historical artworks influenced their artistic designs and provided them with opportunities to share their perspectives on peace.

**FIGURE 9.2** Students paint a Kids' Guernica Peace Mural. Denmark.
*Source: Author, Isaac Larison, Lone Bodæker, and Anna Trolles Skole (School) faculty, teachers.*

**FIGURE 9.3** Students paint a section of the mural. Denmark.
*Source: Author, Isaac Larison, Lone Bodæker, Maggie Koudelka, Anna Trolles Skole (School) faculty, teachers.*

---

## Spotlight on Student Art #9

### Big Idea: Peace

Fourth-grade Danish students collaborated with American pre-service teachers to learn each other's cultures and create a *Kids' Guernica Peace Mural* the size of Picasso's *Guernica* (11ft 5 in. × 25 ft 6 in./3.49 m × 7.76 m) in remembrance of the bombings of Hiroshima during World War II (Figures 9.1–9.3). The schoolchildren studied Picasso's abstracted interpretation of the attack on Guernica in 1937. Because Denmark is a peaceful society, with its citizens identified as the happiest people in the world (Helliwell, Layard, & Sachs, 2016), the homeroom teacher felt hesitant to introduce middle-childhood students to Picasso's horrific subject matter. However, the principal felt it was appropriate for them to study *Guernica* to understand its history in context.

After examining *Guernica*, the students investigated the meanings of war and peace, and identified symbolic images in Danish culture. They discussed Edvard Erichsen's *The Little Mermaid*

(1912), a bronze sculpture perched upon rocks in Copenhagen's harbor to pay homage to Danish author Hans Christian Andersen and his beloved fairytale; historic Viking ships with carved and painted details; and nearby Legoland, where artists create sculptures entirely out of Lego® bricks that replicate renowned international artworks and architectural designs. Based on their discussions, research, and sketches, the students created a peace mural that included the Danish map and their country's native name, *Danmark*, in the form of colorful Lego bricks; Hans Christian Andersen's portrait, with the *Little Mermaid*; the swan, Denmark's national bird; a Viking ship: and a Danish pastime, bike riding. To summarize the meaning of peace from a Danish perspective, the students added the first line of their country's national anthem: "Der er et yndigt land" ("A Lovely Land Is Ours") and popular Danish symbols of a cross, anchor, and heart representing "tro håb og kærlighed" (faith, hope, and love). Their study of historical artworks from Denmark and beyond inspired their mural's design and development.

# INCLUSIVE ART HISTORY

**Inclusive art history** is the practice of presenting art history from diversified lenses that include creative works and scholarship by artists and art historians who are representative of humanity's cultures, races, gender identities, geographies, and abilities. With inclusive concepts in mind, art historians ask, "Who has a voice in art history today?" (Mattos, 2014, p. 259). This question is significant because, throughout most of art history's existence, scholars have canonized Western art, without acknowledging the majority of the world's artists, who include women and people of color, as well as those who create artworks that are not classified as "fine arts" (Seppä, 2010).

Art historians develop convincing cases through philosophical paradigms, detail-oriented accumulations of data, and precise analytical language (Bätschmann, 2003; Preziosi, 2009; Zwijnenberg & Farago, 2003). Their investigations:

- increase knowledge by asking questions, using established rules and research methodologies, and applying relevant theories to formulate educated interpretations about art;
- identify who made artworks, when they were created, who commissioned them, and what their original purpose was;
- organize artworks to assess the content and context that influenced their production including subject matter, styles, and materials;
- classify artworks by periods and themes; and
- make connections so that people can understand the meanings of art created by the world's cultures.

Art historians and other theorists have expanded the discipline of art history beyond the fine arts to include influences from popular culture and new technologies. Each new generation of art historians continues the practice of investigating how cultural values, social milieus, and philosophical beliefs shape our understandings of art. Their work builds upon previous scholarship. The outcomes of their art historical research connect to present-day society because our understandings of art are influenced by the times in which we live. Art history varies from art criticism in that art history searches for truth based on empirical evidence. Art historians seek facts and art critics judge art. Through art criticism's interpretation phase, students provide their best perceptions (guesses) based on evidence and personal reflections to assess what particular artworks might mean. Art historical inquiry asks students to articulate their understanding of historical knowledge, symbols, cultural contexts, artists' biographical information, artistic styles, and artworks' functions in society.

Societies across the globe have long collected significant artifacts. Evidence of early art collections have been found in Paleolithic excavations, ancient Chinese and Egyptian tombs, and other locations. Art history developed as a discipline in the Renaissance. Giorgio Vasari (1511–1574), an Italian Renaissance artist, was the first art historian. He wrote biographies of artists contemporary to his time and some before him to describe their abilities to produce exceptional artworks that surpassed others before them. Two hundred years later, Johann Joachim Winkelmann (1717–1768) broadened Vasari's perspective on art history by presenting a spectator's position when examining art, rather than an artist's viewpoint. He was the first art historian to classify a society's art to understand its history and culture.

Beginning in the 18th century's Age of Enlightenment, a time of intellectual and cultural change, societies developed museums to give everyday people access to collections of important artworks. Prior to museums, most art was held in private collections belonging to royals and other elites (Preziosi, 2009). Wanting to live in fairer, more open societies, intellectuals appealed for public spaces in which citizens could learn about culture. Their influence led governments to construct public museums throughout Europe. Museum collections also began to spread across the globe. By building museum collections inspired by historical research, art historians helped establish the works that cultures deem most valuable and worth preserving and knowing more about. Humanity's desire to preserve and bring awareness to special artworks, practices, and cultural sites continues with examples including UNESCO's World Heritage Sites and its Intangible Cultural Heritage of Humanity list. These United Nations programs assist us, as global citizens, in preserving civilizations' creative achievements and traditions for generations to come.

Despite scholars' call for greater inclusion in art history, an analysis of publications within a prominent art history journal revealed that most of its articles up until recent times focused on European painting and sculpture (Ambrose, 2016). Even though international scholars from non-Western cultures had submitted research to the journal, the fewest articles featured art created by indigenous peoples from Africa, Oceania, and the Americas (Figure 9.4). A different study revealed that only seven out of every hundred artists depicted in most college art history survey textbooks up until recent decades were female, which limited pre-service teachers' early exposure to diversified artists (Clark & Folgo, 2006). Due to social norms, until the mid-19th century and into the 20th century, women had fewer opportunities to receive formal artistic training. Some obstacles remain in studying female artists because it costs publishers significantly less money to print reproductions of artworks that have been long established in public collections in the public domain than contemporary works that are held in private collections. As a result, many student art history texts focus on a limited number of female artists (Rosenberg & Thurber, 2007).

Similarly, children's and adolescents' art history books have traditionally focused on famous historical artists (most of whom were white males), and offer fewer books on well-known and lesser known female artists and individual artists from diverse ethnicities, community artists, and contemporary artists. Teachers can develop original inclusive art historical instructional resources, including writing newsletters for students and creating posters, by collecting biographical and other pertinent data from books, journals, art magazines, and art websites. When creating art history resources, teachers will need to be mindful of students' development and language abilities as they select content and develop original passages of text so that their students can comprehend all meanings. Artists' Lessons to Thrive! 9.1 presents a painting series by Sisavanh Phouthavong-Houghton, who represents a contemporary artist that people can meet in the community. She exhibits her art and participates in community partnerships to share her skills with others. Model 9.1 presents an art history newsletter for students derived from the Artists' Lessons to Thrive! 9.1 on Sisavanh Phouthavong-Houghton.

# Artists' Lessons to Thrive! 9.1 Sisavanh Phouthavong-Houghton: Displacement Identified

## Big Idea: Displacement

Sisavanh Phouthavong-Houghton emigrated from Laos to Kansas with her family at age 4. While being surrounded by American culture, she and her family maintained their Laotian identity at home—speaking their native language and cooking traditional foods. Despite her participation in both cultures, she felt semi-detached from each one. Like so many immigrants, she became a unique individual, one who felt neither fully American nor entirely Laotian. With this in mind, she created a series of eleven paintings titled *Displacement* to chronicle the stories of Laotian-Americans who legally changed their names to assimilate into American culture (Figures 9.1.1 and 9.1.2).

She began her research by interviewing eleven participants and securing copies of their citizenship certificate photographs. The artist discovered that the participants changed their names for multiple reasons. Some sensed hostility when Americans were unable to pronounce their names.

**FIGURE 9.1.1** Sisavanh Phouthavong-Houghton, *Displacement: Bonita Sphabmixay*, acrylic on canvas, 24 × 36 in. (60.96 × 91.44 cm), 2004.
*Source: Courtesy of the artist; www.sisavanhphouthavong. com.*

**FIGURE 9.1.2** Sisavanh Phouthavong-Houghton, *Displacement: Robert Phetchampone*, acrylic on canvas, 24 × 36 in. (60.96 × 91.44 cm), 2004.
*Source: Courtesy of the artist; www.sisavanhphouthavong. com.*

Others changed them for simple convenience. A final group was assigned new names by other Americans, including their schoolteachers. Over time they became used to being called by their American names and changed them legally. Phouthavong-Houghton transformed each participant's photograph into a 2 ft × 3 ft (61 cm × 91 cm) canvas portrait. The canvases project 5-inches. (12 cm) from the wall to represent physical barriers that prohibit viewers from invading the Laotian-Americans' personal space while simultaneously demanding viewers' attention. Each portrait is filled with Ben-Day dots, a commercial printing technique that American Pop artist Roy Lichtenstein adapted in his works. The collective abstracted dots symbolize a loss of identity, yet as individual dots they represent how all humans are unique individuals. Serving as analogies for the participants, each single dot reminds viewers that people's true identities remain, even when they must adapt to living in a new culture and become one of many.

Phouthavong-Houghton has taken steps to preserve her fellow Laotian-Americans' personal heritage by asking questions, collecting evidence, and safeguarding their distinctive identities through art. *Displacement's* lessons on identity can be applied to all people who have experienced changes in life that have caused them to feel out of place and can help them discover a rejuvenated sense of self.

## Essential/Guiding Questions

1. What does displacement mean to you? Why did Phouthavong-Houghton choose the title *Displacement* to describe this series of paintings?
2. How would *Displacement's* meaning change if Phouthavong-Houghton painted its portraits to look more realistic, with natural skin, wrinkles, and blemishes rather than with abstracted dots?

## Preparation

Students will research how multicultural artists have presented identity in art. They will participate in a class discussion about the meanings of people's names and answer questions, including: Have you ever changed your name or used a nickname? Why did you change your name? Has anyone in your family ever changed their name to make it sound more acceptable in a given society or something else?

## Daily Learning Targets

I can create an artwork that identifies a correlation between my name and my identity.

- I can cite at least one example from art history as inspiration for my design.
- I can show craftspersonship and unity in my completed artwork.

I can make valid interpretations about Phouthavong-Houghton's *Displacement* using this textbook's inclusive art historical inquiry model with guiding targets (Model 9.2).

- I can write at least one paragraph for each: (a) analysis, (b) informed speculation, and (c) validation.
- I can discuss my findings with my peers.

**National Core Arts Anchor Standards** 1, 6, 9, and 11
www.nationalartsstandards.org

# Model 9.1
# Artist Newsletter

**Sisavanh Phouthavong-Houghton**

**FIGURE 9.2.1** Sisavanh Phouthavong-Houghton, *Displacement: Sandra Phengvongsa*, acrylic on canvas, 24 × 36 in. (60.96 × 91.44 cm), 2004.

*Source: Courtesy of the artist; www.sisavanhphouthavong.com.*

**FIGURE 9.2.2** Sisavanh Phouthavong-Houghton. *Displacement: Chris Phouthavong*, acrylic on canvas, 24 × 36 in. (60.96 × 91.44 cm), 2004.

*Source: Courtesy of the artist; www.sisavanhphouthavong.com.*

**Big Idea: Displacement**

**Sisavanh Phouthavong-Houghton** is a painter. In 1976, she was born in a country named Laos. She and her family moved to the United States four years later. They lived in Winfield, Kansas. In the United States, she felt like she belonged to two different cultures. At home she spoke Laotian. She spoke English everywhere else.

In 2004, shortly after earning her Master of Fine Arts degree, Phouthavong-Houghton made paintings titled *Displacement*. They show pictures of Laotian-Americans who changed their names legally. She learned about the people in her portraits by asking them questions about what it was like to live in a different country. She also examined the photographs on their citizenship certificates.

To make people look at her Laotian-American portraits, she built the *Displacement* canvases to project 5-inches (12 cm) away from the wall. She filled their portraits with colorful Ben-Day dots. Printers use these dots to make pictures in magazines and newspapers. The dots give her work the look of cartoon characters. They also abstract the Laotian-Americans' portraits, thereby removing part of their identity.

Through her research she learned that the Laotian-Americans in her study changed their names for different reasons. A few did so because some Americans felt frustrated when they could not say their names. Others changed their names because it seemed easier to do. The rest were given American names by Americans as they were growing up and got used to hearing them.

**What Is Displacement?**

A change, shift, or move that has a bad feeling associated with it. It may make a person feel out of place, foreign, different, misplaced, homeless, and/or cultureless.

**Reading Questions**

1. Who is Sisavanh Phouthavong-Houghton?
2. Where was she born?
3. When did she move to the United States?
4. What does displacement mean?
5. What are *Ben-Day dots*?
6. Why did Phouthavong-Houghton use *Ben-Day dots* in *Displacement*?
7. Why do you think she named her paintings *Displacement*?
8. Have you ever changed your name? Do you go by a nickname? Why do you think people change their names?

**Artist Facts**

- Phouthavong-Houghton was born in 1976 in Vientiane, Laos.
- She moved to Winfield, Kansas with her family at the age of 4.
- She studied painting.
- She created the *Displacement* series in 2004.
- She was inspired by American Pop Artist Roy Lichtenstein's *Ben Day Dots*.

**FIGURE 9.4** The Brooklyn Museum website provides contextual information that describes indigenous artworks, including this Pacific Northwest mask. *Kwakwaka'wakw, Baleen Whale Mask,* 19th century. Cedar wood, hide, cotton cord, nails, pigment, 23 5/8 × 28 1/2 × 81 1/8 in. (60 × 72.4 × 206 cm). Brooklyn Museum, Museum Expedition 1908, Museum Collection Fund, 08.491.8901. Creative Commons-BY

*Source: https://creativecommons.org/licenses/by/3.0/*

When art historians from all regions of our planet participate in constructive discourse and inclusive research practices they work to create a "global art historical canon" that minimizes prevailing misconceptions within the discipline (Capistrano-Baker, 2015, p. 255). Society benefits from art historians' scholarship that describes, analyzes, and interprets art from their own diversified communities. Such scholarship provides the public with insights about works that might otherwise be unavailable or more challenging to understand for people outside of their diversified cultures.

Students of all ages can learn from art historians' inclusive inquiry practices even though they have not yet developed the deep level of introspection and knowledge of subject matter that professional art historians have accrued. As part of their professional practices, art historians seek historical truth, called **verity**. They apply scientific inquiry to study art and use diverse models of art historical inquiry to suit their research needs. Oskar Bätschmann (2003) applied a hermeneutic model to interpret art history. His scientific approach describes the importance of inventorying visual data, identifying relationships, and communicating through effective language. The following steps of analysis, informed speculation, and validation present a framework for art historical inquiry inspired by Bätschmann's and other scholars' work.

1. **Analysis:** Art historians develop initial observations as they formulate guiding questions that will dictate their analysis of art historical meaning. They analyze art by applying their careful observations to categorize art, examine details, attribute artworks to artists, compare iconic symbols, and detect forgeries. Art historians generally prefer to examine original artworks for their studies. However, securing access to original art is not always possible due to the fact that artworks, even ones by the same artist, may be spread across the globe in different collections. When **primary sources** (original works) are unavailable, art historians secure quality art reproductions and other applicable resources called **secondary sources**. They also seek reliable primary and secondary literary sources to conduct inquiry, including artists' letters, documents from patrons, artist interviews, biographies, books, and scholarly articles. Art historians begin with the most applicable or recent examples to enhance their knowledge and reconstruct events. They examine art media, identify context that links an artwork to a time or culture, and compare the diverse resources they have collected to yield a fuller picture of an artwork's meaning within history.

   Art historical analysis includes the study of **icons**, symbols that represent an object or belief deemed important to an individual, group, or culture, to discover meanings and establish if these symbols appear elsewhere, perhaps by other artists within a region or period. Teachers can explain to students that people decode icons to understand part of the story the artist is telling. Depending on the time in which artworks were created, and their iconography, some artworks are easier for art historians to decipher than others. An artwork created in a society that had already written much accurate information about particular artists and their use of established symbols is typically easier to interpret than ones created without the benefit of accompanying texts.

   Art historians may reference **provenance** to establish an artwork's authenticity. Provenance provides a clear record of an artwork's physical location and ownership since its creation (Anderson & Milbrandt, 2005; Preziosi, 2009). Art historians can confirm authenticity when an artwork has remained in one place during its entire existence or when an artwork changes its location, but society has proof (such as validated receipts of purchase) that show exactly when an artwork was transferred to different locations.

An artist's choice of media may make a social statement or disclose the location where an artwork was created, such as the selection of a rare material available only in a particular vicinity (Bätschmann, 2003). It can also reveal a culture's aesthetic preferences for materials and explain an artwork's function. For example, an art historian might consider: Is the work a utilitarian object created with durable media or one produced with ornate materials to be admired at a distance or only handled on special occasions? Art historians can also study art media to date individual works by determining when a particular medium was invented or when artists discontinued using a certain material or technique.

**Internal verity** transpires when art historians examine an original artwork, such as inspecting marks on an artwork's surface to see if they match an artist's style. Or, they might collaborate with technological experts who assist them in finding the answers they need, such as taking X-rays to identify what exists at an artwork's foundations, and commissioning scientists to take a chemical analysis of an artwork's medium to estimate its age or to determine if it matches the compositional formula that an artist always used. **External verity** allows art historians to consider factors outside of an artwork to confirm its authenticity, such as the study of other artworks and literary sources that connect to their investigations. The relationships that art historians identify assist them in making comparisons and correlations between works by the same artist or ones of a similar culture or period. Given their discoveries during an analysis, art historians will determine if they are on the right investigative trail or need to modify their initial questions.

2. **Informed speculation:** With the analysis completed and the initial evidence fully gathered, art historians cultivate educated interpretations to speculate about the artwork's possible meaning(s). Bätschmann (2003) refers to this process as creative abduction: conjectures of meaning. Art historians formulate hypotheses to examine their theories by applying factual knowledge from artworks, literary sources, and their expert intuition. They evaluate the relationships they have identified to answer questions other art historians have not answered before. Their hypotheses may include assumptions about an artwork's style, an artist's decision to alter the look of a certain part of the composition so that it varies from the rest, or the artist's incorporation of icons. A hypothesis may center on formal approaches to design and media as well as context that describes artistic choices, historical times, secular needs, philosophies, functions, and social issues. Art historians may choose to bridge concepts in art from **coexisting temporalities**—the ways in which artworks from similar time periods can have multiple impacts and varied interpretations as time progresses. This expands prior thinking in the field by connecting artworks to themes, which allows art historians to make greater comparisons about how people from different times and cultures have expressed similar perspectives (Arnold, 2009). Using one hypothesis or more, art historians reexamine the artwork in question and seek further research to support, reject, or modify their hypothesis or hypotheses. They call upon their professional writing skills to develop substantial interpretations and present their arguments in narrative form, which produces a binding relationship between their data and hypotheses.

3. **Validation.** As a final step, art historians determine if their hypotheses are valid. They present logical conclusions from relevant facts, which may support the original hypothesis or move away from it. A valid interpretation does not form a single, one-right-answer conclusion. Art historians may form different summative interpretations, each of which may be valid based on the questions they asked as well as the philosophical frameworks and contextual data that guided their research. They provide the best possible evidence to confirm the facts. Although validation is grounded in theory and based on well-established deductions, the art historian's literary audience will ultimately view the interpretations as either correct or incorrect. Validation can support or reject the art historian's findings based on the data and reasoning presented. Unlike art critics, art historians' arguments are not focused solely on persuading audiences, but rather their intent is to share information and possible answers by combining objective data with personal sensitivity towards the subject. Other scholars can follow the art historian's research trail to determine if the research was conducted properly, as well as use the art historian's findings to move the research in a new direction. By opening their discipline to an array of alternative interpretations, art historians welcome different perspectives that add richness to the body of literature within their field.

# ART HISTORY INQUIRY METHODS

Given a foundation in approaches to art historical inquiry, teachers can develop a variety of age-appropriate inclusive art history inquiry tasks for students. When placed in context, art inquiry methods provide a useful format for students to understand art's meanings and functions. Teaching art historical inquiry in context with themes moves students beyond acquiring basic factual knowledge and studying art history in a static, unchanging chronological order. The process challenges students to erase boundaries, investigate new meanings, examine coexisting temporalities, and form enduring understandings. Teachers facilitate the needs of students of all ages as they speak, write, and create about art history with growing accuracy and clarity (Barnet, 2014; D'Alleva, 2005).

This textbook's model of inclusive art historical inquiry (Model 9.2) uses the following learning targets to guide students' studies.

- Analysis: I can inquire.
- Informed speculation: I can support my interpretation(s) with facts.
- Validation: I can present a convincing closing argument.

Students can use Model 9.2's targets as a guide to study global artworks and discover truth based on empirical evidence. Depending on students' abilities, teachers will modify their level of guidance so that students will be able to utilize the most applicable methods independently and/or collaboratively. For example, teachers can facilitate class investigations with age-appropriate artworks and resources. They can develop preliminary guiding questions such as: "Who made this artwork?" "What are its unique features?" and "What does it tell us about the time in which it was produced?" Students will take inventory by looking for details and recording their initial perceptions. Teachers can introduce applicable literary works to guide students. Students will learn to make comparisons and identify relationships with supplemental resources. After this analysis, teachers will ask students to explain their informed speculations and reasons for supporting, rejecting, or modifying their hypotheses. Students will learn to validate their findings based on their analysis and informed speculations to form a convincing closing argument. Even if students do not present previously undiscovered art historical information like professionals, the process develops their inquiry skills and knowledge of art history.

## Model 9.2
## Teaching and Learning in Art Education's Inclusive Art Historical Inquiry Model With Guiding Targets

**I can study global artworks.**

| Analysis: I can inquire. | Informed speculation: I can support my interpretation(s) with facts. | Validation: I can present a convincing closing argument. |
|---|---|---|
| I can:<br>• Develop initial questions to guide my analysis.<br>• Classify an artwork's style.<br>• Analyze icons.<br>• Make comparisons.<br>• Identify relationships.<br>• Secure reliable primary and/or secondary art and literary sources.<br>• Identify context that links an artwork to a time or culture.<br>• Recognize the artist's or a culture's choice of media and its meaning.<br>• Detect an artist's or a culture's aesthetic and philosophical preferences.<br>• Look to internal and external verity.<br>• Refer to provenance.<br>• Secure factual information.<br>• Modify my initial questions as necessary. | I can:<br>• Identify questions to guide my study based on my analysis of the artwork's possible meaning(s).<br>• Use language to develop a clear hypothesis as a declarative statement.<br>• Reexamine the artwork in question in support of my hypothesis.<br>• Conduct further research.<br>• Apply factual knowledge from applicable artworks, literary sources, and my intuition to test my theory.<br>• Incorporate relative context in support of my hypothesis.<br>• Support, reject, or modify my hypothesis based on the evidence.<br>• Present my argument in narrative form to produce a binding relationship between my data and hypothesis. | I can:<br>• Provide a logical summative interpretation based on facts.<br>• Present a summative explanation that validates my hypothesis.<br>• Share possible answers using objective data.<br>• Integrate my personal sensitivity towards the subject that I support with evidence.<br>• Incorporate details to validate my position further.<br>• Provide others with clear pathways to follow my inquiry methods. |

Early childhood students are developing emergent writing and language skills as they learn about art history. Because so much information is new to them, teachers should check students' understanding regularly. Young children can point to visual evidence in artworks, name objects, apply new art vocabulary words, recall content, and identify possible big ideas. At the end of an art history discussion or reading, students can collaborate with the teacher to summarize what they have learned. Teachers might simultaneously write down the children's statements and repeat them to the class to demonstrate how art, writing, and language come together. They can utilize their word lists in subsequent lessons to review the information and add new vocabulary as students study additional artworks. Teachers can reinforce what students learn by linking their art history studies with related art production and inquiry tasks.

Middle-childhood students have increased reading and writing skills and are better able to remember facts than in early childhood. They have a greater aptitude for recalling key information presented in art history discussions and readings. Compared to earlier years, they have augmented their listening skills and are more responsive to non-fiction art history books and documentaries. Middle-childhood students are becoming more acquainted with the world and are eager to learn about global cultures and their art and traditions. They can independently compare works from the same artists or art movements and write about their discoveries. With guidance, they can participate in short research tasks and incorporate supportive evidence in their writing and artworks. They can employ art history terminology appropriately, cite references, and integrate quotes into their writing and class discussions to make a point. Class reviews and hands-on learning activities will reinforce their understanding of new art history concepts. Teachers might also introduce art history manipulatives, including art history games and museum invitation cards, to stimulate learning.

Early adolescents prefer art history tasks that relate to real life. Studying art history in context through in-depth discussions, readings, research assignments, and creative productions offers students safe outlets to communicate their unique perspectives on issues that interest and concern them. Given a strong elementary foundation in art history, students can identify artists, artworks, artistic influences, art production techniques, and the components that make up an artwork.

Early adolescents are able to make cogent analyses, cite evidence, and form interpretations using visual and literary sources. They can apply their developing knowledge to explain how different philosophies have shaped art history and identify similarities and differences in artists, art historians, and authors' presentations of information. Teachers can involve early adolescents in short research projects and have them write art history essays that contain an introduction, transition paragraphs, and a conclusion. Students will be able to strengthen their writing by selecting credible sources to support their arguments and make revisions and edits.

Given a strong pre-K–8 foundation, adolescents will continue to augment their art history creative, writing, and research skills and can make deep historical, cultural, and social connections. Teachers can challenge them to apply their investigative skills to identify societies' various uses for art and explain concepts in art history from their own perspectives. Students can generate hypotheses for short and extended research projects. They have the ability to cite evidence from multiple literary sources and art to compose oral, written, and visual products that include sensory details that capture a mood and/or persuade audiences. Using thematic inquiry, they can make connections between disparate creative products including artworks, creative writings, media arts, and visual culture to understand a topic more fully. Teachers can encourage them to publish their art history–inspired writings and creative works publically, such as on a class art history blog and at an exhibition space. Their studies should also address career possibilities within the profession, including art historians and conservationists.

Pre-K–12 art history lessons typically include reading and writing tasks, which may be challenging for some English learners, students with learning disabilities, and students with at-risk tendencies. All students should be encouraged to participate using their existing skills and receive accommodations to acquire new skills and reach learning targets. Teachers might adapt writing tasks into group and class discussions and games. Teachers and advanced learners can model reading and writing tasks for students learning grade-level language skills to emulate. Students needing assistance will work towards completing written tasks independently. When available, teachers can also request the help of media specialists and lead teachers specializing in language arts for extra assistance to teach students reading and writing skills. Their support helps teachers with limited art instruction time by extending art history into the language arts curriculum.

## Interactive Discussions and Games

Using this textbook's inclusive art historical inquiry model is an excellent way to encourage art history discussions. Some discussions can include artworks that connect to students. For example, students might describe their collections of toys as they examine Figure 9.5. The class can continue the discussion to identify the ways that people have taken care of and preserved the objects that they consider valuable. Students can read art history books and discuss their content with teachers and students asking questions and citing evidence. Playing art history games are another way to stimulate student discussions. Younger children might play a telephone game and older students can record a video chat session in which they discuss an artwork's historical qualities. A pantomime game has a teacher or student read a story from art history to the class, with the class experiencing the story by acting out its scenes through intuitive body gestures. Figure 9.6 prompts students' discussions about art history with a teacher wearing clothing she made to replicate artist Piet Mondrian's paintings.

**FIGURE 9.5** Gloria Caranica. *Rocking Beauty Hobby Horse*, designed 1964–1966. Plywood, solid wood, pigment, 20 1/4 × 25 1/4 × 11 3/4 in. (51.4 × 64.1 × 29.8 cm). Brooklyn Museum, Bequest of Laura L. Barnes and gift of Mrs. James F. Bechtold, by exchange, 2007.38. Creative Commons-BY.
*Source: https://creativecommons.org/licenses/by/3.0/*

**FIGURE 9.6** Cassie Stephens wears a Mondrian-inspired outfit she created.
*Source: Stella Blue Photography.*

## Journaling

Students can use their art journals to record art historical information that they have researched. Entries may answer questions such as: "Who created this artwork?" "When was it made?" How was it made?" "Why was it made?" and "What predominant theme is presented in this artwork and/or series of artworks? Students can augment their responses with original sketches and by collaging art reproductions in their journals. When journals are combined with class readings and discussions, students can transform newly found information into detailed writings about art. They can use their journals to collect data for inclusive art historical inquiry writings. As extension activities, students might develop art history inspired artworks, brochures, pamphlets, poetry, lyrics, slogans, posters, timetables, biographies, and invitations using notes and data collected in their journals.

## Block Comparison Paper

A two-paragraph block comparison art history paper compares two artworks. It hones students' observation and inquiry skills. Students will begin by listing similarities and differences between the artworks. Then, in the first paragraph, students will write an introductory sentence that identifies the two different works of art. They will use the remainder of the paragraph to describe the characteristics of the first artwork. Next, they will describe the second artwork in a second paragraph and address the same characteristics mentioned in the first paragraph. Students can use their comparisons to answer who, what, how, and where questions, as well as to explain how characteristics in the second artwork are similar to or different from the ones identified in the first one. Model 9.3 presents an example block comparison paper using artworks from Sisavanh Phouthavong-Houghton's *Displacement* series.

## Model 9.3
## Art History Comparison Paper

FIGURE 9.3.1 Sisavanh Phouthavong-Houghton, *Displacement: Katherine Phouthavong*, acrylic on canvas, 24 × 36 in. (60.96 × 91.44 cm), 2004.
*Source: Courtesy of the artist; www.sisavanhphouthavong.com.*

FIGURE 9.3.2 Sisavanh Phouthavong-Houghton, *Displacement: Tom Phaophongsavath*, acrylic on canvas, 24 × 36 in. (60.96 × 91.44 cm), 2004.
*Source: Courtesy of THE artist; www.sisavanhphouthavong.com.*

**Similar**: Style, Laotian-Americans, Ben-Day Dots, Colors (Red, Yellow, Black, Blue, and White)
**Different**: Facial Expressions, Face Tilt, Man/Woman, Hair, Clothing

| | |
|---|---|
| 1. Both portraits (*Katherine Phouthavong* and *Tom Phaophongsavath*) belong to Sisavanh Phouthavong-Houghton's *Displacement* series. The *Katherine Phouthavong* painting presents a Laotian-American woman with a wide, friendly smile. She has long black hair with blue highlights. Her red shirt, red lips, and white teeth show emphasis. Her head is tilted at a slight angle. Her face is made of *Ben-Day dots* and has black outlines. | 2. *Tom Phaophongsavath* is a painting of a Laotian-American man. His hairstyle is more angular and shorter than Katherine's hair, yet it still has the same blue highlights. Tom looks more serious in his portrait than Katherine does. He stares directly at the viewer. A red background frames his face—making it the painting's focal point. Tom's face is filled with *Ben-Day dots* and has black outlines, just like Katherine's face does. |

## Essay

Students begin to develop essay-writing skills in 3rd grade. Teachers can augment students' art history essay writing skills by assisting them with grammar, vocabulary, and organization. With guidance, they can create outlines, conduct research, and make the necessary revisions to develop quality final drafts. Students will need to study the details within artworks and select appropriate literary sources as applicable to make convincing evidence-based arguments. Teachers can model how to use quotations and difficult terminology effectively. Working with a checklist, students should read their completed essays aloud to check that their sentences flow naturally and that they have justified their positions clearly before submitting them for teacher assessment. To share their art historical findings, students can present their essays in class and through multimedia presentations.

## Exhibition Catalogue Entry

Many museums and galleries create catalogues with beautiful art reproductions and accompanying texts that explain prominent artworks to visitors. They describe an artwork by identifying the artist's name; the artwork's title, size, and medium; its owner or collection name; and pertinent contextual and analytical information. Students will write a descriptive paragraph that connects the artwork to the time in which it was created, explain its context, and define key art terminology for audiences to understand. Like professional art historians, they may need to keep their written descriptions to a predetermined word count to fit within the catalogue's page dimensions. Model 9.4 presents an example art history catalogue entry based on Sisavanh Phouthavong-Houghton's *Displacement* series.

## Model 9.4
## Exhibition Catalogue Entry

FIGURE 9.4.1 Sisavanh Phouthavong-Houghton, *Displacement: Melinda Vilayphone*, acrylic on canvas, 24 × 36 in. (60.96 × 91.44 cm), 2004.
*Source: Courtesy of the artist; www.sisavanhphouthavong.com.*

**Sisavanh Phouthavong-Houghton**
*Displacement: Melinda Vilayphone*
(2004)
Acrylic on Canvas
24 × 36 in. (60.96 × 91.44 cm),
Collection of the Artist

-------------------------------------------------

Melinda Vilayphone's portrait is one of eleven artworks in Sisavanh Phouthavong-Houghton's *Displacement* series. It depicts a Laotian-American who legally changed her native name as a means to enculturate into American society. Although Vilayphone's new name aligns with the collective group, she remains an individual. Phouthavong-Houghton symbolized this by designing the painting's frame to project the portrait's 5-inches (12 cm) away from the wall. Its protruding structure demands viewers' attention because it invades their physical space. Phouthavong-Houghton's choice of *Ben-Day dots* (a printing technique made of individual dots) for the portrait, further represent Vilayphone's distinct individuality, as she is one among many.

## Museum and Community Art Resources

Museums are excellent resources that bring students in contact with original works of art and offer students opportunities to participate in learning activities about exhibitions that curators and museum educators have developed. Teachers and students can utilize museums' virtual art collections to study art and explore interactive information on artists and their works. Some non-art museums, including natural history and science museums, feature arts and crafts collections that can guide interdisciplinary art history learning tasks. Each community includes people who make art, including professional artists, folk artists, and hobbyists. Some local and state art organizations provide grant funding to pay practicing artists to collaborate with teachers and students (Figure 9.7). Successful grant proposals typically explain how a teacher's class would benefit from learning about an artist's particular skill in context and connect the proposal to standards.

FIGURE 9.7 During studio visits, students learn how Pablo Cano collects found objects to produce his art.
*Source: Courtesy of the artist.*

## Art Production

Many teachers align art history studies with art production learning tasks. Teachers may read art history books, essays, and handouts to students or have them do so independently; demonstrate with art posters, reproductions, and/or original artworks; and show art history videos or movie segments. Students will typically spend the majority of class time developing studio art projects related to art history because they are usually the most time- and labor-intensive learning tasks. Art history–infused studio art projects may reference particular artworks, artists, or styles. Figure 9.8 presents a train ride with Pablo Picasso that passes a painted and collaged *Guernica* landscape. Figure 9.9 invites viewers into a student constructed interpretation of Romare Bearden's studio. Teachers will teach

**FIGURE 9.10** Nirel Kadzo, 14-years-old, Kenya.
*Source: Lisa Wee, teacher.*

students how artists select from various art production materials and techniques to produce explicit meanings, rather than having students passively copy artworks. For example, if students want to express a particular mood or meaning through patterns, teachers can have them compare and contrast artists' choices and applications of patterns to help them communicate their ideas most effectively. Figure 9.10 illustrates how a student applied Gustav Klimt's patterning.

## BEST PRACTICES FOR TEACHING ART HISTORY

Best practices for teaching and managing art history share many similarities with teaching and managing aesthetics and art criticism. Teachers place the focus on student inquiry rather than lecturing to students. Quality artworks are essential. Teachers should build a collection of original artworks and reproductions in the form of digital images, posters, books, handouts, and multimedia presentations to guide learning tasks that have personal significance to students and broadens their current understandings (Figures 9.11–9.13). Teachers should reinforce proper etiquette for looking at art and seeing original artworks on display in community settings.

Two main concerns may arise when teaching art history: how to introduce religious subject matter, and when and if to present nudity in art. Some schools and organizations have policies that prohibit teaching religious doctrine. This has been established so that students do not experience preference for one religion over another due to authority figures, including

**FIGURE 9.8** Laura Bartošová, 15-years-old, Občianske združenie art SLNEČNICE, o.z., Bratislava, Slovak Republic.
*Source: 45th ICEFA Lidice.*

**FIGURE 9.9** Savanna Hudson, early adolescent, United States.
*Source: Lydia Horvath, teacher.*

**FIGURE 9.11** These Native American artifacts have been in the teacher's family for generations. United States.

*Source: Amanda Bryant, teacher.*

**FIGURE 9.12** This teacher uses manipulatives to teach art history. United States.

*Source: Cassie Stephens, teacher.*

**FIGURE 9.13** These classroom bookcases contain a collection of art history books. Their teacher created sculpted crayons and pencils to enhance the space. United States.

*Source: Janet Malone, teacher.*

teachers, expressing that their personal religious beliefs are the only correct ones. As a result, some teachers might feel prohibited from integrating art historical works with religious context into the curriculum. In other communities, studying religious artworks is not controversial. Whether or not a school practices a separation of church and state, teachers are typically free to show religious works from varying cultural perspectives as long as they do not use them to inculcate their religious beliefs or teach singular truths. Through a choice-based art curriculum that treats artworks from different religions equally and uses big ideas to make connections and build enduring understandings, teachers teach students how religious artworks broaden people's understandings of human diversity.

Despite how beautiful and non-explicit an artwork containing nudity may be, some individuals may always be opposed to nudity in art. Art historian Leppert (2007) explained how the nude in art history differs from nakedness because an artist creates a nude using a model who is staged into a certain position to depict a mood or moment. The artwork has contextual meaning that extends beyond the model's nudity. Teachers should use professional judgment, administrator guidance, and school/organizational policy to determine if particular artworks and/or subject matter may be off limits, as they know students and their maturity levels, parents, and communities' best. They should consider if the nude subject is necessary to instruction and/or if it would be best to view nude artworks in a museum, rather than a classroom. Some children's art history books contain classical nudity. Many parents, teachers, and administrators feel comfortable sharing these images in context with children, while others do not. Some teachers choose or are required to conceal nude figures' genitals. When teachers have justified the inclusion of classical nudity in the curriculum, they must teach students how to approach the subject responsibly, remain understanding of students' concerns, and never tolerate off-task behaviors and comments. They should plan alternative assignments for students who do not wish to or cannot participate due to parental/guardian objections.

Teachers must also consider potential controversies that may arise during and/or after showing nude artworks (Poling & Guyas, 2008). For example, when planning a field trip for kindergarteners to an exhibition on Auguste Rodin that contained a large collection of his nude bronze figures, many of which showcased human torsos that were missing heads, full arms, and

**FIGURE 9.14** Auguste Rodin, *Marsyas (torso of The Falling Man)*, circa 1882–1889, this cast 1970. Bronze, 40.31 × 29 × 18 in. (102.24 × 73.66 × 45.72 cm). Gift of B. Gerald Cantor Art Foundation (M.73.108.5). LACMA Public Domain. *Source: www.lacma.org*

legs (similar to Figure 9.14), museum staff were concerned about the students' possible reactions to the nudity. To their surprise, the young children did not focus on the sculptures' nudity, but were concerned with their distorted bodies—revealing that children can view art differently than adults anticipate. In different circumstances, teachers may show an artist's age-appropriate artworks. Students may look up the artist online after class and unexpectedly locate examples by the same artist that are inappropriate due to their subject matter. When this is reported, administrators and parents might question why the artist was introduced in the school curriculum and may take disciplinary actions against teachers. While studying religious and classical nude artworks in context can correlate with learning tasks in the choice-based art curriculum, depictions of graphic sexuality and excessive violence never belong because they are not age-appropriate. Teachers must use caution and research artists before deciding to include them in the curriculum.

## OUR JOURNEY TO THRIVE CONTINUES . . .

In this chapter we learned inclusive approaches for teaching art history. In the next one, we will learn strategies for teaching visual culture inquiry. We will identify how visual culture studies build upon our comprehensive teachings of aesthetics, art criticism, and art history.

## CHAPTER QUESTIONS AND ACTIVITIES

1. Describe how you plan to teach inclusive art history as part of a choice-based art curriculum. Which art history learning tasks will you introduce to students? In which ways might students' ages and learning communities impact your curricular content?
2. Develop ten original inclusive art history posters for classroom use. The heading on each poster must be clearly visible at a distance. The posters can include smaller supplemental text for viewers to read up close. All parts will have a professional and unified design.
3. Continue to build your art inquiry card collection (Model 7.1). For this chapter's assignment, create 25 well-designed index cards filled with art history questions, issues, and art reproductions that are appropriate for pre-K–12 students. (Note: The finished box (based on activities from Chapters 7–10) will include a total of 100 cards with 25 aesthetic cards, 25 art criticism cards, 25 art history cards, and 25 visual culture cards for classroom use.)
4. Answer Artists' Lessons to Thrive! 9.1's essential/guiding questions in written form or as part of a group discussion. Complete its daily learning targets.

---

## References

Ambrose, K. (2016). Perspectives on art history. *Art Bulletin, 98*(4), 415. doi:10.1080/00043079.2016.1216667

Anderson, T., & Milbrandt, M. (2005). *Art for life*. Boston: McGraw Hill.

Arnold, D. (2009). Art history: Perspectives on method. *Art History, 32*(4), 657–663.

Barnet, S. (2014). *A short guide to writing about art* (2nd ed.). Upper Saddle River, NJ: Pearson.

Bätschmann, O. (2003). A guide to interpretation: Art historical hermeneutics (T. Brouwers, Trans.). In C. J. Farago (Ed.), *Compelling visuality: The work of art in and out of history* (pp. 179–210). Minneapolis, MN: University of Minnesota Press.

Capistrano-Baker, F. H. (2015). Whither art history? Whither art history in the non-Western world: Exploring the other('s) art histories. *Art Bulletin, 97*(3), 246–257. doi:10.1080/00043 079.2015.1015883

Clark, R., & Folgo, A. (2006). Who says there have been great women artists?: Some afterthoughts. *Art Education, 59*(2), 47–52.

D'Alleva, A. (2005). *Look again!: Art history and critical theory.* Upper Saddle River, NJ: Prentice Hall.

Helliwell, J., Layard, R., & Sachs, J. (2016). *World happiness report 2016, update* (Vol. 1). New York, NY: Sustainable Development Solutions Network.

Leppert, R. (2007). *The nude: The cultural rhetoric of the body in the art of Western modernity.* New York, NY: Routledge.

Mattos, C. (2014). Whiter art history: Geography, art theory, and new perspectives for an inclusive art history. *Art Bulletin, 96*(3), 259–264. doi:10.1080/00043079.2014.889511

Poling, L. H., & Guyas, A. S. (2008). Removing the fig leaf: Issues and strategies for handling nudity in the art room. *Art Education, 61*(1), 39–43.

Preziosi, D. (2009). *The art of art history: A critical anthology* (2nd ed.). New York: Oxford University Press.

Rosenberg, M., & Thurber, F. (2007). *Gender matters in art education.* Worcester, MA: Davis Publications.

Seppä, A. (2010). Globalisation and the arts: The rise of new democracy, or just another pretty suit for the old emperor? *Journal of Aesthetics & Culture, 2*(1). Retrieved from www.aestheticsandculture.net/index.php/jac/article/view/5410/6295

Zwijnenberg, R., & Farago, C. (2003). Art history after aesthetics: A provocative introduction. In C. J. Farago (Ed.), *Compelling visuality: The work of art in and out of history* (pp. vii–xvi). Minneapolis, MN: University of Minnesota Press.

# Chapter 10

# Visual Culture

## Wiser Ways of Seeing and Knowing

**FIGURE 10.1** K. Mahipal Reddy, 13-years-old, Young Envoys International, Hyderabad, India.
*Source: ICEFA Lidice, 37th Exhibition.*

**Visual culture** studies examine the possible meanings of all images within our global society. Each day humans build upon the world's vast collection of images and introduce new ones in the forms of artworks, photographs, crafts, graphics, advertisements, websites, gaming, mass-produced products, and more. Visual culture influences people through its sensory appeal, multimedia innovations, cultural styles, and aesthetic designs. Given society's wealth of visual data, students need to be able to recognize the diverse meanings and purposes of visual products. We can teach students to identify how images interconnect with everyday life and influence social understandings. Through ongoing visual culture instruction, students learn to identify when hidden and overt meanings are present and see other people's perspectives. We challenge them to look through the lenses of cultural observers who can analyze people's roles as consumers and producers of objects.

We will meet the following objectives by participating in this chapter:

- Define visual culture and explain its purpose in the choice-based art curriculum.

- Identify best practices for teaching students visual culture inquiry methods.
- Develop instructional resources for teaching visual culture.

Spotlight on Student Art #10 (Figure 10.1) demonstrates how visual culture inspired a student's artwork focusing on the big idea of exploration. The student applied existing cultural images to produce the artwork's dynamic design.

---

## Spotlight on Student Art #10

### Big Idea: Exploration

Three Indian astronauts float through space among vibrant stars, cratered surfaces, and rockets in a painting by 13-year-old Mahipal (Figure 10.1). His artwork identifies some of humanity's technological advancements in space exploration. Generations of people have marveled at the night sky with its sheer vastness, brightly shining stars, and unknown qualities. Humanity's interest in the night sky sparked astronomy, one of the world's oldest forms of science, beginning in ancient cultures including Indian, Mayan, and Greek. Carrying tools in hand, Mahipal's astronauts focus their attention straight ahead, on the serious work they have to do.

Mahipal made the artistic decision to alter traditional white spacesuits and rockets. Each of his astronauts wears a different colored spacesuit featuring green, blue, red, and yellow hues. They mimic stylish silk and satin Indian fashions, such as the sari and angarkha, which have been prevalent in Indian culture (including Bollywood). Mahipal's gem-like display shares similar characteristics with high-resolution photographs captured by the Hubble Space Telescope. Such a kaleidoscopic depiction of the universe presents us with the illusion of a hospitable space environment suitable for human advancement that moves away from the feeling of a deep, cold void. It also reinforces how the mystery of space has been ingrained in visual culture. Despite the fact that very few individuals have entered outer space, children and adult artists have the know-how to capture its qualities in their creations. They have seen a vast amount of visual data to guide their artistic products, including photographs from high-powered telescopes, blockbuster movies, astronomy websites, entertaining cartoons, and architectural/industrial designs.

---

## VISUAL CULTURE

Early societies originated visual culture when they began making adaptations to the natural environment by manipulating objects, creating functional products, forming aesthetic designs, and inventing advanced symbols. Since humanity's beginnings, people have continued to appropriate others' ideas to replicate products and improve what has already been invented. Generations of artists and designers augment predecessors' changing perspectives of art and design. Their visual statements, which may address universal themes and include new media, provide unique viewpoints for others to contemplate. Like artworks, products, and designs before them, newer works become a part of our collective visual culture for others to emulate and expand upon (Mirzoeff, 1998, 2002; Trafi-Prats, 2009). For example, although the student artwork shown in Figure 10.2 was created decades after the embroidered infant hat shown in Figure 10.3, it shares similar stylistic designs.

FIGURE 10.2 Xiong Chin Wing Elodie, 7-years-old, Simply Art, Hong Kong, China.
*Source: ICEFA Lidice, 39th Exhibition.*

FIGURE 10.3 Han people of China, *Embroidered Infant Hat With Double Tigers*, 1940. The Children's Museum of Indianapolis. CC BY-SA 3.0 via Wikimedia Commons.
*Source: https://creativecommons.org/licenses/by-sa/3.0/*

Some images in visual culture have earned prominence in our collective consciousness because they relate to the human condition through our shared histories, advancements, and concerns. People recall iconic images of real and fictitious events because they are continuously repeated in visual culture. Through **semiotics**, students learn to read symbols in visual culture and interpret their meanings and roles within given societies. Symbolic icons sometimes function as metaphors that represent the things that humans value. When students become informed viewers, they can read and interpret key information quickly by using the semiotic signs that society has taught them to understand. For instance, to demonstrate this concept teachers can ask students to identify the meaning of a red octagonal sign on a

street corner (a stop sign) and recognizable product logos, such as a cartoon character on a cereal box (Heussner, 2011).

A main component in visual culture studies is teaching students how to recognize that images have different meanings and intents. Visual imagery combined with effective storylines and multimedia technologies have the power to influence people's beliefs and behaviors. Students can identify visual culture images as fun, positive, and productive. However, when they are looking at advertisements, which are prevalent in society, young people often do not understand the full meanings of the messages that advertisers use to promote products by targeting specific audiences such as themselves. Many visual images result from marketing campaigns and products designed for profit. Successful campaigns reinforce the idea that purchasing advertised products will help consumers lead better lives, feel happy, look beautiful, fit in, and have their needs met. Advertisers are skilled at creating a "need" for their products and may hire celebrities to endorse them. Celebrities include real people, mascots, and designed fictitious characters, including the ones in movies and cartoons. Celebrities set beauty standards (Briggs, 2007). Students often incorporate these celebrities in their art, especially works they create in their free time. While celebrities may be entertaining, students need to understand that celebrity beauty may result from multiple cosmetic procedures, surgeries, and stringent diet and exercise regimens. When people cannot match established beauty standards, some form negative opinions and feel dissatisfied with their physical characteristics. They may replicate extreme measures that some celebrities use to obtain idealized beauty. Unrealistic media depictions can also lead children struggling with obesity to be teased or bullied, as well as cause some young children to act out adult sexual behaviors, despite their underdeveloped bodies and cognitive skills.

Visual culture is saturated with examples of around-the-clock spectatorship made possible through digital devices, social media, reality television, and gaming. All of this can present a false sense of "reality," and information presented as reality may be manipulated or staged (Farhi, 2008; Freedman, 2003; Rogoff, 2002). Children as young as elementary students have been exposed to explicit, graphic images. Some are made by and for adolescents on social media sites or through sexting, the act of sending and receiving explicit text messages in the form of videos and/or photographs (Hoffman, 2011). Teachers can teach students about the dangers associated with explicit images and demonstrate how to approach safe adults if they come in contact with harmful images. They can develop art learning tasks that center around big ideas including respect, dignity, and self-esteem to teach students positive ways to get attention and be valued for who they are. Teachers can also work with students to brainstorm ways to move away from passive spectatorship and identify how they might combine technology and advocacy to bring public awareness to valid societal concerns, as students have done to address gun violence in schools.

Gaming can play a substantial role in altering students' reality. Some games allow users to develop alter egos through digital characters called *avatars* that can achieve everything from the mundane to super heroic tasks. The visually stunning fantasy worlds that games present, with their thrilling sound effects, can be more stimulating than real life. At their best, games entertain audiences and offer harmless temporary escapes from the world; at their worst, these false realities cause destruction to users' personal relationships, school/employment, psyche, and health because people spend more time focusing on imaginary realities than their own lives. Students are aware of these concerns. While producing a collaborative artwork during a visual culture lesson, one early adolescent student explained: "It can make all of the important things in your life seem to disappear. Although it may seem fun at first, don't let it control your life" (Figure 10.4). Youth gamers might be popular in a virtual world, but unpopular at school. They might use games to numb hurtful feelings. Male players who crave games' social environments and competitive features are the most likely to become addicted (Hussain, Williams, & Griffiths, 2015).

Through critical examination, the choice-based art curriculum teaches students how to recognize the messages behind visual culture so that they become aware of the ways in which individuals and cultural groups choose to act upon, remain neutral to, or disregard distinct imagery according

**FIGURE 10.4** Early adolescent Regan Zahn and her peers created visual culture–inspired artworks and discussed the meanings of their productions. United States.
*Source: Mike Muller, teacher.*

to their personal perspectives and given contexts. Students will learn that some individuals in popular culture are placed in the limelight due to their attainment of "the ideal" as judged by decision makers. Comprehensive lessons teach students how to identify the "invisible" in visual culture by noticing the ways in which individuals and groups of people have been marginalized, forgotten, censored, left out, and/or stereotyped. These can be based on socioeconomic status, physical ability, race, gender, age, religion, political beliefs, sexuality, and cultural mores (Duncum, 2006; Freedman, 2003; Keifer-Boyd & Maitland-Gholson, 2007; Mitchell, 2002; Stuhr, Ballengee-Morris, & Daniel, 2008).

This textbook's Model 10.1, "WISER Consumer Model for Visual Culture Studies," consists of three sections—<u>w</u>ise <u>i</u>nvesting, <u>s</u>ales, and <u>e</u>nd <u>r</u>esults—to teach students how to examine all types of images within visual culture as wiser consumers and viewers of visual data. Model 10.2 presents a list of guiding questions to stimulate students' creative inquiry as they utilize the WISER Consumer Model for Visual Culture Studies. Students will answer its questions to make detailed observations, address corresponding questions, and identify big ideas and design concepts to become informed and ethical viewers, producers, and consumers. Teachers can adapt the questions to accommodate students' ages and abilities.

## Model 10.1
## WISER Consumer Model for Visual Culture Studies

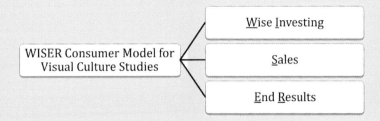

## Model 10.2
## WISER Consumer Model Questions for Visual Culture Studies

### Wise Investing Guiding Questions

1. What is the product or idea?
2. What are its key features?
3. What big idea is presented?
4. What is the product's or idea's purpose?
5. Who is its target audience?
6. Whose perceptions do you see?
7. Who and what are presented? Who and what are left out? What does this presence and absence mean?
8. Who has control?
9. To what end does it persuade its audience?
10. Is its depiction accurate? Is it informative? Is it ethical?
11. How do people's stereotypes impact their initial (or ongoing) interpretations of what they see? How might stereotypes or assumptions provide a limited understanding of the situation presented?
12. What perspectives do you bring with you as you examine this product? In which ways might your age, race, gender, social status, education, and socioeconomic status shape your perspectives?

### Sales Guiding Questions

13. How effectively does the product or idea convey its message?
14. What components make the product's or idea's message easy or difficult to follow?
15. Were high-pressure or low-pressure selling tactics involved?
16. Does the product or idea appear so natural that it seems to sell itself?
17. What makes it appealing, unappealing, or indifferent? In which ways does it engage or disengage one's senses?
18. How convincing are the objects, people, and lifestyles presented?
19. What is the purpose of showing certain images and concepts more or less frequently?
20. Who or what possesses power within an image about the product or idea? Does it empower viewers? Does it cause spectators to feel subjugate to those who have power?

21. Does the product or idea speak directly to viewers? How does it connect with people on a personal level? Why might it appear irrelevant or neutral to others?
22. Which words, phrases, or ideas sell its message?
23. How do multimedia components (such as logos, sounds, and hyperlinks) tell a fuller story?
24. Which key benefits, lifestyle enhancements, and/or guarantees were presented?

### End Results Guiding Questions

25. Would you recommend this product or idea? Why? Why not?
26. What criteria have you set to identify these end results?
27. Given your experience analyzing this work, did this particular image, idea, campaign, or series of works empower audiences and/or manipulate them? Did your beliefs change at any time during your analysis?
28. What role did your prior knowledge and research play in forming your final judgment?
29. What qualities make it feel powerful, weak, or indifferent to you knowing what you now know?
30. In your opinion, was this product or idea effective in doing what it said it would do?
31. Given its combined qualities, did the work meet the needs of its targeted audience?
32. What are the benefits of this product or idea? Does it produce any negative outcomes?
33. In which ways might it have been more effective in reaching its target audience?
34. How have external factors influenced your final judgment?
35. Should this product or idea be endorsed, banned, or censored?
36. In which ways could you communicate your informed knowledge about this product or idea to others?

1. **Wise investing** calls upon students to identify persuasion in visual culture in order to interpret imagery critically from a consumer's perspective, as a possible purchaser or user. Purchasing includes the act of investing in a product or an idea, such as a public service announcement, an advertisement, or a call to action. As part of their initial examination, wise student consumers identify a work's content to determine whom and what are present and left out. They contemplate the possible reasons for represented and missing content used to market a product or idea. They learn to recognize that marketers, who are expert sellers of products or ideas, take deliberate steps to appeal to viewers' perceived needs, emotions, and senses. Consumers' responses will vary according to their life experiences and external circumstances. For example, people develop moral and ethical ideals about how things should be, what things should look like, and how individuals and groups of people should behave. Producers and marketers keep consumers' plausible perceptions, assumptions, and biases in mind because consumers view visual content from different perspectives.

2. **Sales** focuses on the presentations and possible manipulations of media to sell a product or idea. Marketers develop multimedia sales pitches to encourage potential consumers, especially ones with doubts, to go ahead and purchase their products or believe in their ideas. Their marketing tactics direct viewers' attention to the immediate benefits of their commodities. They may also overshadow, ignore, deny, or redirect possible consequences associated with their goods or ideas. Marketers seek people's immediate guttural reactions to produce greater sales or recognition. They understand that people take pleasure in viewing certain types of imagery, even when its content may shock, surprise, and conflict with their ideals and values.

   Marketers may intentionally manipulate people's understandings of visual culture by producing multiple modes of instruction to promote mass-produced products or ideas (Duncum, 2010). Wise student consumers learn to recognize the industry's tricks of the trade by analyzing products' effective designs and marketing concepts. Multimedia campaigns attract audiences through visual and sensory appeals. Successful products' designs are unified and not cluttered or confusing. Designers select optimal color palettes, repeat important content, and emphasize objects, people, or places to create an immediate sense of desire and/or instant recognition. Their quality logos, slogans, jingles, and spokespersons lead consumers to believe that their products are necessary and beneficial.

Retailers sell products using pleasing displays, fashionable packaging, and encouraging salespersons who demonstrate product usage and key benefits. They may offer special deals or giveaways for greater appeal. Similarly, artists develop personal websites that include digital galleries, written statements about their art, critics' favorable reviews, and descriptions of current happenings to drive public interest and generate art sales. When consumers consider downloading online music, they type in, click on, or touch the music selection of their choice. Migrating from link to link in a virtual world stimulates them to locate the resources they need. They can view album art, listen to song clips, and read music reviews. They may link to a music video that depicts the musicians' idealized lifestyle, which was designed to remind consumers of their own desires. The online site offers other music selections to suit consumer tastes based on the choices of customers who purchased the same songs they just browsed.

Each of these forms of communication is designed to speak directly to potential customers. Memorable products can result in customers' enthusiasm and beliefs in products' desired outcomes. Marketers drive key concepts by explaining product advantages over similar products and how they improve one's lifestyle, such as making one more beautiful (Figure 10.5), financially successful, and/or intelligent. A product may also tout that it is of better quality, cheaper, faster, or more convenient than its competition. Given this information as a whole, wise student consumers may feel strongly about a particular product or idea, accept it out of habit, or know of no other better choices that they purchase or accept it—or the intended "sale" may not go through because they feel indifferent about or reject a product or belief altogether.

3. **End results** move consumers beyond the present moment to identify what they will gain or lose from purchasing (believing in) or not purchasing (not believing in) a product or idea. As part of their investigation, students apply research methodology

**FIGURE 10.5** Joy Malaika, middle childhood, paints a glamorous pink-haired female wearing a stunning dress.
*Source: Kenya. Lisa Wee, teacher.*

and personal life experiences to determine if the product's or idea's benefits and/or consequences are short term, long term, or a mixture of the two. They use documentation based on their journal entries, artworks, photographs, sketches, and interviews or testimonials to summarize ideas. They explain their judgments and share their knowledge with others. Their summative findings are based on conscious reasoning and include supportive evidence. As applicable, teachers encourage students to articulate how they moved away from impulsive decisions and took steps to avoid stereotypical perceptions. If they choose to "purchase" products and ideas that may not have represented the best choices, they need to be able to defend their decisions in conjunction with the end results they identified.

## VISUAL CULTURE INQUIRY METHODS

At the onset of the 21st century, visual culture gained popularity in art education because it broadened the visuals that students could study beyond art history. Visual culture learning tasks became well-suited for a new generation of students that owned home computers with realistic gaming software and Internet access; these tasks have continued with society's use of technologies on the go. Much of children's exposure to visual culture is based on their everyday habits, such as surfing the Internet, watching television, taking trips to the grocery store, and being exposed to other children's possessions. Like adults, children of all ages form attachments to and preferences for certain products based on their sensory appeal and the value they add to their lives.

Quality visual culture lessons combine stimulating visual resources with relevant big ideas to equip students of all ages with the knowledge they need to make informed decisions and develop 21st century skills. Many of the learning tasks presented in this textbook's aesthetics, art criticism, and art history chapters (Chapters 7–9) are applicable for teaching visual culture. For example, students can write and sketch about visual culture in their journals, as well as develop comparison papers to analyze images from visual culture. Students can participate in discussions and write essays using the WISER Consumer Model for Visual Culture Studies. Referencing the aesthetic category pragmatism, students can analyze visual culture images and write about and/or discuss the actions or inactions particular images promote. Instead of ranking art, they can rank visual culture works according to their effectiveness in conveying intended messages to target audiences.

This chapter's Artists' Lessons to Thrive! 10.1–10.3 link visual culture studies with contemporary art. "Robert Lungupi: I Need You in My Life—I Really Do!" (10.1) presents Lungupi's portrait of Dolly Rathebe and discusses some of her experiences during South Africa's apartheid. Lungupi's artwork references visual culture iconography from Rathebe's times as a celebrity. "Kimsooja: Where Do We Go From Here?" (10.2) showcases Kimsooja's *Cities on the Move* for students to contemplate diverse reasons for human migration. It demonstrates how Kimsooja repurposed a cultural artifact that is significant in her life into an art form that communicates meanings about the human condition. "Kathy Vargas: The Beauty of Remembrance" (10.3) features a photograph by Vargas that pays tribute to her mother's memory. It examines beauty from a sentimental perspective, rather than what is typical in popular culture. Through these comprehensive art lessons and the chapter's learning tasks students will have opportunities to make critical decisions about products, lifestyle choices, equity, and local and world events.

## Artists' Lessons to Thrive! 10.1 Robert Lungupi: I Need You in My Life—I Really Do!

### Big Idea: Making a Positive Difference

Robert Lungupi, a Tanzanian artist based in South Africa, transformed a functioning radio into a carved and painted artwork depicting legendary South African singer Dolly Rathebe (Figure 10.1.1). Lungupi's sculpted design features Rathebe at a microphone, singing passionately with her eyes closed. Wearing a pink polka dot dress and bright jewelry, Rathebe is placed at center stage. Lungupi portrays Rathebe's iconic status by proportioning her figure much larger than the accompanying jazz musicians.

Many young people and adults surround themselves with cherished mass-produced artifacts of their favorite celebrities. Whether they are real people, actors portraying fictional characters, or cartoon/ digital characters, images of these iconic personalities appear on clothing, pins, posters, lunch boxes, and more. Mass-produced items with celebrity representations can provide fans with an imagined sense of ownership of the famous personality.

Rathebe became a legend in 1949 when she starred in the first South African feature film with an all-black cast, *Jim Comes to Jo'burg* (Johannesburg), and appeared on the cover of *Zonk! Magazine*. Her fame expanded beyond South Africa. Never before had the pan-African community seen a glamorous African woman portrayed on the cover of a glossy picture magazine. Her image departed from the common presentation of African women in domestic and agricultural roles during South Africa's apartheid, a time of racial segregation. Rathebe's talents and beauty brought pleasure to an African audience during a time of extreme oppression. With the government's development of harsher apartheid laws during the 1950s, Sophiatown—a multiethnic cultural community in the center of Johannesburg, and Rathebe's hometown—was destroyed. As a result, Rathebe could no longer pursue her artistic career. Apartheid displaced millions of South Africans and forced them into segregated residential zones. It denied personal

FIGURE 10.1.1 Robert Lungupi, *Radio With Portrait of Singer Dolly Rathebe*, 2002. 13 3/16 × 18 7/8 × 8 1/4 in. (33.5 × 48 × 21cm). Tropenmuseum, part of the National Museum of World Cultures.
*Source: CC BY-SA 3.0 via Wikimedia Commons.*

freedoms, multiracial discourse, and equal access to education and social services (Jaji, 2014). In 1994, apartheid ended with the election of Nelson Mandela as South Africa's president. Rathebe's career flourished once again. Her life story was presented in the 2002 exhibition: *Group Portrait South Africa: Nine Family Histories*, which documented family narratives through their material possessions to explain some of the consequences and complexities that resulted from apartheid (Faber, 2007). The exhibition included artworks inspired by Rathebe's celebrity status, as well as her furnishings, modeled publicity portraits for *Drum* magazine by photographer Jürgen Schadeberg, and personal snapshots. In 2004, just before Rathebe passed away, the South African Government awarded her its Order of Ikhamanga in Silver for excellent achievement in the performing arts and for promoting democracy.

## Essential/Guiding Questions

1. Why is a radio an effective medium for Robert Lungupi to use for Dolly Rathebe's portrait?
2. How has Robert Lungupi's *Radio With Portrait of Singer Dolly Rathebe* captured a moment in time? What is the historical value of this artwork?

## Preparation

Generations of people accrue collections of their favorite celebrity products. Students will reflect on the celebrity products they know. They will discuss how Dolly Rathebe symbolized beauty and hope during the apartheid era. Students will consider her example to select a historic or contemporary individual who has applied his/her fame to make a positive difference in society.

## Daily Learning Targets

I can repurpose an existing object to develop an artwork that tells a story about a celebrity who has made a positive difference.

- I can integrate the celebrity's image, symbols, and cause into my design.
- I can complete all sides of my repurposed object to show unity and craftspersonship.
- I can explain how the object I repurposed correlates with the celebrity I selected.

I can take an inventory of my own or someone else's collection of iconic celebrity imagery to answer the WISER Consumer Model for Visual Culture Studies' guiding questions (Model 10.2).

- I will answer these questions in complete sentences.
- I will integrate art vocabulary in each of the model's three sections.

**National Core Arts Anchor Standards** 2, 6, 8, and 11

www.nationalartsstandards.org

---

### Artists' Lessons to Thrive! 10.2 Kimsooja: Where Do We Go From Here?

#### Big Idea: Migration

People relocate for different reasons. Some people are forced to move because of circumstances such as their jobs, political circumstances, available resources, personal responsibilities, and the search for a better life. Born in Korea, Kimsooja is a contemporary artist who creates sculptural pieces, performances, installations, and videos. As a child, Kimsooja moved around from place to place due to her father's military profession. She regularly packed her belongings in the traditional Korean bundle called a **bottari**, a colorful silken sheet embroidered with symbols of fortune, hope, and fertility that families save as keepsakes throughout their lives. Korean women tie their belongings securely inside of bottaris to protect them. One day Kimsooja viewed her personal bottaris for storing fabrics in a different light. She recognized them as sculptural forms and conceptualized her bottaris as art.

To create *Cities on the Move* (1997), Kimsooja collected used clothing and bedding from flea markets (Figure 10.2.1). She assembled them into multiple bottaris and stacked them onto the bed of a pickup truck. Sitting perched on top of her great stack of bottaris, Kimsooja journeyed through 2,727 kilometers (approximately 1,695 miles) of South Korean cityscapes and landscapes over an eleven day period. She transformed her experience into a 7 minute and 3 second documentary, which served as a metaphor to bring awareness to the emotional conditions of people who have been forced to migrate. The *Cities on the Move* video portrays Kimsooja's figure at a distance from behind. Her form feels unpretentious next to the vast cityscapes and landscapes. Kimsooja's performance illustrates the passing of time in conjunction with changing physical and emotional spaces. As a symbol, her bottaris embody a nomadic way of life, as they represent migration and dislocation. Since developing *Cities on the Move*, Kimsooja has continued to produce bottari-inspired performances and has also installed them as sculptural forms in distinct locations including vaulted interiors, pristine museums, and countrysides (Figure 10.2.2; Malsch, 2005). She continues to travel to different global regions to collect other persons' discarded, donated, and sold possessions that are left in transition to become someone else's property. Kimsooja uses these

**FIGURE 10.2.1** Kimsooja, *Cities on the Move*, 1997, performance, 2,727 kilometers (approx. 1,695 miles) on a bottari truck, 1997, 11 days journey throughout South Korea.

*Source: Photo by Lee Sang Gil, Courtesy of Kimsooja Studio; www.kimsooja.com*

**FIGURE 10.2.2** Kimsooja, *Bottari*, 2009/2012, digital C-print, 22.36 × 30 in. (56.8 × 76.2 cm).

*Source: Courtesy of Kimsooja Studio; www.kimsooja.com*

cultural artifacts to portray diverse aspects of humanity within people's distinct cultures (Art 21, 2009).

## Essential/Guiding Questions

1. Why do familiar objects that have societal value sometimes appear to be overlooked, despite their prominence in everyday life? Do you think Kimsooja was able to maintain the traditional role of the bottari in *Cities on the Move* while communicating her artistic vision?
2. How did Kimsooja's recording of her journey across South Korea on a bottari truck further articulate her message about migration? How is this presentation different than seeing her bottaris in isolation in a museum setting?

## Preparation

Kimsooja uses multimedia art forms to provide richer context to her work. Students will conduct a multimedia search of news items and artifacts that bring awareness to migration. They will include international housing examples in their collection. Students will identify how their collective body of information on migration comes together to communicate an idea more fully.

## Daily Learning Targets

I can answer the following questions in my journal to research migration.

1. What is migration?
2. What is the meaning of home? Is home a feeling, a place, both, or something else?
3. Should having a sense of personal space (perhaps a home) be a given right for all people?
4. How do the look and feel of homes vary across our planet?
5. How might your examination of international homes and representations of their inhabitants' beliefs, customs, and values change and/or enhance your perception of migration and your own home?
6. How do the media present people who carry their possessions with them because they do not have a home compare to their depictions of people who carry some of their belongings for business and/or pleasure?
7. What role should discussions about migration and homelessness play in society and the school curriculum?

I can develop an artwork that focuses on the big idea of migration.

* I can identify an original symbol to signify the meaning of migration.
* I can explain how the material(s) and object(s) I selected for my artwork impact the meaning of my visual message in written form.
* I can orally summarize how my artwork and ideas underwent transformations.
* I can demonstrate unity, emphasis, and craftspersonship in my design.

**National Core Arts Anchor Standards** 3, 5, 8, and 11
www.nationalartsstandards.org

# Artists' Lessons to Thrive! 10.3 Kathy Vargas: The Beauty of Remembrance

## Big Ideas: Natural Beauty and Remembrance

**FIGURE 10.3.1** Kathy Vargas, "My Mother, Susie Salcedo Vargas, on Her Way to Work," from the series *Este Recuerdo*, 2001, hand-colored gelatin silver prints, 24 × 20 in. (60.96 × 50.8 cm).
*Source: Courtesy of the artist.*

Historic family photographs serve as inspirations for understanding concepts of natural beauty that extend beyond what people see in popular culture. Contemporary photographer Kathy Vargas produced "My Mother, Susie Salcedo Vargas, on Her Way to Work" (Figure 10.3.1) as part of her *Este Recuerdo* ("this remembrance") series. The series contains hand-painted double-exposure photographs that Vargas designed to remember family members who had passed away. To produce the work, Vargas photographed an itinerant (street) photographer's vintage photograph of her mother navigating a San Antonio sidewalk with fellow pedestrians.

Vargas added to this moment in time by taking a second photograph of a torn Polaroid frame. The frame is intended to mimic the feeling of a tombstone. Using a film camera, Vargas superimposed the photograph of her mother with the second image to produce a double-exposure photograph. In her artist statement about the series, Vargas wrote: "The overlapping double-exposures imply that moments can co-exist, occupying the same space in time." The past and present are united. Although her mother is no longer living, she appears as vivacious and energetic as she did in the 1940s, when the photograph was originally taken. While Vargas selected the framed Polaroid to symbolize the physical barrier that separated her from her mother, she also gave the work a physical presence. She added soothing touches of love to the printed portrait of the mother she misses dearly by hand-painting the photograph with soft hues.

Reflecting on the artwork, Vargas explained how her grandmother helped at home while her mother worked. As is customary in Chicano culture, Vargas' grandmother taught the family that death marks a reunification with loved ones. Instead of fearing death, families honor the memories of loved ones through celebrations and personal altars. Vargas expanded this concept by creating her mother's portrait for society to share. Her artwork pays tribute to the artist's mother, Susie Salcedo Vargas, and invites audiences to admire and keep her memory alive just like they would with their own family members.

## Essential/Guiding Questions

1. What is remembrance? How has Vargas presented her mother as a source of beauty and remembrance for herself and others?
2. What can society learn about humanity's conceptions of natural beauty and remembrance from *My Mother, Susie Salcedo Vargas, on Her Way to Work*?

## Preparation

Students will discuss the meaning of beauty and remembrance. They will collect historic photographs that they find naturally beautiful, which can include family portraits. They will also assemble examples of idealized beauty presented in contemporary products. They will compare and contrast contemporary and historic perspectives on beauty.

## Daily Learning Targets

I can select a contemporary product that depicts idealized beauty to answer the WISER Consumer Model for Visual Culture Studies' guiding questions (Model 10.2).

- I can answer questions in complete sentences.
- I can include the concept of natural beauty based on the whole person in my response.
- I can integrate art vocabulary in each of the model's different sections.

I can research the big idea of natural beauty surrounds us to manipulate a historic photograph.

- I can select a historic photograph that represents a realistic view of beauty.
- I can integrate a framing device and narrative text into the photograph's altered design.
- I can show effective balance, craftspersonship, and unity in my completed design.
- I can orally articulate my opinions about my artwork and compare them to what I learned studying a contemporary example of idealized beauty.

**National Core Arts Anchor Standards** 1, 6, 7, and 10

www.nationalartsstandards.org

*Quoted artists' statements not listed in the reference section result from personal communications with the author (personal communications, 2014–2018).*

## Early Childhood and Visual Culture Inquiry

Children's introduction to visual culture begins at a young age. Early childhood visual culture lessons should engage young learners' bodies and minds. Students can role-play visual culture scenarios, act out skits with handmade puppets and dolls, and create jingles and dances for their visual culture–inspired products. Teachers can apply young children's exposure to everyday events—including playing with friends and toys, going swimming, and visiting the park—to prompt visual culture learning tasks. For example, Figure 10.6 illustrates a boy's interest in playing with his collection of toy dinosaurs. Young children can use their imaginations to analyze the plastic dinosaurs' different personalities and possible behaviors based on their designs. As shown in Figure 10.7, students can identify the visual qualities that they see when going swimming, including analyzing designs on floats, beach towels, and bathing suits. At this age, young children are just beginning to understand the meaning of symbols. They can recognize product branding and discuss strategies to adapt, manipulate, or redesign familiar products. To teach kindness, students could transform a villain action figure into a benevolent superhero. Young learners can recognize certain apps and computer icons. Teachers can present students with a sampling of icons and images that link visual culture with art history. When studying an icon of a computer trash/recycle bin, teachers could discuss how it protects the computer by deleting unwanted information and saving memory space. Students could make connections to *Sesame Street's* Oscar the Grouch and his beloved garbage-can home. The class could further link the trash icon and Oscar's protective garbage can with Nick Cave's sound suits (Artists' Lessons to Thrive! 1.1), which are also symbols of protection.

## Middle Childhood and Visual Culture Inquiry

In middle childhood, students are becoming more susceptible to outside influences from friends and the media. Teachers can introduce the topic of ethics and ask students to determine if influencing friends and pestering parents to purchase products is right, fair, and/or expected. Students can talk about purchasing's consequences, including lack of funds, and the joys of shopping, including fulfilling a need and togetherness (Figure 10.8). Students will identify how advertisers may use people's influences over others to earn greater profits. They will apply their knowledge to develop an awareness campaign using the media of their choice. Students can manipulate words and language to create metaphors. For a different visual culture lesson, students can collect slogans in popular culture that grab their attention and analyze how slogans sell products and ideas. Students can apply what they learned about effective slogans and font designs to create a visual metaphor that advocates for a cause of their choice. At this age, students start to build collections and will store personal items (i.e. trinkets, games, media devices, and snacks) in their desks and backpacks. Teachers can introduce students to storage spaces including treasure chests, dowry chests, ancient Egyptian tombs, and Kimsooja's Korean bottaris (Artists' Lessons to Thrive! 10.2 and Figure 10.9). Students will discuss the contents within these items and their cultural significance. They will collect items from each of their desks or backpacks to temporarily place in a storage device. They will take an inventory of their collection and identify what their choices tell others about their classroom culture. Students can select an object from their collection, such as a card game, to create an original artwork and describe its meaning and purpose (Figure 10.10).

**FIGURE 10.6** Khaled Al Kodsi, 7-years-old, Private Atelier M. Sibai, Homs, Syria.
*Source: ICEFA Lidice, 39th Exhibition.*

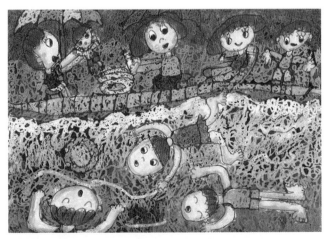

**FIGURE 10.7** Almeira Anindita, 5-years-old, Ananda Visual Art School, Bandung, Indonesia.
*Source: ICEFA Lidice, 45th Exhibition.*

**FIGURE 10.8** Amir Homayoon Ansarifard, 11-years-old, Kanoon–Institute for Intellectual Development of Children and Young Adults, Tehran, Iran.
*Source: ICEFA Lidice, 39th Exhibition.*

**FIGURE 10.9** Kimsooja, *Bottari*, 2011/2017, Used Korean Bedcover and Used Clothing, 21 × 22.5 × 21 in. (53.34 × 57.15 × 53.34 cm)
*Source: Courtesy of Kimsooja Studio; www.kimsooja.com*

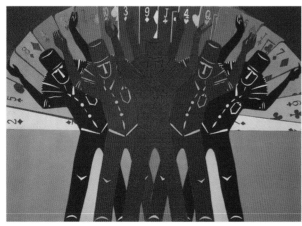

**FIGURE 10.10** Josef Susík, 11-years-old, ZŠ, Nový Jičín, Czech Republic.
*Source: ICEFA Lidice, 40th Exhibition.*

# Early Adolescence and Visual Culture Inquiry

Early adolescents are susceptible to the idealized physical appearances featured in visual culture. Some students are developing physical attraction to others and look to media sources to purchase trendy products to enhance their looks, such as hair gels, acne treatments, and hip clothing. Young adolescents are seeking independence and may feel that adults far outside of their age group do not understand them. They turn to peers, music, and other forms of popular culture to express their identity. The choice-based art curriculum can encourage students to talk about the qualities they and their peers admire in performers. Students can study the designs of logos, tools, instruments, costumes, and/or performance environments of traditional and contemporary international artists and make associations to performers with whom they identify (Figures 10.11 and 10.12). Teachers can explain that many performers appropriate ideas

**FIGURE 10.11** Mithuni Theshika Perera, 13-years-old, Sampath Rekha International Art Academy, Gothatuwa, Sri Lanka.
*Source: ICEFA Lidice, 41st Exhibition.*

**FIGURE 10.12** Juan Rafael Soto Perez, 13-years-old, Casa de Cultura Suez Jorge Sean, Quemado de Guines, Cuba.
*Source: ICEFA Lidice, 40th Exhibition.*

FIGURE 10.13 Dandysh Gumarova, 13-years-old, MBU DO Detskaia khudozhestvennaia shkola No. 1 im. I. I. Shishkina, Elabuga, Russia.
*Source: ICEFA Lidice, 44th Exhibition.*

from other cultures to produce hybrid designs to produce their looks, sounds, or performances. Given their studies, students can create a marketing product about an imaginary performer that integrates at least one aspect of global culture in its design. Although many young adolescents enjoy pop culture, gaming, and social media, they are also experiencing greater school demands and may not think about how they are passing time. Using gaming images, social media snapshots, and artworks and photographs of young adolescents (Figure 10.13), teachers can discuss time management skills. They can ask students to identify how they spend their leisure time, using probing questions such as: "When do you experience quiet, self-reflection times and meaningful interactions with family and friends?" "Do you spend equal or more time participating in gaming, text messaging, and online networking?" Students can develop an art project relating to time management, such as a public service announcement or film. If students continue to struggle with time management skills, they can develop a participatory action research project on practical time management applications.

## Adolescence and Visual Culture Inquiry

Adolescents often want instant gratification and desire greater independence and responsibility. They may dream of adventurous trips to exciting times and places with peers. Teachers can introduce the concept of a dream road trip to study travel-inspired content in visual culture and explain how trips usually require

detailed planning to make getting from place to place more efficient. Each individual student or team of students can select a different travel adventure. Students can research the assortment of visual images they could discover on their trip, including maps, signs (perhaps in different languages), architectural features, forms of transportation (Figure 10.14), license plates, foods, packaging, and clothing. Students might also consider what they would bring on their trip. For example, in an original film one student described his connection to his backpack as he travels through life (Figure 10.15). Students might also decide to travel to a different era. Figure 10.16 shows nostalgia for traveling in a 1960s Volkswagen van. Another visual culture project would call upon students to study a current event of their choice, and to collect images and data from credible Internet sites and reputable social media platforms to be well-informed about

FIGURE 10.14 Kader Goktepe, 14-years-old, OVA Secondary School, Antalya, Turkey.
*Source: ICEFA Lidice, 41st Exhibition.*

FIGURE 10.15 Daniel Orozco Juárez, 14-years-old, Secundaria General Federalizada No. 72 "Presidente Juárez", Tultitlan, Mexico.
*Source: ICEFA Lidice, 45th Exhibition.*

FIGURE 10.16 Kristýna Sumcová, 13-years-old, Viktorie Sumcová, 15-years-old, ZŠ Sedmikráska o.p.s., Rožnov pod Radhoštěm, Czech Republic.
*Source: ICEFA Lidice, 45th Exhibition.*

FIGURE 10.18 *Career Panel: Preparation.* United States. MTSU Public Service Grant.
*Source: Author, Michael McGoffin, and Stephanie Roberts, teachers.*

FIGURE 10.19 *Careers for Careers Mural.* High school students. United States. MTSU Public Service Grant.
*Source: Author, Michael McGoffin, and Stephanie Roberts, teachers.*

their chosen topic. Such an investigation allows high school students to contemplate their place in the world. Students can decide what art media best suit their communication needs. They will integrate related visual culture images into their final artistic design to enhance their message about the event. Another possible unit of study is to teach students necessary career skills through visual culture. Figures 10.17 and 10.18 demonstrate how high school students developed theme-based wooden panels illustrating skills needed to gain and maintain employment. They also painted a mural that taught about different vocations (Figure 10.19). Their designs appropriated van Gogh's *Starry Night*, comic book features, and silhouettes.

## BEST PRACTICES FOR TEACHING VISUAL CULTURE

Many images in visual culture are exciting for pre-K–12 students and stimulate their desire to produce and talk about art in class and in their free time. In the classroom, best practices in visual culture identify people's varied values and beliefs. People can see the same information differently and may not know that some images have hidden meanings or agendas behind them. Teachers skilled in teaching visual culture as part of the choice-based art curriculum address topics with sensitivity and select only age-appropriate resources for instruction. In addition to inviting works that students value, teachers integrate real-world issues through visual culture. They provide students with ample opportunities to digest class information, ask questions, learn other people's opinions, and find commonalities. Before presenting new subject matter, teachers consider how to handle situations when students might introduce related visual culture topics

FIGURE 10.17 *Career Panel: Teamwork.* United States. MTSU Public Service Grant.
*Source: Author, Michael McGoffin, and Stephanie Roberts, teachers.*

that seem unusual, off-task, or too controversial. For example, teachers could redirect a conversation to bring it back on-task or place a topic on hold to talk to a student one-on-one to address the student's individual concerns. They might also meet with a school guidance counselor, nurse, and/or administrator to brainstorm possible solutions to problems. These practices set the stage for promoting open, developmentally appropriate communications about the concerns that students have about healthy relationships, self-worth, bullying, and media and peer pressures.

Although most educators are not health experts, early intervention by positive role models can help students overcome feelings of insecurity and poor self-esteem that may be influenced by media and peer pressures, which can severely impact students' physical and emotional wellbeing. Reflective journals, secure class discussion boards, and student-driven artworks can be resources that assist students who feel shy or uneasy speaking in front of a group to communicate ideas about content in visual culture (Lai, 2009). Their art can serve as catalysts for other students to address relevant issues in their own art and class discussions with greater confidence. Comprehensive curricular tasks and discussions can also reinforce how inappropriate behaviors come with negative consequences. Knowledge of the facts and having a support network can encourage some students who may be engaging in or considering harmful behaviors to seek adult help. Given their effective teachings, teachers can assist fellow educators in managing visual culture instruction by sharing the meaningful topics they addressed with students. Well-managed experiences can inspire teachers with less exposure to or fear of visual culture instruction by seeing concrete examples of students' successful learning outcomes, such as the ones presented in this chapter.

## OUR JOURNEY TO THRIVE CONTINUES . . .

As we move into Part IV of this textbook, we will learn how to teach developmentally appropriate studio art methods to pre-K–12 students. We will address ways to integrate diverse art inquiry methods through aesthetics, art criticism, art history, and visual culture into choice-based studio art lessons.

## CHAPTER QUESTIONS AND ACTIVITIES

1. Define visual culture and its functions in society and the choice-based art curriculum. What is your plan for addressing possibly controversial subjects in a safe, effective, and age-appropriate manner?
2. Develop an original comprehensive visual culture lesson that integrates an artist of your choice. Your lesson will include a studio art activity and age-appropriate questions using the WISER Consumer Model for Visual Culture Studies (Model 10.2). Use the lesson plan template provided on the textbook's companion website and refer to Chapter 2 for more information on lesson plan development.
3. Complete your art inquiry card collection (Model 7.1). For this chapter's assignment, create 25 well-designed index cards filled with visual culture questions, issues, and reproductions that are appropriate for pre-K–12 students. (Note: The finished box (based on activities from Chapters 7–10) will contain a total of 100 cards with 25 aesthetic cards, 25 art criticism cards, 25 art history cards, and 25 visual culture cards for classroom use.)
4. Answer Artists' Lessons to Thrive! 10.1–10.3's essential/guiding questions in written form or as part of a group discussion. Complete the daily learning targets.

## References

Art 21. (2009). *Segment: Kimsooja in "systems"*. Retrieved from https://art21.org/artist/kimsooja/

Briggs, H. (2007). Celebrity, illusion, and middle school culture. *Art Education, 60*(3), 39–44.

Duncum, P. (2006). Introduction: Visual culture as a work in progress. In P. Duncum (Ed.), *Visual culture in the art class: Case studies* (pp. ix–xviii). Reston, VA: National Art Education Association.

Duncum, P. (2010). Seven principles for visual culture education. *Art Education, 63*(1), 6–10.

Faber, P. (2007). Making the *Family Stories* exhibition. In P. Faber, C. Rassook, & L. Witz (Eds.), *South African family stories: Reflections on an experiment in exhibition making* (pp. 7–47). Tropenmuseum Bulletin 378. Amsterdam: KIT.

Farhi, P. (2008). Cable's clout. *American Journalism Review, 30*(4), 18–23.

Freedman, K. (2003). *Teaching visual culture: Curriculum, aesthetics and the social life of art.* New York, NY: Teacher's College Press.

Heussner, K. M. (2011). Iconic icons. *Adweek, 52*(4), 15.

Hoffman, J. (2011, March 26). *Sexting turns explicit, altering young lives.* Retrieved from www.nytimes.com/2011/03/27/us/27sexting.html?pagewanted=1&_r=2

Hussain, Z., Williams, G. A., & Griffiths, M. D. (2015). An exploratory study of the association between online gaming addiction and enjoyment motivations for playing massively multiplayer online role-playing games. *Computers in Human Behavior, 50,* 221–230.

Jaji, T. E. (2014). *Africa in stereo: Modernism, music, and pan-African solidarity.* New York: Oxford University Press.

Keifer-Boyd, K., & Maitland-Gholson, J. (2007). *Engaging visual culture.* Worcester, MA: Davis Publications.

Lai, A. (2009). Images of women in visual culture. *Art Education, 62*(1), 14–19.

Malsch, F. (2005). *The bottari as time capsule: Thoughts accompanying the exhibition, "Kimsooja—Bottari Cologne 2005", Kewenig Galerie, Cologne 29.1–23.4, 2005.* Retrieved from www.kimsooja.com/texts/malsch.html

Mirzoeff, N. (1998). What is visual culture? In N. Mirzoeff (Ed.), *The visual culture reader* (pp. 3–13). New York, NY: Routledge.

Mirzoeff, N. (2002). The subject of visual culture. In N. Mirzoeff (Ed.), *The visual culture reader* (2nd ed., pp. 3–23). New York: Routledge.

Mitchell, W. J. T. (2002). Showing seeing: A critique of visual culture. In N. Mirzoeff (Ed.), *The visual culture reader* (2nd ed., pp. 86–101). New York, NY: Routledge.

Rogoff, I. (2002). Studying visual culture. In N. Mirzoeff (Ed.), *The visual culture reader* (2nd ed., pp. 24–36). New York, NY: Routledge.

Stuhr, P. L., Ballengee-Morris, C., & Daniel, V. A. H. (2008). Social justice through curriculum: Investigating issues of diversity. In R. Mason & T. Eça (Eds.), *International dialogues about visual culture, education, and art* (pp. 81–95). Chicago, IL: Intellect Books, the University of Chicago Press.

Trafi-Prats, L. (2009). Art historical appropriation in a visual culture-based art education. *Studies in Art Education, 50*(2), 152–166.

# PART IV

# Creating Art

# Chapter 11

# Drawing

**FIGURE 11.1** Natasha Brown, 15-years-old, St. Stithians Girls College, Johannesburg, South Africa.
*Source: ICEFA Lidice, 40th Exhibition.*

**Drawing** is the process of creating pictorial products that include fine artworks, sketches, and industrial designs through the act of intentionally producing marks on paper and other surfaces using dry, wet, and technological media. It can stand on its own as a quick communication tool or develop into a time-consuming finished product. Artists apply their training and intuition to manipulate the look, feel, and meaning of their drawings. They communicate ideas through themes, media, and formal qualities including line, volume, tone, proportion, and emphasis. People draw as a hobby, as part of the thinking process when planning

projects, and within their professions. Students make drawings because they are enjoyable and necessary activities that inform others about their inspirations, inner thoughts, and ways of knowing.

Drawing fosters students' visual literacy skills and builds upon art inquiry presented in the choice-based art curriculum through aesthetics, art criticism, art history, and visual culture. Continuing on our journey to thrive, we will teach students how drawings communicate their makers' ideas beyond spoken and written words. We will also teach students how to work through personal drawing challenges by demonstrating multiple pathways to reach learning targets. Students will apply artistic behaviors as they engage in diverse drawing processes and experiment with drawing media.

We will meet the following objectives by participating in this chapter:

- Describe drawing and its qualities, functions, and meanings in society.

- Identify best practices for teaching drawing.
- Create instructional resources for teaching drawing.

Spotlight on Student Art #11 identifies how a student created a drawing with markers and decorative patterns to illustrate the need for a free and just society. The student combined drawing and writing to communicate her message.

---

## Spotlight on Student Art #11

### Big Idea: Freedom

Freedom is a precious human right that grants all people with access to civil liberties. When humanity's basic freedoms are taken away, many people search for a better way of life. Fifteen-year-old Natasha, from South Africa, articulated this perspective in her marker drawing, which contains a central landscape, a bold patterned border, and a handwritten poem (Figure 11.1). The poem begins by stating that freedom is within people's reach. Natasha presents this concept through a bright yellow butterfly that soars freely over a vast landscape—a new world. Yet, the poem also identifies that these people have lost their voices and bear scars. Despite their past hardships, they maintain a positive outlook to repair a broken world. Each individual smiles and expresses joy although their mouths appear to be sewn shut.

The poem further describes how love remains within the world in spite of prior hardships. The people in the picture have a new sense of hope and optimism. Natasha portrays this concept by drawing a couple holding hands and surrounded by a heart. On the horizon, a smiley-faced character rounded with crosshatching marks informs the people that they are in a safe environment. The poem concludes by paying homage to a serene world filled with possibilities and dreams. Rolling hills are speckled with trees and pleasing geometric forms. A wide trail welcomes people into this utopian world. It gradually becomes narrower in the distance to show the vastness of the landscape. Gentle clouds linger above. The areas of white sky that Natasha left uncolored add a sense of tranquility. The puzzle pieces and the many patterns within this hospitable landscape indicate that life is made up of multiple components. When all parts come together, humanity has a sense of order and stability. As a society, people have the ability to put the broken pieces back together and start anew. Within this drawn world, all individuals can soar with the butterfly, sit under shade trees, hold hands, and feel welcomed.

---

## UNDERSTANDING DRAWING IN CONTEXT

Drawing is a communication tool that has aided humanity for millennia. It correlates with available technologies and cultural preferences. Drawings come in many forms, spanning from realistic (Figure 11.2) to abstract (Figure 11.3). Humans achieved sophisticated drawing skills in prehistoric times. Early societies drew on nature's available surfaces, including sand, rock, and bark. Before written language, societies created **pictographs**, simple drawings that represented common objects or ideas within their communities. For example, about 1,500–2,000 years ago, the Nasca culture in present-day Peru produced large drawings of animals and geometric patterns in the dirt called **geoglyphs** by removing darker stones from the surface and scratching into the ground. The Nasca created these drawings for ceremonial purposes in response to their need for water (Hall, 2010). The Aborigine culture in present-day Australia, which dates at least 50,000 years, has a long tradition of producing sacred sand drawings and has continued its sand drawing methods in contemporary times. When introducing these examples and others, teachers can ask students to recall the physical sensations of creating drawings with sticks in sand and with rocks on concrete. Such recall can help students make personal connections as they study geoglyphs and sand drawings in context.

Most of history's early drawings have vanished or deteriorated. Conservation has played an important role in preserving some of the historic drawings that have survived. For instance, due to the fragility of many drawings, museums exhibit them less frequently than other art media and store them in dark, protected shelving units. Paper drawings are sensitive to damage from harsh lights and/or acidity in paper. Many artists use archival drawing papers that are acid free and are less prone to discolor and deteriorate. Their quality drawings result from their abilities to notice subtle differences in objects and transform what they see or think into effective areas of positive and negative space on drawing surfaces called **supports** or **grounds,** which include sand and archival paper. Artists' Lessons to Thrive! 11.1 presents artist Carol Prusa (Figure 11.4), who creates three-dimensional drawings on acrylic spheres. Her example teaches students how contemporary drawings can extend beyond paper.

**FIGURE 11.2** Bai Hui Qian, 13-years-old, Hangzhou Youth and Children's Center–Fine Art Dept., Hangzhou, China.
*Source: ICEFA Lidice, 42nd Exhibition.*

**FIGURE 11.3** Andrej Jurík, 6-years-old, ZUŠ Ivana Ballu, Dolný Kubín, Slovak Republic.
*Source: ICEFA Lidice, 43rd Exhibition.*

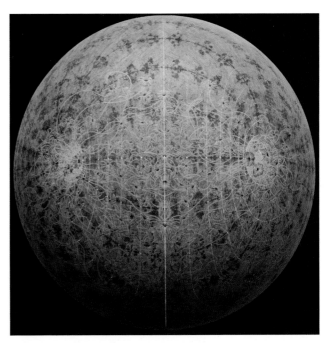

**FIGURE 11.4** Carol Prusa, *Bridge*, 2012, 60 × 60 × 12 in. (152.4 × 152.4 × 30.48 cm) Silverpoint, graphite, titanium white pigment with acrylic binder on curved acrylic with lights.
*Source: Courtesy of the artist; www.carolprusa.com.*

# Artists' Lessons to Thrive! 11.1 Carol Prusa: The Mindful Universe

## Big Idea: Mindfulness

Artist Carol Prusa creates sculpted drawings inspired by the universe and her scientific and medical knowledge. Holding a degree in biocommunication arts, Prusa decided to pursue the visual arts when she became aware of the commonalities between scientific and artistic thinking. She is intrigued with the ways that mathematic and scientific principles bring order to what can be a chaotic world. Out of this passion, Prusa has produced a body of mixed media artworks using specially manufactured acrylic domes. She coats the domes with up to fifteen layers of gesso and sands their surfaces smooth to prepare the ground for her silver stylus drawings. Her domes symbolize human knowledge. She compares the dome form to the cranium, which houses the brain, as well as human creations such as innovative architectural dome structures and the petri dish used to culture microorganisms. Once Prusa completes each meticulous drawing, she layers the entire surface with a wash of crushed graphite and acrylic medium. She carefully outlines select objects with a thin brush of white acrylic paint to produce highlights on the toned graphite surface. For a finishing touch, she drills holes in the dome to attach fiber optic lighting.

Her artwork *Multiverse* (Figure 11.1.1) illustrates the scientific theory that our universe may consist of many universes, known in total as the multiverse. Prusa's dome in *Multiverse* takes on an additional meaning because its dome form correlates with scientific inflation theory. Bubble theory is

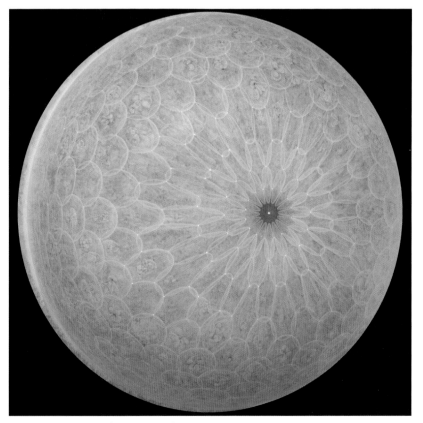

**FIGURE 11.1.1** Carol Prusa, *Multiverse*, 48 × 48 × 24 in. (121.92 × 121.92 × 60.96 cm), Silverpoint, graphite, titanium white pigment with acrylic binder on acrylic hemisphere with fiber optics, 2008.

*Source: Courtesy of the artist; www.carolprusa.com.*

one example of inflation theory. It suggests that our universe is one of many universes that sit on the skin of a bubble caused by a big bang. Our universe—filled with galaxies, stars, black holes, and life—is an example. The artist explained: "In this work I contemplate the magnitude of our universe and the bubbles we each live in while reading contested cosmologies offered from physicists."

Physicist Michio Kaku (2008) presented one interpretation of a possible inflation theory and applied the analogy of a bubble bath. Each separate bubble is located adjacent to another, forming a rich lather on the water's surface. The big bang theory represents the energy that colliding bubbles produce. The different bubbles join together or break apart like they do in a bubble bath. As a result, each bubble universe continues to expand and grow. Scientific research on the big bang theory states that our universe developed approximately 13.8 billion years ago. This process created all of the matter in the universe, including the matter that forms human bodies. The multiverse theory offers numerous possibilities, in which different laws of physics apply to disparate bubbles.

In reference to bubble theory, Prusa considered the meaning of multiple possibilities and alternate realities as she designed the bubbles on *Multiverse's* surface using the principles of divine geometry. This mathematical construct produces the work's harmonious frothing bubble forms. Symbolically, each of us can choose to stay in a particular bubble or move into a different one to create a new way of life. Prusa left many of *Multiverse's* bubbles empty or with developing forms to represent our infinite choices. Such thinking correlates with our metacognition and our mindful awareness of self. As individuals, we have choices to make. We may venture into the unknown and begin a new bubble in life using the information that we have accrued to make successful choices. We can also make incorrect choices in life. Prusa illustrated this reality by appropriating the sorrow in Masaccio's *Expulsion of Adam and Eve from Eden* from circa 1424–1427 (Figure 11.1.2). Ultimately, Prusa offers humanity hope, because humans can grow from the experience of being expelled from paradise and form an entirely new one. To conclude her design, Prusa strategically placed fiber optic lighting at intersecting bubbles to reiterate that we are connected to our personal decisions, cultural mores, and the physical world that surrounds us. It is our responsibility to question who we are and where we are going.

**FIGURE 11.1.2** Carol Prusa, *Multiverse* detail, 48 × 48 × 24 in. (121.92 × 121.92 × 60.96 cm), Silverpoint, graphite, titanium white pigment with acrylic binder on acrylic hemisphere with fiber optics, 2008.

*Source: Courtesy of the artist; www.carolprusa.com.*

## Essential/Guiding Questions

1. How has human knowledge, including scientific theory, inspired Prusa as an artist? Which scientific facts and theories inspire you?
2. Prusa dedicated several hundred hours to completing *Multiverse*. Why did she choose to dedicate so much time to create a single work? Would *Multiverse's* impact be the same if Prusa saved time by simply drawing *Multiverse* on paper? What does Prusa's process for creating *Multiverse* say about her dedication and mindfulness?

## Preparation:

The class will research bubble theory, identify its main qualities, and analyze Prusa's interpretation of bubble theory in *Multiverse* as part of this STEAM lesson. The class will review the meaning of mindfulness and metacognition.

## Daily Learning Targets:

I can create a three-dimensional drawing inspired by bubble theory using the media of my choice.

- I can incorporate at least two bubbles that represent times when I have made wise choices. One bubble will depict a mindful moment in my past and another one will show a mindful moment in my present life.
- I can show line variety, contrast, emphasis, unity, and craftspersonship in my completed design.
- I can apply metacognition to describe why I selected the mindful moments presented in my artwork to peers during a class critique.

**National Core Arts Anchor Standards** 1, 5, 8, and 10
www.nationalartsstandards.org

*Quoted artists' statements not listed in the reference section result from personal communications with the author (personal communications, 2014–2018).*

## Observational Drawing

Artists develop **observational drawings** to record accurate depictions from life. Observational drawings document artists' impressions of people, places, and things. Knowledge of observational drawing is beneficial when people cannot acquire the information or qualities they need through appropriated and digitally manipulated images alone. For example, professionals in anthropology, archeology, law, and art history rely on observational drawing skills to record artifacts and disseminate information. Visual artists and others who draw achieve the greatest visual accuracy by assessing the marks they have made and comparing their actual relationships to the objects they are drawing. This requires them to become self-critical as they focus on minute details. Teachers can encourage students to stop periodically and look carefully to self-assess their observational drawings, as artists' do. This is effective even with younger students who are not yet able to draw with realistic proportions, because it develops their visual literacy skills. Students might also use a viewfinder (an open-framed sighting tool) to see size relationships as they draw a composition. The **grid method** assists students in creating proportional drawings to scale by making grid marks on an inspiration source, such as an original photograph, and enlarging or reducing its scale to produce a drawing (Figure 11.5).

Despite observational drawing's longevity and practicality, in recent decades, emphasis on observational drawing has shifted due to the production

**FIGURE 11.5** Waiyaki Njoroge Regeru, 11-years-old, used the grid method to draw his self-portrait. He then erased the helpful grid marks after drawing the figure to his satisfaction. Kenya.

*Source: Lisa Wee, teacher.*

of contemporary artworks that excluded realistic drawing in favor of installations, performances, digital technologies, and mixed media productions. This transformation caused some members of the art world to believe that observational drawing skills are no longer necessary (Fava, 2010; Gheno, 2015). Others, however, have argued that eliminating drawing instruction places students at a disadvantage because of the skills they teach. Fava (2010) implored educators to redirect the focus from teaching students how to produce only highly realistic objects using a formalist art for art's sake approach to utilizing observational drawing as a means to develop students' greater "cognitive sophistication." Through comprehensive drawing lessons that describe artists' choices and integrate big ideas, students activate higher order cognitive thinking skills as they analyze visual information to produce creative products

(Anderson et al., 2001; Hetland, Winner, Veenema, & Sheridan, 2013).

## Contour Drawing

A **contour drawing** is a rendering created using one or more continuous free-flowing lines that show the inner and outer edges, or outlines, of one or more objects. Quality contour drawings contain smooth, flowing, and varied line qualities that depict mass and volume without shading. Artists bring contour drawings to life by slowly moving their drawing instrument over the paper and looking directly at the objects they are drawing. During this tactile process, the artists' hands and eyes become one with their drawing instrument as they record subtle changes in line qualities amongst different edges (Curtis, 2002; Edwards, 1999). Like artists, students can produce a variety of creative outcomes by producing pure contour drawings from direct observations and combining contour drawing with abstractions. The bicycle contour drawing shown in Figure 11.6 integrates additional colorful patterning (not produced with contour lines) and addresses big ideas about freedom, transportation, and youth. As an added learning task, students can develop **blind contour** drawings: in this task, students do not look at their papers as they draw a subject's contours. While the process rarely results in realistic artworks, it challenges students to acquire a tactile feel for the lines and shapes within a composition and develop their hand–eye coordination.

**FIGURE 11.6** Savannah Hudson, 6th grade, United States.

*Source: Lydia Horvath, teacher.*

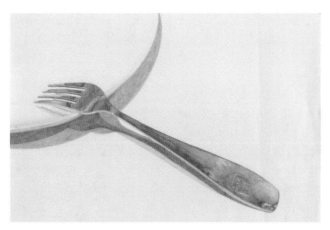

FIGURE 11.7 Chang Jing Mei, 16-years-old, EverDay Art Studio, Selangor, Malaysia.
*Source: ICEFA Lidice, 43rd Exhibition.*

FIGURE 11.8 Truman Boyd, 7th grade. United States.
*Source: Lydia Horvath, teacher.*

## Object Drawings and Still Lifes

Artists' observational drawings may come in the form of object drawings and still lifes. An **object drawing** consists of a single non-moving object (Figure 11.7). A **still life** is an artwork that depicts a visually pleasing arrangement of several non-moving objects. Artists arrange objects of different heights, sizes, and textures to create visual interest through variety and incorporate lights and shadows into their designs to add volume. Historically, artists' created still lifes to illustrate a person's wealth and abundance. Students can make contemporary connections to people posting photographs of their belongings on social media. Artists often focus on drawing a particular section of a still life instead of capturing each object. Teachers and students will prepare still life displays by considering artistic and visual inspirations. Students will locate the best angles to draw their still life's composition and examine how the various edges of objects within the still life come together and overlap to illustrate areas of space (Edwards, 1999). When teaching object drawings and still lifes, teachers can show students how artists explore themes, subject matter, media, and formal qualities to produce their works. Figure 11.8 illustrates how a student was inspired by Janet Fish, who saturates her still life compositions with bright lights reflected on transparent surfaces. The 19th century artist Paul Cezanne altered the picture plane to represent still lifes from multiple angles. Audrey Flack applied 17th century *vanitas* still life subject matter that referenced human mortality to produce *Marilyn* (1977), a still life filled with symbols indicating Marilyn Monroe's untimely death and the passage of time (Rollyson, 2005).

## Figure Drawing

**Figure drawing** is the act of rendering the human form and has been prevalent since prehistoric times. Throughout the ages, artists have stylized and altered the human form to communicate their perspectives on humanity. Artists and designers can render the human body realistically as well as stylize it to suit their artistic needs and preferences. Figure drawings capture human interest because they inform viewers about people's personalities, social conditions, and life experiences. A figure can represent a generic person, whereas a **portrait** identifies a particular individual, and a **group portrait** presents more than one identifiable person. A **self-portrait** is an artist's drawing of him/herself. David Y. Chang (Artists' Lessons to Thrive! 11.2) creates realistic portraits and group portraits using pastels that give his works a lush painterly feel and opulent richness. Studying historic and contemporary portrait drawings teaches students about artists' varied representations of people's personalities, unique expressions, and social circumstances.

Most teachers introduce figure drawing lessons by teaching students how to draw the face (Figures 11.9–11.10) and/or body in a frontal position. Students then progress to more complex poses that include profiles and three-quarter views (Figure 11.11). Generations of artists have learned figure drawing by working with live models and studying human anatomy, paying close attention to the body's bone and muscle structure. Many artists apply mathematical body proportions based on the "eight heads tall" adult figure model

FIGURE 11.9 Sindy Golgata, 14-years-old, produced a stipple drawing. Kenya.
*Source: Lisa Wee, teacher.*

FIGURE 11.10 Martin Tulis, 10-years-old, ZUŠ Vladislava Vančury, Háj ve Slezsku, Czech Republic.
*Source: ICEFA Lidice, 43rd Exhibition.*

FIGURE 11.11 Emily Avaritt, 6th grade. United States.
*Source: Lydia Horvath, teacher.*

FIGURE 11.12 A middle-childhood student draws a manikin.
*Source: Frist Art Museum.*

identified during the Classical Greek period (Sterling Publishing Company, 2004). In addition to live models, students can draw from manikins to practice rendering accurate proportions (Figure 11.12). Figure drawing lessons might integrate props, costumes, and body positioning to present a mood. As with all forms of observational drawing, young artists benefit from studying details to draw what they see rather than what they know. Students should learn how to identify the contours of a body's convex form and its volume and mass. Further lessons on foreshortening and action poses will add complexity and visual interest to students' figure drawings. As part of their studies, students can discuss how the rise of digital gaming has created a demand for skilled artists who can design action figures and other gaming characters using the human form (Wilson, 2015).

### Artists' Lessons to Thrive! 11.2 David Y. Chang's *Joie de Vivre* Through the Arts

#### Big Idea: Joy of Living

David Y. Chang produces pastel drawings that represent the *joie de vivre* (joy of living) through his depictions of sentimental beauty in the arts. Growing up in Shanghai, China, Chang developed his passion for the arts from his parents, who were nationally recognized for their work in Chinese ballet and theatre. He earned a Master of Fine Arts degree from Shanghai Jiaotong University and did postgraduate fellowships at the Cambridge University and the École des Beaux-Arts in Paris, France. Chang utilizes his observational drawing skills to render dramatic portraits, landscapes, and still lifes. He explained: "Art comes from life and transcends it as it captures the transitory moments in life and nature through personal temperament." When holding a pastel in his hand, Chang adjusts the amount of pressure he places on the drawing surface to build up rich, layers of purely pigmented color that record distinct moments in time in artworks including *Duet* (Figure 11.2.1), which chronicles the timelessness, grace, and elegance of two Chinese musicians.

Similar to the sounds of the traditional Chinese instruments that the poised musicians in *Duet* play, their portraits capture Chang's meaning of the *joie de vivre*. Chang stated: "The tranquility and

**FIGURE 11.2.1** David Y. Chang, *Duet*.
*Source: Courtesy of David Y. Chang, artist.*

elegance of the music performed through ancient Chinese musical instruments have always inspired me." In *Duet*, one musician plays an **erhu**, a two-string instrument referred to as the "Chinese violin," and the other blows gently into a **zhudi**, an ancient bamboo Chinese flute. To accurately depict the musicians' concentration and love of their art form, Chang studied their unique, expressive qualities through their body positioning and facial expressions as he drew the live models. He applied his expert knowledge of pastels and outstanding rendering skills to place emphasis on the female musicians by contrasting the dark, empty backgrounds that surround them with the warm, radiating light that reflects off of their skin and silken gowns. While their physical beauty and enchanting music captivate audiences, the musicians seem unaware of the audience's presence as they focus on the striking sounds that their instruments produce. Chang compared such a moment to "a beautiful song frozen in time [as] its melody melts through space." In essence, Chang's dramatic interpretation of the musicians' soothing, yet dramatic, melodies leave audiences wanting more. They feel how music, and all of the arts, bring the *joie de vivre* and a sense of purpose to humanity. Chang's art evokes an emotional response from viewers and reminds society how the arts have the power to touch people's lives and produce deep and meaningful aesthetic responses.

## Essential/Guiding Questions

1. How does the combination of the fine and performing arts inspire Chang's portrayal of the *joie de vivre* in *Duet*? What inspires your joy of living?
2. What visual qualities did Chang use to represent beauty and elegance in *Duet*? In your opinion, does art have to be realistic to be beautiful? Explain your answers.

## Preparation

Students will listen to sound clips of the erhu and the zhudi, then identify the role of the visual and performing arts in eliciting joy. Students will locate research that describes the positive effects of joy on the human psyche.

## Daily Learning Targets

I can create a portrait or self-portrait that represents *joie de vivre*.

- I can select the drawing medium of my choice.
- I can draw a portrait/self-portrait that has accurate proportions.
- I can show value, unity, and craftspersonship in my completed design.

### National Core Arts Anchor Standards 2, 4, 9, and 11

www.nationalartsstandards.org

*Quoted artists' statements not listed in the reference section result from personal communications with the author (personal communications, 2014–2018).*

## Environmental Drawing

**Environmental drawings** illustrate artists' interpretations of realistic, idealized, and imaginary worlds that include landscapes, seascapes, and cityscapes. Many artists like to draw on location because they can experience sites with their senses and integrate their perceptions in their art. **Concept artists** design both realistic and fantasy environments, using their drawing skills for gaming, movies, animation, and comics. Studying environmental drawing can teach students how to become more aware of local and global environments by paying attention to details and their surroundings. Students can participate in comprehensive STEAM lessons that link geography, climate, and sustainability to environmental drawing.

Artists apply specialized techniques to render space and perspective to produce environmental drawings. **Aerial perspective** is the process of diminishing the size of objects as they recede into the distance (Figure 11.2). Artists make areas of space look both hazier and brighter as they fade into the background. Distant objects appear brighter because they are more saturated with light. Before adding details in environmental drawings, artists may block out areas of space using a horizon line, foreground, middle ground, and background. This process can be helpful for students who prematurely concentrate on small details before thinking about the full composition. **Linear perspective** is an illustration technique to represent space and distance through geometric measurements by drawing one or more points on an axis line to portray environments, architectural structures, still lifes, and interiors. Artists draw parallel lines that meet in the distance at the horizon line, or **vanishing point**, located at eye level. Images located further away in a picture plane become smaller. Italian architect Filippo Brunelleschi was the first to use geometric perspective in 1413. Shortly after, in 1427, Masaccio achieved true linear perspective in his fresco *Trinity*. Masaccio's arched structure in *Trinity* looked so lifelike that viewers had the impression that it was an actual three-dimensional environment rather than a two-dimensional illusion. Drawings in linear perspective remain popular today. They appear in video games and cartoons. Learning how to produce linear perspective drawings is an age-appropriate technique for many students beginning around upper elementary or early middle school years, after students feel comfortable incorporating overlapping, shading, aerial perspective, and sighting in their work (see this textbook's companion website for additional resources for creating linear perspective drawings).

## Technical Drawing

**Technical drawing** combines drawing with precise measurements to produce designed products. It makes up much of the world's contemporary drawings, as designers and engineers draw most of the objects we use on a daily basis. "Without such drawings it is hard to see how there could be a modern world. For there would be neither the kinds of technological thinking nor the kinds of manufacture that make industrial and post-industrial societies possible, nor their use and maintenance" (Maynard, 2005, p. 7). Students will learn that companies develop technical drawings to assess if their designs meet performance needs before investing in their costly mass production. Artists continue to refine their drawings until they produce optimal designs. The better industrial drawings' designs and functions, the more likely consumers will purchase their end-results, the manufactured products themselves. Technical drawings are drawn with accurate mathematical precision from multiple angles, and their subjects range from simple to elaborate products. Manufacturers include package instructions with illustrations and clear instructions that simplify the assembly process for products that require home assembly. Technical drawing lessons connect the visual arts with STEAM learning tasks and expose students to the product design profession. Figure 11.13 and Artists' Lessons to Thrive! 14.2 on Christopher Williams illustrate how he creates technical drawings to scale before producing three-dimensional products.

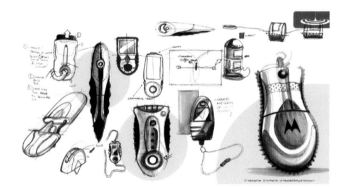

**FIGURE 11.13** Christopher Williams, Ideation Sketches for *Motorola Shield.*
Source: Project sponsored by Motorola.

## APPLYING DRAWING MEDIA IN CONTEXT

Comprehensive drawing lessons teach students about the unique qualities and design limitations of drawing media. The medium impacts an artwork's design and meaning. Some lessons will emphasize teaching students how to use drawing media. Others augment students' existing drawing skills. Through class demonstrations and exposure to materials, students will become competent in choosing diverse drawing media and supports to reach choice-based learning targets and communicate personally-driven messages with artistic fluency.

## Pencils, Coloring Pencils, and Color Sticks

The **pencil** is a primary drawing medium that consists of graphite mixed with clay. Pencils contain no lead. The term "leaded pencil" comes from the pencil's predecessor, the **stylus**, which was originally a leaded drawing and writing instrument that dated to ancient Roman times and is still in use today by artists, including Carol Prusa. Drawing pencils span from **hard-leaded** 8H pencils to **soft-leaded** 8B pencils, with **mid-range** pencils numbered HB, B, and 2B. The higher the number the H pencil is, the harder its lead and the lighter its color. The higher the number the B pencil is, the softer its lead and the darker its color. Pencil drawings span from basic sketches with contour lines to shaded artworks filled with details and patterns (Figure 11.14) Many students like working with pencils because they can erase their mistakes. Teachers should discourage students from erasing too much as this can cause them to lose valuable class time and/or accidentally rip their papers.

**Colored pencils** consist of colored pigment bound in kaolin, a fine white clay, with trace amounts of wax. They function like pencils but do not contain graphite. They are suited for sketching and for creating time-consuming drawings. Quality colored pencils produce fine transparent hues. They lie flat and have a symmetrical center that is encased in wood and looks the same on all sides. As a result, quality colored pencils sharpen more evenly and produce less waste than poor-quality color pencils that have an uneven core. Poor-quality colored pencils contain more wax, do not blend as easily, and produce a clouded, rather than transparent, design (Gildow & Newton, 2006). Drawing with colored pencils, students can apply lighter hues first and add darker ones to blend and build up layers of color. As an alternative to colored pencils, artists may choose **color sticks**. These blend just as readily as colored pencils, but do not have wood around them. They are useful for

filling in large areas of color quickly. Students can combine color sticks and colored pencils with other drawing media such as pencils, markers, and ink, as well as draw on colored papers for added visual

**FIGURE 11.14** Gabrielé Glodenyté, 5-years-old, Viekšniai Kindergarten Liepaite, Viekšniai, Lithuania.
*Source: ICEFA Lidice, 40th Exhibition.*

**FIGURE 11.15** Nastya Asanova, 12-years-old, Detskaya khudozhestvennaya shkola, Ust-Kamenogorsk, Kazakhstan.
*Source: ICEFA Lidice, 42nd Exhibition.*

interest. Figure 11.15 presents a student's colored pencil drawing on black paper.

## Crayons

The **crayon** is a transparent medium that consists of wax and pigment. Most crayons are made with paraffin wax. Finer crayons are made with organic beeswax or soy wax. Crayons are well-suited for drawing, but do not blend as readily as colored pencils and other drawing media. When drawing, students should begin with thin layers of the lightest hues and add darker ones until the paper is saturated with wax. Early childhood learners and some students with special needs may benefit from easier to hold thicker Crayon Rocks® compared to standard elongated crayons. Some manufacturers produce opaque **construction paper crayons** that keep their original hues on colored papers, as transparent crayons work best on white paper and only black keeps its true color on colored papers.

A **crayon engraving** is a drawing that students create by coloring a paper's surface with a layer of bright crayon colors, then covering it with a topcoat of black crayon or paint, and finally etching a design to reveal the bright colors beneath the surface (see Model 11.1). This is an alternative to purchasing manufactured **scratchboard**, which has a black surface and a white background, or can come with multicolored, sparkled, and metallic backgrounds. Students gently etch away parts of the black surface with scratch-art knives, wood styluses (Figure 11.16), penholders, coins, or plastic knives. They can shade areas by integrating hatching and cross-hatching lines into their designs. Figure 11.17 depicts a group project for which each student created a square crayon engraving from a grid to form the tiger's face. In addition to producing crayon engravings, students can create a **crayon resist,** a drawing that combines crayons with watercolors (Figure 11.18), to give their crayon artworks a different appearance. Students color their designs with crayons while leaving some sections of their paper uncolored. They then fill their designs with transparent watercolors, which seep into the uncolored areas of the paper. The liquid cannot penetrate the wax surface created with the crayons, as the watercolor beads up and leaves small dots of color on top of the wax surface.

**FIGURE 11.16** A student draws with a wood stylus. United States. NPS photo by Dana Belcher. Flickr, CC BY 2.0.
*Source: https://creativecommons.org/licenses/by/2.0/*

**FIGURE 11.17** Early adolescents created a collaborative crayon engraving. United States.
*Source: Natsumi Kajisa, teacher.*

**FIGURE 11.18** Kevin Arya, 4-years-old, Ananda Visual Art School, Bandung, Indonesia.
*Source: ICEFA Lidice, 45th Exhibition.*

# Markers

**Markers** are drawing utensils that come in transparent and opaque colors with tips ranging in size from fine point to wide chisel. They are popular amongst fashion designers, professional illustrators, and cartoonists because of their versatility and ability to fill in blocks of color. **Watercolor markers**, which are transparent, are common in schools and work best on white paper (Figure 11.19). Using markers requires little preparation and cleanup time. When drawing with transparent markers, students should leave parts of their white papers uncolored to represent the white areas in their designs. They may also draw black outlines to separate areas of color and show contrast. **Permanent markers** differ from watercolor markers in that they do not run with water. Students can use them to mark on most surfaces, including fabric, plastic, and metal. Drawing on alternative supports with permanent markers adds interest to class assignments and encourages students to express their ideas in new ways. For respiratory safety, teachers should select only brands that bear the AP safety label.

**FIGURE 11.19** Viktor Iliyanov Ivanov, 9-years-old, Art School GEYA, Lovech, Bulgaria.
*Source: ICEFA Lidice, 40th Exhibition.*

# Charcoal, Chalk, and Pastels

**Charcoal, chalk, and pastels** are dry drawing media that allow artists to apply quick line foundations and build large areas of space. These gritty media produce a range of applications from sketching to rendering detailed drawings. **Vine charcoal** comes from burnt vines and has a dark gray tone. It is suited for quick sketches

and base drawings for paintings because students can readily wipe away sections that they wish to rework. **Compressed charcoal** produces a more permanent and darker color than vine charcoal and is harder to erase from the paper's surface. Charcoal is an effective medium for teaching observational drawing because its thicker drawing surface does not require students to focus on fine details (Figure 11.10; Rolg, 2006).

**Chalk** is an inexpensive drawing medium that is available in white and multiple colors. Students can apply chalk to paper, chalkboards, sidewalks, and textiles such as burlap. It is practical for producing preliminary sketches on fabric. **Pastels** are made of colorful pigment and binder, and are of higher quality than colored chalk (Figure 11.20). Pastels are available in soft, medium, and hard consistencies. They work best on paper that has a **tooth** (a rough surface) because the paper holds more pigment and allows students to build deeper layers of color. Artist-grade pastels contain expensive pigments that are comparable to those in quality paints.

When using charcoal, chalk, and pastels, teachers should distribute damp paper towels for students to wipe their hands at their desks to reduce trips to the sink. Students can also place damp paper towels at the base of their drawings to collect dust. Teachers will need to monitor that students do not blow dust from their drawings into the air, because these dust particles can be inhaled. For select finished artworks, teachers might apply a CL-safety-labeled **fixative** in a well-ventilated area to prevent the pigment on the drawing surface from smearing.

**FIGURE 11.20** Nikita Sharapov, 14-years-old, Artschool No. 2, Severodvinsk, Russia.
*Source: ICEFA Lidice, 39th Exhibition.*

## Oil Pastels

**Oil pastel** is a blendable drawing medium that consists of pigment, wax, and a small amount of oil. Its heavy, creamy consistency feels like lipstick. Oil pastel never dries fully because it does not form a hardened surface as with oil paint. Artists can produce a range of textures with oil pastels. In the 1940s, Pablo Picasso inspired the invention of oil pastels when he met with Henri Sennelier, a chemist who owned the Sennelier® art store. Picasso desired the richness of oil paints combined with the ability to cover improvised drawing supports such as glass, canvas, and metal. Given Picasso's criteria,

Sennelier developed oil pastels as a new, fast-setting art medium that would not crack and does not require the time needed to set up an oil painting (Elliot, 2002; Sennelier, 2002). Students can blend oil pastels with their fingers and saturate the paper's surface with compacted layers of oil pastel to give their drawings a polished look (Figure 11.21). The appearance of this slick drawing medium will change according to the papers they select. Oil pastels are suitable for drawing on white and colored papers (Figure 11.22). Students can also combine oil pastels with watercolors on white paper to produce an oil pastel resist, as well as create an engraving using oil pastels and black tempera paint (Model 11.1).

**FIGURE 11.21** Bengisu Boyraz, 10-years-old, Kocaeli Bahcesehir Koleji, Kocaeli/Kartepe, Turkey.
*Source: ICEFA Lidice, 39th Exhibition.*

**FIGURE 11.22** Samreen Sayyad, 10-years-old, Udayachal Primary School, Mumbai, India.
*Source: ICEFA Lidice, 42nd Exhibition.*

## Model 11.1

### Crayon and Oil Pastel Engravings

Use the following steps to produce a crayon or oil pastel engraving.

1. Select a sturdy piece of white drawing paper that can handle drawing pressure, as non-sturdy papers will rip when pressure is applied.
2. Place a stack of newspapers underneath the drawing paper.
3. Press down heavily with brightly colored crayons or oil pastels and fill the entire page with color.
4. Smooth away any crayon or oil pastel flakes with a clean cotton rag.
5. Mix one teaspoon (4.9 ml) of liquid soap into each pint (1/2 l) of black tempera paint.
6. Paint the entire surface of the paper filled with crayon or oil pastel with black tempera paint. (It may require multiple layers of paint to cover the surface completely.)
7. Allow paint to dry fully.
8. Use scratch-art knives, wood styluses, penholders, coins, or plastic knives to scrape away selected areas of the black paint and reveal the colorful designs in crayon or oil pastel.

# Ink

**Drawing ink** contains dye pigments and has a thin, watery consistency. It is available in a wide range of colors. Artists dilute inks with water to create values (Figure 11.23). The more water an artist adds, the lighter the color becomes. Artists apply ink with brushes (watercolor or bamboo), pen points (called **nibs** or **quills**), or twigs. They draw with ink on rice paper or heavy-weight papers that can withstand the wet consistency. The Chinese invented the first ink, which came to be called **India ink**, to produce calligraphy and drawings (Nice, 2005; Smith, 1992). Permanent India ink consists of black particles bound in water, mixed with latex or shellac. Students will need to practice making marks with brushes and diluting ink with varying amounts of water to change its value. Ink drawings are suited for observational drawings, anime drawings, illustrated stories, and poster designs.

# Digital Drawing Tools

**Digital illustration** is a form of drawing made possible through computer technologies (Figure 11.24). Teachers and students have access to many free and inexpensive digital applications. School systems may also purchase professional software programs for the classroom such as Adobe Illustrator. Depending on the hardware available, students can draw with their fingers, a **stylus pen** (a digital drawing tool) on

**FIGURE 11.23** Liu Jia Qi Jacqueline, 11-years-old, Simply Art, Hong Kong, China.
*Source: ICEFA Lidice, 46th Exhibition.*

**FIGURE 11.24** See Allyssa, 12-years-old, South View Primary School, Singapore.
*Source: ICEFA Lidice, 40th Exhibition.*

a drawing tablet or directly on a screen, and/or with a mouse. They might also choose to scan their original art to make manipulations and form new works. They can appropriate Creative Commons licensed images that give students permission to manipulate other people's existing drawings, photographs, and other works using digital and other creative media to produce new creations.. Working digitally provides artists with creative freedoms. They can select from diverse software tools that simulate the look of art papers, drawing tools, and design media. Digital layers allow artists to move, transplant, add, enhance, and delete objects during the design process. If design choices do not match the artists' intentions, they can make revisions until they achieve the desired outcomes (Nalven & Jarvis, 2005). Illustrating drawings digitally can be a constructive process for students who have developed art blocks, because the digital format allows students to fix mistakes with greater ease (Greh, 2002).

# BEST PRACTICES FOR TEACHING DRAWING FROM PRE-K THROUGH HIGH SCHOOL

While drawing begins as an innate human activity, students can only go so far in their visual expression without formal drawing instruction. Students become proficient at drawing with continued practice, access to age-appropriate drawing media, and awareness of diverse drawing processes. Without support students may become blocked and learning is stalled. Comprehensive drawing lessons, like all art production lessons, should address topics including social ethics through art, artistic concepts, behaviors, techniques, and multidisciplinary study (see Chapter 1). Teachers should emphasize artists' behaviors to facilitate student learning during instruction. Students can reference David Y. Chang's patience as he studies the human figure to produce observational drawings and Carol Prusa's persistence and mindfulness when creating mixed media drawings on three-dimensional surfaces. Because some students may struggle when their drawings do not look as they had planned, teachers can help them find solutions by slowing down to see details, articulating their intentions, and making revisions to move forward. They can also teach students independence by showing them how to use quality resources including student-friendly video tutorials, how-to-draw books, drawing apps, and drawing websites. Teachers should also provide students with access to quality printed and digital images to reference as needed for diverse drawing tasks.

Before kindergarten, many children have had some experience with basic drawing media such as crayons and some have already drawn on digital devices. Early childhood students enjoy drawing about their lives (Figure 11.25). Teachers can provide students with opportunities to draw, talk, and write about their daily experiences and special events. Talking about drawings encourages students to articulate their experiences and recall details. Teachers can harness students'

curiosity as they teach young children how to notice differences in the objects they see before them when creating observational drawings. While young children cannot draw the images they see from observation with accurate proportions, they will be able to describe some of the qualities they see. By 2nd grade, students have developed a drawing repertoire through schematic symbols, and they can create more recognizable objects and human and animal figures and illustrate them from different positions. Students can also present a greater sense of space in environmental drawings and still lifes.

In middle childhood, students want teachers to challenge them with more complex drawing media and curricular topics. They enjoy drawing and writing about their hobbies and personal interests. Many create cartoons in their free time. They appreciate class learning tasks that integrate storytelling, which can be based on fantasy or popular culture, and teach important topics (Figure 11.26). They have better control of their

**FIGURE 11.25** Oskars Léconis, 6-years-old, BJC IK. Auseklis, Riga, Latvia.
*Source: ICEFA Lidice, 39th Exhibition.*

**FIGURE 11.26** Deng Bo Yu, 11-years-old, Dongguan Youth and Children's Center, Dongguan, China.
*Source: ICEFA Lidice, 42nd Exhibition.*

hand muscles and can produce greater details, illustrate textures, and blend colors using drawing materials such as oil pastels and coloring pencils. Teachers can develop contour drawing assignments to continue to build students' observational drawing skills. By the upper elementary grades, students have the ability to incorporate aerial perspective into drawn environmental spaces. Given this foundation, teachers can teach them linear perspective drawing. Students can also create multimedia drawings that are abstract or ones that combine abstraction and realism to communicate big ideas. They have a better understanding of global topics, which assist them in producing environmental drawings that focus on local and international themes. They can identify how artists' realistic and abstracted representations change drawings' messages.

Early adolescence is an appropriate time for students to research professions that include drawing (fine arts, product design, concept art, video game design, art history, and more). At this age, students can be self-conscious about how they appear to others, especially peers. Teachers can provide support for students who might struggle with drawing skills by integrating students' personal interests into drawing learning tasks to help them feel more comfortable. For example, early adolescents typically enjoy drawing their names and fancy designs, as seen in Figure 11.27,

a mixed media drawing of a student's first initial "L" surrounded by organic and geometric patterns. Teachers can also encourage students to integrate personally selected items into still lifes and choose inspirational big ideas for choice-based learning tasks. Many early adolescents play video games and know cartoon characters. Teachers can design art criticism activities that include linear perspective drawings from such examples to inspire students' original perspective drawings. Students will also enjoy interpreting art forms including album art, anime, comic books, and **zines** (handmade magazines using photocopied and appropriated imagery) through drawing. Because students also want to work with peers, teachers can implement collaborative drawing projects that focus on social justice topics of students' choices that may include their original designs, text, and references to popular culture.

By adolescence, students can employ a range of artistic behaviors and are well-versed in drawing media, given their participation in comprehensive pre-K–8 drawing tasks. Their drawings show more variety than in previous years and they have a greater ability to represent aerial and linear perspective. Teachers should implement lessons that challenge students to develop product designs, technical drawings, and animations to learn professional design skills. Students can apply their drawing knowledge to produce comprehensive art journals that combine art subject matter, professional skills, and their personal interests. Figure 11.28 shows a student's clever illustrations that document transformations between origami paper and a bird. Teachers can plan lessons that relate to fantasy, imagination, storytelling, and personal memories to encourage adolescents to interpret the meanings behind their past experiences, current hopes, and future aspirations. Additionally, students

**FIGURE 11.27** Lydia Kuhr, 8th grade, repousse and colored pencil. United States.

*Source: Lydia Horvath, teacher.*

**FIGURE 11.28** Noor Majida Albarudi, 16-years-old, Johannesburg, South Africa.

*Source: ICEFA Lidice, 45th Exhibition.*

appreciate the challenge of investigating difficult subject matter related to big ideas by researching related artworks, participating in substantial conversations, answering essential questions, and designing creative drawings (Figure 11.1). These processes teach students how to prepare for their future roles as adults as they independently and collaboratively seek alternative solutions to problems.

## OUR JOURNEY TO THRIVE CONTINUES . . .

By learning how to teach drawing in context, our journey to thrive has demonstrated how students of all ages can gain proficient drawing skills given quality learning tasks, practice, and our genuine support and encouragement. Chapter 12 builds on drawing's foundation and describes stimulating comprehensive learning tasks using rich paint media and techniques. It continues to augment students' visual literacy, creative, and cognitive skills.

## CHAPTER QUESTIONS AND ACTIVITIES

1. Describe drawing's qualities, functions, and meanings from historic and societal perspectives. How will you integrate drawing into the choice-based art curriculum?
2. Practice using the diverse drawing media and methods described in this chapter to compare and contrast their qualities. Summarize what you learned in a group discussion or in writing.
3. Develop an original comprehensive drawing lesson that integrates the drawing medium, process, and big idea of your choice. Use the lesson plan template provided on the textbook's companion website and refer to Chapter 2 for more information on lesson plan development. Integrate inquiry tasks inspired by Part III of this textbook.
4. Answer Artists' Lessons to Thrive! 11.1 and 11.2 essential/guiding questions in written form or as part of a group discussion. Complete the daily learning targets.

# References

Anderson, L. W. (Ed.), Krathwohl, D. R. (Ed.), Airasian, P. W., Cruikshank, K. A., Mayer, R. E., Pintrich, P. R., . . . Wittrock, M. C. (2001). *A taxonomy for learning, teaching, and assessing: A revision of Bloom's Taxonomy of Educational Objectives* (Complete ed.). New York, NY: Longman.

Curtis, B. (2002). *Drawing from observation: An introduction to perceptual drawing*. Boston: McGraw Hill.

Edwards, B. (1999). *The new drawing on the right side of the brain*. New York, NY: Jeremy P. Tarcher and Putnam.

Elliot, J. (2002). *Oil pastel for the serious beginner: Basic lessons in becoming a good painter*. New York, NY: Watson-Guptill.

Fava, M. (2010). What is the role of observational drawing in contemporary art & design curriculum? In E. Norman & N. Seery (Eds.), *IDATER Online Conference: Graphicacy and modeling* (pp. 129–141). Loughborough, England: Design Education Research Group.

Gheno, D. (2015). *Figure drawing master class: Lessons in life drawing*. Cincinnati, OH: North Light Books.

Gildow, J., & Newton, B. B. (2006). *Colored pencil solution book*. Cincinnati, OH: North Light Books.

Greh, D. (2002). *New technologies in the art room*. Worcester, MA: Davis Publications.

Hall, S. S. (2010). Spirits in the sand: The ancient Nasca lines of Peru shed their secrets. *National Geographic, 217*(3), 56–79.

Hetland, L., Winner, E., Veenema, S., & Sheridan, K. (2013). *Studio thinking 2: The real benefits of visual arts education*. New York, NY: Teacher's College Press.

Kaku, M. (2008). *Physics of the impossible: A scientific exploration into the world of phasers, force fields, teleportation, and time travel*. New York, NY: Doubleday.

Maynard, P. (2005). *Drawing distinctions: The varieties of graphic expression*. Ithaca, NY: Cornell University Press.

Nalven, J., & Jarvis, J. D. (2005). *The practice and vision of digital artists*. Boston, MA: Course Technology.

Nice, C. (2005). *Creating textures with pen and ink with watercolor*. Cincinnati, OH: North Light Books.

Rolg, G. M. (2006). *Drawing with charcoal, chalk, and sanguine crayon*. New York, NY: Barrons.

Rollyson, C. (2005). *Female icons: Marilyn Monroe to Susan Sontag*. Lincoln, NE: iUniverse.

Sennelier, D. (2002). Forward. In J. Elliot's (Ed.), *Oil pastel for the serious beginner: Basic lessons in becoming a good painter*. New York, NY: Watson-Guptill.

Smith, J. A. (1992). *The pen and ink book: Materials and techniques for today's artist*. New York, NY: Watson-Guptill.

Sterling Publishing Company. (2004). *Art of drawing the human body*. New York, NY: Sterling.

Wilson, V. L. (2015). *Classic human anatomy in motion: The artist's guide to the dynamics of figure drawing*. New York: Watson-Guptill.

# Chapter 12

# Painting

FIGURE 12.1 Tanrudee Kanokpol, 7-years-old, Kolor Me Art School, Pakred, Thailand.
*Source: ICEFA Lidice, 41st Exhibition.*

**Painting** is the process that artists use to apply layers of pigment suspended in minerals and liquids, including water or oil, to two- or three-dimensional surfaces using mark making tools such as paintbrushes, palette knives, fingers, sticks, and sponges. Paint's rich pigment compounded in liquid makes it a smooth and distinctive art medium. Through comprehensive art instruction, we will teach students how to mix and manipulate paint and identify paintings' qualities, including the themes, inspirations, and materials artists use to create them. We will also explain how artists cultivate ideas for paintings using available technologies, dialogue, and metacognition. Students will be able to produce paintings by applying subject matter they learned in drawing lessons, including the human figure, still lifes, environments, and abstractions.

We will meet the following objectives by participating in this chapter:

- Describe painting and its qualities, functions, and meanings in society.
- Identify best practices for teaching painting.
- Create instructional resources for teaching painting.

Spotlight on Student Art #12 (Figure 12.1) presents a student's dynamic paint applications that align with the big idea of rejuvenation. It illustrates how painting is a layering process and how artists apply different painting methods to produce visual statements.

## Spotlight on Student Art #12

### Big Idea: Rejuvenation

Seven-year-old Tanrudee selected paint as an effective medium to depict the dynamic energy of Northern Thailand's Yi Peng festival (Figure 12.1). To represent people's sense of rejuvenation in the celebration, the young artist applied multiple layers of color using paintbrushes, splatters, drips, and splotches of paint blown through a straw. These visual qualities recreate the sense of fervor that Yi Peng festival participants might experience. The Yi Peng festival takes place in conjunction with the full moon, marking the twelfth month of the country's lunar calendar. Based on Buddhist tradition, it marks a time of annual rejuvenation. In contemporary society, crowds of people join simultaneously after a day of ceremonies to release rice paper lanterns called *khom loi* into the sky. When individuals discharge the *khom loi* they make a wish. As depicted in Tanrudee's painted cityscape, the lanterns gently rise and move further away into the atmosphere. In life, they resemble a school of jellyfish floating through calm waters. By lighting up the darkness, the *khom loi*'s light serves as an analogy to remove a person's worries and hardships. The lanterns allow people to dream of a brighter future.

The water below the evening sky in the painting mirrors the energy of the festival. Tanrudee produced areas of variety and visual contrast by building up a painted base of blue tints and shades. The young artist then added kinetic splashes of water through white paint to mimic the fireworks' designs. The resulting image shows how painting remains a valuable tool in contemporary society for artists to articulate their ideas, as Tanrudee did to illustrate the concept of rejuvenation.

## UNDERSTANDING PAINTING IN CONTEXT

Early humans began painting at least 400,000 years ago by applying colored pigments to their skin to clarify their role in society and portray communal beliefs (Himelfarb, 2000; Schildkrout, 2004). Prehistoric societies also spread paint on natural surfaces including rocks, leaves, tree barks, and animal hides. Over the centuries, humans advanced painting technologies and applied paint to flat structures including wooden panels, walls, paper, metal, and stretched canvas. Some artists began using easels as supports to produce paintings within interior and exterior spaces. Although color remains one of paint's most recognizable features, it is an artist's distinct application of paint to a surface that has the power to render narrative accounts of the human experience. The physical act of painting becomes a gateway to become acquainted with artists' thought processes and feelings about subject matter (Jarvis, 2009). Artists spend a lifetime refining their artistic knowledge of paint and its unique qualities to render their artistic visions convincingly.

Before the inventions of photography and film in the 19th century, painting was a primary medium for artists to create accurate portraits, landscapes, and narratives with lifelike details and coloring. With photography, artists no longer needed to produce solely mimetic designs. Abstraction encouraged generations of artists to experiment with paint applications and design qualities. Artist Jaune Quick-to-See Smith combines abstract painting techniques with realistic renderings and collage. Her layered designs are formed from multiple painting techniques that students can apply to create their own artworks. Smith's paintings are rich with symbols that bring awareness to the ongoing effects of American colonialism on Native Americans and the environment (see Artists' Lessons to Thrive! 12.1). Following Native American spiritual beliefs about the interconnectedness of the land and sky, Smith represents natural environments using open picture planes with rich colors and textures. Josef Zedník paints abstractions to communicate his feelings and cognitive reflections about nature's transformations. Zedník's inspirations from the natural world, particularly his garden, provide him with a chance to focus on the painting process and escape from the chaos of digital technologies that permeate life (see Artists' Lessons to Thrive! 12.2). His paintings provide positive examples for students to see how artists can attain tranquil feelings through painting.

Like Zedník, painter Katharina Grosse is aware of how much our world is inundated with screened images. She values painting as a contemporary practice that enables her to work with textures and tactile qualities that do not exist in digital works (Sawyer, 2018). Instead of painting with a brush at arm's reach like many artists do, Grosse uses industrial spray guns that broaden her reach to generate vivid, larger-than-life painted installations on materials that include oversized draped canvases and whole tree trunks (Petersen, 2010). Her work teaches students how artists can create entire painted environments, using traditional and nontraditional painting surfaces.

Many contemporary artists move through electronic media sources that they may reproduce, combine, and alter before arriving to finished paintings (Weibel, 2010). They determine if evidence of technological inspirations will remain evident in their completed painted products, which may extend beyond the canvas, easel, and frames to include digital installations, displays, and performance pieces. Digital technologies provide artists with supplemental opportunities to integrate context, social influences, knowledge of history, and visual culture into their paintings. Artist Carole Kirk (2014) presented audiences with videos that revealed how she produced collaged paintings. Her videos brought awareness to areas that she wanted audiences to examine closely. She had audiences take reflective notes in participant sketchbooks and share in conversations about what they saw and experienced. Her processes deconstructed traditional barriers between artists, artworks, and audiences, as audience members became an integral part of the artistic process. These multimedia, collaborative painting practices can be helpful in classroom settings because they encourage students to interact with peers to study meanings within their own artistic creations.

Painter Barbara Bolt (2004) studied how painting connects to human nature and metacognition by self-assessing her painting processes. Although her body of work contains realistic renditions from live models, she determined that her painting experience was not about capturing recognizable likenesses. She equated painting with a performance through which both humans and artworks undergo changes. Artists' intuitive painting becomes a core component of the artmaking process and helps determine what each painting will become. The painting experience reaches beyond semiotics (painted symbols), because the physical act of painting ultimately shapes painters' knowledge in ways that words alone cannot. When creating paintings such as those shown in Figure 12.2 as part of a unit of study on the Holocaust

and Figure 12.3 that centers on the sensory pleasures of nature's beauty, students can self-assess their painting processes by recording their feelings, thoughts, and physical movements in journals while making notes of the media and processes they used to create their designs.

**FIGURE 12.2** Nicole Goryachy, 11-years-old, Studio of Art–Ruta Kreitser, Jerusalem, Israel.
*Source: ICEFA Lidice, 41st Exhibition.*

**FIGURE 12.3** Yeung Sze Nga, 7-years-old, Kids Palette Creative Art Workshop, Hong Kong, China.
*Source: ICEFA Lidice, 45th Exhibition.*

### Artists' Lessons to Thrive! 12.1 Jaune Quick-to-See Smith: *Have You He(a)rd?* Setting Higher Standards Through Art, Education, and Activism

### Big Idea: High Standards

Jaune Quick-to-See Smith is an acclaimed contemporary artist, educator, activist, and member of the Confederated Salish and Kootenai Nation. Over her career she has produced a large body of artworks that respond to enduring implications from colonialism and Manifest Destiny, which fueled white settlers' westward expansion that forced Native Americans from their ancestral lands. *I See Red: Herd* (Figure 12.1.1) illustrates the importance of bison in Native American history and addresses complex issues of race, identity, and stewardship. Smith's bison travel through a minimalist landscape with color fields implying land and water masses. The background contains repetitive images of collaged bison that form new herds, replacing just a small fraction of the millions of bison that once roamed North America's grasslands. The white settlers' massacre of bison herds in the 19th century was intended to halt Native Americans' independence forcing them to assimilate, give up valuable lands, and adopt agriculture. Bison had long nourished North America's indigenous peoples and their thick hides offered protection from the cold. Transitioning to agriculture from a nomadic lifestyle forced some Native American nations to sign unfair treaties that gave away their sacred lands in exchange for basic survival goods.

Moving forward, the bison in Smith's artwork head in the direction of a collaged text that presents the title of Paul Gauguin's painting: *Where Do We Come From? What Are We? Where Are We Going?* The bison begin to cross a blue vertical zone that gives the impression of water. Bodies of water along travel routes represent vital sources of life but can also be difficult barriers to cross. A closer examination of the painting's title and layered background reveal additional barriers presented by the artist. For instance, the inclusion of the word "red" in the title has multifaceted meanings (Kastner, 2013), as it is known as a pejorative racial label that refers to Native American skin color and identity. Smith's painting also presents the widely popular concept of "cowboys and Indians" through collaged images. Generations of children played cowboys and Indians with pretend fights among "good guys" and their "enemies." The children's games were rooted in real battles for the American landscape. Echoing the gaming theme, Smith collaged sports ball icons in the painting to signify how Native Americans have been commoditized as team mascots to entertain audiences and sell memorabilia. Over parts of the painting's surface and collaged items, Smith dripped red ochre and burnt sienna earth tones. At the painting's forefront, the drippings symbolically block and repair

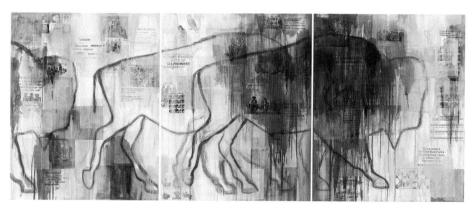

FIGURE 12.1.1 Jaune Quick-to-See Smith, *I See Red: Herd*, 1993 Mixed Media on Canvas 60 × 150 in. (152.4 × 381 cm); signed and dated, verso (Inv# QTSPT026).
*Source: Courtesy the artist and Garth Greenan Gallery, New York.*

the past wrongdoings and stereotypes that have remained. Smith revealed her sanguineness within *I See Red: Herd*, by including Shawnee Chief Blue Jacket's statement (1795): "A single twig breaks but the bundle of twigs is strong." Through art, education, and activism, Smith has dedicated a lifetime of efforts to urge society to come together as a team to learn from past mistakes so that they can collectively set higher standards as good humanitarians and stewards of the earth.

## Essential/Guiding Questions

1. What does it mean to set higher standards? How does Smith demonstrate a need to set higher standards through art (such as *I See Red: Herd*), education, and activism?
2. Smith applied abstract expressionist methods including dripping paint, collaging appropriated images, and repeating objects and design features to produce *I See Red: Herd*. How do these combined qualities add meaning to the painting?

## Preparation

For this group project, students will locate *I See Red: Herd's* painted and collaged images and contemplate Smith's possible reasons for including them during art inquiry tasks. For example, next to the Gauguin title, Smith included a symbolic self-portrait in the form of a coyote inscribed with 7173, her government identification number that authenticates her as an enrolled Salish member (Kastner, 2013). In Native American culture the coyote is viewed as a teacher and is connected to creation (Guarino, 2018). Students will also discuss how societies can set higher standards to grow from past mistakes. Using the prompt: "Have you heard?" students will brainstorm past events (decisions, laws, etc.) that impact contemporary society.

## Daily Learning Targets

We can create an artwork with the theme of setting higher standards that is inspired by a past event that has implications today.

- We can research and analyze the past event to create visual symbols for our artwork that represent the event's meaning.
- We can utilize paint and at least one layering technique (i.e. dripping, splattering, collage) to produce our artwork.
- We can create a unified design that shows repetition and craftspersonship.

**National Core Arts Anchor Standards** 2, 6, 7, and 11

www.nationalartsstandards.org

### Artists' Lessons to Thrive! 12.2 Josef Zedník: Living Transformations

#### Big Idea: Transformation

Josef Zedník is a beloved artist in his native Czech Republic who is known for his positive outlook on life and his artistic creations, which include paintings, woodcarvings, drawings, glassworks, and works in other art media. In 2008, Zedník left his busy lifestyle behind him and moved to the countryside. He wanted to experience a slower lifestyle away from social media, television, and ringing phones. The artist focused on his garden as an alternative to spending too much time using technology. This physical and mental transformation influenced his art. Being in nature and producing art has served as a means for the artist to cleanse "clogged channels" and "perceive new impulses." In particular, slowing down offered Zedník more frequent occasions to observe and interpret the beauty that surrounded him. This included paying attention to quiet moments, listening to birds singing, and taking in nature's fragrances—including the smell of compost in his garden. He describes these experiences as previously undreamed and unimaginable possibilities.

Zedník's *Gates* series provides insights into his transformed lifestyle. New figurative gateways have opened and some of the doorways from the past have closed. His *Gates* series includes optimistic titles that reveal Zedník's positive transformations, including *Gateway to Power* (Figure 12.2.1) and *Gateway to Pleasure* (Figure 12.2.2). Other works within the series reference Zedník's interpretations of time, including *Gateway to Summer* (Figure 12.2.3). The artist explained his motivation for the series: "From time to time, here and there happen to me. That which is before me opens to a new unknown space. It is a kind, yet unrecognized gate. And I can enter." Zedník moves freely throughout these unfamiliar spaces. He takes ownership of the figurative gates because he has imagined them and given them significant meaning. His metacognitive and visionary impressions become real through his trained artistic intuitions and painting processes.

Zedník's works exemplify how an artist can create original abstract painted compositions based on cognitive dispositions. He has the trained ability to transform the realistic environments he sees and the feelings that drive his daily living into symbols, color schemes, line qualities, and tactile textures. By departing from realism and painting abstracted representations, the artist has brought to life accessible gateways to his inner feelings. Like nature itself, which constantly changes and grows, Zedník has made personal and artistic transformations that augment his previous ways of knowing about himself and the world that surrounds him.

**FIGURE 12.2.1** Josef Zedník, *Gateway to Power*, acrylic, 2013.
*Source: Courtesy of the artist.*

**FIGURE 12.2.2** Josef Zedník, *Gateway to Pleasure*, acrylic, 2012.
*Source: Courtesy of the artist.*

**FIGURE 12.2.3** Josef Zedník, *Gateway to Summer*, acrylic, 2012.
*Source: Courtesy of the artist.*

### Essential/Guiding Questions

1. Zedník creates paintings to document and reflect upon his transformation of pursuing a slower paced life. How are these manifestations presented in his paintings? Why do people sometimes feel a need to slow down?
2. In your opinion, how might Zedník's decision to paint abstractions rather than realistic images impact the meaning of his art?

### Preparation

Students will reflect on a moment in which they or someone they know underwent a transformation to obtain a positive result. They will share their reflections with the class.

### Daily Learning Targets

I can create a painting focusing on transformation using the paint medium of my choice.

- I can select a color palette, shapes, and textures to communicate my transformation.
- I can create a unified design that shows effective craftspersonship.
- I can present my process for creating my design to an audience and collaborate with audience participants to interpret other alternative meanings to the artistic symbols I have produced for my painting.

**National Core Arts Anchor Standards** 1, 4, 7, and 10
www.nationalartsstandards.org

*Quoted artists' statements not listed in the reference section result from personal communications with the author (personal communications, 2014–2018).*

## APPLYING PAINT MEDIA IN CONTEXT

Each paint medium has unique qualities that require different artistic skills. **Water-soluble paints** include tempera paints, watercolors, finger paints, and acrylics. They are the most common in schools, compared to oil paints and wax-based encaustics. Comprehensive art lessons present paint media in context. As part of the choice-based curriculum, students can work with an individual paint medium to produce desired results, as well as combine paint with other art media, processes, and technologies. With continued practice, students learn how painting, in its many forms, reaches far beyond compositional qualities and the rudimental characteristics of liquid, pigment, and other applicable media applied to surfaces (Elkins, 2000).

The types of surfaces that students paint upon will vary according to the paint medium/media they have selected and the design concepts they have in mind. These include influences from current practices identified in the previous section and historic ones. For example, students can create **polyptychs**, paintings on multiple conjoined flat panels with distinct framed areas to depict multiple scenes within a picture plane. A **diptych** is a polyptych that consists of two panels and a **triptych** has three sections that include a central panel and two outer panels called wings that cover a central panel, the work's interior space, when the triptych is closed (Figure 12.4). During the Gothic and Renaissance periods, churches used triptychs to communicate important religious messages. Each panel told a different story, yet connected to the overall triptych's theme. A **retablo** is a devotional painting on industrial iron covered with tin that was popularized by Mexican folk artists beginning in the 19th century. The name *retablo* originates from the Latin phrase "behind the altar" as historically church altars had wooden screens embellished with religious images (Zarur, 2001, p. 18). Studying this art form, students can paint directly on prepared metal sheets with dull edges or on cheaper and more accessible tooling foil or heavy-duty aluminum foil (Figure 12.5).

FIGURE 12.4 Agnolo Gaddi's *Madonna Enthroned With Saints and Angels*, 1380/1390, Tempera on Panel. 80 5/16 × 31 1/2 in. (204 × 80 cm). Open Access.
*Source: Courtesy National Gallery of Art, Washington D.C.*

FIGURE 12.5 A. J. Sickler, Early adolescent repoussé retablo. United States.
*Source: Author, teacher. Richard Sickler, photo.*

## Tempera Paint

**Tempera paint** is an opaque paint also known as **poster paint** (Figure 12.6). It is valued in schools for its bright colors, versatility, and affordability. Tempera paint adheres to surfaces including drawing paper, construction paper, butcher paper, cardboard, cotton fabric, and burlap. It comes in liquid, powdered, and cake forms. **Liquid tempera** has a convenient premixed formula. **Powder tempera** must be mixed with water. **Tempera cakes** come in pans of color. Students will moisten their paintbrushes and glide them back and forth in the cake pans to transfer the pigments to their brushes. The color from tempera cakes is not as vivid as that in liquid tempera paints. However, tempera cakes cost less than liquid tempera paints and require less cleanup time. School-grade tempera paints in its liquid, powdered, and cake forms differ from the high-quality tempera paints that Renaissance artists formulated by blending mineral pigments with egg yolks. The Renaissance formula (a predecessor to oil paint) produced a smooth and rich paint that was suitable for application to wooden panels, canvas, and wall surfaces.

Flat and round synthetic brushes are ideal for building up areas of color with tempera paints. While students can apply wet tempera paints to add fresh layers on top of dried colors, they may experience challenges if they try to conceal a dark background section with light and transparent colors, as the darker colors may remain visible after the new paint layers have dried. When this occurs, students might try applying multiple layers of a lighter colored paint to cover up a

FIGURE 12.6 Zarif Hasan Ayman, 6-years-old, Children Painting Workshop, Dhaka, Uttara, Bangladesh.
*Source: ICEFA Lidice, 42nd Exhibition.*

darker hue below, or they may apply liquid starch on top of the darker bottom layer, allow it to dry completely, and then add the lighter color (Brommer & Kinne, 2003). Once students have a feel for tempera painting, students can practice creating textures by applying tempera paint to surfaces using rollers, sponges, and found objects (Figure 12.7). Tempera's consistency is also conducive for creating paint splatters by blowing it through a straw in its original consistency or watered down (Figure 12.8). In addition to painting on paper and fabric, students can apply tempera paints to tooling foil or heavy-duty aluminum foil. Once the surface is prepared, students will mix their selected colors of tempera paint with a drop of liquid soap to help the paint stick to the aluminum surface to produce their designs.

**FIGURE 12.7** Siana Nyachae paints with a roller. Kenya.
*Source: Lisa Wee, teacher.*

**FIGURE 12.8** Mali Nyachae blows paint through a straw. Kenya.
*Source: Lisa Wee, teacher.*

## Watercolors

**Watercolors** are transparent, semi-moist paints in tubes, pencils, or sets filled with pans of colors comprised of pigment bound in a gum base. Artists select special brushes and papers to produce watercolor paintings. **Watercolor brushes** come in a range of sizes and have soft, natural bristles that hold greater amounts of water than less-expensive synthetic brushes. Watercolor paper is white or light cream in color to accentuate the paint's transparent hues. Manufacturers identify watercolor paper by the amount of pounds of water pressure a sheet can hold. The higher the number, the stronger the watercolor paper is, and the less likely it will warp. Common school-grade weights are 90–120 pounds. When working with a single sheet of watercolor paper, students can tape down the edges of the paper to a board or table surface to prevent the edges from curling as they dry.

Artists, teachers, and students alike value watercolors for their portability and the visual effects they produce (Grant, 2010). Watercolors are well-suited for indoor and outdoor painting, as well as creating works that feature reflective lights and transparent layered textures. Students will vary the amount of water on their brushes to produce transparent visual effects with watercolors. The more water a paintbrush has on it, the lighter in intensity the color will be. In comparison, a brush with little moisture will produce the darkest colors. Students can dampen their paper with a sponge or sopping paintbrush to cause the watercolor on a brush to bleed and have a lighter hue when it comes in contact with the watercolor paper. This creates a **wash**, a watery base coat of paint that produces a light, pastel hue. To produce the watercolor shown in Figure 12.9, the student applied a wet brush to form the landscape. When artists apply watercolor on a dry surface it does not spread as much as does watercolor on a moistened surface.

Watercolor artists intentionally leave sections of their paper unpainted that will later become the white objects within their compositions (Figure 12.10).

FIGURE 12.9 Khurshid Matmuradov, 10-year-olds, Children's School of Art, Dashoguz, Turkmenistan.
*Source: ICEFA Lidice, 46th Exhibition.*

Some may use a knife to scratch away painted surfaces on watercolor paper and reveal fresh areas of white paper, which yields added contrast, highlights, and depth between the colored and white sections. For added variety, students can apply salt, cellophane, aluminum foil, or leaves on top of wet paintings to produce interesting textures when dried. Teachers will need to monitor and assist students (especially younger ones) as they paint with saturated paintbrushes so that their paints remain clean. They might prepare one water container for students' brush rinsing only and a second for students to add clean water for brushing the paper's surface.

## Finger Paint

As the name implies, **finger paint** is a thick, tactile paint that children apply with their fingers onto finger painting paper, special paper with a glossy surface and enough weight to hold in moisture and keep the painting intact. Finger paint is an inexpensive art medium typically used in early childhood classrooms. Modern finger painting came to life in the 1920s after a teacher named Ruth Faison Shaw saw one of her students gleefully smear iodine on the bathroom wall after getting cut (Marabel, 2006; Shaw, 1947). To invent finger paint similar to the ones that children use today, she referenced children's delight in using their bodies and hands to produce marks on a surface. Shaw believed that finger painting involved the whole body. She stressed that artists of all ages should stand while finger painting to activate the force of their bodily motions. They should also press and smear their forearms and elbows into wet finger paint to produce dynamic rhythms while reaching outwards to all four corners of their papers. Figure 12.11, a mixed media artwork, presents the tactile excitement of the student's swirling finger marks in the painting's background and also contains collaged imagery in the foreground. Due to finger painting's hands-on application, teachers may have students paint in small-group learning centers wearing protective clothing, and may prepare damp cloths and large water containers for students to clean their hands and arms.

FIGURE 12.10 Lim Luen Gui, 16-years-old, Yeow Chye Art Centre, Penang, Malaysia.
*Source: ICEFA Lidice, 39th Exhibition.*

FIGURE 12.11 Natálie Hierschová, 4-years-old, MŠ Zdraví, Ostrava—Zábřeh, Czech Republic.
*Source: ICEFA Lidice, 40th Exhibition.*

## Acrylic and Oil Paints

**Acrylic paint** is a permanent paint medium comprised of pigment and a polymer binder (see Figure 12.12 for a painting in acrylics). Most school-grade acrylic paints come in squeeze bottles for convenient pouring. They are thinner than professional-grade acrylics, which have a higher percentage of pigment and are packaged in tubes. Acrylic paint has become a leading artist's paint medium. In addition to its ability to dry quickly, acrylic paint is relatively odorless and does not require harsh solvents to dilute. It already has a smooth sheen, unlike tempera paints that have a chalky texture and must be sealed with a glossy layer to have a shiny appearance. Students can apply acrylic paint with quality synthetic brushes and natural bristle brushes. Acrylic paint covers other colors much better than does tempera paint, and it hides mistakes more readily. Acrylic paint adheres to nearly all surfaces, including canvas, paper, wood, metal, stone, fabrics, and cardboard. Students, like artists, can alter its look by (a) giving it a thick, **impasto** texture by mixing it with a thickening medium or painting with it directly from the tube; (b) diluting it with water to give it the appearance of watercolors; (c) mixing it with additives such as gloss medium or matte medium to augment or reduce the reflective quality of the paint; and (d) using it as a thin base coat when working with

FIGURE 12.12 Polina Rusakovich, 13-years-old, CDODiM Mayak, Minsk, Belarus.
*Source: ICEFA Lidice, 43rd Exhibition.*

other types of paint, such as watercolors and tempera paints (Reyner, 2007).

**Oil paint** is a slow-drying paint medium that remains moist for many hours (or days) and is regularly used by professional painters. In the 19th century, American painter John Rand invented the paint tube with a removable cap, which allowed artists to keep paint colors wet longer (Hurt, 2013). Prior to buying premixed oil paint in factory-made tubes, artists hand-mixed ground pigments with oil. They could only produce small amounts of a few colors at a time to prevent paint from drying out prematurely. Oil painting is less common in schools due to its expense, slow drying time, students' young ages or skill levels, and the potential for working with harsh solvents that are harmful to students' developing bodies. When students have opportunities to use oil paints, teachers should purchase only products with

AP and/or CL safety seals and have students paint in well-ventilated areas. Teachers can provide walnut oil or other safe substitutes for students to thin paint and clean brushes as alternatives to harmful solvents with irritating fumes, such as mineral spirits and turpentine. Like professional artists, students will gradually build up layers of oil paint to produce effective color schemes. Students can use quality synthetic brushes, natural bristle brushes, and palette knives to apply oil paint to canvas.

**Gesso** is a thick, most often white, priming material that artists apply by painting directly onto a canvas, paper, stone, or wood surface before adding acrylic or oil paints. Similar to rough specialty papers, a coat of gesso provides a tooth for the paint to adhere to a surface. If students will be painting on canvas, it is more convenient to purchase pre-gessoed, primed canvas. However, some professional artists prefer to gesso their own canvases, and it is a valuable skill for mature painting students to learn.

## Encaustics

**Encaustic**, which comes from the Greek word *encaustikos* ("to burn") is a form of painting created by melting beeswax or synthetic wax with colored pigment and applying it to a surface with a paintbrush, medicine dropper, or spatula (Womack & Womack, 2008). Encaustic painting is an ancient art form that dates back 3,000 years when Greek shipbuilders used beeswax to seal ships (Mattera, 2001). What began as a practical solution for waterproofing vessels turned into an art form as ship builders added color to the wax sealant and created aesthetic designs. Encaustic painting spread from ship decorations to waxed artworks on pieces of wood and even patina on three-dimensional works. The art form eventually reached Egypt, where ancient Egyptians from 100 BCE to 200 CE created realistic encaustic mummy portraits on attached wooden boards to preserve wrapped bodies.

In the 20th century, Abstract Expressionist Jasper Johns applied encaustics to give his artworks three-dimensional qualities by layering textures of paint and wax (Mattera, 2001). Contemporary artists continue to build on this process. Some incorporate photocopy transfers when producing encaustic designs. Most fine artists purchase professional-grade encaustic paints produced from beeswax, resin, and fine pigments.

Some teachers develop encaustic lessons using leftover broken crayons if they cannot afford encaustic paints (Figures 12.13 and 12.14). Students brush layers of melted crayon wax into artistic designs onto surfaces such as thick pieces of paper, mat board, cardboard, wood, and smooth stone. Due to the hot temperature, encaustic learning tasks are best suited for responsible upper elementary and older students in classrooms with pre-established classroom management procedures in place. Overheated wax can produce irritating

**FIGURE 12.13** Ailee Sickler, 6th grade. United States.
*Source: Author, teacher. Richard Sickler, photo.*

**FIGURE 12.14** Ailee layers melted crayons with paintbrushes and a medicine dropper to create her encaustic. United States.
*Source: Author, teacher. Richard Sickler, photo.*

fumes, so these tasks require well-ventilated work environments, and teachers must monitor the heating element closely. Teachers can organize students in small-group learning centers and work with responsible adult volunteers to make supervision of students and heating elements more manageable.

## Murals

**Murals** are commonly large public artworks that individuals or groups of people paint on walls, panels, and canvas. The paint media artists select will depend on a mural's surface. Some recurring themes in the history of murals include community, sacred teachings, significant moments in time, and sociopolitical commentaries. Like billboards, murals capture audiences' attention because of their large size and effective use of visual imagery to communicate messages. A **fresco** is an ancient form of mural painting in which artists apply paint pigment directly to an area of wet plaster on a wall. The pigment is embedded into the plaster surface. Some **graffiti** art is considered to be a contemporary form of mural painting. Street artists create graffiti murals using spray paint on a wall or other large surface.

In the choice-based art curriculum, mural making is a shared art activity often involving teachers and/ or artists leading and assisting groups of students as they paint. Leaders of a mural project secure appropriate permissions before beginning their work. Mural participants initiate their project by collectively brainstorming ideas. The best murals correlate with community sites and the populations they serve. To promote a sense of shared ownership of the work, groups can integrate aspects from each participant's sketches into the final mural design, as occurred when students created a canvas mural displayed in Bali, Indonesia for an international Kids' Guernica celebration (Figure 12.15). The Kids' Guernica Peace Mural Project (Spotlight on Student Art #9) is an exemplary model for introducing students to theme-based murals. When teachers teach students how to create theme-based murals, students have opportunities to collaborate with adult mentors, learn new skills, resolve unexpected challenges, and communicate their viewpoints through paint and dialogue about their chosen themes (Kaneda & Fischer, 2010; Sickler-Voigt, 2006, 2007).

**FIGURE 12.15** United States elementary and middle school students created an international Kids' Guernica peace mural that was displayed in Bali.
*Source: Author and Suzanne St. John, teachers. Tom Anderson, photo.*

## BEST PRACTICES FOR TEACHING PAINTING FROM PRE-K THROUGH HIGH SCHOOL

The choice-based art curriculum includes the study of traditional and contemporary painting processes that range from quick painted sketches to in-depth projects using paint media. Students learn how artists sometimes incorporate mixed media methods and technologies to produce paintings on traditional and nontraditional surfaces. They will study how artists communicate meaning through painting, including Jaune Quick-to-See Smith, who manipulates paint and builds up layers to teach others about Native American culture, and Josef Zedník, whose paintings put him in touch with nature's transformations. In managing painting tasks, best practices call upon teachers to prepare paint distribution and cleanup guidelines to promote greater efficiency. Before painting, student should understand the procedures for using paint media, refilling paint colors and water, and storing paintings. Following are practices that teachers commonly use for painting lessons:

- Organize paint into pre-made table sets. Teachers can assemble paint tubes and/or collect plastic baby food jars for storing paint colors and place the different colored paints inside of a large plastic storage bin with a lid that seals tightly. If teaching back-to-back painting lessons, teachers may ask students to prepare paint supplies for the next class.

- Place materials at students' tables before instruction begins to save distribution time. Materials might include paper, canvas, covered paint palettes, and water containers. Teachers will pass out the paintbrushes and ask students to remove palette lids when ready. Holding off on passing out paintbrushes and using covered paint palettes reduce temptations to touch the paint prematurely.
- Have students write their names on the back of their paper or canvas before applying wet paint.
- Establish a rule that only one student from one table at a time is allowed at the paint storage area to refill paint colors for their table, which minimizes student traffic. Teachers can have small groups simultaneously place wet paintings on the drying rack.
- Demonstrate how to pour small amounts of a paint color at a time. Teachers will show students how to mix light colors first and then add small amounts of darker colors to their mixture to cut down on waste produced by large batches of unwanted hues.
- Oversee students to ensure that they respect painting materials. This includes using paints and water containers without splashing and gently dipping paintbrushes. Jabbing brushes harshly causes them to lose their shape and destroys the bristles.

If pre-K–12 students are off-task at any time during the painting process, teachers will immediately stop the behaviors and review correct painting procedures. With procedures in place, teachers are prepared to guide age-appropriate painting tasks.

In early childhood, students' first painted strokes appear labored and expressive because they are developing fine motor skills. Learning tasks in painting should introduce common themes in young children's daily lives and recalled events. Students can examine how artists have painted about common experiences they understand, including feelings; celebrations; modes of transportation; and friends, family, and pets (Figure 12.16). With each lesson, teachers should introduce and review painting vocabulary so that painting terms become a regular part of students' discussions and class critiques. Lessons and demonstrations should teach students how to hold and operate paintbrushes, as well as dip their hands in finger paint so that they can form more controlled

**FIGURE 12.16** Anastasia Rusinova, 7-years-old, Gorogskaia Shkola Iskusstv, Kharkiv, Ukraine.
*Source: ICEFA Lidice, 40th Exhibition.*

marks. Painting on large pieces of paper and mixing paint promote young children's kinesthetic learning. Students stretch their arms outwards as they angle brushes to produce brushstrokes and apply circular motions to mix paint. Given studies of children's artistic development, teachers recognize that young children paint using imaginative color choices. Teachers should provide them with opportunities to choose the colors they desire for painting activities and also teach them how to mix new colors to begin developing their knowledge of color theory. Teachers can also show them examples of artists' assorted color palettes. Teachers may create assignments in which students paint with just a few colors at a time. Limited color palettes can help students avoid mixing too many colors together, which results in muddied colors. The painting shown in Figure 12.17 has a limited color palette with the student choosing red to paint the eyes, lips, and clothing.

In middle childhood, students have developed their manipulative skills so that they can control a paintbrush better and illustrate finer details in their paintings than they did in early childhood. Teachers will continue to augment students' knowledge of painting vocabulary, painters, and painting materials and processes. Teachers might notice that students can become frustrated when different paint colors accidentally run together because they want the painted hues to look just right. Teachers can help reduce students' feelings of frustration by explaining how painters apply their intuitive knowledge to correct mistakes and produce dynamic results.

Building on years of prior painting instruction, students will be able to select from different brushes and brushstrokes to produce aesthetic marks, including the linear designs shown in Figure 12.18. Beginning in 4th grade, students paint baselines less frequently than they did in the 2nd and 3rd grades. Painting lessons can build students' observational painting skills and abilities to depict details in a painting's foreground, middle ground, and background. Students want to represent the illusion of space by painting objects in the distance that diminish in size and show how objects overlap in space. For example, the animals and foliage in the work shown in Figure 12.19 give the appearance of moving into the distance. Students can portray aerial perspective in their work by gradually changing the value of the colors of painted surfaces in the background. They can mix and layer colors to make paintings appear more three-dimensional and combine varying proportions of primary colors, black, and white to produce dynamic secondary colors, tints,

**FIGURE 12.18** Lilia Margaryan, 10-years-old, Art School Studio Vardges Gulikyan, Yerevan, Armenia.
*Source: ICEFA Lidice, 45th Exhibition.*

**FIGURE 12.17** Miruna Toba, 4-years-old, Scoala Albestii de Arges, Arges, Romania.
*Source: ICEFA Lidice, 39th Exhibition.*

**FIGURE 12.19** Lau Kin Gi. 11-years-old, Simply Art, Hong Kong, China.
*Source: ICEFA Lidice, 45th Exhibition.*

and shades (Figure 12.20). Additionally, teachers can develop lessons that challenge middle-childhood students to integrate abstractions into their designs or

FIGURE 12.20 Kennard Alvaro Hadinata, 9-years-old, Nirvana Visual School, Surabaya, Indonesia.
*Source: ICEFA Lidice, 46th Exhibition.*

FIGURE 12.21 Iryna Firko, 13-years-old, Shkola Dekoratyvno-Uzhytkovogo Mystetstva, Sambir, Ukraine.
*Source: ICEFA Lidice, 42nd Exhibition.*

FIGURE 12.22 Lee Ji Hyeon, 13-years-old, Busan Middle School of Arts, Busan, South Korea.
*Source: ICEFA Lidice, 44th Exhibition.*

combine realism with abstractions like Jaune Quick-to-See Smith. This encourages students to experiment with painting processes and techniques, and it also frees them from the pressure of thinking that their paintings must always look realistic. Up through elementary school, students most regularly paint with tempera paints and watercolors because they are affordable and clean up more readily than other paints.

Early adolescents are prepared to participate in more advanced painting processes and work with painting media such as acrylics, oils, and encaustics on various painting surfaces. When students first enter middle school, teachers can pre-assess their knowledge of painting skills to identify what students already know, then later conduct a post-assessment to demonstrate individual growth over an academic period. The choice-based art curriculum and instructional methods encourage students to take chances to build upon their existing repertoires, move out of comfort zones, and develop new skills. Class learning tasks should include experimental mark making and applications of non-realistic expressive colors to add excitement to the curriculum and remove possible stress for students experiencing creativity blocks as they build up surface areas with layered colors, textures, and creative designs (Figure 12.21). Using big ideas, students apply refined painting skills they learn in class, including producing subtle color changes to show greater value and depth within a composition (Figure 12.22). Collaborative painting activities are well-suited for early adolescents because they promote a sense of belonging and accomplishment as students create works beyond what they could produce individually, such as murals, and interact constructively with peers to reach painting learning targets. Class collaborations may also include visiting artists.

With early adolescents' increased abstract thinking skills, teachers can challenge students to analyze meanings presented in representational and non-representational paintings through class discussions and reflective exercises. Teachers will ask students to cite evidence to make convincing cases as they analyze their own and others' paintings. Using the examples of contemporary painters, early adolescents may wish to present their own painting experiences to audiences using video footage of their production methods and gather audience feedback to build on the meaning of the works they have already created. They can also use journal entries and photographs to document the steps they took to produce finished painted designs, such as a drip painting, and share this information with peers and public audiences as a teaching tool and for self-reflection (Figure 12.23). During summative class critiques, teachers can ask students to identify if they achieved the results they wanted and contemplate how they can make revisions as necessary and augment current skills based on successful learning outcomes.

By adolescence, students should have had substantial experiences manipulating paint media and tools, given comprehensive instruction in elementary and middle school. Teachers can pre-assess students' painting knowledge to develop learning targets that meet student's personal needs. The choice-based art curriculum will provide adolescents with opportunities to build new strengths while working with painting techniques, media, and styles with which they are less familiar, and combining existing skills in new ways. The work shown in Figure 12.24 demonstrates

FIGURE 12.24 Liang Lim Yong, 16-years-old, Yeow Chye Art Centre, Penang, Malaysia.
*Source: ICEFA Lidice, 41st Exhibition.*

a student's ability to paint realistic subject matter in watercolors while integrating textured abstractions to produce shadows and architectural features. Given their building maturity and sense of responsibility, students should also have access to professional-grade painting materials, including absorbent watercolor papers, canvas, professional-grade encaustic wax, and finer brushes. If teachers are working with a smaller budget these might be limited for use on special projects and/or funded by a grant. In addition to providing studio lab experiences, teachers can take students to outdoor environments to paint from life, called **plein air** painting. Like Josef Zedník, students can study transformations in the environment and in their lives through paint. This topic is applicable as students are experiencing personal transformations as they progress into adulthood. The choice-based art curriculum will have students study the content

FIGURE 12.23 Lorna Fida, early adolescent, drips paint. Kenya.
*Source: Lisa Wee, teacher.*

**FIGURE 12.25** Gordey Murashko, 14-years-old, GBOU School No. 1955, Moscow, Russia.
*Source: ICEFA Lidice, 46th Exhibition.*

in paintings to identify some of the ways that paintings have preserved aspects of history and culture. Given contextual background information, students will analyze the commonalities and dissimilarities that paintings share. Teachers will have students review paintings within their portfolios to decide pathways for expanding upon their current ideas, making revisions, and producing future works. The artwork shown in Figure 12.25 presents a historic ship battle that has effective fluid forms, which are based on the student's regular plein air painting experiences. Students will orally describe and write about the meanings of their works and artistic inspirations through artist statements that describe the intended displays, care, purposes, and functions of their works.

## OUR JOURNEY TO THRIVE CONTINUES . . .

In the next chapter, we will learn how to teach paper arts, printmaking, and book arts to pre-K–12 students. We will develop comprehensive learning tasks that motivate and challenge students as they create original paper arts products, prints, and book arts. As we teach students these meaningful art forms, we will be able to integrate some of the drawing and painting techniques we have studied.

## CHAPTER QUESTIONS AND ACTIVITIES

1. Describe painting's qualities, functions, and meanings from a historic perspective. How will you integrate painting into the choice-based art curriculum?
2. Practice the diverse painting media described in this chapter to compare and contrast their qualities. Summarize what you learned in a group discussion or in writing.
3. Develop an original comprehensive painting lesson. Use the lesson plan template provided on the textbook's companion website and refer to Chapter 2 for more information on lesson plan development. Integrate inquiry tasks inspired by Part III of this textbook.
4. Answer Artists' Lessons to Thrive! 12.1 and 12.2 essential/guiding questions in written form or as part of a group discussion. Complete the daily learning targets.

## References

Bolt, B. (2004). *Art beyond representation: The performative power of the image.* London: I. B. Tauris.

Brommer, G. F., & Kinne, N. K. (2003). *Exploring painting* (3rd ed.). Worcester, MA: Davis Publications.

Elkins, J. (2000). *What painting is: How to think about oil painting, using the language of alchemy.* New York: Routledge.

Grant, D. (2010). More watercolor classes are needed in art schools. *American Artist, 74*(811), 74–75.

Guarino, E. (2018). *And the ship sails on: More of Jaune Quick-to-See Smith's Trade Canoe series.* Retrieved from https://kinggalleries.com/and-the-ship-sails-on-more-on-jaune-quick-to-see-smiths-trade-canoe-series/

Himelfarb, E. J. (2000). Prehistoric body painting. *Archaeology, 53*(4), 18.

Hurt, P. (2013). Never underestimate the power of a paint tube. *Smithsonian.* Retrieved from www.smithsonianmag.com/arts-culture/never-underestimate-the-power-of-a-paint-tube-36637764/#QTzQSRQ34rldaVgl.99

Jarvis, M. (2009). Francis Bacon and the practice of painting. *Journal of Visual Arts Practice, 8*(3), 181–193.

Kaneda, T., & Fischer, H. (2010). The Kids' Guernica Peace Mural Project: A vehicle for social justice. In T. Anderson, D. Gussak, K. Hallmark, & A. Paul (Eds.), *Art education for social justice* (pp. 195–200). Reston, VA: National Art Education Association.

Kastner, C. (2013). *Jaune Quick-to-See Smith: An American modernist*. Albuquerque, NM: University of New Mexico Press.

Kirk, C. (2014). "Painting" as emergent knowledge: A practice-led case study of contemporary artistic labour. *Journal of Visual Art Practice, 13*(2), 114–129.

Marabel, D. (2006). Ruth Faison Shaw: First lady of finger painting. *The World and I, 21*(9), 22.

Mattera, J. (2001). *The art of encaustic painting: Contemporary expression in the ancient medium of pigmented wax*. New York: Watson-Guptill.

Petersen, A. R. (2010). Painting spaces. In A. R. Petersen, M. Bogh, H. Dam Christensen, & P. N. Larsen (Eds.), *Contemporary painting in context* (pp. 123–138). Copenhagen: Museum Tusculanum Press.

Reyner, N. (2007). *Acrylic revolution: New tricks and techniques for working with the world's most versatile medium*. Cincinnati, OH: North Light Books.

Sawyer, D. (2018). *Katharina Grosse rejects your idea that painting is archaic*. Retrieved from www.documentjournal.com/2018/05/katharina-grosse-rejects-your-idea-that-painting-is-archaic/

Schildkrout, E. (2004). Inscribing the body. *Annual Review of Anthropology, 33*, 319–344.

Shaw, R. F. (1947). *Finger-painting and how I do it*. New York: Leland-Brent.

Sickler-Voigt, D. C. (2006). From out of sight to "outta sight!": Collaborative art projects that empower children with at-risk tendencies. *Journal of Social Theory in Art Education, 26*, 156–175.

Sickler-Voigt, D. C. (2007). Inclusion in our global community: The International Kids' Guernica Peace Mural Project. *Focus on Inclusive Education, 5*(1), 1–8.

Weibel, P. (2010). Pittura/immedia: Painting in the nineties between mediated visuality and visuality in context. In A. R. Petersen, M. Bogh, H. D. Christensen, & P. N. Larsen (Eds.), *Contemporary painting in context* (pp. 49–66). Copenhagen: Museum Tusculanum Press, University of Copenhagen.

Womack, L., & Womack, W. (2008). *Embracing encaustic: Learning to paint with beeswax*. Portland, OR: Hive.

Zarur, E. N. C. (2001). Introduction. In E. N. C. Zarur & C. M. Lovell (Eds.), *Art and faith in Mexico: The nineteenth-century retablo tradition* (pp. 17–29). Albuquerque, NM: University of New Mexico Press.

# Chapter 13

# Paper Arts, Printmaking, and Book Arts

FIGURE 13.1 First-grade through seventh-grade student exhibition. Norway.
*Source: Author, pre-service educators, and Flåm Skule (School) faculty, teachers.*

Paper arts, printmaking, and book arts produce artistic and utilitarian products that hold importance in daily life. Most people think of paper, prints, and books as mass-produced resources, yet they began as handmade creations that humans developed and refined over time. Contemporary artists continue the art of creating paper, prints, and books. Their works can be made entirely by hand or with the assistance of technologies. As part of the choice-based art curriculum, students will learn the functional applications of paper, printmaking, and book arts and the reasons why artists create these products. We will teach students that **paper** is a material derived from plant and vegetable fibers. Its primary ingredient is

cellulose, an insoluble component contained within plant and vegetable cells that makes paper strong and flexible. **Paper arts** refer to two- and three-dimensional creative works crafted with handmade, recycled, and manufactured papers. **Printmaking** is the method of creating one or more original artworks by applying pressure to transfer a pigmented design or an impression to a new surface, which is often paper. The materials that printmakers select impact the look, feel, and meanings of their works. **Book arts** is the creative practice of constructing and designing artworks in book form as well as the process of manipulating existing books to produce artist's books. Artists create books using diverse art processes and media. Many of their designs contain paper and printed content.

We will meet the following objectives by participating in this chapter:

- Describe paper arts, printmaking, and book arts and their qualities, functions, and meanings in society.
- Identify best practices for teaching paper arts, printmaking, and book arts.
- Create instructional resources for teaching paper arts, printmaking, and book arts.

Spotlight on Student Art #13 explains how students studied an illustrated fairytale as inspiration to create book arts projects about resiliency (Figures 13.1–13.3). Their unit of study combined book arts procedures, paper arts techniques, and printed resources to communicate stories about how they were able to overcome personal challenges.

FIGURE 13.3 Fifth-grade book arts project. Denmark.
*Source: Author, pre-service, and Anna Trolles Skole (School) faculty, teachers.*

FIGURE 13.2 Lars Mykkeltvedt Buene, 6th grade. Book arts project. Norway.
*Source: Author, pre-service, and Flåm Skule (School) faculty, teachers.*

## Spotlight on Student Art #13

### Big Idea: Resiliency

Inspired by the big idea of resiliency and the Norwegian fairytale *East of the Sun and West of the Moon*, Scandinavian students in two countries created handmade books with assorted papers and mixed media techniques that included printmaking and collage (Figure 13.1). Before forming their handmade books, the students identified personal hardships that they wanted to share with the group and made references to the fairytale's characters and the difficulties they overcame to become resilient. Students' obstacles included long hospital stays due to necessary operations, missing a father who lived in a far-away country, breaking a bone while snowboarding, and losing the family home to a fire. Their books served as vehicles to communicate their stories visually.

One group of students created a collaborative book that consisted of individual pages of complementary sheets of colored paper glued together with a piece of ribbon in between. The students tied their individual book pages together to unify their designs and demonstrate how overcoming hardships is an integral part of the human experience. A second group created books using recycled paper that they folded into an accordion pattern and pasted into repurposed cardboard boxes with lids (Figure 13.2). This construction method provided students with a format to present their works' internal and external stories. A third group of students worked in small teams and transformed discarded hardcover books into altered books (Figure 13.3). Collaboratively, they redesigned their book's exterior casing and utilized the book's carved interior compartment to hold individual accordion books. Upon completion, all students exhibited their works internationally and created written stories to accompany their artist's books so that gallery audiences would have deeper understandings of resiliency in their lives.

## UNDERSTANDING AND APPLYING PAPER ARTS IN CONTEXT

Paper arts begin with paper production. Paper's invention around 200 BCE resulted in humanity's increased knowledge due to the many products it produced, including expansive collections of literary works. Students are often excited to watch papermaking in action and learn about the development of this process. Papermakers strive to produce uniform products for consumers and do not typically view their work as fine art (Hubbe & Bowden, 2009). To create paper, they smash cellulose fibers into a pulp from products including wood, recycled rags, and leftover textiles. They pour the pulp onto a framed screen surface that allows added liquid to pass through, leaving a smooth layer of matted fibers on the screen. Then, they remove the excess water from the pulp using a thick absorbent sheet called a **blotter** and allow it to dry (Bloom, 2001).

The pulp paper making process is attributed to Cai Lun in 105 CE, who recommended using rags, bark, and other textile materials as alternatives to bamboo and silk for paper production. Students may be surprised to learn that paper's primary function was to wrap goods. In the 9th century after its introduction in the Middle East from China, paper became widely used as a durable writing surface that individuals could fold into books. In 1009 CE, trade brought papermaking to Europe. As paper journeyed from Asia to Europe, papermakers experimented and applied their available resources to improve papermaking techniques. Because quality paper equated with financial success, artisans at paper guilds and mills kept their papermaking procedures, fibers, and finishes secret so that others could not replicate their products (Avella, 2011; Bloom, 2001; Hubbe & Bowden, 2009; Martin, 2011). Beginning in the mid-15th century, the need for paper increased dramatically when Johannes Gutenberg invented the printing press. His invention reduced the price of books significantly. Prior to the printing press, monks and other skilled individuals created handwritten books, often produced on costly sheets of **parchment,** made from treated sheep and goat hides, or **vellum,** an even thinner and smoother writing surface created from calf skin. Papermaking processes remained relatively unchanged until the Industrial Revolution, when manufacturers sped up paper production with machinery and innovative processes. These resulted in the development and widespread circulation of newspapers, magazines, and books.

Paper production remains a booming business, even with digital reading resources. Artists and consumers alike have become more aware of the negative impacts of industrial papermaking, including deforestation, waste, and the introduction of bleaching agents in the environment. Some paper manufacturers produce eco-friendly products created solely from recycled materials. Handmade paper artisans are the most likely to apply sustainable practices and use greener materials, fewer natural resources, and fewer or no chemicals. Such environmental awareness has also prompted contemporary artists, students, and educators to work with postconsumer paper products. For example, Japanese-born artist Yuken Teruya cuts delicate tree forms directly from everyday waste products, including fast-food bags, pizza boxes, sneaker boxes, and toilet paper rolls (Avella, 2011). Like professional artists, students can use diverse papers such as repurposed materials to produce paper arts.

## Papercutting and Paper Manipulations

**Papercutting** is an early form of paper art that dates to 6th century China and remains a popular practice in today's classrooms. Over China's 1,500-year history, the Chinese have designed artistic papercuts for decorations, celebrations, and religious purposes. Some designs are so intricate that they replicate the look of lace. Mothers passed papercutting traditions to their daughters. Because of papercutting's continued practice throughout China, in 2009 UNESCO honored the artistic tradition by including it in its Intangible Cultural Heritage of Humanity list. Students can study well-known papercutting traditions including Japanese stencil designs, *ketubot* (Jewish marriage contracts), *wycinanki* (Polish Easter decorations), and *papel picado* (decorative Mexican holiday banners). Many students are familiar with Danish author Hans Christian Andersen's fairytales. He is also known for the original papercuts that he created while narrating his fairytales to patrons (Figure 13.4). Contemporary Danish artist Karen Bit Vejle (see Artists' Lessons to Thrive! 8.1.) has been inspired by both Chinese papercutting traditions and Andersen's papercuts.

FIGURE 13.4 Hans Christian Andersen, *A Whole Cut Fairy Tale*. (Danish, Odense 1805–1875 Copenhagen). circa 1864. Paper cutout. Sheet: 13 9/16 × 13 1/4 in. (34.4 × 33.7 cm). Cut paper. The Metropolitan Museum of Art. Mary Martin Fund and The Elisha Whittelsey Collection, The Elisha Whittelsey Fund, 2012. Accession Number: 2012.379. CC0.

*Source: www.metmuseum.org.*

**Silhouettes** are paper cutouts (often black) that reveal only the outlines of a form. They date to 16th century France and became popular in the 18th and 19th century United States amongst middle-class families who made or had their portraits commissioned as silhouettes. Contemporary American artist Kara Walker has continued this art form with her production of silhouette papercut installations that combine antebellum iconography with silhouettes to narrate historically inspired tales about race and prejudice (Art 21, 2003).

Understanding global papercutting practices is particularly useful for a generation of young people living in a technology-driven world: "Paper cutting puts us back in touch with the need to 'make,' to use our hands creatively and escape the pixelated imagery that is everywhere in our screen-dominated lives" (Avella, 2011, p. 9). Students become skilled in cutting and folding paper with practice. They can also experiment with diverse paper manipulation methods including: twisting, braiding, weaving, punching, scoring (making one or more incisions into the paper's surface without cutting through it to produce folded and patterned designs), mosaicking (arranging small

pieces into a pattern with balanced, negative spaces in-between; see Figure 13.5 for an example), and quilling (forming coiled designs). Figure 13.6. shows how students created a collection of sea urchin shells by punching patterns in paper and tearing the edges. In addition to working with scissors and making tears, advanced students with skilled hand–eye coordination may cut with an X-ACTO knife—provided that they follow safety directions, wear cut-resistant gloves, and use cutting mats to protect work surfaces.

FIGURE 13.5 Emily Avaritt, 8th grade, United States.
*Source: Lydia Horvath, teacher.*

FIGURE 13.6 Group project, 12–15-years-old, ZUŠ, Nové Město pod Smrkem, Czech Republic.
*Source: ICEFA Lidice, 46th Exhibition.*

# Collage

A **collage** is an artwork created by pasting cut (Figure 13.7) and/or torn papers (Figure 13.8), as well as other objects, to a background surface to form a design. Pablo Picasso and Georges Braque were the first artists to use collage as an innovative art method.

Jona Lassahn, 11-years-old, Gemeinschaftsschule an der Waldwies, Saarwellingen, Germany.
*Source: ICEFA Lidice, 43rd Exhibition.*

Kateřina Klimešová, 11-years-old, ZUŠ Vladislava Vančury, Háj ve Slezsku, Czech Republic.
*Source: ICEFA Lidice, 42nd Exhibition.*

They adhered materials including newspaper, postage stamps, rope, and fabric to their paintings (Ward, 2008). Fellow 20th century artists followed suit and expanded collage's possibilities with different applications and media. Kurt Schwitters and Hannah Hoch combined collage and photography to produce **photomontages,** collages made with two or more photographs. Collage reaches beyond fine art and includes advertisements, fashion spreads, and album art. In the 21st century, collage's definition and appearance expanded due to the mass production of images in visual culture and digital software's cut and paste capabilities. Some artists create purely digital collages and others combine traditional and technological media (Bereton & Roberts, 2011; Poynor, 2011). Artists regularly integrate manipulated paper techniques into collages, including paper weaving and mosaicking. While working with diverse papers and other materials can produce magnificent designs, art critics have observed that some collages by professional artists appear as "mismatched clutter" because their designs integrate too many visual options (Poynor, 2011). The same result occurs when students overuse heavily patterned and/or shiny papers and lose sight of how to bring emphasis to key components within their designs. To eliminate this concern, teachers can instruct students to sketch their ideas and plan the papers and paper processes they want to use before cutting. Teacher should also encourage students to pause before gluing pieces to their collages to make sure that all parts are arranged where they want them to be.

# Paper Sculptures

**Paper sculptures** include three-dimensional artworks and built environment displays that artists and designers produce by bending, folding, and manipulating two-dimensional paper products. Chinese lanterns are an early example of paper sculptures and date to 230 BCE. For centuries, the Japanese have produced origami by folding a single piece of paper into forms such as cranes. They also create kirigami, which combine folded and cut paper techniques. In the 20th century, artists designed paper sculptures for department store window displays, which were photographed and published in printed advertisements. Contemporary artists use new and repurposed paper products and technologies to create sculptures. Paper sculptor Sher

Christopher recreates fairytale characters using quality artist's papers (see Figure 13.9 and Artists' Lessons to Thrive! 1.3). Diana Beltrán Herrera sculpts lifelike birds in paper (see Artists' Lessons to Thrive! 13.1). She produces realistic bird proportions by using vector line drawings and gives paper the appearance of feathers by applying skillful cutting and folding techniques. These artists' works demonstrate to students how paper transforms from a two-dimensional to a three-dimensional medium.

Paper sculptures can be freestanding, mounted to a base, and hung. Teachers can integrate STEAM subject matter by teaching students how to create paper sculptures using three-dimensional forms that include mathematical cubes, cones, cylinders, and planes as possible structures to form their designs. They should also demonstrate how to score paper to make paper forms easier to bend by gently gliding the edge of a closed pair of scissors along the desired trajectory without breaking through the paper's surface. Like artists, students can integrate paper manipulations into their designs, including paper curls, quilling, and braiding. Students may choose to leave the paper sculpture surfaces undecorated (Figure 13.10) or enhance them with paint and mixed media.

FIGURE 13.9 Sher Christopher. *Little Red Riding Hood* ©.
*Source: Courtesy of the artist; www.sherchristopher.com.*

FIGURE 13.10 Valerii Lichosherstov, 15-years-old, Children Art School, Sarov, Russia.
*Source: ICEFA Lidice, 38th Exhibition.*

## Artists' Lessons to Thrive! 13.1 Diana Beltrán Herrera: Sculpting the World's Birds—An Immersion Into Artistic Practice

### Big Idea: Immersion

Diana Beltrán Herrera creates compelling life-sized paper sculptures of the world's birds. As a child growing up in Colombia, she was exposed to her country's rich biodiversity and spent time admiring nature, imagining what life was like for its flora and fauna. Years later, when Herrera was studying industrial design in the city, she sought a connection to nature and noticed how certain avian populations thrived in urban environments, places that at first impression appear void of wildlife.

She recognized that wild birds were quick to fly away and always remained out of reach. Sculpting their likenesses served as a means for the artist to become closer to the birds she admired. The artist immersed herself in researching the qualities of paper and birds to understand their physical characteristics and particular behaviors. She augmented her existing knowledge and consulted with ornithologists and bird club members to produce anatomically correct avian designs. By delving deeply into her artistic practice, Herrera built a collection of works that includes more than 100 avian species.

Herrera describes her construction techniques as simple, even though creating organic forms accurately in paper is challenging work. She has mastered the processes of cutting, folding, and bending papers to form complex three-dimensional bird forms. The processes she applies have become second nature due to her ongoing artistic practice, detailed studies, and extensive knowledge of subject matter. Each work becomes a tangible product based on the artist's determined efforts with paper, glue, and scissors to replicate the natural look and textures of birds' features. Herrera's *Greater Bird of Paradise* (Figure 13.1.1) is an example of how she captures avian movements and wingspans. As an alternative to her freestanding birds and birds in flight, Herrera has appropriated existing stamp designs and replicated them into three-dimensional paper sculptures for her series *Official Mail* and *Bird Stamps All Around the World*. Herrera's international stamps portray native birds, including the critically endangered Philippine Cockatoo (Figure 13.1.2) and Colombia's common Green-backed Trogon (Figure 13.1.3). Each sculpted bird remains the center of attention among details including the stamp's value, the country's name, and its decorative foliage.

The artist invests much time planning each meticulous design. A single bird can take several weeks to create. As part of her artistic process, Herrera transforms photographs of birds in flight or in resting positions into vector line drawings. These scale drawings reveal each bird's proportions and assist her in constructing the birds precisely in paper. She begins sculpting a bird's body by constructing an armature that has a circular structure with woven parts. She frequently sculpts with Canson paper, but will select

FIGURE 13.1.1 Diana Beltrán Herrera, *Greater Bird of Paradise*, 2014.
*Source: Courtesy of the artist; www.dianabeltranherrera.com.*

FIGURE 13.1.2 Diana Beltrán Herrera, *Official Mail: Philippines*, 2015.

*Source: Courtesy of the artist; www.dianabeltranherrera.com.*

FIGURE 13.1.3 Diana Beltrán Herrera, *Bird Stamps All Around the World: Colombia*, 2015.

*Source: Courtesy of the artist; www.dianabeltranherrera.com.*

papers with different textures, weights, and visual qualities to achieve the aesthetic looks she desires. She adds layers of highly concentrated watercolor pigment to decorate the birds' feathers and uses wire to form the birds' legs and give them stability. As final touches, she sculpts the birds' eyes and beaks.

Herrera's avian works inform society about nature's essential role in our everyday lives. Paper is an ephemeral material, less enduring than stone and metal. Its fragility reiterates the artist's message about our need to pay attention to and preserve the earth's natural resources so that living beings can thrive. Through her detailed paper designs, Herrera causes audiences to remain still and take notice of what would normally be a fleeting moment in time.

## Essential/Guiding Questions

1. Herrera creates beautiful paper sculptures to teach society about nature's value. Why does she feel that people are disengaged from nature? How might her art help reconnect people to nature?
2. In your opinion, how does Herrera's immersion into the artistic practice of sculpting in paper influence the quality of the art she creates?

## Preparation

Students will select an animal or plant to study in depth as inspiration to construct a paper sculpture. They can look to vintage stamps, book covers, and illustrated nature maps in the public domain as possible resources to form their designs.

## UNDERSTANDING AND APPLYING PRINTMAKING IN CONTEXT

Artists create different types of prints. Each has a rich historical background. Printmakers produce prints that are traditional, digital, or combine traditional and digital technologies. Some contemporary printmakers use only traditional methods because they believe that hand-made artworks add special qualities that mass-produced machine-generated visuals cannot replicate (MacPhee, 2009; Stern, 2007). Studying printmaking in context, students will learn its specialized methods, techniques, and vocabulary. For example, printmakers use a surface called a **matrix** to form printed designs. They apply ink (or other pigment) directly to a matrix that may include a printing block, plate, stone, or screen. Most printmaking methods require artists to create matrix designs in reverse. Students may find it challenging to design numbers and letters as mirror images, but will improve with practice. A **substrate** is the surface, such as paper or fabric, on which printmakers produce prints. When creating multiple original prints, printmakers sign their completed works (Figure 13.11). Printmakers use a pencil to write the edition number on the left side of the substrate beneath the inked design (such as 10/12 to indicate it is the tenth print in a series of twelve prints), the print's title in the center (or left), and the artist's name and year on the right.

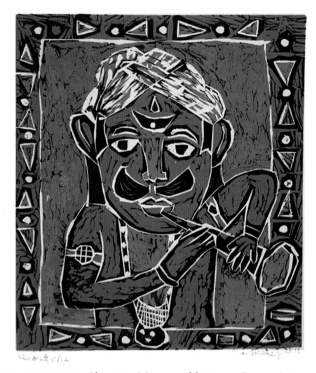

FIGURE 13.11 A. Shreetej, 10-years-old, Young Envoys International, Hyderabad, India.
*Source: ICEFA Lidice, 40th Exhibition.*

### Relief Print

Artists create a **relief print** by carving away components of a block surface (a matrix such as wood and linoleum) to form a design, then inking the raised elements to transfer the design to a substrate. Artisans in the Han Dynasty used the relief process to stamp silk fabrics (Zhao, 2015). By the 8th century the Chinese utilized block printing to print text (Ebrey, 2010). A **woodcut** is a form of relief printing that printmakers produce by inking a wood matrix's raised surface. It is an advanced printmaking process for students due to the need to carve into soft wood to produce a relief design. Woodcuts became popular in Europe during the 15th century, about the same time that paper mills opened in Germany (Thompson, 2003). Artists produced woodcuts for illustrated books, as printmakers could simultaneously print text using Gutenberg's moveable typeset technology with carved woodblocks on a single sheet of paper. Woodcuts' thick inked surface areas retain the imprint of the wood grain from the matrix. During the Edo Period, Japanese artists produced woodcuts that had vivid colors and striking illustrative designs called **Ukiyo-e**, which means "floating world" and references the merchant class' access to arts, entertainment, the beauty of nature, and everyday life (Harris, 2010; Figure 13.12). Ukiyo-e inspired Impressionists, who appropriated its style into their art. Woodblock printing was also a popular medium for German Expressionists. Contemporary artists continue to practice this traditional art form. For example, Taring Padi (an Indonesian printmaking group) develops woodcut prints to advocate for social causes including farmers' rights, fair labor practices, reforestation, and humanitarian aid (Peet, 2007).

A **linocut** is a relief print using a piece of linoleum or similar material that is designed for printmaking (Figure 13.13). Linoleum was originally developed as a flooring material; it became a printmaking medium at the end of the 19th century when art educator

FIGURE 13.12 Utagawa Hiroshige II, *Yoroi Ferry* (1862). Series: *Thirty-six Famous Views of the Eastern Capital,* color woodblock print. LACMA Public Domain.

*Source: www.lacma.org*

FIGURE 13.13 Syafiaah Siti, 15-years-old, Si Ling Secondary School, Singapore.

*Source: ICEFA Lidice, 40th Exhibition.*

Franz Cižek invented Lino cutting for his students as an alternative to carving woodcuts (Morley, 2016). Professional artists soon adopted Cižek's technique. Linocuts and woodblock printing are best suited for students with developed fine motor skills who are able to manipulate linoleum cutters or wood cutting gouges safely, using a **bench hook** or bench plate, which holds a block matrix in place when carving into its surface and inking. Teachers should demonstrate how to carve into linoleum or wood matrixes using linoleum cutters or gouges with cutter blades in assorted sizes to produce various line qualities. As a safer alternative, today's students can use soft rubber carving blocks that are easier to carve. Their softer surfaces do not provide the same quality of detail that the harder linoleum and wood blocks produce. For an even softer surface without the need for specialized carving tools, students can carve into the surface of flat pieces of recycled Styrofoam® with a pencil tip to produce relief prints.

In all forms, relief prints emphasize a work's positive and negative spaces, showing contrast between the inked design and the paper. Ink does not adhere to the recessed surfaces. Artists typically use a handled rolling device called a **brayer** to spread a thin coat of printing ink to block surfaces and run the matrix and substrate through a printing press. In classrooms without a printing press, students can utilize a clean, non-inked brayer or a **baren** (flat disk-shaped printmaking tool) and apply pressure while rubbing all areas of the backside of the substrate to form diverse relief prints.

## Intaglio and Lithography

The 15th century brought a greater demand for printed images. Artists sought methods to introduce grayscale values and further details into prints, qualities that are difficult to produce with woodcuts (Thompson, 2003). They developed a new form of printmaking called **intaglio,** which includes engravings and etchings. Instead of applying the ink on the surface as in relief printing, artists either carve into metal plates using a sharp tool called a **burin** to produce engravings. They create **etchings** by drawing with an etching needle on a metal plate treated with a waxy acid-resistant solution. When this drawing is complete, they place the plate into an acid solution

to burn the exposed designs into the metal surface. This process leaves the rest of the treated plate intact, but the printer's design is the only part that holds ink. To print **intaglio** designs, artists rub ink into the crevices on metal plates—removing excess ink from the surface—and then feed their plate and paper through a press (Elisha, 2009).

At the end of the 18th century Alois Senefelder invented **lithography**, a printing process in which artists draw with a greased lithographic crayon on a treated limestone surface that absorbs grease (Pogue, 2012). His invention became a popular medium for advertising. Given examples of artists at work, students will be able to recognize that lithography's design process is similar to drawing on paper. After drawing an image, the artist seals the stone, wets it with water, and applies oil-based ink that adheres only to the stone's oiled design as it runs through the press to produce a print. Printmakers creating lithographs with more than one color require one or more additional stones to ink their designs. They must carefully align the print's registration marks before running each inked stone through the printing press to produce even results. Due to the need for specialized equipment, both intaglio and lithography are less commonly created by schoolchildren. However, teachers can select these prints to prompt inquiry tasks about artist's techniques and behaviors. For example, students could contemplate how Meghan O'Connor (Artists' Lessons to Thrive! 7.2) transformed a lithograph (Figure 13.14) into a three-dimensional collage (Figure 13.15).

## Stencil Print, Screen Printing, and Serigraph

Printmakers **create a stencil print** by cutting designs into an impervious sheet made from thick paper, plastic, wood, or metal called a **stencil**. They firmly attach the stencil to a substrate and apply pigment by sponging, squeegeeing, brushing, rolling, or spraying (Figure 13.16). The pigment that passes through the stencil's negative space forms the printed design. In 1914, John Pilsworth developed the first multicolor **screen printing** process. Printmakers tightly stretched silk or nylon fabric onto a frame and used a squeegee to spread ink through the open areas of a stencil to pass through the fabric screen onto the substrate.

FIGURE 13.14 Meghan O'Connor. *Disambiguative Communications,* Lithograph.
Source: *Courtesy of the artist; www.curlymeg88.com*

FIGURE 13.15 Meghan O'Connor. *Disambiguative Communications,* Lithograph Collage.
Source: *Courtesy of the artist; www.curlymeg88.com.*

FIGURE 13.16 Benjamin Péter, 13-years-old, Homokbödögei Müvészeti Alapiskola, Homokbödöge, Hungary.
Source: *ICEFA Lidice, 42nd Exhibition.*

Screen printing was built on prior innovations including 19th century Japanese screen printing with paper stencils and the long tradition of Chinese silk stencils. Stencil prints and screen printing differ from many other types of printmaking because they do not require a printing press and are not printed in reverse. Beginning in the late 19th century, screen printing became popular in Europe for manufactured goods and signage. Artists who wanted to differentiate their products from industrial designs, named their form of silkscreening the **serigraph**. Developments in silkscreen technologies enabled artists to integrate photographic imaging by applying a **photo emulsion** solution to the screen, drying it, and using a light to burn an image printed on acetate onto the screen before printing. Classes can work with traditional screen printing techniques that require silkscreen frames, silkscreen ink, squeegees, and screen fillers that block designs on the screens. Like artists, students can make serigraphs to create fine art, print on fabric, and create posters.

## Monotype

A **monotype** is a unique print created without an existing matrix by transferring pigment from a flat surface. Monotypes produce immediate results and are practical for the classroom because they do not require special printmaking supplies and can produce a variety of outcomes. As articulated by artist Jasper Johns who has created monotypes for more than fifty years, monotypes "invite playfulness" (Belcove, 2016, 10th para.). To begin, students will spread block printing ink or paint onto a flat surface, forming a design. Surfaces can include tabletops, plexiglass, Mylar® plastic sheets, and gelatin. Teachers and students can produce gelatin monoprinting plates by mixing gelatin packets and letting the mixture harden on cookie sheets with edges. Manufactures also sell durable, ready-to-use gel printing plates for the classroom. Once students have decided on their printing surface, teachers will encourage them to experiment with their designs. Monotypes can have a painterly feel when students apply color with a brush. Students can also use their fingers, rags, cotton swabs, and brushes to scrape areas of color away from the surface to produce patterns. They can create textures and shapes by stamping found objects into the pigmented surface. They might also integrate original stencils into their designs to produce layered effects. Students will need to work quickly so that their pigment remains moist. Then, they will center their substrate over the monotype matrix. Students can print on diverse papers (including existing artworks that they wish to rework) and fabric. They will rub the entire surface with enough pressure so that the pigment transfers evenly. They will carefully lift the substrate away from the matrix to complete the process and reveal their printed image. Figure 13.17 shows a student preparing a monotype design on a tabletop with a layer of shaving cream painted with liquid watercolors.

## Collagraph

Artists create a **collagraph** by building layers of sturdy collage materials that they glue to a matrix to produce prints with textured patterns (Figure 13.18). This technique originated in the 19th century. Early collographs include works by the sculptor Pierre Roche, who built up embossings by layering adhesive to a metal plate. An **embossing** is a relief print with three-dimensional designs that rise from printed papers' surfaces when run through a printmaking press, as seen with the feather imprint in Figure 13.19. In 1956, artist Glen Alps was the first to name the collagraph process, even though other artists had already employed the art form for decades. For instance, Cubists had expanded the collagraph's artistic possibilities and paved the way for the collagraphs that society knows today (Hughes & Vernon-Morris, 2008). Students can select materials including mat board, tag board, cardboard, recycled file folders, foam sheets, yarn, and other relatively flat and durable objects to build a collagraph matrix with multiple layers. Once the glue on

FIGURE 13.18 Viktoria Angelova, 6-years-old, Children Painting Group, Gabrovo, Bulgaria.
*Source: ICEFA Lidice, 38th Exhibition.*

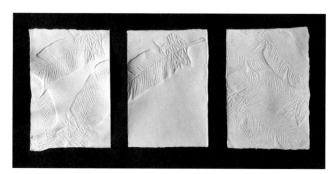

FIGURE 13.19 Adéla Kopečná, 14-years-old, ZUŠ M. Stibora, Olomouc, Czech Republic.
*Source: ICEFA Lidice, 42nd Exhibition.*

FIGURE 13.17 An adolescent student prepares a monotype. United States.
*Source: Author and Monica Leister, teachers.*

the matrix has dried, with all parts firmly attached, students can ink the matrix to produce collagraphs. As an alternative they can transform their collagraph matrixes into **rubbings** by placing a sheet of paper over the collagraph matrix and holding a crayon or other drawing instrument firmly on its side and rubbing its entire surface until the full design appears.

## UNDERSTANDING AND APPLYING BOOK ARTS IN CONTEXT

In a time when people acquire much information through digital print, some contemporary artists view book arts as a new artistic medium. Holding a book provides people with opportunities to experience physical and aesthetic sensations that digital works cannot deliver (Salamony, Thomas, & Thomas, 2012). While students have access to physical books, many are unfamiliar with book making's origins and how long it took for societies to develop book forms similar to the ones used today. Teachers can explain that although humans developed writing in 3,200 BCE, only a few people could read or write for several thousand years. Those who could write usually produced less important texts on temporary surfaces, including dirt and leaves. Societies preserved important written information on stone, wood, papyrus, animal skins, and bones. Beginning in late antiquity, Western societies produced illuminated manuscripts that combined handwritten text and illustrations. The art form reached its peak during the medieval era, when monks created religious holy books on vellum with ornate lettering, page borders, and religious iconography. During the 14th century, artisans in the Middle East had access to larger sheets of paper than were available earlier, and they produced books with sizable illustrations, which became known as Persian miniature paintings (Bloom, 2001). With the industrialization of affordable paper and printing, avant-garde artists began creating books as artworks to communicate their beliefs about art to the greater public.

Artist's book designs range from simple to complex. Figure 13.20 shows a student's book in a bound form. In Figure 13.21, multiple students' original prints are combined into a book; and in Figure 13.22, an entire class tied individual collages they designed with ribbons to form a collective book. Some artist's books contain signatures. A **signature** is a collection of pages that artists fold together and sew or glue to form a book's spine. A **series** is a section in a book.

FIGURE 13.20 Josef Doubrava, 10-years-old, ZUŠ, Mšeno, Czech Republic.
*Source: ICEFA Lidice, 41st Exhibition.*

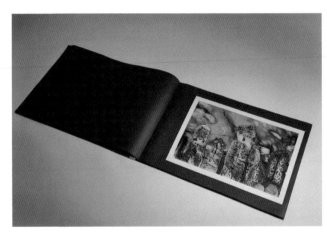

FIGURE 13.21 Group project, 7–14-years-old, ZUŠ, Plzeň, Czech Republic.
*Source: ICEFA Lidice, 42nd Exhibition.*

FIGURE 13.22 Collaborative early childhood book arts project from Spotlight on Student Art #13. Norway.
*Source: Author, pre-service, and Flåm Skule (School) faculty, teachers.*

## Handmade Artist's Books

Handmade artist's books challenge students to create a familiar product in new ways. Their designs can range from purely abstract to figurative—with or without words. An **accordion book** is a basic book design. It has folded pages that produce a zigzag patterned form when opened (Figure 13.2). Paper sizes to produce accordion books can vary. Students can create a 6 × 24 in. (15 × 60 cm) accordion book using the following steps: (1) Fold a long sheet of 6 × 24 in. (15 × 60 cm) paper in half so that it measures 6 × 12 in. (15 × 30 cm) after folding. (2) Fold the right side of the top layer to the left hand side and crease the paper. This will become the top page. Do not pick up the bottom layer in step two. (3) Fold the right sides of the bottom layer to the far left on the backside. This will become the back page. The closed book will measure 6 × 6 in. (15 × 15 cm). If students desire a longer book, they can extend their book's length by creating a new single-sheet book, then overlapping the first new page with the last page and gluing the two pages together to continue the accordion pattern. If students wish to add pockets to their accordion books, they can use taller sheets of paper and fold the bottom third of the page into a pocket before making the accordion folds (Figure 13.23). Once students become proficient in making basic accordion books, they can learn more advanced folded book techniques. Figure 13.24 shows an antique **tunnel book** with a peep hole on its cover design that encourages viewers to look through and admire its multilayered design in perspective. It has accordion folds on its edges that add layers and depth to the book's design. Figure 13.25 showcases a

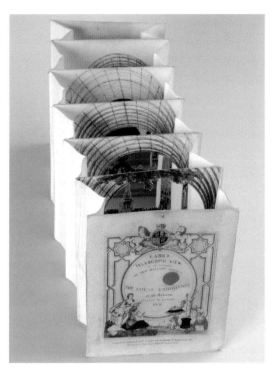

FIGURE 13.24 Thomas Rawlins (1851). *Lane's Telescopic View: The Ceremony of Her Majesty Opening the Great Exhibition* (open).
*Source: Hopkins Rare Books, Manuscripts, and Archives. Flickr, CC BY 2.0. https://creativecommons.org/licenses/by/2.0/*

FIGURE 13.23 Lucia Kostolná, 8-years-old, ZUŠ, Žilina, Slovak Republic.
*Source: ICEFA Lidice, 40th Exhibition.*

FIGURE 13.25 Star fold books, early adolescents. Denmark.
*Source: Author, pre-service, and Flåm Skule (School) faculty, teachers. Photo by Brittany Gardner.*

FIGURE 13.26 Timotej Lučenič, 8-years-old, ZUŠ, Svätý Jur, Slovak Republic.
*Source: ICEFA Lidice, 40th Exhibition.*

collection of folded star books that students created by combining solid, bright colored papers with durable white paper that they marbled into rainbow colors.

**Popup books** have moving features that rise from page surfaces when opened, pulled, or lifted. They were first developed around the 13th century for purposes that included teaching astronomy and telling fortunes. Popup books can have simple or complex designs. Students can create basic popups using scissors, paper, and glue (Figures 13.26). Advanced students may work with sharp X-ACTO blades and cut-resistant gloves, like book artists do, to create intricate, multilayered designs. Teachers can build a classroom library that contains commercial and teacher/artists' original popup books to assist students in learning the processes involved in book arts. Students benefit from studying the structures of these books to determine how artists designed their features and made folds and cuts at specific locations to fit their designs within a book's closed form.

## Altered Books

Artists form an **altered book** by cutting, gluing, augmenting, and manipulating existing books and found objects. Some altered books retain their original book

FIGURE 13.27 Laura Button, 14-years-old, Chancy School, Herts, Great Britain.
*Source: ICEFA Lidice, 40th Exhibition.*

forms (Figures 13.27) and others become sculptures that extend beyond the book's form. Contemporary artist Lesley Patterson-Marx creates altered books using original books and found objects. Artists' Lessons to Thrive! 13.2 teaches students how Patterson-Marx utilized a vintage paint tin to house her colorful selection of handmade miniature books. When creating altered books, students can try the following artist's techniques.

- Gluing sections: Artists can use bulldog clips to hold different pages intact and then brush glue on to the edges to form a solid section (a series) that becomes a sculpted form. This process saves time compared to gluing one page at a time.
- Carving spaces/niches: Artists may choose to cut or carve multiple pages to form shapes, letters, frames, specialized designs, and niches for storing objects inside the book's form. After they have carved the desired depth of pages, they will glue the cut page designs together to form solid edges.
- Forming drawers: Artists collect found objects including mint tins and earring boxes to use as drawers. Using scissors or an X-ACTO knife, they will cut a space into the book pages and glue the edges to fit the dimensions of their intended drawer.

These processes take practice to learn. If making cuts into multiple book pages, students should have extra books on hand for practicing before working on final products.

### Artists' Lessons to Thrive! 13.2 Lesley Patterson-Marx: Book Arts as Passages in Time

#### Big Idea: Time

Lesley Patterson-Marx's studio is filled with intimate collectables that reference passages in time. They include antique photographs, old books, vintage magazines, glass jars filled with notions, and specialty papers. She compiles nostalgic products such as shiny harmonicas, delicate handkerchiefs, and attractive containers to use as structures to design original mixed media book arts projects, prints, and collages. By arranging other people's discarded and forgotten memorabilia, Patterson-Marx creates original artworks whose consolidated parts extend beyond their initial meanings.

Due to her competence in creating with various art production processes and trust in her artistic intuition, Patterson-Marx has developed an ability to design complex arrangements that feel mysterious and fun. For each artwork, the artist invests substantial time to make her designs unified. She spends hours finding, purchasing, and categorizing found objects. She thumbs through old books and magazines to locate just the right images to incorporate into her works. During daily walks, she collects natural resources, including dried leaves and insect wings, to add authentic organic components to her designs. She then assembles and overlays her selection of sundry materials with different colors, textures, and patterns to develop rich layers of information. Each carefully chosen object adds a special touch and meaning to her creations.

For her artwork *Radiant Paint Box* (Figures 13.2.1 and 13.2.2), Patterson-Marx appropriated a watercolor paint tin to house eight miniature books. The paint tin is reminiscent of a book in that it

FIGURE 13.2.1 Lesley Patterson-Marx, *Radiant Paint Box* (Interior), 2012, mixed media, 9 × 3 in. (22.86 × 7.62 cm).
*Source: Courtesy of the artist; lesleypattersonmarx.com.*

FIGURE 13.2.2 Lesley Patterson-Marx, *Radiant Paint Box* (Exterior).
*Source: Courtesy of the artist; lesleypattersonmarx.com.*

opens and closes. Its structure adds a sense of nostalgia to the work because it references a bygone era of American manufacturing with its old-fashioned package design. Through its miniature books nested in the box's empty paint pans, Patterson-Marx made visual references to what the original paint tin would have look like when it was new and saturated with pigment. Each miniature book has a nature inspired theme: white represents light; yellow glistens like the sun; green looks like grass; blue mimics the sky; purple symbolizes flowers; red signifies birds; brown suggests trees; and black embodies the earth.

Patterson-Marx formed *Radiant Paint Box's* miniature books using materials including colored paper, wood, and the shells of robin eggs. She integrated old photographs and sewn drawings to form their designs. Many of the artwork's miniature books have accordion folds and delicate embroidery thread ties. Patterson-Marx applied decorative papercutting techniques to form her light, sun, and sky books. To reinforce the artwork's nature theme, she collaged printed foliage from an old botanical book to its interior spaces, paintbrush, and exterior casing. All parts interconnect, thereby resulting in *Radiant Paint Box's* harmonious design.

As *Radiant Paint Box* indicates, Patterson-Marx constructs intimate artworks that have contemporary value using old collectables. The qualities of her artworks invite audiences to want to hold them, look at them more closely, and admire their distinct components. Her mindful creations become sentimental spaces that summon viewers to ask questions about their parts' origins and invent their own storylines that expand upon the works' intended meanings.

## Essential/Guiding Questions

1. Patterson-Marx refers to her artworks as having a strong feminine crafting tradition, even though she applies fine art production skills including bookmaking, printmaking, and collaging. How might Patterson-Marx's use of crafting materials and fine art processes shape the meaning of the works that she produces?
2. In your opinion, how do materials and memories from the past teach us about who we are today? Why do you think that Patterson-Marx chooses to create contemporary art using vintage materials?

## Preparation

Students will research time idioms including "time flies," "turn back time," and "behind the times," to discuss their meanings. They will collect found objects and historic memorabilia to prepare for their art production activity.

## Daily Learning Targets

I can create a book arts project, print, or original collage that focuses on the big idea of time.

- I can form my design using found objects, historic memorabilia, and a time idiom that I have researched.
- I can integrate a balanced and unified design that shows effective craftspersonship.
- I can display my artwork and create signage that explains the meaning and intent of my artwork and its time idiom.

### National Core Arts Anchor Standards 2, 6, 8, and 11
www.nationalartsstandards.org

## BEST PRACTICES FOR TEACHING PAPER ARTS, PRINTMAKING, AND BOOK ARTS FROM PRE-K THROUGH HIGH SCHOOL

Best practices for teaching paper arts, printmaking, and book arts call upon teachers and students to explore the variety of creative processes they have to offer. Each has rich historic backgrounds and contemporary applications that can stimulate student learning and inquiry as part of the choice-based art curriculum. Because some tasks in paper arts, printmaking, and book arts require multiple steps and specialized equipment to complete, teachers should present all procedures clearly and monitor students and their use of resources so that they can reach learning targets. Teachers can facilitate students' independence during tasks by displaying written and illustrated procedures for paper arts, printmaking, and book arts in visible locations for students and provide access to video/online tutorials as applicable for students to reference as they work. Students will need to learn procedures for cleanup and storing works, which include glued papers, wet prints, and artist's book projects.

In early childhood, lessons in the paper arts, printmaking, and book arts increase students' psychomotor skills and dexterity because they give students muscular memory experiences. Students can begin with basic collage methods including tearing papers and cutting with scissors. Lessons should also stimulate children's imaginations. Studying Diana Beltrán Herrera, students can pretend to replicate her birds' kinesthetic movements and sounds as they practice making folds in paper to produce three-dimensional forms for paper arts projects and artist's books. Students can learn how to create monotypes and transfer their designs to substrates. They can combine their building collage and printmaking skills to produce collagraphs (Figure 13.18). If students feel challenged by learning new procedures, teachers can accommodate their needs by being patient and understanding as they assist them in achieving tasks independently.

In middle childhood, students continue to develop their coordination as they learn techniques in paper arts, printmaking, and book arts. Students should practice working with art materials to make effective cuts and folds to form collages, paper sculptures, and artist's books. Teachers can encourage students to develop prints by selecting from diverse processes, matrixes, and substrates to produce a body of works that center on big ideas. They will develop artist statements that explain the meanings of their paper arts, prints, and artist's books. As students are forming their personalities, they can research artworks that discuss character-building skills, including resiliency (as described in Spotlight on Student Art #13) and wisdom (as in Artists' Lessons to Thrive! 8.1 on Karen Bit Vejle's *Ballerina Bulldog* series).

Early adolescents are interested in people in popular culture and want to share their knowledge with others. Studying Sher Christopher's paper sculptures (Figure 13.9. and Artists' Lessons to Thrive! 1.3) and artists' tunnel books, students can collaborate with peers to produce a series of works focusing on character studies. Tunnel books offer a stage-like environment for students to design characters in particular environments. As inspiration for their own works, they could analyze how Sher Christopher presents character moods in three-dimensional forms. Building on the idea of theatres and audiences, students may wish to design an original series of printed posters that involve characters in music and other popular culture genres. They could research posters by Hatch Show Print to learn how their printmakers created effective works for the music industry.

Given their greater dexterity, maturity, and an ability to concentrate, adolescents will be able to utilize many of the same paper, printmaking, and book arts materials as professional artists. They will apply firsthand experiences to answer essential questions relating to artists' health and safety associated with paper arts, printmaking, and book arts methods. With their ability to understand abstract ideas, teachers can challenge adolescents to produce nonrepresentational paper arts, printmaking, and book arts creations and describe the meanings in their designs. They can also explore how artists like Patterson-Marx integrate nontraditional materials in art to produce altered books. Referencing O'Connor, who turned a lithograph into a three-dimensional collage (Figure 13.15), students can contemplate creative ways to transform their original prints into other art forms.

## OUR JOURNEY TO THRIVE CONTINUES . . .

This chapter has presented paper arts, printmaking, and book arts in context. It demonstrated some of the exciting ways that artists create these works using two- and three-dimensional art production methods. Chapter 14 builds on what we have learned and identifies how we can teach students to create meaningful three-dimensional designs using age-appropriate sculpting materials and processes.

## CHAPTER QUESTIONS AND ACTIVITIES

1. Describe the qualities, functions, and meanings of paper arts, printmaking, and book arts from historic and societal perspectives. How will you integrate paper arts, printmaking, and book arts into the choice-based art curriculum?

2. Practice the diverse paper arts, printmaking, and book arts processes described in this chapter to compare and contrast their qualities. Summarize what you learned in a group discussion or in writing.

3. Develop an original comprehensive lesson plan on paper arts, printmaking, or book arts that focuses on a big idea of your choice. Use the lesson plan template provided on the textbook's companion website and refer to Chapter 2 for more information on lesson plan development. Integrate inquiry tasks inspired by Part III of this textbook.

4. Answer Artists' Lessons to Thrive! 13.1 and 13.2 essential/guiding questions in written form or as part of a group discussion. Complete their daily learning targets.

## References

Art 21. (2003). *Kara Walker*. Retrieved from https://art21.org/artist/kara-walker/

Avella, N. (2011). *Introduction*. In L. Heyenga, R. Ryan, & N. Avella (Cont.), *Paper cutting book: Contemporary artists, timeless craft*. San Francisco: Chronicle Books.

Belcove, J. L. (2016, February 9). Artist Jasper Johns on the process behind his monotypes. *Wall Street Journal Magazine*. Retrieved from www.wsj.com/articles/artist-jasper-johns-on-the-process-behind-his-monotypes-1455033251

Bereton, R., & Roberts, C. (2011). *Cut & paste: 21st-century collage*. London: Laurence King.

Bloom, J. M. (2001). *Paper before print: The history and impact of paper in the Islamic world*. New Haven: Yale University Press.

Ebrey, P. B. (2010). *The Cambridge illustrated history of China* (2nd ed.). New York, NY: Cambridge University Press.

Elisha, D. (2009). *Printmaking + mixed media: Simple techniques and projects for paper and fabric*. Loveland, CO: Interweave Press.

Harris, F. (2010). *Ukiyo-e: The art of the Japanese print*. North Clarendon, VT: Tuttle.

Hubbe, M. A., & Bowden, C. (2009). Handmade paper: A review of its history, craft, and science. *BioResources, 4*(4), 1736–1792.

Hughes, A. D., & Vernon-Morris, H. (2008). *Printmaking bible: The complete guide to materials and techniques*. San Francisco: Chronicle Books.

MacPhee, J. (2009). Politics on paper. In J. MacPhee (Ed.), *Paper politics: Socially engaged printmaking today* (pp. 6–10). Oakland, CA: PM Press.

Martin, S. (2011). *Paper chase*. Retrieved from www.ecology.com/2011/09/10/paper-chase/

Morley, N. (2016). *Linocut for artists and designers*. Ramsbury, Marlborough: Crowood Press.

Peet, R. (2007). Taring Padi: Under Siege in Indonesia. In J. MacPhee & E. Reuland (Eds.), *Realizing the impossible: Art against authority* (pp. 120–127). Oakland, CA: A K Press.

Pogue, D. (2012). *Printmaking revolution: New advancements in technology, safety, and sustainability*. New York: Watson-Guptill.

Poynor, R. (2011). Cut and paste. *Print, 65*(3), 34–38.

Salamony, S., Thomas, P., & Thomas, D. (2012). *1,000 artists' books: Exploring the book as art*. Minneapolis, MN: Quarry Books.

Stern, M. (2007). Subversive multiples: A conversation between contemporary printmakers. In J. MacPhee & E. Reuland (Eds.), *Realizing the impossible: Art against authority* (pp. 104–119). Oakland, CA: A K Press.

Thompson, W. (2003). The printed image in the West: History and techniques. In *Heilbrunn timeline of art history*. New York: The Metropolitan Museum of Art, 2000. Retrieved from www.metmuseum.org/toah/hd/prnt/hd_prnt.htm

UNESCO. (2009). *Chinese paper-cut*. Retrieved from www.unesco.org/culture/ich/index.php?lg=en&pg=00011&RL=00219

Ward, G. W. R. (Ed.). (2008). *The Grove Encyclopedia of materials and techniques in art*. New York, NY: Oxford University Press.

Zhao, F. (2015). Lecture 2: Looms and fabric varieties. In Y. Lu (Ed.), *A history of Chinese science and technology* (Vol. 2, pp. 404–458). Berlin, Germany: Springer.

# Chapter 14

# Sculpture

A **sculpture** is a three-dimensional artwork that has volume and mass. Artists produce sculptures by carving, molding, and constructing materials. Sculptures can be heavy, feel light as a feather, remain static, and move in space. Some sculptures fit into people's pockets. Others dominate the spaces they inhabit, including environmental sculptures that beautify landscapes. The act of sculpting satisfies the human sense of touch and need to manipulate objects into something special. Many of us can remember constructing with building blocks, twigs, and found objects in childhood. Our studies of drawing, painting, paper arts, book arts, and printmaking have set useful foundations as we learn how to produce a range of sculpted artworks and teach these skills to students. Comprehensive sculpture lessons encourage students to create diverse three-dimensional artworks, study the people who have made sculptures throughout time, and research the big ideas that drive sculptors' creations in context.

We will meet the following objectives by participating in this chapter:

- Describe sculpture and its qualities, functions, and meanings in society.
- Identify best practices for teaching sculpture.
- Create instructional resources for teaching sculpture.

Spotlight on Student Art #14 (Figures 14.1–14.3) describes how students collaborated with intergenerational participants to create a wetland-inspired sculpture garden as part of a STEAM unit of study. Their collection of larger-than-life sculptures became informative artworks that beautified the school environment.

FIGURE 14.1 *Wetland Garden.* Middle-childhood students, United States.
Source: Author, teacher. MTSU Public Service Grant. Pamela McColly, photo.

FIGURE 14.2 *Wetland Garden Red-Eared Slider Turtle.* Middle-childhood students, United States. *Source: Author, teacher. MTSU Public Service Grant. Pamela McColly, photo.*

FIGURE 14.3 *Wetland Garden Frog.* Middle-childhood students, United States. *Source: Author, teacher. MTSU Public Service Grant. Pamela McColly, photo.*

### Spotlight on Student Art #14

### Big Idea: Wetland Protection

Under the guidance of a wetland expert, on a museum field trip 5th-grade students put on rubber boots and stomped through the water to learn about their local wetland's plants and wildlife. They identified the sounds of the wetlands and made sketches of its flora and fauna. They used microscopes to view the water samples they collected, and they interacted with the museum's pet corn snake and turtles. Upon returning to school, they demonstrated their understanding of the local wetlands through the creation of a wetland-themed sculpture garden on their school campus (Figures 14.1–14.3).

Working with pre-service teachers, professors, senior citizens, and veterans over a two-week period, they transformed their school's drainage ditch into art. The intergenerational community experts had extensive backgrounds in construction, landscaping, horticulture, and wetland preservation. To see this project through to its completion, groups of children applied sculpture techniques including crushing cinderblocks to fill in the excavated ground; digging 12-inch (30.48 cm) holes in the soil to prepare ten forms of oversized concrete wetland animals; and mixing concrete in a concrete mixer and pouring it over the cinderblocks. Wearing rubber gloves, students spread the moist and pliable concrete with their gloved hands and sponges to create the surface texture of their three-dimensional forms of Canada geese, Mallard ducks, a beaver, a green frog, a coral snake, and a red-eared slider turtle. After the group completed the challenge of constructing the large sculptures, they planted native trees and bushes that could survive partially submerged in water as the drainage ditch flooded after heavy rains. Their construction of the sculpture garden became a creative project that took learning beyond the classroom and demonstrated the children's knowledge of local wetland flora and fauna.

## UNDERSTANDING SCULPTURE IN CONTEXT

Sculptures vary according to artists' and society's needs. In prehistoric times, societies formed sculptures by manipulating natural resources such as mud, wet sand, clay, wood, rock, bone, and ivory into aesthetic forms to express meanings. Archeologists have long studied sculptural artifacts to learn about historical cultures' beliefs, customs, and daily activities. Many early sculptures had utilitarian functions, including weapons, containers, and musical instruments. Some sculptures served religious and ceremonial purposes. As the world became industrialized, contemporary artists began making sculptures out of found objects including tools and plastics. Like professional artists, students also use these materials to produce sculptures (Figures 14.4 and

FIGURE 14.5 Dominik Šimara, 15-years-old, ZUŠ, Uničov, Czech Republic.
*Source: ICEFA Lidice, 43rd Exhibition.*

FIGURE 14.4 Daniela Berezová, 13-years-old; Michaela Chlachulová, 12-years-old; Lucie Kolaříková, 14-years-old; Dominika Laníková, 14-years-old; Jakub Oulehla, 16-years-old; ZUŠ Vladimíra Ambrose, Prostějov, Czech Republic.
*Source: ICEFA Lidice, 40th Exhibition.*

14.5). In all of its shapes and sizes, sculpture communicates stories about life. The choice-based art curriculum describes sculpting methods and materials from past and present times so that students can identify how and why sculptors design three-dimensional artworks. For example, Ashanti tribe members have longed carried totems to group discussions to facilitate their clans' collective decision-making processes. Students will learn how contemporary Ghanaian artist Kojo Bambil continues his culture's tradition of carving clan totems, each of which has symbolic meanings (see Artists' Lessons to Thrive! 14.1). Red Grooms depicted the meaning of city living in his walk-through sculpture *Ruckus New York*. His interactive artworks feel like theatrical productions and contain pulsating caricatures of people, cars, and buildings (Bland, 2008). Many of his sculptures have moving parts that invite audiences to crank, turn, and spin them into action. Mike Kelley developed sculptures that revolved around the theme of abuse. He addressed this painful and serious subject by assembling vibrant stuffed animals, symbols of childhood, and transforming them into enormous sculptural forms that fill rooms with rainbows of color (Art 21, 2005). Judy Pfaff focused on the meaning of loss to create *Buckets of Rain*, an installation that contained black-and-white sculptures that she constructed using roots, plaster, foam, and florescent lights (Art 21, 2007).

## Artists' Lessons to Thrive! 14.1  Kojo Bambil: Carving Strength in Numbers

### Big Idea: Strength in Numbers

Kojo Bambil has been internationally recognized as a master woodcutter from Central Ghana. Born in 1917, Bambil pursued his family tradition of woodcarving throughout his lifetime. As a young man, Bambil worked alongside his brothers and later passed on his exceptional carving skills to his sons. Bambil received recognition for his woodcut totem staffs, which play a significant role in Ghanaian culture. In the country's Ashanti region, clan leaders bring totem animal staffs to community meetings. Each clan has a different totem animal perched on top of its staff. It signifies the clan's defining characteristics and functions as a vehicle to call upon the wisdom of its maternal ancestors. Clans do not worship their totem animals. Rather, they utilize their totem animal's perceived strengths and identify the ways in which the animal might invoke trepidations upon others. The Asakyire clan's lion represents vigilance (Figure 14.1.1). The nocturnal lion remains watchful throughout the night. Therefore, the Ashanti people say that it sleeps with its eyes open, referencing how it is alert when most others are sleeping. The Asenie clan's fish symbolizes diplomacy and effective bargaining skills because it can navigate through rough waters with ease (Figure 14.1.2). With these traits, the fish can traverse all sides of an issue. The Bretuo clan's leopard identifies its tenacity (Figure 14.1.3). As a predatory animal, it hunts with a determined will. It represents the clan's resolve to pursue an issue or a concern fully (Tropenmuseum, 2018).

In Ashanti culture, the concept of family runs deep because it includes all clan members. When carrying their animal totem staffs, selected clan representatives apply their high status within their family group to convey their cohesive messages to the community. By bringing the totem staff to a public gathering, other community members understand that the representative has the clan's full support and is speaking on its behalf. Clan representatives also bring the animal totem staff to funerals. They tie a red ribbon around the animal's neck to symbolize collective mourning for the loss of an individual. Given their strong and historic communal bonds, individual clan members have strength in numbers through shared identity, heritage, and group belonging. Their animal totems serve as a means for them to physically carry their ancestors' strength as a unified collective and assist them in making important judicial and political decisions that impact their lives.

FIGURE 14.1.1 Kojo Bambil, *Painted Wooden Clan Staff with a Lion as a Totem—Asakyire Abusua Poma*, 1999–2000. 60 1/16 × 3 9/16 × 7 11/16 in. (152.5 × 9 × 19.5 cm). Tropenmuseum, part of the National Museum of World Cultures. CC BY-SA 3.0 via Wikimedia Commons.
*Source: https://creativecommons.org/licenses/by-sa/3.0/deed.en*

FIGURE 14.1.2 Kojo Bambil, *Painted Wooden Clan Staff with a Fish as a Totem—Asenie Abusua Poma*, 1999–2000. 61 13/16 × 3 9/16 × 9 1/16 in. (157 × 9 × 23 cm). Tropenmuseum, part of the National Museum of World Cultures. CC BY-SA 3.0 via Wikimedia Commons.
*Source: https://creativecommons.org/licenses/by-sa/3.0/deed.en*

FIGURE 14.1.3 Kojo Bambil, *Painted Wooden Clan Staff with a Leopard as a Totem—Bretuo Abusua Poma*, 1999–2000. 60 1/4 × 3 9/16 × 8 11/16 in. (153 × 9 × 22 cm). Tropenmuseum, part of the National Museum of World Cultures. CC BY-SA 3.0 via Wikimedia Commons.
*Source: https://creativecommons.org/licenses/by-sa/3.0/deed.en*

## Essential/Guiding Questions

1. Why do people maintain customs? What role do Kojo Bambil's woodcut animal totem staffs play in preserving Ashanti customs?
2. How do the woodcut animal totem staffs represent strength in numbers?

## Preparation

For this group project, the teacher and students will collect materials to produce sculpted totem staffs. Students will explain how belonging to the class as productive members creates a better class environment. The teacher and students will further review how having a sense of belonging correlates with their classroom management plan and its positive actions and consequences. The class will divide into groups to form their staffs.

## Daily Learning Targets

We can create a sculpted totem staff.

- We can select a totem symbol that represents what group belonging means to us.
- We can create a unified design that emphasizes our chosen symbol and shows effective balance and craftspersonship.
- We can explain how each team member's individual concepts about belonging came together to produce a unified totem symbol and describe how we selected the best sculpting processes to complete our staff.

**National Core Arts Anchor Standards** 1, 6, 8, and 10
www.nationalartsstandards.org

Artists design most sculptures **in the round**, meaning that people can walk around a freestanding sculpture and see it from all different angles (Figure 14.6). Michelangelo's *David* and August Rodin's *The Thinker* are sculptures in the round that have become integral parts of visual culture because of their prevalence as reproduced artworks. Artists also create sculptures in **relief**, meaning a sculpture has a raised surface that projects forward from a background surface (Figure 14.7). A relief sculpture differs from a

sculpture in the round because viewers cannot see the backside of the images in relief. Reliefs vary by the amount of depth artists use to raise the figures from the background plane. A **bas-relief** sculpture has a low relief, just like the images on cast coins. In contrast, a **high-relief** sculpture projects at least 50% of its form from the background. A high-relief sculpture might show a carving of a person's body emerging from the background, with arms and legs reaching out into space. Teachers might prepare class identification games in which students classify works as in the round, bas relief, and high relief as they learn how to create sculptures in these forms.

Sculptors join different parts together to build an **additive sculpture** (Figure 14.8). They may construct additive sculptures on an **armature,** a skeletal frame located at the core of a sculpture to support it. To produce a **subtractive sculpture**, artists take away mass by cutting, scraping, carving, chiseling, and drilling into an object to reveal the sculptural form within (Figure 14.9). Many sculptors plan what their subtractive sculptures will look like before carving,

FIGURE 14.6 Hassän Mwalago, 12-years-old, toy car. Kenya. Tropenmuseum, part of the National Museum of World Cultures. CC BY-SA 3.0 via Wikimedia Commons.
*Source: https://creativecommons.org/licenses/by-sa/3.0/deed.en*

FIGURE 14.7 Gagik Aleqsanyan, 7-years-old, Kasakh, Armenia.
*Source: ICEFA Lidice, 41st Exhibition.*

FIGURE 14.8 Amálie Gajdová, 6-years-old; Ema Gojtková, 8-years-old; Jolana Juráňová, 6-years-old; Magdaléna Kyšáková, 8-years-old; Eliška Rozsypalová, 9-years-old; Markéta Skalková, 8-years-old; Jiří Vašenka, 8-years-old; ZŠ Sedmikráska o.p.s., Rožnov pod Radhoštěm, Czech Republic.
*Source: ICEFA Lidice, 42nd Exhibition.*

to create numerous sculptures with the same forms. For example, Sandy Skoglund creates installations that contain repetitive molded objects in crowded and surreal domestic spaces to address hidden and unusual topics in society.

Technology plays an important role in contemporary sculpture design and production. Artists may integrate digital screens and interactive computer devices within their three-dimensional sculpted forms and installations to communicate the works' meanings and invite audience participation. Some artists and media entertainment companies rely on a highly accurate model-making process called **subtractive manufacturing**. In this process, high-definition laser scans are made of small-scale designs, which are then transformed using computer numerical controlled (CNC) machining into large-scale sculptures in the media of the artist's choice. This high-tech process, which involves 3D computer-aided design (CAD) and computer-aided manufacturing (CAM), saves creative clients time and money because sculptures that would normally take artists several months to produce through traditional methods are completed with technological assistance within just a few days. Sculptures are also developed as models for designed products, including toys, figurines, home appliances, and architectural structures. These models assist manufacturers and designers in making necessary corrections to their products before sending them into production. Artists' Lessons to Thrive! 14.2 on product designer Christopher Williams (also see Chapter 11, Figure 11.13) demonstrates how he combined drawing, sculpture, and technology to produce 3D models. Teaching students how sculptors utilize technologies and create designs to scale are excellent ways to integrate STEAM lessons into the curriculum.

because once they remove mass from their carving blocks they cannot replace it. They may make preliminary sketches of sculptural designs and model prototypes in clay. Artists produce sculptures from a **mold** by filling a hollow vessel with damp materials (such as plaster or concrete), or by placing damp materials that harden (such as plaster gauze strips) over a surface to reconstruct its existing sculptural form. Just like printmaking, with which artists can make multiple original prints, sculptors can use molds

## Artists' Lessons to Thrive! 14.2 Christopher Williams: Designing Awareness

### Big Idea: Awareness

While working toward a Bachelor of Fine Arts degree, product designer Christopher Williams learned how to develop hip three-dimensional products based on trends in visual culture, art production, youth interests, and global concepts. As part of his studies, Williams participated in a service learning project to develop a socially responsible product for human good. He decided to produce a model of a warning device that would bring awareness to the fatalities and injuries caused to African villagers, especially children and fishermen, by territorial hippopotami and predatory crocodiles as they enter the Nile River to collect water, search for food, and wash. Working with the industry leader who sponsored his class project, he named his device the *Motorola Shield* (Figure 14.2.1). Williams' concept was for villagers to tie his *Motorola Shield* to a tree and toss it into the water to scan for submerged wildlife (Figure 14.2.2). If potential danger lurked nearby, it would begin beeping to sound an alarm.

Williams' design was inspired by Maasai shields, urban sleekness, and comic book coloring. Product designers combine visual art, science, math, and technologies to produce functional designs that meet clients' specifications and/or serve a public need. Designing a final product takes many steps. Williams researched his subject and created ideation sketches with CAD software to

FIGURE 14.2.1 Christopher Williams, *Motorola Shield,* 3D model.
*Source: Project sponsored by Motorola.*

How to use Motorola Shield

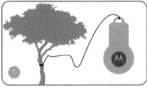

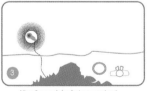

FIGURE 14.2.2 Christopher Williams, *Motorola Shield Instructions.*
*Source: Project sponsored by Motorola.*

illustrate all sides of his shield (see Chapter 11, Figure 11.13). He constructed mockup 3D models sculpted by hand with materials including matboard, clay, and plastics. The mockup models gave him a physical feel for his prototype designs and assisted him in making further refinements using the CAD modeling software. Once his designs met his satisfaction, he used a 3D printer that followed the design's exact mathematical measurements to produce an accurate model of what it would look and feel like.

Eleven years prior, when Williams had been an elementary student, his teachers were well aware of his artistic talents (see Chapter 6, Figure 6.13). He was already talking about how he wanted to become an artist for his future profession. Although Williams earned excellent grades in art, he had lower grades in some other subjects. Surrounded by the support of his family and teachers, Williams reflected on how much he wanted to attend arts magnet secondary schools that required good grades and advanced artistic abilities for admission. In 4th grade he began to improve his grades. In 9th grade he was accepted into a nationally recognized magnet high school for architecture and design. Each school day he woke up at 4:30 a.m. and returned home at 6:00 p.m. after a long commute and a full day of studying. Williams graduated high school with honors and earned a full scholarship to college. He participated in a professional internship with a leading manufacturer to learn product design in practice. His hard work, exceptional art and design skills in two- and three-dimensions, and the support network of family and teachers, demonstrate how students with at-risk tendencies can become problem solvers who use their imaginations, creativity, and life experiences to make positive differences in society.

## Essential/Guiding Questions

1. How has art influenced Williams' life? How did his awareness of the person he wanted to become help him make positive changes as a child and lead him to becoming a product designer?
2. In which ways did producing a sculpture mockup influence Williams' final *Motorola Shield* design? How do three-dimensional prototypes help clients understand designers' intentions?

## Preparation

Students will discuss the meaning of awareness and state ways in which people use awareness to make positive changes in their personal lives and in society. They will identify a cause that they want to make others aware of and create preliminary sketches to illustrate their perspectives. Students will refine their ideas to prepare three-dimensional designs.

## Daily Learning Targets

I can create an artwork that brings awareness to a cause that I care about using the sculpted media of my choice and present my completed artwork and research.

- I can integrate my research on my cause, using at least two sources in my artistic design.
- I can identify at least one possible solution in my artwork.
- I can show craftspersonship, balance, and unity in my design.

**National Core Arts Anchor Standards** 3, 5, 8, and 11
www.nationalartsstandards.org

# APPLYING SCULPTURE METHODS IN CONTEXT

Comprehensive sculpture learning tasks provide means for students to communicate their ideas three-dimensionally while working individually and in teams. Like contemporary artists, students can create additive sculptures, subtractive sculptures, and molds. Students will learn processes that include bending, folding, slicing, joining, pouring, constructing, and carving. The sculpted designs they produce can be realistic works inspired from life observations, be abstracted, or combine realism and abstraction.

## Papier-Mâché

**Papier-mâché** is an art form that artists create with torn, shredded, or pulped paper mixed with glue, flour, or starch (Figures 14.10. and 14.11). Its name

translated from the French means "masticated paper," as it is believed that the French literally chewed on paper to turn it into pulp and mold it into forms to ornament architectural structures (van der Reyden & Williams, 2006). While the name *papier-mâché* originated in France, the Chinese created the first papier-mâché products nearly 2,000 years ago by combining recycled pieces of scrap paper with layers of lacquer to form helmets. Over the centuries, artists from around the world have used papier-mâché to create masks, furniture, jewelry, globes, and home decorations, as well as floats for parades and carnivals. Renowned papier-mâché artists include Juan Alindato from Puerto Rico, who produced carnival masks, and Pedro Linares from Mexico, who invented *alebrijes*, imaginary animal forms inspired by his dreams (Figure 14.12; Congdon & Hallmark, 2002, 2012).

Artists enjoy working in papier-mâché because it is an affordable sculpting method that they can adapt into various forms to achieve the looks they desire. In the classroom, students can construct individual sculptures and work in teams to create large group projects. While papier-mâché is predominately an additive sculpture process, teachers can demonstrate how to manipulate papier-mâché sculptures by cutting away parts or adding on new layers and pieces. Construction of a papier-mâché sculpture begins with a sturdy armature. Students can create their desired forms by balling up pieces of newspaper and taping them into place;

FIGURE 14.10 Ailee Sickler, 5-years-old. United States.
*Source: Author, teacher. Richard Sickler, photo.*

FIGURE 14.11 Group project, 6–10-years-old, ZŠ Sedmikráska o.p.s., Rožnov pod Radhoštěm, Czech Republic.
*Source: ICEFA Lidice; 43rd Exhibition.*

FIGURE 14.12 Pedro Linares, *Alebrije* papier-mâché sculpture, 1986, The Children's Museum of Indianapolis, Michelle Pemberton, photographer. CC BY-SA 3.0 via Wikimedia Commons.
*Source: https://creativecommons.org/licenses/by-sa/3.0/deed.en*

covering pre-formed objects such as blown up balloons, cardboard cylinders, and containers; and forming wire into three-dimensional designs. They can adhere additional sections of newspaper to manipulate parts and fill in areas with added bulk. Once their structure is complete, they will layer the entire surface as smoothly as possible with cut or shredded newspaper dipped in glue (see Model 14.1). The sculpture's surface might have a few small lumps and bumps after the papier-mâché glue mixture dries. Students can sand its surface to make it smoother, if desired, and then decorate it with paint and/or found objects.

## Model 14.1

### Creating With Papier-Mâché

| | |
|---|---|
| Developing the papier-mâché form with balled-up newspaper | • Ball up newspaper, either loosely or tightly, to create a desired form. Apply masking tape to hold the newspaper form in place. If creating with multiple pieces, join the sections of balled up newspaper with masking tape to create a single form. |
| Developing the papier-mâché form with paper cylinders | • Collect empty paper cylinders (such as paper towel rolls) to use as armatures. Stack, cut, and slice paper cylinders to produce desired forms. To make a paper cylinder thinner, slice the roll down the middle, curve it inward, and tape it in place. |
| Developing the papier-mâché form with balloons | • Select a balloon of the appropriate shape and size to create a specific form. For example, long and slender balloons are suited for lengthy cylindrical forms. Petite water balloons can form small heads, and standard 9-inch (23 cm) balloons can form large heads or torsos. (Check for latex allergies before distributing balloons to students.)<br>• Apply a small amount of pressure to attach two or more balloons together with masking tape to achieve the desired form. Place the balloon ties facing inwards so they will not appear in the final form. |
| Developing the papier-mâché form with wire | • Use wire cutters to cut sections of chicken wire, wire mesh, and/or plain wire. Wear safety gloves and goggles when working with wire. Bend the wire with hands and/or pliers.<br>• Join pieces of chicken wire by tying or "sewing" different sections with thin wire.<br>• Bend stray wires towards the structure's interior to avoid cuts when adding papier-mâché strips to the armature. |
| Attaching pieces to the papier-mâché sculpture with masking tape | • Join sculptural parts with masking tape, avoiding unnecessary lumps and bumps in the tape's surface. Apply masking tape vertically to support attached parts. (Using longer strips of tape provides better support between different sections.) Add a second horizontal layer of tape to make the sculpture sturdier. |
| Applying papier-mâché strips | • Rip a section of newspaper, following the grain of the newspaper, into strips that are approximately 1–1 1/2-inch (2.5–4 cm) wide. Tear the strips into smaller sections as needed.<br>• Place a strip of newspaper into a bucket with a glue mixture and saturate it with glue. (Papier-mâché paste, also known as art paste, is the most convenient adhesive to use. It comes in a powder form, mixes with water, and has a smooth consistency. Other options include liquid starch; a 50% school glue and 50% water mixture; or flour paste.)<br>• Remove the newspaper strip from the glue mixture and hold it above the bowl with one hand. With the other hand, squeegee the excess glue between two fingers so it will drop back into the bowl.<br>• Apply at least three or four layers of papier-mâché strips using a crisscross pattern. (The crisscross pattern gives the sculpture's surface added strength.) Layer the strips as smoothly as possible to avoid lumps and bumps. Adhere an optional layer of newsprint or classroom-quality brown paper towels as a topcoat to help conceal newspaper text and images from showing through. (Connect joined parts with papier-mâché strips vertically for added strength. If a balloon is part of the form, apply at least two coats of papier-mâché before setting it aside, as the balloon may deflate within a short period of time and alter its form.)<br>• Set the sculpture aside and allow it to dry. (To expedite this process, place it in front of a running box fan.) The sculpture's surface should feel solid and not cave in once it has dried. If some areas feel weaker than others, apply another coat or two of papier-mâché strips. Add additional textures to the sculptured form as desired after the base coats of papier-mâché strips have dried. |
| Decorating the papier-mâché sculpture | • Paint two layers of tempera or acrylic paint to coat the surface. (If working with economical tempera paint, add a coat of Mod Podge® to soften its chalky texture and prevent cracking. An optional base layer of gesso conceals unwanted newspaper text and images from showing through areas of light-colored tempera and acrylic paint.)<br>• Apply decorations (i.e. assorted fabrics, papers, and notions) as desired with tacky glue or a low-temperature glue gun. |

## Assemblage

Sculptors create **assemblages** by arranging found objects in a pleasing design to produce three-dimensional, additive sculptures (Figure 14.13). Assemblages vary according to artists' styles and preferences for materials, as seen in works by Yoruba sculptors and by Deborah Butterfield, Marisol Escobar, Louise Nevelson, and Joseph Cornell. Assemblages made with found and recycled objects connect to Earth Education lessons as students transform common household materials and found objects (such as blocks of wood, twigs, toy parts, and wire) into art. Students may choose to have the original found objects remain visible in their completed designs.

Comprehensive lessons call upon students to make connections between different artists' assemblages as inspirations to produce creative works. For example, a lesson (adapted from Gray, 2010) titled "I've Got a Secret Assemblage" available on this textbook's companion website teaches about Joseph Cornell's assembled boxes and Sepik tribesmen's secret ceremonial houses. Cornell designed assemblages by setting found objects in framed boxes covered with glass. His artworks centered on themes that included memories, fantasies, and dreams (Sommers & Drake, 2006). The Sepik River Tribe in Papua, New Guinea collected, carved, and crafted items significant to their culture, including yams and natural woods, to complete men's ceremonial houses (Anderson, 2004). The contents of their ceremonial houses remained secret to uninitiated members, which included women and

children. Young males of age were allowed to enter the ceremonial houses to learn the men's customs and secrets. Given the artists' examples, students will identify a secret that they are willing to share with the class. The secret can be silly such as: "I dress my dogs in tutus" or "I want to live in a fairytale" (Figure 14.14). Students will construct a box out of cardboard or wood and decorate all parts. The box will contain at least two shelves as well as a frame, doors, and hidden compartments. The finished assemblage will incorporate at least five different found and handmade objects related to the student's secret, all presented as a unified design.

## Carving

Given clear instruction and careful supervision, students can learn to carve in soft materials such as soap, foam, and wood. The process of carving can encourage students to pay attention to the environment by

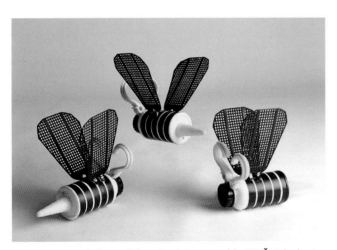

FIGURE 14.13 Sabina Pilcová, 14-years-old, ZUŠ Vladimíra Ambrose, Prostějov, Czech Republic.
*Source: ICEFA Lidice, 42nd Exhibition.*

FIGURE 14.14 J. Quinton Creasy, pre-service teacher. United States.
*Source: Kelly Gray and author, teachers.*

spending time outdoors to find pieces to carve from nature, and/or recycling wood scraps and Styrofoam. As a subtractive sculpture method, the carving process teaches students how to plan ideas and work through challenges such as accidental breakages (Sickler-Voigt, 2003, 2006).

Soap carving originated in Thailand and is a popular art form in schools due to the medium's soft density and affordability. Teachers can introduce students to Thai floral soap carvings, Aztec jade carvings, and Inuit bone carvings to learn the reasoning behind their artistic productions. Contemporary artist Janine Antonie utilized soap as an art medium for her sculpture titled *Lick and Lather*, which consists of two self-portrait busts, one from chocolate and the other from soap. Instead of using traditional carving techniques for the busts, Antonie licked away parts of the chocolate sculpture to alter its form. She used bathwater as a creative resource to manipulate the soap sculpture's exterior (Art 21, 2003). Her performances with the chocolate and soap self-portrait busts served as analogies for erasing one's outer surface. White Ivory Soap® has a consistency that is favorable for carving with plastic knives, which is a safe alternative to carving with blades. Students can also carve glycerin soaps, which come in multiple colors and have bright and semitransparent hues (Figure 14.15). Green soap bars replicate the look of jade sculptures. Teachers will demonstrate how to transfer preliminary sketches to soap bars using a toothpick, carving tool, or the edge of a recycled plastic knife, to prepare for deeper carvings. Because soap is more delicate and brittle than stone, students need to be careful not to break off soap chunks accidentally by pressing

down too hard on the bar's surface. One way to ease the carving process is for students to submerge their knives into warm water before cutting, because the water acts as a lubricant between the soap and knife (Simon, 2013). Students can use soap flakes to fill in small carving mistakes by pressing the flakes into the desired area and molding them into place with their fingers. Students will complete their carvings by rubbing the surface gently to give it a smooth finish and adding contrasting textures with carving tools.

Just like soap, manufactured plastic foams such as Styrofoam and balsa foam have a softer consistency than wood and are a safer alternative for students who are developing manipulative skills. Students can carve these products with recycled plastic knives, stylus tools, and toothpicks. An eco-friendly choice is to repurpose Styrofoam packaging that comes in shipped boxes (Figure 14.16). Students should begin with less dense pieces of Styrofoam, as condensed consistencies are more difficult to carve. As an alternative, teachers can purchase balsa foam, which has a finer grain than Styrofoam and is easier to carve. Whether working with Styrofoam or balsa foam, students have the option of enhancing their carvings with paint and found objects.

**Woodcarving** is a rewarding activity for responsible students (Figure 14.17). Societies around the world produce woodcarvings in many different forms as contemporary and traditional works. Historic examples include African Bambara Chiwara headpieces for rituals, Oaxacan woodcarvings for fiestas, and Viking

FIGURE 14.16 These Styrofoam sculptures combine carving and additive sculpture methods. Štěpánka Jánošíková, 12-years-old; Eliška Jarošová, 14-years-old; Emma Líhová, 11-years-old; Julie Marečková, 12-years-old; Karolína Slavíková, 12-years-old; Valerie Šulcová, 11-years-old; ZUŠ, Mšeno, Czech Republic.
Source: ICEFA Lidice, 43rd Exhibition.

FIGURE 14.15 Ailee Sickler, 10-years-old, United States.
Source: Author, teacher. Richard Sickler, photo.

FIGURE 14.17 Hasitha Gallella, 15-years-old, Kandy, Sri Lanka.
*Source: ICEFA Lidice, 45th Exhibition.*

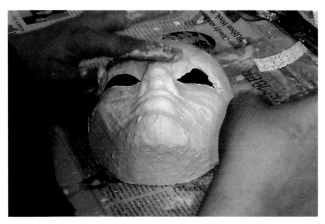

FIGURE 14.18 An early adolescent student creates a plaster of Paris gauze mold. United States.
*Source: Cara Brown, teacher.*

carvings that adorned ships and stave churches. While experienced woodcarvers advocate teaching wood-carving to children as young as 4-years-old (Trudel, 2006), such instruction is rare in classrooms. It would be possible only with direct one-on-one supervision between an adult and skillful child rather than whole classes with less adult supervision. Students who experience difficulties operating a pencil will be unable to control a carving knife. Most students in upper elementary will have enough control of their hand muscles to handle a blade properly, but would still require direct supervision. Teachers should select soft pieces of wood, such as balsa wood and white pine, with a grain that moves in one direction and that have enough moisture in them so that they do not snap apart during carving lessons (Lubkemann, 2005). Pieces with knots, sap, and forks will be more difficult to carve. As woodcarving is a specialty, teachers might look for grants to fund artists-in-resident woodcarvers who can teach students carving skills.

## Molds

Societies have long used molds to make sculptural forms and utilitarian goods such as candles, soaps, toys, and plastic furniture. In the classroom, students often work with plaster of Paris gauze and tape molds. **Plaster of Paris gauze** has a white, powdery texture and comes in strips. This medical material, used for making casts, is also useful for making molds (Figure 14.18). Artist George Segal made this material a popular art medium by using it to produce sculptures of the human figure. Some teachers use plaster of Paris gauze as an alternative to papier-mâché. It dries quicker, but costs more. Students can form molds of static objects such as plastic and clay with plaster of Paris gauze by following these steps:

1. Cut the gauze into strips and dip one piece at a time into warm water, without crumpling it.
2. Place the flat side directly on the desired surface, starting with the outer edges. The bumpy side will face upwards.
3. Without adding additional water, rub the damp plaster on the gauze gently into a creamy consistency.
4. Repeat the process to apply a second coat.

Students must work quickly as the plaster of Paris gauze becomes hard to the touch in about ten minutes. While some artists use plaster of Paris gauze to make molds of human body parts, manufacturers warn against using it on raw skin, hair, and faces. They recommend that students wear safety goggles, gloves, and dust masks when working with plaster products.

As an alternative to plaster of Paris gauze strips, students can use clear packaging tape to produce life-size molds (Figure 14.19). While plaster of Paris gauze has a heavy, solid feel, molds from clear packaging tape have a transparent hue and light feel. Once students complete their initial molds—either plaster of

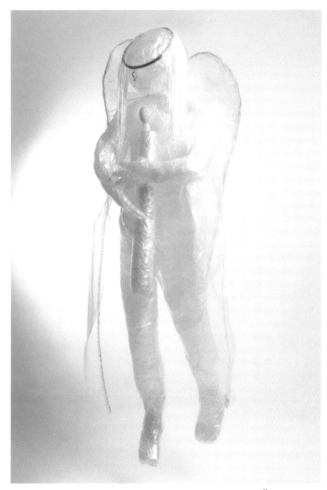

FIGURE 14.19 Anna Kraváčková, 15-years-old, ZUŠ Vladimíra Ambrose, Prostějov, Czech Republic.
*Source: ICEFA Lidice, 43rd Exhibition.*

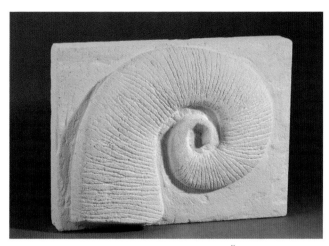

FIGURE 14.20 Anna Ihmová, 12-years-old, ZŠ, Praha 1, Czech Republic.
*Source: ICEFA Lidice, 44th Exhibition.*

Paris gauze or tape—they can leave them undecorated or enhance them with paint, yarns, wires, and raffia. Depending on their size and weight, students can hang these sculptures from the ceiling, mount them to a bulletin board, or use them as props in school plays.

Students can combine mold making with carving by creating plaster molds (Figure 14.20). Many teachers and students collect pint-sized (0.5 l) milk cartons and plastic cups to use as small molds for wet plaster. With supervision, students will follow the package directions, wearing protective gloves, respiratory masks, and eyewear. To mix the ingredients, students will gradually pour the dry plaster mixture into a mound so that it peaks above the water's surface, then and gently mix it into the water. To make carving easier, teachers and students can create a mixture of three parts vermiculite (a landscaping material) or sawdust to two parts plaster, and one to two parts water (Brew, 2004). Once the plaster mixture has a creamy consistency, students can pour the wet plaster into their mold. Because pouring plaster down the sink will clog and damage the drain, students should line their plastic mixing buckets with recycled plastic bags and dispose of them when finished.

The plaster mixture will need to set, so that it becomes firm to the touch, yet remains slightly damp. Plaster becomes more difficult to carve as its moisture evaporates. To keep it moist when carving over multiple days, students will cover their plaster carvings with damp paper towels or rags and store them in individual sealed plastic storage bags with their names on them. Students can use sandpaper and rasps to smooth away unwanted lumps from their plaster forms. If students accidentally break off pieces of their sculptures, they should wait until the plaster has dried fully, then glue their pieces back in place.

## Wire and Aluminum Foil Sculptures

Artists use wires and aluminum foil to make static and kinetic sculptures. With an interest in movement and engineering, Alexander Calder designed and performed *Calder's Circus*, a sculpted artwork that contains wires and mechanized parts with props including a high wire, a trapeze, and clown, acrobat, and animal characters (Whitney Museum, 2018). Some contemporary South African artists create wire sculptures for tourists in the shapes of toys, baskets, animals, and musical instruments. Examples of these works relate to concepts about ecotourism and fair trade. Vannoy Streeter's wire sculptures focus on community and play (see Artists'

Lessons to Thrive! 2.1). Some culinary artists enhance the look of food by twisting aluminum foil into fanciful forms. Their culinary presentations shape society's perceptions about food aesthetics.

Teachers and students have access to many different types of foils and wires (Figures 14.21 and 14.22). These include aluminum foil, colorful plastic-coated wire, pipe cleaners, metal hangers, and soft and flexible aluminum wire. Manufacturers sell wires by their **gauge**, such as 12-gauge or 18-gauge. The number refers to the thickness of a wire; the larger the gauge number is, the thinner the wire. Students can manipulate wire and aluminum foil by rolling, bending, coiling, twisting, folding, pinching, and cutting it. They can alter the texture with modeling tools and

FIGURE 14.21 A. J. Sickler, 6th grade, raised her aluminum manatee sculpture by rolling up a piece of blue paper as a ledge and cutting out green paper to represent the sea grass that manatees eat. United States.
*Source: Author, teacher. Richard Sickler, photo.*

FIGURE 14.22 Vannoy Streeter created *Tennessee Walking Horses* and other sculptures with ordinary wire coat hangers (see Chapter 2, Artists' Lessons to Thrive! 2.1).
*Source: Jonathan Griffith, photo.*

combine wires with aluminum foil to add variety to their work. Wire is an effective medium for designing mobiles. Students can choose from materials such as aluminum foil, tooling foil, cardboard, plastic, and cans to hang from mobiles, while making sure that all parts are well-balanced so that they can move freely.

## BEST PRACTICES FOR TEACHING SCULPTURE FROM PRE-K THROUGH HIGH SCHOOL

Quality sculpture lessons come to life in regular classrooms, specialized studio spaces, and school woodshops (Figure 14.23). Teacher preparation is key to fostering safe learning experiences for students in all types of classroom environments. Students will need to know how to use sculpture equipment and materials that can be potentially dangerous, including carving knives, hot glue guns, hammers, and nails. Students require ample time to practice and experiment with sculpting tools, equipment, and media to gain the confidence and skills needed to produce desired results before completing projects for summative grades. For example, students' practiced using different tools and construction processes before they were able to complete the pencil sculptures shown in Figure 14.24. To assist in maintaining safety and producing quality outcomes, teachers can pre-assess students' knowledge of sculpture safety procedures. Informal pre-assessments include students demonstrating proper technique to teachers and peers and summarizing steps. Students can complete short quizzes and written responses as

FIGURE 14.23 Flåm Skule's (School's) woodshop. Norway.
*Source: Courtesy of Flåm Skule (School), Astrid Hassel, principal.*

FIGURE 14.24 Group project, 9–15-years-old, ZUŠ, Mšeno, Czech Republic.
*Source: ICEFA Lidice, 44th Exhibition.*

formal pre-assessments. When sculpture learning tasks break with normal class routines due to their large sizes and/or need for special equipment, teachers prepare students for these changes by informing them of new or atypical procedures before projects begin. They post instructional resources and signage that explain sculpture production and cleanup methods.

Through class inquiry discussions and their application of sculpture methods, students will be able to explain how studying sculpture augments their understanding of STEAM topics including space, balance, movement, and weight. As part of the choice-based art curriculum, students will learn how their selection of size relationships, proportions, and materials impact the appearances, meanings, and functions of their sculptural designs. Teachers check for understanding by monitoring the class and equipment throughout lessons. They look to see that students are focused on their work and are using materials and safety equipment properly. They provide support to students who need extra guidance and additional demonstrations. If students are experiencing difficulties forming or balancing in-process sculptural works, teachers and students will discuss strategies to make necessary corrections. During cleanup, teachers will check that all students have individually written their names on a piece of paper and placed their name next to their drying sculpture, as some sculptural projects may not be individually recognizable in early stages. Teachers will remind students not to put clogging materials, including plaster or papier-mâché pulp, down the sink and show them how to wipe desktops and countertops with damp sponges to capture particles, such as plaster dust, to avoid inhalation.

In early childhood, the production of sculpture correlates with children's desire to manipulate their environment physically. Young children often enjoy forming mounds with damp sand, assembling collections of twigs and stones, and building with sculptural toys and fabricated blocks. Early childhood students can produce simple sculptures using papier-mâché and wire. With guidance, children learn how to bend, twist, coil, and shape soft wires in different directions to produce dynamic forms. They can roll and layer newspaper to create papier-mâché sculptures inspired by life, as well as produce abstracted works. Given young children's fascination with moving objects, teachers can develop a lesson for which each student creates an individual part of a collaborative class mobile that focuses on an art concept and a big idea and display them together as a finished product (Figure 14.25).

FIGURE 14.25 Kindergarten group project. United States.
*Source: J. Quinton Creasy and Janet Malone, teachers.*

When producing wire sculptures, students can look for inspiration to artworks such as *Calder's Circus* and Vannoy Streeter's *Tennessee Walking Horses* (Artists' Lessons to Thrive! 2.1) to create an environment filled with characters and props using assorted sculpture media. Students can act out their sculpted characters' roles within the environment and discuss how the inspiration artists' influenced their production ideas.

In middle childhood, students have acquired the manipulative skills needed to combine objects to produce more complex sculptures than they could in early childhood. They can safely carve soft surfaces, including soap, foam, and clay. These media do not require sharp knives and will give them the foundational skills to move onto more advanced carving processes. Middle-childhood students like to build collections of objects that interest them. They can study assemblages and identify the diverse materials that artists select to create their works. For example, they could examine three assembled cat sculptures (Figure 14.26) from Pablo Cano's *Blue Ribbon Production* that were inspired by Goya's portrait of a young boy, Manuel Osorio Manrique de Zuñiga, and his pets. Students can name the materials Pablo Cano assembled to produce the cat sculptures and generate ideas to create sculpted designs using personally chosen objects. Teachers can also develop learning tasks in which students participate in class research and scavenger hunts using books and educational websites that teach sculpture in context. Given what they learn, students can produce original designs from wire sculptures, papier-mâché, molds (Figure 14.27), and other sculpting methods. They can apply diverse sculpture processes to create an installation or a **diorama** (miniature environment display), like Sandy Skoglund, and focus on a big idea.

FIGURE 14.26 Pablo Cano. *The Blue Ribbon Marionette Production*, 2009.
Source: Jose Rodriguez, photograph.

FIGURE 14.28 Barbora Kulhánková, 13-years-old, ZUŠ, Mšeno, Czech Republic.
*Source: ICEFA Lidice, 42nd Exhibition.*

FIGURE 14.27 Group project, 10–12-years-old, ZUŠ, Zlín–Malenovice, Czech Republic.
*Source: ICEFA Lidice, 36th Exhibition.*

By early adolescence, students have an advanced knowledge of sculpture vocabulary and can write in detail about sculptors and their work. For example, they can review how technologies aid in three-dimensional design by studying the steps that Christopher Williams takes to create product designs (Artists' Lessons to Thrive! 14.2). Additionally, they can cogently present their opinions about sculptures in oral and written forms. Early adolescents have greater strength in their hand muscles than they did when they were younger and can produce sculptures with some of the same equipment that professional sculptors use. Assemblage lessons challenge students' minds as they work with tools and combine non-traditional art media to produce aesthetic forms (Figure 14.28). Teachers can call upon early adolescents' preferences for working with peers to form interactive sculpture lessons, including collaborative papier-mâché sculptures (Figure 14.29) and environmental sculptures. Students might apply Kojo Bambil's clan totems as inspirations to develop totems to guide class debates and aesthetic and art criticism discussions (Artists' Lessons to Thrive! 14.1).

In adolescence, students can produce more sophisticated sculptural forms given their years of training using sculptural tools and methods. If they have not had prior experiences, teachers can provide new opportunities for students to work with specialized artists' tools to create sculpted designs such

FIGURE 14.29 Džeina Gutaroviča, 12-years-old, Una Laizāne, 12-years-old, Inčukalna novada muzikas un makslas skola, Vangaži, Latvia.
*Source: ICEFA Lidice, 44th Exhibition.*

as woodcarvings and mixed-media wire sculptures (Figure 14.30), as well as refine their skills using more traditional classroom sculpting methods such as papier-mâché and assemblage. As part of the

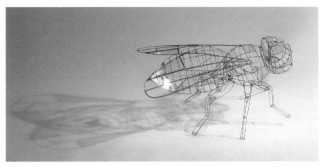

FIGURE 14.30 Tomáš Mravec, 16-years-old, ZUŠ Antonína Dvořáka, Lipník nad Bečvou, Czech Republic.
*Source: ICEFA Lidice, 43rd Exhibition.*

choice-based art curriculum, students will select sculptors they admire to study in greater detail. They can use their journals to write and sketch about their selected artists and build a virtual collection of their works. Teachers can ask students to identify how the artists that they use for inspiration expressed big ideas through sculpture, then have students make connections between their own sculpted products and the ones that they studied. Students will analyze artists' choice of sculptural materials and methods, and the functions of their designs. Students can also apply their understandings of sculptural concepts to consider possible professions that require knowledge of working in three dimensions, including the visual arts, construction, mechanics, set design, and engineering. Teachers can invite specialists in these professions into their classes as guest speakers to talk about their work. They should also identify the role of sculptures in private collections and public places including city spaces, lobbies, campuses, and gardens. They might have students work in collaborative teams to plan and create sculpted designs that could be transformed into large-scale public artworks, as sculptors do when competing for public and private art commissions. For example, Figure 14.31 could serve as a model for a large-scale public artwork.

## OUR JOURNEY TO THRIVE CONTINUES . . .

This chapter presented comprehensive methods for students to build aesthetic forms using diverse sculpture media and processes. In the next chapter, we will learn how to teach students clay and mosaics in context. We will apply three-dimensional design methods

FIGURE 14.31 Eduard Korbel, 15-years-old, Pavel Neumann, 16-years-old, Tomáš Toms, 16-years-old, ZUŠ Fr. Kmocha, Kolín II, Czech Republic.
*Source: ICEFA Lidice, 43rd Exhibition.*

to teach students how to create clay forms and attach mosaics to sculptural works.

## CHAPTER QUESTIONS AND ACTIVITIES

1. Describe sculpture's qualities, functions, and meanings from historic and societal perspectives. How will you integrate sculpture into the choice-based art curriculum?
2. Practice the diverse sculpture processes described in this chapter to compare and contrast their qualities. Summarize what you learned in a group discussion or in writing.
3. Develop an original comprehensive lesson on sculpture that focuses on a big idea of your choice. Use the lesson plan template provided on the

textbook's companion website and refer to Chapter 2 for more information on lesson plan development. Integrate inquiry tasks inspired by Part III of this textbook.

4. Answer Artists' Lessons to Thrive! 14.1–14.2's essential/guiding questions in written form or as part of a group discussion. Complete their daily learning targets.

## References

Anderson, R. (2004). *Calliope's sisters: A comparative study of philosophies of art.* Upper Saddle River, NJ: Prentice Hall.

Art 21. (2003). *Janine Antonie.* Retrieved from www.pbs.org/art21/artists/janine-antoni

Art 21. (2005). *Mike Kelley.* Retrieved from www.pbs.org/art21/artists/mike-kelley

Art 21. (2007). *Judy Pfaff.* Retrieved from www.pbs.org/art21/artists/judy-pfaff

Bland, B. F. (2008). *Red Grooms: In the studio & the bookstore.* Yonkers, NY: Hudson River Museum.

Brew, C. A. (2004). The big heads: Sculptures that know it all. *Arts and Activities, 135*(4), 18–19.

Congdon, K. G., & Hallmark, K. K. (2002). *Artists from Latin American cultures: A biographical dictionary.* Westport, CT: Greenwood Press.

Congdon, K. G., & Hallmark, K. K. (2012). *U.S. folk artists of the twentieth century.* Santa Barbara, CA: ABC-CLIO.

Gray, K. (2010). *I've got a secret: A study of the Sepik River Tribe and American artist, Joseph Cornell.* Unpublished lesson plan.

Lubkemann, E. C. (2005). *The little book of whittling: Passing time on the trail, on the porch, and under the stars.* East Petersburg, PA: Fox Chapel.

Sickler-Voigt, D. C. (2003). Out of the woods and into the light: O. L. Samuels on mentoring children with at-risk tendencies through personal history and carving lessons. *Journal of Cultural Research in Art Education, 21*(1), 60–67.

Sickler-Voigt, D. C. (2006). Carving for the soul: Life lessons from self-taught artist O. L. Samuels. *Journal of Art Education, 59*(3), 25–35.

Simon, E. (2013). *Soap sculptures.* Retrieved from www.landscapesmag.com/teachers/lessonplans/Aboriginal%20lesson%20plans/Soap%20Sculptures.pdf

Sommers, J., & Drake, A. (2006). *The Joseph Cornell box: Found objects, magical worlds.* Kennebunkport, ME: Cider Mill Press.

Tropenmuseum. (2018). *Kojo Bambil.* Retrieved from https://collectie.wereldculturen.nl/#/query/b96bee93-467b-41dc-ab09-03d01124c850

Trudel, R. E. (2006). *Carving for kids: An introduction to woodcarving.* Fresno, CA: Linden.

van der Reyden, D., & Williams, D. (2006). *The history, technology, and care of papier-mache: Case study of the conservation treatment of a Victorian "Japan ware" chair.* Retrieved from www.si.edu/mci/downloads/RELACT/papier_mache.pdf

Whitney Museum. (2018). *Calder's circus: 1926–31.* Retrieved from www.whitney.org/WatchAndListen/1094

# Chapter 15

# Clay and Mosaics

**FIGURE 15.1** First-grade students, United States.

*Source: Author and Suzanne St. John, teachers. Bailey Ingram, photo.*

**Clay** consists of fine soil particles, water, and minerals such as phyllosilicate, quartz, feldspar, and iron oxide. Many of us remember the tactile sensation of squeezing clay between our fingers and the excitement of molding clay forms in our hands. On a daily basis we see clay in utilitarian designs, including ceramic mugs and terracotta clay pots for plants. Natural clay is most commonly found along riverbeds, streambeds, and lakebeds. The highest quality clays are pure and free from impurities such as small stones and vegetation. Like clay products, mosaics can also have functional purposes. Artists create **mosaics** by attaching small individual pieces of tile made from clay, glass, and other materials called **tesserae** to a background surface including a floor, wall, or three-dimensional form. They construct mosaics by arranging traditional and/or nontraditional tesserae pieces in non-touching designs. We can use the analogy of a puzzle with a mosaic design to explain how its different parts come together to produce a design for students to understand. Artists bring many different pieces together to form a completed work that comes to life as a single unified design.

Our curriculum will teach students about humanity's time-honored traditions of producing utilitarian and aesthetic artworks with clay and mosaics that enhance the environment. We will meet the following objectives by participating in this chapter:

- Describe clay and mosaics, as well as their qualities, functions, and meanings in society.
- Identify best practices for teaching clay and mosaics.
- Create instructional resources for teaching clay and mosaics.

Spotlight on Student Art #15 (Figures 15.1–15.3) demonstrates how a class combined ceramic, mosaic, and printmaking techniques to design an original board game. Their collaborative artwork teaches healthy living skills.

**FIGURE 15.2** Ceramic game pieces, first-grade students, United States.

*Source: Author and Suzanne St. John, teachers. Bailey Ingram, photo.*

**FIGURE 15.3** A first-grader prints with a clay stamp. United States.

*Source: Author and Suzanne St. John, teachers. Bailey Ingram, photo.*

## Spotlight on Student Art #15

### Big Idea: Olympic Values

A first-grade class of high-ability learners created an original game with handmade ceramic pieces and a mosaic board that focused on Olympism, the philosophy dedicated to maintaining a healthy mind, body, and spirit (Figure 15.1). The students' studied the meaning and history of the Olympic games, as well as the value of healthy living skills. They also identified prominent symbols in popular winter Olympic advertisements. Through these activities, they learned how the Olympic Games extend beyond the thrill of the sport. The Games promote core values including excellence, peace, respect, and friendship.

The class paired into five teams to create the board game. Each team represented a color of the Olympic rings: blue, yellow, black, green, and red. The students modeled moist earthenware clay by rolling and manipulating small pieces in their hands to create individual ceramic game pieces in the forms of polar bears (Figure 15.2). When all of the moisture evaporated from their clay figures, their teachers fired them in a kiln, which gave the figures a hardened ceramic consistency. They painted their polar bear game pieces with acrylic paint and added details with fine-tipped black permanent markers. Each polar bear wore a winter accessory that matched its team's Olympic color. The students used leftover moist clay to create stamps of the Olympic rings that they dipped in tempera paint to decorate game cards (Figure 15.3). Each group of students developed a section of the game board with a mosaic pattern. The colored paper and glittered foam mosaic designs symbolized winning a gold medal on a clear winter day. Once the children completed their ceramic and mosaic work, they played the game. The students rolled a die and pulled game cards that required them to participate in kinesthetic learning activities and answer questions about the Olympics and health to move their game pieces forward. The first polar bear that reached the finish line won a gold medal for their team.

## UNDERSTANDING AND APPLYING CLAY IN CONTEXT

Early humans first discovered clay's ability to hold a form by shaping it in their hands and drying it in the sun. In time, humans placed clay figures into fires during religious ceremonies because they believed the figures had spiritual powers and aided their chances for survival (Cooper, 2000). Additionally, hunter-gatherers lined fire pits with clay to prevent extra moisture from seeping in and destroying their fires. Scholars believe that these separate fire-related acts caused prehistoric societies to discover that when they heated clay in a red-glowing flame (to approximately 1,100 °F, or 600 °C) it underwent a chemical reaction that caused it to harden. Fired clay retains a solid ceramic surface, whereas unfired clay disintegrates in water.

Evidence of the first ceramic cookware dates to China around 18,000 BCE (Wu et al., 2012). The rise of agriculture about 10,000 years ago marked the period in which humans began producing ceramic vessels to store food and liquids. Because of increased demand for ceramic goods, farmers split their time between tending their crops and developing ceramic pottery (Cooper, 2000). They mastered the art of firing clay and produced beautiful ceramic artifacts by shaping them into sensuous forms, scratching designs into their surfaces, and coloring them with different clays and **glazes**, which are vitreous (glass-like) coatings that color and seal ceramic pieces (for example, Figure 15.4 shows a functional glazed ceramic vessel). The ancient Greeks, who had access to fine-quality clay, mastered the art of vase-making techniques by designing excellent aesthetic forms. Olympic athletes received large vases filled with costly olive oil as prizes for winning events.

Contemporary ceramicists build on past practices and beliefs. Robert Arneson developed realistic ceramic portraits on pedestals that pushed the boundaries between fine art and craft. As a traditional high-art form, artists typically sculpted important portraits in marble. Alternatively, Arneson utilized crafting materials (clay and inexpensive glazes) and depicted satirical subjects (Foulem, 2005). Rose Pecos-Sun Rhodes (Artists' Lessons to Thrive! 15.1) added a new twist to established Pueblo crafting practices by producing ceramic storytelling dolls. Students will learn how Pueblo artists like Rhodes have used local clay and pigments as direct links to the earth and their ancestors. Technologies also impact contemporary ceramic design and production. Some artists integrate ceramic transfer printing decals to add text, photographs, and original drawings to ceramic

**FIGURE 15.4** Tamara Bogdanova, 11-years-old, MBOU DOD Detskaya Khudozhesvetnaya Shkola, Eniseisk, Russia.
*Source: ICEFA Lidice, 41st Exhibition.*

products. Dutch industrial designer Olivier van Herpt reformed ceramics through 3D printing technologies. Unlike typical 3D printers that extrude plastics to produce sculpted products, his hardware extrudes eco-friendly clay. Van Herpt's food-grade ceramic vessels mimic the look of handmade works with woven patterns and textures. He programs in small imperfections to give his technological products a hand-crafted feel. Students can compare van Herpt's computer-generated works with the realistic handmade student ceramic sculptures shown in Figure 15.5 and discuss how artworks' meanings can change according to how they are produced.

Ceramic forms are sometimes included in art installations. Judy Chicago's *The Dinner Party* contains

FIGURE 15.5 Group project, 8–10-years-old, Césu BJC, Césis, Latvia.
*Source: ICEFA Lidice, 45th Exhibition.*

thirty-nine place settings that represent significant real and mythological female characters, paying homage to their historical contributions (Chicago, 1979). Chicago applied the lost art of lace draping to produce *The Dinner Party's* Emily Dickenson ceramic plate. She drenched lace in porcelain **slip**, a clay paste that consists of water, clay, and sometimes vinegar, then fired it to give it a glass-like appearance. Because the plates in Chicago's collection had different depths, she and her team sometimes fired individual plates five times so that each would be durable and communicate what she intended. Presenting Chicago's example of working through challenges shows students how artists take great efforts and make revisions to produce the results they desire. Artists Kat Hutter and Roger Lee created a collaborative installation called *Another California Day* inspired by their travels across California. They used time-lapse video to document how they formed their installation (Pasadena Museum of California Art, 2016). Over a week, Lee, a ceramicist, threw multiple pots on a potter's wheel and arranged them into sculpted designs. His ceramic sculptures remained unfired and dried naturally over the course of the exhibition. The unfired clay referenced California's desert. At the same time, Hutter painted abstracted patterns on the installation's walls that signified California's climate. Students can discuss how the artists' decision to document their work through video provided audiences with insights into their collaborative practices and has extended the life of their installation.

 **Artists' Lessons to Thrive! 15.1 Rose Pecos-Sun Rhodes: Collective Storytelling in a Physical Form**

**Big Idea: Storytelling**

Pueblo artists create dolls for ceremonial purposes and to pass down wisdom and cultural traditions. A Pueblo singing mother doll portrays a mother sharing stories with her children as she holds them. *Kachinas* are devotional dolls that families give to children to teach them spiritual beliefs. In 1964, Helen Cordero of the Cochiti Pueblo created the first storyteller doll by expanding upon traditional singing mother dolls. Instead of sculpting a mother, she modeled a male character in clay, representing her grandfather, who was a great storyteller. She surrounded his figure with many children, as youngsters would eagerly gather around to listen to his lively tales. Being an accomplished storyteller is a high honor in Pueblo society. Since Cordero invented storyteller dolls, Pueblo ceramicists have had the freedom to produce storytellers in male, female, and animal forms. Rose Pecos-Sun Rhodes' *Storyteller*

**FIGURE 15.1.1** Rose Pecos-Sun Rhodes, *Storyteller Under Sunny Skies*, 1993. Children's Museum of Indianapolis. Wendy Kaveney, Photo. CC BY-SA 3.0 via Wikimedia Commons.
*Source: https://creativecommons.org/licenses/by-sa/3.0/deed.en*

*Under Sunny Skies* (Figure 15.1.1) is a ceramic storyteller doll that draws inspirations from Pueblo figurative sculptures.

Rhodes' selected a female figure as her artwork's storyteller. Her ceramic design incorporates Navajo fashions, including the flowing skirt that the artist selected as a base to support the ranch children. The skirt is reminiscent of a grandmother's soft blanket. The storyteller's relaxed body positioning welcomes the children to story time. Sitting comfortably beneath a purple umbrella, the storyteller sings her melodies by heart. With full rounded lips she shuts her eyes and concentrates on this extraordinary moment. Her song captures the younger generation's imaginations. The children simultaneously give hugs, nurture a baby, pet animals, and play games. Rhodes' storyteller figures include her trademark, a little boy wearing a cowboy hat (White Buffalo, 2017). The hat serves as an analogy to reference how her husband endearingly placed his large hat on their young son's head as he was growing up.

Storyteller dolls combine modern life experiences with ancestral wisdom. Indigenous clay and pigment for storyteller dolls connect the Pueblo to the land. For 2,000 years the Pueblo people have created ceramic vessels from local clay, minerals, and plants to hold food and water. The clay symbolizes life, as the earth provides nourishment. Their songs foster spiritual wellbeing. As the earth nourishes the people, Rhodes' ceramic storyteller nourishes future generations who desire to know more about life and their culture's rich traditions.

## Essential/Guiding Questions

1. Why do you think Rhodes selected clay to create her storyteller? What does *Storyteller Under Sunny Skies* teach us?
2. How do learning stories and cultural traditions benefit society? Which stories and experiences have shaped your life?

## Preparation

The class will research storytelling practices from various cultures, including the Pueblo.

## Daily Learning Targets

I can create a ceramic form about storytelling.

- I can select a symbolic color scheme to decorate my ceramic form.
- I can produce a balanced and unified design that is realistic and/or abstract.
- I can integrate a personal storytelling experience that accompanies my presentation of my ceramic form.

**National Core Arts Anchor Standards** 1, 4, 8, and 11
www.nationalartsstandards.org

Students can produce designs with natural and/or manufactured clays when studying the works of historic and contemporary ceramicists. Natural clays require use of a **kiln**, a high-temperature clay oven. For example, the ceramic busts in Figure 15.6 were fired in a kiln. Synthetic clays do not require use of a kiln and have different consistencies than natural clay. Figure 15.7 illustrates how students integrated synthetic clay into a mixed-media artwork. The following examples describe common natural and synthetic clays for classroom use:

- **Earthenware** is a low-fire natural clay that remains semi-porous when it is fired in a kiln. This kiln-fired clay is most common in classrooms. White earthenware has a smoother consistency than **terracotta**, a red earthenware clay that gets its color from its rich iron-oxide content. White earthenware is favorable for glazing because it shows glaze colors more vividly than do terracotta and brown earthenware. Teachers, students, and artists utilize low-fire glazes to glaze this clay.
- **Stoneware** is a natural clay that is stronger than earthenware due to its high firing temperature.

Teachers, students, and artists use high-temperature glazes with stoneware clays. It becomes non-porous after firing, so it is well-suited for serving food and beverages.

- **Grog** consists of particles of fired clay that artists add to moist earthenware and stoneware to give them greater structural strength. This additive makes the clay more porous and reduces cracking.
- **Modeling clay** (plasticine) is a synthetic clay made with oil that comes in multiple colors. The oil keeps the clay's consistency smooth and prevents it from drying so that students can use it repeatedly. This type of clay is not baked.
- **Polymer clay** is a synthetic plastic clay that is pliable and comes in many colors. Teachers and artists bake it in conventional ovens. Students can use polymer clay to cover armatures due to its low baking heat and minimal shrinkage.
- **Play dough** is a reusable synthetic clay that is most often made from flour, water, salt, and tartar; it is not baked. Teachers can make play dough or purchase Play Doh®. It stays malleable when stored in a sealed container.

- **Flour clay** is a synthetic clay that consists of eight cups of non-rising flour (1,892 grams), four cups of salt (946 gm), six tablespoons of oil (88 ml), and four cups of water (946 gm). Students can add color by mixing in food coloring while the clay is still moist or by painting their completed clay forms after baking. Teachers can bake modeled flour clay forms in a conventional oven at 300–350 °F (149–177 °C) for 30–60 minutes. Students can reuse unbaked, moist flour clay stored in airtight containers.

- **Air dry clay** is a soft synthetic clay that hardens in the air. It must be stored in an air-tight container to remain malleable. Students can press decorative materials into it while it is still moist. They can paint it or color it with markers once it has dried.

**FIGURE 15.6** Group project, 12–15-years-old, ZUŠ, Český Krumlov, Czech Republic.
*Source: ICEFA Lidice, 40th Exhibition.*

## Clay Stages

Natural clay transforms from soft and malleable to a hardened ceramic product through five stages. **Plastic** is its first stage, meaning that the clay is moist and easy to manipulate. It has just the right amount of water for small clay particles to join together so that students can form it into various designs. Students benefit from kneading their plastic clay at the onset of a project to remove any possible air bubbles that might damage their pieces when fired in a kiln. Students should also form ceramic pieces with equal wall thicknesses so that their structures become sturdier and will fire more evenly. **Leather hard** is clay's second stage, with the clay becoming firm to the touch. Some of the clay's moisture has evaporated and it has the appearance of leather. Ceramicists connect attachments to clay sculptures, such as handles, when they are leather hard. If attachments will be added, teachers need to demonstrate how to **score** the leather-hard clay surfaces by scratching into all parts that will be joined together. This process gives the clay rough edges to hold the slip. Students will attach the parts by pulling clay across from each side to the other side in even, balanced motions using their hands or clay modeling tools. They will smooth the surface so that the slipped seam line disappears. The melded pieces cannot have different moisture levels because they will dry at different rates and break. Therefore, teachers must carefully monitor and assist students as they add attachments. To produce the artwork shown in Figure 15.8, the student carefully scored and slipped

**FIGURE 15.7** Group project, 4–6-years-old, 24. MŠ Úsměv, Chomutov, Czech Republic.
*Source: ICEFA Lidice, 40th Exhibition.*

**FIGURE 15.8** Eliška Vaňková, 8-years-old, Dům dětí a mládeže Praha 3–Ulita, Praha 3, Czech Republic.
*Source: ICEFA Lidice, 43rd Exhibition.*

the sculpture's different parts including the owls, walls, handle, and decorative features. Additionally, teachers should make sure that students poke a small pinhole in their sculptures when creating closed forms to prevent built up air pressure, which causes clay to explode when fired in the kiln.

When students are working on a project over multiple days, they will need to store their in-progress natural clay sculptures securely in a plastic bag to keep the clay plastic or leather hard until they are ready to dry their sculptures. The clay sculptures should be freestanding and not touch other clay forms because they might stick together. Spraying water on them with a squirt bottle and covering the sculptures with damp paper towels or rags keeps them moist because the added dampness penetrates the clay. Teachers may need to repeat this process to keep students' clay forms moist for extended periods. Students may or may not add water to forms that they want to become leather hard. This will depend on when they will be working on them again as well as climate conditions that impact drying times.

The third stage is **bone dry**, signifying that all moisture has evaporated from the clay. The clay's arid mass has shrunken slightly and has become fragile. Clay cannot be safely fired in a kiln until it is bone dry. Many ceramicists prefer a slower kiln firing for ceramic ware because it gives bone dry clay time to set and reduces the risk of explosion. Once clay has been fired, it undergoes a chemical transformation and enters its fourth stage, called **bisque**. Bisqueware has a rock-hard surface and can no longer return to its plastic stage with water (like leather hard and bone dry clay can). Teachers and students should be mindful not to open the kiln while it is firing. The glowing red flame can cause eye damage and the change in heat can damage the kiln walls. Ceramic pieces should not be removed until the kiln has cooled fully.

Depending on a piece's function, students can leave the bisqueware's natural color or decorate it with glaze or paint. When bisqueware has been coated with glaze and re-fired in a kiln, it becomes **glazeware**, the fifth stage of clay. Glazes have a glossy, satin, or matte finish. The sculpted backpack in Figure 15.9. has bright glossy colors. When firing glazeware, teachers should line the kiln's refractory shelves with **kiln wash**, which prevents glaze from sticking to the shelves during firing. Glazed pieces should never touch each other during firing, as the glaze will fuse the pieces together. Teachers can place glazeware on **refractory stilts** that slightly raise ceramic pieces from the shelf surfaces to

FIGURE 15.9 Ernests Kuplis, 9-years-old, Tukums Art School, Tukums, Latvia.
*Source: ICEFA Lidice, 44th Exhibition.*

prevent sticking. As an added protection, some teachers may ask students not to glaze the base of their bisqueware. In addition, they might have students apply a ceramic product called **wax resist** over bases or lidded areas before glazing. Students will wipe off any extra glaze that may drip on the wax resist.

## Handbuilding Techniques

**Handbuilding techniques** (sculpting clay by hand) produce hollow forms, cylindrical pieces, and flattened surfaces. Knowing how to form basic structures assists students in designing clay sculptures of various shapes and sizes to depict the concepts they have in mind. When connecting pieces of clay to form designs, students will use scoring and slipping methods so that the pieces will form a strong bond when joined together. Ceramicists use different methods to produce slip for natural clay. A common classroom method is to mix equal parts water and vinegar to crushed dry clay particles and stir the mixture until it forms a creamy consistency. Teachers should wear a respiratory mask to avoid breathing in clay particles and store the slip in an airtight container to preserve it. As an alternative to slip, AMACO Brent (2016) recommends combining equal parts of water and vinegar in a spray bottle. Students will spray the mixture directly on the clay's scored surfaces and join the clay pieces together. Students can also score some non-oil-based synthetic clays using the sprayed water and vinegar mixture to join parts together.

FIGURE 15.10 Raku pinch pot, high school. United States.
*Source: Jonathan Griffith, teacher. Jonathan Griffith, photo.*

FIGURE 15.11 Mia Ella Chlebovská, 6-years-old, Anastázie Ginkulová, 6-years-old, Adéla Jančurová, 4-years-old, MŠ Zdraví, Ostrava—Zábřeh, Czech Republic.
*Source: ICEFA Lidice, 41st Exhibition.*

**Pinch pots** are usually small sculptures that students form by shaping a ball of clay in their hands to produce a hollow, cylindrical form (Figure 15.10). Students can transform pinch pots into containers, animals, baskets, and hats. Teachers can demonstrate how to create a pinch pot with students by following these steps.

1. Roll the clay into a smooth ball.
2. Hold the ball of clay in one hand. Use the other hand and point the thumb in a downward motion. Push the thumb into the base of the clay ball, making sure not to pierce through the entire ball.
3. Take the index and middle fingers from the same hand that pushed into the clay and press against the outer ball of the clay while the thumb is still inserted in the clay. Gradually rotate and pinch the pot to form its sidewalls. The walls will become thinner with each rotation and pinch. Finished walls should measure about 1/4 in. (.6 cm) thick for stability. If a flat base is desired, set the pinch pot on a flat surface and rub the base's interior with a thumb.
4. Smooth all unwanted lumps and bumps out of the clay.

A **coil** is a long, cylindrical form that ceramicists twist, braid, roll, and layer to construct forms and give their works a decorative look (Figure 15.11). Teachers will show students how to make a coil by holding a ball of clay between their hands and rolling it back and forth, like a pencil. The more that the clay is rolled, the longer and thinner the coil becomes. For a more even coil, students can roll the

cylindrical piece of clay on a smooth, flat, nonstick surface. They will place their hands in the middle of the coil and gradually work their hands outwards to elongate the clay. Teachers can demonstrate how artists form objects including arms, legs, and handles with coils (Figure 15.12). Students can also create pots and vases with coils. First, they will flatten a ball of clay into a disk. The width of the disk should be the same size as the desired base of the coil pot or vase. If they will be firing their work in a kiln, they will need to score and slip all connective parts. Next, they will roll a coil and press it into the base. They will continue to build coils until they reach the desired height of the pot or vase and tuck each end of a coil into the starting point of the previous coil to form smooth joints. They can place coils directly

FIGURE 15.12 Agáta Bortlová, 14-years-old, Dům dětí a mládeže Praha 3—Ulita, Praha 3—Žižkov, Czech Republic.
*Source: ICEFA Lidice, 40th Exhibition.*

FIGURE 15.13 Group project, 14–16-years-old, ZUŠ, Sedlčany, Czech Republic.
*Source: ICEFA Lidice, 40th Exhibition.*

FIGURE 15.14 Polina Zujeva, 9-years-old, Spogu Mūzikas un Mākslas Skola, Spogi, Latvia.
*Source: ICEFA Lidice, 45th Exhibition.*

on top of each other for a straight edge or develop a curved silhouette by gradually moving coils inward for a narrower edge and outwards for a wider one.

There are multiple ways for students to create a **sphere**, a ball-shaped form, in clay (Figure 15.13). Students can combine two pinch pots by slipping and scoring to form the ball shape. As an alternative, they can begin with a pinch pot base and construct the second half by adding layers of coils, slipping and scoring as they work, and then smoothing the clay to remove the ridges. They can also make a sphere entirely from a coil. Finally, teachers can purchase spherical ceramic molds to produce larger forms using slip. When firing a closed sphere, students will need to poke a small pinhole to act as an air vent.

A **slab** is a flat, even piece of clay that can be used to produce tiles, masks, decorative shapes, cylinders, plaques, boxes, and flat puzzles (Figure 15.14). Students can make basic slabs by pounding clay against a flat surface with their fists or using a rolling pin. A slab-rolling machine produces the most even slabs. A typical slab measures 1/4 in. to 1/2 in. (0.6 to 1.3 cm) thick. Students can construct new forms with slabs or use them to produce decorative shapes. They should avoid working with preformed decorating materials and tools such as manufactured cookie cutters, which might prohibit them from applying problem-solving skills associated with cutting and designing clay. Rather, they should create original forms with modeling tools (Bartel, 2002). When constructing a slab box with natural clay, students

will need stable, leather-hard slabs, because soft plastic clay will collapse during construction. Students will score and slip the different slabs together to form their boxes. If they want a lidded box, they can use a wire cutter to separate the lid from the rest of the box once their slabs are secured in place. Figure 15.15 depicts a room constructed with a slab design.

FIGURE 15.15 Eliza Mickus, 7-years-old, Martins Mickus, 10-years-old, Pamatskola Ridze, Riga, Latvia.
*Source: ICEFA Lidice, 39th Exhibition.*

Some artists select natural and synthetic clays to produce jewelry. People wear jewelry for personal beautification and social purposes, including identifying a religious affiliation or marital status. Ceramicists design jewelry that flows with the form of the human body. Clay jewelry can be functional or purely decorative. Teachers can connect jewelry design with big ideas including beautification, status, and function. They can demonstrate how to add textures to manipulate clay and draw designs on its surface with modeling tools. If students use natural clay to create jewelry, their forms will shrink in size as they dry. Polymer clay generally keeps its original size. Students can use skewers to punch holes for clay beads before they harden. They may want to add color to their clay designs with glaze or paint or select pre-colored polymer clay. To create the polymer clay artwork shown in Figure 15.16, the student studied real flowers.

## Wheel Throwing

Given students' understanding of handbuilding procedures, they can begin wheel throwing to produce hollow, rounded ceramic vessels on a pottery wheel. Wheel throwing began in Mesopotamia around 4,000–3,000 BCE as a faster alternative to the coiling construction method (Cooper, 2000). Teachers must be proficient at throwing clay on a wheel or bring in a professional ceramicist as a visiting artist to teach students this skill (Figure 15.17). A highly skilled potter may provide introductory exposure to the wheel to young children with one-on-one guidance; however, early adolescence is a common age to begin class wheel-throwing lessons (Bartel, 2002). The class will need at least one throwing wheel. Manufacturers sell different wheels—including electric wheels and manually powered kick wheels, small tabletop wheels, and wheelchair accessible wheels. Wheel throwing requires effective hand and body posturing and much practice for consistent outcomes (Leach & Dehnert, 2013). Students must learn how to center the clay on the wheel's central axis so the clay can develop into aesthetic forms including bowls, platters, and vases. Water lubricates the clay during the throwing process. Potters carefully guide the right amount of water with their fingers and/or a sponge to the appropriate locations. They apply controlled pushing and pulling motions to create forms. Potters vary the wheel's speed according to tasks they are performing. As the wheel has moving parts, students will need to follow safety procedures under teachers' close supervision.

**FIGURE 15.16** Ailee Sickler, 5th grade, United States.
*Source: Author, teacher. Richard Sickler, photo.*

**FIGURE 15.17** Art educator Jonathan Griffith has a ceramic studio and demonstrates wheel throwing to his classes.
*Source: Jonathan Griffith, photo.*

# UNDERSTANDING AND APPLYING MOSAICS IN CONTEXT

During antiquity, Greek artists made the first mosaics by arranging different colored pebbles into a pleasing design to create durable floors. Pebbles were the best material for constructing floors because they could withstand everyday wear and tear. As Greek artists became better skilled in mosaic design, their floors became more ornamental and began including images from everyday life and mythology. Around the 4th century BCE, mosaicists began placing mosaics on walls and **vaults**, arched ceiling structures. At this time, the Romans invented ceramic and glass tesserae, which were thinner and easier to cut than stone. Glass and highly glazed ceramic tesserae have a lighter feel than stone, and they beautifully reflect light, which make them well-suited for decorating walls and vaults in churches and mosques. Such qualities enabled mosaicists to design mosaics with religious themes that replicated the look of paintings. Due to these technological innovations, mosaics became the leading art form in Byzantium up until the 14th century.

Mosaics are commonly produced for public and private art commissions as well as home decoration, with designs on sculptural forms (Figure 15.18), walls (Figure 15.19), floors, tabletops, and countless other surfaces. Antoni Gaudí conceived Güell Park (1900–1914), as a prestigious housing and park complex in Barcelona, Spain. In 1978 after visiting Güell Park, artist Niki de Saint Phalle created *Il Giardino dei Tarocchi*, a monumental mosaic garden that features twenty-two walk-through mosaic sculptures based on the tarot. Contemporary artists Julee Latimer (Artists' Lessons to Thrive! 5.1), and Carlos Alves and JC Carroll, produce a range of mosaic forms that adorn interior and exterior spaces. Artists' Lessons to Thrive! 15.2 describes how Alves and Carroll transformed a

FIGURE 15.18 Julee Latimer ©. *Kat, mosaic sculpture,* 16.52 × 10.23 × 15.74 in. (42 × 26 × 40 cm.)
*Source: Photo by HONE photography. Courtesy of the artist; www. juleelatimer.com.*

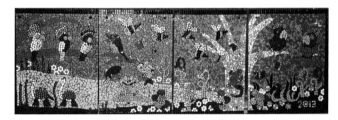

FIGURE 15.19 Early childhood students at Thornbury Kindergarten created this collaborative mosaic. Australia.
*Source: Julee Latimer ©, artist-in-resident. Courtesy of the artist; www. juleelatimer.com.*

fountain into a beautiful public artwork that represents their community's aquatic life with mosaic tesserae and clay figures. When working as artists-in-residence, they teach their mosaic and ceramic skills to pre-K–12 students (see Spotlight on Student Art #6).

---

## Artists' Lessons to Thrive! 15.2 Carlos Alves and JC Carroll: Beautifying the Urban Environment One Piece at a Time

### Big Idea: Beautification

"Chip it, crack it, smash it. Put it back together and give it a whole new life" is a motto that drives artists Carlos Alves and JC Carroll, who combine ceramic tesserae, recycled crockery, and original clay figures to create vibrant, tropical mosaics. In the late eighties Alves opened his first art studio on

**FIGURE 15.2.1** Carlos Alves and JC Carroll, *Save Our Reefs*, mosaics and clay, 2004.
*Source: Courtesy of the artists; carlosalvesmosaics.com.*

Miami Beach's world famous Lincoln Road Mall and began working with his future wife, JC Carroll. Through ongoing beautification efforts, artists like Alves and Carroll transformed the quiet mall—which had its heyday during the 1930s–1950s—back into a thriving hot spot for art, fashion, music, food, and entertainment. Their mosaics adorn public and private spaces throughout Miami Beach's Art Deco District and have helped define South Florida's artistic culture.

Alves and Carroll regularly receive grants and commissions to enhance public sites, because people enjoy their lush creations and positive messages. One of their most recognizable artworks is a public fountain on Lincoln Road Mall titled *Save Our Reefs* (Figure 15.2.1). The City of Miami Beach commissioned Alves and Carroll to redesign the existing Art Deco fountain with an ocean theme to promote the importance of preserving South Florida's coral reefs. The artists beautified this fountain with an original mosaic design that includes ceramic sea life forms. Alves and Carroll selected tesserae and glazes that are vibrant and expressive in color, like the Florida sun and skyline. They applied hues ranging from iridescent turquoise to deep cobalt blues to form the fountain's background. The artists produced the sea life using molds so that they could repeat their ceramic figures throughout the fountain. Their three-dimensional fish, shells, and sea vegetation in yellow, orange, green, and red contrast against the mosaicked tropical seawater. Their forms project a few inches away from the background surface and give the fountain an added visual and tactile appeal.

Alves and Carroll's fountain represents more than chipping, cracking, and smashing ceramic tiles because it teaches audiences, radiates joy, and beautifies the community. Through *Save Our Reefs*, Alves and Carroll convey the importance of preserving the ocean. Their fountain symbolizes how humanity can take something that is broken, including damaged coral reefs, and take steps to make them healthy and beautiful again.

## Essential/Guiding Questions

1. What do Alves and Carroll mean when they say that they are giving broken pieces of tile new life by arranging them into artworks?
2. In what ways have Alves and Carroll's South Florida surroundings influenced the look of *Save Our Reefs*? Why do you think that public and private patrons commission them to install mosaics on their properties?

## Preparation

The students will examine Alves and Carroll's mosaics and discuss how artistic beautification efforts enhance a community.

## Daily Learning Targets

I can create a mosaic to beautify a space.

- I can select the form and tesserae of my choice to produce my mosaic.
- I can create a unified design that shows pattern, positive and negative spaces, and craftspersonship.
- I can explain how I designed my mosaic and made revisions to my work to produce a final product that beautifies a particular space.

**National Core Arts Anchor Standards** 3, 5, 7, and 10

www.nationalartsstandards.org

*Quoted artists' statements not listed in the reference section result from personal communications with the author (personal communications, 2014–2018).*

## Mosaic Tesserae

When creating mosaics, students can construct mosaic forms that range from individual artworks with found objects to collaborative large-scale public displays using fine glass and ceramic tesserae. The first step in preparing a mosaic is for the artists to identify the mosaic surfaces and types of tesserae necessary for their designs. Like contemporary artists, students can select traditional and non-traditional mosaic tesserae, including pebbles, shells, game pieces, plastic caps, buttons, trinkets, found objects, and small items such as beans (Figure 15.20). Manufacturers sell traditional ceramic and glass tesserae in square and rectangular shapes. These preformed tesserae work best for beginners because they do not require cutting and are well-suited for linear designs. Teachers can introduce more advanced students to the challenge of cutting tesserae using a cutting tool called **nippers**. Large ceramic pieces, including repurposed chipped dinner plates, may be too large to cut with nippers. If students wish to integrate ceramic dinnerware pieces in their designs, they can hammer them into broken pieces, which will produce random sizes

**FIGURE 15.20** Mosaic self-portrait. Ailee Sickler, 6th grade. United States.
*Source: Author, teacher. Richard Sickler, photo.*

and patterns. Students must wear protective eyewear and gloves and concentrate fully on their work while hammering. Teachers should have students place the ceramic pieces in a heavy-duty clear plastic bag and wrap the bag inside of a thick folded towel before hammering to prevent shattered pieces from flying.

## Mosaic Surfaces, Adhesives, and Grout

Artists select the best adhesives and tesserae for their work surfaces. Mosaic surfaces include cardboard, wood, frames, stepping stones, furniture, and walls. For beginners and teachers with limited budgets, an inexpensive cardboard base can be an ideal surface on which to adhere lightweight tesserae and found objects. Students will glue the tesserae to the cardboard surface in an aesthetic design. If they wish to have a decorative background, they can paint or collage the surface to alter the look of the work's negative spaces before adhering tesserae. Plywood boards can hold the weight of glass, stone, and ceramic tesserae. Students can use mastic or another appropriate glue to attach tesserae to a wood surface such as plywood for interior mosaics. Outdoor projects on walls or concrete furniture will require **thinset** (a cement-based construction material) to adhere ceramic and/or glass tesserae. When adhering mosaics to a wall surface (Figure 15.21), teachers should seek the advice of a tile expert for professional tips and guidance. Students can create original, preformed mosaic shapes on screen at their desks rather than working directly

**FIGURE 15.22** Fifth- and sixth-grade students arrange mosaic tesserae. United States.
*Source: Author, teacher. Pamela McColly, photo.*

on a wall to save time and make the learning process easier to manage (Figure 15.22). After arranging the tiles for placement on a wall into position they will fill the negative spaces with a mixture of glue and water. The glue mixture will dry and hold the mosaic tesserae in place. Then, the students will attach the mosaic design to the wall with thinset.

Once the appropriate adhesive (thinset, mastic, etc.) has dried fully and the tesserae are firmly set into position, students will add **grout**, a porous, cement-based, nontoxic material. Grout secures mosaic tesserae in place on hard surfaces such as wood, walls, frames, and cement, and adds visual appeal to mosaic designs (DuVal, 2004). Cardboard designs will not require grout. Grout is either **sanded** or **non-sanded**. Typically, artists use non-sanded grout on wall surfaces, but sanded grout is necessary when the spaces between tiles are greater than 1/8 in. (.3 cm). Teachers and students should follow the grout's package directions before applying it to a surface. Depending on the color that an artist selects, grout can contrast sharply against tesserae or blend with them harmoniously. Teachers can purchase different colored grouts or have students tint white grout with powdered grout pigment, food dye, or acrylic paint. Grout should have a thick peanut butter consistency to spread evenly into the cracks between individual tesserae. **Grouting squeegees** and **rubber trowels** assist artists in applying thinset to a surface and spreading grout into cracks between tesserae. Once students have filled all of the cracks, the grout will set for about 15 minutes. Afterwards, they

**FIGURE 15.21** Ballerina figures with mosaic details. Fifth- and sixth-grade students. United States.
*Source: Author, teacher. Pamela McColly, photo.*

will use a lint free cloth to wipe away excess grout particles and clean the tesserae with a one-part white vinegar to ten parts water solution to remove the grout's dull film and bring out the mosaic's shine.

## BEST PRACTICES FOR TEACHING CLAY AND MOSAICS FROM PRE-K THROUGH HIGH SCHOOL

Comprehensive art lessons provide students with ample opportunities to study the works of global ceramic and mosaic artists. Teachers can introduce students to clay and mosaic discoveries in anthropological excavations and compare them to contemporary works. Learning about artworks in context, students will compare and contrast ceramic and mosaic artworks' functions and meanings. For example, students might study Carlos Alves and JC Carroll's mosaic artworks within the built environment and compare them with historic wall and floor mosaics to discuss why societies beautify public and private spaces with mosaics. Teaching clay and mosaics requires teachers and students to use specialized equipment. Teachers should use formative assessments for students to acclimate to the physical qualities of clay and mosaic materials, tools, equipment, and procedures before they submit works for summative grades. For example, students will need to practice holding nippers at their base to break tesserae or centering on a pottery wheel before they can do so independently. Some students may feel uncomfortable touching squishy clay and grout. Teachers can demonstrate their understanding for students' concerns by providing gloves and plastic bags to assist students when working. In circumstances in which teachers have kiln access, but do not know how to operate a kiln safely, they can read packaging directions; locate online tutorials; and contact a district art supervisor, ceramicist, or mentoring art teacher for assistance so that students will be able to create kiln-fired clay products (Figure 15.23).

Throughout the learning process, teachers will monitor students to assess that they are on-task, wear proper safety equipment, and refrain from pouring clay water, grout, and adhesives down the sink. Teachers and students will cover work surfaces with canvas. This protects tables from tesserae scratches and prevents clay from sticking to the tables. Each table should also have a bucket filled two-thirds full

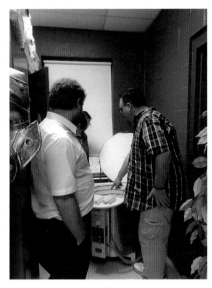

FIGURE 15.23 This art teacher shows pre-service teachers how to load and operate a kiln. United States.
*Source: Ted Edinger, teacher.*

with water, a stack of paper towels, and sponges for students to add additional water to their work, moisten their hands, and clean at their tables as necessary to reduce trips to the sink. Because some clay and mosaic activities require pounding with fists or a hammer, teachers will show students how to pound without using excessive force. Teachers will demonstrate how to use caution when handling glass and ceramic tesserae, which may have sharp edges.

Teachers may need to make accommodations to teach the lessons they desire because quality clay and mosaic supplies can be costly. For example, some teachers substitute metal flatware and plastic utensils for clay modeling tools. They might also have students paint bisque-fired clay as an alternative to glazing. For mosaic projects, teachers can assemble found objects and donated goods including broken china plates and cups, ceramic floor tiles, broken costume jewelry, utensils, and buttons to use as tesserae. Once teachers have materials secured, they will need to plan how and where they will store students' clay and mosaic projects. Some classrooms are equipped with clay storage cabinets. When these are not available, teachers might collect old plastic cafeteria trays and supermarket bread carts and line them with canvas sheets or small wooden boards on which to store clay. Teachers can store mosaic tesserae in sturdy clear plastic containers with lids.

In early childhood, children's introduction to clay often begins with exposure to synthetic clay products like Play Doh. Working with clay, tesserae, and beads

FIGURE 15.25 Markéta Kremerová, 5-years-old, Tomáš Payne, 6-years-old, MŠ, Praha 3, Czech Republic.
*Source: ICEFA Lidice, 40th Exhibition.*

FIGURE 15.24 Šmejkalová Bára, 5-years-old, Dům dětí a mládeže „ULITA" Praha 3, ul. Na Balkáně 100, Czech Republic.
*Source: ICEFA Lidice, 34th Exhibition.*

FIGURE 15.26 Johana Anna Hladíková, 10-years-old, Barbora Kalianková, 11-years-old, Adéla Malíková, 10-years-old, DDM, Český Krumlov, Czech Republic.
*Source: ICEFA Lidice, 44th Exhibition.*

satisfies young children's desire to manipulate objects with their hands. Students learn how to manipulate materials through repetitive actions and like to arrange tactile clay and mosaic materials in personally pleasing ways. To create the sculpture shown in Figure 15.24, students used repetitive rolling actions to form coils to produce the dragonfly's figure. Teachers can also have young learners roll a string of beads from natural, polymer, or colorful air dry clay and push them onto dull skewers to dry as a stimulating repetitive tactile learning task. Given teacher demonstrations and practice, students can learn how to string handmade beads independently onto pieces of yarn, string, or elastic to create necklaces and bracelets. Young students are inquisitive and appreciate I Spy games. Teachers can have them identify traditional and non-traditional tesserae and their various textures on artworks and examples from visual culture. They can look to Rose Pecos-Sun Rhodes' *Storyteller Under Sunny Skies* as well as other ceramic and mosaic artworks as inspirations to participate in storytelling activities. For example, the ceramic sculpture shown in Figure 15.25 is inspired by a fairytale. For all lessons, teachers will select age-appropriate clay and mosaic products only, and will monitor the class to see that students do not put clay and mosaic pieces in their mouths.

Middle-childhood students are developing observational skills, and they can model clay sculptures inspired

by textures that they see and touch (Figure 15.26). Teachers can introduce students to mosaicists' projects as inspirations for designing individual and collaborative mosaics. Because middle-childhood students have developed hobbies and collect objects that interest them, teachers can teach lessons in which students form an original clay slab box or add a mosaic to an existing container to hold a special collection of objects. They can add decorations to their boxes and containers that showcase their hobbies and interests. They might also create a ceramic puzzle that they could use to play with classmates (Figure 15.14). Their designs can be original or appropriated from art history. Upper elementary students have a greater ability to empathize with other people's emotions.

Teachers can have students identify feelings portrayed in ceramic sculptures. Students can research mythological characters on Greek vases and identify characters whose stories interest them, including Herakles, the hero, or Aphrodite, the goddess of love. Middle-childhood students are also skilled at organizing and classifying information. Teachers can augment students' knowledge of ceramics and mosaics with flashcards. Students can match similar artworks, such as a pair of mosaics by the same artist or ceramic forms from a particular culture.

If early adolescents had limited exposure to ceramics in elementary school, teachers will need to accommodate their learning needs by teaching them basic clay construction techniques before requiring them to complete more advanced designs. This will make the ceramic process less intimidating and more enjoyable for students who may feel self-conscious about their work. Early adolescents can be eager to try something new and to learn adult skills. Teachers may invite a professional ceramicist to teach students how they produce ceramic vessels on the wheel, either in a classroom that has throwing wheels or at a clay studio. Some teachers take wheel throwing classes so that they can teach wheel throwing to students. For handbuilding techniques, teachers can have early adolescents blend construction techniques and incorporate various surface textures to add visual interest to their clay designs, like artists do (Figure 15.27). Participating in mosaic learning tasks is equally exciting for early adolescents. The curriculum should give students opportunities to create a full range of mosaic products. Teachers might invite mosaicists

as artists-in-residence or a parent who lays tile for a living to teach students how to arrange, adhere, and grout tesserae. Students may be interested in filming documentary videos that show how they created community art projects and/or installations that include clay and mosaics. Because early adolescents are more aware of social issues, they might donate their clay, mosaic, and jewelry products to a favorite charity. They can also create these products as special gifts for people they care about.

Adolescents who have ongoing comprehensive clay and mosaic experiences in elementary and middle school will enter high school ready to participate in more in-depth learning tasks. For example, with teacher guidance they could construct an original three-dimensional form and add a mosaic to its surface like Julee Latimer does with her sculpted forms (Figure 15.18) and furniture pieces (Artists' Lessons to Thrive! 5.1). Teachers might pair students who had fewer opportunities to acquire basic ceramic and mosaic techniques with student mentors who can teach them basic skills. Lessons might have students combine figures that normally do not belong together to produce interesting designs, such as the musical portraits in Figure 15.28, or mix clay figures with sculpting materials to produce additive sculptures like that shown in Figure 15.29. Students can investigate postmodern principles that demonstrate why crafts and fine art are equally valuable and necessary in society. They can identify how

FIGURE 15.27 Natálie Kuklová, 13-years-old, ZUŠ Jana Zacha, Čelákovice, Czech Republic.
*Source: ICEFA Lidice, 43rd Exhibition.*

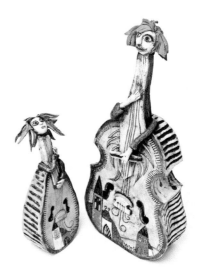

FIGURE 15.28 Veronika Kolářová, 15-years-old, Dům dětí a mládeže Praha 3–Ulita, Praha 3–Žižkov, Czech Republic.
*Source: ICEFA Lidice, 40th Exhibition.*

**FIGURE 15.29** Zaur Gamkrelidze, 16-years-old, Oni Public School, Oni, Georgia.
*Source: ICEFA Lidice, 43rd Exhibition.*

artists and craftspersons share many of the same materials and processes, then debate the distinction of what constitutes fine art and crafts. Students can extend this activity by researching the work of local artists who produce clay and mosaic products.

## OUR JOURNEY TO THRIVE CONTINUES . . .

This chapter presented effective means to teach comprehensive clay and mosaic processes to students. In the next chapter, we will expand our knowledge by learning how to teach textiles and puppetry in context. Like clay and mosaics, these art forms have deep historic roots and add meaning to the choice-based art curriculum and provide students with quality learning experiences.

## CHAPTER QUESTIONS AND ACTIVITIES

1. Describe the qualities, functions, and meanings of clay and mosaics from historic and societal perspectives. How will you integrate clay and mosaics into the choice-based art curriculum?
2. Practice the diverse clay and mosaic processes described in this chapter to compare and contrast their qualities. Summarize what you learned in a group discussion or in writing.
3. Develop an original comprehensive lesson plan on clay and/or mosaics that focuses on a big idea of your choice. Use the lesson plan template provided on the textbook's companion website and refer to Chapter 2 for more information on lesson plan development. Integrate inquiry tasks inspired by Part III of this textbook.
4. Answer Artists' Lessons to Thrive! 15.1–15.2's essential/guiding questions in written form or as part of a group discussion. Complete their daily learning targets.

# References

AMACO Brent. (2016). *Don't slip! Joining clay without slip.* Retrieved from https://www.amaco.com/clay_how_tos/200

Bartel, M. (2002). Clay and kids: The natural way to learn. *Studio Potter, 30*(2), 60–63.

Chicago, J. (1979). *The dinner party: A symbol of our heritage.* Garden City, NY: Anchor.

Cooper, E. (2000). *Ten thousand years of pottery* (4th ed.). Philadelphia, PA: University of Pennsylvania Press.

DuVal, E. (2004). *Beyond the basics: Mosaics.* New York: Sterling.

Foulem, L. (2005). Arneson and the object. *Ceramics-Art And Perception, 61,* 20–25.

Leach, S., & Dehnert, B. (2013). *Simon Leach's pottery handbook: A comprehensive guide to throwing beautiful, functional pots.* New York, NY: Stewart, Tabori, & Chang.

Pasadena Museum of California Art. (2016). *Kat Hutter and Roger Lee: Another California day.* Retrieved from http://pmcaonline. org/exhibitions/another-california-day/

White Buffalo. (2017). *About the artists.* Retrieved from www. whitebuffalo1.com/artist.htm

Wu, X., Zhang, C., Goldberg, P., Cohen, D., Pan, Y., Arpin, T., & Bar-Yosef, O. (2012). Early pottery at 20,000 years ago in Xianrendong Cave, China. *Science, 336*(6089), 1696–1700.

# Chapter 16

# Textiles and Puppets

FIGURE 16.1 Defne Görgülü, 12-years-old, Ted Istanbul Koleji, Istanbul, Turkey.
*Source: ICEFA Lidice, 40th Exhibition.*

**Textiles** are the products that people produce by spinning or felting natural or synthetic fibers into yarn and then interlacing the yarn through the process of weaving, knitting, sprang, or crocheting to form cloth. When artists arrange fibers in an aesthetic and pleasing fashion they create textile designs. Early humans began creating textiles to protect their bodies and later developed innovative textile processes, with different styles and functions to suit their geographical regions and

design preferences. Just like textiles, cultures across our planet have produced puppets in many forms. **Puppets** are typically inanimate objects that appear to come to life as puppeteers physically manipulate their parts with their hands, bodies, strings, and/or rods to give them recognizable characteristics that are similar to living beings. Many of us are familiar with the likeable bright green Kermit the Frog puppet made from fabric and other materials. His creator, Jim Henson (2008), once said: "If you care about what you do and work hard at it, there isn't anything you can't do if you want to." We can apply his positive message as we teach students how to create textile products and puppets, and discuss their historical functions and meanings. Our textile and puppet lessons will teach students how to explore diverse media and apply individual and combined art processes to form quality designs.

We will meet the following objectives by participating in this chapter:

- Describe textiles and puppets and their qualities, functions, and meanings in society.
- Identify best practices for teaching textiles and puppets.
- Create instructional resources for teaching textiles and puppets.

Spotlight on Student Art #16 (Figure 16.1) presents an example of how a student produced a quality collection of puppets using textiles and art production methods. The works exemplify how puppets can convey storytelling traditions.

## UNDERSTANDING AND APPLYING TEXTILES IN CONTEXT

Textile production began in the prehistoric era when humans needed to protect their bodies from the elements. Early civilizations learned how to sew different pieces of fur and animal skins together to form clothing and blankets by making needles from bones and thorns. They produced thread from leather, plants, and twine. Societies eventually transformed wool, silk, and cotton into fabrics. Over the centuries, humans developed more complex and decorative stitches and fabricated fancier threads, fabrics, materials, and textile processes. They produced textiles using available flora and fauna that were either accessible in their vicinity or obtained through trade routes, such as the Silk Road that bridged Asia with the Mediterranean (Gillow & Sentance, 2005). As is true for early paper products, contemporary society has few surviving examples of early textiles due to their fragility. Archeological excavations have uncovered some textiles in excellent condition because they were preserved in burial sites that protected them, in dry areas and in bogs. In other

---

### Spotlight on Student Art #16

#### Big Idea: Storytelling Traditions

Welcome to the show! With their warm smiles, these puppets by 12-year-old Defne from Turkey invite audiences to listen to what they have to say (Figure 16.1). Created in response to a call for ICEFA's exhibition on storytelling and puppetry, these contemporary, student-made puppets add to Turkey's rich storytelling traditions and its century-old puppet theatre performances. The trio looks like they belong together because the young artist made the conscious decision to design their forms with matching clothing and physical features. Dressed in black and white, the puppets are part of a team. They share similar bodily proportions to interact with each other eye-to-eye during performances. Defne formed the puppets with papier-mâché and textiles. She sculpted the puppets' distinct facial features, which include eyelids, protruding noses, and open mouths. After constructing their heads with papier-mâché, she painted their faces with natural skin and eye colors, eyebrows, and eyelashes to make them appear more lifelike. The puppets' open mouths add personality and make them seem as if they were fully engaged in conversation. She adhered yarn to the top of the puppets' heads to form the characters' unique hairstyles. Despite their similarities, each puppet is an original. The young artist achieved this by creating small variations in the puppets' designs. One puppet has shorter hair than the others, one has green eyes and wears a red bowtie with polka dots, and one has light hair and wears a black bowtie with polka dots. Each individual puppet looks formal in his dress attire. All three puppets wear large shoes that are proportionally balanced with the puppets' prominent heads. They give the puppet figures a unified look. Performing with puppets such as these invites young audiences to become the next generation of storytellers in their communities.

circumstances, conservationists took great care to preserve highly valued textile products that were deemed important when they were originally produced.

Before the 19th century, people sewed everything by hand including clothing, bedding, curtains, ship sails, and canvases on covered wagons (Carlson, 2003). Sewing by hand required many hours of labor. As a result, people, including the wealthy, possessed fewer textile products. Isaac Singer forever changed textiles in 1850 when he introduced an affordable mechanical sewing machine. Mechanical sewing machines, Eli Whitney's invention of the cotton gin, and automated machines for producing fabrics greatly expanded the textile market (Raizman, 2004). The fashion industry grew because it cost less to produce textiles with these technologies. People also became more conscious of their dress and could more readily purchase and replace textile products. Because of the industrialization of clothing and its cheaper costs, some people readily dispose of textile products to purchase new ones. This desire places greater demands on available natural resources.

Textile production is associated with ethics, labor practices, and sentiment. For example, the cotton gin's rapid ability to separate cotton from its seeds resulted in greater demand for cotton products and expanded slavery during the 19th century (Eli Whitney Museum and Workshop, 2018). In today's society, sweatshops and child labor practices are global concerns. Some factory owners strive for greater profits and force underpaid workers, some of whom are children, to produce textiles and other products by working long hours in deplorable conditions. As an alternative, some consumers purchase fair-made textile products, including those produced by Oleana, to ensure that textile workers are treated fairly (see Artists' Lessons to Thrive! 4.1). People also value handmade textiles passed down in their families (including quilts, tablecloths, scarves, and plush figures) for their sentimental value. They hold these products dear to their hearts because of the people who made them. They continue to cherish them even when they are no longer in mint condition. For example, Figure 16.2 shows a detail of an appliqué tablecloth from the 1940s. The family heirloom has brown food and weather stains as well as small tears that the artist repaired. It was a handmade family artifact created by a grandmother and regularly used at meals with her family members. Teachers can use Figure 16.2 as a guide when asking students to

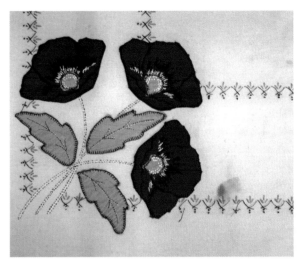

FIGURE 16.2 Aileen Niemi Joyner, tablecloth detail.
*Source: Richard Sickler, photo.*

FIGURE 16.3 Edith Meusnier, *Sortilège Festival Artec La Ferté Bernard*, gift ribbon. 2010.
*Source: Courtesy of the artist; www.edithmeusnier.fr.*

describe the sentimental textile products they have in their homes and when and how they use them.

Today's textiles can be part of an installation or a performance piece. For example, French artist Edith Meusnier uses an ancient textile technique to produce environmental land artworks in urban and natural spaces to teach about sustainability (Figure 16.3). In

Artists' Lessons to Thrive! 16.1 students will learn how Meusnier's textile designs transform the environments in which she places them. Kimsooja fills environmental spaces with silk Korean bottaris as sculptural forms that expand their utilitarian functions (see Artists' Lessons to Thrive! 10.2). As part of Norway's Slow TV movement, a million viewers watched a live twelve-hour broadcast of its National Knitting Night. The broadcast showed participants producing a sweater from "sheep to sweater," shearing the sheep on site, spinning its wool by hand, and knitting a complete sweater. Anonymous groups of people also come together to produce street artworks called *yarn bombings*, also known as *knit graffiti*. They transform objects in public spaces such as trees, light posts, and benches with their soft and colorful designs. These examples allow students to see textiles in ways that they might not have previously considered. In addition to learning how past and contemporary textile artists and designers present their works, the choice-based art curriculum will teach students how to produce appliqués, quilts, molas, weavings, tapestries, yarn paintings, and batiks.

## Artists' Lessons to Thrive! 16.1 Edith Meusnier: Sustainable *Sprang* Installations in the Environment

### Big Idea: Sustainability

FIGURE 16.1.1 Edith Meusnier, *Artifact (Artefact)*, Bois de Belle Rivière, Québec. 2010–2012, Gift ribbon and stainless steel threads.
*Source: Michel Dubreuil, photo. www.edithmeusnier.fr*

French textile artist Edith Meusnier creates environmental artworks using an ancient technique called *sprang*. Through this process, she forms long, plaited textile designs using only warp threads interlinked together. Meusnier explained: "Sometimes I plait just giftwrap ribbon for colors and lightness. At other times, I plait just stainless steel threads to play with light and relief." She also combines giftwrap ribbon with stainless steel thread to add more resistance to her designs. Meusnier has transformed the functions and meanings of the sprang technique and how people can use plastic gift ribbon beyond its intended purpose. She expanded sprang's role as a crafting technique and applied ephemeral gift ribbon to produce fine artworks that bring awareness to the environment and sustainability issues. The sprang method, which dates to the Bronze Age, has great flexibility. It looks similar to netting and has been used to produce utilitarian products including hairnets and cord. Gift ribbon also has a utilitarian function. It is an affordable decorative medium available in assorted colors. People give each other gifts in attractive packaging that often includes gift ribbon, which many dispose of immediately after opening instead of repurposing. As a sculptural material, gift ribbon is lightweight and can withstand strong winds.

Each of Meusnier's artworks is site-specific. She produces environmental pieces for natural and built environment spaces. To begin an artwork, she studies a distinct location, such as a park, castle, or city space. She takes photographs, makes sketches, and produces test pieces before constructing a final artwork for installation. She selects the appropriate gift ribbon colors and forms module structures to match each chosen environment. At first sight, Meusnier's installations appear to be in full harmony with the environment. In a natural setting, however, the artist's choice of plastic gift ribbon serves as an analogy for humanity's impact on the environment because the gift ribbon is an artificial medium disconnected from nature. When she produces art forms for prestigious human built environments, the gift ribbon represents a disposable product that contrasts against the longevity of the fineries preserved within such spaces.

*Artifact* is one of Meusnier's forest installations (Figure 16.1.1). Its eleven pieces span across treetops and are similar to a spider web in nature. *Artifact* has a double meaning, as does her art production method and choice of gift ribbon. An artifact is a human-made product from a specific time period and culture that is not a natural part of the environment. Meusnier does not intend for her seasonal environmental artworks to become long-lasting artifacts. *Artifact* and her other installations interact with the earth's elements during their short life spans. The warp threads become kinesthetic objects that invite nature into its positive and negative spaces. Drops of water rest on their warp threads after rain showers and reflect the natural light. In the winter, warp threads collect patches of snow. Like the setting sun and the changing seasons, Meusnier's environmental works eventually disappear. As this occurs, she continues to create new artworks that impact different spaces, bring awareness to sustainability issues, and touch people's lives.

## Essential/Guiding Questions

1. How does Edith Meusnier create environmental artworks about sustainability?
2. Why do you think the artist chooses to design temporary artworks rather than ones that could be preserved? In your opinion, does the temporality of her artworks add greater meaning and value?

## Preparation

The students will review Edith Meusnier's environmental artworks and discuss how art can play a valuable role in teaching others about sustainability.

## Daily Learning Targets

I can create an artwork about sustainability using a textile material and/or process.

- I can design a unified artwork that demonstrates craftspersonship and conveys its message about sustainability through my choice of design elements.
- I can select an appropriate natural or built environment in which to display or install my artwork.
- I can explain how I developed and revised my ideas during the artmaking process to teach others about sustainability.

## National Core Arts Anchor Standards 3, 5, 8, and 11

www.nationalartsstandards.org

*Quoted artists' statements not listed in the reference section result from personal communications with the author (personal communications, 2014–2018).*

## Sewing and Embroidery

Some students will enter class knowing how to sew. For others, it will be their first time threading a needle. Many students have sewing kits in their homes to repair basic tears and replace lost buttons. Through comprehensive instruction, teachers will teach students how the art of sewing moves beyond these basic skills. Students will improve their hand-sewing techniques by watching demonstrations, practicing, and experimenting. They will learn how to operate needles safely and select from different types of threads to bind fabrics together. Teachers might also encourage students to hand-sew buttons and trims (Figure 16.4). Teachers will introduce various embroidery stitches and teach students how to distinguish the qualities of textile products, including when to use fine thread and when to work with coarse yarn. Once students have practiced hand-stitching techniques, they will be ready to move into more complicated textile processes and combine diverse textile media to produce art. For example, the face in Figure 16.5. incorporates different sewing methods and textiles.

FIGURE 16.5 Eliza Alexandra Enache, 8-years-old, Primary School Vasile Conta, Iasi, Romania.
*Source: ICEFA Lidice, 41st Exhibition.*

FIGURE 16.4 Fardeen Ayub Asghar, 4-years-old, The City Kindergarten IV, Karachi, Pakistan.
*Source: ICEFA Lidice, 41st Exhibition.*

## Appliqué

Artists create an **appliqué** by sewing one or more layers of material onto a base layer (Figure 16.6). As an art form, appliqué is similar to a collage. Instead of gluing objects to a surface, artists bind layers of fabrics together through sewing. Some artists use a process called a **reverse appliqué** in which they cut holes into a piece of fabric and then sew a different piece of fabric underneath it. A *mola,* which means "blouse" or "shirt," is an example of a reverse appliqué that has at least two layers of fabric and contains patterned imagery. Teachers will explain that the Kuna people of Panama design molas in reference to their spiritual beliefs (Singer & Spyrou, 2000). Before creating molas, the Kuna had initially painted their bodies in primary colors with images of stylized birds, sea animals, spirits, and people to warn off evil spirits. They switched from painting to producing molas on shirts because of

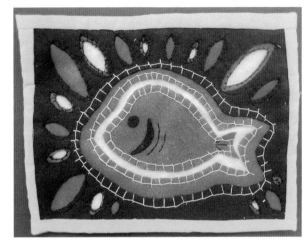

FIGURE 16.6 Emily Avaritt, early adolescent, United States. *Source: Lydia Horvath, teacher.*

FIGURE 16.7 *Sampler Friendship Quilt.* United States, probably Pennsylvania, circa 1860–1880. Textiles; quilts. Pieced, quilted, and embroidered cotton. 75 3/4 × 75 3/4 in. (192.4 × 192.4 cm) LACMA Gift of "To a Friend's House" Project (M.88.68). LACMA Public Domain. *Source: www.lacma.org*

their exposure to European fabrics and embroidery skills. Their designs often incorporate a top layer of red fabric with a contrasting colored fabric underneath. Simple appliqué and mola patterns will be easier to cut and sew for beginners. Students may choose to make a preliminary sketch on paper and transfer their design with chalk to the background fabric. If one is available, teachers can provide an embroidery

ring or a wooden frame to stretch and hold the fabric in place. Students' fabric needs to be taught and free from wrinkles and dimples. Teachers should demonstrate how to leave a 1/4 in. (0.6 cm) seam allowance when they cut out fabric shapes. Teachers will show students how to pin and stitch the fabrics securely in place as they sew.

**Quilting** is the most popular appliqué form and can include both traditional (Figure 16.7) and reverse appliqué processes. Quilters place **batting**, an insulating material, in between the outer layers of fabric to add warmth and soft comfort to their designs. Originally, quilters sewed full-size fabrics together with a running stitch. In the 18th century, quilters developed the **patchwork quilt** method in which they arranged small pieces of varying fabrics in a pleasing design and sewed them together. Highly recognized quilts include Amish quilts, Hawaiian quilts, Underground Railroad quilts, Gee's Bend quilts, and Faith Ringgold's story quilts. Although many people think of quilts as blankets, artists also produce them as wall hangings, rugs, and clothing. Teachers can design learning tasks in which students work on individual quilt squares, collaborate to produce full quilts, and/ or create quilts in hanging and other forms.

## Soft Sculpture

A **soft sculpture** is a three-dimensional artwork that has a soft consistency and is made from materials such as textiles and pliable plastics. Artists produce soft sculptures with traditional sewing techniques, using sculpture methods, and by assembling nontraditional mass-produced objects. Soft sculptures range from small artworks to large-scale installations. For example, Japanese artist Yayoi Kusama creates installations filled with minimalist polka dot patterns that cover all surfaces, including her original soft sculptures as well as wall, ceiling, and floor spaces. American artist Claus Oldenburg and Korean artist Choi Jeong Hwa have formed enormous replications of everyday objects as moveable soft sculptures that inflate and deflate. Students can select from a variety of materials to create soft sculptures. Teachers can demonstrate how to augment soft sculpture designs with paint, permanent markers, and found materials, as well as incorporate Poly-Fil® to add bulk and softness (Figure 16.8).

FIGURE 16.8 Anna Šulcová, 14-years-old, ZUŠ, Blatná, Czech Republic.
*Source: ICEFA Lidice, 42nd Exhibition.*

## Weaving

People create **weavings** by arranging threads in a crossing pattern on a **loom,** a weaving device that holds vertical threads in place so that the horizontal threads can pass through. Looms range from simple handmade devices, such as ones students produce from sturdy paper plates or pieces of cardboard, and manufactured looms that range from small to large pieces of equipment. When weavers tightly wrap yarn around the vertical notches on a loom, they create a **warp.** Teachers often purchase rug yarn for the warp because of its strength. Weavers create a **weft** by moving their yarn across the warp horizontally, from left to right. Depending on the look they desire, they can choose from a variety of yarns, ribbons, fibers, and found objects for weft threads. Some weavers select filler yarn for the weft because it requires fewer rows of weaving than thinner rug yarn. They can also use a thin device called a **shuttle** to roll up excess weft yarn and prevent it from tangling as it passes through the warp. Students can create individual weavings or collaborate with peers to produce larger, more detailed works. They can augment reading assignments with woven bookmarkers and book covers (Figure 16.9) or weave accessories including purses and backpacks (Figure 16.10). For added variety they might design a radial (circle loom) weaving (Figure 16.11). As students create weavings they will study global weaving

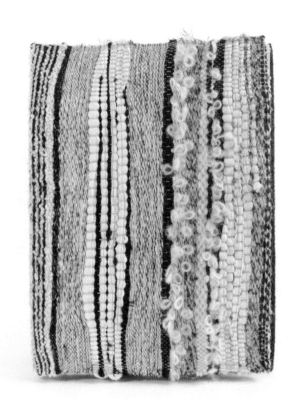

FIGURE 16.9 Gagne Tuče, 12-years-old, Maltas BJC, Malta, Latvia.
*Source: ICEFA Lidice, 44th Exhibition.*

FIGURE 16.10 Group project, 8–12-years-old, Pamatskola, Latvia.
*Source: ICEFA Lidice, 44th Exhibition.*

traditions and make connections to their own works. For example, Navajo mothers pass weaving traditions to their daughters, who learn how to create weavings with intricate geometrical patterns. Male weavers in Ghana produce **kente cloths,** long vertical textiles with vividly colored stripes, to wear on special occasions.

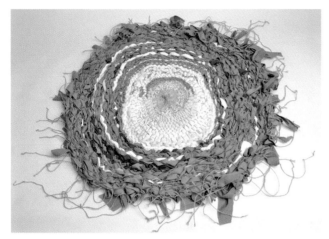

FIGURE 16.11 Bára Zapletalová, 13-years-old, ZUŠ Uherské Hradiště, Uherské Hradiště, Czech Republic.
*Source: ICEFA Lidice, 43rd Exhibition.*

## Tapestries

Since Greek antiquity (300 BCE), artists have created embroidered and woven wall hangings called **tapestries**. They generally differ from traditional weavings in that weavings have a balanced warp and weft. Tapestries conceal the warp threads to emphasize the weft designs. Tapestries are similar to paintings in that they can contain many colors (sections of yarn) and have detailed designs. The Bayeux Tapestry (circa 1082) is an early tapestry that artists created by passing embroidery stitches through a fabric's warp. Tapestries reached their peak during the Middle Ages when Europeans used them to cover and insulate cold, stone castle and cathedral walls. Some of the most recognizable tapestries include the seven-loom woven Unicorn Tapestries (see Figure 16.12). Artists' tapestries can take months to years to complete. For example, Bjørn Nørgaard designed eleven painted tapestry designs that documented Denmark's history for the Queen's Tapestries at Christiansborg Palace. Le Mobilier National et les Manufactures Nationales de Gobelins et de Beauvais required ten years to transform Nørgaard's designs into intricate tapestries (1990–2000). Teachers can bring in an artist-in-residence for students to learn advanced tapestry techniques and utilize its specialized equipment (Figure 16.13). Figure 16.14 presents Emi de Graeve's in-progress tapestry. Its warp threads are white. Its weft's colored yarns hang on tapestry bobbins.

FIGURE 16.12 *The Unicorn in Captivity* (from the Unicorn Tapestries), 1495–1505. Wool warp with wool, silk, silver, and gilt wefts. Overall: 144 7/8 × 99 in. (368 × 251.5 cm). CC0 1.0.
*Source: www.metmuseum.org*

FIGURE 16.13 Belgian artist Emi de Graeve teaches tapestry and weaving skills to students.
*Source: Živé Muzeum Gobelínů.*

FIGURE 16.14 Emi de Graeve, *Anonymous Muse* tapestry in progress.
*Source: Courtesy of the artist.*

FIGURE 16.15 Colin Amos, early adolescent. United States.
*Source: Lydia Horvath, teacher.*

## Yarn Painting

Most people associate painting with brushes. **Yarn painting**, however, does not involve paint or paintbrushes. Instead, artists adhere pieces of yarn to a hard surface in a pleasing design. The Huichol people of Mexico developed yarn paintings in ancient times and continue to make them to express religious beliefs. They place beeswax on top of a board in the sunlight, spread it evenly over the board, and press pieces of yarn into selected surface areas to create their designs. Once the wax cools, it holds the yarn in place. To produce original yarn paintings, students may replicate the original process or substitute school glue for beeswax and work inside to save time and money (Singer & Spyrou, 2000). As an alternative to working on a flat board, students may create a yarn painting on a three-dimensional surface, such as a mask form (Figure 16.15)

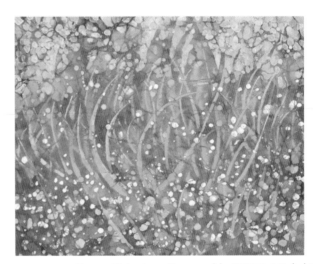

FIGURE 16.16 Darya Kalugina, 9-years-old, GUDO Vitebskii oblastnoi dvorets detei i molodozhi, Vitebsk, Belarus.
*Source: ICEFA Lidice, 46th Exhibition.*

## Batik

**Batik** (meaning "dot") is a wax resist process that artists originally created by applying areas of beeswax to form patterns to decorate textiles. Figure 16.16 shows a flat textile batik, whereas the batik in Figure 16.17 has been transformed into a pillow. Batik most likely originated in China; however, early examples of batik

FIGURE 16.17 Hana Vacková, 7-years-old, ZUŠ, Mladá Boleslav, Czech Republic.
*Source: ICEFA Lidice, 39th Exhibition.*

were also present in Egypt, India, and Japan (Stokoe, 2000). Around the 13th century, batik came to Java. The Javanese improved its production by developing a tool called a **tjanting needle**, which is a wax-releasing pen that produces intricate designs (Figure 16.18). The tjanting needle has a handle, like a paintbrush, and a metal reservoir that stores hot wax. Artists simply lean the tip forward to release the wax from its reservoir onto white fabric (they select white fabric because it reveals the transparent dye colors best). Then, they draw the outlines of their design onto the fabric, covering the areas they want to remain white with wax. This process prevents the dye from pigmenting the fabric beneath the wax. They start with the lightest dye colors and then repeat the waxing and dying process for each additional deeper color they include in their designs (Burch, 2011).

As an alternative to traditional batik processes, some teachers teach students how to create cold batiks using school glue (Dick Blick, 2007). Using a board lined with aluminum foil as a work surface, students will attached a piece of fabric to the board and sketch a batik design with a light-colored watercolor marker. After drawing their design, they will apply a steady stream of glue to produce a solid and even glue line on the marker outlines. When the glue has hardened and formed a relief surface, students will mix two parts acrylic paint with one part textile medium and then paint the areas between the glue outlines with selected colors. For deeper colors, students can paint the backside of their designs with the same colors

FIGURE 16.18 Third-grade students draw with tjanting needles. United States.
*Source: Janet Malone, teacher.*

and allow them to dry. They will remove their fabric from the board and run warm water over the fabric to loosen the glue, using their fingers to peel away any remaining glue lines or pieces of aluminum foil. Some paint color may wash out during the rinse. Students will remove the fabric from the water once the glossy glue has washed out. Students (or teachers) will iron the completed dried batiks.

## UNDERSTANDING AND APPLYING PUPPETS IN CONTEXT

Prehistoric societies used campfires to cast shadow silhouettes of their contorted hands and bodies as puppets to enliven stories and perform as characters. Over time societies created different types of puppets using available resources. When people came in contact with other societies over the millennia, they exchanged techniques for producing and performing with puppets. Puppeteers became skilled in augmenting their performances by developing storylines and adding music, dramatic movements, and distinct character voices. Although many people think of puppets as child's play, history shows that puppet performances have long addressed important societal issues. Teachers can explain to students that puppeteers have used their performances to act out rituals, convey necessary life skills, bring good fortune to their communities, express political and spiritual beliefs, and entertain others. Tribal societies used puppet performances to pass down secrets and guarantee the survival of their clan. In America, the Hopi peoples produced puppets to help grow healthy crops to nourish their families. In Mali, an artist named Mamari Fane (Artists' Lessons to Thrive! 16.2) designed puppets for his community's Bamanan masquerades. Students will learn how adult mentors use puppets and masquerade performances to teach younger generations their cultural traditions. Artists continue to create puppets to teach about survival. For example, contemporary Togolese artist Danaye collaborated with a women's organization to produce an original puppet production that teaches community members about aids prevention (Figure 16.19). Some puppets—including ones that archeologists have discovered in Mexico, Egypt, and China—guided the deceased in the afterlife. Puppets are also vehicles for everyday people to communicate political views. They can be so powerful that different

FIGURE 16.20 Pariksit shadow puppet, *Wayang Kulit* (Before 1914). Java, Indonesia. Tropenmuseum of the Royal Tropical Institute (KIT). Tropenmuseum, part of the National Museum of World Cultures. CC BY-SA 4.0.
*Source: https://hdl.handle.net/20.500.11840/180830*

leaders have tried to ban puppetry because puppeteers could sway disheartened crowds into taking action against oppressors (Blumenthal, 2005).

Certain types of puppets have remained relatively unchanged over the centuries and remain popular today, including abstracted Javanese shadow puppets made from gilded leather (Figure 16.20). Television brought puppets to the forefront of pop culture in the later half of the 20th century (Currell, 2004). Jim

FIGURE 16.19 Danaye, *AIDS! If I Had Known!* Marionette, 1993. Story by Danaye and Members of the Togolese Association of Women Against AIDS (ATFS). Tropenmuseum, part of the National Museum of World Cultures. CC BY-SA 4.0.
*Source: https://hdl.handle.net/20.500.11840/166747*

## Artists' Lessons to Thrive! 16.2 Mamari Fane:
## Sogo Bo Masquerade Traditions

### Big Idea: Tradition

Mamari Fane, a Malian blacksmith, produces puppets for his culture's Bamanan masquerades, which are called *Sogo Bo*. The Bamana is an agricultural community that produces annual masquerades in June that last three nights and two days. The Sogo Bo's activities teach moral stories and pass on cultural traditions. The Bamana use these ceremonies to initiate children into adulthood and to celebrate the harvest. The Sogo Bo masquerades fuse the visual arts with the performing arts through their exquisite array of puppets and masks, which are accompanied by live drumming, dancing, and singing. The puppets and masks appear in the forms of bush animals, people, and spirits. The name *Sogo Bo* means "grass animals coming out from the bush" and references the dry grasses that the

Bamana use to create some of their puppets and masks. For evening performances, the puppets, called *binsogo*, are covered with these traditional grasses. In the daytime, large puppets called *finisogo* appear in the forms of powerful animals and have bodies covered in fabric.

Sigi is a wild buffalo rod puppet consisting of a carved head mounted on a rectangular cuboid framed body draped in cloth (Figure 16.2.1). The fabric frame measures about 6 feet in length (2 m) and conceals three puppeteers underneath. One puppeteer operates Sigi's head. Fane designed Sigi with a sitting monkey chewing a corncob on his head and two birds pecking at food bowls on his horns. Sigi symbolizes a time in Bamanan culture when the animals roamed the lands freely. He is a strong animal that hunters fear. Bamanan puppeteers, dancers, and musicians work in unison to portray his great strength and elegance through slow, majestic movements.

The remaining puppeteers operate smaller rod puppets called *maaninw* (Figures 16.2.2–6.2.4). They are located behind Sigi's head and perform on his back. Most of these characters represent people and animals from everyday life. The *maaninw* wear traditional Malian mud cloths that cover the rods that the puppeteers use to perform their movements. A farmer puppet holds an iron hoe to till the soil. Two women face each other as they grind millet to the beat of the drums. Some of the puppets pay homage to the Bozo, a neighboring fishing society that shares masquerade traditions with the Bamana. A crocodile puppet with a moving snout and tail represents a respected animal from the nearby Niger River. Faaro, a female water spirit puppet with flowing dark hair and large eyes, references Bamana's ancient creation story. She performs next to a patterned canoe puppet that supports two oarsmen and a woman holding a freshly caught fish.

FIGURE 16.2.1 Mamari Fane, *Sigi, Wild Buffalo*, 1994. Tropenmuseum, Part of the National Museum of World Cultures. CC BY-SA 4.0.
*Source: https://hdl.handle.net/20.500.11840/167215*

FIGURE 16.2.2 Mamari Fane, *Grinding Millet,* 1994. Tropenmuseum, Part of the National Museum of World Cultures. CC BY-SA 4.0.
*Source: https://hdl.handle.net/20.500.11840/167273*

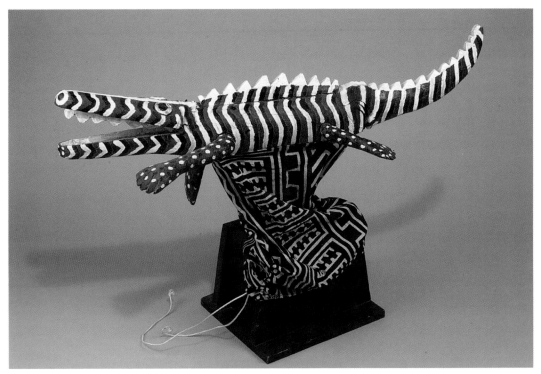

FIGURE 16.2.3 Mamari Fane, *Crocodile,* 1994. Tropenmuseum, Part of the National Museum of World Cultures. CC BY-SA 4.0.
*Source: https://hdl.handle.net/20.500.11840/167274*

FIGURE 16.2.4 Mamari Fane, *Canoe*, 1994. Tropenmuseum, part of the National Museum of World Cultures. CC BY-SA 4.0.
*Source: https://hdl.handle.net/20.500.11840/167277*

The puppeteers remain concealed underneath the buffalo's fabric body throughout the performance. A guide directs their movements by ringing a hand bell and giving them oral cues. The masquerades are passed down from generation to generation. With each new celebration, the Bamana continue to pay homage to their cultural origins and integrate aspects of contemporary life into their performances. Young people learn these art forms and the meaning of their stories from their elders (Arnoldi, 1995; Den Otter, 2015; Du Preez, 2011). Bamanan youth have their own masquerades that prepare them to take leading roles in the Sogo Bo as adults. For example, children who are the offspring of blacksmiths and woodcutters use these experiences to learn how to create puppets from a skilled parent. They also participate in puppet, song, and dance performances.

### Essential/Guiding Questions

1. How do Mamari Fane's puppets contribute to the Sogo Bo?
2. What does the Sogo Bo tell you about Bamanan traditions? How do Bamanan artists and performers share these traditions with youth in their community?

### Preparation

For this group project, students will learn the following contextual information. The Malian Government has taken efforts to preserve its country's rich and historic masquerade traditions due to its significant role in its cultural heritage. However, challenges that can replace and/or change Bamanan traditional ways of living include youth migration to urban areas, limited finances, religion, and access to formal education. Den Otter (2015), an anthropologist who has researched Bamanan masquerades, has also expressed concerns that global tourism for economic profit—which incentivizes producing trivial performances on demand—might eventually reduce or eliminate the symbolic meanings and traditions rooted deep in Bamanan culture. The teacher and students will discuss the meaning of tradition and its role in the Bamanan Sogo Bo. They will brainstorm various ways that people share traditions, as well as the meaning of a loss of tradition.

## Daily Learning Targets

We can create a puppet production about tradition.

- We can create unified puppets with fabric costumes that show effective balance, rhythm, and craftspersonship.
- We can write an original script about tradition. We can integrate performance activities into our production including sound effects, music, dance, and/or a procession to communicate our story.
- We can evaluate the quality of our work and how we communicated the meaning of tradition through our performance.

**National Core Arts Anchor Standards** 2, 6, 9, and 11
www.nationalartsstandards.org

Henson created some of the world's most beloved puppets for *Sesame Street* and *The Muppet Show*. Since 1969, Henson's characters have entertained families and taught children valuable educational skills. In addition to television broadcasts, current technologies have shaped what puppets have become. For example the French performing arts company Royal de Luxe creates international street performances using giant hydraulic-driven marionettes. Their marionettes stand approximately 50 ft high (15.24 m), towering over audiences. Thousands of spectators line the streets to see these giant marionettes in action.

## Puppet Construction

Students can choose from numerous possibilities to perform tales, stories, and social histories with the original puppets they create (Figures 16.21. and 16.22). Comprehensive puppet lessons will teach students about different cultures' puppets and their histories. Teachers might introduce a class to Japanese Bunraku puppet theatre, named after the 18th century puppeteer Uemura Bunrakuken. Bunraku puppets stand about 4 ft tall (1.2 m) and wear traditional Japanese clothing. Their faces have the appearance

of porcelain, as artists layer them with fifteen coats of paint. Puppeteers change the puppets' heads during performances to portray different facial emotions (Kaplin, 2001). Given this information, students may desire to design different heads for their puppet characters. They can create simple puppets by decorating spoons, plates, tag board, and paper bags with markers, paint, textiles, and paper. Teachers can also teach them how to form puppets' figures with papier-mâché and have them sew puppets' costumes as the papier-mâché parts dry to utilize class time effectively.

For more than 1,000 years, Javanese puppeteers, called *dalangs*, have performed wayang kulit performances with **shadow puppets** (Figure 16.20). Dalangs project light onto puppets to produce shadows on a sheet or screen. Becoming a dalang takes years of training. Dalangs are responsible for simultaneously manipulating puppets' movements, narrating a story, and projecting convincing character voices. Students can create shadow puppets by cutting shapes out of sturdy paper and attaching paper binders to join leg and arm segments. They can add emotional impact to their puppet performances by moving puppets closer and further away from the light source to manipulate shadow sizes.

FIGURE 16.21 Réka Helmli, 8-years-old, Kozármislenyi Alapfakú, Kozármisleny, Hungary.
Source: ICEFA Lidice, 40th Exhibition.

FIGURE 16.22 Early childhood students, Czech School Without Borders London, Great Britain.
Source: ICEFA Lidice, 40th Exhibition.

FIGURE 16.23 Elementary group project. ZŠ, Praha 1, Czech Republic.
Source: ICEFA Lidice, 40th Exhibition.

As an alternative puppet construction method, students can form **soft textile hand puppets** using pre-existing textiles including socks, gloves, and sheer stockings. Figure 16.23 shows a collection of puppets created with soft glove bodies and ceramic heads. Students can also cut and sew patterns from fabric to produce original puppets. Kermit the Frog is an advanced hand puppet. Jim Henson modified his design by attaching rods to better control the movement of Kermit's hands during performances. Students will need to leave a 1/2 in. (1.3 cm) seam allowance as they cut and prepare to sew soft textile puppets from fabric. They will also need to check that their designs are large enough to fit their hands. If they are working with sheer stockings, students can knot the stockings into different segments and stuff them with Poly-Fil to create a puppet's body as well as pinch sections of stuffed fabric and sew them in place to form noses, dimples, wrinkles, and lips.

**Marionettes** are puppets operated with strings and a control bar (Figure 16.24). Researchers believe that marionettes evolved from early civilizations' masks with moving jaws that they manipulated with strings. Greek literature suggests that their culture used marionettes as early as 800 BCE. Some ancient religions used marionettes to inspire audiences with awe and wonder as they watched the marionette's "magical" movements. Other cultures banned the use of human actors because they objected to live impersonations. They permitted marionettes as a suitable substitution for human performances. Over the centuries, marionettes remained popular in religious centers, community settings, and aristocrats' private properties. During

FIGURE 16.24 Anna Lajšnerová, 14-years-old, ZŠ Sedmikráska o.p.s., Rožnov pod Radhoštěm, Czech Republic.
*Source: ICEFA Lidice, 44th Exhibition.*

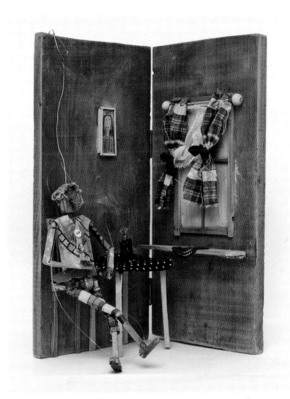

FIGURE 16.25 Hanka Škripeňová, 10-years-old, ZUŠ, Dunajská Lužná, Slovak Republic.
*Source: ICEFA Lidice, 40th Exhibition.*

the 18th century, audiences watched marionette operas set to Mozart's compositions. In the 20th and 21st centuries, marionettes' popularity transferred to television, film, the Internet, and larger-than-life street performances. Like artist Pablo Cano (see Artists' Lessons to Thrive! 1.2 and 7.1), students can combine different techniques, including papier-mâché, soft textiles, and found objects to produce marionettes. They will need to practice manipulating marionettes with control bars before attempting live performances.

## Puppet Stages and Performances

A class can work with pre-made puppet show stages, have a handyperson with a jigsaw construct one from plywood, or create their own using materials such as cardboard, science board, or boxes (Figures 16.25 and 16.26). As necessary, teachers can place a dowel or PVC pipe into cut openings to hang scenes. Another

FIGURE 16.26 Cody Hale, a pre-service teacher, created a puppet stage using a science board. United States.
*Source: Author. teacher.*

option is to select a table, an open doorway, or a space under a classroom loft. Students can tape a piece of fabric or decorated butcher paper over the front of the stage area, cut out a space for the puppets to perform, and design a background setting.

## BEST PRACTICES FOR TEACHING TEXTILES AND PUPPETS FROM PRE-K THROUGH HIGH SCHOOL

Textiles and puppets enable hands-on learning activities that engage students' minds, bodies, and emotions. Teachers can begin comprehensive textile studies by having students identify the many forms of textiles in the daily environment, including those used in clothing and backpacks, and introduce quality textile products from around the world. By analyzing textiles in art history and visual culture in context, students will see how textiles can provide clues about people's tastes, customs, and resources. Their studies can integrate language arts, history, and social studies. As part of the curriculum, students will study global puppet productions and investigate puppeteers' choice of subjects. As they build their knowledge, students will be able to explain how societies have used puppetry to share their beliefs on universal themes that impact humanity. On an emotional level, teachers can encourage students who feel upset or are experiencing dilemmas to work out their thoughts constructively through puppets. They can also show students how to take up textile products such as weaving and sewing when they feel troubled, because these tactile activities offer repetitive kinesthetic actions that can feel therapeutic. The choice-based art curriculum will encourage students to combine sewing techniques, textile production methods, and puppetry with other art processes to make multimedia artworks. For example, the artwork shown in Figure 16.27 blends textiles with painting, and Figure 16.28 shows a weaving created on a ceramic silhouette. Like contemporary artists, students might also create textiles and puppets for installations and special performances. They can utilize technology to present their creations to wider audiences and/or document how they created them.

Teachers should collect fabrics, notions, found objects, and sewing supplies and organize these materials into labeled containers for easy student access. If they are working with a limited budget,

FIGURE 16.27 Group project, 10–14-years-old, La Rosierre Primary School, Mahe, Seychelles.
*Source: ICEFA Lidice, 40th Exhibition.*

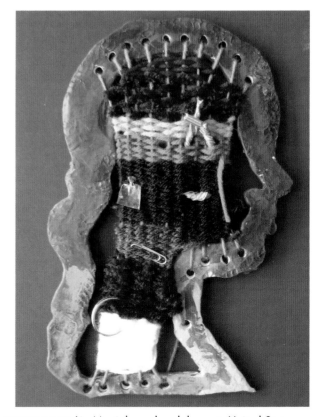

FIGURE 16.28 Liz Maniak, early adolescent. United States.
*Source: Lydia Horvath, teacher.*

teachers might purchase remnant fabrics, repurpose unwanted textile products, and seek donations of supplies. Teachers should make available instructional resources that reinforce textile and puppetry processes. For example, they might draw an illustration on the board that distinguishes a weaving's warp from its weft. They might integrate age-appropriate videos that show contemporary textile artists and puppeteers at work to reinforce production procedures. When introducing textile lessons, teachers will emphasize that needles and scissors are sharp, and will demonstrate how to keep sharp instruments away from body parts. Teachers can show students how to thread a needle with pieces of thread that are no longer than the distance between their hands and elbows when knotted. This makes the thread easier to manage and less likely to tangle. If the class is working with traditional batik processes, teachers will watch that the wax does not become too hot and possibly produce irritating fumes or burns. Teachers will place warning signs next to heating devices to emphasize safety. Reflecting on class instruction, students will review key artists, vocabulary, techniques, and big ideas. If students are creating puppets, teachers can ask them to explain in their own words how quality puppet productions keep audiences' attention and communicate ideas. Teachers will teach students how to plan all aspects of their puppet performances and discuss the importance of all participants contributing to the group's efforts.

Early childhood students want to learn how to manipulate tools and appreciate working with tactile objects. Given these students' inquisitive learning styles, lessons will explain how textile artists and puppeteers make their creations. Teachers will give clear demonstrations so that students can learn new procedures one step at a time. As young children are developing manipulative skills, some may experience difficulties threading a needle and tying a knot. Teachers will assist students so that they learn to achieve these tasks independently. Skilled peers can also help fellow students learn these processes. Students will find it easier to thread blunt **tapestry needles** because they have large eyes. Introductory lessons might have students use tapestry needles to stitch yarn directly on loosely woven materials, such as burlap, or sew on embroidery canvas. In addition to learning how to sew, teachers will teach students how to form their first puppets (Figure 16.29). Young

**FIGURE 16.29** Anna Řeháčková, 5-years-old, ZUŠ, Postoloprty, Czech Republic.
*Source: ICEFA Lidice, 43rd Exhibition.*

children will actively tell stories and listen to other people's tales through puppetry. Teachers can encourage students to manipulate their handmade puppets to tell original stories and perform puppet shows using children's literature as inspiration.

In middle childhood, students have increased hand–eye coordination. Building on their practice in early childhood, students will be able to sew with regular needles and design products using embroidery stitches. They can sew more complex designs, form soft sculptures using hand-batiked fabric (Figure 16.30), and construct puppets with greater detail. They can participate in guided research about different cultures' textile and puppet productions. For example, students can employ art criticism to analyze historical textile artifacts. They can study textiles portrayed in artworks, including paintings and sculptures, as part of aesthetic discussions about these products' functions

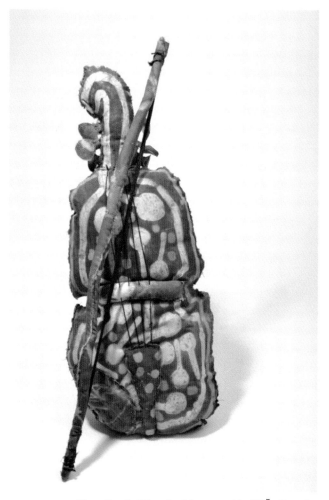

FIGURE 16.30 Veronika Lešáková, 11-years-old, ZUŠ, Postoloprty, Czech Republic.
Source: ICEFA Lidice, 44th Exhibition.

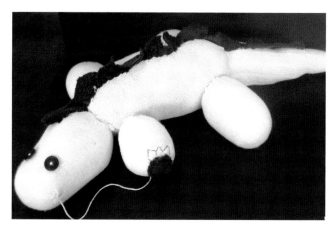

FIGURE 16.31 Madison Littin, early adolescent. United States.
Source: Lydia Horvath, teacher.

and meanings. In middle childhood, students have opinions about what is right and wrong. Teachers can challenge them to brainstorm ideas to produce a puppet show about an ethical decision. They might develop a participatory action research project about overcoming a class struggle through puppetry or textiles. Working as a team, class members can study the qualities of Bamanan masquerades and puppets by Mamari Fane to design a school or community puppet procession focusing on a valuable life skill they learned from an elder.

In early adolescence, students can apply greater concentration skills and dexterity to produce yarn paintings and wax batiks with fine details. Some might prefer forming sculpted yarn paintings as alternatives to working on flat surfaces or designing soft sculptures (Figure 16.31). Students can create individual wax batiks or work together to form a quilt or wall

hanging. Young adolescents write in greater detail, are interested in friendships, and can perform in front of audiences. They can combine these characteristics to generate puppet productions with original puppets, character voices, and narratives about friendship or group identity. For such learning tasks, to promote a broader social base teachers can pair different students together who might not normally interact. Young adolescents can also debate social justice issues that correlate with current topics and trends in the textile industry, including growing green products for textile designs or creating fair working conditions for factory workers (Artists' Lessons to Thrive! 4.1). They can look to Edith Meusnier's installations that focus on sustainability as part of their studies.

Adolescents have a great interest in popular culture. They want to know about contemporary artists and careers in the textile and entertainment industries. Fashion and interior designers have an excellent knowledge of textile design. Professional artists use sewing to make quilts, puppets, and handmade books. Filmmakers commission artists to develop textile products and puppets that enhance movies' storylines and scenery. In addition to studying these examples, students can analyze international clothing advertisements and compare and contrast them to fashions they see in their communities. They can identify the trends and visual qualities that make different fashion designs appealing. Students can also research contemporary puppeteers who create puppets for the entertainment industry, theatre performances, community celebrations, art exhibitions, and for educational purposes and learn how they started their careers and what steps they took to become successful. As adolescents are more socially conscious, they can create puppets and textile products using repurposed materials. For example, they may study Pablo Cano's marionette productions and develop marionettes using recycled and found objects. Figure 16.32 illustrates how weaver Emi de Graeve produces woven designs from bark and plastics. As an alternative, students might select an ideal space and/or object to produce a collaborative yarn bombing.

**FIGURE 16.32** Emi de Graeve creates experimental weavings with wood and plastic in a studio space.

*Source: Courtesy of the artist.*

## OUR JOURNEY TO THRIVE CONTINUES . . .

This chapter described best practices for teaching textile and puppet methods in context. In the next chapter, we will learn about the built environment and the many ways in which it shapes daily life. Students can apply the skills that we teach them about textiles and puppets to recognize the utilitarian and creative functions of these products in a broad range of built environment spaces that include their schools, homes, and communities.

## CHAPTER QUESTIONS AND ACTIVITIES

1. Describe the qualities, functions, and meanings of textiles and puppetry from historic and societal perspectives. How will you integrate textiles and puppetry into the choice-based art curriculum?
2. Practice the diverse textile and puppetry processes described in this chapter to compare and contrast their qualities. Summarize what you learned in a group discussion or in writing.
3. Develop an original comprehensive lesson plan on textile and/or puppetry that focuses on a big idea of your choice. Use the lesson plan template provided on the textbook's companion website and refer to Chapter 2 for more information on lesson plan development. Integrate inquiry tasks inspired by Part III of this textbook.
4. Answer Artists' Lessons to Thrive! 16.1–16.2's essential/guiding questions in written form or as part of a group discussion. Complete their daily learning targets.

## References

Arnoldi, M. J. (1995). *Playing with time: Art and performance in Central Mali.* Bloomington, IN: Indiana University Press.

Blumenthal, E. (2005). *Puppetry: A world history.* New York: Harry N. Abrams.

Burch, P. E. (2011). *How to batik.* Retrieved from www.pburch.net/dyeing/howtobatik.shtml

Carlson, L. (2003). *Queen of inventions: How the sewing machine changed the world.* Brookfield, CT: Millbrook Press.

Currell, D. (2004). *Making and manipulating marionettes.* Marlborough, Wiltshire: The Crowood Press.

Den Otter, E. (2015). *The secret comes forth: The depiction of Bozo and Bamanan animals in Malian puppetry.* Retrieved from www.elisabethdenotter.nl/site1/Homepage_of_Elisabeth_den_Otter/Publications_files/depiction_of_animals_in_Malian_puppetry.pdf

Dick Blick. (2007). *Easy fabric "batik"*. Retrieved from www.dick-blick.com/lesson-plans/easy-fabric-batik-with-glue/

Du Preez, P. (2011). The tall tale of *Tall Horse*: The illusion (or manifestation) of African cultural and traditional aesthetics in hybrid performances. In K. Igweonu (Ed.), *Trends in twenty-first century African theatre and performance* (pp. 139–170). New York: Rodopi.

Eli Whitney Museum and Workshop. (2018). *The cotton gin*. Retrieved from www.eliwhitney.org/new/museum/eli-whitney/cotton-gin

Gillow, J., & Sentance, B. (2005). *World textiles: A visual guide to traditional techniques*. Boston: Bulfinch Press.

Henson, J. (2008). *The Jim Henson Company: Homepage*. Retrieved from www.henson.com/

Kaplin, S. (2001). A puppet tree: A model for the field of puppet theatre. In J. Bell (Ed.), *Puppets, masks, and performing objects* (pp. 18–25). Cambridge, MA: The MIT Press.

Raizman, D. (2004). *History of modern design*. Upper Saddle River, NJ: Prentice Hall.

Singer, M., & Spyrou, M. (2000). *Textile arts: Multicultural traditions*. Worcester, MA: Davis Publications.

Stokoe, S. (2000). *Practical batik: A contemporary approach to a traditional art*. New York: Lorenz Books.

# Chapter 17

# The Built Environment

FIGURE 17.1 Dagnis Timofejevs, 10-years-old, Riga Juglas Vidusskola, Riga, Latvia.
*Source: ICEFA Lidice, 44th Exhibition.*

The **built environment** consists of constructed and open spaces that include architectural structures, landscape design, city planning, streets, interior spaces, earthworks, public monuments, nature preserves, and other areas that are constructed or maintained by humans. Its visual appearance and aesthetic appeal are influenced by the location, people's tastes, and economic factors, including choice of building materials. Building design and its innovations impact people's sense of community and quality of life. The choice-based art curriculum teaches students how to become critical thinkers who investigate topics presented in the built environment. Students will compare and contrast historical and contemporary global built environment trends to develop understandings of the built environment in context. Like built environment professionals, class activities challenge students to find solutions to built environment problems. The real-world learning tasks we develop can plant seeds to inspire future generations of design professionals, including architects, interior decorators, landscape architects, and artists, who will have the potential to make positive changes in the built environment and design spaces that are sustainable and accessible.

We will meet the following objectives by participating in this chapter:

- Describe the built environment and its qualities, functions, and meanings in society.
- Identify best practices for teaching the built environment.
- Create instructional resources for teaching the built environment.

Spotlight on Student Art #17 (Figure 17.1) presents a glass-fused sculpture created in response to a school

fire. It demonstrates how students can create artworks that depict real events related to the built environment.

## UNDERSTANDING THE BUILT ENVIRONMENT IN CONTEXT

Built-environment structures appear in children's artworks beginning at young ages and are an integral part of their play. Children play with dollhouses and in tree houses, hide under makeshift tents, sculpt sandcastles, and construct with building blocks. The choice-based curriculum will expand students' existing awareness of the built environment to teach them about its history and functions. For example, scholars believe that humans began constructing rounded housing structures, similar to bird nests, because they were easier to build with their hands and basic tools and required fewer natural resources (Bartuska, 2007; Moffett, Fazio, & Wodenhouse, 2004). The earliest known housing fragments appear approximately 400,000 years ago in France, where humans erected homes from branches as an alternative to dwelling in protective caves. A more complete example dates to 14,000 BCE, when hunter-gatherers in Europe assembled shelters from mammoth bones and leather hides.

### Spotlight on Student Art #17

### Big Idea: Shelter

Buildings provide people with shelter and make them feel safe. When structures become damaged and unstable they no longer protect people the way they were designed to. Dagnis, a 10-year-old student from Latvia, created a fused glass (kiln-formed glass) artwork representing his three-story school building (Figure 17.1). This artwork brings to life the concerns that he and his classmates must have felt when their school's roof caught fire due to combustible roofing material. Fortunately, the 1,312' (400 meter) fire was contained on the roof and all 155 occupants, mostly schoolchildren, evacuated the building safely.

The young artist carefully arranged multiple pieces of cut glass to form the built environment structure. The kiln's heat bonded the artwork's stacked pieces of glass together to create its distinct architectural features and flames. The kiln firing also added a handcrafted touch to the artwork by producing slightly rounded edges and small surface bubbles on the glass school structure. Using a tap fuse design, Dagnis' work was fired in a kiln at a low temperature (about 1,350 °F/732 °C) so that its different pieces of glass would fuse together to create relief areas on the artwork's windows, roof, and flames. To emphasize the emotional impact of the experience, Dagnis applied colored frit (pigmented glass powder) to make the roof's red, orange, and yellow flames the focal point of his school building. These jagged flames contrast against the building's calming linear features.

Some contemporary cultures have retained early building styles such as the Sami lavvu and Mongolian yurt. Figure 17.2 presents a student's rendering of activities within a yurt's rounded interior.

With the development of agriculture, people had the luxury of staying in one location and developing larger communities. The oldest known ancient urban community is Jericho (in present-day Israel), where in 8,000 BCE humans constructed a walled community filled with huts. Another ancient example is the Catal Hüyük settlement in present-day central Turkey (6,500 to 5,700 BCE), which contained mud-brick homes with conjoined walls that formed an exterior barrier to protect its residents. Although at that time Europeans had not yet developed urban centers, they transported and transformed heavy boulders and stones called **megaliths** (*megalyth* means "great stone") to form burial chambers as well as mark astrological occurrences for their calendars and religious purposes. Stonehenge (2,900 to 1,400 BCE) remains the best-known megalith. Its builders used basic tools and collaborative efforts to stand stone pillars that weigh up to 20,000 tons (18,143.7 Mg) each in a symbolic design. Similarly, Easter Island Polynesian settlers (from 500 to 1650 CE) carved volcanic stone into *moai* that weighed as much as 100 tons (907 kg) each and stood up to 40 feet (12 m). These abstracted human figures with oversized heads and angular jawlines represent ancestral chiefs who served as intermediaries between the living and the spiritual worlds.

From these innovative concepts and designs, humans developed the field of **architecture**, the art and design of buildings that takes into consideration mathematical, scientific, and aesthetic principles to create structurally sound buildings. The oldest surviving architecture book comes from the Roman architect Vitruvius, who practiced architecture in the 1st century CE; however, many great architectural structures dated centuries before the common era (Moffett et al., 2004). Significant architectural structures that have survived the centuries include Egyptian pyramids (circa 3200 BCE), the Parthenon in Greece (447–432 BCE), the Roman Coliseum (70–80 CE), the Great Wall of China (7th century BCE–16th century CE), Chartres Cathedral (mostly 13th century), Mesoamerican pyramids (1497 CE), and the Taj Mahal (1632–1653 CE). In addition to historic works, students can study prominent contemporary architectural structures such as Frank Gehry's (1997) Guggenheim Bilbao Museo in Spain. They can also examine how artists utilize historic and contemporary built environment works to communicate meaning. Figure 17.3 presents a still from Kimsooja's *Migrateurs* performance, for which she traveled on a bottari truck towards Place de la Bastille's July Column (1835–1840 CE), a monument commemorating the French Revolution that signifies freedom from oppression. (See Artists' Lessons to Thrive! 10.2 for more information on Kimsooja.)

Architects design buildings and structures to suit particular purposes, spaces, budgets, and community or client wishes using styles and materials ranging from the traditional to contemporary to dictate the look,

FIGURE 17.2 Tsengelbayar Mendsaikhan, 16-years-old, National Laboratory Secondary School No. 1, Khentii Province, Mongolia.
*Source: ICEFA Lidice, 44th Exhibition.*

FIGURE 17.3 Kimsooja, *Migrateurs*, 2007, bottari truck, performance/single channel video, 10:00, loop, silent.
*Source: Courtesy of Kimsooja Studio; www.kimsooja.com*

space, and flow of their work. They utilize software programs to create architectural designs and commission three-dimensional models of their proposed designs to give clients realistic views of what their finished products would look like. The best architectural structures have a pleasing design and are built to last. While a single architect may work alone on a small project, groups of architects and designers collaborate in teams to design large-scale projects. Team members contribute to the overall design by applying their diversified specializations. For example, a team of architects, interior designers, landscape architects, and other professionals specializing is sustainable design would work together to design all components of an eco-friendly school with features that include sustainable building materials, solar panels, energy efficient insulation, and a roof garden. Karen L. Braitmayer (Artists' Lessons to Thrive! 17.1) collaborates with fellow built-environment professionals to create accessible spaces for all people to navigate. Students studying her designs learn to differentiate between accessible and non-accessible spaces and explain how accessible designs improve people's quality of life.

After architects and designers have produced their final designs, they collaborate with contractors and construction workers (Figure 17.4), who build the architects' buildings. Contractors and carpenters work with detailed, two-dimensional design plans in

FIGURE 17.5 Photo by Solveig Hisdal, Oleana©.
Source: https://en.oleana.no

FIGURE 17.4 Nikita Golozov, 13-years-old, MOU DOD Deskaya khudozhestvenaya shkola No. 3 im. E. V. Gurova, Omsk, Russia.
Source: ICEFA Lidice, 39th Exhibition.

FIGURE 17.6 Isidor Canevale, architect and Johann Georg Leithner, carver. Boiserie from the Palais Paar, 30 Wollzeile, Vienna, Austria, circa 1765–1772, with later additions. Carved, painted, and gilded pine; plaster; gilt bronze; mirror glass; oak flooring. CC0 1.0.
Source: www.metmuseum.org

printed form or high-resolution digital files that precisely transform an architect's design into functional three-dimensional spaces.

Whereas architecture focuses on a building's structure, **interior design** is the aesthetic and purposeful arrangement of objects within the space of a built environment. Interior designers plan for space efficiency, function, and comfort levels. They make effective design decisions by determining how to utilize the space available within an architectural structure best. Interior designers collaborate with construction workers, electricians, upholsterers, and artists to make

their designs a reality. They prepare formal presentations of their proposed designs for clients with the aid of computer technologies and display boards that may include lighting choices, fabrics, pictures of furniture, artworks, paint chips, flooring samples, and a **floor plan**, a scaled drawing or computer-generated plan of a single room or an entire building. This process allows clients and interior designers to make necessary changes to the designs before implementation. Students can compare and contrast how the design of the rooms shown in Figures 17.5. and 17.6 impact the rooms' functions and feelings.

## Artists' Lessons to Thrive! 17.1 Karen L. Braitmayer: Invisible Accessible Design

### Big Idea: Accessibility

Seattle-based architect Karen L. Braitmayer's passion for crafting and constructing began in her childhood. A career aptitude test identified her ability to visualize three-dimensional spaces and guided her to pursue a Master of Architecture Degree. When Braitmayer was working as a general architect, fellow colleagues repeatedly approached her for advice on how to design accessible spaces for people utilizing wheelchairs, given her architecture expertise and lifelong experience using a wheelchair. Braitmayer's interest in accessibility design burgeoned and she became an expert on the laws and guidelines relating to developing accessible spaces (Figure 17.1.1). In 1993, she co-founded Studio Pacifica, where her work has since focused on providing consultation and design services to clients in the public and private sectors. Her career achievements include shaping Washington's State Accessibility Code and being appointed by President Barack Obama to the U.S. Access Board to lead the nation in setting accessible design standards in compliance with the Americans with Disabilities Act and other guiding laws.

Braitmayer's work as an architect, consultant, and advocate teaches people to become more aware of the spaces they inhabit and the role of the built environment in daily life. She explained that most built environments are designed for the average male between the ages of 25 and 32. The physical dimensions of built-environment structures and the placement of countertops, sinks, and light fixtures suit the average man's physical stature and abilities. These "standard" designs do not take into account children's smaller body proportions, people moving in wheelchairs, women, the elderly (whose bodies begin to decline), and people with other impairments. Braitmayer collaborates with fellow built-environment specialists to design spaces that are suited for all people. Her designed spaces enable people to share the same natural flow of movement. In this regard, Braitmayer describes her work as having a sense of invisibility. "We would like a project to look useable to everyone without any segregation or specialized design. Rather than thinking that is where the wheelchair goes, that is where EVERYONE goes! Everyone is able to follow the same path." The only obvious clues to Braitmayer's invisible designs is signage, including signs that indicate family-friendly restrooms with adequate space, privacy, and support for people who use wheelchairs, the elderly, and parents with young children.

FIGURE 17.1.1 Karen L. Braitmayer, project, Magnolia Mid Mod; owner, Erskine/ Braitmayer; architect, Rom Architecture, and photographer, Kathryn Barnard.
*Source: Courtesy of the architect; studiopacificaseattle.com.*

Through her work, Braitmayer has made unseen and unnoticed injustices relating to the built environment visible by advocating for what is right, working to implement better laws, and creating socially and physically accessible environments for all. She is a strong activist who volunteers and mentors young people about accessibility and the built environment. She organizes workshops that teach students with disabilities about career possibilities in design and encourages them to seek out architectural training camps and college design programs.

## Essential/Guiding Questions

1. What qualities make Braitmayer's accessible design spaces appear "invisible?"
2. In your opinion, why do built-environment specialists typically design spaces for only one type of person? How does accessible design move beyond this practice?

## Preparation

Students will identify spaces in their homes and the community that are accessible and ones that are not. They will brainstorm possible strategies to make non-accessible spaces accessible.

## Daily Learning Targets

I can create an artwork that teaches about accessibility in the built environment.

- I can select the most effective medium and design elements to communicate my idea.
- I can create an artwork that demonstrates craftspersonship and unity.
- I can explain the meaning of my artwork and identify the ways that it can augment people's understandings of the need for accessible spaces in the built environment.

**National Core Arts Anchor Standards** 2, 4, 8, and 11

www.nationalartsstandards.org

*Quoted artists' statements not listed in the reference section result from personal communications with the author (personal communications, 2014–2018).*

FIGURE 17.8 David Patchen, *Gold Bloom,* blown glass, 23 × 18 × 10 in. (58.42 × 45.72 × 25.4 cm).
*Source: Courtesy of the artist; www.davidpatchen.com.*

FIGURE 17.7 Michael Špitálský, 10-years-old, DDM Praha 2, Výtvarná dílna Vinohrady, Praha 2, Czech Republic.
*Source: ICEFA Lidice, 40th Exhibition.*

Interior designers combine all of the visual arts to develop functional and decorative spaces. For example, societies initially created ceramic pots and bowls to store food and later used ceramics to produce planters, sinks, and other items for the home. Weaving led to the development of pillows, rugs, curtains, tapestries, and baskets. Furniture builders design products with wood, stone, metal, plastic, and textiles to accommodate interior and exterior spaces. Figure 17.7 shows how a student transformed an ordinary chair into a giraffe to give its design added appeal. It is an ideal furniture piece for a jungle-themed classroom learning center. Artistic accessories enhance the feel of public and private spaces. Interior decorators augment bare walls and spaces with artists' stretched canvases, framed art, scenic murals, tapestries, hanging fountains, and sculptures. Artists' Lessons to Thrive! 17.2 teaches about Merete Rein's production of functional glass sculptures for use within the built environment. She designs artworks that make people feel cozy within the spaces they inhabit. David Patchen designs decorative glass sculptures for display in interior spaces (Figure 17.8). His colorfully patterned *Bloom* designs promote a sense of visual elegance with their organic forms and smooth textures.

 **Artists' Lessons to Thrive! 17.2 Merete Rein: Hand-Blown Glass and the Comforts of Daily Life**

**Big Idea: Cozy**

Norwegian glassblower Merete Rein creates decorative and functional glass sculptures that include ornaments, candleholders, drinking glasses, and bowls. For her portfolio and website, she uses photography to reference her works' organic forms by surrounding them with snow, fjords, and

FIGURE 17.2.1 Merete Rein, *Bowls,* glass.
*Photo: Trond Are Berge.*

ferns. The organic qualities of Rein's artworks bring a sense of the outdoors and nature into built environment spaces. People cherish the soothing sensations and atmospheres that her products exude. The experiences they generate reference a Norwegian concept called *koselig,* which has a similar meaning to "cozy." People achieve *koselig* when objects, environments, moments, and close friends and family come together. *Koselig* moves beyond cozy in that the term encompasses one's full senses, feelings of pleasure, and overall well-being. Walking into Rein's rustic red wooden studio and shop provides visitors with a sense of *koselig.* Vibrant glass sculptures fill bright white shelves that invite people to touch the sculptures carefully and to hold them close. At a window, glass shelving showcases Rein's sculptures against a picturesque fjord view.

In a separate space, visitors can look down into Rein's studio and watch her in action as she creates glass forms using a free-blowing method. Powerful furnaces produce bright orange 2,000 °F (1,093 °C) molten glass. Seeing Rein working in close contact with molten forms and furnaces shows visitors just how hot and dangerous her work can be. The artist gathers a thick mass of molten glass she has just prepared and utilizes a process called *inflation* to blow through a blowpipe and expand the molten glass figure. She repeats the processes of blowing, rolling, and reheating the molten glass to create her desired form. She adds decorative features and a flat base as necessary. Once she has created a final product, Rein cools the glass object slowly in a lehr furnace to maintain even levels of heat and avoid shattering.

Her artworks, simply titled *Bowls*, are organic spheres that reference the look and feel of Norway's ice and bodies of flowing water (Figure 17.2.1). The artist prefers creating small, intimate sculptures. Large-scale works require glass artists to work in large teams. Rein explained that her small-scale design philosophy is typical Norwegian, meaning that many people in her culture favor simple, less cumbersome objects. The artist mostly works alone in her studio; however, her husband assists her with processes that require additional hands. Rein's great efforts result in beautiful, sensuous products. People who purchase her glass art for their homes or receive them as gifts add a touch of *koselig* to their lives by making their environments and moments in time all the more special.

## Essential/Guiding Questions

1. Which influences shape Rein's design philosophy?
2. In your opinion, why would people want and need to experience *koselig* in their lives?

## Preparation

Students will discuss Rein's art and the meaning of *koselig*. They will provide examples of times in their lives when they experienced such feelings.

## Daily Learning Targets

I can create an artwork about *koselig* to enhance a particular built environment space.

- I can select the medium of my choice to design my artwork.
- I can create a unified design that demonstrates craftspersonship.
- I can explain how my design correlates with the concept of *koselig*.

**National Core Arts Anchor Standards** 1, 6, 7, and 10

www.nationalartsstandards.org

**Landscape architecture** is a field of design that unifies nature and architectural structures to enhance, beautify, preserve and/or rehabilitate external environments, including parks, gardens, trails, and playgrounds. Like architects and interior designers, landscape architects have a solid knowledge of design and planning skills, and they compliment these skills with their knowledge of plants, water structures, and other products to enhance a landscape by including decks, patios, gazebos, fountains, bike trails, and walkways. Figure 17.9 shows a student's representation of how people and a pet use a pathway in a park setting. Landscape architects sometimes alter the land by excavating and elevating the ground to

FIGURE 17.9 Alina Gontova, 11-years-old, MAOUDOD Tsentr detskogo tvorchestva, Birobidjan, Russia.
*Source: ICEFA Lidice. 45th Exhibition.*

suit their design needs. This process dates back thousands of years, as exemplified by Native American ceremonial mounds. Unlike most artworks, which are typically static, a landscape is in a constant state of fluctuation as it is impacted by weather conditions and growth patterns. Students can readily imagine how plants may wilt without a sprinkler system and weeds may take over a flowerbed if gardeners do not remove them. Because of nature's dynamic qualities, the best landscape architects have hands-on experience working with plants, know their growth habits, understand their pruning needs, and can explain all aspects of the project to the crew who installs and maintains their sites.

## APPLYING STEAM TO TEACH THE BUILT ENVIRONMENT IN CONTEXT

Built-environment specialists apply STEAM concepts to produce creative and innovative designs suited for particular functions and behaviors. Students will investigate, analyze, and interpret meanings associated with the built environment as presented through the study of architecture, interior design, landscape architecture, earthworks, monuments, public artworks, and community spaces. Educator John Dewey (1934) identified how societies do not always put forth full efforts to design built environments, even though they have the technical capacity to produce excellent designs and have access to quality building materials. His criticism serves as a worthy class inquiry topic about why a society may not always use its best intellectual resources and materials to construct healthier environments for all people. For example, built communities can discourage people from living physically active lifestyles. Developers might design spaces for cars without considering pedestrians' and cyclists' needs. As regular practice, some developers have built new communities and shopping plazas, while leaving older ones empty and rundown. Urban sprawl can result in economic hopelessness, crime, segregation, loss of health care, financial insecurity, and fewer job opportunities (Bartuska, 2007; Hughey, Speer, & Peterson, 1999; Lippard, 1997; Longo, 2007; Maziak, Ward, & Stockton, 2007; National Institute of Environmental Health Sciences, 2004).

Healthy communities are places where residents care about fellow inhabitants' well-being and provide substantial resources to meet community needs, including public safety, health care, educational opportunities, cultural events, family support, and open recreational spaces. They offer residents access to safe walkways, bike paths, natural resources, the arts, and quality food choices that lead to better health (Figure 17.10). Teachers can explain to students that at their best, architects, interior designers, landscape architects, and artists design the built environment to aid quality of life. Well-planned and maintained built environments promote a healthy sense of community in which people learn, develop, and share experiences. Having learned how reflective glass on buildings kill up to a billion birds annually in the United States alone, some architects are designing bird-safe buildings (American Bird Conservatory, 2015). For example, they construct buildings using fritted glass with ceramic dots or stripes that give the glass an opaque appearance, which reduces fatal bird collisions. Students can also contemplate Artists' Lessons to Thrive! 7.3 on Maya Lin and how she shaped the earth to form the Vietnam Veterans Memorial. As visitors physically move into the memorial, they are reflected onto the names of fallen soldiers—building a connection between the past and present. Additionally, students can look to Artists' Lessons to Thrive! 17.3, which presents Martin Homola's photographs documenting a reconstructed Czech landscape that had been annihilated by war. His example teaches students about the importance of reconstruction and survivors' forgiveness.

FIGURE 17.10 Derick Ma, 13-years-old, Linda Yorba, United States. *Source: ICEFA Lidice, 42nd Exhibition.*

On a cold, damp November morning, photographer Martin Homola traversed the Lidice Memorial grounds in the Czech Republic to photograph a story that he needed to tell. In preparation, Homola reflected on the site's history. He selected black-and-white photography and chose a foggy day with frost-covered fields to capture the mood he had envisioned. These decisions resulted in a collection of photographs that illustrate the Lidice Memorial's landscape, veiled in a gray mist and speckled with the ruins of stone foundations and deep-rooted trees (Figure 17.3.1). Homola's opaque photographs feel stark and lonely, yet render a sense of grace and elegance. After spending six hours crossing expansive fields of ice-coated terrain, Homola's feet felt "terribly frozen." The artist's discomfort extended beyond the physical. He explained: "even though 73 years have passed, it is still painfully alive."

Homola was referring to World War II events. On June 10, 1942, the Nazi regime ordered the complete annihilation of the Lidice village in retaliation for a fatal attack on one of its high-ranking officers. Lidice villagers were falsely accused of the assault because two of its residents served in the British resistance that fought against the Nazis. With the intention of erasing the village from history, Lidice's 102 homes and its school, church, and cemetery were set on fire. The Nazis blew up and bulldozed all that remained after the horrific blaze. Most tragically, they massacred 340 of its 500 residents. This included 82 of Lidice's children.

Hearing of the village's destruction, Sir Barnett Stross, a British politician, physician, and arts patron, coined the term "Lidice shall live!" After the war, he raised money to erect a new Lidice village that included a memorial and a rose garden that would be a place of peace for all of humanity. Under the direction of Czech architect František Marek, the community constructed 150 new homes for Lidice's survivors.

When he began this three-year project, Homola had been closely connected with the Lidice Memorial through his freelance work photographing its grounds, events, and annual ICEFA Lidice exhibitions. The Lidice massacre's 75th anniversary was approaching and Homola wanted to document the survivors' stories. He knew that time was of the essence due to their advanced ages. He chronicled portraits of the survivors in their present homes to show how they lived. He also took them back to the sites of their childhood homes on the memorial grounds. In Figure 17.3.2, Homola photographed Eva Bullock (who had emigrated to Canada in 1948) pointing to the location where her family home once stood. She was only five-years-old when her father was executed, her house was destroyed, and her mother was sent to a concentration camp with other women from Lidice. Looking at the land that marked her former home, Bullock explained: "I feel my roots here. And although everything was destroyed and there's only grass, there's still life thanks to nature" (Homola, 2018, p. 52). For the photograph shown in Figure 17.3.3, childhood neighbors Milada Cábová and Marie Šupiková demonstrated to Homola how they used to talk to each other at the fence line that once divided their homes.

Reflecting on his work and deep personal connections with the survivors, Homola noticed how his perceptions of the Lidice Memorial transformed from considering it as a place of sadness to seeing it as a site that represents the strength, courage, and power of forgiveness. Through his photographs, Homola brings to light the survivors' courage and asks us to recognize how they have shown true humanity by forgiving those who harmed them and their loved ones. Homola described how, as ambassadors of goodwill, Lidice's survivors met with German students at the memorial many decades after the war and explained to them: "if we can admit it [the atrocity] [happened] and become friends there is a chance that history, hatred, xenophobia and racism will not be repeated." New generations

FIGURE 17.3.1 Martin Homola, *Landscape of Pain: Horák Farmhouse Remains*.

Source: Courtesy of the artist; www.abcphoto.cz.

FIGURE 17.3.2 Martin Homola, *My Home: Testimony of Portrait, Eva Bullock*.

Source: Courtesy of the artist; http://www.abcphoto.cz.

FIGURE 17.3.3 Martin Homola, *My Home: Testimony of Portrait, Milada Cábová and Marie Šupiková*.

Source: Courtesy of the artist; http://www.abcphoto.cz.

will continue to learn about Lidice thanks to the diligent efforts of the many people who helped to rebuild some of what was lost, preserved Lidice's memories, and demonstrated that kindness prevails.

## Essential/Guiding Questions

1. What mood has Homola presented through his series of photographs about the landscape of the Lidice Memorial and its survivors? How did he capture his thoughts and feelings about the site's history and its people through his camera?
2. Why was reconstructing Lidice necessary? In which ways can reconstruction help people forgive?

## Preparation

The class will identify the meanings of Homola's photographs through art inquiry. Teachers and students will discuss the impact of war on people, nature, and the built environment. If teachers are working with younger students, they will simplify and soften the details about war by gently explaining how war hurts people and the places in which they live. Older, more mature students can delve into deeper historical content about the Lidice Memorial.

## Researching and Planning for the Built Environment

Research and planning play significant roles in the design of built environments. Built-environment professionals learn clients' needs, examine sites, conduct research, analyze statistical data, acquire applicable technological skills, and select appropriate resources and materials to suit projects' requirements and budgets. They make estimates and predictions, plan structural designs, and assess and reassess products and ideas before implementing final designs. Applying the practices of built-environment professionals, students will learn to do the following:

- Recognize structures in the built environment and analyze their designed spaces according to their functions.
- Name construction methods, parts, structures, and materials.
- Identify key features, textures, supplies, and lighting sources within built spaces.
- Study the life span and/or durability of products.
- Understand how different parts come together to form unified products.
- Apply research methodologies to plan built environment spaces by posing questions, collecting data, making interpretations, and sharing their findings with others.

The choice-based art curriculum integrates concepts about functional design, historical preservation, sustainable design, and managing (sub)urban sprawl. Students can contemplate how built-environment spaces accommodate or impede physical, emotional, professional, educational, and social needs. Considering people's responses to the built environment assists designers in bettering their products (Lee & Breitenberg, 2010; Pizarro, 2009). With this in mind, students can document their sensory perceptions within the built environment by recording the sights they see and sounds they hear, writing down the smells they notice, and describing the tactile feel of materials.

A review of architectural structures and their interiors can reveal how the best-designed interior spaces complement architectural structures. Students can begin by generating relevant images and literary sources to guide their studies. Depending on students' ages and abilities, they may complete this work independently or with teacher assistance. Learning tasks include:

- selecting images of quality built environments;
- acquiring literature from local resources, including newspapers, magazines, commercials, real estate booklets, and the news;
- taking digital pictures, making video clips, and producing sketches;
- collecting floor plans, satellite images, maps, street photographs, and illustrations;
- comparing and contrasting aerial views of land that reveal changes in development (students can apply them to estimate the proportions of built and natural spaces and/or study loss of natural habitat as development occurred);
- identifying how climate and environmental conditions impact built-environment designs;

- studying the characteristics of built-environment advertisements, which may be persuasive and/or biased due to the nature of their publication;
- obtaining data from city hall to learn historical facts and statistics;
- assembling data from professional websites (i.e. built-environment associations and architectural firms) that present current trends and issues in design concepts and provide biographical information about leading built environment professionals; and
- research how globalization and technologies impact community design.

Students' communities can serve as springboards to understand trends and issues relating to the built environment (Argiro, 2004). They will learn that built-environment specialists sometimes combine traditional styles in their communities with global ones to form hybrid designs (Anderson, 2004). People's access to visual images has resulted in built-environment designs moving further away from communities' unique styles. Students can brainstorm the qualities that make a community unique and contemplate how outside influences may have impacted local designs. Teachers can show historical examples of the built environment and have students make comparisons between the styles they see today.

Students benefit from meeting with built-environment experts and asking them questions about their work. Adolescents might participate in field studies to learn the realities of built-environment professions. Given adult supervision, students can interview people related to particular locations, including residents, visitors, and people responsible for maintaining spaces. When students develop personally-driven questions they begin to make real-world connections that build enduring understandings. This process also builds students' communication and interpersonal skills. Teachers will need to assess students' interview questions beforehand to ensure that they ask safe and fair questions. Based on their interviews and observations, students can determine how locations have particular meanings given people's associations with them.

After students have asked questions, collected data, and conducted a review of literature, they can use their research journals to organize their thoughts, review key information, make personal reflections, and determine if there is any additional information they need to collect. Once they have analyzed their data, they will create related art projects, presentations, and other resources to disseminate what they have learned. For example, Figure 17.11 portrays a student artwork showing an aerial view of the land from the perspective of skydivers. The student's built-environment design shown in Figure 17.12 simultaneously depicts highrises, roads, and natural spaces. Along with these finished products student creators could prepare reports that include factual information and interview quotes about these sites to accompany their art presentations.

FIGURE 17.11 Tulqin Ziyodullayev, 15-years-old, Republic Specialized Academic Licey of Music and Art, Tashkent, Uzbekistan.
*Source: 4ICEFA Lidice, 5th Exhibition.*

## Art Production, Design, and the Built Environment

Some STEAM lessons have students construct models that teach balance and size relationships—including height, length, volume, weight, and proportions—but lack creative design. The visual arts open pathways for students to acquire these skills while developing understandings about how and why built environment professionals make design choices that are practical and aesthetically pleasing. As curricular inspirations, teachers can look to visual arts performance standards and ones in other subjects as well as the UNESCO International Years and Decades that bring global awareness to STEAM topics that relate to humanity's usage, preservations, and protection of built and natural spaces. Through the choice-based art curriculum students can produce products inspired by built environments using an array of art media and two- and three-dimensional design processes. Built-environment specialists, artists, natural environments, and content in visual culture may influence students' creative designs. Students might create artworks with moving parts such as mobiles and popup books focusing on their built-environment studies. Learning tasks can have students work with rulers and grids to produce projects to scale. Students can construct real and imagined model built-environment spaces using clay, papier-mâché, foam board, cardboard, and other materials. Students can work individually and in groups to build environments such as a residential dwelling, city block, town, or playground. Figure 17.13 presents students' ceramic interpretations of decorative manhole covers. Students might also represent the built environment through dioramas and assemblages.

Students will learn that communities sometimes allocate 1% of a building project's budget towards funding public artworks. As part of the choice-based art curriculum, students can research issues related to public art and the built environment. They might calculate the costs of public artworks, as well as participate in class debates and/or write position papers that identify if art experts and/or citizens should have a say in selecting public artworks and whether a public artwork should always satisfy the majority of the population. This is necessary because some artworks have been controversial and removed from public sites because the greater public did not appreciate artists' and patrons' tastes. Given what they have learned, students can design school and community installations. For example, Figure 17.14 shows a mock hanging chandelier made from repurposed water bottles and paint, influenced by Dale Chihuly's blown-glass sculptures. Teachers might also collaborate with students and community experts to develop community art projects that enhance the built environment, including painted and mosaicked wall murals, sustainable school gardens, and installed sculptures. Community art projects assist children in taking shared ownership of their schools and communities and feeling positive about their group accomplishments.

FIGURE 17.14 Elementary students. United States.
*Source: Janet Malone, teacher.*

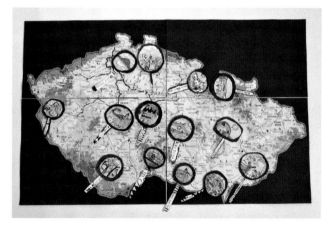

FIGURE 17.15 Group project, 7–11-years-old, Studio Experiment z.s., Olomouc, Czech Republic.
*Source: ICEFA Lidice, 45th Exhibition.*

**Mapping** is a learning task in which students use existing maps and/or develop their own maps to identify features and topics within the built environment (Figure 17.15). Teachers and students will collect maps and use the images they assembled of places within a community. Teachers will reinforce that people sometimes have dissimilar experiences about the same places

(Dennis, Gaulocher, Carpiano, & Brown, 2009; Hicks & King, 1999; Powell, 2008). Class members exploring the same locations may feel differently about the sites based on their life experiences. Perhaps one student might have a positive view of a location for sentimental reasons, while another may feel indifferent or have negative feelings about it. All student perspectives should be respected. When students are ready to create, they can write on, collage, and decorate maps to identify information (i.e. community spaces, safety and danger zones, and ideal places for bike riding). Preliminary mapping tasks can inspire students to create further artistic works based on what they have learned. As extension mapping activities, students can also develop small- and large-scale participatory action research projects. For example, mapping can become a tool for students to make a classroom design more efficient by rearranging furniture, decorating the room, and developing learning centers based on their needs and interests. To produce large-scale, service learning mapping projects, students might collaborate with a transdisciplinary team of adult professionals to determine how child-friendly or accessible a community's built environment is and take action to improve it. Transdisciplinary teammates can give their expert opinions about the built environment and use their combined knowledge to improve the quality of a particular space.

## BEST PRACTICES FOR TEACHING THE BUILT ENVIRONMENT FROM PRE-K THROUGH HIGH SCHOOL

Best practices for studying the built environment extend beyond memorizing names, dates, and styles. Students learn to make personal connections as they study the built environment in context. Class inquiry tasks involving aesthetics, art criticism, art history, and visual culture encourage students to slow down and notice details, similarities, and differences in local and global built environment spaces. Students learn to identify built-environment functions and designs, including size relationships and selection of materials. Art production tasks about the built environment are tools to augment students' spatial reasoning skills and understandings of geometric modeling. When they have become aware of creative design solutions, students can address personally-driven desires and concerns they have associated with the built environment. If students plan to implement specific actions in real life, the best results occur when they feel that they can find answers to the problems at hand. Taking action may include students organizing and/or consulting with groups and individuals that share their same beliefs, have specialized knowledge, and/or know how to find solutions to problems. Taking action may also include communicating their concerns and possible solutions to elected officials and other responsible persons. Students need to recognize that: "Taking action need not mean only changing the environment. It can also mean sharing one's own perceptions and views" (Adams, 1999, p. 190). This perspective can broaden students' understandings of what successful outcomes can be. For example, when problems in a built environment are too great for students and communities to solve at a particular time, students will still have benefited by learning how to identify their concerns and teaching others. They can also use these early life experiences to implement positive changes in the future.

Early childhood learners' play includes constructing three-dimensional forms using building blocks, empty containers, found objects, and art supplies. Teachers can augment young children's enthusiasm with daily opportunities to practice and experiment with building manipulatives. Young children also enjoy looking for clues and learning new information through I Spy games. Working with images representing built-environment designs and observations from life, students can learn to identify the components they see in architectural and design features. Students can use them as inspirations to make artworks. During class critiques, they can describe their designs' functions and identify information including who uses them. For example, teachers might have young learners look to the playground and discuss the qualities that exemplary playgrounds have. Students can brainstorm the qualities that make playgrounds fun and design a playground using sculpting materials. When studying castles, students can create a folded-paper design of a defensive stone castle, built to protect the people inside (Figure 17.16). They can use it as a set to perform a puppet show about living in the medieval era. When studying airports, students can learn about features such as airport control towers that direct airplane traffic and airport terminals. They can use their bodies to simulate planes coming in for landing on a runway and create artworks about planes arriving and departing at the airport (Figure 17.17).

FIGURE 17.16 Jan Klapetek, 6-years-old, ZUŠ Ant. Doležala, Brno, Czech Republic.
*Source: ICEFA Lidice, 40th Exhibition.*

FIGURE 17.17 Takahashi Ayumu, 6-years-old, Kamon Children Art School, Tokyo, Japan.
*Source: ICEFA Lidice, 39th Exhibition.*

Middle-childhood students recognize built-environment spaces and can contemplate their functions and meanings. The choice-based art curriculum can introduce a mapping activity in which students identify key characteristics within their communities. Students could begin by exploring overlooked places including public artworks, monuments, and buildings

(Coutts, 2004). They can discuss the qualities that make places memorable. They can create written journal reflections and develop artworks that portray their interpretations of community. For example, the ceramic building featured in Figure 17.18 is rich with architectural features such as doorways, stairways, fencing, and landscaping that give the

FIGURE 17.18 Kristýna Kocourková, 11-years-old, Dům dětí a mládeže Praha 3–Ulita, Praha 3–Žižkov, Czech Republic.
*Source: ICEFA Lidice, 39th Exhibition.*

impression of quality living. The charming design in Figure 17.19 gives viewers the feeling of comfort with its hot tea, fresh fruits, and bright textiles. Such works link the study of environmental aesthetics in which people identify life's sensory pleasures in everyday moments (see Chapter 7) and Merete Rein's art, which promotes coziness (see Artists' Lessons to Thrive! 17.2). Middle-childhood students are aware of products in the media and can identify designs intended for children and adults. They can assemble magazine clippings, information from websites, and media clips as inspirations for their own built-environment designs and identify their visual qualities. Given what they have learned, students can develop an artwork in which they pretend they were commissioned to design a room for a documentary or a magazine. Students can consider how others will use their designed spaces, such as having a hangout zone for friends, a workstation, an arts-and-crafts area, and/ or place to enjoy meals together. They can integrate special touches to enhance their designs, including furnishings and other decorative features.

Early adolescents can classify and identify the different functions of the built environment and explain how the built environment and utilities protect people from the elements. For example, the students depicted in Figure 17.20 paint comfortably in a climate-controlled classroom as snow falls outside. Students can also create artworks that present their understandings of the built environment within their communities. Figure 17.21 presents beautiful illustrations of a country's historic architecture that

FIGURE 17.19 Marjona Abdullajonova, 9-years-old, 36-sonli Umumtalim Maktabi, Namangan viloyati, Uzbekistan.
*Source: ICEFA Lidice, 39th Exhibition.*

FIGURE 17.20 Milena Kocharian, 12-years-old, Detskaia khudozhestvennaia shkola O. Sharambeiana, Dilizhan, Armenia.
*Source: ICEFA Lidice, 44th Exhibition.*

FIGURE 17.21 Martina Zapletalová, 12-years-old, ZUŠ F.X. Richtera, Holešov, Czech Republic.
*Source: ICEFA Lidice, 39th Exhibition.*

criticism debate. Students can research professions relating to the built environment and present their findings in class presentations. Their data collection might include informative Internet links and examples of exceptional design in their community, or places they have visited. They may also produce related artworks, such as designing a built environment within a repurposed briefcase (Figure 17.22) or painting a community waterscape (Figure 17.23) in response to their research. Adolescents enjoy problem-solving activities that challenge them. Students might play the roles of built-environment professionals and clients. Teachers can divide students into pairs and have students take turns being the design professionals and clients. When students role-play clients, they can describe their desired goals for built environment spaces and commission built environment specialists to develop digital presentations and/or display boards that represent their projects' specifications. They can consider both large and small projects and can decide upon subject matter. For example, they might focus on eco-friendly

demonstrate how the student artist is a special part of her community and the broader world. Students can review accessible designs by Karen L. Braitmayer (see Artists' Lessons to Thrive! 17.1) and conduct research to determine how and if identified environments meet the needs of all people. Early adolescents value having extra responsibilities. Teachers can seek the advice of local architects, landscape architects, designers, artists, and other professionals and hobbyists to develop community art installations, such as a mural, sculpture installation, or art garden. Each student can have assigned responsibilities for creating the project. Young adolescents want to make a positive difference and help others. They can participate in a community beautification day. Students can take photographs that capture before and after images of their work and describe the transformation in their journals. Students can use their data, which can include onsite interviews, to write an article or blog entry accompanied by their photographs and artworks using the cleaned recycled products they collected.

Adolescents can articulate their preferences in art. Students can compare and contrast works relating to the built environment with diverse design qualities. They can defend their preferences through an art

FIGURE 17.22 Nikola Zanášková, 14-years-old, ZUŠ, Pelhřimov, Czech Republic.
*Source: ICEFA Lidice, 42nd Exhibition.*

FIGURE 17.23 Ong Chin Wei, 15-years-old, Chung Ling High School, Georgetown, Malaysia.
*Source: ICEFA Lidice. 39th Exhibition.*

tourism and consider ways to develop structures and transportation routes that respect the environment and local cultures and limit human's impact on the natural environment. Or, they might look to built-environment spaces that have been impacted by poor planning or human destruction and identify ways to repair them. They can analyze how Martin Homola captured meanings associated with the built environment's destruction and reconstruction through photography (see Artists' Lessons to Thrive! 17.3).

## OUR JOURNEY TO THRIVE CONTINUES . . .

This chapter has presented ways to teach students about the built environment, its meanings, and its associated professions. In the next chapter, we will study technology and its many uses in teaching, learning, and creating in classroom spaces and beyond. Its content builds on what we have learned about artists and designers uses of technologies in their creative productions and its many applications in the choice-based art curriculum.

## CHAPTER QUESTIONS AND ACTIVITIES

1. Describe the built environment's qualities, functions, and meanings from historic and societal perspectives. How will you integrate the built environment into the choice-based art curriculum and STEAM learning tasks?
2. Develop an original comprehensive lesson on the built environment. Use the lesson plan template provided on the textbook's companion website and refer to Chapter 2 for more information on lesson plan development. Integrate inquiry tasks inspired by Part III of this textbook.
3. Answer Artists' Lessons to Thrive! 17.1–17.3 essential/guiding questions in written form or as part of a group discussion. Complete their daily learning targets.

## References

Adams, E. (1999). Art and the built environment: A framework for school programs. In J. K. Guilfoil & A. R. Sandler (Eds.), *Built environment education in art education* (pp. 184–193). Reston, VA: National Art Education Association.

American Bird Conservatory. (2015). *Bird-friendly building design.* Retrieved from https://abcbirds.org/wp-content/uploads/2015/04/Bird-friendly_Building_Guide_WEB.pdf

Anderson, R. (2004). *Calliope's sisters: A comparative study of philosophies of art.* Upper Saddle River, NJ: Prentice Hall.

Argiro, C. (2004). Teaching with public art. *Art Education, 57*(4), 25–32.

Bartuska, T. J. (2007). The built environment: Definition and scope. In W. R. McClure & T. J. Bartuska (Eds.), *The built environment: A collaborative inquiry into design and planning* (pp. 217–228). Hoboken, NJ: John Wiley & Sons.

Coutts, G. (2004). Multimedia, curriculum, public art. *Art Education, 57*(4), 19–24.

Dennis, S. F., Gaulocher, S., Carpiano, R. M., & Brown, D. (2009). Participatory photomapping (PPM): Exploring an integrated method for health and place research with young people. *Health & Place, 15,* 466–473.

Dewey, J. (1934). *Art as experience.* New York: Capricorn.

Hicks, L. E., & King, R. J. H. (1999). Mapping a sense of place: A contextualized approach to designed environments. In J. K. Guilfoil & A. R. Sandler (Eds.), *Built environment education in art education* (pp. 10–17). Reston, VA: National Art Education Association.

Homola, M. (2018). *My home: Testimony of portrait.* Lidice, Czech Republic: Pamatnik Lidice.

Hughey, J., Speer, P., & Peterson, A. (1999). Sense of community in community organizations: Structure and evidence of validity. *Journal of Community Psychology, 27*(1), 97–113.

Lee, H. K., & Breitenberg, M. (2010). Education in the new millennium: The case for design-based learning. *The International Journal of Art and Design Education, 29*(1), 54–60.

Lippard, L. (1997). *The lure of the local: Senses of place in a multicentered society.* New York: New Press.

Longo, N. V. (2007). *Why community matters: Connecting education with civic life.* Albany, NY: State University of New York Press.

Maziak, W., Ward, K. D., & Stockton, M. B. (2007). Childhood obesity: Are we missing the big picture? *Obesity Reviews, 9,* 35–42.

Moffett, M., Fazio, M., & Wodenhouse, L. (2004). *A world history of architecture.* London: McGraw Hill.

National Institute of Environmental Health Sciences. (2004). Fighting obesity through the built environment. *Environmental Health Perspectives, 112*(11), A616–A618.

Pizarro, R. E. (2009). Teaching to understand the urban sensorium in the digital age: Lessons from the studio. *Design Studies, 30,* 272–286.

Powell, K. A. (2008). ReMapping the city: Palimpsest, place, and identity in art education research. *Studies in Art Education, 50*(1), 6–21.

# Technology

## Media Arts, Photography, and Graphics

**FIGURE 18.1** *Peace Is in the Air,* early childhood students, United States.
*Source: Author, Monica Leister, Suzanne St. John, pre-service, Angela Bunyi, and Julia Hudson, teachers. Original song by Brian Shind and music production by Dwayne Russell.*

**Technology** is the invention of products based on scientific and creative knowledge that humans have developed throughout history to solve problems, achieve goals, manipulate the environment, and communicate with others. The term *technology* dates to the Greek word *technología*, with *techne* meaning the arts and *logos* meaning thought. Artists throughout history have linked the arts with cognitive thought and creativity to produce technological innovations, including ceramic vessels to hold liquids. The rise of the Industrial Revolution with its scientific technologies and enhanced machinery that replaced handmade products broadened people's understandings of what technology could be. Every day, we are surrounded with new technologies. As we have studied throughout this textbook, artists call upon technology to produce artworks in various forms. Media arts, photography, and graphics represent some of the ways that the arts align with technology. The choice-based art curriculum will teach students how to employ technologies to create art, research, and interact with others. We will encourage students to participate in discussions about the role that technology plays in their daily lives and raise awareness of the benefits and problems associated with technology.

We will meet the following objectives by participating in this chapter:

- Describe technology, media arts, photography, and graphics and their qualities, functions, and meanings in society.
- Identify best practices for teaching technology, media arts, photography, and graphics.
- Create instructional resources for teaching technology, media arts, photography, and graphics.

This chapter's Spotlight on Student Art #18 (Figures 18.1–18.3), explains how elementary, middle, and high school students created a stop-motion film using STEAM learning tasks. Their goal was to communicate characteristics of peaceful living.

**FIGURE 18.2** *Peace Is in the Air* still, early childhood students, United States.

*Source: Author, Monica Leister, Suzanne St. John, pre-service, Angela Bunyi, and Julia Hudson, teachers. Original song by Brian Shind and music production by Dwayne Russell.*

**FIGURE 18.3** *Peace Is in the Air* still, early childhood students, United States.

*Source: Author, Monica Leister, Suzanne St. John, pre-service, Angela Bunyi, Julia Hudson, teachers. Original song by Brian Shind and music production by Dwayne Russell.*

---

## Spotlight on Student Art #18

### Big Idea: Peaceful Living

First- through 12th grade students from two different schools collaborated to create an international Kids' Guernica stop-motion animation, filled with colorful hot air balloons and a collaged sky, called *Peace Is In the Air* (Figures 18.1–18.3). Their teachers taught animation techniques to the students using an app designed for tablet computers. Elementary and middle school students from a state school for the blind planned the stop-motion animation's storyline. They identified playing, cooking, resting, and spending time with family as their favorite peaceful activities. Next, they created vibrant hot air balloons with plasticine clay and found objects as the main characters for their animation. The students wrote an original script and recorded their voices reading the script using a microphone connected to a laptop computer. Throughout the project, students referenced a storyboard to review their animation's main scenes. The school's adolescent students added to the project by creating drawn and collaged props to accompany the hot air balloons. Teachers assisted both groups of students in locating the shutter button and framing the composition on the tablet using a stop-motion animation application.

Three 1st grade classes from a school for high-achieving students created additional art for the project and photographed the next phases of the stop-motion animation. They needed practice to learn how to move the objects in small increments. They reviewed their stop-motion animation in real time through a wireless connection to a classroom smart board. This instant feedback served as an ongoing self-assessment tool for students to revise and alter their stop-motion animation in progress. Once the students' work was complete, a volunteer professional producer edited their animation's sound and music in a recording studio as a public service.

## UNDERSTANDING TECHNOLOGY IN CONTEXT

Modern technologies have greatly impacted our world. The 20th century brought the Internet, home computers, laptops, and cellular phones, providing society with access to instant global communications and digital information through online videos, chat rooms, podcasts, and blogging sites. These advances were made possible through **digital technologies** that code recorded data into numbers stored on computers and other digital devices and transform the code into text, sound, and visual images. Digital technologies evolved from electronic **analog** signals that convey information within an original structure with voltage flowing at a continuous rate. Today's high-resolution digital visuals were impossible to create on early computers because they did not have the graphic capabilities that contemporary computers have (see Artists' Lessons to Thrive! 3.1 on Lawrence Gartel). Initial computer imagery was so rudimentary that graphic geometric shapes were limited to **alphanumeric images**, which were created by aligning letters or simple contour lines into shapes. **Nanotechnologies** (technologies that are small in size) resulted in the compact smartphones and tablets that flooded the 21st century consumer market. The products that resulted from these powerful technologies are the ones with which students are most familiar.

**Media arts** define the wide range of screen-based products that inventors and designers develop using various technological components. They include interactive designs, mobile/desktop technologies, animations (Figure 18.4), films, videos, virtual designs, software development, apps, and special effects. Media arts make possible time-based motions and offer multiple sensory stimuli through content such as recorded and live images and sounds. Media arts differ from static **graphic technologies**, including

FIGURE 18.4 Elementary and secondary students developed a stop-motion animation about an adventure. United States, *Source: Author, Monica Leister, and pre-service, teachers.*

FIGURE 18.5 Natalie Robinson, 17-years-old, United States. *Source: Jonathan Griffith, teacher.*

photography (Figure 18.5) and graphic design (Figure 18.6), because they are time-based, moving products. Screens that range from small smartphone to billboard sizes permeate the human environment and transmit multimedia data to people seeking or passively receiving information, communicating with others, playing games, and/or passing the time.

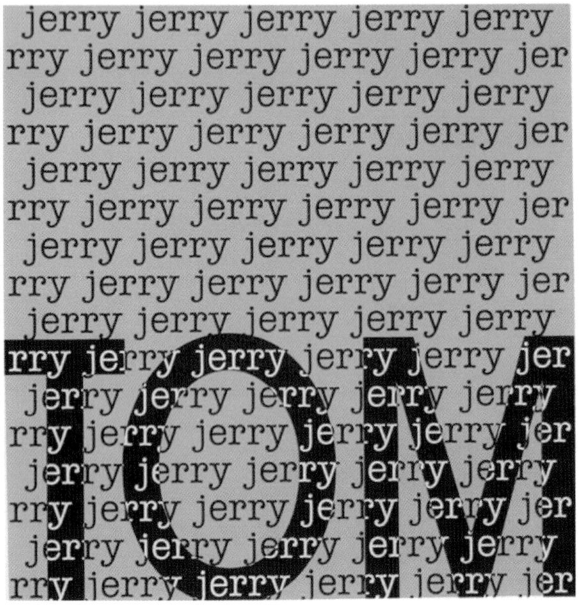

FIGURE 18.6 Irina Viktorovna Kuzminyh, 13-years-old, Detskaya Khudozhestvennaya Shkola, Ust-Kamenogorsk, Kazakhstan.
*Source: ICEFA Lidice, 40th Exhibition.*

Students will be able to identify the many places where they see screens and the types of information they project. Media artists regularly integrate static graphic components, including photographs, lines of designed text, and illustrated symbols into their productions. Unlike previous art forms that remained relatively unchanged for centuries, media arts evolve continuously and result in new technologies and products. Through well-designed code and interfaces artists and technological innovators push boundaries and try things that have not been attempted before.

As a subject of study, media arts expand beyond digital technologies that began in the latter half of the 20th century. Students will learn how distinct historical and cultural factors from humanity's complete history have led to today's technological developments and will continue to impact future ones (Cubitt & Thomas, 2015). For example, Louis Jacques Mandé Daguerre and Henry Fox Talbot invented the first permanent forms of **photography**, the process of capturing photographic images on a light sensitive (photosensitive) surface (Sandler, 2002). In 1839, Daguerre developed a reliable photographic process, called a **daguerreotype**, using a copper plate treated with silver. Talbot invented the **calotype** process in 1841 by coating quality paper with layers of silver iodide. Before the advent of

photography, only skilled artists could document people's likenesses and past events. Fine artists in the 19th century were the first to use photography as an innovative tool to capture realistic images for their paintings and sculptures.

In 1878, photographer and scientist Eadweard Muybridge took photography to the next level when he produced a series of photographs called *The Horse in Motion*. Muybridge applied the horse's galloping movements to activate the tripwires on his cameras' **shutters**, devices that allow light into cameras to take pictures. The movements he captured through photography occurred too quickly for the human eye to process. Muybridge rapidly projected these sequential photographs using a machine called a **zoopraxiscope** that gave his photographs the illusion of a fast-running horse in continuous motion (Figure 18.7). In 1924, painter Fernard Léger combined fine art with technology to produce *Ballet Mécanique*, an experimental film symbolizing a dance between machines, manufactured products, text, and human forms. Ansel Adams elevated photography as an art form with his dramatic black-and-white toned landscapes that depicted nature's pristine beauty. His photographs became persuasive tools to advocate for protecting the environment and developing national parks (Figure 18.8).

Until the latter half of the 20th century, most photographs, films, and television shows were monochromatic. Sarah Acland was an early pioneer of color

FIGURE 18.7 Eadweard Muybridge, *The Zoopraxiscope, Horse Galloping*, 1893.
*Source: Library of Congress. LC-DIG-ppmsca-05947.*

FIGURE 18.8 Ansel Adams, *The Tetons and Snake River,* 1941.
Source: *U.S. National Archives and Records Administration.*

photography. In 1900, Acland photographed portraits and travel landscapes using the Sanger Shepherd process. Acland took three consecutive black-and-white photographs with alternating red, green, and blue filters to create a single color photograph. This process was much slower than typical black and white photography. A few decades later, the film industry became modernized through the combination of Technicolor (all three primary colors) and sound, which resulted in colorful traditional animated films such as *Snow White and the Seven Dwarfs* (1937) and the musical film *The Wizard of Oz* (1939).

In 1973, Na June Paik created an innovative video art production called *Global Groove.* This electronic video collage fused psychedelic colors with the performing arts, international advertisements, and kaleidoscopic marks to present a futuristic vision about the possibilities of global television communications. Such creative innovations—combined with advances in graphics and computer technologies—impacted the art, film, and entertainment industries. For example, filmmakers use computer graphics to invent convincing imaginary worlds. In the 1980s, they began commissioning game designers to transform epic and animated movies into marketable electronic games for children and adults to earn greater profits (Brown, 2008; Dixon & Foster, 2008). New-media arts festivals have become popular events across the planet. They bring thousands of people together to interact with and enjoy digital artworks. Some technology specialists apply four-dimensional presentation methods to

synchronize physical sensations such as movement, smells, and water and wind elements with films, theme park rides, and interactive works to give audiences greater sensory experiences. Students may recall some of their personal engagements with these technologies.

Contemporary artists, photographers, graphic designers, and hobbyists use software to view, create, edit, draw, and manipulate images on a screen using a mouse, digital stylus, and their fingertips or bodies. Artists can shade their creations, add painterly qualities, apply textures, stretch forms into different directions, construct virtual structures, incorporate text, layer images, and more. Technological productions may be screen-based or extend beyond the screen to become physical products including art installations, three-dimensional printings (see Artists' Lessons to Thrive! 14.2 on Christopher Williams), and interactive art forms. Leslie Patterson-Marx (Artists' Lessons to Thrive! 13.2) photographed the processes of her drawing on a vintage photograph to create a stop-motion animation and an artist book (Figure 18.9). With a wide range of resources available, creative

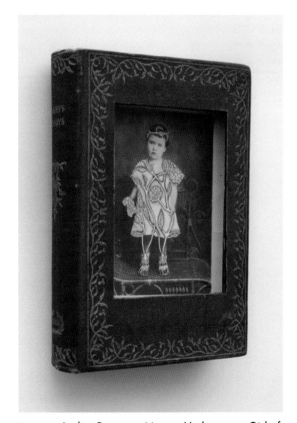

FIGURE 18.9 Leslie Patterson-Marx, *Hydrangea Girl,* found book, found photograph, acrylic ink, graphite, Plexiglas, 6 × 4.25 × 1.25 in. (15.24 × 10.79 × 3.17 cm), 2013.
Source: *Courtesy of the artist; lesleypattersonmarx.com*

technological professionals may work independently or as part of multidisciplinary teams. Madalyne Marie Hymas (Artists' Lessons to Thrive! 18.1) worked independently to create *Dyslexic Advantage*, an interactive artwork. Students will learn how she overcame obstacles and applied resiliency to pursue a career in graphic design. Artists Dan Goods, Nik Hafermaas, and Aaron Koblin (Artists' Lessons to Thrive! 18.2)

collaborated to produce a suspended art installation inspired by real-time weather data. Students will learn how their design is suited for an airport terminal. Some artists invite the greater public to assist them in developing technological artworks. **Open source software** gives public audiences permission to produce, alter, and share content including storyline trajectories and visual images.

---

# Artists' Lessons to Thrive! 18.1 Madalyne Marie Hymas: *The Dyslexic Advantage*

## Big Idea: Advantage

**FIGURE 18.1.1** Madalyne Marie Hymas, *The Dyslexic Advantage*, 2013, installation, 9 × 7 × 3 ft (2.74 × 2.13 × 0.91 m).

*Source: Courtesy of the artist; madalyne.com.*

---

Madalyne Marie Hymas' portfolio includes elegant logos, packaging designs, and advertisements for leading corporations. In addition to marketing renowned designers' merchandise, Hymas has applied her graphic design skills to teach society about important causes. *The Dyslexic Advantage* is an art installation that Hymas developed to educate viewers about dyslexia, the world's most common learning disability (Figures 18.1.1 and 18.1.2). She received an award of excellence from the prestigious Kennedy Center's VSA Emerging Young Artists Program for *The Dyslexic Advantage*. VSA recognizes talented visual artists with disabilities between the ages of 16–25 and introduces their works to the public through its exhibitions and community events.

**FIGURE 18.1.2** Madalyne Marie Hymas, *The Dyslexic Advantage* detail, 2013, installation, 9 × 7 × 3 ft (2.74 × 2.13 × 0.91 m).

*Source: Courtesy of the artist; madalyne.com.*

Twenty-percent of the world's population has dyslexia. *The Dyslexic Advantage* makes a profound impact because Hymas has integrated her personal life experiences of being diagnosed with the condition into its design. Her artwork emphasizes words and phrases associated with the condition and defines dyslexia as "a structural brain variation that changes how one recognizes, processes, and organizes information." Signage in *The Dyslexic Advantage* explains how people diagnosed with dyslexia typically have average or above-average cognitive skills. Hymas reiterated this fact by listing the names of famous individuals with dyslexia, including Albert Einstein, John F. Kennedy, and Walt Disney.

Despite dyslexia's prevalence in society, many people have misconceptions about what dyslexia is and how individuals with dyslexia process information. Dyslexia is often discovered in schools when capable children experience difficulties with reading, writing, sounding out words, and spelling. In a section of her installation titled "Insults & Misconceptions," Hymas selected phrases that identify the common stereotypes and lack of understanding that individuals with dyslexia like herself have heard simply because they process information differently:

- "MADALYNE, I'M GOING TO HAVE YOU READ OUT LOUD DURING CLASS TODAY TO SEE IF YOU CAN FINALLY GET OVER YOUR DYSLEXIA."
- "YOU WILL BE LUCKY IF YOU EVEN GRADUATE FROM HIGH SCHOOL.
- "IT'S GOING TO BE HARD FOR YOU TO BE GOOD AT GRAPHIC DESIGN!"
- "SHE IS ONE OF OUR SPECIAL STUDENTS."

Given this information, viewers can see how Hymas developed *The Dyslexic Advantage* to shift society's perspective from what people with dyslexia cannot achieve to identifying their personal strengths. In particular, her artwork explains how individuals with dyslexia have excellent reasoning skills and can see the big picture. They visualize objects from a variety of perspectives and process information more rapidly than individuals without dyslexia. They have excellent problem-solving abilities and can visualize both memories and fantasies with exquisite details. Hymas has called upon these skills to become the accomplished graphic designer she is today. Her creations, including *The Dyslexic Advantage*, inspire audiences. She uses her professional knowledge to teach society to look to the advantages of the conditions that individuals with disabilities have and seek ways to use them to achieve quality results, experience new possibilities, and better society.

## Essential/Guiding Questions

1. How have Madalyne Marie Hymas and other individuals with dyslexia used their condition to their advantage? In which ways have you transformed what appeared to be a personal disadvantage into an advantage?
2. Why do you think that Hymas felt the need to teach others about dyslexia? What have you learned by studying *The Dyslexic Advantage*?

## Preparation

The students will research dyslexia. They will examine Madalyne Marie Hymas' website to compare and contrast the content in her graphic design products with *The Dyslexic Advantage*.

## Daily Learning Targets

I can create an artwork that identifies how I or someone else transformed what appeared to be an obstacle into an advantage.

- I can select the media of my choice.
- I can integrate text into my artistic design using an appropriate font to convey my message.
- I can emphasize my ideas by producing a balanced composition showing craftspersonship and unified parts.

**National Core Arts Anchor Standards** 1, 4, 9, and 11
www.nationalartsstandards.org

## Artists' Lessons to Thrive! 18.2 Dan Goods, Nik Hafermaas, and Aaron Koblin: *eCloud*, A Real-time, Innovative Art Installation

### Big Idea: Innovation

Every day, individuals look up to the sky to watch the clouds. Innovative contemporary artists Dan Goods, Nik Hafermaas, and Aaron Koblin merged people's interest in cloud gazing with interactive design to develop *eCloud*, a 108 foot (33 m) polycarbonate installation with the volumetric mass of a natural cloud (Figure 18.2.1). Their artwork is suspended from a tensile structure within a concourse in the San Jose Airport in California. The trio applied their combined artistic and technological strengths to develop *eCloud's* interface, which connects real-time meteorological data with their fine art installation. *eCloud* consists of 3,000 individual liquid crystal planes called *smart glass* that the artists arranged in hanging panels. Each square plane represents an individual pixel, with the combined pixels forming a low-resolution

**FIGURE 18.2.1** Dan Goods, Nik Hafermaas, and Aaron Koblin, *eCloud*, 2007–2010.
*Source: Spencer Lowell, photo.*

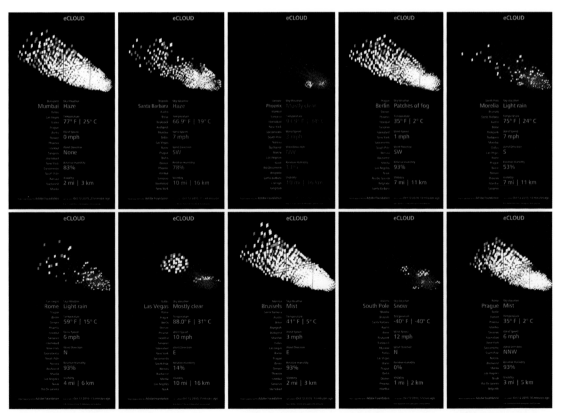

**FIGURE 18.2.2** Dan Goods, Nik Hafermaas, and Aaron Koblin, *eCloud* (screen capture), 2007–2010.
*Source: Spencer Lowell, photo.*

mosaicked screen. The artists programmed 100 custom circuit boards to pass electronic currents to *eCloud's* pixels at different intensity levels, so that they would range from fully opaque to crystal clear. Without programming to activate its electric currents, *eCloud's* liquid crystal planes would simply remain opaque.

ECloud's master computer translates instant data from the National Oceanic and Atmospheric Administration into abstract weather projections showing conditions from 100 different flight destinations. The electronically activated artwork mimics the look and ephemeral behaviors of a perfect cloud as *eCloud's* animated designs travel throughout the installation in distinct patterns to represent changing weather conditions. Every 20 seconds, *eCloud* rotates to a different location. If it is snowing in the South Pole, *eCloud's* shimmering animations replicate the look and wind direction of an Antarctic snowfall in real time. For lightly cloudy weather in a different region, a cluster of opaque tiles located next to activated clear tiles would give the illusion of a small cloud traveling through the atmosphere. Instead of revealing the name of the projected city on *eCloud's* suspended installation, curious onlookers must walk up to a separate display board to view a location's name, sky weather, temperature, wind speed, and wind direction (Figure 18.2.2). The display also presents a digital thumbnail of *eCloud's* animated behaviors. By separating the suspended installation from the display board, the artists have maintained the artwork's luminous appearance.

Goods, Hafermaas, and Koblin's transformation of weather conditions into a perpetually changing artwork in real time required great technological and artistic skills. Through *eCloud's* hanging panels and fluctuating data visualizations the artists have moved audiences beyond simply looking at a flat computer screen, which had been common practice with technological works, and provided them with digitally inspired spatial experiences that beautify and add sensory interest to the airport. As a result, *eCloud* displays the weather like no others have done before. The artists' appealing design encourages people to look at the radiant electronic cloud, contemplate the meanings of the visual weather patterns *eCloud* projects, and experience wait time at the airport in a whole new light.

## Essential/Guiding Questions

1. How have Goods, Hafermaas, and Koblin applied technological and art innovations to create *eCloud*?
2. In your opinion, how would the meaning of *eCloud* change if Goods, Hafermaas, and Koblin designed the work without the suspended installation and only developed its display panel?

## Preparation

The students will discuss how artists' curiosity can lead to creative, innovative designs. The teacher will inform students that when creating *eCloud*, Goods worked for the National Aeronautics and Space Administration's Jet Propulsion Laboratory, Hafermaas taught at Art Center College of Design, and Koblin headed Google's Data Arts Team. The class will identify how artistic innovations impact society.

## Daily Learning Targets

I can portray an innovative idea through art.

- I can select the media of my choice to form a design that incorporates a pattern or value.
- I can produce an artwork using effective balance, unity, and craftspersonship.
- I can present my completed project and preliminary designs during a class critique or post it on a discussion board forum.

**National Core Arts Anchor Standards** 3, 5, 8, and 11
www.nationalartsstandards.org

## APPLYING STEAM TO TEACH TECHNOLOGY IN CONTEXT

The choice-based art curriculum is rich with STEAM learning tasks that unite technology and the visual arts. Students will learn how technological products including video games, animations, and apps (applications) contain artistic designs to boost their appeal. Like artists, students apply technologies to learn, communicate, research, and create. Students may produce completely digital artworks or form hybrids by merging traditional art processes with technology. Some of the most common classroom technological art production methods include photography, digital art and edits, video productions, animations, and gaming.

## Photography

Before digital photography, photographers worked with film cameras to capture photographic images. Some photographers continue to use film cameras to achieve looks and qualities that differ from digital photography. Traditional photography can also work in conjunction with digital technologies. For example, students can download light meter apps on their phones and tablets to measure the amount of light to adjust the camera settings and achieve quality exposures. Photographers who use film cameras and want more control, develop their photographs in a **darkroom**, a darkened room for processing film and developing prints (Figure 18.10). They manipulate the

**FIGURE 18.10** High school darkroom. United States, Jonathan Griffith, teacher.

*Source: Jonathan Griffith, photo.*

look of photographs in the darkroom by adjusting the amount of light exposure, cropping the composition, and choosing photographic papers. After processing film into negatives, photographers use an **enlarger**, a device that projects images of negatives onto photographic paper to expose pictures. They soak light-exposed photographic papers in a series of chemical baths, rinse them with water to remove the chemicals, and dry them. School darkrooms are most prevalent in secondary schools and are typically used by art and photography specialists.

Developing film in a darkroom is a valuable learning opportunity for students as they experience the magic of watching pictures come to life. For schools and community art spaces that do not have darkrooms and film cameras, digital cameras, smartphone cameras, and tablet cameras can be the most viable means to acquaint students with photography. Digital cameras, smartphone cameras, and tablet cameras require no film, making film processing unnecessary. They are equipped with a **charge-coupled device** (CCD) and an image sensor, which together translate pictures into electronic signals that a digital camera, computer, smartphone, or tablet can recognize. Students can achieve instant results with digital photography and take large quantities of photographs without concerns for running out of film (Barron, Ivers, Lilavois, & Wells, 2006).

Teachers will introduce students to a variety of photographic processes and have them plan what they would like to achieve through the medium so that they can become skilled photographers (Keyker, 2014). Teachers will explain that photographs range from realistic to abstract. Photographers manipulate photographs through choice of subject matter, lighting, angles, cropping, and other means. As students delve deeper into photography, they will become able to identify the characteristics of photographic genres, including fashion, advertising, photojournalism, nature, and portraiture. Teachers will teach them how photographers apply artistic interpretations to record specialized subject matter and highlight visual qualities. For example, the photograph in Figure 18.11 explores textures and the photograph in Figure 18.12 presents abstracted, reflected light.

Many photographers and artists transform original photographs through **photo manipulations**. Students can learn to edit photographs using basic

FIGURE 18.11 Coley Lee, 13-years-old, United States.
*Source: Mike Muller, teacher.*

FIGURE 18.12 David Tsypris, 12-years-old, Studio of Art–Ruta Kreitser, Jerusalem, Israel.
*Source: ICEFA Lidice, 43rd Exhibition.*

photo editing applications that come with technological devices as well as work with professional editing products such as Adobe Photoshop. A **multiple exposure** is a photograph that photographers create by superimposing two or more exposures on film or a photographic surface. Many photographers achieve this effect using a manually winding film camera and opening the shutter to take two different photographs on a single frame without advancing the film to the next frame. Kathy Vargas differs in that she uses a 4 × 5 camera to create multiple-exposure photographs. Her series *I Was Little/They Were Big* (Figure 18.13) contains a multiple-exposure portrait of her father's age-ravaged lawn chair fused with a photograph of her childhood backyard. She designed it to preserve and commemorate family memories. (See Artists' Lessons to Thrive! 10.3 for more information on the artist). For the image shown in Figure 18.14, students created a multiple exposure with film of a local mountain and school playground equipment to document places they enjoy in their community. As an alternative to using film, students can achieve a multiple exposure effect using photo editing software to superimpose two or more photographic images.

FIGURE 18.13 Kathy Vargas, *I Was Little/They Were Big,* 1998, hand-colored gelatin silver prints, 24 × 20 in. (60.96 × 50.8 cm).
*Source: Courtesy of the Artist.*

**FIGURE 18.14** Group project, 5th grade. Norway.
*Source: Brittany Gardner and Author, teachers.*

**FIGURE 18.16** A high school student uses his pinhole camera. United States.
*Source: Jonathan Griffith, teacher. Jonathan Griffith, photo.*

**FIGURE 18.15** Matko Meštrović, 16-years-old, Hrvatski Fotosavez, Zagreb, Croatia.
*Source: ICEFA Lidice, 43rd Exhibition.*

Students can create **light painting photographs** or light trail photographs by leaving a camera shutter open long enough to capture moving light within the picture frame's composition (Figure 18.15). The photograph records the light trails the students form. Students can work with flashlights and LED lights to achieve a greater range of effects. The shutter speed they use will vary according to the length of their light paintings, and might be open 10–20 seconds compared to a photograph's normal fractions of a second exposure time.

Living in a digital age, students benefit from learning less-familiar historic photographic procedures. For example, they can construct a **pinhole camera**, which does not have a lens (Figure 18.16). A pinhole camera consists of a darkened box chamber free of light that can open and close. Students add an aperture to the camera by puncturing a small hole on the front side of the box and covering it with a moveable protective covering. When opened, the aperture allows light into the box to produce an exposure on film or photographic paper that students place inside the camera chamber opposite of the pinhole. The exposure time for each photograph depends on the amount of available light. Another option is to create a **cyanotype,** a monochromatic Prussian blue print made with a solution of ammonium iron citrate and potassium ferricyanide (Figure 18.5). Students can study 19th century cyanotypes by Anna Atkins, who created the first book with photographic images called *Photographs of British Algae: Cyanotype Impressions*. Students can work with pretreated cyanotype papers and fabrics, or mix their own solutions with teacher supervision to produce cyanotypes on a wider range of surfaces. Students can also produce a **photogram**, a photograph on photosensitive paper taken without a camera and using the light of the sun or a darkroom enlarger. The light exposes objects arranged on photosensitive paper and result in a black-and-white photograph with the objects represented as silhouettes with tonal details (Figure 18.17). In the early 20th century, the artist Man Ray experimented with photograms as an art form by arranging everyday objects into abstract compositions and exposing the objects on a photographic surface for various amounts of time to show

**FIGURE 18.17** Alžběta Suchá, 15-years-old, ZUŠ M. Stibora, Olomouc, Czech Republic.

*Source: ICEFA Lidice, 42nd Exhibition.*

greater values among the disparate objects. He called his process a **rayograph**.

The validity of digital art as fine art has not always been recognized by the art world. Fine art has long been associated with quality art supplies and the artist's significant time commitment in creating a product, whereas people typically view computers as time-saving devices that make life easier (Nalven & Jarvis, 2005). Innovative contemporary artists have recognized the liaison between digital art and fine art production. For example, fine artist David Hockney, known for his 20th century paintings, helped correlate digital art with fine art with his 21st century solo exhibition called *Me Draw on iPad*. Hockney created hundreds of artworks that mimicked traditional painting and drawing media using a stylus and an inexpensive app called Brushes and displayed them on Apple iPads for the exhibition (Louisiana Museum of Modern Art, 2011).

Students can use digital technologies to produce fine artworks, photographs, commercial designs, interactive designs, and installations. Although digital art cannot mimic the tactile sensations of fine art materials, computer programmers have replicated the look of art media such as watercolors, chalk pastels, oil pastels, ink, pencils, airbrush, and crayons. For example, the artwork shown in Figure 18.18 contains digitally generated black outlines and airbrush qualities. Students can compare the processes and results of working with tactile art media with their digital equivalents.

## Digital Art

**Digital art** embraces the fine arts and graphic design. As part of the choice-based art curriculum, students will learn how to distinguish whether a creation is fine art or graphic design based on the intent of the product. Artists typically create fine art to express ideas and communicate through art media and processes. Graphic designers usually create products for business and industry, including advertisements, logos, printed materials, page layouts, websites, branding, and packaging. They form stylized designs and select the best typography to make products and models look more appealing. Some focus on interface design to make computer software, webpages, and manufactured products easier for users to navigate and understand.

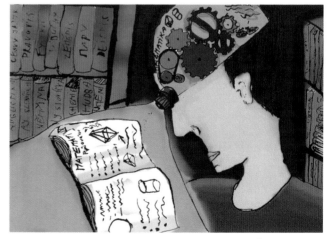

**FIGURE 18.18** Aneta Lišková, 13-years-old, ZUŠ, Praha 5, Czech Republic.

*Source: ICEFA Lidice, 44th Exhibition.*

## Video Production

Contemporary visual culture is saturated with instant videos, personal movies, and eyewitness accounts by everyday people who upload original videos to social media sites. Stemming from traditional filmmaking, video production was originally limited to a few people due to the expensive cost of recording equipment and editing content. With access to mobile technologies, students can record original videos and edit them with free software that comes loaded on devices or work with professional editing applications that their schools may purchase.

The best video productions result when students understand equipment, filming methods, storyline development, and editing skills. Students should plan how they will position the camera to record information within chosen settings and capture desired lighting effects. Students will learn how to hold the camera steady and use a tripod to avoid shaky footage when filming. Classes benefit from informative online tutorials and class demonstrations to learn how to apply editing features that come with specific applications. If students are working with a tablet or smartphone, they may wish to import video footage onto a computer rather than editing it on a recording device because it can be easier and save time. With practice, students will become competent in cropping, splitting, and merging video segments, as well as augmenting video productions with titles, photographs, transitions, sound clips, voice recordings (Figure 18.19), music, and credits.

**FIGURE 18.19** Elementary and middle school students record a script. United States.

*Source: Author, Monica Leister, and Natsumi Kajisa, teachers.*

Students can choose from a variety of formats such as a short film, **vlog** (video blog), and a question-and-answer video or use built-in themes and movie trailers that come with apps. They can develop these works to create art reviews, tutorials, and commentaries on art topics and class themes. Students can make a **documentary film**—a nonfiction movie about a real event, person, place, or thing. Filmmakers create documentaries to preserve information and teach audiences something new. They sometimes present multiple sides of an issue using historical data and expert interviews. When filming is complete, filmmakers carefully select from available content including interviews, images, and sound clips to make edits and arrange data to present a coherent storyline. The end result shows the filmmaker's personal touch with all parts of the documentary coming together to present a clear and meaningful work. As an alternative, students can develop a **mockumentary,** a film that appears to be a real documentary but is actually a satire work that presents a humorous interpretation of what appears to be normal or not so normal events. Mockumentaries include scripted or improvised fake interviews with specialists in the field.

## Animation

**Animation** is the process of making a movie or artwork using a series of static images created through drawing, photography, and/or computer graphics that appear to move when activated due to small incremental variations in their sequential designs. A **flip-book** is the most basic animation technique. Artists create flip-books by binding consecutive artworks in book form and rapidly flipping the pages to animate the artworks. Animators created most 20th century animated films with transparent celluloid sheets, called *cels*. They layered background scenery with sequential cels to show character actions without having to repaint the background for each change of movement. Computer animators later replaced this time-consuming process with 2D animations of vector and bitmap images. This process made transitions between images even smoother than had been possible with cel animations. In 1995, Pixar created the first 3D-animated film, *Toy Story*, using geometric modeling to produce lifelike characters. This type of animation requires complex mathematical coding and is more difficult to process than 2D animation.

Filmmakers and artists produce **stop-motion animations**, or stop-motion films, by physically moving non-moving objects in small increments and photographing them frame by frame to convey the illusion of independent movement when the video is played back (Figure 18.20). Like professionals, students can assemble found objects such as Legos (Figure 18.21) and toys to create stop-motion animations or construct original artworks to serve as characters and props for their films. For example, schoolchildren working with the artist collective Tiny Circus used collage materials and their own bodies to form a stop-motion animation (see Spotlight on Student Art #19).

**FIGURE 18.20** This image shows a still from *Be Good Beach*, a stop-motion animation created by elementary and secondary students. United States.
*Source: Author, Monica Leister, Eric Breedlove, Tammy Mason, and Cullen McMackins, teachers. 46th ICEFA Lidice.*

**FIGURE 18.21** Students review their in-progress stop-motion animation created with Legos. United States.
*Source: Author, Monica Leister, and pre-service, teachers.*

**Claymation** is a stop-motion animation made with hand-molded plasticine or polymer clay figures positioned in various action poses to show independent movements. When constructing claymation figures, artists create balanced forms using wire armatures and heavier bases so that their figures will stand upright and remain intact during filming.

Animations, stop-motion animations, and claymations appear in popular culture as fine artworks, commercials, music videos, television programs, and movies. Like regular film projects, animations commonly include a title, narrative text, film credits, and sound clips. Animators and filmmakers use a **storyboard**—an illustrated graphic organizer with rectangular forms—to plan an animation's key frames in sequential order. Animations work well for group projects. Students share the responsibilities of developing a storyline; preparing a set; taking photographs; drawing, constructing, and/or assembling character figures and props; moving characters into various action poses; and editing and presenting the film. Students should plan for smooth animation transitions by moving characters in small increments. They will need consistent camera angles to photograph frames and might find it easier to work with a tripod. They can produce digital artworks for two-dimensional animations and edit them with movie editing software or an animation app. For stop-motion animations and claymations, students can take photographs with a camera and insert them into editing software. Or, they can download an app to create stop-motion animations and claymations directly on a smartphone or tablet. When editing animations, students may repeat frames to slow down particular actions or duplicate a series of frames to show repetitive movements such as walking and waving. For classrooms with limited technology, students can insert photographs or drawings into a presentation software program and loop its slideshow feature to indicate continuous movement. Students can also form flipbooks with or without technology, using only hand-drawing methods or photographs and/or computer drawings.

## Game-Based Learning

**Game-based learning** is a method of integrating into the curriculum educational games that students want to play. Many art museums offer free interactive games that teach students about art history and provide opportunities for students to create. The best educational games are interactive and encourage students to experiment and make decisions. They place students in the role of active digital creators who produce knowledge (Beavis, 2012). Minecraft: Education Edition is a virtual gaming world made of blocks; it is suitable for students ages 5 and up. Within its virtual spaces, students collect resources to build architectural structures. In the game's creative mode, students might use its blocks to create a virtual art gallery, transform a two-dimensional artwork into a three-dimensional space, and/or design an original built environment (Overby & Jones 2015).

Students can also design original video games. Some apps allow students to construct games without coding. Games with original student coding may require the assistance of a technology specialist and additional time to develop. When planning gaming projects, teachers should pre-assess students' knowledge to identify their current abilities and use this knowledge to partner students with classmates so that they can apply their strengths to game construction (Alexander & Ho, 2015). Students need to agree upon unifying game concepts. In the professional world, game designers work in teams to bring their products to the marketplace. Successful games look great and are entertaining. Game designers select the best color palettes, fonts, music, and sound effects to create quality products. They plan multiple tasks for game characters and integrate short- and long-term reward systems within their games to motivate people to continue to play. Completed class video games can come in many different styles. For instance, students can select artworks in the public domain to create a digital art memory matching game or create an environment where a lead character must find stolen artworks and return them to their owners.

## BEST PRACTICES FOR TEACHING TECHNOLOGY FROM PRE-K THROUGH HIGH SCHOOL

Given many young people's access to stimulating technologies in their free time, students appreciate learning and creating with technology as an integral part of their education. Students' technical abilities will vary according to their ages and access to instructional technologies. Students with fewer technological skills

and/or disabilities may require supplemental instruction and additional time to complete learning tasks. Advanced students may have more knowledge and experience working with certain technologies than their teachers and peers. As this occurs, teachers should encourage students to work as co-educators in the classroom and teach others new skills. When available, teachers and students may also benefit from working with an onsite computer technician who can assist with class technology needs.

**Blended learning** is a hybrid instructional approach that combines regular classroom instruction with online resources and activities to augment student learning. Teachers and administrators must take precautions to protect students' identities, with teachers monitoring students' online behaviors during instruction. Schools and youth organizations must comply with Internet safety laws, such as the **Children's Internet Protection Act (CIPA)**, which requires parental consent when online companies collect and share personal information on children under the age of 13. To keep students safe, schools purchase software that prevents students from entering potentially harmful sites and **learning management systems** that provide students with secure interactive virtual environments to participate in blended learning tasks (Tucker, 2012). They differ from public websites (like free social media ones) that collect users' personal data, feature distracting ads, and offer communications with strangers.

A learning management system is an excellent place to post instructional resources and reinforce classroom teaching. Online learning management systems contain organized spaces for students and teachers to message each other, write on discussion boards, create blogs, participate in videoconferencing, access instructional resources, and view assessments. They can use learning management systems to store digital art portfolios. Teachers can post online video tutorials for students to watch in the non-school hours and apply what they have learned in class. This **flipped classroom** approach teaches students the responsibility of learning new material independently and encourages them to make decisions to prepare for forthcoming class activities. Teachers can also provide students with links to content on museum, educational, and professional websites. Class discussion boards provide students with additional time to process questions and answers and can be helpful to students who feel shy about talking in class and/or are learning English.

When using online technologies, teachers will emphasize proper **netiquette**, so that students avoid hurting and antagonizing others on online environments.

Through comprehensive technology tasks, students will learn how to produce projects inspired by multimedia technologies, apply technological vocabulary, and recognize how the arts influence the technological products they use on a daily basis. To facilitate learning, teachers should troubleshoot anticipated technological problems that may arise before starting assignments. They will plan how students will charge, store, and protect technological devices. In circumstances when a classroom may not have adequate technology, teachers may be able to reserve a computer lab or incorporate a **bring your own device (BYOD)** policy in which students bring a personal mobile device to participate in learning tasks, while making accommodations for students without personal devices. Teachers will also reinforce the importance of saving and backing up completed and in-progress works so that students will not lose important information. Beginning with young learners, teachers will demonstrate how to conserve paper and print only what is necessary.

In early childhood, students enjoy looking at images, taking pictures, and creating digital artworks. Teachers can demonstrate how to operate tablets with protective casing or kid-friendly cameras to show students how to take pictures. While arranging found objects into a design, students could photograph their progress (Figure 18.22). This process combines necessary tactile learning with digital technologies. With teacher assistance, they could transform their documenting photographs into a stop-motion animation, like Leslie Patterson-Marx (Figure 18.9). Teachers can also design lessons for students to experiment and create art with studio apps. Teachers may limit students' drawing and painting tools during demonstrations and gradually introduce more options in sequential lessons to prevent students from becoming overwhelmed. When students are creating with educational computer games that require typing, teachers can create word banks to assist young children and teach them how to spell key words. Young children can compare and contrast technological artworks presented in books and animations. For example, they might compare and contrast the qualities of traditional animations with contemporary 3D animations. They could investigate the visual qualities of app icons designed especially for kids and compare them to ones designed for adults.

**FIGURE 18.22** Kindergarten students arranged found objects into a heart design. United States.
*Source: Author and Abbey Logan, teachers.*

In middle childhood, students have greater finger span and muscle strength in their hands, so they can begin learning formal typing skills. Teachers can align typing activities with lessons that demonstrate how artists and graphic designers incorporate digital text into art. Students can integrate different fonts to show meaning in traditional and digital artworks. During class critiques, students will explain how their chosen fonts augment artworks' meanings. Students at this age are more familiar with navigating websites and like to collect and organize information. They can complete online learning tasks, including ones found on museum education pages, and begin a digital collection of theme-related artworks to inform others about a particular topic. Students can manipulate original drawings, collages, paintings, and photographs with design software to create entirely digital works (Figure 18.23). They will experiment with various visual effects to manipulate the look of final products. At around age 11 children become more engaged in social networking (Ofcom/Sherbert Research, 2014). Although many social networking sites are developed for adults and older teens, middle-childhood

**FIGURE 18.23** Kristýna Kovalová,10-years-old, ZUŠ, Praha 5, Czech Republic.
*Source: ICEFA Lidice, 44th Exhibition.*

**FIGURE 18.24** This claymation by elementary through high school students teaches about global warming. United States.
*Source: Author, Monica Leister, and pre-service, teachers.*

students may ignore required age limits. As students desire more frequent group interactions, teachers can develop blended classroom learning discussion boards and blogs through which students can build social skills while remaining safe. Students can collaborate as a team to create an original educational video game. Given their familiarity of digital photography on mobile devices, students can broaden their knowledge to create stop-motion animations and claymations. They can also explore traditional photography methods such as creating photograms and cyanotypes, and constructing pinhole cameras.

By early adolescence, students have developed special interests and hobbies. They seek group belonging and many are fully engaged in social networking sites. As part of a comprehensive art curriculum, students can research and identify strategies to maintain privacy and online safety and present them in the form of creative works. Teachers might work with students to develop a participatory action research project that teaches about Internet safety and cyber bullying, because many young people have been exposed to mean and hurtful comments on the Internet (Hinduja & Patchin, 2015). As early adolescents can articulate cohesive points of view, students can develop persuasive videos focusing on current events. Students can also create collaborative animations, stop-motion animations, or claymations (Figure 18.24) based on big ideas that are relevant to them. With ongoing exposure to lessons that link art and technology, students can identify and incorporate the qualities that technology specialists integrate into their works

to influence people to view and/or purchase their products. Students can also investigate technology professions that interest them as possible career choices, such as graphic design. They can study how Madalyne Marie Hymas applied professional graphic design skills to inform society about dyslexia (see Artists' Lessons to Thrive! 18.1). Students can also examine Kathy Vargas' photographic series as inspirations to create theme-based multiple exposures (see Artists' Lessons to Thrive! 10.3). and Ansel Adam's use of photography as an advocacy tool.

Adolescents have an interest in digital media and can see the long-term benefits of developing and maintaining a discussion forum, class blog, or vlog. Students will determine the best content for these platforms, such as teaching art skills, presenting and responding to questions about contemporary art issues, and providing critiques of public art exhibitions. They will apply increased analytical and vocabulary skills to express their thoughts cogently and teach others. As adolescents appreciate social interactions, they can discuss the qualities that make new media festivals entertaining for the public. They can also identify how artists create interactive technological installations that inspire strangers to interact with each other. In preparing for future career skills, students will identify how technology specialists work in teams, as Dan Goods, Nik Hafermaas, and Aaron Koblin did to create *eCloud* (see Artists' Lessons to Thrive! 18.2). Students will work in groups to design collaborative technological art projects based on big ideas, including games, animations, documentaries, mockumentaries, art installations, and interactive artworks. The class will break into teams with individual members applying their skills to take the lead on distinct components for each project. By high school, students should have opportunities to work with professional products to create, edit, and manipulate images to produce comprehensive projects. If the school or learning facility does not have a darkroom, teachers who use film cameras might be able to arrange a class visit to a darkroom and studio and watch professional photographers in action. Figure 18.25 shows how Martin Homola photographs student artworks in a studio setting.

**FIGURE 18.25** Martin Homola uses specialized equipment to photograph ICEFA Lidice Exhibitions.
*Source: Martin Homola, photo.*

## OUR JOURNEY TO THRIVE CONTINUES . . .

This chapter addressed comprehensive strategies for integrating technology into the choice-based art curriculum. It completed Part IV on creating art through drawing, painting, paper arts, printmaking, book arts, sculpture, clay, mosaics, textiles, puppetry, and technology. Moving into Part V of this textbook, we will discover effective means to make the most of our teaching careers. Chapter 19 describes the many benefits of arts advocacy.

## CHAPTER QUESTIONS AND ACTIVITIES

1. Describe technology's functions and meanings from historic and societal perspectives. How will you integrate technologies including media arts, photography, and graphics into the choice-based art curriculum and STEAM learning tasks?
2. Practice the technology activities described in this chapter to compare and contrast their qualities. Summarize what you learned in a group discussion or in writing.
3. Develop an original comprehensive lesson on technology. Use the lesson plan template provided on the textbook's companion website and refer to Chapter 2 for more information on lesson plan development. Integrate inquiry tasks inspired by Part III of this textbook.
4. Answer Artists' Lessons to Thrive! 18.1–18.2's essential/guiding questions in written form or as part of a group discussion. Complete their daily learning targets.

## References

Alexander, A., & Ho, T. (2015). Gaming worlds: Secondary students creating and interactive video game. *Art Education, 68*(1), 28–36.

Barron, A. E., Ivers, K. S., Lilavois, N., & Wells, J. A. (2006). *Technologies for education: A practical guide* (5th ed.). Westport, CT: Libraries Unlimited.

Beavis, C. (2012). Video games in the classroom: Developing digital literacies. *Practically Primary, 17*(1), 17–20.

Brown, H. J. (2008). *Video games in education.* Armonk, NY: M. E. Sharpe.

Cubitt, S., & Thomas, P. (2015). The new materialism in media art history. In V. Catricalà (Ed.), *Media art: Towards a new definition of arts in the age of technology* (pp. 19–38). Rome, Italy: Fondazione Mondo Digitale.

Dixon, W. W., & Foster, G. A. (2008). *A short history of film.* Piscataway, NJ: Rutgers University Press.

Hinduja, S., & Patchin, J. W. (2015). *Bullying beyond the school-yard: Preventing and responding to cyberbullying* (2nd ed.). Thousand Oaks, CA: Corwin Press.

Keyker, K. (2014). *Teaching digital photography: The ultimate guide to "tween and teen learning"*. Santa Barbara, CA: ABC-CLIO.

Louisiana Museum of Modern Art. (2011). *David Hockney: Me draw on iPad*. Retrieved from www.louisiana.dk/uk/Menu/Exhibitions/David+Hockney%3A+Me+Draw+On+iPad

Nalven, J., & Jarvis, J. D. (2005). *Going digital: The practice and vision of digital artists*. Boston, MA: Course Technology.

Ofcom/Sherbert Research. (2014). *Children's online behaviour: Issues of risk and trust*. London, UK: Ofcom. Retrieved from http://stakeholders.ofcom.org.uk/market-data-research/medialiteracy/childrens/

Overby, A., & Jones, B. L. (2015). Virtual LEGOs: Incorporating Minecraft into the art education curriculum. *Art Education, 68*(1), 21–27.

Sandler, M. W. (2002). *Photography: An illustrated history*. New York: Oxford University Press.

Tucker, C. R. (2012). *Blended learning in grades 4–12: Leveraging the power of technology to create student-centered classrooms*. Thousand Oaks, CA: Corwin Press.

# PART V

# Making the Most of Your Teaching Career

# Chapter 19

# Arts Advocacy

**FIGURE 19.1** Tiny Circus, *Elephant Trap*. United States. Tiny Circus, artists-in-residence.
*Source: Sarah Fitzgerald, teacher.*

**Arts advocacy** is the act of informing others about the value of the visual arts and their roles in providing students and society members with exemplary learning experiences. Similar to effective advertisers who create valuable public service announcements to teach about significant issues through enthusiastic tones, quality visuals, and descriptions of their meanings, teachers with strong advocacy skills cogently explain how the visual arts benefit students and society. Their art education campaign promotes the value of the visual arts to students, parents, administrators, and the community. It articulates why students need the visual arts in schools and in the non-school hours. Arts advocates know their audience and speak to them directly to ensure that they understand and appreciate the need for a quality education through the visual arts in schools and communities. Like the individual frames that form a completed stop-motion animation, diverse arts advocacy methods come together to present a clear picture about the many benefits of teaching and learning in the visual arts.

We will meet the following objectives by participating in this chapter:

- Explain the qualities that make teachers effective arts advocates.
- Generate a plan for an arts advocacy campaign.
- Develop an art budget and write a grant proposal for teaching art.

Spotlight on Student Art #19, and Figures 19.1 and 19.2, present a school-wide arts project that provided students with exceptional learning experiences that extended beyond typical class instruction. This

**FIGURE 19.2** *Elephant Trap* still. Students manipulate their bodies into the form of a sailboat.
*Source: Tiny Circus, artists-in-residence; Sarah Fitzgerald, teacher.*

community art education project is a superb example of arts advocacy because of the substantial efforts the teachers applied to bring a stop-motion animation to life that involved students, professional artists, and the greater community.

## Spotlight on Student Art #19

### Big Idea: Arts Advocacy

Under the evening sky, community members watched the premiere of *Elephant Trap*, a three-minute stop-motion animation created by 527 pre-kindergarten through fourth-grade students and the Tiny Circus artists' collective. *Elephant Trap* (Figures 19.1 and 19.2) features an elephant blissfully munching on peanuts that have been strategically placed on a seesaw. Its motions activate cranking gears, a spinning windmill, and a sailboat that trap the elephant as part of an innocent game. This project represents arts advocacy, the act of informing others about the valuable role of the visual arts in students' education. *Elephant Trap* came to fruition because of the art teacher's vision and effective planning with the school's music teacher, administration, and parent–teacher organization. The art teacher sought the expertise of Tiny Circus to provide students with an exemplary learning experience that extended beyond what occurs during a typical week at school.

The students designed *Elephant Trap*'s collages, took its photographs, and added digital effects under the supervision of Tiny Circus and their art teacher. Art students from the neighboring middle school helped the younger students photograph aerial scenes, which required using a 40-foot (12 m) scissor lift. Simultaneously, the music teacher worked with students to develop an original music score that enhanced the film's visuals and added excitement to the storyline. The art teacher invited the local media to document the learning experience. In addition to the animation's premiere, Tiny Circus presented *Elephant Trap* and the processes of creating it on social media sites. All participants received accolades from the community for their work on *Elephant Trap* and the school administration invited Tiny Circus back the following year to create a new animation.

# ARTS ADVOCACY AND TEACHER LEADERSHIP

Arts advocacy and teacher leadership go hand in hand. Teachers who are arts advocates apply their leadership skills to generate quality learning outcomes for all students. Leadership includes teachers' professionalism, knowledge of the visual arts, enthusiasm for subject matter, genuine care for students, and the extra steps they take to inspire others. Teachers who are arts advocates continuously augment their understandings of art content and teaching methodologies. They recognize how the visual arts have intrinsic values (ones that make art a unique subject of study) and extrinsic values (that demonstrate how art connects to diverse aspects of life). They organize and develop meaningful arts experiences for students in which students are engaged and value the learning process (Figures 19.3 and 19.4). They inform administrators and the greater public about students' achievements and their professional

**FIGURE 19.4** Middle school students talk with their teacher about their work. United States.
*Source: Mike Muller, teacher.*

**FIGURE 19.3** Keiya Sumaria, 6-years-old, experiences the joys of creating art. Kenya.
*Source: Lisa Wee, teacher.*

accomplishments as well as share other significant information and statistics about the importance of the visual arts in society. They seek administrative/organizational support, form community partnerships, and take steps to secure sustainable program funding (National Coalition for Core Arts Standards [NCCAS], 2014; Rolling, 2011).

## Communications

Regular communications are an essential component of arts advocacy. Many teachers perform diligent work and produce effective results with students; however, they may not inform others about their achievements (Shin, 2012). If parents, administrators, and policy makers are not aware of results, they will not know what teachers and students have accomplished (Freedman, 2011). Arts advocates use multiple forms of communication as advocacy tools to communicate their messages. These include face-to-face communications, websites, emailing, letter writing, texting, and posting information on school and district/organization social media pages. Arts advocates use communication to highlight student and program achievements, raise awareness, seek guidance, and ask for support. Teachers who are arts advocates often develop multimedia resources to present quality student works, demonstrate art

**FIGURE 19.5** This paper mural and bench welcome elementary school visitors. United States.

*Source: Cassie Stephens, teacher.*

processes, teach art in context, and showcase students' artist statements and portfolios on websites and social media sites that reach broad audiences. They also display original student works with informative signage in high-traffic areas at their school/organization and within the broader community so that others will take notice and experience them firsthand (Figure 19.5).

Arts advocates inform the media about special art happenings by writing **press releases** that include contact information, images (as applicable), appropriate credits, and brief descriptions of important information, such as what a project is about, its date, time, place, and participants (see Model 19.1). The most effective press releases have catchy titles. As good practice, arts advocates send press releases a few weeks before events and contact the media about a week after sending them as a reminder (Council for Art Education, 2015).

## Model 19.1
## Press Release

Name: Quality Teacher                                                   Today's Date
Address: 123 Art Street
         Art City, My State 12345
Phone: (000) 000-0000
Email: My Email Address

### Students Paint Beautiful Teamwork Mural

During the academic school year, students at _____ (name of school) designed and painted a mural centering on the theme of teamwork. This large mural has three walls that depict children participating in collaborative learning activities including (a) performing on stage as dancers and musicians; (b) playing tug-of-war on field day; and (c) painting a mural and cleaning up their art supplies at the sink. This project was created under the guidance of _____ (teacher name, etc.) and received support from community volunteers, the school PTO, and a $1,000 grant from _____ (name of grantor). We cordially invite you to our opening reception on _____ (date) at _____(time) so you can view the mural and meet the students who created it.

## Everyday and Special Events

Teachers who are arts advocates recognize the importance of everyday events and special ones. Daily events establish the routines of what is to be expected as normative quality practices. Organizing and participating in art-centered special events increase program visibility and align with arts advocacy practices. Teachers who are arts advocates invite parents, community members, business leaders, members of community organizations, administrators, and policy makers to their arts events. The quality experiences they share can be vehicles to recruit their support in advocating for the visual arts. They may work together to plan **Youth Art Month (YAM)** events. YAM activities articulate the value of art in students' lives and the need for quality arts programming. YAM calls upon educators and community members to advocate for art at schools, within communities, at the state level, and nationally to gain support for the arts (Council for Art Education, 2018). Arts advocates may develop exhibitions, performances, seminars, and panel discussions (Figures 19.6 and 19.7). They might write grants to bring artists-in-residents to their learning sites. They may also participate in a school-wide or community career day to teach about visual arts professions. Many people do not know that there are nearly six million jobs in the arts and that this represents a $166 billion industry (Dean et al., 2010). Such facts can impress parents and policy makers.

FIGURE 19.7 Nick Peña, *From Sea to Shining Sea*, 2018, 30 in. (76.2 cm) diameter, watercolor, acrylic, sintra mat
Source: Courtesy of the artist; www.nickpena.net.

Sponsoring an art club is also an excellent means to advocate for the visual arts because it offers in-depth art instruction with specialized projects for visual arts students who want to expand their knowledge beyond classroom instruction and devote more time to studying art. Students in sixth through twelfth grades can become members of the **National Art Honors Society**, established by NAEA. Its purpose is to support talented students who want to pursue advanced art opportunities, participate in community service, and take leadership roles (NAEA, 2018). Student efforts often result in special activities that bring awareness to the art program.

## Community Art Education

Many arts advocates establish deep roots within the community through **community art education**, the practice of developing extraordinary projects and events with community partners that extend beyond regular classroom learning experiences. This chapter's Spotlight on Student Art #19 (Figures 19.1, 19.2, and 19.8) is one example of many community art education possibilities. Another example, presented in Artists' Lessons to Thrive! 19.1, teaches about the Tiny Circus film *Creativity* and the participants' work with adults in the community for the purpose

FIGURE 19.6 Pre-service art educators and art teacher Eric Breedlove give a panel discussion on arts advocacy while surrounded by original artworks by Nick Peña.
Source: Author, teacher.

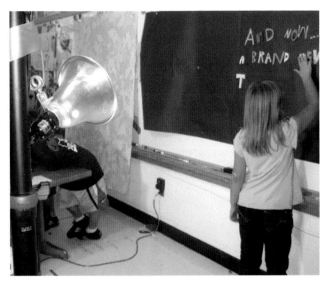

**FIGURE 19.8** Students developing *Elephant Trap*. Tiny Circus, artists-in-residence.

*Source: Sarah Fitzgerald, teacher.*

**FIGURE 19.9** Students and intergenerational participants formed concrete sculptures for a wetland themed art garden. United States.

*Source: Author and Suzanne St. John, teachers. Funded by MTSU Public Service Grant. Pamela McColly, photo.*

of identifying the meaning of creativity in daily life. It serves as a model for students to see how artists learn other people's opinions and ideas when creating artworks with the community. In addition to the stop-motion animations, community art education projects featured in this textbook include murals and an art garden. To implement community art projects, teachers take advantage of existing partnerships and establish new ones. Community art projects integrate special partners including teachers, professional artists, university students, and members of organizations. They put students in touch with people with whom they may not normally have contact, such as senior citizens, for intergenerational learning opportunities; male role models; people of different racial, ethnic, and sexual orientations; individuals facing hardship; people with disabilities; and individuals with specialized skills (Figure 19.9). Working with intergenerational and differentiated groups can provide a more accurate

representation of humanity and bring a greater sense of community to schools. Community partners apply their diversified life experiences to inspire students and teach them new knowledge (Reese, 2006; Sickler-Voigt, 2010; Tollefson-Hall & Wightman, 2013).

Working with partners, certified art educators apply their professional teaching methodologies and knowledge of curricular standards and assessments to reach students' needs (Gee, 2007; Stankiewicz, 2001; Trafi-Prats & Woywod, 2013). They prepare students to participate in community art education partnerships. Their preparation provides students with ideas to draw upon as they work on their project with artists and community members. Closure is equally important for community art education projects. Reflecting on their creative acts and learning processes are essential components of their efforts. Teachers and students should assess what they have learned and plan strategies to move forward (Carpenter, Taylor, & Cho, 2010).

 **Artists' Lessons to Thrive! 19.1 Tiny Circus: *Creativity***

**Big Idea: Creativity**

"Come and Join the Circus" is the alluring call of the Tiny Circus artist collective that produces stop-motion animations. Founded in 2008, its membership includes a small cast of full-time collaborators and more than 1,000 everyday people who come from all ages and range from novice producers of art to highly experienced professionals. Community members join the circus by participating in collaborative

**FIGURE 19.1.1** Tiny Circus, *Creativity* still, stop motion animation, 2012.
*Source: Courtesy of the artists; www.tinycircus.org.*

workshops that last from a few days to several weeks. As a team, circus members agree upon a theme and develop a storyboard for each film. They photograph multiple frame shots to illustrate a sequence of movements, edit their work, and add special effects.

Advocating that creativity belongs to everyone, the stop-motion animation *Creativity* tackles society's significant questions about creativity and adds a sense of playfulness through spinning objects, bright colors, and kaleidoscopic designs (Figure 19.1.1). Rather than focusing on the faces of people who tell their stories about creativity, the film presents viewers with scenes of circus members arranging and rearranging objects such as plates, books, and Scrabble® pieces, into aesthetic designs. These visual references serve as analogies that reveal how creativity surrounds us, even in what can be very simple and common forms. In essence, people need not have special tools or equipment to radiate creativity.

Although many people associate creativity with artistic products and performances, Tiny Circus broke through preconceived notions and asked everyday people to describe a creative act and recall a time in their lives when they made something. The group received sundry responses including making cream puffs, writing, dancing, and crocheting. The development of open-ended, non-assuming questions prompted individuals to explain that there are many ways in which people can be creative. For example, one elderly gentleman described how he felt creative in his youth when he played football. Delving deeper into the meaning of creativity, some participants identified how being creative is a time-consuming venture because small products can require a great deal of effort and time to produce to one's satisfaction. One interviewee expressed that he wanted other people to see him as creative, but would never actually call himself creative. His confession brings to light some of the stereotypes and pressures that can arise from society's preconceived perceptions of creativity, such as the concept that relatively few individuals are creative. Indeed, Tiny Circus' *Creativity* brings a much-needed dose of reality to society by identifying how creativity belongs to each of us and encompasses a range of tasks.

## Essential/Guiding Questions

1. The Tiny Circus slogan "Come and Join the Circus" invites new members into its collective. Why do you think that Tiny Circus cast members choose to work with all kinds of people, rather than only highly skilled artists and technological experts?
2. What is creativity? In which ways do you use creativity in your daily life? How have your own creative acts and/or products benefited you and others?

## Preparation

Students will view Tiny Circus' stop-motion animations online, including *Creativity*, and discuss the qualities and meaning of these works.

## Daily Learning Targets

I can create a mixed media artwork or stop-motion animation that advocates how creativity and the visual arts belong to everyone.

- I can assemble common objects to produce my artwork.
- I can create a unified design that includes repetition and demonstrates effective craftspersonship.
- I can present my completed work to an audience and explain how the different parts came together to communicate my message.

**National Core Arts Anchor Standards** 1, 5, 7, and 10
www.nationalartsstandards.org

## Teacher Research

Teachers know their programs best as they design art curricula, assess student learning outcomes, and evaluate the goals they have set. When teachers ask "what if" and "why" questions they seek to know more about their teaching methodologies, students, and programs. The NAEA Research Commission (2014) developed a research agenda to assist teachers in researching their programs and teaching. It provides sample questions in the areas of assessment and evaluation; social justice; emerging technologies; and demographic data. While its list is not meant to be all-inclusive, it helps teachers generate questions and understand the need for research that focuses on current art education theories, practices, and advocacy methods. Through self-guided research, teachers assume leadership roles and work as agents of positive change (Buffington & McKay, 2013). A team of educators (and students) can work alone or collaborate with university faculty and other knowledgeable community members to research specific issues through participatory action research and other methods. For example, the mural shown in Figure 19.10 is the result

of a partnership between an afterschool program and a university. Its purpose was for elementary students to participate in a participatory action research project for students to learn and express the meaning of respect from their own perspectives. Based on their findings, they developed a mural titled *Planet Respect*.

**FIGURE 19.10** *Planet Respect*. Elementary students. United States.

*Source: Author and Suzanne St. John, teachers. Funded by MTSU Public Service Grant. Pamela McColly, photo.*

The research process assists teachers and students in making connections and discoveries that they have not made before (McKay, 2006). Plus, it prompts teachers and students to take actions and feel empowered as they learn how to make positive changes. When teachers and students present the results of research findings in publications, teacher blogs, and conference presentations, they share their knowledge with other teachers and students who face similar challenges. Their research-driven advocacy efforts shape theory and best practices in art education (Klein, 2003; Stout, 2006).

## BUILDING AN ARTS ADVOCACY CAMPAIGN

This textbook provides quality exemplars for building arts advocacy campaigns. Arts advocacy must remain ongoing to stay current in people's minds. Many people support the arts. High-quality art programs and learning experiences satisfy parents who want the best education for their children. Students want to participate in high-quality visual arts programs due to the intrinsic and extrinsic benefits they provide (Rademaker, 2003). NAEA (2016) emphasized the importance of being visible and knowledgeable when advocating for the visual arts. Its website provides rich information on contemporary arts advocacy theories and practices through its downloadable promotional materials, white papers, advocacy discussions, and external links that showcase how other organizations have advocated for the arts. NAEA members regularly update the organization's strategic vision to identify the direction of art education. To stay current and relevant, art educators redesign standards, policy, curricula, and assessments as necessary so that all students will continue to have access to high-quality visual arts programs and experiences.

When building an arts advocacy campaign, teachers need to form lasting partnerships with people who understand the work that they do and are ready to step forward and take actions to support learning in the visual arts. This includes involving supervisors and specialized arts supervisors when available (Freedman, 2011). Community members' participation in art advocacy campaigns is also essential because there is strength in numbers. They broaden an art program's reach by aligning teachers and students with external partners. Working as a unified team their collaborative

advocacy efforts serve as reminders to policy makers and administrators about what the arts can do to benefit students and the reasons why students need the arts each and every day, even when budgets are tight and standardized testing plays a prominent role in schools. They may schedule times to meet with administrators and elected officials to advocate for the visual arts and describe how teaching the visual arts aligns with standards and a school's, district's or organization's mission statement. They may participate in phone call and letter writing campaigns. Teachers, students, and volunteers might send postcards and/or original artworks to decision makers and the general public to gain their support. In circumstances when policy and educational cuts become extreme, arts advocates take even greater measures through their arts advocacy campaigns to promote the value of a quality education in the visual arts. If art instruction time is reduced at their school or program, or if a school requires a full-time certified art educator, teachers and supportive parents may decide to join forces with members of community arts organizations and other partners who can assist in communicating (and ultimately satisfying) students' needs for sufficient art education programming to the administration, school board, and other policy makers (Stankiewicz, 2001; Trafi-Prats & Woywod, 2013). Throughout their advocacy campaigns, teachers regularly take steps to recognize the people and policy makers that have supported their cause.

## ADVOCACY AND VISUAL ARTS FUNDING

Arts advocacy can have a direct impact on available resources for teaching art because principals and other administrators control art budgets, class facilities, and scheduling. When they witness the benefits of the visual arts firsthand through advocacy methods, they are more likely to continue to support them (Luehrman, 2002). The art budget relates directly to program operations. Using an approach that is similar to planning through backwards design, teachers must predetermine how available resources impact what and how they teach for students to meet learning outcomes (NCCAS, 2014). While teachers have a reputation for being resourceful individuals who can turn recycled trash into repurposed treasure, they require adequate funding to teach comprehensive art lessons, such as

**FIGURE 19.11** Tereza Hejlová, 5-years-old, ZUŠ, Plzeň, Czech Republic.
*Source: ICEFA Lidice, 41st Exhibition.*

**FIGURE 19.12** Nare Vartanovna Arutiunian, 14-years-old, National Children's Library after Khnko-Aper, Yerevan, Armenia.
*Source: ICEFA Lidice, 41st Exhibition.*

those represented by the examples in Figures 9.11 and 9.12. Unlike the materials used in many other academic disciplines, most art supplies are consumable. Teachers must constantly replenish the majority of class products, including crayons, paint, and specialty papers. Classrooms for teaching art should also be furnished with specialized equipment, including a paper cutter, drying rack, kiln, and computer devices.

## Art Budget Planning

Administrators allocate a predetermined financial amount to fund the visual arts each school year. Programs receive varying funding amounts based on available resources and/or administrators' and policy makers' commitment to the arts. Some teachers receive no funding and others have substantial budgets to cover student needs. In planning their budgets, teachers should estimate how much it will cost to teach curricular content to meet standards. Many pre-service, beginning teachers, and non-arts administrators can be surprised by the expense of art materials and equipment, especially when teaching hundreds of students each week. When planning supply needs, teachers should consider how many students they will be teaching and list the supplies that they require. Larger school districts have distribution centers that store bulk art supplies for schools to purchase at discounted prices. Teachers might also use art catalogues and shop sales to supplement what the distribution center does not carry. When the essential supplies that students need cost more than the budgets allocated, teachers can request an appointment with their administrators to explain how their programs require specific art media and equipment for students to meet standards and other relevant learning needs. They can also have ready a list of necessary supplies and their prices. If they have made a convincing case, but their schools or organizations do not have the necessary funding, they can ask their administrators for guidance in finding alternative sources.

## Fundraising

**Fundraising** is the act of soliciting monetary or material contributions through organized events designed to support a program, project, or event. Many school systems, organizations, administrators, and teachers participate in fundraising activities to supplement their budgets. Some teachers hold annual art auctions for which artists, teachers, and students donate art to raise money for their causes. Special events such as these can be utilized as arts advocacy to showcase program happenings and their quality outcomes. Some teachers sell artistic products for a profit, such as ceramic mugs. Teachers may select from fundraising businesses that specialize in selling students' products, such as frames to display students' original artworks and reproductions of students' artworks on products including key chains and magnets. Teachers might ask parents and students to clip coupons to redeem cash or goods for their programs. The funds that teachers generate vary according to teacher time investments, school support, and parents' ability to afford such products. Regardless of the type, the best fundraisers involve many supportive individuals (Ellison, 2003; Schachter, 2005).

## Grant Writing

**Grants** are financial awards that government agencies, businesses, and foundations offer to support specific purposes. They come in all shapes and sizes. They vary in financial amounts, may be limited by geographic regions, and target certain audiences. Funding agencies develop grants to align with their organizational goals. For example, they may focus on the arts, dropout prevention, or children's healthy living habits. **Grantors** (funders) most often support educational and nonprofit organizations because of their tax-free status and their ability to perform projects that benefit society. In return, grantors demonstrate their funding agency's commitment to the community (Wason, 2004).

Bringing in grants to support the visual arts is an excellent advocacy strategy. Successful grant writers allow adequate time to plan and write grants, as grant writing can be time consuming. Teachers can learn how to write successful grants through workshops and university courses. Throughout an academic year, teachers can receive notices about grants for which their programs qualify. Teachers also can conduct Internet searches to locate grants and see what their art and teacher organizations have to offer. If their school districts or organizations have a grants office, they can contact its personnel for assistance in finding grants that suit their project needs and ask to be placed on a grant listserv. Because grants have different goals and target audiences, teachers need to search for the best match for their project ideas and student populations. For example, the children's organization that created the mural shown in Figure 19.13 received grants that supported their student population, which included children and adolescents with at-risk tendencies.

**FIGURE 19.13** *Lift Every Voice and Sing.* Early childhood through adolescence. United States.
*Source: Jill Harper, director.*

**FIGURE 19.14** *Teamwork Mural: Ballet Wall.* Elementary students. United States. Funded by Arts for a Complete Education/Florida Alliance for Arts Education.
*Source: Author, teacher. Pamela McColly photo.*

Successful grant writers structure their projects around a specific need rather than a want, because funders will only provide financial assistance to solve specific problems, not to fancy an individual's personal desire. A sample want might include: "I want students to paint a mural." However, when describing a need, a teacher would use the mural as a means to solve a specific problem. The need might be: "My students are having difficulty collaborating with one another" and the solution might be: "Through the creation of a mural focusing on teamwork, the students will brainstorm the meaning of teamwork based on their study of teamwork in daily life, home, school, and artists' creations. They will apply collaborative learning skills to plan, implement, and complete their mural." Figures 19.14–19.16 present a teamwork mural funded by a grant.

Teacher applicants should follow all directions carefully when they write a grant and fill out its application. Those who do not follow directions may have their proposals discarded by the grantor without considering their content. Some grant agencies may have teachers insert information into fixed templates, while others ask applicants to create an original document using their guidelines. Although formats vary,

**FIGURE 19.15** *Teamwork Mural: Mural Painting Wall.* Elementary students. United States. Funded by Arts for a Complete Education/Florida Alliance for Arts Education.
*Source: Author, teacher. Pamela McColly photo.*

**FIGURE 19.16** *Teamwork Mural: Tug of War Wall.* Elementary students. United States. Funded by Arts for a Complete Education/Florida Alliance for Arts Education.
*Source: Author, teacher. Pamela McColly photo.*

most grant proposals include (a) an introduction that summarizes the project and addresses its need and goals; (b) its objectives, written so that the grantors can understand measureable student actions, such as "The student(s) will" + measurable behavior + stimulus + criteria; (c) project methods; (d) an evaluation; (e) a timeline; and (f) a budget. In addition to these, teachers may need to submit résumés and letters of support from their administration and other key decision makers and participants.

Strong grant proposals are well written, professional, personable, and have a logical flow, as this makes reading grants more engaging and attractive to grantors, who may have a large selection of grants from which to choose. Effective grant writers use their proposal's introduction to explain the project's need, identify project participants, and state its goals. They incorporate relevant research and statistics to support the cause. Next, they define the project's objectives, which measure the actions that participants will take to reach the project's goals. They identify how the proposed project connects to the funder's goals and their school or organization's mission.

For the project methods section, teachers describe the project's activities and how they will guide participants in reaching its goals and objectives. They identify participants' responsibilities and their instructional strategies and resources to meet the grant's need. They make sure that the grantors understand what they have described, rather than assume that grantors know what they mean. They explain terminology and avoid jargon. Quality grant proposals include a plan to evaluate what students will learn from the experience. For example, students can create a project portfolio, as well as participate in summative critiques to discuss how they reached their final product. Teachers might interview participants to identify their perspectives on the combined learning experiences. For example, if a project revolved around teamwork, they could check to see if participants introduce the words "teamwork" and "we" during their interviews without prompting.

Successful grant writers plan their budgets by determining if a funding agency will pay for their project in full, or if the grantor funds only partial requests and anticipates contributions from other sources. Some grants require **matching funds** that necessitate that grant writers obtain equal amounts in cash from another source to match the funds the grantor will award. For example, if such a grant has a maximum value of $2,000, the grant writer must secure another $2,000 in cash from other sources. Grantors often request matching funds to verify that the grant writer is invested in the project. Matching funds double the project's budget and permit participants to achieve more. Another form of support is called an **in-kind contribution**, which includes non-cash goods and services from other sources. For instance, a company may donate materials for a project, such as a paint company that contributes remnant paint colors. Teachers can also include materials, instructional resources, and equipment that they already have (including markers, books, and computers) in their in-kind funds. In-kind support can include people's salaries calculated at an hourly rate for their donated services. For example, teachers may volunteer their time to work on a project, as well as bring in parents and community members with special skills necessary to the project's goals. If a participant earns $25/hour and will volunteer on the project for 10 hours, teachers would calculate $250 in in-kind support. Like matching funds, grantors want to see that teachers have generated in-kind support from people, businesses, and organizations because it shows a greater commitment to the project, as well as teachers' abilities to make community connections. Even if grants do not require matching funds and in-kind support, teachers can list them on a grant if they are available to let funders know how these contributions will help them reach their proposed grant's goals. If a grantor requires matching funds and/or in-kind support, and a grant writer cannot obtain them, the grant will be rejected.

Many successful grant writers choose to communicate with funding agencies as they develop their grant proposals. This process introduces their project ideas, answers important questions, and assists them in determining if their projects align with grantors' goals. It also lets the grantors see their passion for a proposed project (Wason, 2004). With this in mind, teachers ask valid questions when contacting a grantor, rather than basic questions that they can find the answers to on grant applications and websites. They check deadlines and review previously funded grants (when available) on grantors' websites to assist in developing proposals. They finalize the grant by reading the proposal carefully and have a qualified colleague or administrator proofread the grant to catch mistakes and other necessary information they might have missed. Depending on the grantor's requirements, they will submit the grant online, deliver it in person, or send it through certified mail to confirm its safe arrival.

After efforts to submit a quality proposal, all teachers like to receive this news: "Congratulations! We've funded your grant!" Once a grant proposal has been funded, teachers will document evidence of student learning throughout the grant's duration. Grantors integrate these data for the grant's final report, which is required by most funders. They often publish the data from final reports on their websites or in newsletters to demonstrate how their financial support has made a positive difference and solved a need. In circumstances in which a grant proposal does not receive funding, teachers can politely contact the grantor to learn how they could have improved a submission. In some cases teachers may have written a quality grant proposal, but the grantor may have had limited funds, or a different grant was closer to its goals. Striving to become successful grant writers, they do not give up when they do not receive funding. They keep trying and continue to build their grant writing skills. See the sample teacher proposal for a mini-grant in Model 19.2.

## Model 19.2
## Teacher Mini-Grant

### Describe Your Project and Its Need in 100 Words or Less

The purpose of this project is to design a mural that focuses on teamwork. While people need to possess teamwork skills in daily life, many of our school's students have shown frustration when it comes to forming collaborative projects due to not knowing practical strategies for working together effectively. Instead of telling students that they must demonstrate teamwork, this project will teach students how to utilize teamwork through the creation of a school mural that represents teamwork in action. Students will identify how artists, society members, and people like themselves have applied teamwork to solve problems in diverse situations.

### Identify the Project's Objectives

1. Given class discussions and preliminary sketches, the students will create a 6-foot × 60-foot (2m × 18m) mural using exterior wall paint and mosaic tiles that represents three different examples of teamwork. Their mural will have an effective composition and show craftspersonship.
2. Given learning tasks relating to teamwork, the students will create a portfolio that contains at least four artworks in the media of their choice about teamwork, a one-page paper on what teamwork means to them, and at least three different art inquiry responses to the artworks they studied.
3. The students will present their in-progress and completed teamwork projects on the school website and write reflective statements to describe their processes for creating the mural.

## List the Procedures to Meet the Stated Objectives

- The teacher will introduce the big idea of teamwork and the project to the students.
- The teacher and students will investigate the ways in which diversified artists have depicted teamwork in art.
- The class will participate in discussions about the role of teamwork at home, school, work, and society. Students will make choice-based artworks related to each of these subcategories.
- The students will create a portfolio and use the class website to assemble and reflect upon their sketches, readings, and writings.
- Once the students have demonstrated a foundational knowledge of teamwork, they will continue to create artworks using the media of their choice to identify teamwork's different characteristics.
- The students will make sketches to plan the design of their teamwork mural.
- The students will draw their mural design on the walls with chalk and paint their mural with exterior latex paint.
- The students will listen to fellow students' ideas as they work to develop solutions to problems related to creating the mural.
- The students will apply mosaic tiles to the mural wall.
- Throughout the mural and art making processes, class members will assess the quality of their work and make revisions as necessary.
- Upon completion of the mural, the students will participate in a class critique to discuss teamwork and the mural making process. They will post images of their completed mural on the class website.

## Identify How You Will Evaluate the Project

- The teacher will write a summative report that includes photographs and identifies what students learned from creating the mural and its related projects. Students will address how they can continue to grow after completing the project.
- To assess the student portfolio, the teacher will use a holistic scoring rubric to measure the quality of its contents.
- The students will use self-assessment during formative and summative class critiques to discuss their progress and what they have learned about teamwork.
- The teacher will utilize a checklist to assess the process of students working together to document that they are cooperating with one another and working to the best of their abilities.
- Throughout the project, the teacher will meet with students individually and in small groups to assess their progress formatively.

## Provide the Project Timeline

- **September**: The teacher will introduce the teamwork mural project to the students. The class will discuss the importance of teamwork and how artists have represented it. They will examine murals in art history through class discussions and written inquiry activities. The class will create monthly online postings to document the project and their insights.
- **October**: The students will apply their research on teamwork to begin designing the mural. They will create a large-scale drawing of the mural.
- **November**: The students will begin painting the mural. They will continue to work on their teamwork portfolio and discuss their study of teamwork.
- **December–February**: The students will continue painting and developing their portfolios. They will contemplate the meaning of teamwork given what they have learned.

- **March**: Students will incorporate mosaic tiles into the mural. They will continue to study teamwork's meanings and purposes.
- **April**: Students will complete the mural and their portfolios. They will participate in a final critique and discuss how teamwork enabled them to create the mural. The school will hold an opening reception and recognition ceremony.

## Budget Detail

| Item and Description | Amount Requested | In-Kind Contributions (Supplies and Services) | Total |
|---|---|---|---|
| Exterior Latex Paint 20 Gallons @ $25 | $500 | $100 (The paint store will donate remnant paint.) | $600 |
| Three-Piece Paintbrush Set 5 @ $10 | $50 | $50 (Our school will supply small paintbrushes.) | $100 |
| Sanded Grout (for Mosaics) 2 Bags @ $12.50 | $25 | | $25 |
| Thin Set (for Mosaics) 1 Bag @ $25.00 | $25 | | $25 |
| Tile Nippers 4 @ $12.50 | $50 | | $50 |
| Mosaic Tiles Bag of 24 30 @ $5.00 | $150 | $150 (The tile store will donate remnant tiles.) | $300 |
| Canvas Drop Cloth 4 @ 12.50 | $50 | | $50 |
| Grouting Trowels 4 @ $12.50 | $50 | | $50 |
| Rubber Gloves | | $25 (The school will supply the gloves.) | $25 |
| Sponges, Smocks, and Rags | | $25 (The school will supply these materials.) | $25 |
| Paper | | $25 (The school will supply the paper.) | $25 |
| Paint Buckets | | $25 (The school will supply the buckets.) | $25 |
| Books on Art History and Mosaics 4 Books @ $25.00 | $100 | $200 (The school will supply additional books.) | $300 |
| Total | $1000 | $600 | $1,600 |
| TOTAL FUNDS REQUESTED | $1000 | | |

## OUR JOURNEY TO THRIVE CONTINUES . . .

This chapter provided practical information on arts advocacy. Our effective advocacy efforts maintain the visual arts as strong and vital components of school and community life. As arts advocates, we communicate about arts' intrinsic and extrinsic values. We teach others how to recognize the many ways that the visual arts are meaningful to students' whole development. In the next and final chapter of this textbook, we will learn how to apply our ongoing arts advocacy efforts to make the most of our teaching careers and provide students with quality learning experiences that last a lifetime.

## CHAPTER QUESTIONS AND ACTIVITIES

1. Describe the qualities that make teachers effective arts advocates. Develop a plan to implement an arts advocacy campaign by listing the steps you (and others you recruit) will take to advocate for the visual arts in schools and the community.
2. Develop $500 and $1,000 art budgets (in table format) that accommodate 150 to 500 students, with classes that have approximately 30 students each. In planning your budgets, include basic materials (paper, scissors, glue, paint, markers, masking tape, etc.) that will accommodate two- and three-dimensional projects. Your budget table will include four columns: (a) material/equipment name, (b) price per unit, (c) quantity, and (d) total price for material/equipment. Reflect on the materials in your final budgets. What materials would you have liked to purchase at the $500 and $1,000 amounts that you could not afford?
3. Write a $1,000 grant proposal to fund a community art education project. You may not exceed this amount, but can include additional in-kind contributions and/or matching funds. Use Model 19.2 as a guide to (a) describe your project and its need in 90–100 words, (b) state its objectives, (c) list its procedures, (d) identify how you will evaluate your project, (e) develop a timeline, and (f) create a detailed budget.
4. Answer Artists' Lessons to Thrive! 19.1's essential/guiding questions in written form or as part of a group discussion. Complete its daily learning targets.

## References

Buffington, M. L., & McKay, S. W. (2013). T(Res)ea(r)cher. In M. L. Buffington & S. Wilson McKay (Eds.), *Practice theory: Seeing the power of art teacher researchers* (pp. 1–8). Reston, VA: National Art Education Association.

Carpenter, B. S., Taylor, P. G., & Cho, M. (2010). Making a (visual/visible) difference because people matter: Responsible artists and artistic responses to community. In T. Anderson, D. Gussak, K. K. Hallmark & A. Paul (Eds.), *Art education for social justice* (pp. 60–66). Reston, VA: National Art Education Association.

Council for Art Education. (2015). *How to submit a press release.* Retrieved from http://councilforarteducation.org/wp-content/uploads/2015/10/How-to-Write-a-Press-Release.pdf

Council for Art Education. (2018). *Youth art month.* Retrieved from http://councilforarteducation.org/youth-art-month/

Dean, C., Ebert, C. M. L., McGreevy-Nichols, S., Quinn, B., Sabol, F. R., Schmid, D., . . . Shuler, S. C. (2010). *21st century skills map: Arts.* Tucson, AZ: Partnership for 21st Century Skills.

Ellison, S. (2003). $chool fundraising. *Scholastic Parent & Child, 11*(3), 13.

Freedman, K. (2011). Leadership in art education: Taking action in schools and communities. *Journal of Art Education, 64*(2), 40–45.

Gee, C. B. (2007). Valuing the arts on their own terms? (Ceci n'est pas une pipe). *Arts Education Policy Review, 108*(3), 3–12.

Klein, S. R. (2003). Introduction. In S. Klein (Ed.), *Teaching art in context* (pp. ix–xviii). Reston, VA: National Art Education Association.

Luehrman, M. (2002). Art education and attitude toward art education: A descriptive study of Missouri public school principals. *Studies in Art Education, 43*(3), 197–218.

McKay, S. W. (2006). Living the questions: Action research in art education. *Art Education, 59*(6), 47–51.

National Art Education Association. (2016). *Advocacy made simple.* Retrieved from https://www.arteducators.org/advocacy/articles/51-advocacy-made-simple

National Art Education Association. (2018). *National Art Honor Society: National Junior Art Honor Society: 2017–2018 chapter handbook and resource catalog for new chapters.* Retrieved from www.arteducators.org/community/national-art-honor-societies/handbooks-and-forms

National Art Education Association Research Commission. (2014). *NAEA research agenda.* Retrieved from www.arteducators.org/research/articles/168-naea-research-agenda

National Coalition for Core Arts Standards. (2014). *National Core Arts Standards: A conceptual framework for arts learning.* Retrieved from www.nationalartsstandards.org/sites/default/files/NCCAS%20%20Conceptual%20Framework_4.pdf

Rademaker, L. L. (2003). Community involvement in arts education: A case study. *Arts Education Policy Review, 105*(1), 13–24.

Reese, S. (2006). The art of mentoring. *Techniques: Connecting Education & Careers, 8*(6), 14–19.

Rolling, J. H. (2011). *Art education as a network for curriculum innovation and adaptable learning.* Retrieved from www.arteducators.org/advocacy/NAEA_AdvocacyWhitePapers_1.pdf

Schachter, R. (2005). Fundraising grows up. *District Administration, 41*(2), 39–43.

Shin, R. (2012). The business of art education: Friend or foe? *Art Education, 65*(2), 33–39.

Sickler-Voigt, D. C. (2010). Unsung heroes: Making a positive difference through intergenerational learning. In T. Anderson, D. Gussak, K. K. Hallmark, & A. Paul (Eds.), *Art education for social justice* (pp. 84–90). Reston, VA: National Art Education Association.

Stankiewicz, M. A. (2001). Community/school partnership for the arts: Collaboration, politics, and policy. *Arts Education Policy Review, 102*(6), 3–10.

Stout, C. J. (2006). With all due respect: A second look at action research. *Studies in Art Education, 47*(3), 195–197.

Tollefson-Hall, K., & Wightman, W. (2013). Enhancing teacher preparation through intergenerational-based service learning. *Journal of Art for Life, 4*(1). Advance online publication. http://diginole.lib.fsu.edu/jafl/vol4/iss1/2

Trafi-Prats, L., & Woywod, C. (2013). We love our public schools: Art teachers' life histories in a time of loss, accountability, and new commonalities. *Studies in Art Education, 55*(1), 7–17.

Wason, S. D. (2004). *Webster's New World® grant writing handbook.* Hoboken, NJ: Wiley.

# Chapter 20

# Making the Most of Your Teaching Career

Great teachers are easy to identify. Their positivity and enthusiasm are contagious! They continuously strive to improve their teaching practices and advocate for students and best educational policies. Great teachers understand that the teaching profession has its rewards and challenges, and they take conscious steps to maintain personal and professional well-being at all stages of their careers (Figures 20.1 and 20.2). Educators' rewards come in many forms. The most meaningful accomplishments for many teachers include the joys of sharing their knowledge with others and knowing that they have positively impacted students' lives. This requires teachers to invest their time and their belief in students, especially when

**FIGURE 20.2** Vsevolod Romankov is a great teacher who creates and exhibits his plein air paintings internationally.
*Source: Courtesy of the artist.*

**FIGURE 20.1** Marynn Robinson is on her way to becoming a great teacher. As a pre-service teacher she developed a quality teaching portfolio that includes an original curriculum she designed to teach students the values of school and community pride.
*Source: Author, teacher.*

students feel that the odds are stacked against them. Great educators also take measures to reduce personal stress when challenges arise and use productive means to make the most of their teaching careers.

We will meet the following objectives by participating in this chapter:

- Identify how teachers express creativity and explain how lifelong learning results in career enhancement and personal satisfaction.
- Develop personal resources to prepare for job searches in the teaching profession.

- Reflect upon this book's teachings about best practices in teaching art and identify how to apply them to our personal teaching careers.

## TEACHER CREATIVITY

Teacher creativity comes in many forms to suit individual educators' needs. It includes the visual arts as well as activities such as creative writing and performances. For some, teacher creativity might center on designing original instructional resources, lesson plans, and assessments. Some teachers study their own professional practices and may publish their findings in journals and/or share their creations on social media. Teachers' own artistic creations may focus on a particular concept, medium, or process. Some teachers exhibit their works; others keep their creations private. Teacher creations can span from small products to elaborate public commissions. Teachers who simultaneously work as practicing artists and teach are called **teacher artists** (Booth, 2003). Their teaching influences their art, and their art-making practices inspire their teaching (Graham & Zwirn, 2010; Smilan, 2016). The following narratives demonstrate how teaching artists fuse artistic and pedagogical skills to teach students and the broader community; these narrative include quotes that resulted from communications with the author (personal communications, 2018). The teacher artists' exemplars offer insights to the diversified ways that educators combine artistry, effective teaching methodologies, and life lessons as integral components of their professional practices. Similarly, this chapter's Artists' Lessons to Thrive! 20.1 features Lorinne Lee, a retired teacher artist and lifelong learner, who continues to expand her creative horizons and inspire others through her ongoing service to the profession.

---

### Artists' Lessons to Thrive! 20.1 Lorinne Lee: Setting the Stage for Leadership in the Visual Arts

#### Big Idea: Leadership

Lorinne Lee is an experienced leader in art education who has dedicated four decades of outstanding service to the profession. Her painting *Bluegrass Banjo* serves as an analogy for her leadership as a teaching artist and advocate for the visual arts. The artwork belongs to *Rhythmic Melody*, Lee's series that features street musicians, called buskers, performing at Seattle's famous Pike Place Market. Lee designed the series for *Artistic Voices: Teachers as Artists*, an exhibition that she curated. *Bluegrass Banjo* is unique to the series because it integrates art advocacy statements. One reads: "ART MATTERS: Support visual arts education in your community." Its inclusion references a NAEA convention that took place in Seattle just before Lee painted it.

*Bluegrass Banjo* contains a second advocacy statement that urges art educators to tell the world about the value of an education in the visual arts. It asserts "Your voice and vision matter!" Lee's selection of visual arts advocacy statements aligns with the Pike Market Place buskers' campaign of providing public platforms for performers as a fundamental societal right. Just as performers require public spaces to perform, all students deserve access to a quality education in the visual arts to communicate their ideas, learn about others, and shape the environment. A strong advocate for all arts, Lee expressed: "Art and music together engages us to express our emotions, stories, ideas and opinions regarding life."

Lee composed *Bluegrass Banjo* by layering brushstrokes to form deep colors and textures. She described their meanings: "The lines, brushstrokes, colors and materials may appear raw, fluid and spontaneous, but they are specific as one's own handwriting and message." Her layered painting processes parallels the commitment needed to construct a career rich with rewarding experiences

**FIGURE 20.1.1** Lorinne Lee, *Bluegrass Banjo,* 2018.
*Source: Courtesy of the artist.*

for students, teachers, and community members. Examples of Lee's commitment include building professional partnerships and seeking grants to support students. In addition to teaching, she has worked as a district art supervisor and mentored teachers, led professional development activities, and developed art curricula and assessments for her district and state. Similar to the banjo player's concentrated facial expression, Lee's commitment to art education is equally focused and has resulted in quality outcomes. She continues to mentor art educators and students. She even curated an exhibition that featured artworks by her former students, who work as professionals within and outside of the visual arts. She described the experience as "one of the most rewarding projects" since retiring.

In sum, Lee's *Artistic Voices: Teachers as Artists* exhibition reached 18,000 visitors a month with its strong visual arts advocacy message. Like fine and performing artworks that make people feel good and lead them to positive actions, Lorinne Lee's leadership style inspires others. Dedicated to the love of teaching, she welcomes everyone to the visual arts, demonstrates how to lead by example, and always thanks people for their diligent efforts. Her lifetime of achievement and her positive disposition encourage others to get involved and invite students and young professionals to become the next generation of leaders.

## Essential/Guiding Questions

1. What qualities make an effective leader? Which of Lorinne Lee's leadership qualities stand out to you the most?
2. Why did Lee include the statements "Art matters" and "Your voice and vision matter!" in *Bluegrass Banjo*? How does their inclusion promote leadership in the visual arts?

## Preparation

Students will brainstorm the qualities of effective leaders and identify leaders within their communities. They will discuss ways to visualize leadership skills and convey meanings through art. For example, in addition to including advocacy statements within *Bluegrass Banjo* Lee wrote a haiku poem to accompany the series:

Rhythmic Melody
Happiness Is Hearing Notes
Awakes Me from Sleep

## Daily Learning Targets

I can create a self-portrait that represents my abilities as an effective leader.

- I can integrate key words, poetry, and/or inspirational leadership quotes into my artwork's composition and/or as part of my artwork's display.
- I can select appropriate art production methods, symbols, and materials needed to construct a unified artwork that shows effective craftspersonship (i.e. two- or three-dimensional design; realistic and/or abstract symbols).
- I can develop a visual and written plan that describes how and where I would want to exhibit my artwork.

**National Core Arts Anchor Standards** 1, 6, 7, and 10
www.nationalartsstandards.org

*Quoted artists' statements not listed in the reference section result from personal communications with the author (personal communications, 2014–2018).*

## Cassie Stephens: Making Magic Happen in the Classroom and Beyond

Cassie Stephens is a compelling ambassador for art education because of her ongoing advocacy efforts in the classroom and community. Social media followers eagerly await her postings on best teaching practices and the creative classroom fashions that she produces from scratch and with repurposed thrift store finds (Figure 20.3). While Stephens' multimedia blog inspires followers with its quality visuals, useful tips, and her sense of humor, her elementary students have the greatest benefit of learning and creating under her close supervision within the magical classroom atmosphere that she designed with mesmerizing artistic and educational displays. Students attentively participate during instruction as she wears themed outfits that reinforce lesson content. Stephens also integrates exciting character voices and a full range of manipulatives to spark students' imaginations and stimulate learning.

## Vsevolod Romankov: Building Mutual Trust as Artists and Travelers

Vsevolod Romankov is an internationally acclaimed teaching artist recognized for his exceptional plein air paintings (Figure 20.4). For decades he has taken middle and high school students to national and

**FIGURE 20.3** Cassie Stephens' handmade crayon-inspired outfit matches her classroom.
*Source: Stella Blue Photography.*

**FIGURE 20.4** Vsevolod Romankov, *Evening in Moscow,* watercolor, 23.62 × 31.49 in. (60 × 80 cm.)
*Source: Courtesy of the artist.*

**FIGURE 20.5** Weather is rarely a limiting factor. Romankov and his students paint on cold winter days. Russia.
*Source: Vsevolod Romankov, teacher.*

international destinations to paint, visit cultural sites, and participate in art competitions (Figure 20.5). Excursions last up to fourteen days. His instructional methods encourage students' creative choices and are designed to dissolve communication barriers. Students observe Romankov's expert techniques as they paint side-by-side with their teacher. He never imposes his opinions about how students should paint. He simply helps them find their own creative and technical solutions. Sharing their mutual respect and trust for each other, Romankov explained "both the teacher and the student reveal themselves as individuals" and added, "in the open air we all are artists and travelers." These interactions demonstrate their authentic camaraderie. Their diligent art practices and positive attitudes produce outstanding results. Each year Romankov's students win prestigious awards and receive invitations to exhibit their paintings.

## Melanie Anderson: Stepping Out of One's Comfort Zone

Melanie Anderson has painted an impressive collection of dog portraits. Her vivid artworks reinforce her belief that dogs "brightly color our world." They love to play and be in the present moment. Sometimes her painted dogs wear bowties or carry a ball or two as part of their play routines (Figure 20.6). *The Sunbathers* (Figure 20.7), with its gray undertones, differs from Anderson's usual paintings. She stepped out of her comfort zone to paint it using a historic method called *grisaille* that consists of gray tones and thin glazes. Anderson developed the artwork in preparation for teaching a grisaille lesson to understand the potential difficulties that her high school students might encounter. She shared her

FIGURE 20.6 Melanie Anderson, *Eat, Sleep, Play, Repeat.*
*Source: www.melanieanderson.net*

FIGURE 20.7 Melanie Anderson, *The Sunbathers.*
*Source: www.melanieanderson.net*

production experiences with students so they could identify with her struggles and experimental efforts. By seeing how Anderson worked through challenges, students were motivated to take creative risks as they explored a new art production method.

## Mike Muller: Delivering One-to-One Instruction

Mike Muller generates artworks in his middle school classroom that align with the lessons he teaches. He simultaneously produces videos that document the

FIGURE 20.8 Mike Muller, *Self-Portrait.*
*Source: Courtesy of the artist.*

artistic procedures he uses to make art. One time-lapse video shows how he transferred ink to paper using printmaking tools to create self-portrait prints (Figure 20.8). The videos supplement his live classroom demonstrations at the beginning of instruction. He revisits the videos during lessons with students to strengthen their understandings. Because students can further review class tutorial videos as needed, Muller and his students have the benefit of increased one-to-one instruction time. This provides him with additional opportunities to focus on each student's individual needs and identify all students' unique learning goals.

## Romana Štajerová: We Learn Together

Romana Štajerová teaches at an arts academy for students ages 5–20. Reflecting on her teaching, she explained how students are aware of teachers' perceptions of them. Štajerová says that she and her students

**FIGURE 20.9** Romana Štajerová, *Perseids*.
*Source: Courtesy of the artist.*

**FIGURE 20.10** Nichole Dawson Rich, *Inner Peace*, acrylic, 20 × 30 in. (50.8 × 76.2).
*Source: Courtesy of the artist.*

learn together. She views students as creative partners and promotes equality between the teacher and students. Her students produce exceptional results without feeling the pressure to be perfect because she applies an effective instructional style and her knowledge of art to inspire them (Figure 20.9). They regularly participate in meaningful conversations and exchange ideas. Students recognize her love and enthusiasm for teaching art. She encourages them to relax their minds and bodies so they can unwind and enjoy creative practices. Given these combined methods, Štajerová skillfully prepares students to explore diverse media and processes, develop a heightened aesthetic awareness, respect their own and other artists' creations, and understand the value of art in society.

## Nichole Rich: Cultivating a Positive, Self-Reflective Mindset

Nichole Rich's triptych, shown in Figure 20.10, represents her conscious choice to begin each day with meditation and exercise to generate positive thoughts about teaching and learning. She believes that such awareness promotes a sense of inner peace and personal satisfaction. Rich strives to help her elementary students become better people through the choice-based art lessons she develops and the artistic

mindsets she teaches. She emphasizes that educators need to be self-reflective when challenges arise: "You have to do a lot of reflection. It is not just about you. The students make up the class. You have to think about what is going right and what is not and reflect on how to fix things."

## Sasha Burnette: Yes I Can, Overcoming Obstacles Through Art

Sasha Burnette designs painted shoes called *shoescapes* (Figure 20.11). The shoes' exteriors are blank canvases for her to decorate with motivational statements and designs that reflect customers' hobbies

**FIGURE 20.11** Sasha Burnette painting shoescapes.
*Source: Courtesy of the artist.*

and interests. Each time she creates new designs she feels inspired by her customers' ideas. Prior to painting shoescapes, she felt hesitant about sharing her creations publicly. She overcame her initial reluctance due to her love of art, the tactile joy of painting shoes, and knowing that she is creating something meaningful for others. Her resiliency in overcoming her fear of showing her artwork in public serves as a concrete example for teaching her elementary (and other) students that all people experience challenges and can find productive ways to overcome them.

## Gerald Obregon: Opening Doors to Possibilities

Gerald Obregon teaches gifted and talented secondary art students. Obregon is a voice of reason and encouragement when students feel parental resistance to pursuing the visual arts as a profession: "I tell them that it is a career choice and legitimate." His curriculum pushes students beyond taking the easiest pathways. He emphasizes the importance of idea development, producing quality products, and networking to build professional contacts. After many years of teaching, he utilized part of a summer break to study abroad in France. He painted where famous artists once painted. This experience made him even more passionate about his teaching and painting practices (Figure 20.12). An advocate who pays it forward, Obregon is eager to impart what he has learned as a professional with students and fellow teachers.

He shares his enthusiasm and knowledge so that others like him have the option to open their own doors to new creative possibilities.

## Nan Liu: Researching and Teaching Diversified Artistic Practices

Nan Liu studied art in China and the United States, and is skilled in Eastern and Western art traditions (Figures 20.13 and 20.14). Given his education, life experiences, and work in higher education, he is interested in sharing his knowledge about Eastern and Western painting methodologies with his students and the broader community. He regularly gives live painting demonstrations to show others his specialized techniques. Some of his paintings are in a purely Eastern or a Western style, while others result in hybrid designs. His passion has inspired his textbook, which explains to Chinese art educators the diverse ways that Western art educators teach students art production methods and philosophies (Liu, 2019).

**FIGURE 20.13** Nan Liu demonstrates traditional Chinese art techniques.
*Source: Courtesy of the artist.*

**FIGURE 20.12** Gerald Obregon participating in an art festival.
*Source: Courtesy of the artist; www.gerasco.com.*

FIGURE 20.14 Nan Liu, *Climbing Up*, 2014, 68 × 60 in. (152.4 × 152.4 cm) oil on canvas.
*Source: Courtesy of the artist.*

Educators can utilize his body of works to reflect on how they might combine familiar cultural norms with the exchange of diversified ideas to augment their teaching practices.

## Janet Malone: Let's Get Involved

Janet Malone advises pre-service and beginning teachers: "Don't be afraid to get involved in your school." Malone does just that by taking on special projects that showcase her students' many achievements and her professionalism as a teacher. When she is not busy creating the next special project, professional development for teachers, or student exhibition, she uses her free time to produce beaded artworks and other creative products. She describes the repetitive beading process as tedious, yet relaxing (Figure 20.15). Malone brings her art-making passion to her teaching by showing elementary students how to develop the artistic behaviors needed to create detailed artworks. She explains to students that they must learn to concentrate, tune others out, and persevere to achieve quality results.

FIGURE 20.15 This artwork is one of Janet Malone's many beaded canvases.
*Source: Courtesy of the artist.*

## Jonathan Griffith: Honing Students' Creative and Professional Skills

Jonathan Griffith organizes annual studio art tours for students so that they can watch live demonstrations of artists' techniques and talk to artists about their careers. These experiences result from his personal interactions with the community artists with whom he exhibits and sells his works at juried craft fairs. His low-relief ceramic sculptures with hardwood elements balance craft and fine art methodologies with his love of the outdoors (Figure 20.16). Focusing on depth, texture, and craft, Griffith takes great efforts to produce harmonious products that reflect his passion for daily living. He applies his expert knowledge as a practicing artist to teach high school students the differences between exceptional and poor craftspersonship to assist them in making informed judgments about art and to hone their creative skills. Given the experiences Griffith provides, his

FIGURE 20.16 Jonathan Griffith, *Mirage*, 2018, 31 × 9 × 2 in. (78.74 × 22.86 × 5 cm), Clay/Teak/zebra-wood/tiger-maple.
*Source: Courtesy of the artist; www.jonathanlgriffith.com.*

FIGURE 20.17 Teaching artists Martin Homola and Romana Štajerová practice woodcarving in their free time at the home of fellow teaching artist Josef Zedník.
*Source: Courtesy of Romana Štajerová.*

students secure proficiencies that they can apply to produce diverse art forms and understand viable career pathways in the visual arts.

## LIFELONG LEARNING

Lifelong learning is the ongoing pursuit of knowledge and skills. Great teachers, including those just described, are lifelong learners who exchange ideas with peers, students, and community members to add intrinsic value to their teaching and learning practices. They are self-motivated and inquisitive. They look to inspirational people who are excellent at what they do. Learning takes place in formal and informal environments. Their pursuit of knowledge occurs as independent and collective practices. For example, Figure 20.7 resulted from the teacher-artist independently learning a new art method and Figure 20.17 shows teacher-artists practicing woodcarving together. Lifelong learners self-reflect on their planning, instruction, management, and assessment, and they build on existing proficiencies to become even better teachers. Their self-reflection comes in many forms including asking questions, making anecdotal notes, talking to others, reviewing literary and visual sources, and developing teacher journals and other creative products. By taking an active role in analyzing their teaching practices and dispositions a few minutes each day, teachers can set realistic goals, navigate their career pathways, and continue to grow.

Professional development and specialized trainings for teachers are designed to improve their knowledge and skills about art, education, and other topics. Teachers may participate in professional development to earn credentials, recertification, and advanced degrees. Some professional development opportunities are mandatory and others are selected by teachers because they align with their goals and/or interests (as with Gerald Obregon, shown in Figure 20.12, who studied painting in France). Participating in professional development opportunities helps teachers stay informed about best pedagogical practices and theories for teaching art. Many professional development activities are group centered, including seminars, workshops, university courses, and professional learning communities. Online trainings can be designed for collaborative and independent study. School districts, museums, and professional art, education, and art education organizations at local, state, national, and international levels, provide professional development for teachers. Larger organizations, including NAEA, develop quality resources and events such as scholarly journals, conventions, online forums, workshops, grants, and more. Art education organizations offer an assortment of professional development opportunities taught by art educators and/or professional artists for members to learn new skills and practices, as well as create artworks. Participants might visit museums and cultural venues at their conventions that can serve as inspirations for developing grade level curricula and their own creative works.

Like professional development, mentoring is an important component of lifelong learning. Each of us can identify mentors who positively influenced our personal and professional lives. Teacher mentors impart their skills, knowledge, and care to help others achieve. The quotes within this section are based on teacher communications with the author (personal communications, 2018). Serving as a mentor for her school district and university students, Janet Malone observed how in-service teachers are frequently alone without peer supports because they are busy teaching students in their classrooms. Malone begins her mentoring role with friendly conversations. She invites teachers to let her know if there is anything they need and does all that she can to help. Reflecting on the mentors who helped her as a beginning teacher, she stated: "I don't know where I would have been without that support." Lorinne Lee (Artists' Lessons to Thrive! 20.1) views mentoring as a continuous source of inspiration. In her roles as a teacher, supervisor, and volunteer working, on non-profit organizations' advisory boards, Lee has utilized her professional expertise to share lessons that she learned along the way: "My past and present art education experiences and collaborative teamwork made me realize how important it is that we continue to be role models for the next generation of art educators." Ted Edinger ("Mr. E.") views mentoring as a personal responsibility (see Chapter 15, Figure 15.23): "Taking on university students allows me to feel more fulfilled in my profession. I love teaching children. However, I also love teaching young adults the "craft" of art education." Edinger sees the relationship between mentor and mentee as an exchange: "I feel I get as much as I give in these relationships. The future educators bring in fresh ideas and refreshing perspectives. I am constantly able to reflect on my practices as I help them reflect on theirs." As a parent and educator, Edinger wants the best teachers for all children: "If I can positively influence future art educators, I'm also influencing the students, faculty, and communities they will be serving. This allows me to have a greater impact in our field and our world."

## TEACHING PHILOSOPHY

Teachers articulate their beliefs about teaching and learning by developing a teaching philosophy in essay form using rich, descriptive language with active verbs and concrete examples to articulate their professional strengths and knowledge (Stephens, 2007). A teaching philosophy provides insights into teacher and student dispositions, anticipated goals, and successful outcomes. An effective teaching philosophy is constructed with unified content that has a natural and captivating flow. Its terminology is approachable without confusing jargon so that employers can understand and stay connected to its intended message. Most teaching philosophies are one-page, single-spaced documents with an introduction and a summary that are usually each one paragraph in length. Its body, written in one or more paragraphs, describes goals, methods, leadership, and advocacy.

A teaching philosophy should capture an audience's attention immediately at its introduction by having a hook that aligns with teachers' qualifications and/or aims. This can be in the form of a motivational quote, a brief anecdotal story, or an inspirational question or thought. Teachers should contemplate personally-driven responses to broad questions about teaching such as: What does it mean to be a quality teacher? What should students know and be able to do given their involvement in a comprehensive art program? (See Model 20.1 for a list of guiding questions.) Teachers can construct the teaching philosophy's main body by describing significant theories and methods that guide their teaching, planning, and assessment practices. This textbook's Model 20.2, "Teaching Philosophy," provides concrete examples to support given statements. A philosophy's narrative needs to show teachers' flexibility, open-mindedness, and willingness to work through obstacles. Teachers should reflect on their professional development experiences and the positive attributes of those who mentored them. Some educators have been motivated by obstacles that hindered their growth and incorporated them in their philosophies to demonstrate how they could do better. When educators choose to address an adversity, they must craft their statements carefully so that they remain positive and promote opportunities for success without appearing negative. After the body is developed, the summary reinforces teacher qualifications and includes future professional aspirations as a lifelong learner that will help teachers and their students grow. A well-written teaching philosophy will leave readers with an impression that they know who teachers are and what they value.

## Model 20.1
## Guiding Questions for Developing a Teaching Philosophy

1. What are your professional teaching qualifications?
2. What attributes and experiences make you highly qualified to teach art?
3. What inspires you as a teacher and/or a creator?
4. What is a driving concept that guides your teaching?
5. How do you cultivate student learning and achievement?
6. Which theories and practices have shaped your teaching?
7. How do you create a positive learning environment?
8. What will your classroom environment look like? How will it promote learning, experimentation, and risk taking?
9. How do you utilize instructional methods and assessments to cultivate student growth?
10. What role do standards play in your teaching?
11. How do you accommodate diversified learners?
12. How do you teach students to work through challenges and achieve quality learning outcomes and dispositions?
13. How do the learning experiences you provide have value in the classroom and beyond?
14. What steps do you take to improve your teaching practices? How do they align with your short- and long-term goals?
15. How do you utilize assessments and evaluations to enhance teaching and learning?
16. How do teacher research and professional development shape your teaching practices?
17. How do you demonstrate leadership?
18. What additional skills and capabilities do you bring to the profession?
19. How do you go above and beyond what is expected?
20. What will students know and be able to do by participating in your class?
21. How do you motivate students, including ones who may resist teacher support and encouragement?
22. How do you view yourself as a colleague?
23. How can your services benefit administrative, parent, student, and/or community needs?
24. What makes your teaching style unique?
25. How do you demonstrate a commitment to lifelong learning?

## Model 20.2
## Teaching Philosophy

As a young child, I was surrounded by creativity with family members who taught me how to work with tools and make things. They challenged me to take creative risks and work through mistakes to learn problem-solving techniques. Their mentorship instilled my lifelong passion of exploring and creating. Throughout my life, I have held on to these early inspirations and have applied them to my journey in becoming a certified art educator who has the knowledge and skills to inspire diversified student populations. I view students as active learners and problem solvers who can utilize the art curriculum to study topics that shape humanity and influence our many ways of knowing about the world.

During my undergraduate studies I had the opportunity to study curriculum and assessment methodologies and apply them to teaching pre-K–12 students art production methods and inquiry skills. I felt motivated by the choice-based art curriculum model in which I can serve as a facilitator who assists students in gaining skills and utilizing research methodologies to learn new information and transform what they learn into personally-driven outcomes. An example of this occurred when my class and I went to teach children at a school for the blind and we introduced a STEAM (science, technology, engineering, arts, and mathematics) lesson with a conservation theme. Each student identified the meaning of conservation in daily life. They developed an original narrative and a stop-motion film to tell a story about the importance of conservation. I was amazed with their ideas and the works that they produced. In addition to teaching students with disabilities, I have experience teaching English language learners in the local community and during a study-abroad semester in Scandinavia. These experiences instilled in me a deep desire to help students work through communication barriers that arise during instruction. In all of my teaching endeavors, using formative assessments has benefited me in knowing where students are at and helping them reach learning targets. They allow me to assist students who work on grade level as well as prepare accelerated tasks for gifted and talented learners and to find pathways for students with special needs who require modifications and accommodations.

As I continue to grow in the teaching profession, I am highly interested in professional development opportunities to augment my current practices. I plan to explore innovative ways to integrate the National Visual Arts Standards' essential questions that address topics including creativity, persistence, and personal decision making into comprehensive art lessons in which students will talk, write about, and create art. Additionally, I aspire to implement a school art club and engage students in community art education experiences that bring them in contact with inspirational community members and provide them with firsthand glimpses of the value of the arts in daily life. Ultimately, I strive to foster positive relationships and learning experiences that students will remember for years to come and feel proud of their many achievements given their active participation in the visual arts.

## SECURING THE RIGHT TEACHING JOB

The broad field of education provides numerous career pathways for teaching professionals. Great teachers work in classrooms and other community settings. Many teach in pre-K–12 positions or are employed in related fields that require advanced degrees including (arts) administration, art therapy, museum education, and higher education. Securing the right teaching job is work. Teacher job candidates should be aware that positions offer rewards and incentives that they might not have previously imagined without going in and seeing them for themselves. Teacher job candidates must convince employers that they are the best person for the position given their qualifications. Employers also want to see winning dispositions that align with their school's or organization's needs, such as being a team player, having effective organizational skills, and taking leadership roles. The teaching philosophy, portfolio, résumé, and cover letter are resources that illustrate teachers' unique stories as educators. (See this textbook's companion website for more information about cover letters.) Collectively, they document teachers' professional knowledge and skills at a given time and will need to be updated as teachers grow within the profession.

## Teaching Portfolio

A **teaching portfolio** is a collection of artifacts that represent an educator's planning, teaching, and assessment abilities. Many pre-service teachers are required to develop portfolios for performance assessments and university courses. They can integrate this content into a broader teacher portfolio (Sickler-Voigt, 2018). In the visual arts, teaching portfolios include original instructional resources, lessons, and assessments; images documenting pre-K–12 teaching; photographs of displays/exhibitions; and quality student artworks. Other pertinent artifacts include letters of recommendation, certificates, video clips documenting effective teaching, and evidence of professional accomplishments. In all forms, quality portfolios are neat, organized, professional, and labeled with headers and brief descriptions of content as applicable to make navigation easier. Online portfolios have the advantage of being viewed from a distance by hiring committees before an interview. Binder portfolios and artist case portfolios are suited for presenting artifacts in person.

In Figures 20.1 and 20.18, pre-service teachers are shown practicing navigating their portfolio content during formal presentations. This exercise teaches future job candidates how to be selective in their choice of materials and gives them practice making their usage more natural during interviews. For instance, if a principal were to ask about budget planning, teachers might have a sample budget prepared with a list of necessary art materials and equipment. Or when asked to describe how they would integrate the visual arts with another subject, teachers might pass around a well-crafted teacher-made puppet from their portfolio and tell employers how the students

they taught learned literacy skills through writing and performing their own puppet shows. By holding the handmade puppet, employers can make tactile connections to the actual work.

## Professional Teacher Résumé

**Résumés** highlight teachers' significant work experiences, educational background, and professional qualifications (see Model 20.3). They provide an overview of teachers' skills and help determine if teachers will be invited to interview. Although pre-service teachers lack some professional experiences that in-service educators have acquired, they can emphasize their pre-service teaching experiences such as practicum and residency placements, teaching internships, tutoring, volunteer work, and employment at summer camps and extended school programs. They can also identify professional development experiences including presenting educational workshops and participating in community art projects.

Teacher résumés are usually one page long. Some employers may also request a résumé of two or more pages in length that provides greater details about teaching experiences. Most employers quickly skim résumé content to weed out candidates and reject those with inaccurate information and poor designs (Fredericks, 2017). Therefore, résumés should have appropriate headers, wording, and content to showcase teaching proficiencies and move beyond passively mimicking content on standardized templates. All information on résumés must be accurate and represent teachers' actual professional experiences. Effective résumés identify the skills employers expect for a position, including teaching qualifications and proficiencies in curriculum development, assessment, art production methods, and classroom management. Experiences unrelated to teaching and the visual arts do not belong on art teaching résumés.

To begin a résumé, teachers should review a job description's key words and determine how their qualifications match a position. They should select strong action verbs written in past tense to identify experiences, such as *facilitated* or *implemented*. Employers appreciate teacher job candidates who write out full phrases before using acronyms so that they can understand their meanings. When résumés contain all necessary content, teacher job candidates

FIGURE 20.18 Eric Breedlove created a professional website, binder portfolio, and artist case portfolio to showcase his abilities as an educator. United States.
*Source: Pamela Catania, photo.*

should reread and edit them to ensure that all qualifications are clearly stated and error free.

When résumés are informative and well-designed, employers will often invite teacher job candidates to interview so that they can ask questions to identify the qualities that the candidate might bring to their position. Many books and websites offer sample interview questions. Practicing answers to some of these questions while listening actively in the interview will help teacher job candidates' answers sound prepared and not rehearsed. One common interview question is "Why should we hire you?" (Fredericks, 2016, p. 160). As basic as this question appears, when nerves kick in, it might feel challenging to answer. As important as words are during an interview, principals agree that teacher job candidates' body language must radiate confidence without being arrogant. They recommend that teachers wear professional clothing, smile as appropriate, provide firm and welcoming handshakes, and make proper eye contact to give positive impressions. They must listen attentively to what employers have to say and come prepared to ask important questions, such as: How are the arts supported? With this information in mind, teacher job candidates are on the way to having the necessary skills, dispositions, and resources to secure the right teaching job.

## Model 20.3 Teacher Résumé

### Name
[Street Address] [City, State, and ZIP Code]
[Phone] [Website] [Email]

## Objective

Teach in a school environment as a certified art educator.

## Education and Licensure

### Bachelor of Science, Art Education                                        [Insert Dates]
University Name, City, State, Grade Point Average (GPA)
### K–12 Visual Art, Educator License [Insert Location]                       [Insert Dates]

## Teaching Experience

### K–12 Residency                                                            [Insert Dates]

- Developed and taught standards-based visual art lessons to diversified K–12 students using formative and summative assessments to measure student attainment of learning goals.
- Collaborated with mentoring elementary teacher during a school-wide campaign to raise reading scores by developing lesson plans and instructional resources that teach literacy skills through the visual arts.
- Supervised high school students' personally-driven capstone projects that centered on an essential question identified in the National Visual Arts Standards and displayed completed projects in the school arts advocacy night exhibition.

### International Teaching in Scandinavia                                      [Insert Dates]

- Taught comprehensive book arts lessons during a study abroad semester to English learners (grades 1–7) in Norwegian and Danish schools using the theme of resiliency as identified in Scandinavian folklore.
- Facilitated group discussions and art critiques with classroom teachers in English and their native language to assist students in making personal connections and self-assessing their work.

### K–12 Practicum                                                    [Insert Dates]

- Instructed K–12 students from a state school for the blind to create an original stop-motion animation about environmental conservation.
- Created a theme-based mural with mosaics about respect with middle school students.

### Art Museum                                                        [Insert Name]
### Summer Camp Instructor                                            [Insert Dates]

- Designed and taught theme-based lessons to children (Ages 5–12) inspired by the museum's exhibitions.
- Facilitated hands-on activities for children and families in studio workshops for the summer art extravaganza.

## Skills

**Curriculum and Instruction:** standards-based lessons; quantitative and qualitative assessments; art research and inquiry methods; classroom management; accommodations for diversified learners; academic art vocabulary

**Art and Technology:** 2D and 3D techniques (including drawing; painting; collage; puppetry; sculpture; mosaics; clay; mixed media); journaling; murals; community art education; stop-motion animation; claymation; ePortfolios

**Professional Development:** National Art Education Association member; presented a STEAM (science, technology, engineering, arts, and mathematics) workshop to student chapter art education association; attended a National Art Education Association convention in [Insert Location]

## OUR JOURNEY TO THRIVE CONTINUES: MAKING THE MOST OF YOUR TEACHING CAREER . . .

Maintaining positive a disposition and professional behaviors makes teaching and learning genuinely rewarding. The steps that great teachers take to ensure best practices, as advocated throughout this textbook, come together in dynamic, well-managed learning environments in which students and teachers have ongoing opportunities to share in healthy dialogue and take productive risks. As a great teacher, you will apply your knowledge of the visual arts, artists' ways of knowing, effective pedagogical models, advocacy methods, and assessments to cultivate students' full potential. You will take steps so that the art curriculum you develop generates excitement for students and yourself because it incorporates your expertise as a teacher, creator, and human being who possesses a range of abilities (Jaffe, 2012). As a lifelong learner, you will continue to learn new processes and build on your current knowledge. By working through your creative struggles like other great teachers do, you will develop an understanding of the challenges students experience as they create art and problem solve.

As in all professions, teachers face challenges during their careers. However, they recognize the value of their ongoing efforts in investing in students' education. You can strive to become a teacher whom students will thank for many years to come because of your passion, commitment, and ability to provide diversified learners with the skills they need to thrive and succeed in school and beyond. If at any point you start to question your effectiveness in the profession, you can reflect on the students and teachers who have inspired you. You might consider special moments when students gave you sentimental drawings and/or thanked you for caring. These rewards serve as refreshing reminders of why teachers love to teach art and how the work we do makes a positive difference in students' lives and benefits the broader community.

## CHAPTER QUESTIONS AND ACTIVITIES

1. Describe how you plan to make the most of your teaching career. What roles will teacher creativity, lifelong learning, and applications of best practices and theories in teaching art play in your personal and professional development?
2. Refer to this chapter's resources for developing a teaching philosophy, résumé, and teaching portfolio to showcase your current teaching skills and beliefs (Models 20.1–20.3). Present your works as if you were talking to a hiring committee. Describe your plans for augmenting your résumé and portfolio through additional teaching and learning opportunities.
3. Reread Artists' Lessons to Thrive! 20.1. Answer its essential/guiding questions in written form or as part of a group discussion. Complete its daily learning targets.

## References

Booth, E. (2003). What is a teaching artist? *Teaching Artist Journal, 1*(1), 5–12.

Fredericks, A. D. (2016). *Ace your teacher interview: 149 fantastic answers to tough interview questions* (2nd ed.). Indianapolis, IN: Blue River Press.

Fredericks, A. D. (2017). *Ace your teacher résumé (and cover letter)*. Indianapolis, IN: Blue River Press.

Graham, M. A., & Zwirn, S. G. (2010). How being a teaching artist can influence K–12 art education. *Studies in Art Education, 51*(3), 219–232.

Jaffe, N. (2012). A framework for teaching artist professional development. *Teaching Artist Journal, 10*(1), 34–42.

Liu, N. (2019). *Art education in the United States*. Changsha, China: Hu Nan Fine Arts Publishing House.

Sickler-Voigt, D. C. (2018). *Changing mindsets about edTPA: From test anxiety to demonstrating teacher competencies through authentic teaching and assessment practices*. Retrieved from www.arteducators.org/learn-tools/assessment-white-papers-for-art-education

Smilan, C. (2016). Developing visual creative literacies through integrating art-based inquiry. *Clearing House, 89*(4/5), 167–178.

Stephens, P. (2007). *Writing a philosophy of art teaching*. Retrieved from www.davisart.com/Promotions/SchoolArts/PDF/STSG207.pdf School Arts

# Index